The 2nd Earl of Rosse in the robes he wore at the coronation of George IV in July 1821, from a portrait (1820–1) by Thomas Foster (1798–1826). Reproduced by kind permission of the Earl and Countess of Rosse, and with the assistance of Mr William Laffan. See Foster to Rosse, 5 June 1820 (E/34/35 in text) and William Laffan and Brendan Rooney, 'The death and life of Thomas Foster', *Irish Architectural and Decorative Studies*, vii (2004), pp 91–4.

CALENDAR

of

THE ROSSE PAPERS

CALENDAR

of

THE ROSSE PAPERS

A.P.W. MALCOMSON

IRISH MANUSCRIPTS COMMISSION

DUBLIN, 2008

In memory of

Peter Jupp (1940–2006)

and of

Des Scott (1940–2007)

ISBN 978-1-874280-69-9

Irish Manuscripts Commission © 2008
A.P.W. Malcomson © 2008

45 Merrion Square, Dublin 2
www.irishmanuscripts.ie

Printed by Betaprint
Typeset in Adobe Garamond by Carole Lynch

CONTENTS

G/1-69   Papers (almost exclusively estate and financial), *c.* 1540–2001, of the
              Wilmer Field family of Heaton Hall, Bradford, Yorkshire, whose co-
              heiress, Mary Field, married in 1836 Lord Oxmantown, later 3rd Earl
              of Rosse, including a few papers about the Heaton estate after its merger
              with the Rosse estates in Ireland.

H/1-130   Papers of the Hawke family, Lords Hawke, 1682–1824 and 1832-2006,
              present among the Rosse Papers because of the marriage in 1870 of the
              Hon. Frances Cassandra Hawke, heiress of her father, the 4th Lord
              Hawke, to the 4th Earl of Rosse; including some naval, administrative
              and political papers of Admiral Sir Edward Hawke, K.B., 1st Lord
              Hawke, victor of the Battle of Quiberon Bay in 1759, and First Lord of
              the Admiralty, 1766–71.

J/1-31   Correspondence and other papers of the 3rd Earl of Rosse, 1829, 1832
              and 1840–2003, as President of the Royal Society, Chancellor of Trinity
              College, Dublin, Lieutenant of King's County, leading landowner there,
              and general public figure, excluding where physically possible
              correspondence of the sort concentrated in Section K.

K/1-40   Correspondence of the 3rd and 4th Earls of Rosse with fellow-
              astronomers or about the Birr and other observatories, including
              correspondence of the 5th and 6th Earls about the Birr Observatory,
              1840–1909, 1913–14, 1938 and 1964–84.

L   Journals containing astronomical observations, drawings of nebula,
              drafts for articles and speeches on astronomy, and other papers
              (excluding correspondence) of the 3rd and 4th Earls of Rosse on the
              subject of astronomy, [pre-1828–1908].

M/1-42   Correspondence and other papers of the 4th and 5th Earls of Rosse,
              [1860]–1956, on subjects other than astronomy, including estate and
              other King's County affairs, the 4th Earl's contributions to public life as
              a representative peer, Chancellor of T.C.D., etc.

N/1-46   Letters and papers, 1739–1995 (mainly 1876–1962), of the Lister Kaye
              family, of Denby Grange, near Wakefield, Yorkshire, one of whom,
              Frances Lois, second daughter of Sir Cecil Edmund Lister Kaye, 4th Bt,
              married in 1905 the 5th Earl of Rosse.

O/1-66   Maps, plans and drawings, [*c.* 1610], 1638, [*c.* 1690] and *c.* 1750–1970,
              mainly of a size which makes it physically convenient to form them into
              a separate section.

P   Twelve photograph albums, ranging in size from folio to small octavo,
              five bundles of loose photographs, and other material, *c.* 1870–*c.* 1945,
              all deriving from Mary Countess of Rosse, the 3rd to the 6th Earls of
              Rosse, the Hon. Geoffrey L. Parsons and the Lister Kaye family.

Detailed calendar   195

APPENDIX: by Aoife Leonard   509

A descriptive list of the 17th–century material within the archive (placing it in an 'ideal' arrangement which the format of the originals does not permit).

INTRODUCTION AND
ACKNOWLEDGEMENTS

'Intellectual is not a word that springs to mind in describing the Anglo-Irish gentry of the 18th and 19th centuries. One thinks of them as, at their best, brave, dashing and witty; at their worst, drunken, dissipated and illiterate. But there has, of course, always been a leavening of less typical families, and of these none are more interesting than the Parsonses of Birr. To have produced, in three generations, a patriot statesman, two leading astronomers, and an inventor of genius is by any standard an impressive achievement. ...' Thus Mark Girouard, at the outset of a four-part article on Birr published in *Country Life* in 1965. While it could be argued that this assessment rates the generality of the Anglo-Irish gentry too low, there can be no doubt that the Parsonses deserve to be singled out as a family of unusual and unusually sustained ability.

THE PARSONS FAMILY AND BIRR, 1590–1791

Girouard continues: '... The fortunes of the Parsons family in Ireland were founded by two brothers, William and Laurence, who came over from England about 1590. Like the great Earl of Cork (with whom they had marriage connections), they were members of the group of tough and capable Englishmen that pioneered the resettlement of the country after the wars of the 16th century. William, the elder, ... obtained large grants of lands, mostly in Wexford, and was created a baronet in 1620. He was the ancestor of the Earls of Rosse of the first creation whose line died out in 1764. ...' The offices conferred on or acquired by him (most of which gave him opportunities for building up a large landed estate) included those of Surveyor-General of Ireland (1602), Commissioner of the Plantations in Leinster, Ulster and Connaught (1604), Joint Supervisor and Extender (with his younger brother, Laurence) of Crown Lands in Ireland (1611), and Master of the Irish Court of Wards (set up in 1621 on his recommendation to the all-powerful royal favourite, George Villiers, 1st Duke of Buckingham). Sir William Parsons retained his offices and some of his influence after the assassination of his patron, Buckingham, in 1628. He served, controversially, as one of the two Lords Justices of the kingdom, 1640–43, was imprisoned for a time in Dublin Castle, and died in England in 1650.

Sir William's younger brother, Laurence, the ancestor of the Earls of Rosse of the second (1806) creation, lived initially at Youghal, Co. Cork, before his participation in the plantation of Co. Longford caused him to establish himself at Birr after 1622. His offices, too, were mainly Munster-based. A lawyer by training, he was Clerk of the Crown, Peace and Assizes for Munster, 1604–16, Attorney-General for Munster, 1612–24, Judge of the Admiralty and a deputy Vice-Admiral for Munster, 1619–28, and Second Baron of the Irish Exchequer, 1624–8.[1] The first of the brothers to attach himself to the rising star of the Duke of Buckingham, he was knighted in 1620 and died – much earlier than his elder brother and in the same year as Buckingham – in 1628.

Like Sir William's, Sir Laurence's official career was (in the words of Mark Girouard) '... more successful than meritorious; and it is his activities as a coloniser and developer of plantation lands that are interesting. In 1620 he acquired 1,000 acres of arable land and 277 of wood and bog in the territory in central Ireland known as Ely O'Carroll. This acquisition centred on the town and castle of Birr; on June 26 of the same year it was constituted a manor under the new name of Parsonstown. Parsonstown and Birr have remained alternative names for the town up till recent years. [Indeed, in 1968, Eamon De Valera wrote to Anne, Countess of Rosse, with surprising courtliness, that he scarcely recognised the name 'Birr' which she had used in a letter of invitation, because he always thought of it as Parsonstown!²] ...

By the early 17th century the tribal system of Ely O'Carroll had disintegrated and the territory was in a state of chaos, with four different O'Carrolls disputing for the lordship. On the death of Sir Charles O'Carroll in 1619 the territory was declared (understandably, if on rather tenuous grounds) to have become crown property and a Royal Commission for the Plantation was set up on September 30, 1619. A very considerable proportion was regranted to the old proprietors; but a number of new English settlers were introduced, who, it was hoped, might bring an element of stability into this disturbed area. Among the new settlers the Parsonses rapidly became the most prominent.

Sir Laurence Parsons proved himself a vigorous and capable developer of his new estates. The town grew and flourished under his benevolent autocracy ... . [When he] ... acquired Birr it was little more than a village. All that survive visually from the Middle Ages are the bridge that carries Main Street across the River Camcor, picturesquely built up with houses, like a miniature version of old London Bridge, and the ivy-clad walls of the main body of the church, surrounded now by the overgrown tombstones of the old Birr families. The actual tower of the church was probably built by Sir Laurence and is decorated with his arms; perhaps he built it from the first with defence in mind, and it certainly played its part, as a defensive outpost, in the two sieges of the castle in 1643 and 1690. This church tower and his work at the castle are the sole architectural remainders of Sir Laurence's time, but in fact he did much to establish the prosperity of the town, which he ruled autocratically, but benevolently. He started a glass factory, under a Huguenot family of the name of Bigo; it was, for a time, prosperous and well known, and used to supply Dublin with window and table glass. He acquired for the town the right to have two weekly markets, and laid down a number of ordinances that show a sense of civic amenities in advance of their time. The sidewalks were to be paved at the inhabiutants' expense, Sir Laurence having paved the main road at his. A 4d. fine was exacted from anyone who "cast any dunge rubbidge filth or sweepings into the forestreet". Anyone who lit fires in their house other than in stone chimneys was to be banished from the town. He had a prejudice against barmaids, and no woman was allowed to serve beer "uppon payne to bee sett in the stocks by the constable for 3 whole markett dayes". ...

[Sir Laurence also] ... substantially enlarged the castle, and his work remains the core of the building that is there today. ... The original castle of the O'Carrolls was a great square tower, known as the Black Castle. It stood about 60 yards north-west of the present building, where smooth lawns now lead from the entrance front towards the park. ... Between 1620 and 1627 Sir Laurence made considerable alterations and additions ... . He put two English masons in charge, and paid them 2s. a day each. The most important piece of work undertaken was the building or rebuilding of a gatehouse 46 feet by 25 feet, which forms the hall and centre of the present building; the archway of the gatehouse ran through what is now the basement under the main entrance, and the long and rather narrow shape of the present entrance hall is due to the fact that it was the room above this archway. This new gatehouse was steadily enlarged until it became the main house. At some, on the available evidence, undatable stage it absorbed what appear to have been originally two free-standing towers set diagonally to either side of the main gatehouse and known, in the military language of the day, as "flankers". The linking of these flankers to the central block produced a very curious and individual plan – a central block with two bent arms hooked on to it – which can really only be explained visually, by an aerial view or a plan. Immediately south of the house the ground drops steeply down to the Camcor River, a lively mountain river still clear and turbulent from the Slieve Blooms where it has its source. Seen from the west the house and its wings extend in a long embracing sweep; as one moves round to the south they contract into a high and compact silhouette hunched up above the river. Perhaps this is the aspect of Birr that sticks most firmly in the memory. To the east the town jostles straight up against the castle walls, as it has always done – an intimate relationship between great house and town found comparativelys seldom in England and even less often in Ireland. ... In the course of time the defensive importance of the castle dwindled, but it still played a leading part in the life of the town – economically and socially because the growth of the town was actively stimulated by the Parsons family, physically because the barrier of the castle and its demesne on the west forced the town to expand to the north, east and south. ...

Sir Laurence Parsons died in 1628, fourteen years before the castle entered on one of the two most stormy episodes in its history. In 1641 the Irish Catholics rose in rebellion. Sir Laurence's grandson, William, was made Governor of Ely O'Carroll and garrisoned it for the crown. His diary survives at Birr, together with a large number of other contemporary documents, part of a collection of family papers of a size rare for Ireland. On April 13, 1642, the Molloys, Coghlans and Ormonders appeared in force together, and at ten in the evening set the town on fire and burnt almost every house in it to the ground. "And when they saw the Towne on fire, they blew up their Bagpipes, and beat up their drums and fell a Dauncinge on the hills." Then followed a difficult time for the castle, culminating in a rigorous five days' siege on January 16–20, 1643. Among the besiegers was a mason who had worked on the building of the castle; under his instructions a mine was laid under its west side, and the threat of this forced the garrison to capitulate on honourable terms. William Parsons withdrew to join the English army in Dublin; Birr was for a time garrisoned by the Catholics, but in the end they abandoned it, having burnt it out first.

William Parsons died in 1653, and never re-occupied the castle. This was left to his son, Laurence, who was created a baronet in 1677. In 1681 the English topographer Thomas Dineley was in Ireland and entered in his journal the following information: "Lord of this town is Sir laurence Parsons, where there is much plenty of Ewe-Timber, that of his House the Windows, Staircases, Window Cases, Tables, Chairs, Benches, Stooles and Stooles [sic] are formed therewith. Here is sayd to be the fairest staircase in Ireland." ... A few years after Dinely made his entry, Birr was once again in trouble – as a result of the disturbances provoked by the reign and expulsion of James II. In the late 1680s, Sir Laurence Parsons and his family removed for a time to London, leaving an agent at Birr by the name of Heward Oxburgh. Oxburgh soon proved himself a far from faithful servant, whose ultimate ambition appears to have been to supplant his employer's family altogether. The rents due to be remitted to London failed to arrive, and when Sir Laurence returned to Birr he found himself little more than a prisoner on his own estates. In 1689 Oxburgh seized the castle on the grounds that it was being held as a garrison for William of Orange; Sir Laurence and two others were put on trial as traitors to King James, and condemned to death by a packed jury. Fortunately they managed (in the teeth of Oxburgh's opposition) to obtain a reprieve, and were ultimately rescued by Williamite forces before the sentence was put into effect.

But troubles at Birr were not over. It was garrisoned by the Williamites, and in 1690 was hotly besieged by the Duke of Berwick and an Irish Jacobite army – in which the relentless Oxburgh was a colonel. Various accounts of the siege survive. One of the garrison wrote of the besiegers that "their great guns never ceased, but continued without intermission like a continued thunder; only now and then a little comical discourse, and scolding would happen from our men, bidding them go home and dig their potatoes, and calling them rapparees, which they took as a great affront." The garrison were in the end reduced to making their own bullets: "they cut and melted a leaden cistern belonging to Sir Laurence in which his lady used to salt her beef for hanging and was so large it would hold the carcases of 5 or 6 beeves." The "great guns" of the Jacobites seem to have been placed to the north-west of the castle "and as good luck would have it played at the flanker next them, which we judge to be the strongest part of the house." This must have been the north flanker, which still carries cannonball scars; a number of the actual cannonballs are preserved in the house. But the enemy artillery never succeeded in making a breach, though "three great bullets missed the flanker and came in at the parlour window, which hit the wainscot, two of which stick yet in the wall." Ultimately, in the course of a night, their army slipped away and marched on south to Limerick. This was the only occasion on which the Duke of Berwick was forced to raise a siege, excusably perhaps, as he was in his first independent command, dependent on untrained Irish levies, and only nineteen years of age.

The castle then became a Williamite military hospital. Four hundred sick and wounded men were in it from August 9 to the end of September 1690, and left it in a filthy condition. "The stairs and floors of the house, which to my knowledge used to be neatly and cleanlily kept, were so thick with dirt one could not see what they were made of, and the rooms so full of vermin both black and white, there was no coming near them." The corpses of entire horses were disinterred from the muck-heaps in the stable yard – or so the steward wrote to Sir Laurence Parsons ... . It remained a source of bitterness in the Parsons family that they never received any kind of recompense for the losses they sustained through their support of Charles I and William III. The disasters of the 17th century were probably responsible for the relative lack of incident in the history of the castle in the 18th century – it was a period of recovery, ended by the burst of building activity that started in or soon after 1800.

Nevertheless, within the old walls a certain amount of decoration took place in the Georgian period. What little is known about the Parsonses of these years suggests that they had civilised tastes. An engraved walking-stick presented to Sir William Parsons, the 2nd Baronet (died 1741), by Handel passed through the sale-rooms some years ago. This Sir William sent his son Laurence (1712–56) on the Grand Tour, and a surviving bill from the time of the latter contains payments connected with the construction of a ballroom having "2 square ceilings" and a "cumpass ceiling", and of a "Cumpass Ceiling in the Room next the River." ... [This bill is a rare exception in an archive which is unusually rich by Irish standards for the 17th century, but inexplicably blank for the period *c.* 1690– *c.* 1775.] Sir Laurence's son, another Sir William (1731-91), laid out the park, but at the expense of the "Black Castle" or "Black Tower" of the O'Carrolls. According to Thomas L. Cooke, a local historian and the author of *A Picture of Parsonstown* (Dublin, 1826), Sir William initially converted the top of this tower "... into a sitting room and he and his friends occasionally, after dinner in summer-time, used to drink their wine there." But in about 1778 the same Sir William swept [it] away ... [along with the adjoining] stables, kitchen and courtyard, and replaced them by the lawns and parkland that are still there today, making the original arrangements almost impossible to visualise. ...

[Major changes also took place in the town of Birr at about this time] ...; for the town reached its greatest prosperity in the 18th and early 19th centuries, and most of its buildings date from then. Expansion started in the 1740s, when, to commemorate the Battle of Culloden, Duke Square and Cumberland Street were laid out, as a northward extension of the Main Street. In the centre of Duke Square the Duke of Cumberland, imperiously pointing down Main Street, was elevated on a handsome stone column [designed by Samuel Chearnley, a cousin and protégé of Sir Laurence, 3rd Bt]; the statue was supplied from London, carved by Sir Henry Cheere in 1747. This grandiloquent example of Hanoverian propaganda could not be expected to weather the changes of this century; the Duke has been unseated, and only his head, much battered, ... survive[s]; Duke Square has become Emmet Square and Cumberland Street is now Emmet Street. ...

Sir William Parsons ... played an enthusiastic part in the Volunteer movement of the 1770s and '80s, in the course of which the Volunteer army, raised by the local gentry and aristocracy to defend Ireland from possible invasion from France, were used to prise substantial concessions to the Irish parliament and Irish trade from the English government. As a young man ... [his son, Laurence Parsons (1758–1841), later the 5th Baronet and the 2nd Earl of Rosse] served as a subaltern in the Parsonstown Volunteers, the embroidered banner of which, together with various other Volunteer relics, are still preserved at Birr. ...

SIR LAURENCE PARSONS, 5TH BT AND 2ND EARL OF ROSSE

The 2nd Earl of Rosse is a man who holds a decided place in Irish political and cultural history of the late 18th and early 19th centuries, even if he is in neither respect a figure of the first rank. But the archive in the Muniment Room at Birr Castle, and the castle itself and the town of Birr, are dominated by the contribution and legacy of the 2nd Earl. A good deal has been written by and about him, whether in manuscript, thesis or printed form. First and foremost, he is the subject of an unpublished Ph.D. thesis by N.D. Atkinson, 'Sir Laurence Parsons, 2nd Earl of Rosse, 1758–1841' (Dublin University, 1961). This work is inevitably dated, and perhaps from the outset, it suffered from the fact that the author obviously succumbed to the charm of the then Lord and Lady Rosse, and from the more serious defect that only a small minority of Parsons's papers had then come to light and were available to Atkinson. Nevertheless, his work provides a solid bed-rock and includes many perceptive insights. Other writers – Mark Girouard, Peter Jupp and R.B. McDowell – have addressed aspects of Parsons's career. More recently, the present writer published, in William Nolan and Timothy O'Neill (eds.), *Offaly History and Society ...* (Dublin, 1988), Chapter 14, a piece entitled 'A Variety of Perspectives on Laurence Parsons, 2nd Earl of Rosse'. This draws very heavily on the previous work of these other scholars (as indicated by the quotation marks in the text). What now follows is an abridged version of that article,[3] and the reader should refer to it for detailed citation of the passages drawn from Atkinson, Girouard, Jupp and McDowell.

'Sir Laurence Parsons, 2nd earl of Rosse (1758–1841), eldest son of Sir William Parsons of Birr, and Mary, only daughter and heiress of John Clere of Kilbury, was born on 21 May 1758. He graduated B.A. of Trinity College, Dublin, in 1780, and in the same year published a pamphlet denouncing the Irish mutiny bill. ... In July 1782 he was elected one of the representatives of the university in parliament, in the place of Walter Hussey Burgh, created Chief Baron of the Exchequer. He disclaimed party politics, but his intimacy with Henry Flood, for whom he had a profound admiration, seems unquestionably to have coloured his political views. He followed him [in 1782–3] in the matter of the Renunciation as opposed to Simple Repeal, advocated retrenchment by reducing the army, and cordially supported the Volunteer bill for the reform of parliament. His friendship for Flood rendered him naturally hostile to Grattan who, he insisted, had more than once sacrificed the public welfare to private pique, and on a notable occasion [he] taunted him with having bungled every great public measure that he had ever undertaken. ... He opposed Pitt's Commercial Propositions (1785) from the beginning; but on the question of the regency (1789) he went with the minority, arguing strongly in favour of following the example of England. To do otherwise, he declared, would be "only an assumption of a power which we never could put in practice, an idle gasconade which may alarm England and cannot by any possibility serve ourselves". ...' '...The outbreak of the French Revolution had a decisive influence on his political development. As he later wrote, in 1822: '... When first I came into parliament, I was led into an approbation of ... [parliamentary reform] by the example of Mr Pitt. But when the French doctrines of the Revolution began to prevail, I changed my opinion, and [in 1793] wrote a pamphlet entitled *Thoughts on liberty and equality* ...'.[4] In the intervening period between 1789 and 1793, '... Flood's two objectives, of financial retrenchment and constitutional reform, still underlay much of Parsons's political thought, ... [and] they were asserted now with a sense of urgency not evident before. ...

Yet, it is clear that he had no revolutionary changes in mind. He opposed any extension of the franchise, since "the poorer the voter, the more liable is he to be easy to corrupt". He was anxious to preserve the ascendancy of the propertied classes, who he believed were alone fit to rule, and he was prepared to build up an "artificial superiority" in the constitution to preserve them from the physical superiority of the lower classes. ... "'Tis better for a people that those who have been educated with the expectation of enjoying fortune and power should possess them than those who have not." ...' In subsequent private correspondence he made the point even more explicitly. '... As to the general principle of appointment, I confess, I have a partiality for gentlemen. I would rather associate with them; I would rather deal with them; I would rather see them put into places of trust and power. Those who are raised much more above their native sphere seldom I think demean themselves altogether suitably. ...'[5]

'... The reasons which led Parsons to remain aloof from his colleagues [who formed the Irish Whig Club in June 1789] are not difficult to find. He had already formed the opinion that an organised opposition was undesirable and worked against the efficiency of parliament. ... He was still preoccupied with the teachings of Flood, and could not be expected to view with much sympathy a movement so strongly influenced by Grattan. Moreover, the events in France impelled him to take a course of action more drastic than that envisaged by the other members of the opposition. ... [His] position was revealed in the course of two speeches which he delivered during the early days of the session of 1790 ... [and in which] he warned the government to come to terms with the popular demand for reform, and subjected the entire system of privilege in Ireland to the most crushing attack it had yet received in parliament. ... These two speeches marked a decisive change in the development of Parsons's political career: ... he spoke in tones that were unmistably threatening and full of anger, and seemed to offer a large measure of justification for the growing strength of popular unrest. ...'

'... Having represented Dublin University from 1782 to 1790, he was returned, on the death of his father in 1791, for King's County, which he continued to represent in the Irish Parliament till 1800, and afterwards in the Imperial Parliament till his elevation to the peerage in 1807. ... [In the period 1791–3, he opposed] any alteration in the method of collecting tithes, but supported the demand for a place and pension bill as the only adequate check on the system of parliamentary corruption practised by the crown. During the debate on the Catholic Relief Bill of 1793 he took a broad and statesmanlike view of the whole subject ..., [arguing] that the elective franchise should be given to no catholic who had not a freehold of £20 a year, and that it should be accompanied by the admission of catholics into parliament. ...' He also '... proposed that the measure for Catholic Relief should be united with one for moderate constitutional reform. For the first time, he made a statement of his own aims in the matter of reform, and introduced a number of definite proposals. These showed no revolutionary features, but were obviously designed to bring about only so small a change as the circumstances of the present emergency seemed to require. They had three main features. A plan already suggested by Pitt, to increase the number of county members, should be adopted, and two additional members given to each county and two to the city of Dublin; all large towns (such as Belfast) should be made into open boroughs, with a grant of the franchise to all freeholders; the total numbers of members of parliament should remain unchanged, by the abolition of a sufficient number of "rotten" boroughs. ... The House gave the speech a poor reception. Members of the government did not bother to make any formal answer to Parsons's suggestion. One government supporter (Hon. D[enis] Browne) spoke derisively of his "multiplicity of matter" and dismissed his arguments as "very finely confused, and very alarming, and really above my recollection or powers of answering". ...'

Understandably, the independent line he took exposed him to the resentment of government and opposition alike. In July 1791, the Chief Secretary wrote in exasperation: '... Every attention was shown to Sir Laurence Parsons at the close of the regency business. He was *given* a pension for his uncle, and offered a place at the Accounts, £800 per annum, for himself, which he declined, and abused us at the opening of the next session as much as he had Grattan the session before. You are not therefore to be surprised at my not entertaining much hope of his support. ...'[6] '... When, early in 1792, George Ponsonby attempted to bring in a measure to allow free trade between Ireland and the East, Parsons treated him to a scathing reproof, to the accompaniment of government applause and manifest disappointment from the opposition. ...' The resentment of government and opposition fused to a considerable extent during the period 1793–5, when Grattan was to be found supporting the measures, particularly the wartime emergency measures, of Dublin Castle. In February 1794, Edward Cooke, under-secretary at the Castle, wrote waspishly: '... Sir L. Parsons, a disciple of Flood, with much of his policy and little of his ability, and bearing much hated to Grattan, and full of lofty pretensions as a justification for ingratitude to government, thought he saw an opportunity of making himself of some importance. ... [So] Grattan had a fine occasion to show his sincerity and to expose Parsons, which he did with much ability. ...'[7]

In 1794 he ... professed to question the sincerity of [Earl] Fitzwilliam's administration but, having elicited from Grattan a promise that the measures advocated by him in opposition would find a place in the ministerial programme, he offered government his cordial support. He was the first to notice the disquieting rumours in regard to Fitzwilliam's recall, and on 2 March 1795 moved for a short money bill. He attributed the existence and strength of the United Irish conspiracy to the misgovernment that followed Fitzwilliam's recall, and on 5 March 1798 moved for a committee to inquire into the state of the country, and to suggest such measures as were likely to conciliate the popular mind and to restore tranquillity; but his motion was rejected by 156 to 19. ... . According to Lord Cornwallis, Parsons originally declared in favour of a Union upon "fair and equitable principles".[8] The charge, Parsons declared, was unfounded, and he was certainly a most uncompromising opponent of that measure in parliament. On 24 January 1799 he moved an amendment to the address to the crown to expunge a paragraph in favour of a Union, which was carried by 109 to 104; but a similar amendment to the address on 15 January 1800 was defeated by 138 to 96; and he weakened his position by failing to substantiate a charge he preferred against the government of having dispersed a meeting of freeholders in the King's County by military force.

[During the eighteen years for which Parsons sat in the Irish parliament, he] '... made a total of 54 speeches, intervening on every major question of the period except the regency bill. Yet he could not claim even one decisive victory. ... The explanation of his failure is to be found in his unwavering loyalty to the teachings of Henry Flood. Before the French Revolution, Parsons's advocacy of financial retrenchment and parliamentary reform was a wise attempt to extend the integrity and independence of the Irish parliament. Yet the Revolution introduced new elements in Irish political life, the significance of which he never fully appreciated. He failed to see that the opposition must achieve a far greater measure of cohesion and common purpose, if it were to justify itself in the eyes of newer and more extreme forces of popular unrest. By standing apart from the more organised opposition which emerged from the Whig Club ... and owed its leadership to Ponsonby and Grattan, Parsons was weakening the best chance of winning a measure of reform, and impeding the formation of a strong united opposition, the absence of which was, in the last resort, the real reason for the government's success in the Union controversy. The results on his own career were disastrous. Although for a brief period he found himself the head of a small minority group who opposed the war, he continued for the remainder of his days in the Irish parliament isolated and with very little influence. Even during the Union controversy, he never really identified himself with his colleagues of the opposition. ...'

Some other, broader reasons for his isolation may be suggested (and are implicit in the already-quoted comments of Denis Browne). '... In a smaller sphere ... [he was] not unlike his [older] contemporary, Lord Shelburne [with whom he corresponded[9]]: though able and intelligent, he was a somewhat solitary figure, whom his fellow landowners tended to think too clever for a gentleman. He had what they considered odd ideas: he refused to send his sons to a public school, and instead educated them (with startling success) at home; he took no interest in sport; he was reluctant to flog his soldiers, and because of this one of his officers had him ejected (on the grounds of "mistaken lenity") from the command of the King's County Militia in the critical year of 1798. At a time when the divine right of Greek and Latin was taken for granted in polite society, he came to the defence of Celtic literature – in support of an abortive legacy to found a chair for the study of the ancient literature of Ireland, left to Trinity College, Dublin, by Henry Flood ... . It is not surprising to find that he was also a friend of Maria Edgeworth, whose letters to him survive at Birr;[10] for the Edgeworth family had the same kind of cosmopolitan outlook and intellectual curiosity as the Parsonses.'

His defence of Celtic literature, which took the form of a short book called *Observations on the bequest of Henry Flood Esq. to Trinity College, Dublin, with a defence of the ancient history of Ireland* (Dublin, 1795), deserves particular examination. Though it is his most celebrated publication, it '...was and still is greatly misunderstood. ... The book begins with a recital of Flood's will, dated 27 May 1790. The principal provisions of the will were that all the estates in Kilkenny City and County settled by Flood's marriage settlement were to belong to his widow for her life, and thereafter were to pass in fee to Dublin University, which was to use the proceeds from them to found a professorship of Erse, to endow an annual Irish language prize, and to buy up books and manuscripts in that language. After this recital, Parsons goes on to make the following 'Observations': '... It has been said most untruly, and believed most absurdly, that it was Mr Flood's design, in his legacy to the College of Dublin, to bring the Irish language again into general use in this country. But his will shows that his only object was to have it studied by some men of letters, there being many curious and valuable records in that language which would throw a considerable light upon a very early era in the history of the human race, as well as relieve this country from the most unjust charges of ignorance and barbarism at a time when it was by far more enlightened and civilized than any of the adjacent nations. ... He has ordered by his will that, after all the manuscripts in the Irish language that can be purchased have been obtained, then those books and manuscripts in the languages that have an immediate affinity to the Irish shall be likewise purchased; thereby showing the great chain of thought that moved through his mind upon this subject ...'.

In the second part of the book, 'Defence of the ancient history of Ireland', Parsons entered on more contentious ground. But he '... did not contend that there was any direct contact between the two countries [Ireland and Ancient Greece], and he showed himself to be well aware that the Greek sailors did not venture so far from home. He suggested that knowledge of Ireland reached them by way of the Phoenicians ..., [and argued] that the trade of the Phoenicians was carried on, not merely with the tin mines of Cornwall, but also with the lead mines of Ireland. The implications of this suggestion have never been answered. ... It would seem, even now, that Parsons had a strong case. ... He was less convincing, however, when he made the suggestion that the Irish were themselves a Phoenician colony. ... The arguments of those who denied the antiquity of the Irish nation were [also] passed by with a reticence which is very disappointing. Nevertheless, he made a number of telling points against them. He believed that references hostile to Ireland in the classical authors were of no significance: the Irish civilisation was undoubtedly of a lower order than the civilisations of Greece and Rome, but this in no way detracted from its richness and antiquity. ...

This treatise was the first major work of scholarship in which Parsons engaged. His purpose had not been primarily academic, but merely to defend the honour of his friend. ... [The book] has the merit, rare amongst historical writings of the 18th century, of presenting a well-knit central argument, unimpaired by literary embellishment and over-description. It is founded upon a historical knowledge which, though nowhere profound, is proof of surprising industry during a time when the author was busily occupied with affairs in parliament. ...' As Parsons himself unassumingly concludes: '... Being no antiquarian, nor conversant with the history of those early ages any further than is necessary as a foundation for that of the more important ones which succeed, being also unacquainted with Irish language and therefore knowing nothing of these records but from translations and from conversations with those who have read the originals, should I ... have committee any errors, I trust they will be excused. A wish to do justice to the memory of a deceased friend, to vindicate the reputation of the ancient memorials of my country, and to stimulate those who have more leisure for such pursuits to investigate them further, induced me thus to step out of my path and give this brief argument upon this subject.' It must, however, be added that '... there is no evidence that during his active political career Flood ever drew attention to Ireland's Gaelic past ...'.

AFTER THE UNION

'... The Union came as a decisive turning point in ... [Parsons's] political career. His parliamentary activities were not interrupted, since he continued to represent his former constitutency of the King's County in the imperial parliament. Yet he made no further attempt to challenge the new constitution or to oppose the policies of the Irish administration. Henceforward, he co-operated closely with the government and turned his thoughts for the first time towards an appointment to public office. ... Several factors contributed to make him ambitious. His marriage in 1797 ..., and the birth of a young family shortly after the Union, introduced a settling influence into his affairs. More important, he had, since the death of his father [and of Flood] in 1791, come increasingly under the influence of his uncle, ... [the 1st Earl of Rosse, who] was responsible ... for obtaining his first offer of an appointment in the Irish administration. ...'

In many respects, however, Parsons was experiencing a problem common to most leading Irish parliamentarians of approximately his generation following the implementation of the Union. The Irish members who went to Westminster immediately after the Union '... were unusually young: in 1804, the average age of the non-Irish members was roughly forty-six, and that of the Irish members forty-one. ... The Irish members had a sharp eye to "the reversionary interest", were politically unreliable on questions concerning the Prince of Wales, and were therefore likely to have diagnosed ... [the experienced members from among their own ranks] as a bad reversionary bet. For much the same reasons as they were youthful, the Irish members were lacking in policial talent – "inevitable" House of Commons men, for the most part, listlessly performing the political functions of their social station. All but fifteen of the Irish members who sat at Westminster between 1801 and 1820, came from families who had sat in the Irish parliament; and these were the very families which, because of their parliamentary interest, had been widely ennobled. In 1805, Lord Dunlo, who had been considered for the chancellorship of the Irish exchequer in 1803, succumbed to his father's earldom of Clancarty; and in 1807, at the very time he was being considered ... [for the same office], Parsons succumbed to his uncle's earldom of Rosse. ...'[11]

'Parsons was well described by Lord Hardwicke [Lord Lieutenant, 1801–6] as a country gentleman and an M.P. who was eager to take a part "in public business in parliament". ...

Sundry patronage was distributed to his family while Addington was Prime Minister, and his ... [appointment as a Lord of the Irish Treasury] was no doubt his reward for supporting Addington "in the most steady and honourable manner" and then doing the same for Pitt. However, he was not eager to support Lord Grenville and during May and June 1806 ministers were angry at the absence from parliament of one of their leading placemen. There is no indication, moreover, that he came to terms with the government before their resignation ...', and he was swift in declaring his support for the 'No popery' administration which succeeded in April 1807. Indeed, he pointed out to the new Chief Secretary, Sir Arthur Wellesley, that '... my dearest friend, Lord Rosse ..., met his unexpected fate in consequence of a cold he got coming to town to assist in asserting the King's prerogative in a severe season.'[12] In the following year, commenting on Parsons's pretensions to be elected a representative peer for Ireland, Wellesley argued: '... These seats ought to be given to the persons resident in Ireland who have the largest influence and the greatest property and are in themselves of the most respectable character; and on this ground Lord Rosse is the man of all others who ought to be appointed. ...' And, he subsequently added, '... in this case we may hope to derive from the promise the support of three members [two for King's County and one for County Longford] on the first day of the session'.[13] In 1809, Parsons, now 2nd Earl of Rosse, was elected a representative peer, as well as being appointed joint postmaster general.

The member for Co. Longford to whom Wellesley referred had been returned through the influence and freeholder votes of the 1st Earl of Rosse, which continued to be placed by his widow at Parsons's command; the two members for King's County were closely connected with Parsons himself. His '... long defence of the Irish parliament during the Union controversy ... had done much to diminish [earlier local] ill-feeling against him ... . His marriage in 1797 to Alice Lloyd had won the alliance of one of the chief families in the south of the King's County. When he was raised to the peerage, in 1807, he was able to ensure the election of his brother-in-law, Colonel [Hardress] Lloyd, to succeed him as representative for the King's County, and Lloyd voted according to ... [his] directions in all parliamentary divisions. ... [In 1818, Lloyd was succeeded by Parsons's brother and in 1821 by] Lord Oxmantown ..., [who] sat in parliament until 1835 ... . Thomas Bernard, the second member for the county, appears to have also allied himself with ... Parsons, although [owing much to the sponsorship of the earl of Charleville, and] outwardly preserving an appearance of independence. ...' '... The Ponsonbys probably also had some influence: Bowes Daly, [owner of the Philipstown estate and] a representative from 1790 to 1802, was politically connected with their party, and in 1806 George Ponsonby, the Irish chancellor, had some thoughts of setting up his nephew, George, at the general election. This came to nothing and there was no contested election in this period.

Nevertheless, even uncontested elections could be preceded by exciting and significant events. ... [Parsons], for example, later cited the circumstances surrounding the election of 1818 as a "slight shadow" of what would happen in Ireland if Roman Catholics were admitted to parliament: "... My brother [John Clere Parsons] was a candidate for this county. His opponent was Mr Malone, whose mother was a catholic, and though he was a protestant and a peaceable gentleman, we were so threatened with mobs that the freeholders began to be afraid of venturing to the election, unless they voted for Mr Malone ... . A principal inducement to him [Malone] to decline was the preservation of the peace, for [he feared] that the county would soon become a horrid scene of outrage if the election had proceeded ...".' By the time of

Parsons's death, in 1841, the situation had been reached where '... The Roman Catholic tenants on Rosse's estate who live in and near to Birr are allowed to register their families: those at a distance remain unregistered, ... [as] the influence of the agent ... will avail but little when placed in opposition to the will of the priest or to the commands of the agitating agents ...'[14]

Parsons served as Joint Postmaster General from 1809 to 1831.[15] '... The Irish Post Office was ... a comparatively new office. During the greater part of the 18th century the British Post Office, acting under the powers bestowed by the Post Office Act of 1711, functioned in Ireland. But in 1784, consequent upon the constitutional changes of 1782, the Irish parliament passed an act setting up an Irish post office under an Irish postmaster general [and later, for reasons of patronage, under two]. At the beginning of the 19th century the Irish postal establishment comprised about 70 senior officials, clerks and sorters and over 50 porters and letter carriers, all attached to the head office in Dublin. And in addition there were about 260 post towns, each with its deputy postmaster, scattered about the country. ... The routine administration of the office was ... carried on by the secretary, Sir Edward Lees, an experienced official. ... Well paid (his emoluments were over £1,400) he was a zealous official, ready to carry a large load of responsibility and to make improvements in the service. Besides the secretary's office there were nearly a dozen departments in the Dublin post office. ... By 1822 the total post office staff in Dublin amounted to over 100 senior officials, clerks and sorters, over 140 letter carriers and porters, and 85 mail guards. In the country there were over 430 post towns, each with a deputy post-master who might employ a small staff. ... By contemporary standards the Post Office was a large and complex department. The number of post towns increased by sixty per cent between 1797 and 1822 ...', and the Irish Post Office was responsible for mail services between Ireland and Great Britain as well as within Ireland itself.

'... The task which confronted ... [Parsons] at the Irish Post Office was not an easy one. He did not enjoy undisputed authority; ... Post Office affairs were administered by two joint Postmasters General, among whom the senior was his colleague, Lord O'Neill. ... Chief authority was exercised, not by the Postmasters, but by the Secretary, who issued all warrants for payment on his own signature alone. There was no recognised system of accounting. ...'

'... In theory boards [presided over by the Joint Postmasters General] were held, minutes bearing the heading "Present the Earls". In fact, the Postmasters General infrequently came to the office and were rarely, if ever, there together. Indeed, the Secretary asserted in 1824 that he had only once seen Lords Rosse and O'Neill in the same room, and that was at Parsonstown. In practice the Secretary ... ran the office, reporting to the Postmasters General and securing the sanction of one of them. For extraordinary financial expenditure he was careful to obtain their joint signatures in advance, since otherwise he was afraid he might find himself liable. When there were differences of opinion between the Postmasters General, Lees "experienced considerable difficulty", but, he explained, "without apprising the Postmasters General in all cases of the variance which has existed between them, I have endeavoured on my own responsibility to do the best I could". ...'

'... Parsons's first objective was to produce a revised and much more efficient system of account. His arrangements, which came into force on 3 January 1810, appear to have been based on the practice of both the English Post Office and the Irish Treasury. In future all payments were to be subjected to a system of "checks and control". Vouchers must be produced on every occasion, sworn to by the heads of the departments concerned, and laid before the

Commissioners of Accounts at the end of the year. All warrants were to be submitted by the Secretary to one of the Postmasters General for his signature, and this provision was later extended to require the signature of both the Postmasters, since Parsons wished to exercise a personal supervision over all expenses. (On one occasion, while absent in London, Parsons found that O'Neill had made a disadvantageous agreement with contractors, which would result in a loss of £60,000 to the Post Office.) At the same time, he inaugurated a vigorous programme of financial retrenchment, which resulted in an annual saving of £10,000. These measures appear to have been highly successful. ...

In 1813, he endeavoured to improve the arrangements for the conveyance of mail to England; in order to shorten the voyage, mail was to be despatched from Howth instead of Dublin. There were to be three vessels, ... constructed in such a way that there could be no access to the cargo, and coaches were to be provided with an iron safe, for the safety of government despatches. Mail services from Howth were carried on for a period of several months, but ceased when objections were raised by the English Post Office. ... Parsons's efforts to improve internal mail services were more successful. ...' 'In 1815, Bianconi, the proprietor of a great fleet of long cars, the "bians", which travelled regularly and with surprising speed even through the most difficult country in Ireland, began his long association with the Post Office. At first by contracts with the deputy postmasters and later, after 1830, by contract with the Post Office, he carried the mails over a large area in the south and west, his cars being only slowly superseded by the railways. ...' An act of parliament passed in 1818 with Parsons's enthusiastic support required grand juries to levy large sums of money for the improvement of mail-coach roads. As a result of the improvements effected by this act, he was enabled to increase the average speed of the coaches from four to five Irish miles per hour, and make more satisfactory agreements with the contractors.

These reforms met with considerable opposition from the Secretary, Sir Edward Lees. The latter was particularly hostile to Parsons's requirement [of August 1812] that all warrants should bear the signature of both Postmasters General, since this imposed a considerable check on his own authority. ... [So he] took no notice of the regulation, and continued to issue warrants on the authority of one of the Postmasters alone. Early in 1816, it was [also] discovered that Lees had made considerable over-payments to an accomplice amongst the mail-coach contractors ... . In February 1816, Parsons made a formal complaint against Lees's conduct to the Chief Secretary, ... Robert Peel, and demanded an inquiry. "Unless the Postmasters General have a secretary on whose truth, fairness, directness and knowledge of business they can rely", he declared, "this important department cannot be properly conducted". No action was taken against Lees by the government. He remained at his position for the remainder of Parsons's tenure of office. Indeed, there is some reason for believing that the proceedings on this occasion only served to damage Parsons's reputation amongst his superiors. The Chief Secretary [Robert Peel] was also angry that he did not attend parliament more regularly ... .

In 1822, ... among new arrangements of the Irish administration, it was ... [proposed] that the office of postmaster general should be discharged by one person only. It was made clear to Parsons that, as he was junior to O'Neill, he would be expected to resign. Parsons objected strongly ..., [pointing out] that he had been responsible for performing the greater part of the duties of the office, that he had carried out a number of important reforms, and that there must be disastrous results for the Post Office if it were left in the sole charge of O'Neill, since most of the work must then fall on Lees, who was unfitted for responsibility. "I think it is of great importance to the public that a person accustomed to business and with diligent habits should have the control over him." [Parsons] asked for an alternative appointment, in which he might "again endeavour to be useful to the government", adding with a sense of material grievance that, unlike most other revenue officials, he was not entitled to a retiring allowance. ... [Ultimately, however, the old arrangement of Joint Postmasters General, and Parsons's services as one of them, were retained until 1831, when the Irish Post Office was merged with the British.] ...

Parsons's period of office as Postmaster General, while marked by many unhappy incidents, was certainly one of the most significant episodes in his career. ... Moreover, he '... left one lasting memorial ... . The General Post Office in Dublin, the construction of which began during the summer of 1814 to a design by Francis Johnston which Parsons had approved, was completed during his tenure of office. For some time it had been evident that more commodious post office premises in Dublin would have to be found. And the building he erected on Sackville Street in cut Portland stone with an ornamental portico supported by doric columns, was a work of considerable architectural merit ...'.

One of Chief Secretary Peel's grievances against Parsons was the latter's poor attendance record in the imperial parliament, where '... he spoke only infrequently. He disliked travelling to London, since it interrupted both life with his family and the intellectual pursuits with which he was now deeply engrossed, [to say nothing of his administrative labours at the Post Office]. Apart from the Catholic question, his speeches were mainly concerned with economic matters and were marked by a desire to safeguard the interests of Ireland under the Union settlement. In 1811, ... [when] government ... forced through a bill declaring bank-notes to be the equivalent of gold, and punishing refusal to accept them at their face value as a misdemeanour, Parsons stood out as one of the chief government supporters in the House of Lords. ... He wished the government's measure to be extended to Ireland, where many tenants in the north had been forced to pay their rent in bank-notes which were discounted by landlords. ...

In 1826, when there were attempts to repeal the usury laws which limited the rate of interest chargeable on borrowed money, ... Parsons contemplated the proposal with considerable anxiety, since it seemed to be a threat to the security of the landed classes. ... The prosperity of the landed classes, he believed, rested upon two safeguards, both of which must be preserved – the corn and usury laws. Free trade, whether in money or corn, must be resisted. ... His last speech, delivered in 1833, is interesting for the remarkable insight it gives into his feelings during these years in the imperial parliament. The occasion was the debate on the Church Temporalities Bill ... . The Union, he suggested, differed from other statutes in that it was an agreement made between two countries, the inviolability of which had been pledged by the British parliament. To challenge this agreement, was to provide an excuse for the disaffected elements in Ireland to engage in renewed agitation. ... "We who opposed the measure at the time, objected to it because we saw it must increase the number of absentees. ... We saw there were other evils likely to flow from the measure; but we did not anticipate that we should lose our Board of Treasury, our Board of Customs and Excise, our Boards of Stamps, of Imprest Accounts, our Barrack Board, our Board of Inland Navigation, our Board of Works and almost all our public establishments. But least of all did we anticipate that we should lose ten of our

INTRODUCTION AND ACKNOWLEDGEMENTS

bishops. ...." This was the only occasion when ... [he] spoke with a large degree of passion in the imperial parliament, and his speech recalled much of the spirit which had animated the earlier part of his career. ...'

On the two previous great measures affecting Ireland, Catholic Emancipation in 1829 and the Reform Act in 1830–32, he took no part. He gave silent (and constrained) support to the first, and sullenly absented himself from the debates on the second. Writing in September 1831, the Whig Lord Lieutenant, Lord Anglesey, complained: 'Lord Rosse will not stir. I have urged him in every way; and finally insinuated that there was a Ribband [ie. the Order of St Patrick] for him if he went. Nothing would do. ...'[16] It is indicative of changing times that the order of St Patrick, which later was honourably acquired by the 3rd earl of Rosse for his scientific achievements, had been offered to, and declined by, the 2nd earl as an inducement to vote against his political principles.

A less happy indication of changing times is Parsons's progressively hardening attitude on the Catholic question, which from prudential motives he revealed more fully in his private than in his public utterances and which was probably the dominant theme of his post-Union career. An earlier letter, of 1795, contains what are perhaps the first expressions of his disillusionment with the character of Irish Roman Catholicism and had been provoked by a catholic bishop's condemnation of a King's County militiaman for attending a service in a protestant church. The Bishop, wrote Parsons, '... offered to show me documents of his Church to prove that he was not at liberty to act otherwise, as if the ancient rubbish of the Vatican ought to be ransacked in these times for precepts of repulsion between our sects. ... Unless the liberal laity of the catholics trample down the superstitions of their hierarchy, there cannot be that union which I believe they wish among the people of this country.'[17] This episode is particularly significant in that it provides contemporary authority for the change of heart which Parsons later claimed to have undergone about this time. This claim is made in a series of letters of 1822, which include the trenchant passage:

> Were the Catholic Bill now intended, to pass, may it not drive away the upper classes of protestants? If the representation becomes catholic, will not the sheriffs, the grand juries, the officers of militia and of yeomanry corps, be in a few years catholic? Will not the patronage of government flow in the same line necessarily? Will the upper class of protestants brook this longer than until they can escape from it? Will they not, according as they can extricate their property from their family settlements, withdraw it and themselves from this country? I have no doubt that they will. And what security will England have after for the continuance of the connection? For a time, the catholics will be very submissive. They will vote with government until they get us much as possible into place and power, but the first moment that England by war, foreign or domestic, is in difficulty and enfeebled, they will break the connection and set up their own church and a government for themselves. The connection of these islands probably would not last fifty years.[18]

In this view of the threat which the catholics constituted to 'the connection' he was being entirely true to his discipleship, since Flood had never wavered from the principle that catholics must be excluded from political life in every shape or form.

THE PARSONS ESTATES AND THE DEVELOPMENT OF BIRR

'... The instruction for plantation in Ely O'Carroll had ordered that the first Sir Laurence should receive 1,000 acres. Under the patent of 1620 he was granted land in some 21 districts, lying within the O'Carroll barony of Ballybritt and the neighbouring barony of Eglish. Since the names of these districts can almost be identified with places situated a short distance from the town of Birr, it is reasonable to assume that the Parsons estates occupied a compact area extending north and east from Birr. Moreover, the original grant of 1,000 acres was ... [presumably greatly understated and was subsequently augmented by purchase]. The family received an additional 850 acres under the terms of the Cromwellian settlement, although they were subsequently forced to sell some property to pay off debt. Sir William, the 4th baronet, added further estates in Tipperary and Mayo through his marriage with Mary Clere, most of which passed to the younger brothers of ... [the] 2nd Earl ... . We have no accurate measurement of the area of the estates until the middle of the 19th century, when ... [the 3rd Earl] calculated it to be 16,914 acres. ... [The 2nd Earl] had, however, about 1810, estimated the value of his rents at "about £10,000" – a figure which falls remarkably close to that subsequently given by ... [the 3rd Earl], £10,671. ...'

More extensive than his patrimonial King's County estate was the estate which he had expectations of inheriting from his uncle, the 1st Earl of Rosse.[19] This was the Harman family's estate of Newcastle, near Ballymahon, County Longford. In 1742, Anne Harman, ultimate heiress to the Harman estate, had married – as his second wife – Sir Laurence Parsons, 3rd Bt. Sir Lawrence's son by his first marriage succeeded to the baronetcy and the Parsons estate, while his surviving son by the second marriage, the future 1st Earl of Rosse, succeeded in 1784 to the Harman inheritance (amounting, by repute, to nearly £8,000 a year and £50,000 in cash) and assumed the name Harman in lieu of Parsons. The new Mr Harman and his half-brother's son and successor, the future 2nd Earl, were closely allied politically; so much so that in 1792 the Lord Lieutenant successfully recommended Harman for the Irish peerage as '... Lord Oxmantown, with remainder to Sir L. Parsons ..., as by that means ... we got the goodwill of Sir L. Parsons, who is a very troublesome debater.' Another contemporary commentator added: 'Mr Harman has one daughter and is one of the richest men in the kingdom; I suppose he will marry her to Parsons.' This was a somewhat strained supposition. But, since the title of Oxmantown, and the earldom of Rosse to which Lord Oxmantown was promoted in 1806 with the same collateral remainder, had formerly been held by the senior branch of the Parsons family, it might reasonably have been supposed that Lord Oxmantown intended to unite his estates and titles in the person of Sir Laurence Parsons. This supposition, however, was unwarranted. In 1799, the 1st Earl's daughter had married, not his own nephew, but his wife's, the Hon. Robert King. On the 1st Earl's death in 1807, his estates passed to his widow, and on her death in 1838 to the Kings' second son, who double-barrelled his name to King-Harman. What is extraordinary about this affair is that the 1st Earl's intentions, which he had expressed fairly clearly to an outsider in 1799, were not known to the 2nd Earl at the time of the 1st Earl's death. Nor did he find out about them until 1818.[20]

It was possibly because he entertained false hopes of a great inheritance from his uncle that he embarked on a large-scale remodelling of Birr Castle. '... He appears to have been to a considerable extent his own architect ..., though he had a professional assistant, an architect or builder called John Johnston [not to be confused with Francis] ... There is a notebook ... at

Birr,[21] dating from about 1801–2, full of [Parsons's] little sketches of projects for the new work – for castellating the entrance front, for building a grand Gothic staircase at the end of the hall, for a new Gothic entrance gate from the town, and so on. The entrance gate was built much as shown in the sketches; the Gothic staircase was never executed, though a grant Gothic saloon or drawingroom was built along the river; the front was gothicised with a new facing of smooth, grey limestone, and there was further gothicising at the back. The new front was based on the simpler of the sketches, without, for instance, the great central turret shown, in one of them, rising from behind the battlements of the central porch. This porch, with its giant recessed arch, is now the dominant feature of the front; a drawing for it by John Johnston, showing it nearly but not quite as built, survives at Birr and is dated April 1803. It is a skilfully conceived feature, for its striking form diverts attention from the fact that the front of the house is only approximately symmetrical. In fact the wall to the right of the porch is set considerably further forward than that to the left; and the windows of the two sides by no means match each other. The proportions of this front were noticeably altered – not, perhaps, to their advantage – in the 1830s. ...

In undertaking ... [his remodelling] ... Parsons was in the fashion, for in the years after the Union a great deal of castellating was going on in Ireland. At the other end of the county, for instance, ... [the] Earl of Charleville had started in 1800 to build his great new castle at Charleville. This must surely have acted as a stimulus at Birr ... . Lord Charleville – for which posterity, other than his descendants, have every reason to be grateful – all but bankrupted himself by building his great new house. Parsons had ... more sense; he altered rather than rebuilt, and left untouched the 17th-century staircase and a number of Georgian interiors. Even so he spent, as he confessed, more money than he could afford. ...'

With a rental income of about £10,000 a year, *c.* 1810, augmented between 1809 and 1832 by his official income as Joint Postmaster General, but subject to annual interest and annuity payments of £3,000 and annual outgoings of £750 for quit rents and chief rents, he was barely in a financial situation to support an earldom. After the misunderstanding over the Harman estate was unravelled in 1818, the Dowager Lady Rosse consoled him with generous presents of cash, and added £6,000 to the marriage portion of each of his three surviving younger children. All told, her benefactions may have amounted to *c.* £25,000. When his elder son married an heiress in 1836, her marriage portion of £20,000 more than sufficed to pay off the then mortgage debt charged on his estate; and when her father died, she came into landed property valued at £80,000 and ultimately worth far more, and probably much cash besides.[22] Partly because of his mistaken expectations of the Harman estate, partly because of the financial relief afforded him by his aunt, and partly because of the transformation of the Parsons family's financial situation in 1836, Parsons was able to contribute significantly to the early 19th-century development of the town of Birr.

'... In these years ... Birr ... finally assumed the appearance that has remained little altered up to the present day. ... It was the seat of the quarter sessions and the market town of a prosperous countryside. Its glass works had long ago disappeared, and a brisk woolen trade which replaced it did not survive the 18th century; but the town had instead a big corn mill and two large distilleries and breweries. It had a theatre, and assembly rooms in Dooley's Hotel on the square. In the early 19th century, barracks for 2,000 soldiers were built a mile south of the town at Crinkill, and provided a handsome fillip for the local tradesman. The officers in the barracks and the family in the castle formed a social nucleus which, combined with the pleasantness of the town, attracted genteel society to come and settle or retire there. ... The town expanded rapidly; and owing largely to the taste and enthusiasm of ... [Parsons], it also expanded very pleasantly. The first development came in 1810 or '11, when the Protestants abandoned the old church and built a new one north of Duke Square. At the same time new entrance gates were formed to the castle grounds, and a new street laid out leading from the gates to the church. It had a tree-lined mall for evening promenading on its southern side, and the north side filled up quickly with pleasant, solid houses. The new street known as Oxmanstown Place or Oxmantown Mall, neatly expresses the essence of polite Irish provincial society of its time – the spaciousness, the Gothic church at one end and the Gothic gates to the great house at the other and, in between, the trees and houses with their trimly railed front gardens and simple but elegant fanlight. The church was designed by the John Johnston who had assisted ... [Parsons] in his Gothic improvements to the castle; it has slender Gothic pillars, plaster vaults, and an enfilade of galleries; the west gallery, once hung with scarlet drapery, was originally built as the Parsons family pew.

The Catholic counterpart to Johnston's Gothic lifts its slender and elegant spire at the other end of the town, where the Camcor river is crossed by a second bridge designed in the early 19th-century by ... [Parsons]. It was built in 1817, only a few years later than the protestant church, to the designs of Bernard Mullan. ... [Parsons] gave the site on which it was built, the quarry for the stone, and a £100 donation to the building fund; his son, Lord Oxmantown, ... laid the foundation stone. ... [In memory of his second son, John Clere Parsons, who died young in 1828, Parsons ... erected a little schoolhouse, in the form of an Ionic temple desgined by himself. It was built on the ground east of Duke Square, and a broad new street known as John's Place was laid out to the south of it, with a strip of garden in the centre. The new street proved as attractive as Oxmantown Mall had done, and some of the best houses in Birr were built on it. These must date from the 1830s though stylistically they could have been built twenty years earlier. ...'

Parsons's other memorial to his dead son was the last of his published works, *An argument to prove the truth of the Christian revelation* (London, 1834). Although his original purpose was to commemorate John Clere Parsons, '... his work eventually took the form of an extended theological discourse. It was begun during the autumn of 1829 and published almost exactly five years later, in November 1834. During this time, he withdrew himself almost completely from public life and engaged in a vigorous programme of study. His theme ... was no doubt inspired by his efforts to relieve the bitterness of his loss, but the work shows little trace of emotionalism or religious fervour. It draws its main support from the conclusions of contemporary scientific investigators, which he discussed with remarkable confidence and knowledge. The timing of the work is significant. It was published one year after Bakewell's *Philosophical conversations* and fourteen years earlier than Darwin's *Origin of the species*. Thus, it belongs to a period which saw the emergence of the theory of natural evolution, as enunciated by Bakewell and formulated by Darwin. ... Although he [Parsons] accepted the main features of the traditional account of the Christian revelation as given in the bible, he subjected them to a searching examination for scientific truth. In this, he was following directly in the tradition of Malthus, Buffon, Erasmus Darwin, Lamarck and other writers of the late 18th and early 19th centuries, all of whom brought scientific knowledge to bear upon philosophic problems.

His own contribution to that tradition was to make what was probably the first systematic attempt to assemble the evidence of scientific investigations in support of orthodox Christian belief. ...'

THE 3RD, 4TH, 5TH AND 6TH EARLS OF ROSSE

Girouard concludes:

'[In 1836, Laurence Parsons (1800–67), Lord Oxmantown and, from 1841, 3rd Earl of Rosse], ... married Mary, the elder daughter of John Wilmer Field of Heaton Hall, near Bradford, one of two Yorkshire heiresses who brought ... [considerable wealth] to Birr in the 19th century [as well as family and estate archives to enrich the contents of the Muniment Room]. Mary Field seems to have been talented as well as rich. [She was a major and pioneering photographer; and] she is said to have designed, and even helped to make in the estate forge, the splendid Gothic cast-iron gates on the main entrance and the gate-tower at Birr; these were made on the estate from her maquettes, some of which still survive. Generally speaking, the mid-19th-century years at Birr are typical of their period in their cheerful and unselfconscious mixture of the functional and the unfunctional, with pioneer suspension bridges and telescopes coming into existence at the same time as sham fortifications and Gothic embellishments, and the 3rd Earl climbing the ladder to the platform of his observatory, in order to record nebulae from between elaborately crenellated walls. ...'

The 3rd Earl's experiments (continues the 6th Earl, in an article on his great-grandfather published in *Hermathena: A Dublin University Review*, No. CVII, 1968) '... concerning reflecting telescopes started soon after leaving Oxford, the first results being published as early as 1828 in the *Edinburgh Journal of Science*. The previous largest telescope in the world had been that constructed by Sir William Herschel at Slough; but, since he had died in 1822 without ever publishing any details about his methods of casting and polishing specuila, much pioneer work had to be carried out before any actual construction could take place. ... [In view of this, the 3rd Earl's] engineering achievements were as remarkable in their way as his astronomical discoveries. No expert advice of any kind was available to him; he was his own technician and all the work, much of it excedingly complicated and delicate, had to be carried out by local men trained wholly by himself. The very tools and machinery, together with the furnaces in which to fashion them, had necessarily to be produced on the spot. After many experiments, he fixed on an alloy of copper and tin, in proportion of four to one, as the ideal material for a speculum; and he invented in 1828 a steam engine with which to grind it to the correct optical shape with absolute accuracy and then to polish it. The difficulties of such original work were immense, and it was not until 1839 that a 3-foot speculum was finally cast and then mounted similarly to the Herschel instrument. Photographs of this exist today, since it continued to stand beside the Great Telescope for many years, and details of its construction were published by the Royal Society in 1840.

But, though the 3-foot telescope was responsible for some useful observations, the principal result was to stimulate him to go ahead at once with constructing a reflector of double that size, half again as large as the biggest ever before made. The greater the size the greater the strain on the very brittle material during the cooling process; and twice the speculum split. Refusing to be discouraged, he persisted in his efforts, which were finally crowned with success in 1843. Building on the structure with which to manoeuvre it had meanwhile gone ahead. Two solid stone walls 70 feet long and 50 feet high were built on either side, between which was slung a tube 58 feet long, at the base of which was placed the reflector. Owing to its unprecedented size, by the standards of that day, the practical difficulties of working it must alone have been well-night insuperable. It was unquestionably cumbersome to manoeuvre and a whole team of men had to be in constant attendance; and instant precision was essential, since its field of vision was distinctly limited. But its magnifying powers were so spectacularly greater than any previously available that these limitations scarcely mattered.

By the beginning of 1845 the Great Telescope, with its 6-foot reflector, was finally ready for use; and it was formally opened in typically Victorian style by a Church of Ireland Dean, walking throughout the length of the tube wearing a top hat, and with an umbrella raised over his head, to demonstrate its immense size. In March of that year the speculum received its final polishing and two distinguished astronomers, Dr T. R. Robinson of Armagh Observatory and Sir James South, were invited to participate in the first observations. The Irish climate is not exactly renowned for its clear skies and the equinoctial gales were exceptionally provoking that spring; but there was just sufficient time in which to note the spiral character of the "Whirlpool" nebula before the disastrous scale of the Great Famine became evident and all energies had to be diverted to fighting it. ... It is said that my great-grandparents devoted all their time and most of their income to relief work throughout the time of the Famine. Not only did my great-grandfather take the widespread suffering very much to heart, but he had also weighty official responsibility as Lieutenant of the county and Colonel of its militia.

Certain it is that astronomical observation with the Great Telescope only began in earnest in 1848; but after that date it was in almost continuous use. Though a considerable amount of work was done in connection with the planets, especially Jupiter, the main concentration was on the nebulae. Herschel had been able to see these with his telescope and had indeed speculated on the possibility that they might be galaxies, or star systems, outside and altogether separate from our own. But it had not been powerful enough for him to detect their spiral forms. It was reserved for the Birr telescope to make this vital discovery, which led directly to the conclusion, which is now proved to be correct, that these galaxies may be at least as numerous as the 100,000 million stars, or suns if you prefer, which compose our own. So distant are many of them that we do not see them as they are today, but as they were millions of years ago. ... In the mid-19th century all this was totally uncharted ground. It was essential to record the observations accurately and photography was yet in its infancy, though it was to be much used in later recordings. The really exciting discoveries were all made in the early years and the details had necessarily to be drawn by hand at the time. Fortunately my great-grandfather was as able a draughtsman as he was an astronomer – quite surprisingly so when some of his drawings are placed alongside modern radio photographs of the same subject. ... He must have enjoyed unusually fine eyesight as well as powers of deduction. Such aptitude is apparently recorded of a number of noted astronomers of the past, among them Galileo.

Mr Patrick Moore ... points out that "no other telescope in the world at that time could show the spiral shapes, because no other telescope could collect enough light. If astronomers wanted to see the spirals, they had to come to Birr Castle. Let it be added at once that Lord Rosse was only too ready to share his great telescope with others. All were made welcome and a steady stream of visitors came, from all over the world." For more than half a century, to the end of my grandfather's life, Birr became an international scientific centre. Everything of moment achieved there, unlike so much astronomical work of the past, which had been mostly carried out by professionals, often anxious to keep their secrets to themselves, was recorded at once in the various scientific journals of the day, in the *Proceedings of the Royal Irish Academy* and *Royal Astronomical Society*, or in *The Philosophical Transactions of the Royal Society*.

Recognition was not slow in coming. He had become a member of the Royal Astronomical Society as long ago as 1824 and of the Royal Society in 1831. He presided at the British Association meeting in Cork in 1843. He served as President of the Royal Society from 1849 to 1854, and received its Royal Medal in 1851. In that same year he was also a Commissioner of the Great Exhibition, in local celebration of which a memorable firework display was staged in front of Birr Castle, which was pictorially recorded in the *Illustrated London News* at the time. Foreign honours also came his way. He had considerable correspondence with Russian scientists and was elected a member of the Imperial Academy of St Petersburg in 1853. Two years later, on the occasion of the Paris Exhibition of 1855, Napoleon III created him a Knight of the Legion of Honour. But there is reason to believe that, of all the honours bestowed on him, he appreciated the Irish ones most of all. From early years he was a member of the Royal Irish Academy; in 1845 he became a Knight of St Patrick; and in 1862 Chancellor of [Dublin] University. ...

Mathematicians have a reputation for aloofness and austerity, ... but ... my great-grandfather was ... kindly and genial, and inspired affection in his workmen equally with members of his own family. In view of his attainments, he was also singularly unpretentious and simple in his approach. When looking at any portrait of him, probably serenity is the quality that first comes to mind. His wife shone in her own right as a woman of high character and intelligence. ... Among other interests, she was a pioneer photographer and one of the founders of the Irish Photographic Society. The many distinguished visitors who came to Birr on account of the telescope had a uniformly high regard for both her personal and intellectual qualities. She was an equally devoted wife and mother and subsequently showed her conscientiuousness with regard to her sons' education by taking a house in Dublin, when the two youngest entered ... [Trinity] College shortly after their father's death. ...

[The 3rd Earl's] health began to fail at the comparatively early age of 65 and he suffered a good deal during the last two years of his life. In the summer of 1867 a house was taken at Monkstown on the coast of Dublin Bay, so that he could benefit from the fresh sea-air. But a tumour developed on his knee and he died there on October 31st of that year. ...

What importance should be accorded to my great-grandfather's work when it is viewed, as it now can be, in perspective? It has became increasingly evident with the years that he was altogether greatly ahead of his time. Though primarily an astronomer, the range of his scientific interests was extraordinarily wide. His engineering abilities have already been noted. He had an extensive knowledge of chemistry, which he put to good use. Also he was responsible for the first known proposal for the armour plating of warships when he composed an elaborate memoir on the subject for the Admiralty at the time of the Crimean War. By an odd coincidence the Secretary of State for War, to whom it was addressed, was my great-great-grandfather on my mother's side, the Earl of Lincoln. I am sorry to say that the Admiralty treated the proposal as disdainfully as they were later to treat his youngest son's original proposal for the steam-turbine thirty years later.

The tremendous contribution to knowledge of his discoveries in the skies was on the other hand fully and generally recognised in his day. At the same time many other scientists remained sceptical of certain of his more revolutionary deductions. They were inclined to think that he had read more into what he had seen than was actually warranted. It can be fatally easy for scientists to fall into just that error, but, as I have mentioned earlier, he did in fact enjoy outstanding powers of vision as well as of intellect. The advent of radio-astronomy has enabled us to know for certain how justified the deductions made by him from his observations with his telescope were. And quite extraordinarily correct they are mostly now proved to have been, and furthermore absolutely relevant to most of the pioneer work at present being undertaken with the aid of radio telescopes, though carried out more than a century ago. ...

It is Sir Bernard Lovell who first explained to me the relevance of much of my great-grandfather's work to that of today ...: "... The achievements of the 3rd Earl of Rosse will live forever in the annals of astronomy. He succeeded in an almost impossible task, the measure of which can be appreciated when it is remembered that his telescope remained the largest in the world for three quarters of a century, and that in these islands his telescope was only superseded in size a few months ago – although all the resources of modern knowledge and technology and a vast sum of money were devoted to the task for two decades. It is a pleasant thought that this successor to the 3rd Earl's telescope was built by the firm founded by his youngest son. The Birr Telescope is a monument to the 3rd Earl's skill in engineering and optics; the results he obtained with it are a remarkable tribute to his observational skill and to his insight that such a device would record more of the depths of the universe than man had yet conceived. I have before me two illustrations of the nebula in Canes Venatici – a galaxy more than ten million light years away in space. One is a drawing made by Lord Rosse as he saw it in the Birr Telescope. The other, a photograph taken a century later by the 200-inch telescope on mount Palomar. The identity of the two is dramatic and the spiral form of the galaxy is shown with far greater clarity in the drawing. It is to the everlasting credit of Lord Rosse that he discovered the spiral structure of the nebulae, and thereby opened an avenue of exploration which today has led us into the inconceivable depths of space and time."

Scientific discoveries continued to be made at Birr for a further forty years [after 1867], to which brief reference should be made. The four sons of the house were educated at home by private tutors, all of whom were well versed in the sciences and acted also as practical assistants to their father in his astronomical work. One of them later became, as Sir Robert Ball, Astronomer Royal for Ireland. The eldest son, Laurence, who succeeded as 4th Earl of Rosse, carried on the astronomical tradition and was possibly an even more ingenious mechanic than his father. Though he continued to make use of the Great Telescope for demonstration purposes, he concentrated his main energies on discoveries concerning the Moon. He was the first man ever to measure its heat, with an instrument evolved by himself which still exists at Birr; and he also drew the first map of its surface, now seen to be surprisingly accurate. He too ... became in later life the Chancellor of ... [Dublin] University. The second son, Clere, became a highly successful railway engineer and was responsible for constructing railway lines throughout the world, especially in South America ... . Only the third son, Randal, eschewed science altogether and showed his individuality by becoming a Canon of the Church of England. ...' '... His youngest brother', concludes Girouard, 'Sir Charles Algernon Parsons, became one of the great pioneer figures of modern science through his development of the steam turbine. The story is well known of how his turbine-propelled vessel, the *Turbinia*, made rings round the British Navy at the naval review of 1897, leading inevitably to the general adoption of the stream-turbine for the propulsion of ships, and the transformation of the fleets of the world. ...'

Patrick Moore writes (*Ireland of the Welcomes*, vol. 17, No. 1, May-June 1968, pp. 11–12): '... Unfortunately, the intricate, rather cumbersome mounting of the great 72-inch telescope was hard to maintain. It had never been easy to handle, and in the latter part of the 19th century more modern instruments came into use, smaller than the Birr reflector but much more convenient to use. Gradually the mounting became unsafe, and the telescope was used less and less. During the latter stages of its career, its role was mainly in demonstration; its most important work had been done earlier, and it was last turned to the sky in 1908, the year in which the 4th Earl died. Yet the observing work was not confined to the 72-inch, and there were many famous astronomers who worked at the Observatory. Among them were J.L.E. Dreyer, a Dane, who afterwards became Director of Armagh Observatory and who drew up the classical catalogue of star-clusters and nebulae ...; Sir Robert Ball, ...; Dr [Ralph] Copeland, who went from Birr to the premier astronomical position in Scotland, and so on. ...'

The 4th Earl of Rosse followed the matrimonial as well as astronomical tradition established by his father. In 1870 he married Frances Cassandra Harvey-Hawke, only daughter and heiress of the recently deceased 4th Lord Hawke. As a result of this marriage, the Hawke, originally Harvey, seat of Womersley, near Doncaster, and the rest of the Hawke estates in Yorkshire (including the site of the battle of Towton), came into the possession of the Earls of Rosse. The 5th Earl succeeded his father in 1908 and died young – of wounds received in the First World War – in 1918. Mainly because of his short life, he is the least well-documented of the Earls of Rosse, apart from the 1st. In 1911 he sold the remaining Heaton and Shipley estate, outside Bradford, which Mary Field had brought into the family. His wife, too, was from Yorkshire; she was Lois Lister Kaye of Denby Grange, Wakefield. Although she was not an heiress, it was as a result of this marriage that papers of her grandparents, parents, uncle, brother and sister (respectively the 6th Duke and Duchess of Newcastle, Sir Cecil Edmund Lister Kaye, 4th Bt, Lady Adeline Beatrice Lister Kaye, Sir John Pepys Lister Kaye, 3rd Bt, Sir Kenelm Lister Kaye, 5th Bt, and Adeline, Countess de la Feld) eventually came to rest at Birr Castle. They include a distinctly unusual modern archive relating to coal-mining at the Denby Grange colliery in the period just prior to the establishment of the National Coal Board.

The 5th Earl's elder son succeeded in 1918 as a minor, but because of the literary and artistic friendships made by him at Oxford in the 1920s, his correspondence is of historical significance from these early days to his death in 1979. In 1936 he married Anne, daughter of Leonard and Maud Messel of Nymans, Handcross, Sussex, and sister of the painter and designer, Oliver Messel. Together Lord and Lady Rosse became prominent in all manner of architectural, horticultural and conservationist organizations, Irish and British, Georgian and Victorian, and kept up an intimate correspondence with numerous prominent figures in the world of literature and the arts, including Sir Harold Acton, Sir John Betjeman, Robert Byron, James Lees Milne and many more besides. His most significant activities include his share in plant-hunting expeditions to China and elsewhere, his work for the International Dendrological Union/Society, and his various public roles in the U.K. as Chairman and later President of the Georgian Group, Chairman of the Standing Commission on Museum and Galleries, Chairman of the Properties Committee of the National Trust and Deputy-Chairman of the Trust. The friendships, and contribution to artistic and public life, of the 6th Earl and Anne Countess of

Rosse ensure that the Rosse family (and archive) sustains its interest and importance, in U.K. as well as Irish terms, right up to the present day. The 6th Earl died in 1979 and his widow in 1992.

The emphasis of this Introduction has been on the post-1700 Irish content of the Rosse Papers. It remains, therefore, only to point out that what makes them unusual by Irish standards is the wealth of 17th-century and of non-Irish material which they contain. The 17th-century Irish material, as well as being covered by the summary list of Section A, is the subject of a special, descriptive list compiled by Ms Aoife Leonard in 1988–9 and financed by the Carroll Institute. This is printed in full as an appendix. Foremost among the non-Irish material are the scientific papers of the 3rd and 4th Earls (Sections J and K). These are clearly – like some of the papers of the 6th Earl – of international importance, and have already been made available to an international readership. Present also among the Rosse Papers are three (indeed more) distinct family and estate archives relating to Yorkshire (Sections G, H and N) and deriving from the Yorkshire women whom the 3rd, 4th and 5th Earls successively married, the first two of them heiresses or co-heiresses to property in that county. Yorkshire, in fact, comes second only narrowly to Offaly as the best-documented county in the Birr Castle archive.

The present writer's involvement with the archive began as long ago as 1979. From then until his retirement in 1998, work on it was ongoing, if intermittent, and was carried out under the auspices of the Public Record Office of Northern Ireland, the institution best-placed to tackle an archive which so signally straddled the two jurisdictions and the Irish Sea. Since 2003, responsibility for concluding the task of sorting and listing has been assumed by the IMC, which has also contributed to the cost of providing a quantity of additional acid-free boxes for the Muniment Room at Birr Castle. As a preliminary to the publication of this volume, and as a means of updating the text in the future, the IMC has paid for the scanning of the PRONI typescript, much of which dated from an earlier era of PRONI technology.

The task of sorting and listing the archive has been prolonged, not simply because it was carried out on a very part-time basis, but also because the archive has kept on growing. This is due to the energy and activity of its owners, the present (7th) Earl and Countess of Rosse. The section of the archive appropriated to them (Section W) is, not surprisingly, in a state of frequent accrual. Moreover, in a number of instances, archive material held by other family members has been annexed to the main archive at Birr – the most recent being material rendered homeless by the sale in 2005 of the family seat in Yorkshire, Womersley Park, near Doncaster. Within Ireland, legal and estate material unexpectedly came to light because a Dublin firm of solicitors tried, without authority from Lord Rosse, to destroy it. In Birr itself, the former Estate Office, which it was thought held material only of comparatively recent date, turned out to have in its recesses a large quantity of deeds, rentals, etc (the now Section Q), going back to 1604.

As a result, some aspects of the arrangement of the archive are not as logical as might be wished. However, the major inconsistencies have been mitigated by cross-referencing.

Over the years, a number of individuals and institutions have contributed to the sorting and listing of the archive. Mention has already been made of PRONI, the Carroll Institute and

Aoife Leonard. In the early 1980s, the late Professor P.J. Jupp came to Birr Castle on a number of occasions, and helped with the calendaring of the early 19th-century political correspondence – his own area of expertise – of Sir Laurence Parsons, 2nd Earl of Rosse. Much more recently, Emily Turner Simon, an undergraduate at Harvard who worked as an intern under the Practical Work Experience Programme operated by the Birr Scientific and Heritage Foundation, spent over three months in the Muniment Room helping to incorporate the newly arrived additions from Womersley and generally re-arranging the archive and updating the list. Her contribution was invaluable and her enthusiasm infectious. Over the period 2003–7, Mr T.D. Scott of WP Plus, Killinchy, Co. Down, laboured successfully to re-format the list and keep track of the multifarious insertions in it; this involved the scanning of a typescript dating back to 1979, and the correction of the numerous errors which scanning introduced. Over the same period, Dr Cathy Hayes, administrator to the IMC, and Dr James Kelly, one of the Commissioners, gave vital support on the part of the IMC.

Throughout the period 1979–2007, Lord and Lady Rosse have been unstinting in their encouragement, hospitality and help. While they multiplied the work involved by multiplying the archive, they also simplified it because of their knowledge of family history, science, botany, and so forth, and because of their willingness to respond to queries and generally muck in. Genealogical enquirers who wish to trace ancestors who were tenants or employees of the Parsons family, may well find that the documentation they seek is available on microfilm in PRONI; the following sub-sections of the list, all of them chosen for their high genealogical content, were microfilmed by PRONI (MIC/564): Q/16/1, Q/108,Q/128, Q/148,Q/239, Q/271 and Q/316. Researchers who require access to material uniquely available in the Birr Castle Muniment Room, are asked to make a contribution to the costs involved in giving access by taking out an annual subscription as Friends of the Birr Castle Archive. On this basis, Lord and Lady Rosse are able to run what is possibly the only family-operated archive service in Ireland, and administer the archive for the benefit of a growing number of scholars from all over the world. The Birr Castle archive is a considerable success story, for which much of the credit is fairly attributable to Lord and Lady Rosse themselves.

In the time which has elapsed between the completion of this text and its publication as a volume, two of the key contributors have, sadly, died: Professor P. J. Jupp in September 2006 and Mr T. D. Scott in October 2007. In recognition of their respective contributions, I have dedicated the volume to their memory

A.P.W. MALCOMSON

NOTES TO THE INTRODUCTION

1　For the tangled and somewhat conflicting information about the offices held by Sir William and Sir Laurence, see: John Lodge, *The Peerage of Ireland* ... (4 vols., Dublin, 1754), ii, pp. 60–71; and Victor Treadwell, *Buckingham and Ireland, 1616–1638* ... (Dublin, 1998), pp 55–6, 130–47 and passim. Treadwell's bibliography provides up-to-date guidance on further reading.

2　Rosse Papers, K/38.

3 The main difference is that the present writer's 1982 monograph on aristocratic marriage, which was cited at a number of points in the article, has since been re-written and republished as Malcomson, *The Pursuit of the Heiress: Aristocratic Marriage in Ireland, 1740–1840* (U.H.F., Belfast, 2006). The relevant page numbers in the new version of the book are cited in the notes which follow.

4 Parsons to Lord Redesdale, 3 May 1822 (Redesdale papers, Gloucester Record Office; PRONI, T/3030/13). This remarkable run of letters from Parsons, which has been quoted in a number of sources, was transcribed in full in Malcomson (ed.), *Eighteenth-Century Irish Official Papers in Great Britain: Private Collections, vol. ii* (Belfast, 1990), pp 459–68. Redesdale's replies are in D/28 of the Rosse Papers, to which photocopies of the Parsons originals have been added. Both sides of the correspondence are transcribed in the present volume.

5 Parsons to Sir Arthur Wellesley, 1808 (Wellington Chief Secretaryship papers, Southampton University Library; photocopies in PRONI, T/2627/3/2/286).

6 Robert Hobart to Lord Hillsborough, 3 July 1791 (PRONI, Downshire Papers, D/607/B/310).

7 Cooke to Evan Nepean, 7 Feb. 1794 (TNA, H.O. 100/51, ff 161–5).

8 This is difficult to reconcile with Cornwallis's own memorandum of their first, and perhaps only, conversation on the subject (Kent Archives Office, Stanhope/Pitt Papers, U.1590/C.67/8), in which Parsons expressed himself 'Disinclined – did not think he could be reconciled. ...'

9 Rosse Papers, D/1.

10 Rosse Papers, D/21.

11 Malcomson, *John Foster: the Politics of the Anglo-Irish Ascendancy* (Oxford, 1978), pp 446–7.

12 Parsons to Wellesley, 21 Apr. 1807 (PRONI, Wellington papers, T/2627/3/2/6).

13 Wellesley to Duke of Richmond, 11 Nov. 1808 and 18 Jan. 1809 (*ibid.*, T/2627/3/2/282 and 295).

14 Colonel Hardress Lloyd to Lord Downshire, 2 May 1841 (PRONI, Downshire papers, D/671/C/12/783).

15 His Post Office material (Rosse Papers, E/14) has been microfilmed by PRONI (MIC/512/10).

16 Anglesey to Lord Grey, 14 Sep. 1831 (PRONI, Anglesey Papers, D/619/28C, p. 188).

17 Parsons to Peter Burrowes, 1795 (Burrowes Papers, RIA, MS 23 K.53).

18 Parsons to Redesdale, 3 and 9 May 1822 (Rosse Papers, D/28).

19 This paragraph is taken from Malcomson, *The Pursuit of the Heiress: Aristocratic Marriage in Ireland, 1740–1840,* (Belfast, 2006), pp 90–91 and 194.

20 Parsons to Dowager Lady Rosse, 30 Sep. 1818 (Rosse Papers, D/7/97).

21 Rosse Papers, O/16.

22 Malcomson, *Pursuit of the Heiress*, pp 201–2.

ROSSE PAPERS

SUMMARY LIST

A/	DATE	DESCRIPTION
1–26	1595–1699: 1871	17th-century letters and papers of the two branches of the Parsons family, the Parsonses of Bellamont, Co. Dublin, Viscounts Rosse, and the Parsonses of Parsonstown, alias Birr, King's County. [N.B. The whole of this section is kept in the right-hand cupboard of the Muniment Room in Birr Castle. It has been microfilmed by the Carroll Institute, Carroll House, 2–6 Catherine Place, London SW1E 6HF. A copy of the microfilm is available in the Muniment Room at Birr Castle and in PRONI.]
1	1595–1699	Large folio volume containing *c.* 125 very miscellaneous documents, amateurishly but sensibly attached to its pages, and referred to in other sub-sections of Section A as 'MSS ii'. This volume is described in R. J. Hayes, *Manuscript Sources for the History of Irish Civilisation*, as 'A volume of documents relating to the Parsons family of Birr, Earls of Rosse, and lands in Offaly and property in Birr, 1595–1699', and has been microfilmed by the National Library of Ireland (n.526: p. 799). It includes letters of *c.* 1640 from Rev. Richard Heaton, the early and important Irish botanist.
2	1595–1699	Late 19th-century, and not quite complete, table of contents to A/1 ('MSS ii') [in the handwriting of the 5th Earl of Rosse (d. 1918)], and including the following entries: '1. 1595. Elizabeth Regina, grant to Richard Hardinge (copia). ... 7. 1629. Agreement of sale from Samuel Smith of Birr to Lady Anne Parsons, relict of Sir Laurence Parsons, of cattle, "especially the cows of English breed". ... 15. 1636, 19 February. A schedule of the lands and hereditaments for which William Parsons Esq. compounded (5$^1/_2$ pages). ... 17. 1636. Grant of lands of Bogoin, Clonbrany and Shangallagh to Dame Anne Parsons (copy). ... 21. 1638, 15 June. Order for "the remedy of defective titles" to William Parsons, brother of the late Richard Parsons, son of the late Sir Laurence Parsons, Knt, to whom the original grant had been made, concerning lands in the barony of Fermoy, Co. Cork. ... 25. 1639. Royal examination of William Parsons and Capt. William Peisley concerning the finding of arms at the house of John Carroll of Clonlisk. ... 35. 1641, 30 August. Instructions from the freeholders of the King's County to their representatives, William Parsons of Parsonstown alias Birr, King's County, and John Coghlan of Streamstown (original parchment, much strained, and paper copy – numerous autograph signatures). ... 39. 1641. List of properties (forfeited) in the counties Cork, Tipperary, Westmeath, Limerick and Longford, with "proprietors in 1641, denominations and to whom granted, number of acres, and rent received; endorsed, "forfiters [sic] Sir George Preston". ... 59. 1650. A "dunning" letter from William Davys to William Parsons. 71. 1668, October 29. Letter of the Duchess of Ormond[e] to Sir

A/2 *contd.*

George Preston at Dublin concerning his patent for the salmon
weir [in dispute between Preston and the corporation of
Limerick]. ... 125. Dressmaker's bill for "Madam Parshons", 1689.
... 133. Parchment deed -certificate stating the losses of Sir
L[aurence] P[arsons] during the siege of Birr Castle in 1687 and
1688, signed by numerous inhabitants of King's County (gentry),
1690 (on back, list of houses burnt and pulled down). ... 154.
Receipt for £55.12s.0d. by William Parsons's officers, 25 July 1642
(copy). ... [155–189 are all similar documents, 1641–3.] 205. List
of holdings in Cork with proprietors in 1641; endorsed, "A copy
of the lot in which I am concerned". ... 207. Petition by Sir
William Parsons, 2nd Bt, ... to ... parliament; refers (a) to Sir
Laurence Parsons's imprisonment and sentence of death, also to
William Parson's services in 1641; endorsed, "late Duc Ormond
[sic] told me not [to] give [in] this petition, and he'd serve me with
the King". ... 211. 1680/81. Accounts of money lent to and paid
for Sir Richard Parsons (of Bellamont? – 8^1/$_2$ pages foolscap ...). ...
219. Instructions for Capt. [Heward] Oxburgh, March 28, 1686
(7 pages foolscap). [221–247 also concern the Oxburgh affair, for
which see the Introduction.] ... 251. 1641. King Charles I's letter
concerning Concordatum money. 253. 1641. King Charles I's
letter concerning Brian McConnell "of the King's footemen [sic]",
to Sir William Parsons and Sir John Borlase. 255. Order of the
Lords Justices of Ireland [Parsons and Borlase] concerning
contribution for the fortification of Dublin by the parish of "St
Michael's".'

| 3 | 1607 | [?Bond or lease] concerning John Netterville of [Dowth?], Co. Meath, [and probably relating to the senior branch of the Parsons family, as Frances, daughter of the 1st Viscount Rosse, married the 4th Viscount Netterville. For the Nettervilles, see also D/18 and F/11.] |

| 4 | 1612–94: 1912: 1940 | Tattered vellum-bound volume covering the period 1612–94, microfilmed by the National Library (n.5483: p.5650), and containing, according to the *Hayes* description: memoranda about Star Chamber procedure, with notes of cases heard *c.* 1612–16; official letters relating to the plantations of Co. Longford and King's County, 1619–26; orders for the preservation of royal rents and revenues in Ireland, 1623; instructions to officers of the Exchequer as to their duties, 1623; instructions of Sir L. Parsons for his plantation at Birr and for markets in and the government of the town, 1626–7; near-contemporary particulars of the acreage of Ely O'Carroll; rentals of the estates of the Parsonses of Parsonstown, mostly in King's County, 1629–94; medical and kitchen recipés, 1645–52, including some to cure 'the stone'; and details of the births and baptisms of the children born to Sir Laurence Parsons, 1st Bt, and his wife, Frances, 1660–66; together |

A/4 *contd.*

with (and not covered by the microfilm) a lease of 1912 and legal papers of 1940 relating to the tolls, fairs and markets of Birr and reciting earlier grants back to the 1620s.*

5   1617–94

Folio volume similar to A/1 and described in other sub-sections of A as 'MSS i', containing 94 very miscellaneous documents. This volume has been microfilmed by the National Library (n.527: p. 795), and is described in *Hayes* as 'A volume (marked vol. ii [*sic* – i]) of papers relating to the Parsons family of Birr, dealing with private and public affairs, governing the period 1617–1692 [sic], ... mostly dated 1649–49'. In the appendix to the *First Report of the Royal Commission on Historical Manuscripts* (London, 1870), p. 127, it is described (by Sir John Gilbert) as 'A volume in large folio containing about 90 original letters and documents connected with the affairs of Ireland from 1626 [*sic*] to 1694, and having special reference to the transactions in the King's County and its vicinage'. In the appendix to the Second Report of the H.M.C. (London, 1874), pp 217–23, a full description is given. The following is a brief summary of some of the documents in the volume:

Agreement between Richard Roche Fitzdavid and Sir Laurence Parsons for the lands of Shinanagh, Co. Cork, 1620; acquittance from R. Smith and J. Knollis to L. Parsons for £84 for the redemption of two ploughlands in White's Island which Capt. Tent sold, 23 October 1625; order of composition between William Parsons and the Commissioners on Defective Titles, 4 April 1636; certificate of Sir B. Mayart, Justice of the King's Bench, of the acknowledgement by H. Sacheverell of Ballingtagort, Co. Armagh, of £50 due by him to Anne Parsons, 24 June 1636; order to William Parsons concerning Birr and other lands in King's County, signed by Ri. Bolton, Trinity 1636; similar order concerning Newtown and other lands in King's County, 1636; indenture between Lady Anne Parsons of Parsonstown and D. O'Kenedy of Tirreglasse, Co. Tipperary, and E. O'Kenedy of Portlaghan, Co. Tipperary, concerning the lands of Lackenboy, barony of Lower Orrnond, 14 January 1636[/7]; schedule of the lands and hereditaments for which William Parsons compounded with the Commissioners for Defective Titles, 15 June 1638; order by the Lords Justices and Privy Council to Capt. W. Peisley and William Parsons for searching the house of John O'Carroll of Clounlish, 13 November 1639; acquittance from Donnell MacCahirr O'Molloy to Lady Anne Parsons for £100 in redemption of a mortgage, 25 March 1640 [/41]; commission from the Lords Justices and Privy Council to William Parsons for raising footmen and horsemen in the country of Ely O'Carroll, 12 November 1641; letter from Phelem Molloy,

* See detailed calendar.

Catholique [sic] camp, Eglish, to William Parsons asking him
to join the King's [ie. Confederate] party rather than the
Puritans, and offering him protection, 17 March 1641[/2?];
account of sums due to William Parsons for the garrisons at
Birr from November 1641 to January 1642, April 1642; order
by the Lords Justices and Privy Council for 25 horse for Capt.
William Parsons and 100 foot for Capt. Chidley Coote, for the
defence of the castle of Parsonstown and the town and country
thereabouts, 1 April 1642; letter from Farell O'Kennedy to
William Parsons offering to arrange a meeting with Colonel
Richard Butler and discussing the military situation, 28 July
1642; letter from Ro. Moore [a Confederate colonel] to Lady
Anne Parsons discussing her request for the restoration of her
captured coach-horses, 5 September 1642; receipt from
Chidley Coote, J. Williams and Simon Tench for money
received from William Parsons, commander-in-chief of Ely
O'Carroll, 29 October 1642; note of money paid by William
Parsons to the soldiers under Capt. Carroll and to the garrisons
at Parsonstown, Ballyndarrow and Cloynakill from November
1641 to January 1642[/3]; articles of surrender for Birr Castle
signed by T. Preston, the Confederate General of Leinster, and
William Parsons, 20 January 1642[/3?]; order by the Lords
Justices and Privy Council for the repayment to William
Parsons of sums spent by him for Capt. Chidley Coote's
company, 3 June 1643; orders from Ormonde to Capt.
William Parsons to march with his troops to Jobstown,
Monasterevin and Kilgobbane, 3 and 20 June and 5 July
respectively; letter from R. Southwell to Capt. William Parsons
about the land of Ballyage and other lands round Kinsale, 11
June 1647; various papers relating to the military services of
Capt. William Parsons, 164 3–8; debenture under the Act of
Settlement awarding to Capt. William Parsons £1,112-odd for
arrears of pay from November 1641 to September 1643, 10
March 1663[/4]; terms of Birr Castle's surrender to the
Jacobites, signed by Colonel H. Oxburgh and Lieutenant-
Colonel R. Grace, of the one part, and Sir Laurence Parsons,
Bt, of the other, 27 February 1688 [/9?]; warrant from James II
to Francis Coghlan, High Sheriff of King's County, reprieving
for one month Sir Laurence Parsons, James Roscoe and
Jonathan Darby, lately indicted at Philipstown for rebellion,
and sentenced to death, 29 April 1689; further grant of
reprieve, 22 May and 7 August 1689 respectively; Colonel
Garret Moore's certificate to the Duke of Tyrconnell
concerning Sir Laurence Parsons's actions at Birr Castle, 8
March 1689[/90?]; and petition from Sir Laurence Parsons to
the commissioners for the management of the forfeited estates,
with the commissioners' order on it, September 1690.*

A/6	1617–94	Late 19th-century list of contents of A/5, similar to A/2.

7/1–2   July 1619   Document recorded in the *First Report* of the H.M.C. as 'Letters patent on parchment, from George, Duke [recte: Marquess] of Buckingham, Lord High Admiral, dated 28 July 1619, containing grant of Admiralty to Laurence Parsons, with seal and autograph of Buckingham'; together with an earlier deputation to Parsons from George Lowe, Vice-Admiral of Munster and Leinster, 23 July 1619. [George Lowe was one of the four patentees of the farm of the Irish customs. In 1614 he had bought out on their behalf the Irish vice-admiralty (which Buckingham's predecessor, Lord Nottingham, had granted to Nottingham's son). Their object in making this purchase was presumably to enable them to combat piracy and so enhance the proceeds from the customs farm. Lowe appointed one principal deputy, Humphrey Jobson, but seems to have employed a number of local deputies as well, Laurence Parsons being one of the latter. See Victor Treadwell, *Buckingham and Ireland, 1616–1628* (Dublin, 1998) pp 99–100. The 'grant of Admiralty' from Buckingham to Parsons was actually the appointment of Parsons as Judge of the Admiralty for Munster. (Judgeships of the Admiralty in Ireland were in the gift of the Lord High Admiral until 1785, when the patronage was resumed by the Crown.) This patent could not initially be found in Birr Castle (see Treadwell, p. 327, 48*n*), but has since turned up and bears reference A/7/2.]

8   1620–40: 1660–66   Clutch of papers, crudely bound with a parchment cover, microfilmed by the National Library (n.5483: p. 5650), and described in *Hayes* as 'Abstracts of leases of holdings in Parsonstown Manor made by Sir L. Parsons, 1620–40 ...'. The volume was turned upside down and used by the first Sir Laurence Parsons to record accounts for the period 1627–8. These last have been transcribed (1983) by Miss Frances Wilson, and the MS. and typescript of her transcript are included with the volume.*

8A   1620–21   Volume, not at present to be found in Birr Castle and probably missing since the period 1826–75, described in the second edition of Cooke's *Picture of Parsonstown*, which was published in the latter year under the title *The Early History of the Town of Birr or Parsonstown ...*, as an account book kept by Sir Laurence Parsons's steward, Francis Morley, and recording among other things the "... prices of provisions, work and materials for building in Birr and the end of 1620 and beginning of 1621 ...'.*

9   18 Oct. 1641– 20 Jan. 1642[/3]   [Capt. William Parsons's?] diary of the siege of Birr Castle in 1643 and other military events during the early years of the wars of the 1640s, re-bound in half calf in the early 19th century, and some pages of it detached with a view, apparently, to conservation, but without having so far been conserved (these pages have been

---

*   See detailed calendar.

A/9 *contd.*		placed loose between the front end-papers). The diary has been photostated by the National Library (MS. 13667). The rest of the volume consists of 44 pages of copies of deeds relating to the Savage family of Cottenhoe, Buckinghamshire, and to Sir Arthur Savage of Raban Castle (grandfather of Frances Savage, wife of Parsons's son, Sir Laurence, 1st Bt? – see T/1), 1609–35.*
9A	18 Oct. 1641– 20 Jan. 1642[/3]	Late 19th-century transcript of the diary, together with notes on it and other MSS in Birr Castle and elsewhere (all in the 5th Earl of Rosse's hand).
10	1646	Captain's commission in Colonel (Michael) Jones's regiment of horse for William Parsons of Birr, signed by Viscount Lisle.
11	1651: 1653	Copy, made *c.* 1820, of the will of Sir William Parsons, Knight and 1st Bt, the former Lord Justice, proved in the Prerogative Court of Canterbury, together with an incomplete, typescript copy (made by Rolf Loeber, [*c.* 1990]) of the will of William Parsons of Parsonstown, proved 1653, and typescript notes by Loeber on both wills.
12	1652–96	Volume described in the *First Report* of the H.M.C. as 'A thick folio volume of accounts of money, debts, payments, prices of articles, clothes, allowance, and other matters connected with the family of Parsons, from 1652–1696'.
13	1660	Power of attorney from Dame Catherine Parsons of Bellamont, Co. Dublin, mother and guardian of Sir Richard Parsons, 3rd Bt (and future 1st Viscount Rosse), to the Earl of Cork, Lord Digby and Sir John Cole, Bt, apparently to act as guardians on her behalf.
14	1662	Rules prescribed by the mayor and corporation of Galway for the regulation of one of the companies (or guilds) of the town. [The document is badly damaged, and the name of the company, among other things, is missing.]
15	[1666?]	Volume of near-contemporary copies of State Papers, etc, concerning the terms of the Acts of Settlement and Explanation, briefly described in the *First Report* of the H.M.C. as 'A folio volume of 90 pages containing copies of documents concerning Irish matters, from 1641–1666', and calendared in the Second Report.*
16	1668–75	Account book, of uncertain provenance, belonging to one David Johnston of Dublin, recording payments to him for such diverse commodities and services as deal-boards, iron, sugar, indigo, calicoes and funeral expenses; among the clients mentioned are Capt. Claud Hamilton, Thomas Bligh and 'Mr Westenra' (presumably Peter Westenra, ancestor of the Lords Rossmore, as Bligh was the ancestor of the Earls of Darnley).
17	1666[–*c.* 1720]	Small quarto volume containing medical and kitchen recipes, of Dorothy Parsons, daughter of Sir Laurence Parsons, 1st Bt. of Parsonstown, and incorporating some suggestions of 'Lady

* See detailed calendar.

A/17 *contd.*		Elizabeth Parsons', wife of Sir William Parsons, 2nd Bt, of Parsonstown?, with, loose in the fly-leaves, a pen and pencil drawing of 'Parsonstown House, 1668', showing alterations which appear to have been carried out and which, clearly, were intended to render the old castle more amenable to domestic living; the sketch is wittily headed, 'An excellent receipt to spend 4,000 pound [sic]'. [A photocopy of the 1668 drawing is present in PRONI, ref. T/3498/1. For other receipés/receipt books, see E/13A, G/20 and M/18.]
18/1–9	1669: 1671–3: N.D.: 1688: 1692: 1694	Miscellaneous, loose letters and papers of Sir Laurence Parsons, 1st Bt, including a copy of the Chancery bill in Parsons v L'Estrange, 1669, a county treasurer's computation of the number of acres in King's County, N.D., a copy of a letter from Sir Laurence Parsons to the 2nd Duke of Ormonde about money due Parsons out of the estate of Lady Preston [see A/1] 1688, etc. [Much of this sub-section is in a bad state of repair.]
19	1672–9: 1688–9	Parchment-bound volume described in some detail in the First Report of the H.M.C., as follows: 'A book of orders and rules of commissioners for assessment on the King's County, 1672–1679. In this volume are entered particulars of assessments and levies in various baronies [*sic*], including Meath, Dublin, Louth, Ossory, Rathdown, Wicklow, Shillelagh, Salt, Ikeathy and Oughterany. There are also contained rules and orders of the commissioners of array in the King's County, notes of their meetings, copies of letters, accounts of money laid out for exercising and training the militia, distribution of two troops and their companies upon the several baronies of that county allowing 600 acres for a horseman and 300 acres for a foot soldier. Two leaves are filled with a journal narrative, in very small writing, of local transactions of 1688–9.'
20	2 July 1681	Illuminated document recorded in the *First Report* of the H.M.C. as 'Letters patent granting to Richard Parsons of Bellamont in the county of Dublin the dignities of Baron of Oxmantown and Viscount Ross[e], dated at Dublin, 2nd July in the 33rd year of Charles II, 1681'.
21	1682	The same – 'Grant of arms to Sir William [sic – Laurence] Parsons from Richard St George, Ulster King at Arms, 1682'.
22	[*c.* 1688]	Copy of a Chancery bill filed by Richard, 1st Viscount Rosse, and an apparently related memorandum about the disputes within that branch of the Parsons family which engendered the bill.
23	*c.* 1691	Volume, not now to be found in Birr Castle, described in the *First Report* of the H.M.C. as 'A volume in small quarto, of 130 pages, written in a very minute current hand about 1691, containing a narrative of the affairs of Sir Laurence Parsons from April 1687 to 1691, detailing circumstances connected with the wars of James

* See detailed calendar.

A/23 *contd.*   and William in Ireland, the siege of Birr Castle by Jacobites in
                                     1688, and of that castle and town in 1690'.*

24   1685–91: 1695   Folio volume, falling apart, containing a late 19th-century
                                     transcription of A/23; together with a [*c.* 1800?] copy of a 'Plan of
                                     the castle and town of the Burre [*sic*] as besieged by General
                                     Sarsfield in 1691, taken from the account given in Harris's Life of
                                     William III'; a photocopy of the respite of Sir Laurence Parsons's
                                     execution, signed by James II, 8 March 1690[/91; the originals of
                                     two near-contemporary military commissions, one signed by James
                                     II and Lord Sunderland appointing Wentworth Harman a
                                     lieutenant in the Horse Guards, 1685, the other by William III and
                                     the Duke of Shrewsbury appointing Anthony Shepherd (a Harman
                                     connection) a captain in Fairfax's Foot, 1695; etc. [The commissions
                                     are both framed and hanging in the Muniment Room.]

25/1–13 1604: 1611:   Highly artificial bundle of title and settlement deeds: the items of
             1621: 1625:   1611, 1621, 1625, 1627, 1632 and 1643 are King's County title
             1629: 1632:   deeds, three of them to the lands of Ballindarragh and Crinkle,
             1634: 1639:   one of them a deed of settlement on the younger children of Sir
             1643: [1666?]:   Laurence Parsons, and others certified copies of the grants to him
             1680: 1682:   of fairs and markets at Parsonstown; the deeds of 1639 are a post-
             1694: 1696   nuptial settlement on Capt. William Parsons, and a fine of the
                                     lands of Reban, Co. Kildare, the property of Thomas Savage, who
                                     presumably was a brother of Frances Savage, wife of Sir Laurence
                                     Parsons, 1st Bt; the remaining title deeds concern the Co. Wexford
                                     estate, settled in 1634 by Sir William Parsons, the Lord Justice, on
                                     Arthur Parsons of Tomduff, Co. Wexford, and his descendants,
                                     who died out between 1708 and 1711, when this Wexford estate
                                     passed to Sir William Parsons, 2nd Bt, of Parstonstown. There
                                     were two components of this estate: Tomduff (also known as
                                     'Parsonstown'), barony of Ballaghkeen North, near Courtown, and
                                     St John's, barony of Bantry, near Enniscorthy. In the first half of
                                     the century, the Co. Wexford Parsonses seem to have been 'of
                                     Tomduff: the deed of 1696 describes the then Co. Wexford
                                     Parsons, William, as 'of St John's. [For the manorial lordship of,
                                     and other papers about, St John's, see B/12.]

26/1–12 1851: 1871:   Artificial sub-section made up of subsequent communications
             1922: 1955:   concerning the events covered by Section A, as follows: letter
             1973: 1982–6:   from Eliot Warburton (the novelist and minor historian) to the
             1990   3rd Earl of Rosse asking if he possesses any MS. information
                                     about Lord Justice Parsons or can think of any one redeeming
                                     feature possessed by the latter, 1851; letter of 1871 from Sir John
                                     T. Gilbert to the 4th Earl of Rosse about the MS. diary of the siege
                                     of Birr Castle in 1642 [A/9], which had been mislaid at the time
                                     of Gilbert's First Report, but which he will report upon next time
                                     if it has since come to light; photocopies of reminiscences of Leap
                                     Castle, Co. Offaly, 1922, sent subsequently to the 6th Earl of

A/26 *contd.*   Rosse; carbon, typescript copy of Norman D. Atkinson's M.A. thesis, 'The Plantation of Ely O'Carroll, 1619–1693' (T.C.D., June 1955), with accompanying letter; envelope of papers about the O'Carroll castle of Leap, 1973; newspaper cutting and letter about Bellamont/Ballymount, Co. Dublin, seat of the Viscounts Rosse, 1982 and 1985 respectively; typescript dissertation on 'Birr as a landlord town, 1600–1900', by Siobhan McNamara, 1983; typescript notes on references to the first Sir Laurence Parsons in The Lismore Papers, [1985]; and photocopies of articles by Rolf Loeber on Clonony Castle, Co. Offaly, sometime home of the Boleyn and Clere families, 1985, and Tomduff, Co. Wexford, 1986; etc, etc.

[For other papers of a later date relating to the 17th century history of the Parsons family and Parsonstown, see B/12 and 15, F/11, J/17, M/20 and M/28.]

B/	DATE	DESCRIPTION

1–15 1705–1887 Letters and papers documenting the eighteenth-century history of both branches of the Parsons family (the Earls of Rosse of the first creation and the Parsonses of Parsonstown), excluding the papers of Sir Laurence Parsons, 5th Bt, later 2nd Earl of Rosse, which constitute Sections C-F. [Section B, and everything else, unless otherwise stated, is kept on the shelves of the Muniment Room in Birr Castle.]

1/1–13 1705: 1708: 1714–16: 1721: [*c.* 1724]: 1728–9: 1733: 1739: N.D. Letters and papers of Sir William Parsons, 2nd Bt, including: a copy of a letter from him to Ormonde, the Lord Lieutenant, about the financial embarrassments of Parsons's kinsman, 'Mr Phillips,' 1705; a badly damaged deed of settlement, 1708; a copy of a letter from the Lords Justices of Ireland to Parsons, in the absence of the Governor of King's County, Lord Shelburne, about the invasion scare of January 1716; a division list recording the names of the 152 M.P.s (Parsons among them) who voted against the proposed national bank for Ireland, and the 98 who voted for it, December 1721 [a different division list from the one in the Midleton Papers, Guildford Muniment Room, MS. 1248/5, ff105–6, although both are on the same issue]; a copy of Parsons's will, 1733; and a copy of Lady Parsons's his second wife, *nee* Elizabeth St George of Dunmore, Co. Galway, will, 1739.*

2/1–12 1713: N.D.: 1741: 1760: *c.* 1983–6: 1990: 1998 Papers of or about the 2nd Viscount, later 1st Earl of Rosse, and his son and successor, the 2nd Earl, two of them the originals of letters written by the 1st Earl to 'Your Grace [Ormonde?]' seeking guidance about Rosse's career at Oxford, another of them a photocopy of the relevant section of a *c.* 1930s history of the Grand Lodge of Freemasons of Ireland, of which the 1st Earl was the first Grand Master (1725–30), and a notice of the death of the 2nd Earl in 1764 recorded in *The Irish Genealogist* for 1998.

3/1–5 23 Sept. 1715– 22 Oct. 1715 Rolled parchment draft or copy of a bill empowering the 1st Earl of Rosse to charge his estates with a jointure for his wife and to make a settlement on the issue of his marriage on 25 June 1714 to Mary, daughter of Lord William Powlett, which previous family settlements did not permit because he had married her when he was under-age, together with a printed (7 pages) copy of the act, 2 copies of the act as passed, 22 October 1715, and 2 copies of the post-nuptial settlement authorised by the act, 23 September 1715. [The rolled parchment was not originally at Birr Castle, but is docketed as having been '... received from Colonel W.A. King-Harman, Newcastle, Ballymahon, Mullingar, on 11th July 1944'. For further material concerning the Earls of Rosse of the first creation, see B/15 and M/20.]

---

* See detailed calendar.

B/4/1–26 1730: 1732:   Letters and papers of Sir Laurence Parsons of Parsonstown, 3rd Bt,
       1734–41:   including: his commission as a J.P. for King's County, [1732];
       1746–9: 1753: copies of an exchange between the 3rd Viscount Doneraile and the
       N.D.   Bishop of Sodor and Man about Doneraile's profligate way of life,
       1734; some form of licence or official document signed at Madrid
       by Cardinal de Molina, [?1734 – and quite possibly having
       nothing to do with Sir Laurence Parsons]; a letter from Parsons,
       then in Hamburgh, to Trevor Lloyd of Gloster, his King's County
       neighbour and the grandfather of the 2nd Earl of Rosse's wife,
       describing his continental travels, 1737; papers relating to the sale
       of part of the Parsons estate in Co. Tipperary, 1738; short, verbal
       survey of the Sprigge estate, inherited by Parsons's wife Mary, the
       co-heiress of William Sprigge of Clonivoe, King's County
       (Lisclooney, Clonivoe, etc, totalling nearly 2,600 acres in King's
       County with a rental of £281, and lands in Kildare and
       Westmeath with a combined rental of £266), [1738]; a fragment
       of a rental of the Parsons estate, showing a total of £1,304 per
       annum for the Tipperary estate, and at least £1,039 for the King's
       County [possibly this total is incomplete], N.D.; a letter from
       Trevor Lloyd, Gloster, King's County, to Parsons complaining of
       the tyranny of Lords Belfield and Molesworth in invading rights
       secured to Lloyd by royal patent, 1739; estimates from the
       sculptors, John and Henry Cheere of Hyde Park, London, for, and
       other papers concerning the erection of the statue of the Duke of
       Cumberland in Cumberland Square, Birr, 1746–9, including
       copies of an account, in a 19th-century book on Freemasons, of
       the laying of the foundation stone for the column on which the
       statue was to be erected; an extract from a printed copy of the
       Journal of John Wesley, recording his visit to Birr and Gloster, where
       'Sir Laurence Parsons and his lady dined with us, whether coming
       by accident or by design I know not' (Wesley also notes how Miss
       Acton, daughter of William Acton and niece of the 1st Earl of
       Rosse, 'a cultivated lady, had become a Methodist'); a poem about
       the victory of 17 December 1753 on the Money Bill issue; and an
       account for 'Work done for Laurence Parsons, Baronet, by James
       Norriss and Henry Barton at the Castle of Birr ..., [including the
       erection of] 2 square ceiling[s] and a cumpass [*sic*] in the
       ballroom', N.D.

5   Sep. 1745–   Papers [of? and] about William Parsons, younger brother of Sir
     Mar. 1746:   Laurence Parsons, 3rd Bt, including a late 19th-century copy of
     1771: late 19th his will, dated 1771, and late 19th-century notes on his military
     century   career, which show (among other things) that he was gazetted 2nd
      Ensign in Colonel John Folliott's Regiment of Foot on 31 October
      1745, and 2nd Lieutenant in the same regiment on 21 November
      1747. These facts and dates may explain the presence in Birr
      Castle and in this sub-section of the Rosse Papers, of a '45

B/5 *contd.*	Rebellion journal kept by Lieutenant-General Sir Thomas Wentworth, K.B., chief of staff or second-in-command to Field Marshall Wade, who died at Turin in December 1747. The journal, which is partly in shorthand, documents the out-manoeuvring of Wade's Northern Army by Bonnie Prince Charlie, the lack of planning on the part of Wade and his advisers, the failure to move promptly on Hexham when it was realised that the rebels were outside Carlisle, and a rejected proposal that Wade should endeavour to make contact with General Ligonier in Staffordshire. [The attribution to Wentworth, and these comments on the significance of the journal, were made by the British Library in 1958: the suggested association between Wentworth and William Parsons is purely hypothetical, although there would seem to be no more plausible explanation for the presence of the journal in Birr Castle.]
6/1–14 1754–62: 1774: 1787: 1789	Estate and financial papers of Sir William Parsons, 4th Bt, including: a draft or copy of a private act of parliament empowering him to sell part of the Co. Tipperary property of the late John Clere of Kilbury, whose daughter and heiress, Mary, Parsons had married in 1754 [see B/14], in order to clear the debts of Parsons's father-in-law; a small quarto personal account book of Parsons, 1754–61; rentals of Parsons's Birr estate (excluding the townlands comprising the inheritance from the Sprigge family and possibly other parts of the King's County estate), 1760 onwards, giving a figure of £2,096 a year, subject to £660 (the interest on debts totalling £11,000); a bill presented to Parsons for mirrors and other glassware for Birr Castle, 1757; and a schedule of the judgement debts owed by Parsons just before his death, 1788 onwards.
7/1–6 1756–7: 1779: 1782	Formal documents appointing Sir William Parsons to various local offices in King's County, 1756–7, 1779 and 1782, and as a J.P. for Co. Tipperary in 1779, together with a return of his King's County troop of dragoons, *c.* 1757.*
8/1–14 1761: 1768: N.D.: [1774]: 1780–81: 1784–6: 1790–91: 1912: 1963: [1983?]	Letters, poems and other papers of Sir William Parsons concerning personal, political and local administrative matters, including: a letter from his namesake and cousin, William Parsons, elder son of the William Parsons (d. 1771) described in B/5, giving an hilarious description of a banquet held in Robert Adam's fantastically elaborate temporary building erected in the grounds of The Oaks, Epsom, Surrey for the wedding of Lord Stanley later 10th Earl of Derby and Lady Betty Hamilton in 1774; an address of thanks and compliment from the King's County grand jury to the county M.P.s, Sir William Parsons and John Lloyd, September 1780, declining to impose on them any instructions from their constituents; a letter from Major Laurence Parsons, second son of the William who died in 1771, describing social life at Spa, 1781;

B/8 *contd.*   a partly coloured 'Plan of the Volunteer army reviewed by General Sir William Parsons, Bt, at Parsons Town, September 20th 1784'; and a letter from Laurence Parsons, the future 5th Bt and 2nd Earl of Rosse, about prospects for the King's County general election of 1790 at which Sir William Parsons, 4th Bt, who died in the following year, was the successful candidate.*

9/1–4   N.D.: 1778–81:   Four notebooks of Sir William Parsons, all of them containing
         [1783]:   accounts of personal, household and demesne expenditure, and
         1785–90   three of them relating to other things as well: the earliest, and undated, notebook contains a journal of a tour in England, with architectural sketches of, and antiquarian observations on, Stourton, Glastonbury, etc, and the 1783 notebook contains rough minutes of the evidence heard by the committee of the House of Commons appointed to try the Co. Sligo election petition of that year.*

10   1790–91   Original bundle of receipts and vouchers to Sir William Parsons, preserved, presumably, because they became part and parcel of his executorship accounts after his death in May 1791. These papers have not been put in chronological order.

11/1–4   1709: 1742:   Three copies and one original of recoveries suffered by the
         1754: 1779   Parsonses of Parsonstown, giving a good deal of information about the descent of their estates.

12/1–13   1704–5: 1708:   Deeds of mortgage, settlement and conveyance of lands in the
         1711: 1715:   manor of Parsonstown, Co. Wexford [see A/25], which passed
         1718: 1737:   from the Parsonses of Tomduff to the Parsonses of Parsonstown
         1739: 1753:   between 1708 and 1711; the lands named in these deeds are
         1771: 1997   Cullentrough, barony of Gorey, Ballyduff, Mangan, Killenagh, Howell's Lane, and Glascarrig, barony of Ballaghkeen; and all or part of the manor of St John's (Tomnegranoge, Knockmarshal, etc), barony of Bantry. The papers of 1997 relate to the sale, by the 7th Earl of Rosse, of the lordships of the manors of St John's and Tomduff, alias Parsonstown, Co. Wexford.

13/1–7   1716: 1727:   Deeds of settlement, resettlement and assignment in respect of
         1739: 1742:   lands in King's County, Co. Roscommon and Co. Tipperary. The
         1765: 1771:   Tipperary lands are part of the Clere inheritance – the burgage
         1783   lands of Clonmel, 1716 – and a City of Cashel tenement owned by the Lloyd family of Gloster, King's County, 1739; the Roscommon lands are the estate of the Persse family of Roxborough, resettled in 1727 with Sir William Parsons, 2nd Bt, as one of the trustees of the resettlement; and the King's County lands are the manor of Roscomroe and other Parsons estates, 1742, 1765 and 1783.

B/14/1–18 1699: 1707:   Original bundle of deeds, mainly relating to a frequently
1715: 1718:   reassigned mortgage for £2,000 raised on the security of the
1723: 1748:   King's County estate of the Parsonses of Parsonstown, but
1753–4: 1771:   including the settlement made on the marriage of Sir William
1779: 1783:   Parsons, 4th Bt, and Mary Clere, 1754, and a long statement
1785: 1788   of title, 1683–1779, which shows among other things that the
debts of the Parsonses, Cleres and Sprigges were such that the
Parsonses gained little in the way of land from their marriages
to the heiresses of the latter two families.

15   [1619: 1641:]   Box containing an original bundle of deeds not originally at
1754: 1764   Birr Castle, but bought at auction by the 7th Earl of Rosse in
1773: 1785:   2003 relating to the Wicklow estate of one Wentworth Erck of
1804: 1828–87   Herbert Place, Dublin (1862). This property comprised a
small part of the Wicklow estate formerly owned by the Earls
of Rosse of the first creation, particularly the manor of
Croneroe, barony of Newcastle. Because of this Rosse
derivation, the box contains non-contemporary copies of
patents granting or confirming their Wicklow estate to Sir
William Parsons and Richard Parsons, 20 October 17 James I
[1619] and 22 April 17 Charles I [1641]; memorial of the
marriage settlement of the 2nd Earl of Rosse and Olivia
Edwards, 15 February 1754; will of Lord Rosse, 18 July 1764;
and will of Lady Elizabeth Parsons, 16 July 1773. The 19th-
century abstracts of the Erck title also recite various Rosse
deeds and leases, 1698– c. 1780. [For the Wicklow estate of
the Earls of Rosse of the first creation, see also D/18.]

C/	DATE	DESCRIPTION
1–17	1765–*c.* 1820: 1855	Letters and papers of Sir Laurence Parsons, 5th Bt, who succeeded in 1807 as 2nd Earl of Rosse (of the second creation, the earldom in the elder branch of the Parsons family having died out in 1764), reflecting Parson's youthful intimacy with Henry Flood, and consisting of correspondence and speech-notes of Flood, letters to Parsons from and about Flood, and drafts for biographical and historical writings by Parsons on Flood.

1/1–16 1765: [1769]: 1771: N.D.: 1774: [1777]: 1780: 1782–3:

Letters to Flood from miscellaneous correspondents, including Edmund Burke, Edmond Sexten Pery, Speaker of the Irish House of Commons, Denis Daly of Dunsandle. Co. Galway, M.P. for that county, the 1st Earl of Charlemont, etc, etc, about Irish (and British) political affairs.*

Apart from the letters to Flood in Birr Castle, Flood's surviving correspondence consists of *c.* 110 letters in the British Library (Add. MS. 22930), about the provenance of which nothing is known except that they were purchased by the Norfolk botanist, bibliophile and antiquary, Dawson Turner (1775–1858), from a Mr Anderson in February 1833, and subsequently acquired (presumably by the British Library) at Turner's sale on 7 June 1859. Prior to coming into Turner's possession, they were edited and published anonymously, and somewhat inaccurately, in 1820 by T[homas] R[odd], in whose possession they then were, under the title *Original Letters Principally from Lord Charlemont, the Rt Hon. Edmund Burke, William Pitt, Earl of Chatham, and Many Other Distinguished Noblemen and Gentlemen to the Rt Hon. Henry Flood ...* (London, 1820). A collated and corrected copy of this edition, together with a xerox of one letter in Add. MS. 22930 omitted from it, will be found at PRONI, T/3501.

For the next item, in point of chronology, relating to Flood, see F/21, which includes a long (*c.* 30 pages) and very polished draft for a speech opposing the Address, October 1765?, in which Flood maintains that the British ministry is bent on destroying the liberties of America, Ireland and England, warns the House against falling into the trap of exaggerating the gravity of the Whiteboy disturbances, and asserts the pre-Norman antiquity of the Irish constitution and the pre-Norman civilization of the Irish people.

2/1–43 1767–80

Correspondence between Flood and Rev. Dr William Markham, his former tutor at Oxford, successively Bishop of Chester and Archbishop of York, consisting of originals of Markham's letters to Flood [only one other of which is in Add. MS. 22930] and drafts of Flood's letter to Markham, concerning Anglo- Irish relations, Flood's complaints of ill-treatment and neglect in 1774 when he was passed over for the Provostship of Trinity in favour of John

---

*   See detailed calendar, and a transcript of C/1/1–2 published in *The English Historical Review*, 457 (June 1999). An offprint from this publication is present in the envelope.

C/2 *contd.*   Hely-Hutchinson, his subsequent charges against the British
                                    government and justifications of himself, particularly in 1778–80,
                                    when Markham was endeavouring to restrain him and remind him
                                    of the paramount loyalty he owed to the British connection, etc,
                                    etc. [These letters are, even by the generally sorry standards of the
                                    2nd Earl's papers, in urgent need of conservation.]*

3   [*c.* 1770:   One printed copy of a pamphlet by Flood, with MS. corrections
           c. 1778:   in his hand, one poem, and two MS. [and unpublished]
           c. 1784]   pamphlets by Flood, as follows: the first (and printed) pamphlet is
                                    an attack on Lord Townshend, the Lord Lieutenant of Ireland for
                                    the controversial prorogation of the Irish parliament at the end of
                                    1769; the second pamphlet is a MS. 'Answer to Dr Samuel
                                    Johnson's "Taxation no tyranny" ', [*c.* 1778]; and the third
                                    pamphlet is an anti-Pitt the Younger account, by Flood, of 'The
                                    first session of Mr Pitt's administration', 1784.

4   [1770s–1780s] Notes by Flood, and historical extracts made for Flood, concerning
                                    the history of Poynings's Law.

5   [1770S–1783?] Folio volume containing drafts of speeches by Flood, including a
                                    63-page draft for his speech on the Perpetual Mutiny Bill on 28
                                    April 1780, the first 50 pages of which coincide exactly with the
                                    fair copy in C/6, and a 34-page draft for his speech on Poynings's
                                    Law on 11 December 1781 – for this, too, see the versions in C/6.
                                    The last two items in the volume are of only a couple of pages
                                    each: the first is a draft for some tart observations on Grattan's
                                    Declaration of Right, 19 April 1782 – see C/6 ('One would have
                                    thought by Mr G – n's elaborate oration on the 16th of April, that
                                    the Declaration of Rights [*sic*] was a thing that would be
                                    contested. ...'); the second is a draft of some paragraphs in defence
                                    of his political consistency, for use in his rebuttal of Grattan's
                                    charges on 31 October 1781 – see C/6. [This volume is in dire
                                    need of conservation.]

6   1779–84   Reports of a number of Flood's major speeches in the Irish House
                                    of Commons, most of them corrected in his own hand. The
                                    speeches concerned are those on the Short Money Bill, 24–5
                                    November 1779?, on Grattan's Declaration of Right, 19 April
                                    1780, on the Perpetual Mutiny Bill, 28 April 1780, on Flood's
                                    own conduct in retaining the Vice Treasurership while opposing
                                    the Irish administration, October 1781?, on Poynings's Law, 11
                                    December 1781 [one copy of this speech is corrected in Flood's
                                    hand, and there are two other and fairer copies, both entirely in
                                    Parsons's hand and both apparently incomplete], on Renunciation
                                    [this version consisting of a rough draft in Flood's hand for the
                                    latter part of the speech, and notes by him of mistakes made in the
                                    version printed in the first volume of the *Irish Parliamentary
                                    Register*, pp 407–14, 11 June 1782], on Flood's own conduct in

*   See detailed calendar.

C/6 *contd.*

response to Grattan's attack on him, and this version titled by Parsons, 'Second defence', that of 1781 being the 'First defence', 31 October 1783, and 'Speech of Mr Flood on the Address' in effect, on parliamentary reform, in the wake of the rejection of the Volunteer plan, October 1784. Several of these copies are prefaced by a summary of the 'Argument' in Parsons's hand, so that it looks as if he was preparing an edition of Flood's speeches. The later material in this sub-section is in dire need of conservation.*

The collation which has so far been made between these and other contemporary reports shows that the first version of the Poynings's Law speech of 11 December 1781 in C/6, which is in a clerical hand and is corrected extensively in Flood's hand, is verbatim the same as the version in vol. 23, pp 105–94 of Sir Henry Cavendish's MS. reports of debates in the Irish House of Commons (originals in the Library of Congress, Washington: photocopies available in PRONI, MIC/12 and T/3435/A/1). This is an important discovery, on two counts. First, it shows that, given a choice between Cavendish's version and the version which he must have known had been made for publication in the forth-coming first volume of the *Irish Parliamentary Register*, Flood referred to Cavendish's version, presumably because he regarded it as more accurate. Second, a comparison between the Cavendish version, which like almost all the rest of Cavendish's Irish reports remain unedited, with Flood's earlier draft (C/5) and his subsequent corrections and alterations, will provide a unique opportunity to access the accuracy of Cavendish in the eyes of someone whose speech he had reported – although it is probable that Flood may have 'corrected' Cavendish to the point of introducing things which Flood omitted to say at the time! Further comparison with Cavendish shows that the C/6 version of the 'Second defence' (which Cavendish dates as 1 November 1783, presumably because it was delivered after midnight on the 31st) is almost verbation the same as Cavendish's; and that Cavendish's report of the part of the 11 June 1782 speech on Renunciation which exists in rough draft in C/6 follows the draft fairly closely. There is no Cavendish version of the other speeches in C/6. However, from October 1781 there is an *Irish Parliamentary Register* version, except for the 'First defence'. Parsons's 'Argument' states that this was delivered 'in the year 1781 ..., just before he [Flood] was removed from his office' -which can only mean October 1781. Possibly it was delivered in committee, and therefore was outside the scope of both the *Irish Parliamentary Register* and Cavendish.

The draft for the 11 December 1781 speech in C/5, and the first version of the same speech in C/6, have been photocopied by PRONI, T/3498/2–3.

---

* See detailed calendar.

C/7   1785: 1787–8:   Corrected MS. and printed reports of Flood's speeches in the
           1790   British House of Commons, on the Slave Trade, 1787?, the
                                   commercial treaty with France, 15 February 1787, the India Bill,
12 March 1788, and British parliamentary reform, 4 March 1790.
This version of the India Bill speech appears to be in Flood's hand,
and looks more like an autograph draft than a subsequent copy;
the versions of the French commercial treaty and the parliamentary
reform speeches are pamphlet-publications with MS. corrections,
and there are two different printed copies of the latter.

8/1–85 1784–91   Correspondence between Flood and Parsons, consisting of original
letters on both sides, but only a couple of them from Parsons to
Flood. A large portion of the letters relate to Flood's chequered
pursuit of seats in the British House of Commons, in which he
was assisted by or associated with Parsons. The letters supplement
those in Add. MS. 22930 concerning Flood's bitter and protracted
dispute with the Duke of Chandos over the return for Winchester
in 1784, and break new ground by documenting Flood's and
Parsons's ultimately unsuccessful bid to be returned for Seaford,
Sussex, their mustering of witnesses and marshalling of evidence
for production before an election committee, etc, 1784–7. There
are some references to Irish parliamentary affairs, including a
number of cutting comments by Flood about Grattan, and a
discussion of Parsons's attack on Grattan in the aftermath of the
regency crisis in 1789, as a man who had already been paid too
much for selling his country short and now over the regency had
blundered yet again. The concluding letters relate to the hunt for
seats, both for Flood and for Parsons, in the Irish parliament of
1790, which was unsuccessful in Flood's case, because his death
occurred before a seat could be found. Conservation is, again, an
urgent priority.*

9   [1785]   Notes by Flood for speeches in the Irish or British House of
Commons or both? on the Commercial Propositions.

10   1791: 1794:   Letters to Parsons from Edmund Malone, a friend and literary
        1797: 1815   correspondent of Flood, General Charles Vallancey, the then
expert on ancient Ireland, and others about Flood's death, his will
(with its bequest of much of his property to the founding of a
professorship of Erse at Trinity and to the purchase of old
manuscripts in the Irish language), his memory generally, etc. The
letter of 1815 describes the distressing circumstances of the death
of Lady Frances Flood, Flood's widow.

11   [1795]   Papers, not now to be found in Birr Castle, but described in the
First Report of the H.M.C. as 'the MSS of "Observations on the
Bequest of Henry Flood to Trinity College, Dublin, with a
Defence of the Ancient History of Ireland" ', a pamphlet written
by Parsons and published in Dublin in 1795. Since there are a

---

*   See detailed calendar.

C/11 *contd.*   good many MSS in Parsons's handwriting on the subject of Flood,
                                 it is possible that Sir John Gilbert jumped to the erroneous
                                 conclusion that all or some of them related to this particular
                                 publication, the more so as the others, which constitute the
                                 concluding sub-sections of Section C, appear not to have been
                                 published. However, see also F/7.

12   [Paper-marked   Small octavo volume, not quite full, containing an account in
          1813]   Parsons's, now 2nd Earl of Rosse, hand of the life of Flood up to
                               1778, including some unique background information about the
                               Flood family in relation to the parliamentary borough of Callan,
                               over which Flood fought a fatal duel in 1769. This account,
                               though obviously incomplete, seems to be too short to be intended
                               as a publication in its own right: possibly it was intended as an
                               introduction to an edition of Flood's speeches or to the 2nd Earl's
                               work identifying Flood as the author of the *Letters of Junius.**

13   [*c.* 1810–20]   Voluminous rough drafts and jottings, in the 2nd Earl's
                               handwriting and on paper variously marked 1809–19, all on the
                               subject of Flood and Junius.

                               Atkinson gives the following account of the background to these
                               papers ('The 2nd Earl of Rosse', p. 75): '... In 1812 the suggestion
                               of Burke's authorship [of the *Letters of Junius*] was revived by
                               Daniel O'Connell, for reasons of personal enmity. At this point, ...
                               [the 2nd Earl] intervened in the controversy. He wrote to [George]
                               Woodfall in London, who had come into possession of the original
                               letters of Junius [and was about to publish them in an enlarged,
                               three-volume edition], enclosing a manuscript which he declared
                               would establish the true identity of the author and vindicate
                               Burke's character. Although he refused to give Woodfall permission
                               to reveal the author's name, he urged him to make an examination
                               of the manuscript, and intimated that an article on the subject, by
                               a writer named Roche, would shortly be published in the *Quarterly
                               Review*. ... Roche [however] never published his article in the
                               Quarterly Review, although he subsequently made some
                               observations on the matter in an article which appeared in the
                               Cork Magazine in September 1848. ...'

                               At the top of this pile of papers has been placed a copy of another
                               letter from the 2nd Earl, Fulham, to 'Sir' [Woodfall?], 29 June
                               1812, in which he argues ingeniously that Junius must have been
                               an Irishman, because he refers to the repairing 'of a country bridge
                               or a decayed hospital' by means of a lottery, at a time when
                               lotteries flourished in Ireland, but only the state lottery was
                               permitted in England. He then goes on to point out that it is easy
                               to ascertain Flood's whereabouts on the dates on which each
                               successive letter of Junius was published, 'As he was the leader of
                               the opposition at that period, and as it was the custom to appoint

*   See detailed calendar.

C/13 *contd.*   the most distinguished speaker on all great questions teller, [with the result that] his name appears in the [Irish] journals on such occasions', and on other occasions he could easily have been in London. An enclosure in this letter illustrates the striking coincidence between the publication of each letter of Junius and periods when the Irish parliament was not in session; and there are numerous other papers in the sub-section to the same purport. [See also D/2/14.]

14/1–5 [*c.* 1810–15]   Loose-leaf clutch of 300 pages of octavo, consisting of an autograph MS. in the 2nd Earl's hand on the subject of Flood and Junius: together with 4 small quarto volumes, the first 3 containing *c.* 200 pages and the fourth *c.* 100, being a fair, clerical copy of the same work. The 300 pages of autograph are some of them paper-marked 1809, while the paper-mark on the 4 volumes is 1814. Since the 2nd Earl's object was, not only to prove that Flood was Junius, but to repel the assertion that Junius was 'an assassin', much of the material relates to Flood's devotion to the cause of liberty, his attachment to the constitution, etc, and in effect turns into a political biography of, or apology for, Flood.*

15   [*c.* 1820]   Small quarto 20-page series of anecdotes, by the 2nd Earl, of Flood and other contemporary orators and parliamentarians.*

16   [*c.* 1820?]   Duplicate copies of the concluding pages (pp 37–52) of a printed pamphlet [by the 2nd Earl?] on the authorship of the *Letters of Junius.*

17/1–2 1855   Letter, and enclosure, from Telford McDonagh to the 3rd Earl of Rosse about Flood's bequest to T.C.D.

D/	DATE	DESCRIPTION
1–24	1791–1834	Letters to Sir Laurence Parsons, 2nd Earl of Rosse, from his principal correspondents, on all manner of personal, political and business matters, arranged as follows:
1/1–6	1791: 1794–5	Letters to Parsons from the 1st Marquess of Lansdowne (great-nephew of the Lord Shelburne who was Governor of King's County in 1716 – see B/1) about the support given to Parsons by Lord Lansdowne's King's County freeholders in parliamentary elections, about county politics generally, about the Lord Lieutenancy of Earl Fitzwilliam, 1794–5, the war, the state of Ireland, etc.*
2/1–18	1792: 1796–7: 1800: 1804: 1808: 1812: 1814: 1828	Letters to Parsons from Peter Burrowes, his friend and political associate, an Irish barrister and M.P., who as early as 1784 had written a pamphlet advocating the restoration of the Irish Roman Catholics to the franchise on a £50 freehold franchise, as the only means whereby Irish Protestants could secure parliamentary reform; about Catholic Relief and Emancipation, 1792; Co. Dublin politics, 1796; the rapprochement between Parsons and the Irish administration, which was conducted via Burrowes and Richard Griffith of Millicent, Co. Kildare, and which came to nothing because of the complaint brought against Parsons as Colonel of the King's County Militia in 1798, 1797, the Orangemen, and the consequences of the Union as far as the future government of Ireland and the future discussion of the Catholic Question is concerned, 1800, and with references to Lady Frances Flood, the mystery over the authorship of Junius, Sir Frederick Flood, Caesar Colclough (who in 1814 returned from poverty in France to find himself in possession of £6,500 a year in Co. Wexford), 1804–14. [For an earlier letter from Burrowes about Parsons's candidature for Seaford, Sussex, see C/8/36. The letters up to 1800 have been photostated by the National Library (MS. 13840, part), and a second set of Photostats has been placed alongside the originals.]
3/1–3	1793: 1797	Letters to Parsons from Edmund Burke, the letter of 1793 thanking him for and commenting upon Parsons's *Thoughts on Liberty and Equality* (Dublin, 1793), the second, of 1797, discussing the war, the expected French invasion, the fact that Ireland is maintained in a state of siege whilst Europe is conquered, the use to which the British fleet should and should not be put, etc, and the third, also of 1797, asking if Parsons has received its predecessor. [The first two of these letters were photostated by the National Library (MS. 13547), and the second was published in *The English Historical Review*, no. 457 (June 1999), a copy of which will be found at C/1. For Parsons's *Thoughts on Liberty and Equality*, see F/8.]

* See detailed calendar.

D/3 *contd.*

R.B. McDowell writes, in *Ireland in the Age of Imperialism and Revolution, 1760–1801* (Oxford, 1979), p. 360: Parsons's '... *Thoughts on Liberty and Equality* (Dublin, 1793), was published in the wake of the pamphlet warfare over the French Revolution which Burke had opened in 1790. ... One revolutionary dogma, constantly proclaimed in France and fervently assented to by radicals all over Europe, equality, seemed to conservatives to be the root of much political evil. Conservatives perhaps perceived its implications sooner than some radicals, arguing that political and economic equality tended in practice to be closely related. Early in 1793 Sir Lawrence Parsons ... published a clear, compact pamphlet in which he tried to demonstrate that inequality was requisite to social progress. Man, Parsons wrote, was "a progressive animal" and "the great stimulation to progress" was property. Property, acquired by industry and ability, was "the great prime mover everywhere". Obviously all men could not progress equally, and this was just as well, because with a vast number of tasks of varying difficulties and importance to be performed, "a great and various inequality" was absolutely necessary "to sublime man to the highest degree we know he is capable of". Political power was annexed to property because every man had a right to the acquisitions of his own labour, and ought to have the means to protect them. Parsons was also convinced that democracy was absurd. The peasant, who had spent his days digging the earth and who had been educated as "a mere machine", could not be expected to understand political issues. Even a strong radical when he was ill did not "call on the next digger of the earth to feel his pulse". To anybody who thought the lot of the poor hard, Parsons had an answer – "let it be considered the right to political power has been forfeited by their own or their ancestors' imprudence and indolence, but that by contrary conduct they or their children may rise to the enjoyment of such power" ...'

4/1–14 1793: 1797–8: 1804–5: 1807: 1817

Letters to Parsons from the Hon. Robert Stewart, Viscount Castlereagh, the earliest of them written as a back-bench political associate of Parsons in the Irish House of Commons, those of 1797–8 as acting Chief Secretary or Chief Secretary to the Lord Lieutenant, and the rest as a member, in various capacities, of the British government. The topics include the political manoeuvrings of the parliamentary session of 1793, the state of the barracks in which the King's County Militia has been accommodated, 1797; the fate of prisoners in Parsonstown Gaol who, in spite of having surrendered within the terms of a government proclamation of amnesty, have been arrested and incarcerated there, 1798; Parsons's relations with the second Pitt administration and hopes of being appointed to the Chancellorship of the Irish Exchequer under it, 1804–5; and more minor matters of patronage, 1807 and 1817.

*   See detailed calendar.

D/4 *contd.*   [Some of these letters have been photostated by the National
                                   Library (MS. 13840, part), and a second set of photostats has been
                                   placed alongside the originals. The letter of 1805 is in urgent need
                                   of conservation.]*

5/1–62 1798: 1800–02:   Letters to Parsons from his younger brother, Thomas Clere
         1806: 1817:   Parsons (the fourth son of their father, and Assistant Barrister for
         1822: 1824–5   King's County, 1803–25), including a run of blow-by-blow
                           accounts of the rebellion, May-July 1798, and discussion of the
                           Union, family history, estate affairs, etc (Thomas C. Parsons
                           appears to have acted as his brother's head agent up to 1803); also
                           included are other letters and papers of Parsons, now 2nd Earl of
                           Rosse, about the local furore arising out of complaints that
                           Thomas C. Parsons had misconducted himself as Assistant
                           Barrister, 1822, and letters of condolence to the 2nd Earl on, and a
                           printed poem about, Thomas C. Parsons's death, which took place
                           at Tullynisky Park, Birr, the house which he shared with another
                           brother, the Rev. William Parsons, in 1825. [See also F/21. The
                           '98 Rebellion letters, with one exception, have been photostated
                           by the National Library (MS. 13840, part), and a second set of
                           photostats has been placed alongside the originals. Most of the
                           original letters in the sub-section are in urgent need of
                           conservation.]*

6/1–6 1798: 1800:   Letters to Parsons from another barrister-brother, John Clere
        1806   Parsons, Chief Commissioner of the Insolvent Court, 1822–6,
                          whose legal opinions on matters affecting the family estates will be
                          found in E/3, about minor matters of business. [The two letters of
                          1798 have been photostated by the National Library, and a second
                          set of photostats has been placed alongside the originals.]

7/1–173 1800: 1802–34:   Letters to Parsons from his uncle, Laurence Harman (Parsons) of
         1837–8: 1842:   Newcastle, Ballymahon, Co. Longford, 1st Viscount Oxmantown
         1898: 1903:   and subsequently (1806) 1st Earl of Rosse, and, after the 1st Earl's
         1949–50:   death in April 1807, from his widow, Jane, Countess Dowager of
         1976: 1983:   Rosse. The letters concern all manner of family, political and
         1987–8: 1992   financial affairs. At the time of writing, the 1st Earl and his widow
                           were almost invariably in England, either in London or at their
                           successive country houses in various parts of the country (mainly
                           Stretton Hall, Wolverhampton, Staffordshire, where he lived,
                           1806–7, and she, 1807–38), and Parsons almost invariably in
                           Ireland. The 1st Earl's letters relate to: the family's relations with
                           the Addington, Pitt and Grenville administrations; complaints
                           about Parsons's absence from parliament in 1806, on account of
                           his wife's ill-health, when the government expected him, as a Lord
                           of the Irish Treasury, to attend; Co. Longford and King's County
                           elections, particularly in 1806, when the 1st Earl visited Newcastle
                           for electioneering purposes; the 1st Earl's reluctant consent to
                           apply for the earldom, but solely on condition that it was

* See detailed calendar.

D/7 *contd.*   remaindered on Parsons, 1806; etc, etc. The letters from the
                         Dowager Lady Rosse concern the 2nd Earl's taking possession of
                         the 1st Earl's Dublin house in Stephen's Green, 1807; her nearly
                         fatal accident while out driving in her carriage in the same year;
                         King's County and Co. Longford politics and elections (with the
                         2nd Earl acting as the Dowager Lady Rosse's adviser and
                         sometimes spokesman in respect of the latter); the Dowager Lady
                         Rosse's relations with her nephew and son-in-law, the 1st Viscount
                         Lorton; the 2nd Earl's disappointment on discovering in 1818 that
                         he was going to inherit none of the 1st Earl's Harman/Co.
                         Longford property; the intimidation of the Dowager Lady Rosse
                         by some deranged kinsman called William Parsons [see D/24]; etc,
                         etc. Copies of some of the 2nd Earl's letters to the Dowager Lady
                         Rosse are present in the sub-section, whereas only the other side of
                         the correspondence between the 1st Earl and him survives. The
                         papers of 1838 and 1842 (which are subsequent to her death)
                         relate to the provisions of her will, 1838, and an estate bill
                         initiated by Lord Lorton, 1842. The letters and papers of 1898,
                         1903, 1949–50, 1976, 1983, 1987 and 1992 respectively relate to
                         the ruinous state of a monument to the 1st Earl in a cemetery off
                         Hampstead Road, London, a portrait of him painted in 1809,
                         King-Harman family portraits formerly at Newcastle, a portrait of
                         the Dowager Lady Rosse hanging in Rosse Hall, Kenyon College,
                         Ohio, and the 7th Earl of Rosse's visit to Kenyon College in 1987
                         (following which he received from the college photocopies of
                         correspondence, 1824–7, relating to the Dowager Lady Rosse's
                         benefaction to it), and a thesis written in 1992 on Keenagh church,
                         Mosstown, Co. Longford, which was built by her in 1832.*

8/1–22 1802: 1805–6: Correspondence between Parsons, before and after his succession
         1817–20: 1826   as 2nd Earl of Rosse, and Miss Charlotte Burgh (later Mrs
                         Zachariah Cornock, who writes mostly from the house of her
                         cousin, Lord Chief Justice Downes, at Merville, Stillorgan,
                         Dublin), mainly about literary and social matters, but including
                         references to her brother, General Sir Ulysses Burgh, subsequently
                         2nd Lord Downes; to a portrait at Ripley Parsonage, Yorkshire,
                         which may be of Capt. Laurence Parsons (fl. 1673), 1802; and to
                         'the Parsonstown rebellion' of 1820 [see E/11]. Miss Burgh appears
                         to have been regarded by the 2nd Earl as a kind of literary
                         consultant, for example being treated by him to first sight of his
                         thirteen-canto poem, 'The Revolution [of 1688]', in 1820 [see F/1].

9/1–15 1803–8   Accounts and letters to Parsons from Richard Darcy, the
                         steward?, Parsonstown, consisting of one calf-bound, folio volume
                         of accounts, 1803–5, in which building operations at Birr Castle
                         feature fairly prominently, one unbound small quarto volume of
                         accounts, 1806–7, and letters to Parsons from Darcy, 1808,
                         mainly March-April 1808.

* See detailed calendar.

D/10/1–14 May-June 1805: Letters from Parsons to Lady Parsons, with one of November
  Nov. 1806   1806 from her to him, containing many references to political
  and parliamentary matters at Westminster. They are also full of
  humour, affection and sadness, and vividly describe the
  forlornness of the post-Union Irish M.P., possessed of few
  contacts in London, sleeping in a 'bed chamber in the garret' of
  Nerot's Hotel, and eating his 'veal cutlet solitarily'.*

11/1–10 1807–8   Letters to the 2nd Earl from the Rev. Robert Moffett of
  Ballymahon, (agent for the Harman estate in Co. Longford until
  he went off his head in 1818? – see D/7/94), mostly about the
  death of the 1st Earl and its immediate aftermath.

12/1–14 1809: 1816–19: Letters and receipts to the 2nd Earl from his Dublin banker,
  1821: 1824–5: B. Ball & Co.
  1829

13/1–53 1809: 1812: Letters to the 2nd Earl from Morgan Crofton, law agent for the
  1818–19: 1821: Harman estate in Co. Longford, about the 1st Earl's former
  1823: 1825: house in Stephen's Green, Longford politics and elections,
  1827–8: 1830 promotion in the navy for Crofton's son (with letters from the
  2nd Viscount Melville, First Lord of the Admiralty, to the 2nd
  Earl on that subject), and estate and financial business.*

14/1–12 1809: 1817: Letters, together with a printed pamphlet on the state of Ireland
  1822: 1824: in 1822, to the 2nd Earl from the author of the pamphlet, the
  1828 Rt Hon. Denis Browne, younger brother of the 1st Marquess of
  Sligo, about the Irish representative peerage elections of 1809, at
  the second of which the 2nd Earl was the successful candidate,
  Lord Oxmantown's (the future 3rd Earl) prospects of political
  office in 1828, etc, etc.*

15/1–8 1812–14: 1823 Letters to the 2nd Earl from John Legg, the agent, Parsonstown,
  about estate business, including the registering of freeholders.

16/1–14 1817: 1823–4 Letters to the 2nd Earl from Mr and Mrs William Newenham
  of Celbridge, Co. Kildare, about their financial embarrassments.

17/1–7 1817: 1821: Letters, and one bill of costs, to the 2nd Earl from James C.
  1825: 1834 Martin of Ely Place, Dublin, his Dublin attorney.

18/1–14 1818: 1821: Letters to the 2nd Earl and Thomas C. Parsons from the 6th
  1825–6: 1828 Viscount Netterville, a descendant in the female line from the
  elder branch of the Parsons family [see A/3], about family
  portraits of the Parsonses, and Lord Netterville's wish that the
  2nd Earl should purchase the Wicklow property of the elder
  branch [B/15] which had descended to Lord Netterville; also
  included are letters and papers about Lord Netterville's death in
  1826 and will, by which he forbade his representative to sell the
  Wicklow property to anybody but the 2nd Earl, 1826 and 1828,
  together with a long-subsequent letter of 1851 to the 3rd Earl,
  describing the will as 'a very extraordinary and a very voluminous

* See detailed calendar.

D/18 *contd.*   production, manifestly the composition of the testator, and one
                                        which does not speak very favourably for his intellect or
                                        education'. The first of Lord Netterville's letters, of 9 December
                                        1818, mentions that 'The Rosse estate [in Co. Wexford?]
                                        certainly centres in the Boyd family after *the God*son' – implying
                                        that the Boyds of Co. Wexford had come by their property as a
                                        result of illegitimate descent from the extinct Earls of Rosse. [See
                                        also D/5/27 and D/22/18.]

19/1–7   1821–2   Letters and papers of the 2nd Earl about the claim of one
                                        Thomas Bond of Tullamore, King's County, to a fortune of
                                        £100,000 lodged in the Bank of England.

20/1–14 1822: 1827   Letters to the 2nd Earl from the 1st Lord Redesdale, Lord
                                        Chancellor of Ireland, 1802–6, about the state of Ireland,
                                        together with photocopies of the originals, and a copy of
                                        PRONI's calendar, of the other side of the correspondence, the
                                        2nd Earl's letters to Lord Redesdale in reply (Gloucestershire
                                        Record Office, Redesdale Papers, C/34; PRONI, T/3030/13/1–
                                        7, printed in Malcomson (ed.), *Eighteenth-Century Irish Official
                                        Papers in Great Britain: Private Collections, vol ii* [Belfast, 1990],
                                        pp 459–68).*

21/1–16 1823: 1826:   Letters to the 2nd Earl from Maria Edgeworth, together with a
         1826–30   copy of the 7th Earl of Rosse's article in *The Yorkshire Post*, 1963,
                                        describing their contents and the background to the writing of
                                        them; the principal topics are the whip-round to save Abbotsford
                                        and Sir Walter Scott's library, the death of the 2nd Earl's second
                                        son, John Clere Parsons, Irish round towers, Celtic
                                        Zaroastrianism, telescopes, the July Revolution in France, etc.

22/1–33 1826: 1830–31:   Letters to the 2nd Earl from his elder son, Lord Oxmantown,
         1833   M.P. for King's County, who writes from London, where he was
                                        attending parliament, to his father, in semi-retirement at Birr,
                                        about currency and corn, reform of the Irish Post Office, of
                                        which the 2nd Earl was Joint Postmaster General – see E/14,
                                        general politics, etc.*

23/1–13 1828–9: 1831   Letters to the 2nd Earl from Catherine-Maria, Countess of
                                        Charleville, wife of the 1st Earl of Charleville, who lived at
                                        Charleville Forest, Tullamore, King's County, and at this time was in
                                        alliance with the 2nd Earl in county politics, about the death of
                                        John C. Parsons, county politics and elections, the political activities
                                        and prospects of their respective sons and heirs, Lords Oxmantown
                                        and Tullamore, the Catholic and Reform Questions, etc.*

24/1–11 1831–3   Letters to the 2nd Earl from William Parsons, an aggrieved
                                        nutcase, who wrote threatening letters both to the 2nd Earl
                                        and to the Dowager Lady Rosse about William Parsons's
                                        mythical claim to Harman property in Co. Longford [see also
                                        D/7 and E/42].

* See detailed calendar.

E/	DATE	DESCRIPTION
1–42	1791–1841	Letters and papers of Sir Laurence Parsons, 5th Bt, subsequently 2nd Earl of Rosse, including (during his life-time) papers of his first and second sons, Lord Oxmantown and the Hon. John Clere Parsons, arranged as follows:
1/1–93	1791–1801: 1804–10: 1814–21: 1823–32	Tradesmen's accounts and letters to Sir Laurence Parsons, 2nd Earl of Rosse, some of them relating to jewellery and clothes, and some of them to furniture and glassware for Birr Castle and to plants and trees for the pleasure grounds there.
2/1–2	1792–4: 1793–9	Two small quarto account books, one kept on Parsons's behalf by an agent or bailiff?, the other kept by Parsons himself, both recording household and demesne expenditure, and giving some information about rent receipts and rent; the second account book, Parsons's own, also gives information about interest money owed to and by him, King's County Militia expenses, etc.*
3	1792: N.D.: 1806: 1809: 1816: 1818: 1824–6: 1831	Cases for counsel's opinion, legal case papers, and bills of costs, all relating to Parsons's title to parts of his King's County estate, some to the validity or invalidity of leases granted back to the time of Sir William Parsons, 2nd Bt, and some relating to a mortgage raised by Sir William Parsons, 4th Bt, in 1766, and involving his son and successor in the protracted Chancery and House of Lords lawsuit, Rosse v the Rev. James Stirling, which the 2nd Earl claimed elsewhere (D/7) had cost him £16,000 in legal costs by 1818, before it had even reached the House of Lords. For a reconveyance of mortgage, 1826, bringing this lawsuit to an end, see E/28. Several of the counsel's opinions were given by the 2nd Earl's second brother, John C. Parsons, K.C.
4/1–40	1792–1824	Surveys and valuations, mainly non-pictorial and all small in size, of bits and pieces of the King's County estate.
5/1–11	1793: 1808: 1825: 1828–9: 1831–2	Letters and accounts to Parsons concerning Dublin houses: the single item of 1793 relates to his house or villa at Rathmines, and the rest to the Stephen's Green house which he either inherited or purchased from the 1st Earl's estate, in 1809 [see Q/2]. Included in the sub-section is a 'List of kitchen articles', 1828, which may relate to Birr Castle, not Stephen's Green.
6	31 Jan. 1794: 9 Aug. and 16 Sep. 1796: 22 Oct. and 17 Nov. 1801	King's County freeholder's certificate, 1794, and bundle of certificates, 1796 and 1801, recording that each of the undersigning King's County Roman Catholics has taken the oath of allegiance prescribed by the Catholic Relief Acts of 1774 and 1778, and the oath and declaration prescribed by the Catholic Relief Act of 1793.
7	1797: 1806–7: 1809: 1817:	Rentals relating to parts of the King's County estate, principally Corowantill and Lumcloon; the 1809 item is a calculation by the

E/7 *contd.*

1819: 1830	2nd Earl that his rental is over £10,000, charged with over £3,000 a year for interest and annuities, and subject to over £750 for quit and chief rents.

8   1797–1800:   Receipts, letters, bonds, etc., all relating to Parsons's borrowings
         1805–6:   from various people, including his brothers, John C. Parsons and
         1809–12: 1815: Thomas C. Parsons; in 1798, for example, he borrowed £1,000
         1817–25: 1829: from Lady Frances Flood.
         1832

9   Apr.-June and   Issues of *The Courier* and *The Dublin Evening Post*, one of them
         Nov. 1798   carrying a copy of Parsons's resolute reply of 21 April to an address
                       from some of his King's County constituents denouncing his
                       parliamentary and general conduct.

10/1–2 'c. 1799'   Papers, photostated by the National Library (MS. 13842) and
         [*recte: c.* 1820] described in Hayes as 'Alleged oaths and tests of United Irishmen
                       and Caravats, *c.* 1799, with a note [by Sir Laurence Parsons?] on the
                       Catholic lower-class conspiracy'. The note is indeed by the 2nd Earl,
                       and the documents are paper-marked 1811 and 1814 respectively. A
                       second set of photostats has been placed alongside the originals.

11/1–72 1804–5:   Letters and papers of Parsons concerning the town and immediate
         1807–8: 1834: vicinity of Parsonstown/Birr: its Castle, barracks, canal, Protestant
         1912:   and Roman Catholic churches, Sunday school, streets, tolls, mill,
         [*c.* 1975]:   etc, etc. Included in the section are 7 letters from the 1st Earl of
         [1990?]   Norbury, Lord Chief Justice of the Common Pleas, and a local
                       landowner whose seat was at Durrow Abbey, King's County, and
                       one from Sir Jonas Green, later Recorder of Dublin, about 'the
                       Birr rebellion' of 1820, the popular name given to the scare
                       engendered by the forgeries of Mrs Thomas Legg, wife of the local
                       stationer, which for a while deluded the 2nd Earl and everyone else
                       into believing that a repetition of the 1641 rising was about to
                       take place at Birr; two letters of the same year from Thomas Lalor
                       Cooke, a local solicitor and historian, whose *Picture of
                       Parsonstown*, published in 1826, and republished by his son in
                       1875, drew on many original documents then and/or now in Birr
                       Castle, about minor business matters, 1820; and letters and
                       papers, one of the letters from William Conyngham Plunket, Lord
                       Chief Justice of the Common Pleas, about disputes and skirmishes
                       between the followers of the two rival parish priests at Birr, Revs.
                       Patrick Kennedy, later Roman Catholic Bishop of Killaloe, and
                       Michael Crotty, 1824–8 [see also F/21 and 23 and Q/75. For
                       Crotty's subsequent career, see J/8.] Inserted in this sub-section
                       [E/11/60], though not originally among the Rosse Papers, is
                       Thomas L. Cooke's own copy of his *Picture of Parsonstown*,
                       acquired by the 7th Earl of Rosse in 1981. This copy has many
                       extra illustrations and other printed and MS insertions, 1827–*c.*

---

*   See detailed calendar.

E/11 *contd.*		1855, including glosses on ancient Irish place names in the locality, a plan of the battle of Culloden, a letter from Thomas C. Parsons to Cooke about the wording of the book's dedication to the 2nd Earl, and a letter from the 2nd Earl himself thanking Cooke for presenting him with a copy of the book, 26 January 1827. Also added to the sub-section are a typescript extract from the Hamwood Papers (formerly at Hamwood, Dunboyne, Co. Meath, and now in the National Library of Wales, Aberystwyth) describing Birr in 1796, [*c.* 1975], and a modern xerox of a census fragment of 1821 listing those then residing in Birr Castle.*
12	1808: 1812: 1814: 1816: 1819–20: 1822: 1824: 1826: 1828: 1830–32	Receipts and letters to the 2nd Earl of Rosse, from various London and Dublin bankers and stockbrokers.
12A	Jan.-July 1811	54 issues of miscellaneous Dublin newspapers – *Faulkner's Dublin Journal*, *The Patriot*, *The Correspondent*, *The Dublin Evening Herald*, *The Freeman's Journal*, etc.
13	1811–13	Octavo personal account book of the 2nd Earl.
13A	[*c.* 1800–20]	Small quarto recipe book of the 2nd Earl's wife, Alicia. [This book is kept in the small library in Birr Castle. For other recipes/recipe books, see A/17, G/20 and M/18.]
14/1–99	1808–31: 1833	Letters and papers (occupying two-thirds of a box) of the 2nd Earl about the Irish Post Office, of which he was Joint Postmaster General, 1809–30 [see the Introduction], including: papers about the alleged misconduct of the Secretary of the G.P.O., E.S. Lees, 1816 and 1822, among them a letter from Robert Peel,[the Chief Secretary, on the subject; an undated note from Lees lamenting 'It is really too bad to have the Postmaster General's papers missent ...'; returns of balances in the hands of individual postmasters, 1817, 1824–5 and 1829; reports on proposals for contracts to carry the mail, among them a report on a proposal of 1818 from Bianconi; memorials from the merchants and inhabitants of Castletownroche, Co. Cork, of Dublin, etc., mainly N.D.; correspondence about the 2nd Earl's dispute with the other Joint Postmaster General, Earl O'Neill, over a Post Office appointment at Limerick, 1828, and more amicable correspondence over O'Neill's wish for a marquessate in the same year; and correspondence about Post Office reform and the 2nd Earl's resignation on the fall of the Duke of Wellington's administration in 1830. [This sub-section has been microfilmed by PRONI – MIC 512/10. See also D/14, D/22 and 0/11.]*
14A	1990-91	Correspondence of the 7th Earl of Rosse about the launch by him of the Northern Ireland Post Office Board-sponsored publication,

E/14A *contd.*   *Sources for the History of the Post Office in Ireland* in the Market
                           House, Hillsborough, Co. Down, 1991, together with a letter and
                           a note from Victoria Glendinning about her research in E/14 in
                           connection with Anthony Trollope's association with the Irish Post
                           Office.

15/1–5   1813: 1819:   Contemporary copies of the wills of sundry inhabitants of Birr;
         1829:   together with letters of administration of the goods of Rev.
         [*c.* 1829]:   William Parsons of Tullynisky Park, Birr [see Q/56], younger
         1836   brother of the 2nd Earl.

16/1–15 1809: 1815–18:   Letters to the 2nd Earl about the progress and prospects of his
         1822: 1827–9:   sons, Lord Oxmantown and John C. Parsons, the possibility of
         1985   their being sent to Harrow, their studies at Trinity College,
                           Dublin, Magdalen, Oxford, etc, the chemistry books of Lord
                           Oxmantown, Lord Oxmantown's bright suggestion about forcing
                           the Dardanelles and the Duke of Wellington's tart response to the
                           2nd Earl on the subject, 1828, correspondence of the 7th Earl of
                           Rosse about the mystery of why and where the 3rd Earl was born
                           in York, 1985, etc.

16A   1990   Correspondence of the 7th Earl of Rosse with Roger Hutchins of
                           Magdalen about the part which Magdalen played in developing
                           the 3rd Earl's interest in astronomy.

17/1–21 Apr.-Aug. 1818   Letters to the 2nd Earl about the general election in King's
                           County.*

18   1818: 1821:   Copies of wills and codicils of the 2nd Earl and (1864) of his
         1828: 1838–9:   widow, Alicia, Countess of Rosse. [For copies of 2 earlier wills, of
         1841: 1864   1806 and 1813, see National Library, D.24152–4.]

19   1819–21   Fragmentary accounts between the 2nd Earl and his younger
                           brother, Thomas C. Parsons.

20   May 1822   Folio volume containing the observations of William Parsons
                           [not the same William Parsons as E/15 and hardly the same as
                           D/24?], an acknowledged Revenue expert, on the Irish Customs
                           and Excise, submitted to the Commissioners of Enquiry into the
                           Irish Revenue.

21/1–12 1825   Papers concerning Rodolphus Buchanan, distiller, a bankrupt,
                           present in Birr Castle because Buchanan held a lease of Mount
                           Sally, Birr, reassigned to the 2nd Earl in 1825, and a lease of
                           premises near the tuck mill of Birr [see Q/68 and 73]; included in
                           the sub-section are earlier papers of 1781–2, 1806 and 1815.

22   1826–8   *c.* 12 bundles of papers of the 2nd Earl's second son, John C.
                           Parsons, who died young in 1828, consisting mainly of
                           parliamentary papers of his elder brother, Lord Oxmantown, M.P.
                           for King's County and notes by John C. Parsons on these,
                           evidently made with a view to research or a publication on

* See detailed calendar.

E/22 *contd.*		political economy. [These papers have been kept for many years, and possibly since John C. Parsons's death, in a trunk at one end of the first-floor landing in Birr Castle, under a marble bust of John C. Parsons.]
23	1827–9: 1833	Letters and papers of the 2nd Earl concerning the illness and death of John C. Parsons, the sculpting of the bust of him, and the erection of 'John's Hall' (the schoolhouse in Birr) in memory of him [see also Q/85]. Included in the sub-section are John C. Parsons's last letters to his father, an account book kept by him up to the time of his death, letters of condolence to the 2nd Earl on that event [apart from letters written by those who already have 'correspondence' sub-sections to themselves in Section D], and MS. 'Reflections' by the 2nd Earl, which in effect constitute a short life-history of John C. Parsons, whose death affected him deeply, and probably accentuated the religiosity of his later years.
24/1–2	July 1832: Feb. 1833	Two weekly lists of labourers and their wages.
25/1–29	Oct.-Dec. 1832	Letters to the 2nd Earl and Lord Oxmantown, mainly the latter, about the King's County general election, at which Lord Oxmantown was one of the successful candidates.*
26	Nov. 1832– May 1833	Original bundle consisting of receipts to Dr George Heenan, the agent, Parsonstown, for the sums received by him on behalf of the 2nd Earl, and 3 letters from the 2nd Earl to Heenan.
27	Apr.-June 1834	Thank-you letters to the 2nd Earl for presentation copies of his book, *An Argument to Prove the Truth of the Christian Revelation*, published in that year [see F/15], from among others, Lords Arden, Holland and Lansdowne, and the Bishop of Kildare.
28	1808: 1828: 1841	Two letters and a deed relating to the 2nd Earl's role as a trustee of the marriage settlement of the Rev. Henry Mahon of Killegally, King's County, younger brother of Sir Ross Mahon, 1st Bt.
29	8 Jan. 1835	Addressed but unsent printed copies of an election circular from Lord Oxmantown to sundry King's County electors; the theme of the circular is the defects of the present franchise, which have induced Lord Oxmantown to withdraw his candidature rather than solicit support from the enemies of the Union and of the Established Church.
30	1841	Printed poll book for the borough of Brighton, Sussex, where the 2nd Earl died in that year.
31/1–28	1780–91	Miscellaneous political, personal and general correspondence of the 2nd Earl, then Sir Laurence Parsons, from miscellaneous correspondents, including Dr John Jebb, the English parliamentary reformer, the Hon. George Knox, a younger son of the 1st Viscount Northland, the 1st Earl of Charlemont, etc. The

* See detailed calendar.

E/31 *contd.*   topics include the split among the Patriots over the Simple Repeal
of Poynings's Law, with which Grattan and his followers declared
themselves satisfied, and the Renunciation on Britain's part of the
right to legislate for Ireland, which Flood and *his* followers
declared to be essential, 1783; parliamentary reform, 1784; the
Commercial Propositions, 1785; the mode of drawing up the Irish
public accounts, 1788; the regency crisis, 1788–9; and Trinity
College, Dublin, and King's County politics and elections,
particularly Parsons's failure to be re-elected for the former at the
general election of 1790 and his election for the latter at a by-
election in 1791. Also included is an undated, vituperative poem
attacking the 1st Earl of Clonmell, *c.* 1790? [One of the letters
from Dr Jebb has been photostated by the National Library (MS.
13840), and a second photostat copy has been placed alongside
the original.]*

32/1–38 1794–1800   The same. In this continuation of E/31, the correspondents
include John Lloyd of Gloster, Parsons's father-in-law, the 2nd Earl
of Charlemont (son and successor of the 'Volunteer' Earl), John
Foster (Speaker of the Irish House of Commons and, in effect,
leader of the opposition to the Union), Colonel E. B. Littlehales
(private secretary to the Lord Lieutenant, Marquess Cornwallis),
etc; and the topics include the recall of Lord Fitzwilliam in 1795,
the '98 Rebellion, King's County politics and law and order, the
Union, etc. Also included in the sub-section is a long, but
incomplete, MS. pamphlet, in the form of a letter to Parsons,
*c.*1797, and a special licence and a newspaper cutting relating to
his marriage to Alicia Lloyd of Gloster in May of that year [see
E/38. Several of these letters have been photostated by the
National Library (MS. 13840) and a second set of photostats has
been placed alongside the originals. An envelope of papers
including and concerning the 7th Earl of Rosse's *Irish Times* article
of 1963 on the '98 Rebellion has also been placed in this sub-
section, as has a photocopy of a letter from Parsons to Mrs Jane
Lloyd, January–April 1797, about his engagement to her niece,
Alicia (PRONI, D.3897/3).]*

33/1–47 1801–10   The same. The correspondents include Henry Addington (First
Lord of the Treasury and Prime Minister), the Dowager
Marchioness of Downshire (owner of the Blundell estate at
Edenderry, King's County), John Lloyd, Arthur French of
Frenchpark, Co. Roscommon (who complains of ill-treatment at
the hands of the Pitt administration), Sir Thomas Fetherston of
Ardagh, Co. Longford (who sat for that county on the electoral
interest of the 1st Earl of Rosse), and the Dublin Castle powers-
that-were, including the 3rd Earl of Hardwicke (Lord Lieutenant,
1801-6), William Wickham, (Chief Secretary, 1802–4), Alexander
Marsden (Under-secretary, 1801–6) and Sir Arthur Wellesley,

*   See detailed calendar.

E/33 *contd.*
(later 1st Duke of Wellington, Chief Secretary, 1807–9). The topics include both general politics and the local politics of King's County, Co. Longford, Co. Tipperary and Carlow borough, concerning the last of which the 2nd Earl is asked to act as a referee between the 1st Earl of Charleville, the patron of the borough, and Frederick John Robinson, to whom he had sold the seat; Lord Melville's trial; the 2nd Earl's initially unsuccessful aspirations to the Irish representative peerage, 1809; the charges against the Duke of York as Commander-in-Chief, 1809; and various minor patronage matters.*

34/1–41 1811–20
The same. The correspondents include Robert Peel Chief Secretary, 1812–18, and the topics, King's County politics, law and order, agriculture, etc [for a complete sub-section on the King's County election of 1818, see E/17]. Also included in this sub-section is a description, in the form of an original letter from the 2nd Earl to his brother, the Rev. William Parsons of Tullynisky Park, Birr, of a reception in London for the visiting Continental dignitaries in 1814.*

35/1–45 1821–34:
1839
The same, including some letters addressed to Lord Oxmantown. The correspondents include Lord Norbury, the 2nd Earl of Liverpool (Prime Minister, 1812–27), the Marquess Wellesley (Lord Lieutenant, 1821–7), Lord Francis Leveson Gower (Chief Secretary, 1828–30), and Sir Benjamin Bloomfield (later 1st Lord Bloomfield). The topics include King's County patronage, militia, law and order, and elections; the views of Thomas Foster, who had just finished the portrait of the 2nd Earl, in George IV coronation robes, which is in the dining room in Birr Castle, about his painting, 'Mazeppa', and other artistic matters, 1822 [for Foster, see also E/34/35 and D/22/6, 9, and 14]; the desirability of having a pope of 'moderate principles' (in Lord Liverpool's view, expressed in 1823); the financial affairs of the late Capt. Hardress Lloyd of the Gloster family, but not the namesake who was M.P. for King's County, 1807–18; etc, etc. [For other original correspondence of the 2nd Earl relating to the late Capt. Hardress Lloyd's affairs, 1823–5, see National Library, MS. 13885. These particular papers appear not to be of Birr Castle provenance.]*

36/1–9 1788: 1803–8:
1822: 1825:
1828
Letters to the 2nd Earl about his small remaining Co. Wexford estate, from the agent, Benjamin Porter of Raheen, Gorey, Co. Wexford, whose letters enclose rentals and accounts; these show that the estate comprised the lands of Ballyduff, etc, and that the rental, in 1807, was a mere £350. [Confusingly, two of the townlands in the King's County and Co. Tipperary estates of the Parsons family are also called Ballyduff, the King's County Ballyduff being near Birr, and the Tipperary Ballyduff, inherited from the Cleres, being near Clonmel.]

* See detailed calendar.

E/37/1–90	1805–11: 1814–26: 1828–33	Letters to the 2nd Earl about the affairs of his estates elsewhere than Co. Wexford – in King's County, Co. Tipperary and, apparently, Co. Kilkenny. The principal correspondents are fellow-landowners, including the Droughts of Droughtville and Whigsborough, King's County, John Lloyd of Gloster, and the 1st Lord Dunalley (about the disposal in 1805 of some Tipperary property (the Sopwell Hall estate, near Cloughjordan) belonging to Dunalley and adjoining the 2nd Earl's estate in that county), etc, etc; and also sundry tenants of the 2nd Earl, whose letters and memorials will be found in this sub-section unless they relate to the town of Birr [see E/1]. One matter discussed in some detail is a partition, effected in 1806, between the 2nd Earl and John Lloyd of a property in and around Shinrone, King's County [see Q/53] which, for reasons unconnected with the 2nd Earl's marriage to Lloyd's daughter in 1797, they owned jointly.
38/1–8	1791: 1797: 1806: 1820: 1826: 1829–30	Miscellaneous title deeds or deeds of settlement concerning parts of the 2nd Earl's estates in King's County and Co. Tipperary, including the settlement made on his marriage of Gloster, 1797, a non-contemporary copy of the 1806 deed of partition [see E/37 and O/47], a conveyance with Alicia Lloyd by Lord Dunalley to the 2nd Earl of lands in Co. Tipperary (Ballyloughnane, Croghan, Killeen, etc) for £20,000, 1820, and a reconveyance by the heirs-at-law of the late Marlborough Stirling of a mortgage granted by the 2nd Earl [see E/3], 1826.
39/1–6	1836	Series of deeds which together constitute the settlement made on the marriage of Lord Oxmantown, later 3rd Earl of Rosse, and Mary Field. [See G/19 and Section G generally, and also J/19/2.]
40/1–4	1792–3: 1806: 1825	Patents and commissions to the 2nd Earl or to his uncle, the 1st Earl, with remainder to him: grant of supporters to the 1st Earl, after his elevation as Baron Oxmantown, 1792; commission of the peace to the 2nd Earl as a J.P. for Co. Limerick (presumably because the King's County Militia was stationed there?), 1793; patent creating the earldom of Rosse, 1806; and patent appointing the 2nd Earl Custos Rotulorum of King's County, 1825. [The grant of supporters, 1792, and patent of peerage, 1806, are outsize and are to be framed.]
41/1	1807–38	Vellum-bound, small folio volume, tempore the 2nd Earl of Rosse, but of uncertain provenance, recording precedents for various types of legal document – eg. feoffment, will, etc. Though presumably assembled by a law student or solicitor's apprentice, the volume contains almost verbatim transcriptions of various deeds, one of them the marriage settlement of the 5th Earl of Abingdon, [1807], and several others relating to the Imokilly branch of the Ponsonby family, Earls of Bessborough.

* See detailed calendar.

E/42/1 1759: 1775: 1794–1795: 1816–1823

Bundle of letters and papers, not of Rosse provenance but an appropriate addition to the archive at Birr Castle, because they relate to part of the Harman/Parsons estate in Co. Longford and elsewhere. The letters and papers derive from Graves Chamney Swan of Stewart & Swan, land agents, 6 Leinster Street, Dublin. Swan acted for R.B. Deverell, husband of Anne Harman/Parsons, who was the daughter of Wentworth Harman/Parsons, elder brother of the 1st Earl of Rosse. On the death of Wentworth Harman/Parsons in 1794, most of his mother's estates (deriving from Cutts Harman, Dean of Waterford), passed to his younger brother, the future 1st Earl of Rosse. But, according to D/7/142, the 'entailed estates' passed after a lawsuit to Wentworth's daughter, Anne, Mrs Deverell. This bundle of letters and papers relates to those entailed estates, which consisted of a house in Kildare Street, Dublin, the Castlecor estate, Co. Longford (where Dean Harman, who had confined himself to making a grand 'bungalow' addition to Newcastle, Co. Longford, had built a small architectural fantasy based on the duke of Savoy's hunting-lodge at Stupingi, near Turin, which is still recognisable today in spite of subsequent accretions), and the small estate of Millicent, Abbeylands and Clane, Co. Kildare. In 1818, by which time the Kildare Street house was no longer part of the inheritance, these entailed estates were yielding *c.* £1,550 a year, of which *c.* £275 derived from Millicent.

The bundle includes: copy memorials of deeds relating to the Kildare Street property, 1759 and 1795; copy probate (1775) of the will (1773) of Anne Parsons, Lady Parsons (mother of Wentworth and the future 1st Earl of Rosse), and copy probate (1794) of the will (1786) of Wentworth Harman/Parsons; letters, tenants' proposals, etc, to R.B. Deverell (who outlived his first wife, Anne, the heiress, remarried, died at the end of 1820 and was long survived by his second wife) at various addresses in Middlesex and to G.C. Swan, about all manner of estate and financial business; and a rental, with accompanying vouchers, for the entailed estate, 1818. Some of the correspondence relates to the problem of finding a new tenant for Castlecor after the existing tenant went bankrupt in 1818, some to the doubtful probity and solvency of R.B. Deverell's Co. Longford agent, Richard Armstrong, some to the double-dealing of Mr Griffith, tenant of Millicent, and there is one very full report of June 1820 on the Co. Longford estate, with queries about whether Deverell wants to arrest the change from protestant to catholic tenants on the estate in order to keep up his registry of freeholders.

F/	DATE	DESCRIPTION
1–23	[1765?]: *c.* 1775–*c.* 1840	Notes and drafts by Sir Laurence Parsons, 2nd Earl of Rosse, in connection with various subjects: parliamentary precedents, his speeches at College Green and Westminster, his poems, the history and genealogy of the Parsons family, and his miscellaneous writings (published or unpublished), with the exception of those on the subject of Henry Flood [for which, see Section C].
1/1–3	[late 1770s?]	Three folio volumes concerning parliamentary precedent and procedure, the last two in what appears to be the handwriting of a youthful Sir Laurence Parsons and constituting Parts 2 and 3 of some kind of history of the subject, the first in another hand, though possibly it is Part 1 of the same history. At the end of the third volume, and upside down in the book, is a translation of, or variation on, Demosthenes's 'Oration on the letter of Philip of Macedon to the Athenians'.
2	[*c.* 1780– *c.* 1840]	Box containing drafts of poems and other literary compositions by the 2nd Earl, principally his thirteen-canto poem, 'The Revolution [of 1688]', together with extracts from State Papers and other historical jottings in connection with that work.
3	1784–8	Rough sketches by Parsons of some of the events of the Lord Lieutenancies of the Duke of Rutland and the Marquess of Buckingham, including the clashes between John Foster and Sir John Pamell, Chancellor of the Irish Exchequer, on the one hand, and John FitzGibbon, the Attorney-General, on the other, over the bill for lowering the rate of interest from 6 percent to 5 percent*
4		Blank in the sequence.
5	[1780s?]	Small notebook in which Parsons has recorded comments on the populations of various parts of England and Scotland.
6	[*c.* 1789–98]	Extensive jottings and notes by Parsons on the state and constitution of France, French Revolution, the justification for and conduct of the war against the French Republic, etc, etc.
7	[*c.* 1791–5?]	Small notebook containing jottings on the antiquities and ancient language of Ireland, which goes into much greater detail on the subject than his *Observations on the Bequest of Henry Flood to Trinity College, Dublin, with the Defence of the Ancient History of Ireland* (Dublin, 1795), and therefore can hardly be the MS. of that work referred to in the *First Report* of the H.M.C. – see C/11.
8	1792–3	Small notebook containing notes by Parsons for his *Thoughts on Liberty and Equality,* together with a printed copy of that pamphlet which has, attached to the fly-leaves, an MS. copy of Burke's letter of 1793 praising it [for the original of which, see D/3]; also included in this sub-section is a page containing a few much harsher comments, apparently made by an anonymous

* See detailed calendar.

F/8 *contd.*		critic, which would seem to have been implemented, in MS, by Parsons in this printed copy of the pamphlet.
9	[*c.* 1793–8]	Speech notes by Parsons for speeches advocating economical and parliamentary reform, discussing the Catholic Question, urging that the Irish administration adopt measures of conciliation, suggesting counter-propaganda to that of the United Irishmen, etc, etc.
10	[1799–1801]	Speech notes by Parsons for anti-Union orations, including notes for a couple of speeches at Westminster just after the Union and making allusion to that measure and to the future government of Ireland.
11	[*c.* 1800–*c.* 1840]	Fat bundle of notes by Parsons on the history and genealogy of the Parsons family, including various drafts of justifications of the conduct of Lord Justice Parsons in the 1640s; drawings of Parsons coats of arms, including those of '... Anne Malham, the first Lady Parsons of Birr', those of the Parsonses of York, 'Parsons quartered with Sprig [*sic*] and Denny charged with Clere', 'Parsons impaled with Loftus', sketches of the seals of Viscount Rosse (1682), Arthur Parsons, 1708?, and Sir William Parsons, 1734, etc; a two-page account of the Malham family; a ' short notice of [the] family of Colonel Emmanuel Pigott, brother to Miss Pigott, who married [Sir] William Parsons, 1705'; an MS. pedigree (20 pages) of the Clere family, taken from a history of Norfolk, and a late 16th century MS. volume containing Norfolk pedigrees, including that of Clere; extracts from the marriage register for Pontefract, Yorkshire, concerning Parsonses; lists of acts of parliament and extracts from the *Commons' Journals* concerning the Parsonses of Parsonstown and Lord Justice Parsons; pedigrees of the Parsonses of Parsonstown, and lengthy notes on the history of the family and the town, 1620–1802, all by the 2nd Earl; and 4 letters, of 1804–5 and 1828, to the 2nd Earl about Parsons portraits, pedigrees, etc, and the connection between the Parsonses and the Nettervilles. [For this last connection, see A/1 and D/18. For other letters to the 2nd Earl about family history, see D/5 and 8.]
12	[*c.* 1806]	Two sketches by Parsons, one concerning his own indifference to office and power, the other concerning the formation of Lord Grenville's 'Ministry of All the Talents'.*
13	[post 1816]	Incomplete? 'Political recollections' of Parsons, now 2nd Earl of Rosse, covering the years 1777–81. This document has been photostated by the National Library (MS. 13841), and a second photostat has been placed alongside the original.*
14	[1822 onwards]	Speech notes and other jottings of the 2nd Earl, on Catholic Emancipation and the Repeal of the Union, with particular reference to a debate in the House of Lords over the contents of a stolen and published letter from William Saurin, Attorney-General

---

* See detailed calendar.

F/14 *contd.*   for Ireland, to Lord Norbury, in which the 2nd Earl's real
                              sentiments on the Catholic Question had been quoted [see F/21],
                              1822; these notes include references to Daniel O'Connell, Dr
                              James Warren Doyle, Roman Catholic Bishop of Leighlin and
                              Ferns, etc, etc.

15   [Early 1830s?]   Voluminous drafts and notes by the 2nd Earl for works on
                              theological and philosophical subjects, presumably including
                              preliminary notes for his *Truth of the Christian Revelation*
                              (London, 1834) [see E/27].

16   [1775–1812]   Folio commonplace book/scrapbook of the 2nd Earl's, in which he
                              has made apparently youthful notes on 'Embargo', 'Strength of a
                              state external and internal', etc, and notes on speeches in the Irish
                              House of Commons, which must have been delivered prior to his
                              becoming a member of it in 1782, one of them opposing the
                              proposal that a proportion of the troops on the Irish establishment
                              should be replaced by Hessians, 1775, another advocating
                              retrenchment at least back to the far from inexpensive level of the
                              administration of Lord Harcourt, *c.* 1778. The same volume has
                              been turned upside down and used as a receptacle for newspaper
                              cuttings concerning the Battle of Borodino and other events of
                              Napoleon's invasion of Russia in 1812.

17   [*c.* 1778–   The same, consisting of the sort of entries which are characteristic
        c. 1819]   of a commonplace book, under such topics as 'Absentees',
                             'Boroughs', 'Popularity', 'Treason', etc, but also containing, under
                              the headings 'Reform' and 'Regency', notes 'of a much more
                              extensive kind, which appear to be from speeches delivered in the
                              Irish House of Commons on parliamentary reform in 1784 and
                              on the regency in 1789; under 'Anecdotes' there is one of Marshal
                              Suvarov which appears to date from *c.* 1810. [Some of the
                              handwriting in this book may conceivably be Flood's, not
                              Parsons's: Parsons's youthful handwriting is somewhat protean.]

18   1785–93   Similar volume, which is however octavo in size and much
                              slimmer, recording snippets from debates in the British House of
                              Commons and items of Spanish, Turkish, etc, history, 1785–6 and
                              1793.

19   [1794–8]:   Folio commonplace book/scrapbook, which Parsons has begun to
        1938–9   use to record the dates of bills drawn by him or on him, but which
                              is converted to other purposes, particularly to an account of
                              parliamentary and other political transactions involving Parsons,
                              January-March 1794 and January 1795; the book also includes
                              notes for speeches or pamphlets on the corn bounties,
                              parliamentary reform, 'The repeal of the Insurrection Bill', etc,
                              and also the first few pages of some political recollections along the
                              lines of F/13, covering (in a fairly uninformed fashion, since
                              Parsons was very young at the time) the period between the

F/19 *contd.*

passing of the Octennial Act and the outbreak of the American War. The book was the principal element in the Rosse papers drawn on by Stephen Gwynn in his *Henry Grattan and his Times* (London, 1939), so subjoined to it are Gwynn's letters to the 6th Earl of Rosse on the subject, 1938–9.*

20   1791–1819

Quarto commonplace book, bound in red morocco, containing copies (the paper of the book is marked 1811) of poems by Parsons, most of them expressing home-sickness for Birr and Ireland generally, and variously titled 'The Absentees', 1801 (this also contains passages about 'Charleville Castle'), 'Passage from Dublin to Holyhead, March 24 1804', 'Verses on quitting Birr Castle in 1812, written for Lord Oxmantown to turn into Latin verse', 'Passage from Holyhead to Dublin in December 1819', etc, etc; and also including poems in other subjects, particularly on the death of Flood in 1791, and on Parsons's resignation of the command of the King's County Militia in 1798. [The poem on the latter subject is accompanied by copies of the correspondence between Parsons and Lord Camden, the Lord Lieutenant, which will be found in E/3.]*

Of Parsons's poetry, Norman Atkinson writes informatively: most of his poems '... are concerned with the events of his private life. The style of his poetry is heavy and sententious and the author frequently becomes preoccupied with moralisation and sentimentality. There is an impression of deep sincerity, and a more than ordinary appreciation of the pleasures of home life. [But] the effect is often wearisome, and there is a notable absence of the grace and flow which is such a characteristic feature of the work of many early 19th-century poets. Instead, his lines show a sound technical competence, typical of the Augustan poets of the 18th century, who always laid the chief emphasis on form. The effect is not improved by his unfortunate experiment in metre; in place of the ten syllables normally used in the heroic metre of his day, he introduced a greater number of unaccented syllables, leaving only five accented. This system, he believed, must produce a more flowing and varied measure. Yet he failed utterly to achieve this result, since his lines are jagged, graceless and at time of very faulty scantia. The most significant feature of Parsons's poetry, particularly when we compare it with his work on the Christian Revelation, is its strongly expressed belief in men's supremacy over nature. This, unlike his style, is characteristic of the early 19th century. ...'

21   [1765?]:
          1795–8:
          1822–8

Folio commonplace book/scrapbook, which originally must have been Flood's property, as the first item in it is a lengthy (*c.* 30 pages) draft, in Flood's handwriting, for his speech on the Address in October 1765?, in which he maintains that the British ministry

---

*   See detailed calendar.

F/21 *contd.*

is bent on destroying the liberties of America, Ireland and England, warns the House against falling into the trap of exaggerating the gravity of the Whiteboy disturbances, and asserts the pre-Norman antiquity of the Irish constitution and the pre-Norman civilization of the Irish people. The rest of the book contains speech-and other notes by Parsons, together with relevant newspaper cuttings inserted by him. These notes and cuttings particularly concern the work-up to the '98 Rebellion, in King's County and elsewhere, February-April 1798, and include copies of proclamations and circulars from Dublin Castle; there are also comments by Parsons on the 'Bill to prevent seditious assemblies, English parliament, November 17, 1795'. The rest of the book is devoted to the period 1822–8, and contains, among other things, a newspaper publication of the text of the stolen letter from Saurin to Lord Norbury [see F/14], 1822. Also included is a newspaper publication of a King's County address to Lord Wellesley in March 1822, which Parsons, now 2nd Earl, notes was composed by his younger brother, Thomas C. Parsons. There are a couple of papers about the death of Thomas C. Parsons and the local testimonial to him [see also D/5], and also notes and papers on the death of another brother, John C. Parsons, on 1 May 1826 at Roscommon, where he was on circuit with the Insolvent Debtors' Court. On a brighter note, there is a detailed account of an entertainment given in the yellow drawing room in Birr Castle on 4 July 1926. Further detail about the disputes and skirmishes in Birr between the factions supporting the rival parish priests of the 1820s [see E/11] is provided, and a newspaper controversy between Bishop Doyle and the 5th Lord Farnham causes the 2nd Earl to record some interesting notes on Flood's motives at the time of the drawing up of the Volunteer plan of parliamentary reform in November 1783. [One end of this volume is in dire need of conservation.]*

22   *c.* 1796

Almost empty, small quarto commonplace book/scrapbook containing notes by Parsons for a speech against the war, 1796, and jottings on 'Modern history'.

23   [*c.* 1830]

Photocopy of an incomplete account in the 2nd Earl's handwriting of the rival parish priests affairs. [This photocopy was made by the 7th Earl in 1983 from the original in the possession of Mrs Trevor Lloyd, formerly of Gloster.]

G/	DATE	DESCRIPTION
1–69	*c.* 1540–2001	Papers (almost exclusively estate and financial) of the Wilmer Field family of Heaton Hall, Bradford, Yorkshire, whose co-heiress, Mary Field, married in 1836 Lord Oxmantown, later 3rd Earl of Rosse, including a few papers about the Heaton estate after its merger with the Rosse estates in Ireland.

This section of the Rosse archive is particularly complex, because the Field family were themselves heirs or co-heirs of a number of other Yorkshire families: in particular, the Sugers of Goodramgate, York, the Idles of Bulmer and Westow, and the Wilmers of Upper Helmsley. These ramifications are not actually relevant to the Rosse inheritance, which consisted solely of the Field estate of Heaton and Shipley. However, by the accidents of archival descent, it has happened that papers relating to properties which passed, on the death of Mary Field's father, John Wilmer Field, in 1837, either to her sister and co-heiress, Delia Duncombe, or to her father's younger brother, Joshua Field, are present in Section G. The genealogical particulars on which the arrangement which follows is based have been taken, either from the documents themselves, or from the *History of the Wilmer Family, together with some Account of its Descendants*, by Charles Wilmer Foster and Joseph J. Green (Leeds, 1888), pp 138–48. The arrangement is tripartite: G/1–20 contain papers of individual members or branches of the families concerned; G/21–51 contain papers relating to particular properties; and G/52–67 contain rentals, valuations and estate accounts.

1–20		**PAPERS RELATING TO INDIVIDUAL MEMBERS AND BRANCHES OF THE WILMER, IDLE, SUGER AND FIELD FAMILIES,** AS FOLLOWS:
1	1710–49	Deeds drawn up by Randall Wilmer of Staple Inn, London, and York City (1690–1761) in his professional capacity as an attorney in London and subsequently in his native York; the earliest deeds concern property in Essex, the latest property in Yorkshire, including that of the Sugar family of Goodramgate, York, into which Randall Wilmer married in 1749. Mary Wilmer, the second of his two daughters by Jane Suger, married in 1774 Joshua Field of Heaton. The documents in this sub-section have not been arranged in chronological order.
2/1–3	1716–28	Three vellum-bound folio volumes relating to Randall Wilmer's practice at Staple Inn; one of them a writ book, one a bill book, and the third of uncertain character.
3	1742–9	Fat, rolled bundle of case papers drawn up by Randall Wilmer in connection with a wide variety of cases at the York assizes. [Not in chronological order.]

G/4   1735: 1742–55 More or less original bundle of letters and legal case papers of John Idle of Bulmer and Westow, Lord Chief Baron of the Exchequer in Scotland, and a connection of Mrs Randall Wilmer's family, the Sugars, concerning his Yorkshire estate affairs. The papers consist mainly of letters from his agent, John Watson, and case papers in relation to his proceedings against Watson's widow after Watson's death. Also included in the sub-section is a pedigree setting out the connection between the Idles and the Sugers, and a copy of Chief Baron Idle's will of 1755.

5   [1750s–60s] Drafts of sermons by Rev. Zachary Suger, Rector of St Cuthbert's, York, a brother of Mrs Randall Wilmer, who ultimately succeeded to all his property. [Not in chronological order.]

6/1–38 1763: 1767–74: Original bundle, with some additions, of letters and papers of the
        1778: 1788: Suger/Wilmer family. The letters are to Thomas Johnson of York,
        1799 law agent to the late Nicholas Suger of Goodramgate (d.1763), to Suger's widow, Elizabeth, and to his daughters, Miss Martha Suger and Mrs Randall Wilmer. The subject-matter is the affairs of the Idle, Suger and Wilmer estates, jointures and annuities to various widows and dependants, etc; the principal correspondent is one Mrs Barbara Idle. Included among the additions to the bundle are a lease of the house and demesne of Westow, 1771, and a copy of the settlement made on the marriage of Joshua Field and Mary Wilmer, 1774.

7   1681: 1695–8: Bonds, legal case papers, calculations and 1 letter, all of John Field
        1702: 1707–8: of Heaton (d.1713).

8   1732: N.D.: Miscellaneous business letters and papers of John Field of Heaton
        1737: 1739: (d.1772), nephew and successor of Joseph Field, d.1733, who in
        1741: 1743: turn had been nephew and successor of John Field, d.1713. The
        1747: 1754: material includes case papers and correspondence about estate
        1761–2: 1772 and family affairs, a printed subscription list for the new assembly rooms in York, 1732, and a shrievalty document concerning York Gaol and its inmates, 1754.

9   1738–69 Receipts and accounts to, and 3 account books of, John Field of Heaton. [Not in chronological order.]

10   1759–61 Letters and case papers of John Field of Heaton concerning his action for debt against one Christopher Dibb.

11   1753: 1756: Eight, mostly folio, volumes of accounts, etc, deriving from John
        1758 Field, second son of John Field of Heaton, d.1772. The first two of the volumes are mathematics exercise books of 1753 and 1756, inscribed 'John Field'; the other 6 are account books of 1758, in a similar hand, relating to a Wakefield merchant who deals mainly in cloth and sends consignments of it to Barbados, among other places. This John Field died young, in December 1758; so it seems probable that the account books as well as the exercise books derive from him.

G/12	1777: 1785	Papers of Joshua Field of Heaton (1742–1819), elder son and successor of John Field, d.1772, and husband of Mary Wilmer, as a partner, with Henry Wickham and others, in the Leeds New Bank; the sub-section consists principally of draft and executed partnership deeds.
13	1778: 1780: 1783: 1786: 1789–91: N.D.: 1807–9: 1811–12: 1814–15: 1817	Miscellaneous business letters and papers of Joshua Field of Heaton, including his commission as a Deputy Lieutenant for the West Riding of Yorkshire, 1778, and a copy of a printed requisition from the undersigned gentlemen of Bradford and its vicinity (including Joshua Field) for a meeting to congratulate Pitt on the happy outcome of the regency crisis, 1789.
14	1790–c. 1825	Seven quarto children's exercise books; one belonging to J[oshua?] Field, another to 'Ann Field' presumably Mary Anne Field, one of Joshua Field's two sisters, and the 4 Last belonging to Mary Field, his daughter, the future Countess of Rosse.
15	1818–19	Medical prescriptions for Joshua Field during his last illness.
16	1811–12: 1819–34	Miscellaneous business and personal letters and papers of John Wilmer Field, elder son and successor of Joshua Field of Heaton, d.1819, about his father's death and will, his own estate and financial affairs, subscriptions to York Minster in 1830, etc, etc. The correspondents include John Wilmer Field's mother, one of his sisters, Mrs Delia FitzGerald, and his daughter, Mary, the future Countess of Rosse.
17	1819–22	Letters and papers of John Wilmer Field about his snobbish quest for a new coat of arms incorporating the maximum number of quarterings and rectifying the fact that the arms used by his father were bogus. The principal correspondent is William Ratclyffe of the College of Arms, who signs himself as 'Rouge Croix', although he frequently explains that he is currently under suspension from his official situation on a charge of forgery. There are also letters about the coat of arms from Edmund Lodge, Lancaster Herald, and from John Wilmer Field's younger brother. Joshua. The sub-section includes copies of ancient documents concerning the Thwenge and other families, and schedules of deeds transmitted by John Wilmer Field in proof of his various claims, and containing unique information about the genealogy and chronology of the Field family. Belonging in the sub-section, but stored elsewhere (in the top drawer of the old vestment chest in the Muniment Room) are 7 outsize, parchments, one of them John Wilmer Field's new grant of arms, 1821, the others coloured and emblazoned 16th-19th century pedigrees of the Field, Eton, Baskerville and Thwenge families.

G/18	1841: 1843: 1850: 1876: 1885: 1911–13: 1918: 1927	Miscellaneous letters and papers of the 3rd, 4th and 5th Earls of Rosse concerning Heaton, mainly its sale in 1911; including an outsize folder of printed maps, rentals and sale particulars, 1911. [Not in chronological order.]
19/1–15	1624: 1713: 1728: 1772: 1836: 1866: 1872: 1883–4: 1886	Wills and probates of heads of the Field family of Shipley and Heaton, including Mary Field, Countess of Rosse, the settlement of the Heaton estate made on her marriage, 1836, and subsequent re-settlements of 1866 and 1898. [For 1836 settlement deeds, of Rosse not Field provenance, see E/39.]
20	c. 1760–c. 1830	Recipes and poetry composed by members of the Field family.

21–51 PAPERS RELATING TO PARTICULAR PROPERTIES

21/1–15	1548: 1587: 1592: 1596: 1601: 1604: 1614: 1616–18: 1621: 1625	More-or-less original run of title deeds and leases concerning the manor of Allerthorpe-cum-Waplington, then the property of the Myers family of Allerthorpe, and subsequently acquired by the Idles.
22/1–29	1647: 1655: 1664: 1676: 1680–82: 1690: 1694: 1696: 1702–3: 1710: 1712: 1714: 1717: 1720 174 1–2: 1746	Further fat bundle of Allerthorpe title deeds and leases, in continuation of /21.
23	1625–1740	Original bundle of title deeds, leases and bonds, numbered G.1–G.41, relating to Allerthorpe; in numerical order according to the G.1–G.41 sequence, which is not a chronological sequence. [It is purely coincidental that this sequence should bear the prefix 'G', which is the prefix of this section of the Rosse Papers.]
24	1696–1706	Original bundle of receipts and assessments concerning the Myers family and Allerthorpe.
25	1700: 1707: 1709: 1713–15	Leases, etc, of farms in Allerthorpe granted by Thomas Myers.
26	1716	Certificate signed by the Mayor of King's Lynn, Norfolk, in respect of the 'Susanna' of Hull, whose owner is Ralph Myers of Allerthorpe.
27	1736–43	Lease of the capital messuage and several closes in Allerthorpe from Chief Baron Idle and Alderman William Cookson to one William Cell, 1736, together with an original bundle of receipts, mainly to Cookson, for fee farm rents issuing out of Allerthorpe.

G/28   *c.* 1550s–1620s Fat bundle of title deeds and leases relating to the township of Beilby, near Allerthorpe, therefore presumably relating to that property. [Not in chronological order, and some of them in a deplorable physical state.]

29   1596–1686: 1730: 1756   Original bundle, with some additions, of title deeds and leases relating to Bulmer and Welburn, which by 1730 belonged to Jeremiah Idle of Bulmer. The principal additions consist of 4 deeds relating to the other Idle properties of Westow and Tockwith. [Not in chronological order.]

30   1604: 1631: 1659: 1704: 1717: 1721: 1725   Original bundle, labelled 'Title deeds of the house in Stonegate, York, purchased by Mrs Elizabeth Suger', widow of Nicholas Suger of Goodramgate, and mother of Mrs Randall Wilmer.

31A   1655: 1671: 1682: 1709: 1714: 1719: 1733: 1739: 1778: 1783: 1785: 1790: 1792–3: 1798: 1806: 1814   Mainly original bundle of title deeds and leases concerning the Idle, Wilmer and Suger properties of Barnby Moor, Leavening, Burythorpe, Kennythorpe, Marton, Pocklington and Goodramgate.

31B   1660–1760   Two envelopes containing an original run of Burythorpe deeds, leases and related papers (including wills of the Bowers family, from whom Chief Baron Idle bought the property in 1749).

32/1–5   1707: 1744: 1792: 1794: 1797   Title deeds and case papers concerning the inheritance of Randall Wilmer's elder daughter, Ann, who married her cousin, Wilmer Gossip, and concerning the half of the Wilmer manor of Upper Helmsley [see O/2A] which passed to the Gossip family through this marriage, until bought in 1804 by Joshua Field, the husband of Ann Gossip's younger sister, Mary, who inherited the other half of the manor.

33   1756: 1766: 1770: 1777: N.D.: 1822   Leases of parts of Upper Helmsley granted by Randall Wilmer and Jane, his widow, 1756 and 1766, papers about Upper Helmsley Church and a Suger memorial erected there, 1770, 1777 and N.D., and papers of John Wilmer Field about the lapsed manor court of Upper Helmsley, 1822.

34   1624–35: 1684: 1742: 1759–6   Title deeds to the second and adjoining Field manor of Shipley, including mid-18th century King's Bench decrees. [Not in chronological order, and possibly overlapping the documents in the sub-section which follows.]

35   *c.* 1540–1741   Title deeds to Heaton, including a post mortem inventory of 1600. [Not in chronological order; see also G/34.]

G/36/1–37	1622: 1674: 1689: 1704: 1738: 1741–2: 1752: 1759: 1767: 1781: 1789–1803: 1810: 1815–17: 1819: 1822	Large bundle of accounts and papers concerning the township of Heaton and its assessment for land tax [see also G/58], poor rates,church rates, illegitimate children, etc; with papers about localboundaries and roads, amenities provided by the Field family, subscriptions to Bradford charities and religious organisations,etc, etc. The earliest item concerns a boundary dispute betweenHeaton and Manningham, 1622; there is an incomplete run of Heaton Poor Law overseers' accounts, 1789–1819; and the final items include printed reports on Bradford Grammar school, Religious Tract Society and Auxiliary Bible Society, 1819.
37	1735: 1737: 1786: 1789: 1828	Papers about Bradford parish church and tithes, including a history of them back to 1638, and about the Field pew in the church and, later, in the district church of Shipley.
38	1679: 1689–90: 1693: 1702: 1736: 1738: 1753: 1757: 1759: 1762: 1772: 1775–6: 1808: 1817: 1819	Leases of closes, minerals, etc, in Heaton, granted by successive heads of the Field family.
39	1742: 1760–61: 1772	King's Bench writs and decrees, and another case paper, concerning disputes with tenants and actions for trespass at Heaton.
40	1790	Small, original bundle of papers concerning the sale, by R.F. Lister to Joshua Field, of additional land in Heaton.
41	[c. 1820]	'Particulars of lands sold, and of lands now in Mr Field's possession, contained in settlements and conveyed in exchange.' The document itemises the lands of Newsholme, Idle, Eccleshill, Pudsey, Bildon, Chellow, etc, etc, and is included at this point because most of the deeds which follow relate to the lands concerned.
42	1676–94	Original bundle of title deeds and other papers concerning the Field estate in Pudsey, acquired from a family called Lumby. [Not in chronological order.]
43 in	1639:	Fat bundle of title deeds, leases and bonds relating to property
	1687–1805	the town of Bradford, and the settlement on the marriage of Judith Field, sister? of John Field of Heaton, d.1772 and Henry Atkinson of Bradford in 1733. [Not in chronological order.]

G/44	1612: 1677: 1691: 1706: 1752	Title deeds and leases concerning Cullingworth and Hardon, parish of Bingley.
45	1599–1778: [c. 1810]	Title deeds and leases concerning Allerton, Chellow, Clayton, Eccleshill, Oxenhope and Yeadon, parish of Bradford; together with two memoranda'... to show that the Chellow estate is part of the dissolved monastery of Selby', c. 1810.
46	1614–1701	Title deeds and leases concerning Manningham, parish of Bradford. [Not in chronological order.]
47	1605: 1724: 1727: 1733: 1735: 1749: 1779: 1823	Title deeds and leases concerning Bolton and Idle, parish of Calverley.
48	1661–1785	Title deeds and leases concerning Newsholme and Gamster, parish of Keighley. [Not in chronological order.]
49	c. 1600–1771	Title deeds and leases concerning Bildon and Newhall, parish of Ottley. [The earliest document in the sub-section is damaged, and its date illegible.]
50	1599–1708: 1810	Miscellaneous title deeds and leases relating to Yorkshire properties, none of them connected in any obvious way with the other documents in Section G. The sub-section includes documentation of urban properties in Hull, Leeds and Newcastle, and also a post mortem inventory of the goods of Walter Appleton of Goodman, 1602. [Not in chronological order.]
51	1702	Marriage settlement concerning the estate of Sir Thomas Hanbury of Little Martle, Herefordshire. [It is not clear why this document should have been found among the Field papers.]

52–67 RENTALS, VALUATIONS AND ESTATE ACCOUNTS

52A	1640	Terrier or survey of Thomas Myers's manor of Allerthorpe.
52/1–2	1737–1819	Two tall, thin, vellum-bound volumes recording rent receipts for Heaton and elsewhere, including receipts from the lordship of the manor, 1796–1820.
53/1–2	1767–1819	The same, recording miscellaneous household and other accounts of Joshua Field of Heaton.
54/1	1765–74	Slim, small quarto account book recording accounts between James Rothwell and Joshua Field for the building of a new house and offices at Heaton.
55/1	1772–6	Tall, vellum-bound account book for the Mill Stone Hill coalmine near Heaton.

G/56	1781–1817	Fifteen small octavo household demesne and farm account books for Heaton, tempore Joshua Field.
57	1812–35	Nine volumes, ranging in size from tall, thin folio to small, squat octavo, recording household and personal expenditure and the general financial position of John Wilmer Field, including calculations of the income of the Earls of Rosse prior to the marriage of Field's daughter to Lord Oxmantown in 1836.
58	1818–32	Tall, vellum-bound 'Tax book' for the township of Heaton [see G/36], including acreage and valuation particulars.
59	1819–35	Rentals and estate accounts for Heaton, including timber and stone valuations and sale papers.
60	1819–34	The same in respect of Shipley.
61	1828–31: 1872–8	Two octavo volumes, one including jottings of John Wilmer Field about estate and other income and expenditure, both containing a record of stocks and shares in the handwriting of the 4th Earl of Rosse. In view of the provenance, it has been assumed that these stocks and shares derived from the Field inheritance.
62	1837–40: 1849: 1852	Letters, accounts and valuations concerning the estates of the late John Wilmer Field. Collectively, these show that his personal estate, after payment of debts, yielded £8,700 to each of his daughters and co-heiresses, Lady Oxmantown and the Hon. Mrs Arthur Duncombe; that the former took, as her share of the real estate, Heaton and Shipley (valued at £88,000, subject to a mortgage of £10,000), and the latter 'the York estate', consisting of the Idle, Suger and Wilmer properties, minus Upper Helmsley, which passed to John Wilmer Field's younger brother, Joshua; and that the Heaton and Shipley rental was *c.* £3,000 a year in 1849.
63	1858–67: 1869–74: 1878–1907	Tall folio volume containing a rental for Heaton and Shipley, 1858–67; further rentals and accounts, 1869–74; and a fairly complete run of rentals and accounts, 1878–1907. [See also G/18.]
64	1756: N.D.: 1779–80: 1785: 1790: 1802: 1872: 1885: 1897: 1937: 1955: 1972	Maps, plans, drawings and inventories relating to Heaton and Shipley, including the collieries, the garden and the inside of Heaton Hall; the items of 1937, 1955 and 1972 are illustrations of the outside of the Hall. [See also G/18 and O/47A.]
65	1772–9: 1791: 1793: 1796–1819	Four small quarto volumes of accounts and valuations for the Wilmer manor of Upper Helmsley, half of which, as has been seen, was inherited by Mary Wilmer, daughter of Randall Wilmer and wife of Joshua Field, and the other half of which was purchased by Joshua Field from William Gossip in 1804.

G/66/1–2 1772–94   Two folio volumes covering the years 1772–81 and 1782–94 respectively, containing a series of accounts between Timothy Mortimer, the agent, and Mrs Nicholas Suger, Miss Martha Suger and Mrs Randall Wilmer, the heiresses of the Suger and Idle estates of Heworth, Marton, Kennythorpe, Leavening, Burythorpe, Westow, Bulmer, Barnby, Allerthorpe and Waplington, and in York City.

67   1795: 1802:   Five variously sized volumes of accounts for the same estates, in
      1813–19   this period shared among Mrs Randall Wilmer, Joshua Field and John Wilmer Field.

68   1955–6: 1981:   Fairly modern letters and papers, mostly of an historical
      1983–4:   nature, about Heaton and Shipley, including a calendar of
      1988–9:   parts of varioussub-sections of Section G, made by Councillor
      1996–7: 2001   J. S. King of Heaton, September 1981, together with a Field family history published by him in the *Heaton Parish Magazine*, 1955, his 8-page typescript biography of John Wilmer Field, covering his 'Early life and marriage', 'The election of 1825', 'Local activities', 'Social life', and his death in 1837, accompanying letters from Mr King to the 6th Earl and Anne Countess of Rosse, 1955–6, letter from Mr King submitting a copy of his published book *Heaton: The Best Place of* All together with the 7th Earl's comments on it and Mr King's reply, 2001–2, letter from Christopher Robson [brother-in-law of Alison, Countess of Rosse], Richmond, Yorkshire, to the 7th Earl of Rosse, 1984, with enclosures from Lord Feversham, typescript summary, made in 1988, of the contents of the will of Mary, Countess of Rosse, letter to the 7th Earl about the possible sale of the manorial lordship of Shipley, 1989, letters and enclosures from D.R. Sanderson of Readley, Burnley, about Heaton history and a document of 1625 signed by Joseph Field, 1991, etc, etc.

69   1966–78   Letters and papers of the 6th Earl about Bradford civic and historical societies, as well as local Church of England affairs.

H/	DATE	DESCRIPTION

1–130 1682–1824: Papers of the Hawke family, Lords Hawke, present among the
1860: 1869–70: Rosse Papers because of the marriage in 1870 of the Hon. Frances
1891: 1904–11: Cassandra Hawke, heiress of her father, the 4th Lord Hawke, to
1922–2006 the 4th Earl of Rosse.

1–13 **NAVAL, ADMINISTRATIVE AND POLITICAL PAPERS OF ADMIRAL
SIR EDWARD HAWKE, K.B., 1ST LORD HAWKE, VICTOR OF THE
BATTLE OF QUIBERON BAY IN 1759, AND FIRST LORD OF THE
ADMIRALTY, 1766–71.**

1 11–25 Dec. Tall folio volume containing copy minutes of the proceedings of
1688 the Upper House of the Convention Parliament, which met first
at the Guildhall, and then back at Westminster. Inscribed on the
front cover of the vellum binding is the name 'Bladen', which
suggests that the book belonged to Nathaniel Bladen of Lincoln's
Inn, barrister-at-law, father of Colonel Martin Bladen (see H/14–
15) and maternal grandfather of the 1st Lord Hawke.

2 1739: 1742–3: Modern morocco-bound guard-book containing 206 folios of
1747: 1753: letters and papers of the 1st Lord Hawke, [and resembling the
1755–62: work of the British Library, who presumably photocopied the
1765–71: papers at the time of conserving and guarding them, although
1777–81 there is no record of this having been done. They were
subsequently (1983–6) lent to and microfilmed by the National
Maritime Museum, Greenwich (ref. NMM MS. 83/153).] Lord
Hawke's correspondents include: George II; his grandsons, Princes
Edward and Henry, respectively Dukes of York and Cumberland,
who appear to have served under Hawke in the navy; the Prince of
Mecklenburg; the Dukes of Montagu as Commander of the Order
of the Bath, conferred on Hawke in 1749, Bedford, as Lord
Lieutenant of Ireland, and in connection with the three-life
pension on the Irish establishment awarded to Hawke after the
Battle of Quiberon in 1759, Queensberry and Kingston; the 2nd
Marquess of Rockingham; the Earls/Earls of Granville, as Lord
President of the Council, Chatham, as the head of the
administration under which Hawke became First Lord of the
Admiralty in 1766, Suffolk and Rochford, as Secretaries of State
for the Northern and Southern Departments respectively,
Shelburne who appears in D/1 as 1st Marquess of Lansdowne,
Howe and Sandwich, as First Lords of the Admiralty; Admiral
Lord Anson, also as First Lord of the Admiralty; and Admirals
Boscawen, Byng and Keppel. There are a number of papers about
the Battle of Quiberon, and a number of letters and instructions
from the King, the Privy Council and the Southern Secretary of
State during the Seven Years War. Hawke's First Lordship of the
Admiralty papers are in general of a more formal or trivial nature,

H/2 *contd.*

being mostly concerned with patronage. The most delightful document in the guard-book is a letter written just after the Battle of Quiberon, and signed 'Lord Granby's second son, Charles Manners': 'I hear you have beat the French fleet when they were coming to kill us, and that one of your captains twirled a French ship round till it sunk [*sic*]. I wish you was come home, for I intend to go to sea, if you will take me with you.'

3   Aug. 1755   Slim, folio, soft-back volume containing copies of out-letters from Hawke, writing from the 'St George' at sea, to the Secretary of State, Sir Thomas Robinson, and the Secretary to the Admiralty, J. Clevland; with, at the other end of the book, 'A list of ships and vessels taken by the squadron under the command of Sir Edward Hawke', August–September 1755. (NMM MS. 83/122/A/1).

4   1755–62   Folder of letters and papers received or issued by Hawke during the Seven Years' War, particularly communications between him and the Board of Admiralty, the Secretary of State's office and various other naval commanders, including Admirals Boscawen, Lord Howe and Saunders; also included are a draft of a letter from Hawke to Lord Anson, 29 September 1759, a letter from Clevland to Hawke about Belleisle, 9 October 1760, and detailed orders from Hawke for boarding enemy boats in Quiberon Bay, 24 November 1759. (NMM MS. 83/122/A/6 – with additions and subtractions.)

5   1760   Folder containing 2 diagrams and copies of various orders and signals issued by Hawke during the successful attack on Belleisle. (NMM MS. 83/122/A/5.)

6   Sep. 1767   Folder of letters to Hawke, when First Lord of the Admiralty, all received by him while staying at Swathling, near Southampton, and most of them consisting of applications for various appointments in the navy. Included in the bundle are 4 letters about a mayoral election at Rochester, a letter about malpractices at Plymouth Dock, two letters from one John Carter about Portsmouth politics, a letter from Edward Stratford (afterwards 2nd Earl of Aldborough) soliciting promotion for his brother, and a petition from James Grierson referring incidentally to the Battle of Quiberon Bay. (NMM MS. 83/122/A/4 – with subtractions and one addition.)

7   1770   Folder of memoranda by Hawke, made for the purpose of reminding himself about various bits of Admiralty business which had to be done, together with other Admiralty papers, including an Admiralty Office 'List of captains and masters and commanders desiring to be employed', 1 October 1770. (NMM MS. 83/122/A/7 – with one addition.)

8   *c.* 1770   Slim, folio, soft-back volume containing lists of 'Lieutenants recommended to be promoted to the rank of masters and

H/8 *contd.*		commanders' and of people recommended for lieutenancies, 1746–70. (NMM MS. 83/122/A/2.)
9	*c.* 1771	Slim, small folio, soft-back volume containing 'Considerations on the state of the navy from the end of 1766 to the commencement of 1771 (Hawke's period of office as the First Lord of the Admiralty), with an appendix and notes'. (NMM MS. 83/122/A/3.)
10	[1769 onwards]	Very slim folio volume containing copies of the following accounts to do with the navy: 'An account of the number of seamen voted, borne and mustered for each year since the Revolution, with the amount of the several proportions', 'Abstract of the ordinary estimates of his Majesty's navy as delivered each year from the 1 January 1688', and 'An account showing the debts of his Majesty's navy in every year since the Revolution, with the increase and decrease there …'.
11	1751: 1754–5: 1763: 1765	Miscellaneous naval papers of Hawke, including a copy of a letter from him concerning a mayoral election at Portsmouth, 1751, a letter to him from W? Fairfax (presumably a connection via the Bladen family) who writes from Virginia about the state of affairs there, 1754, weekly returns for three ships anchored at Spithead, 11 June 1755, a letter from Lord Sandwich about trying out a time piece, 1763, etc, etc. (The documents of 1751 and 1763 have been transferred from NMM MS. 83/122/6: the rest have not been microfilmed by NMM.)
12	[1768?]: 1770: [1773?]: 1776–80	Naval, patronage and political correspondence of Hawke, several of the letters from this protégé, Captains (later Admirals) Richard Edwards and Francis Geary, and his successor at the Admiralty, Lord Sandwich, and also including: a long recital of the naval service of, and a letter from, Robert Tomlinson, 1768 and 1776; letters about the outcome of legal proceedings over elections in Portsmouth, 1777; a letter from the 2nd Marquess of]Rockingham about the Palliser and Keppel affair 1779; a verse about the first Battle of Cape Finisterre by a chaplain who was an eye-witness of it, 1779; and 2 letters from Augustus Hervey, 3rd Earl of Bristol about the parliamentary motion of censure on Lord Sandwich, 1779. (NMM MS. 83/122/B/5 and 15–17 – with many subtractions and one or two additions.)
13	1754–79	Miscellaneous printed matter deriving from Hawke, including a printed '… Elevation of the north front of the new building for the London Hospital in Whitechapel Road, 1754' and the 'Case of the proprietors of the Coventry Canal', *c.* 1770. (NMM MS. 83/122/B/19–20 –with additions and subtractions.)
13A	1753–76	Photostat and, in one instance, typescript copies of sundry naval papers deriving from Hawke, including a bound photostat copy of

H/13A *contd.*

the naval estimates for 1768. [Found elsewhere, and now associated with these papers, is a letter of 1953 from Henry Thursfield, apparently of the Admiralty, to the 6th Earl of Rosse, almost certainly referring to the 6th Earl's loan of the originals to the Admiralty for studying and copying (presumably with a second copy for the 6th Earl, which these present papers are). In particular, Thursfield comments that the naval estimates for 1768 are of special interest, because the series of naval estimates among the Admiralty papers in the P.R.O. begins only in 1773. Presumably, the originals of this very random selection of Hawke papers were sold to NMM in 1970].

14–26 PERSONAL AND BUSINESS PAPERS OF THE 1ST LORD HAWKE

14   1698–1702   Small quarto volume kept by Martin Colonel Martin Bladen of Hemsworth, Yorkshire, a Commissioner of Trade and Plantations, 1717–46, maternal uncle of Hawke and his first and principal patron, consisting firstly of a short family history of the Bladens, the Fairfaxes of Steeton (York City), the Hammonds of Scarthingwell, near Ferrybridge and other related Yorkshire families, and secondly a diary recording Bladen's doings as a law student at Lincoln's Inn and a young barrister. The diary entries are perfunctory and uninformative up to 1700, but for 1700–02 rather more detail is given of cases in which Bladen was concerned.

15   1732: 1750:
1754: 1759:
1766: 1772:
1780: 1973   Personal letters and papers of Hawke, mainly relating to family events and history, including: a letter of 1732 reporting that Colonel Bladen '… has sent his sister (Hawke's mother) his and his lady's pictures …'; letters from Catherine Hawke, Swaythling, to Hawke (her husband), 1750 and 1754; copies of entries in various registers concerning the births and marriages of Bladens and Hawkes, 1766 and 1768; a letter of 1780 reporting the death of 'Mr Bladen'; and a photocopy of pp.128–35 of A.G. Olson's *Anglo-American Politics, 1660–1775* … (Oxford, 1973), which discuss Colonel Martin Bladen's pre-eminent role on the Board of Trade in the 1730s. (NMM MS. 83/122/B/17–18 and various – with 2 additions.)

16   1760: 1764:
1767: 1776–9   Letters to Hawke from his elder son, the Hon. Martin Bladen Hawke, afterwards 2nd Lord Hawke, with some political comment. (NMM MS. 83/122/B/5 and 14 – with subtractions and one addition.)

17   1768–80   Letters and papers of Hawke and the 2nd Lord Hawke from and about Hawke's third son Cornet Chaloner Hawke, his repeated requests for money to pay his debts and for promotion in the army, some of the letters and papers relating to the clearing up of these debts after Chaloner's early death in 1777. (Almost all of these papers have not been inspected or microfilmed by NMM.)

H/18	1748–64	Medical prescriptions for the 1st Lord Hawke. (NMM MS. 83/122/B/11 – with some additions.)
19	1760: 1762: 1767: 1771: 1776–81	Business letters and papers of Hawke about investments and his erratically paid pension on the Irish establishment, including a letter of 1767 about the decoration of his house in Bloomsbury Square [for tradesmen's bills in this connection, see H/23.] (NMM MS. 83/122/B/10, 16 and various).
20	1749–54	Bills and receipts to Hawke from tradesmen, workmen, rates- and tax-collectors, etc, etc, including a photocopied receipt for Hawke's settlement of an account in respect of plate and cutlery bought from the famous silversmith, Paul de Lamerie. (NMM MS. 85/122/B/13 – with subtractions and additions.)
21	1756–64	Bills and receipts to Hawke. (NMM MS. 83/122/B/7 and 13 – with subtractions and additions.)
22	1765–6	Bills and receipts in connection with alterations and repairs to Hawke's house at Sunbury, Middlesex. (NMM MS. 83/122/B/8.)
23	1766–9	Bills and receipts to Hawke. (NMM MS. 82/122/B/3–4 – with subtractions and additions.)
24	1770–72	Bills and receipts to Hawke. (NMM MS. 83/122/B/3–4 – with subtractions and additions.)
25	1774–8	Bills and receipts to Hawke. (NMM MS. 83/122/9–10 – with subtractions and additions.)
26	1780–81	Bills and receipts to Hawke. (NMM MS. 82/122/B/9 and 12 – with subtractions and additions.)

27–35 PAPERS ABOUT THE HAWKE ESTATE AT SCARTHINGWELL, SAXTON, TOWTON, ETC, NEAR FERRYBRIDGE, YORKSHIRE

27	1702–15	Large bundle of letters, surveys and valuations, accounts, bonds, legal case papers, etc, concerning the Scarthingwell estate, which then belonged to the Hammond family of Scarthingwell, one of whom, William, married Colonel Martin Bladen's sister, Frances, as a result of which marriage the estate ultimately descended, at least in part, to the 1st Lord Hawke. Colonel Martin Bladen features among the legal case papers as a barrister on behalf of one of the Hammonds. [See also H/109.]
28	1726	Correspondence of Colonel Martin Bladen, one letter concerning his application for a job in the excise for someone, the rest consisting of correspondence between him and his sister, F. Harman, and her husband about Scarthingwell. [This F. Harman was presumably the remarried Frances Hammond? See also H/109.]
29	1735–67	Two folders of rentals, accounts, valuations, etc, of the 1st Lord Hawke for Scarthingwell. (NMM MS. 83/122/B/6 – with some subtractions and many additions.)

H/30	1760: 1767: 1776: 1780	Letters to Hawke from Rev.? Thomas Mosley, whose wife was co-heiress with Hawke to all or part of the Hammond estate of Scarthingwell, and whose moiety Hawke appears to have bought out in 1768. (NMM MS. 83/122/B/2, 6 and 16 – with subtractions and additions.)
31	1777: 1779: 1781–2: 1784	Three envelopes of letters of instruction from Martin Bladen Hawke, subsequently 2nd Lord Hawke, to whom the Scarthingwell property had been made over by his father in or before 1774, to his steward at Scarthingwell, William Beck.
32	1779: 1781–2: 1786	Four envelopes of letters from Beck to Hawke.
33	1786	Letters to Hawke from John Davidson, another employee at Scarthingwell Hall, possibly Beck's successor?
34	1782–1804	Accounts, surveys, valuations and other estate papers relating to Scarthingwell, including one of 1790 relating to Sunbury and possibly some relating to the Womersley estate, Yorkshire, it being difficult at times to distinguish between the two Yorkshire properties.
35	1784–1802	Letters to Hawke about Scarthingwell estate affairs.

[For other Scarthingwell estate papers, see H/97, 105 and 108–9.]

PERSONAL LETTERS TO THE HAWKES, PRINCIPALLY TO THE 2ND LORD HAWKE AND HIS WIFE, CASSANDRA

36	1771–81	Letters to the 2nd Lord Hawke from his father, the Admiral. [In date order.]
37	1788: 1797–1801	Letters to Cassandra, wife of the 2nd Lord Hawke, from Miss Sarah Birt, the devoted 'companion' of the Admiral, who had kept house for him and brought up his children after the death of his wife, Catherine, in 1756, and whom, according to one of the letters in this bundle, the house at Sunbury had been left. The letters are written mainly from Sunbury and from Greenwich, and they (together with the many references to Miss Birt in other letters to the Hawkes) show that she remained an intimate member of the family circle until her death. [See also H/111.]
38	1770: 1775: 1784: 1788: 1793	Three envelopes of letters to the 2nd Lord Hawke from his wife, Cassandra, whom he married in 1771. The earliest letters therefore reflect the progress of their courtship, but the explicitly affectionate tone is maintained—on both sides—throughout the correspondence. [In approximate date order. See also H/110.]
39	1770: 1778: 1784: 1788–9: 1796–8	Three envelopes of letters to Lady Hawke from Lord Hawke, discussing (obviously) personal and domestic matters (such as the their second son, Martin, at Cambridge in 1800), family events (such as the threatened divorce misconduct of of Lady Hawke's

H/39 *contd.*		nephew, the 14th Lord Saye and Sele in 1797), and with frequent references to wider social events and politics. [In approximate date order. See also H/110.]
40	1769: 1777–96	Letters to Lady Hawke and her husband from her mother, Cassandra? Turner, daughter of William Leigh of Adlestrop, Gloucestershire, and wife of Sir Edward Turner, 2nd Bt, of Ambrosden Park, Oxfordshire, and from her brothers, Sir John Turner, 3rd Bt?, who subsequently changed his name to Dryden, on marrying a descendant of the poet, John Dryden, and Gregory Page Turner subsequently 4th Bt? [See also H/65.]
41/1–6	1784: 1786–1800	Six envelopes of voluminous letters to Lady Hawke from her sister, Eliza Turner, wife of General Thomas Twistleton, 13th Lord Saye and Sele (d.1788), who lived at Broughton Castle, near Banbury, Oxfordshire. Topics covered include Lord Saye and Sele's death in 1788 and the winding up of his estate, which intimately concerned the Hawkes, as Lord Hawke acted as executor and trustee – see H/83], the elopement of Lord and Lady Saye and Sele's second daughter, Cassandra, with Edward Jervis Ricketts in December 1789 or January 1790, their almost immediate marriage and their divorce by act of parliament in 1799, etc, etc. The 2 items of 1784 seem to be present as a result of an error (probably arising from the executorship); they are letters from Lady Saye and Sele, not to her sister but to her husband. The letters to her sister begin in 1786. On the subject of the elopement, she writes on 25 and 29 January 1790 that the match had been opposed because the young couple will have only £400 a year to live on, Cassandra Twistleton's fortune being small and Ricketts's father being a rich but miserly West Indian. She reports that it was her youngest son who overtook the couple at Dover and brought them back, but agrees with Lady Hawke '... that more of the family *winked* at this continued attachment (if *not* the *elopement*) than we were aware of.' As for her other daughter, Julia, and Julia's husband, she does not think they '... were ever in their *hearts* against the alliance'. In a voluminous letter dated 2 March 1799 about the divorce, she encloses a copy of a letter from Lord Walsingham (Chairman of Committees in the House of Lords) dated 21 December 1798 in which he states '... that it is not the present usage in the House of Lords to insert any allowance to the lady in divorce bills, but that it is left to the injured party to make such allowance as they think fit.' [See also H/110–11.]
42	1786–8	Three letters to Lord and Lady Hawke from her brother-in-law Lord Saye and Sele. [See also H/71].
42A/1–7	1785–7	Seven folders of accounts and receipts from tradesmen, insurance companies, etc., to Lord Saye and Sele (present because of Lord Hawke's executorship role).

H/43	1788–1800	Letters to Lady Hawke and Lord Hawke from three of the Saye and Sele children, Cassandra Twistleton, Gregory William Twistleton, afterwards 14th Lord Saye and Sele and Thomas Twistleton.
44	N.D.: [1786–1800?]	Letters to Lady Hawke and Lord Hawke from her other Saye and Sele niece, Julia Twistleton, who was doubly related to Lady Hawke because she married Lady Hawke's first cousin, James Henry Leigh of Adlestrop and, subsequently, of Stoneleigh, Warwickshire.
45	1786–8: 1792: 1796–1801	Letters to Lady Hawke from another Leigh connection, Elizabeth Leigh who appears to have been married to a Thomas Leigh, possibly a younger brother of Lady Hawke's mother?, together with a letter from Thomas Leigh to Lord Hawke. [See also H/110.]
46	N.D.: 1788: 1795–6	Letters to Lady Hawke from another Leigh connection, Mary? Leigh.
47	1787–8: 1795–8	Letters to Lady Hawke from 'C. Cooke', who writes mainly from Bookham and from Adlestrop, and who is identified as 'Lady Cooke' in a wrapper so endorsed by Lord Hawke, and apparently was another Leigh connection. N.B. The bundle contains a letter dated '1769' which, from internal evidence, must be 1796.
48	1771: [1786]: N.D.	Three miscellaneous letters and papers relating to or deriving from the Leighs, including a poem on the marriage of James Henry and Julia Leigh, [1786], and a crude elevation of Adlestrop, N.D.
49	1784: 1794–8	Letters to Lord and Lady Hawke from their elder son, subsequently (1805) 3rd Lord Hawke, the earliest of them written when he was still a child. Some of the later letters, those of 1794–5, are written from his Grand Tour in Switzerland and elsewhere, and are accompanied by letters from his tutor and companion, M. Mounier. At the end of the bundle is a letter of 1798 about finding an employment for Mounier. [See also H/110.]
50	1790–1800: N.D.	Nine envelopes of letters to Lady Hawke and Lord Hawke from one of their two daughters, Cassandra, who in 1793 married Samuel Estwicke 'of Barbados' (d.1798?), and in 1800 Rev. Stephen Sloane. [See also H/92, 109 and 111.]
51	1798–1801	Letters to Lord Hawke from and about his second son Martin, including a draft of a letter from Lady Hawke to Martin, all concerning Martin's unsatisfactory progress at Cambridge, his promises of amendment, letters proposing settlement terms on behalf of a Mrs Huddleston in consequence of the 'illness' contracted by her as a result of what passed between Martin and her (!), etc, etc. [For other letters from and to the Hon. Martin Hawke, see H/95 and 111.]

H/52	1799: N.D.: 1806	Small, highly artificial bundle of correspondence between Lady Hawke, on the one hand, and on the other her daughter-in-law, Frances Harvey, the heiress who brought the Womersley estate, near Tadcaster, Yorkshire, into the Hawke family through her marriage to the future 3rd Lord Hawke, who double-barrelled his name to Harvey Hawke, and Frances Harvey Hawke's mother, Mrs S. Harvey.
53	1786–99	Letters to Lady Hawke from the Misses Elizabeth and Mary Guy of Richmond, Yorkshire, including a couple of letters to Lord Hawke from the Miss Guys about money he owes to them. (These are the first of a long series of tuft-hunting, female acquaintances of Lady Hawke, who played persistent court to her, and whose letters are largely devoid of significant content.)
54	1789–1800	Two envelopes of letters to Lady Hawke from Mrs Sarah Green, apparently of Hull.
55	1789: 1797–1801: N.D.	Two envelopes of letters to Lady Hawke from Mrs Anne Wolley of York. [In date order.]
56	1790–97	Letters to Lady Hawke from Mrs Anne Wormald, together with one from her husband to Lord Hawke soliciting the postmastership of York, 1795. [For York politics and patronage see also H/71.] Mrs Wormald and Mrs Wolley have uncannily similar handwriting; but as both ladies are busy writing throughout 1797 under their respective names, it seems impossible that they can be one and the same person whose name changed in consequence of a second marriage. In date order.
57	1791–1800	Two envelopes of letters to Lady Hawke from Miss Anne Gibbs, apparently of Hull, though she writes mainly from the successive Hawke town houses in Portland Place and Devonshire Street. The addresses from which most of these letters are written, and the many greetings sent to Miss Gibbs in other letters to Lady Hawke, show that she was very much part of the family or household; there are also references in other letters to the search for a position for Miss Gibbs, so it is possible that she acted as some kind of genteel housekeeper.
58	1796–9	Letters to Lady Hawke from Mrs Bridget Stott of York.
59	1796–1808	Two envelopes of letters to Lady Hawke from Miss Eliza Mosley of Pontefract. This lady, and the other Mosleys of Pontefract, for whom Lord Hawke acted as trustee – see H/87 – were presumably daughters or other relations of Rev. ? Thomas Mosley, whose wife was a co-heiress to the Scarthingwell estate – see H/30.
60	1796–8: N.D.	Letters to Lady Hawke from Miss Anne Mosley.
61	1796–1801	Letters to Lady Hawke from Catherine Maria Mosley, Mrs Perfect, who also lived in Pontefract.
62	N.D.: 1805–6	Letters to Lady Hawke from Frances Mosly, subsequently Mrs Bindloss, also of Pontefract.

H/63	1795: N.D.	Letters to Lady Hawke from Mrs A. B. Mosley (probably a sister-in-law of the foregoing ladies, and wife of P. Mosley of Pontefract – see H/87.)
64	[1770?]: 1785–99	Letters to Lady Hawke from miscellaneous correspondents on personal and domestic matters, including letters about sundry rows and tiffs and about the recommendation and employment of housekeepers and other servants. The first, isolated item is addressed to Lady Hawke prior to her marriage from 'C[atherine] Hawke' (presumably an unmarried sister of her husband?)
65	1805: N.D.	Two personal letters to the 3rd Lord Hawke, one from his wife, Frances Harvey Hawke, and the other from his cousin, Sir Gregory Page Turner, 4th Bt? [See also H/40.]

66–79 PAPERS OF THE 2ND LORD HAWKE ABOUT LOCAL GOVERNMENT, LOCAL AND PARLIAMENTARY POLITICS, AND PUBLIC LIFE IN GENERAL

66	[1769 onwards]	Thick octavo notebook inscribed 'M.B. Hawke' and therefore belonging to the future 2nd Lord Hawke. containing law student's or barrister's notes of 'Heads of cases determined in the House of Lords from 1706–1726 …', and notes on cases heard before the House of Lord, 1758, and 1767–9.
67	[*c.* 1760s–90s]	Notes made or collected by the 2nd Lord Hawke in connection with parliamentary business – the John Wilkes affair, the Royal Marriages Act, the restrictions on the trade and industry of the colonies, the quarrel with the North American colonies, Ramsgate Harbour, 'the Turkey trade', the justification for the war against Revolutionary France, treason and attainder and the reversals of attainders, etc, etc. (NMM MS. 83/122/B/20 – with some subtractions and many additions.)
68	[*c.* 1760s–90s]	Scrappier and more miscellaneous notes by Lord Hawke on history, law, Greek, books he has read, etc, etc.
69	*c.* 1775–97	Notes, papers and printed matter of Lord Hawke about canals and the inland transportation of coal, with particular reference to the Coventry, Trent and Oxford Canals. (NMM MS. 82/122/B/19–20 – with large subtractions and additions.)
70	1786–92: 1796	Letters to Lord Hawke from and about Colonel Robert Kelly and his son, George, mostly concerning Robert Kelly's frustrated ambitions in the East India Company's army, Lord Hawke's endeavours to have his services properly requited, and subsequently his endeavours to advance George Kelly. The papers also include discussions of Tipu and the war in the Carnatic, and give some insights into the East India Company's patronage system. [See also H/110.]

H/71	1787: 1789	Letters and papers of Lord Hawke concerning York City politics, his ambition (or otherwise) to secure a parliamentary seat for York for his son (1787), Lord Saye and Sele's application for a government post in the same year and Lord Hawke's dissociation of himself from this move and declaration of his political independence, the Regency Crisis and local effects on the political clash between Pitt, on the one hand, and Fox and the Whigs on the other, etc, etc. [See also H/108.]
72	1787–91	Accounts kept by Lord Hawke in connection with road-making in Yorkshire.
73	1793–4	Notes made by Lord Hawke on the impeachment proceedings against Warren Hastings – particularly notes on speeches made by Edmund Burke, the principal conductor of the proceedings against Hastings.
74	N.D.: 1795–H	Letters and papers, several of them printed, of Lord Hawke concerning agricultural improvement, principally in the spheres of corn and wool.
75	[*c.* 1795]	Original bundle of detailed notes and statistics made or collected by Lord Hawke in connection with the Duke of Bedford's motion on the state of the navy. (NMM MS. 83/122/B/1.)
76	1795–7: 1800: 1802	Letters and papers of Lord Hawke about local government, the postal service, politics and patronage in Yorkshire, principally about the raising of yeomanry and militia and the taking of other security measures against internal disaffection and possible French invasion. The correspondents include [the 4th Earl] Fitzwilliam, William Wilberforce, and many other Yorkshire notabilities.
77	N.D.: 1790: 1795: 1797: 1803	Letters to Lord Hawke about miscellaneous political and patronage matters.
78	1783–95	Miscellaneous printed matter collected by Lord Hawke, mainly in connection with parliamentary business, but excluding the issues and events already covered.
79	1807	Letter to the 3rd Lord Hawke from Lord Fitzwilliam soliciting his support for Fitzwilliam's son, Lord Milton, in the forthcoming Yorkshire election.

[For further papers of the 2nd Lord Hawke relating to politics or public life, see H/110–11.]

80–97   BUSINESS LETTERS AND PAPERS OF THE 2ND AND 3RD LORDS HAWKE

80	1770–90	Two envelopes of letters and papers of the 2nd Lord Hawke about the Yorkshire estate and the debts of Sir John Ingilby, Bt, for whom Lord Hawke seems to have acted as some kind of trustee,

H/80 *contd.*		but whose estate also lay under a Chancery receivership. Included are printed copies of private acts of parliament to divide lands in the Forest of Knaresborough and otherwise to clarify the Ingilby title and relieve the Ingilby creditors.
81	1782–93	Letters, many of them incorporating receipts, to Lord Hawke from his London stock-broker or man of business, A. Chorley of Titchfield Street.
82	1785–8	Letters and papers of Lord Hawke about his property on Dominica, the condition and sale of negroes owned by him, etc, etc. Included in the bundle are instructions from Lord Hawke that, in the selling of his slaves, husbands and wives are not to be separated or families split up. Also included are 2 printed papers relating to the West Indies generally.
83	1788–95	Three envelopes of accounts, receipts, valuations of property and stock, letters, etc, all concerning Lord Hawke's role as executor and trustee for Lady Hawke's late brother-in-law, Lord Saye and Sele. The principal correspondent, and the name which figures most prominently in the accounts, is Richard Ness, who was agent or man of business for the Saye and Sele family. Also included among the papers are a few papers of earlier date deriving from Lord Saye and Sele himself. [See also H/108–11.]
84	1781–5	Letters and papers of Lord Saye and Sele concerning his family history, which must have got accidentally mixed up with the executorship papers.
85	1785–90	Letters and papers of Lord Saye and Sele as Colonel of the 9th Regiment of Foot. These mainly concern his regimental accounts, and so are directly relevant to the executorship; they also include references to the regiment's sojourn in Ireland, to its recruiting efforts there, to regimental patronage, etc, etc. [See also H/110.].
86	1770–88	Box containing bundles of bills and receipts from tradesmen, workmen, labourers, rates- and tax-collectors, etc, etc, to Lord Saye and Sele. Most of these were parcelled up in wrappers endorsed '… put by April 1792'. [The contents of this box are bound to be of interest to any student of the social, economic and local history of the Banbury area of Oxfordshire, where Lord Saye and Sele's seat, Broughton Castle, was situated.]
87	1793: N.D.	Two letters and a paper of Lord Hawke about the affairs of the Mosleys of Pontefract [see H/59–63], for whom he acted as trustee. The paper may or may not relate to the letters; but as it refers to an estate on Nevis, and as the Mosleys had a debt secured on such an estate, this is probably where it fits in.
88	1795–1802	Two envelopes of letters to Lord Hawke from J. H. Tritton of Messrs Barclay, Tritton & Bevans, his London bankers, including

H/88 *contd.*   references to the limited success of the 'voluntary subscription' to
                           the war effort, 1798, discussion of the giving up of Lord Hawke's
                           townhouse in Portland Place and the finding of an alternative,
                           1800–01, and repeated mentions of the problems besetting the
                           payment of his pension on the Irish establishment, the differential
                           between English and Irish currency, etc, etc, 1801–2.

89   1797–1800   Letters to Lord Hawke about two boys called Houghton, whom
                           he has taken under his care in his capacity as a leading figure in the
                           African Association. Most of the letters relate to the expenses incurred
                           in educating and clothing the boys while on board ship and about to
                           embark for some unspecified destination. The correspondents are an
                           officer on board the ship, the secretary to the African Association, and
                           another leading figure in it, Sir John Hort. There are also a couple of
                           references to Mungo Park and Sir Joseph Banks.

90   1798   Original bundle of letters and papers of Lord Hawke concerning
                           the terms and details of the settlement made on the marriage of his
                           son to Frances Harvey, heiress of Womersley (her two brothers,
                           Stanhope and William having died in 1795–6, and her father
                           Colonel Stanhope Harvey, in 1797).

91   1798–9: N.D.   Letters to Lord Hawke from and about the Vicomte de Bruges,
                           who apparently was some connection of the Harvey family and had
                           some claim against the Harvey estate. This conjecture is supported
                           by a wrapper on which Lord Hawke has written that the Vicomte's
                           letters were 'about Mr Wood's business', since one St Andrew Wood
                           was one of Frances Harvey's trustees. [See also H/110.]

92   1802–4   Letters and papers of Lord Hawke concerning his payment of
                           debts run up by his daughter Mrs Sloane [see H/50].

93   1803–5   Letters to Lord Hawke from H. Collett, a naval officer, whose
                           letters give some information about the naval operations in which
                           he has been involved, but mainly deal with his requests for
                           financial assistance.

94   1788–1802   Miscellaneous business letters to Lord Hawke, one of them from
                           the 2nd Duke of Leinster, October 1798, explaining his inability
                           to pay the interest on his loan from Hawke because of the
                           rebellion, and adroitly comparing Sir John Borlase Warren's recent
                           exploit with that of the 1st Lord Hawke.

95   1800–03   Business, mainly dunning, letters to his errant second son, the
                           Hon. Martin Hawke.

96   1806–13   Miscellaneous business letters to the 3rd Lord Hawke, two of them
                           about the winding up of the 2nd Lord Hawke's estate after the
                           latters death in 1805, several of them about the 3rd Lord Hawke's
                           debts, which ultimately led to the enforced sale of a collection of
                           Poussins and other works of art, silver and jewellery belonging to
                           his wife, Frances Harvey.

H/97   1772–1818   Box of bills and receipts to the 2nd and 3rd Lords Hawke from tradesmen, workmen, labourers, rates- and tax-collectors, etc, etc, many of them for goods and services in connection with Scarthingwell Hall and estate (and therefore rightfully belonging in H/34) and, from 1805 onwards, to Womersley and the Womersley estate as well, and therefore rightfully belonging with H/105 and 111–12. Every attempt has been made to separate out Womersley bills and receipts prior to 1805 (see H/101), but this attempt may not have been completely successful.

The papers include a disbound volume recording the 3rd Lord Hawke's debts, mainly to tradesmen, and the means adopted to pay or at any rate satisfy the creditors, *c.* 1815; but otherwise, in spite of endorsements by Anne Countess of Rosse denouncing the 'rotten' 3rd Lord Hawke, the papers do not throw much light on his debts or on the sales which had to take place in order to clear them. Included in the box are the following items: 'Estimate of a vault in Saxton Church, 1772', by J. Lang; account for sundry books supplied to the future 2nd Lord Hawke by B. White; account for furniture supplied to, the future 2nd Lord at Bloomsbury Square, by John Cobb, 1776, including '…10 mahogany hall chairs with fluted legs and rails complete … [and] painting the arms on the backs of the 10 hall chairs …'; very long and detailed account for carpentry work done by Benjamin Gale at Scarthingwell Hall?, 1782; account from William Smith for pillar stones and 'coaping' stones for chimneys at Scarthingwell?, 1783; estimate for making a table service and a dessert service, 'gilt all over', N.D.; account for bugles and horns, one of them a silver hunting horn, 1809; account from Thomas Wirgman, jeweller and goldsmith of St James's Street, for watches and jewellery, 1811; account from Henry Carr for furniture for Womersley, including '…3 large bookcases, brass locks and fixing up …' and '12 elm chairs', 1812; and account from Mr Linck, painter, of Geneva, for coloured gouaches of Mont Blanc and other Swiss scenes, 1817.

H/98–105 PAPERS OF THE HARVEY, LATER HARVEY HAWKE, FAMILY RELATING TO THE WOMERSLEY ESTATE, NEAR DONCASTER, YORKSHIRE

98   1682–1718   Large bundle of letters, surveys, valuations, rentals, deeds, legal case papers, etc, of Tobiah Harvey of Womersley (1659–1720) relating to his estates at Womersley, Balne, Campsall, Fulham, Norton, 'the manor of Ousefleet', Smeaton, Sutton, Woodhall, etc, including details of the purchases made by him to augment his inherited Yorkshire property. Included in this sub-section is a photostat of an elevation of 'The south prospect of Womersley, the seat of Tobiah Harvey Esq.', [*c.* 1715], the original of which is in the British Library and bears reference P. 33211. Lan. 91.4. [See also H/108.]

H/99	1759–85	Large bundle of similar papers, though mainly consisting of accounts, surveys and valuations, of Tobiah Harvey's grandson], Colonel Stanhope Harvey (1723–97), who succeeded his short-lived father, William (1693–1739) in 1739.
100	1787	Small bundle of surveys of farms on the Womersley estate.
101	1731: 1785–97	Large bundle of bills and receipts to William and Colonel Stanhope Harvey (almost exclusively the latter) from tradesmen, workmen, labourers, rates- and tax-collectors, et, etc. Many of these seem to have been preserved because they were necessary to the executorship of Stanhope Harvey's will. [See also H/110.]
102	1786: 1796: N.D.	Letters and papers about Stanhope Harvey's will and about Harvey finances generally, including: a letter to him from his lawyer, Mr Mellish, bluntly commenting on the provisions of his will, and making reference to Harvey property on Jamaica, 1786; a list of the debts of Harvey and of one of his sons, N.D.; executorship accounts for his estate, 1799; and other letters and papers about family finances.
103	1795: 1797: 1801	Three miscellaneous surveys of parts of the Womersley estate.
104	Feb.-Sep. 1805: Nov. 1806–1809	Two envelopes of letters to the Hon. Edward Harvey Hawke, husband of Frances Harvey Hawke, the Womersley heiress, who succeeded in the course of this correspondence, in March 1805, as 3rd Lord Hawke, from the agent or steward at Womersley, Robert Atkinson. [See also H/111.]
105	1806–13	Letters, accounts, granary returns and other papers of the 3rd Lord Hawke about Yorkshire estate business, principally relating to Womersley (insofar as one estate can be distinguished from the other), but including 2 letters of 1808 about a rumoured sale of Scarthingwell Hall. This may indeed have taken place at this stage, and certainly took place at some time in the 19th century. The other house on the original Hawke estate, Towton Park, was lived in at this time by the Hon. Martin Hawke, and was also subsequently sold.

[For other Womersley estate papers, see H/108 and 110–17.]

106–112 MISCELLANEOUS 17TH, 18TH AND EARLY 19TH CENTURY LETTERS AND PAPERS OF THE BLADEN, HAWKE, HARVEY AND HARVEY HAWKE FAMILIES

| 106 | 1587: 1641: [c. 1725]: 1737 1757: N.D. | Miscellaneous verse and ephemera, including a 'Receipt of killing rats' addressed to William Harvey, c. 1725, 'A copy of a speech spoke by Richard Darley Esq. to his neighbours at the Methodists' meeting, November 6th 1757, in Bishop Wilton', 'Account of the coals and tan used in the kitchen garden at Kew', 1778–82, |

H/106 *contd.*
docketed as having come from the papers of a Sir Francis Drake who was Master of the Household to George III, and the only original document among a couple of others of Drake provenance and association, although what connection the Drake family had with the Harveys or Hawkes is less clear.

107   [*c.* 1790–1800?] Two small, crude designs for houses.

108   1688–1820
Outsize, slim, folio volume (the first of a series of six) into which original documents have been crammed in a random fashion cutting across any logical arrangement of the archive. This first volume is more internally coherent than the rest, in that it consists exclusively of business and estate papers, but for both the Harvey and the Hawke families, including: account of the rents from the manor of Kirkfenton [ie. Church Fenton, part of the Scarthingwell estate], 1684–8; 'Brother John Harvey's release to me [Tobiah Harvey of Womersley] … dated 12 of August at Hamburg [where John Harvey was a merchant], 1690'; 4 rentals of the manor of Broughton [Oxfordshire], the property of the Hon. John Twistleton, 12th Lord Saye and Sele, N.D., 1777 and 1779; abstract of the title of Sir John Berney, Bt, to freehold estates in Hertfordshire, *c.* 1776 (how this relates to either the Harveys or the Hawkes is not clear); bill of costs and receipt to Lord John Cavendish, Charles Turner and Martin Bladen Hawke for legal expenses incurred in a case concerning the freemen of York, 1777 [see H/71]; lease of a farm in the parish of Saxton from Martin Bladen Hawke, 1778; undated plan and elevation for a farm building with residential accommodation above it; surveys, granary return and accounts for the Womersley estate, N.D., 1809 and 1811; and inventory of furniture in the servants' quarters in Womersley Hall, 1820.

109   1689–1795
Small quarto volume, similar in character, but more miscellaneous in content, containing among other things: letters and estate papers of the Hammond family of Scarthingwell, 1701–31, including 3 long letters to Mrs Frances Hammond from her father, Nathaniel Bladen, 1712–13 [see H/27–8]; a slim, disbound Saye and Sele account book, 1784 [see H/83], and three personal or business letters to Cassandra, wife of the 2nd Lord Hawke, one of them from their daughter, Cassandra, the future Mrs Estwicke/Sloane [see H/50], 1787 and 1795.

Pasted in at the end of the volume are 2 printed sale descriptions of the early 20th century both describing, in varying detail, 7 volumes similar in character to the present. Six such volumes are at Birr Castle (H/108–12), and the seventh is probably in NMM, which has among its Hawke Papers a volume containing a mixture of naval correspondence of the 1st Lord Hawke and family letters and papers of his and related families. It would therefore appear

H/109 *contd.*   that these 7 volumes somehow or other became detached from the
                           Hawke/Rosse archive and were bought back early in the present
                           century, probably by the Hon. Geoffrey L. Parsons, whose
                           bookplate is to be found in H/108–12.

109A   1702–1800   Slim, folio volume (slightly smaller than H/108) containing a
                           variety of estate, personal and political papers (none of them of the
                           first importance) of the Harvey and Hawke families, including:
                           early 18th-century estate and financial papers relating to the
                           Scarthingwell and Womersley estates; 2 letters of 1712–13 from
                           Nathaniel Bladen to his daughter, Mrs Hammond, at
                           Scarthingwell; estate, financial, military and executorship papers of
                           Lord Saye and Sele, 1775–88; 2 tradesmen's accounts to the Hon.
                           M.B. Hawke, 1777–8; minor political papers of the 2nd Lord
                           Hawke, 1782–5; letters to him and to Lady Hawke from their
                           elder son, the future 3rd Lord, who writes from Berne, Switzerland,
                           while on the Grand Tour in 1795; and Womersley estate accounts
                           and valuations, 1800 and N.D. [This volume has been inserted as
                           an afterthought because it unexpectedly turned up in the possession
                           of Messrs Christie in 1991, having been in their possession since it
                           was sent there for appraisal in 1970. It presumably would have been
                           sold to NMM at that time, but for the fact that it proved to contain
                           no naval papers of the 1st Lord Hawke.]

110   1774–99   Small quarto volume containing a couple of receipts and accounts
                           to Colonel Stanhope Harvey [see H/101], one of them a recruiting
                           account for his regiment (the 2nd West York Militia), 1774 and
                           1777, but otherwise consisting of business and personal letters to
                           the 2nd Lord Hawke and his wife, 1777–99. The correspondents
                           include Lord and Lady Hawke themselves (ie. further personal
                           letters to each other [see H/38–9]), the future 3rd Lord Hawke
                           when still a child and later when on the Grand Tour [see H/49],
                           Thomas and Elizabeth Leigh [see H/45], Lady Saye and Sele [see
                           H/41], the Vicomte de Bruges [see H/91], etc, etc. Lord Hawke's
                           executorship of the will of Lord Saye and Sele [see H/83–6] is
                           perhaps the biggest single topic covered by the correspondence,
                           and many of the letters are from Messrs James & John Meyrick,
                           army agents, about the accounts of the 9th Regiment of Foot [see
                           H/85]. There are also several letters concerning the claims and
                           disappointments of Colonel Robert Kelly [see H/70], and a letter
                           of 1783 conveying to Lord Hawke a unanimous address of thanks
                           from the proprietors of lands and others interested in the province
                           of East Florida.

111   *c.* 1790–1824   Small quarto volume containing similar letters to Lord and Lady
                           Hawke (whose correspondents include Miss Sarah Birt [see H/37],
                           their daughter Cassandra [see H/50], Lady Saye and Sele [see
                           H/41] and Richard Ness [see H/83]), and more numerous letters,
                           receipts and accounts to the 3rd Lord Hawke, some of them from

H/111 *contd.*		the Womersley agent or steward, Robert Atkinson [see H/104], some from his younger brother, Martin [see H/51 and 95], some from the Vicomte de Bruges [see H/91], and others from Lords Burghersh and Blandford (the former of whom writes about the 3rd Lord Hawke's patronage of a theatre). Also included in the volume is a letter from Sir John Sinclair to the 2nd Lord Hawke about a scheme to bring their friend, Lord Moira, into the Addington administration, 1803.
112	1804–23	Small folio volume containing letters, accounts, valuations and printed matter addressed to the 3rd Lord Hawke, one of them in his capacity as Lt-Colonel of the West Riding Yeomanry Cavalry, 1804, others from Robert Atkinson's successor as steward or agent at Womersley, Samuel Godwin, 1811–12 [see H/104–5]. Included in the bundle are Womersley rentals and accounts, 1806–8 and 1820–23. Also included is a fascinating anonymous letter from 'Veritas' admonishing Lord Hawke: '… notorious and public connections in a *married* man are not even in *this* loose age tolerated with impunity. You have *now* got rid of *that restraint* [Lady Hawke had died in 1810], but still passing your life and dedicating your whole time to opera dancers and performers, and being the *constant* companion of an Irish adventurer ["Colonel O'K?"] is not the proper society for a peer of the realm and a descendant of the *gallant Hawke. …*'

113–117 LATER PAPERS CONCERNING THE HARVEY HAWKE FAMILY, WOMERSLEY AND THE YORKSHIRE ESTATES

113A	1832–68	Box containing six volumes of a diary kept by the 4th Lord Hawke and, apparently, relating almost entirely to his hunting and other local activities at Womersley and elsewhere in Yorkshire.
113	1869: 1886	Two small quarto volumes respectively containing a 'Valuation of the Womersley and Towton estates in the county of York belong to the Rt Hon. Lord Hawke …, by Richard Gouthwaite-Lumby', 1869, and a 'Plan of the Towton estate', 1886. The 1869 volume states the components of the Womersley estate as Womersley, Little Smeaton, Walden Stubbs, Norton, Baln and Whitley, containing a total of 4,432 acres, valued at £5,302 per annum, and the components of the Towton estate as Towton, Saxton cum Scarthingwell, Barkston, Church Fenton, Little Fenton, Biggin and Sherburn, containing 1,786 acres, valued at £2,439 per annum: total 6,217 acres valued at £7,751 per annum.
114	1860: 1870: 1891: 1904–24	Newspaper cutting about the marriage of the Hon. Frances Cassandra Hawke to the 4th Earl of Rosse, 1870 [see also M/38]; miscellaneous letters and pedigrees, mainly about Hawke (and Harvey) family history and genealogy; and wills, settlements and related charges affecting the Hawke estates, including a typescript

H/114 *contd.*		statement concerning Lady Hawke's charge of £14,444 on the Womersley and Towton estates, post-1905.
115	1887–98	Letters and papers of the successive Womersley agents, J. W. Douglas (1887) and L. James Senior (1894–6), and of Cassandra, Countess of Rosse.
116	1903: 1908–16: 1931: N.D.	Original bundle of bills to Cassandra, Countess of Rosse *nee* Hawke, giving information about furniture and pictures then at Womersley, 1908–16; together with papers about money, furniture and other effects left by Lady Rosse to her daughter, Lady Muriel Grenfell, 1921–2, and an 'Inventory of furniture removed from Womersley Hall to Birr Castle, December 1931', with related correspondence and inventories. [For other such inventories, see H/108, M/25 and T/38.]
117	1914: 1952: 1954: 1968	Bound inventories of the furniture and objets d'art belonging to the Hon. G.L. Parsons (which later went to Womersley), 1914, 1952 and 1954, and of the fine art contents of Womersley, 1968.
118	1922–99	Box of correspondence of the 6th Earl and Anne Countess of Rosse about historical, heritage, ecclesiastical, etc., matters pertaining to the Womersley estate (eg. the Hawke papers). The box includes: an essay by Oliver Warner on the 1st Lord Hawke's memorial in North Stoneham Church, 1948, a printed copy of Anne Countess of Rosse's booklet on Womersley Park, 1956, a proof of Sir Nikolaus Pevsner's? entry for St Martin's Church, Womersley, N.D., papers about the 6th Earl's sale in 1968 of the Paul de Lamerie silver ordered by Admiral the 1st Lord Hawke in 1750 [H/20], portraits and pictures relating to the Admiral and to the battle of Quiberon Bay, 1933, 1956 and 1970, newspaper cuttings and other papers about the 6th Earl's sale of the naval papers of the Admiral (apart from those still at Birr Castle) to the National Maritime Museum, Greenwich, 1970, and papers and photographs about the sale of the Hawke emeralds, 1976. Other correspondents include successive Lords Hawke, Ruddock F. Mackay, Julia Ward-Aldham of Hooton Pagnell Hall, Doncaster (about the Hawke papers), Colonel George Howard of Castle Howard, Roger, Bishop of Wakefield (and subsequently of Chichester), etc, etc. [See also N/25 and Q/266 and 392.]
119–120	1922– *c.* 1975	Two boxes of Womersley estate and business correspondence, including letters to and from the trustees during the 6th Earl's minority (Sir Charles Barrington, Bt [see also T/19] and Colonel St A. Ward-Aldham), and letters from L. James Junior and J.H. Tyler, the successive agents for the Womersley estate). H/120 contains printed sale particulars of the Womersley estate, 1922, and of the Towton estate, 1930. [For Womersley accounts, 1961–74, see Q/266.]

H/121	1955–73	File kept by the 6th Earl on Womersley, sub-divided into 'House, church, village, garden, woods, estate, minerals, accounts, local affairs'.
122	1973–9	The same.
123	1977–86	Three files of correspondence of the 7th Earl of Rosse and of Alistair J. Buchanan (his father's executor) about 'Tilcon' (mineral rights at Womersley). [See also T/66B.]
124	1984–6	File of correspondence of the 7th Earl about the manorial lordship of Woodhall and about Womersley affairs generally.
125	1985–6	Correspondence of the 7th Earl and printed sale catalogues, all relating to the manorial lordships of Towton and Womersley.
126/1–3	1987–2001	Three folders of letters and papers of the 7th Earl and his agents about the sale of Spring Lodge Quarry, Womersley.
127	1981–2003	Fat folders of letters and papers of Anne Countess of Rosse and the 7th Earl about the presentation to the living of Womersley.
128	1986–2005	Folder of letters and papers of the 7th Earl about the 'Rosse Trust' set up to help support St Martin's Church, Womersley, and the associated church school.
129	2004–5	Catalogues and correspondence of the 7th Earl about the sale of the contents of Womersley.
130	2006	Correspondence between the 7th Earl and the 11th Lord Hawke about the sale to the latter of the Hawke grants of arms, supporters, etc. [These had apparently been deposited in Coutts Bank, The Strand, London, by the executors of Cassandra, Countess of Rosse, the Hawke heiress (d.1920), and had been stored by Coutts, at the expense of the 6th and 7th Earls of Rosse, from *c.* 1920 until 2006.]

[Papers relating to the 1st Lord Hawke's career in the navy and at the Admiralty (apart from H/2–13), which were formerly part of the Rosse archive, are now in the National Maritime Museum (MS. 70/109); previously, between 1953 and 1955, the NMM had microfilmed these papers (MRF/8a-b and MRF/10–16). They were used extensively in Ruddock F. Mackay's *Admiral Hawke* (Oxford, 1965), and were subsequently edited by him in *The Hawke Papers: a Selection, 1743–1771* (Navy Records Society, London, 1990).]

J/	DATE	DESCRIPTION
1–31	1829: 1832: 1840–2003	Correspondence and other papers of the 3rd Earl of Rosse, as President of the Royal Society, Chancellor of Dublin University, Lieutenant of King's County, leading local landowner there, and general public figure, excluding (where physically possible, but see J/28) correspondence of the sort concentrated in Section K, and including some later material of relevance.
1	1829: 1852: 1862	Letters to the 3rd Earl (and Lady Rosse) from Charles Babbage about government support for his scientific work and inventions; together with photocopied correspondence and printed matter about Babbage and his relations with the 3rd Earl, obtained in 1986 from the British Library and other sources.
2	1841: 1853: 1865: 1867	Wills and codicil of the 3rd Earl.
3	1841–2: 1846–8: 1853–6: 1863–5: 1867	Letters and papers of the 3rd Earl about his King's County estate affairs, including government-financed and Board of Works-supervised drainage, 1855, with a long and detailed explanation by Sir Richard Griffith on that subject; and also including counsel's opinions on various leases, 1846 and 1864–5, copies of speeches made by the 3rd Earl to the Parsonstown Union Farming Society, the first of them 'corrected and reprinted for distribution among his tenants', c. 1840 and 1847, several copies of printed instructions from the 3rd Earl to his tenantry (one copy with long MS insertions in his handwriting), 1847, an account of the annual charges on the Rosse estate in 1848; and a printed pamphlet by the 3rd Earl on the *Relation of Landlord and tenant* (London, 1867).
4/1–12	1842–5: 1851: 1853: 1855: 1866	Letters to the 3rd Earl from the Conservative leaders, Sir Robert Peel and the Duke of Wellington, about elections to the Irish representative peerage, including the 3rd Earl's own, 1842 and 1844, and letters to him from them and other Ministers (Lords Aberdeen, Derby, Palmerston, etc) about miscellaneous political and patronage matters.*
5	N.D.: 1843–4: 1850.	Tradesmen's accounts to the 3rd Earl.
6	N.D. 1843: 1845: 1851–9: 1862–6	Letters to the 3rd Earl about the visits of sundry dignitaries, friends, etc, to Birr, mainly for the purpose of inspecting his 'Great Telescope'; included among the dignitaries are Lord Stanley, the Prince Imperial (son of Napoleon III), and a deputation of the British Association – this last visit, made in 1857, is described in a number of newspaper cuttings, which also provide information about celebrations and other events in the town of Birr [see also J/7 and 22]. To this sub-section have been added (1987–8) typescript and/or xerox copies of accounts by Frances Power Cobbe and Thomas Lefroy of visits to Birr and Birr Castle, early 1840s? and

J/6 *contd.*		March 1846 respectively, and two original letters from the 3rd Earl, one extending an invitation to avail of the 'pretty good fishing' to be had with the 'plenty of large fish' then in the lake at Birr.
7/1–26	1843–4: 1848–9: N.D.: 1851–2: 1854: 1856: 1858: 1860: 1863: 1865: 1867	Letters and papers of the 3rd Earl about Birr and King's County [see also E/25, 29 and 35], including: correspondence between the Rev. Michael Crotty, former parish priest of Birr, who with many of his flock had become a Protestant, and Lord John George Beresford, Archbishop of Armagh, 1843; 2 letters from Sir John Burgoyne about either the fortification of Birr Barracks or the mock-fortification of Birr Castle, supervised and planned, mainly as a Famine relief measure, by Lady Rosse's uncle, Colonel Richard Wharton Myddleton, a Peninsula War veteran – see J/19 and 0/32–4, 1844; the King's County Militia and the strength of the constabulary force stationed in the county, 1854, 1856 and 1867; a captured Russian gun which, at the request of the Birr Town Commissioners, was presented by the government to the town, 1858 [see also J/23]; etc, etc.
8	1845–61	Fat quarto volume, largely empty, containing stuck-in trade cards, letters and accounts from, in particular, the manufacturers of optical and scientific gadgetry, a letter about the Daguerrotype pre-photographic process, 1848, a list of the duties of the kitchen-boy at Birr Castle, 1848, and a series of lists (in the 3rd Earl's handwriting) of labourers employed at Birr, 1855–61.
9	1845: 1862: N.D.: 1866–7	Letters to the 3rd Earl about Irish education, mainly about the National School system, but including a commission appointing him a visitor of Maynooth, 1845; the principal correspondents are Richard Whateley, Archbishop of Dublin, and Lord Mayo, as Chief Secretary, and there is also a printed address from James Carlile, a Presbyterian clergyman, *To the Roman Catholic Members of the Mechanics Institute of Parsonstown*, 1845.
10	1845: 1850–54 1856: 1859: 1866–7: 1982–4	Letters to the 3rd Earl about the conferring of various honours upon him, including honorary degrees at Oxford and Illinois, the Order of St Patrick, the (French) Legion d'Honneur, membership of the Russian Imperial Academy and of the Historical Society of Tennessee, the institution of the Rosse Medals, etc, etc; together with letters of 1982–4 from the Rev. Peter Galloway to the 7th Earl relating to the 3rd Earl's insignia as a Knight of St. Patrick.
11	1845–7: 1867: N.D.	Letters, drafts of speeches or pamphlets, and other papers of the 3rd Earl concerning the condition of Ireland, the Famine, land improvement, etc, including a report on a meeting of the Parsonstown Agricultural Society in 1847, chaired by the 3rd Earl, and held to concert responses to the potato failure, a letter from Sir John Burgoyne, writing from the Relief Office, Dublin, to thank the 3rd Earl for a copy of the latter's *Letters on the State of*

J/11 *contd.*   *Ireland* (London, 1847), a copy of that pamphlet, and letters to
                                    the 3rd Earl from his fellow King's County landowner, H. Darby,
                                    about Tenant Right and Fenianism. [See also J/28.] The sub-
                                    section also contains a photocopy of a page from the *Memoirs of
                                    Georgiana, Lady Chatterton* (London, 1848) in which she recalls
                                    seeing the 3rd Earl looking at blighted potatoes through his
                                    microscope during her visit to Birr, and photocopies and
                                    transcripts of two letters from J. Spain, P.P. of Birr, 11 and 13
                                    January 1847, one of them to the 3rd Earl, about the obstructions
                                    to the dispatch of business by the Birr relief committee created by
                                    the behaviour of its secretary, Capt. Cox.

12   1847–57   Four bank books of the 3rd Earl, with Coutts, the Parsonstown
            1861–7   Savings Bank, and the Parsonstown branch of the Provincial Bank
                                    of Ireland; and 9 other personal and general account books.

13   1849–50: N.D.   Letters to the 3rd Earl from the 1st Lord Brougham, ex-Lord
                                    Chancellor of England, mainly about Royal Society matters.

14   1849–55   Letters to the 3rd Earl, as President of the Royal Society, about his
                                    successive presidential addresses (including his first, for the
                                    purposes of which information had to be collected by him to be
                                    embodied in a tribute to his predecessor, Lord Northampton, the
                                    President of the Royal Society's right of entree at Court,
                                    government patronage for the advancement of science and for
                                    financial assistance to individual scientists [see also K/8], etc, etc;
                                    the correspondents include Michael Faraday (who cannot decide
                                    on a Copley Medallist because of his 'infirm memory'), 25 June
                                    1850, and Lords John Russell and Derby (the latter rejecting the
                                    3rd Earl's application for funds towards the publication of T.H.
                                    Huxley's voyage journal; also included is a rough draft in the 3rd
                                    Earl's handwriting for what appears to be a presidential address
                                    [see also J/28]. To the sub-section has been added photocopies of
                                    the relevant pages of vol. 4 of *The Correspondence of Michael
                                    Faraday ...*, edited by *Frank A.J.L. James* [*and*] *published by the
                                    Institution of Electrical Engineers*, where the text of the Faraday
                                    letter is printed in full, together with the text of two later letters
                                    from the 3rd Earl to Faraday to be found in Faraday's papers and
                                    not in the Birr Castle archive.

15   1849–55   Letters to the 3rd Earl accepting or refusing dinner invitations,
                                    some of them explicitly and most of them probably to the 'soirees'
                                    which he gave as part of his duties as President of the Royal
                                    Society, including also, usually in connection with such
                                    invitations, requests to be allowed to bring along or introduce
                                    distinguished visitors; the correspondents include Dickens,
                                    Hallam, Macaulay and numerous visiting foreigners, and the
                                    letters are largely formal in content and autographic in interest.

16	1849–65	Letters and papers of the 3rd Earl about the Great Exhibition, its sequel in Dublin, and similar exhibitions in Britain and on the Continent, mainly reflecting his role as one of the organisers of the British and Irish Exhibitions, but including a not-very-sensible request that his Great Telescope be shipped to London for inclusion in the British. Associated with the sub-section (but not physically, as it is framed and hanging in the China Passage in Birr Castle) is a formal certificate of 1851, signed by the Prince Consort as President of the Royal Commission for the Exhibitions, attesting that the 3rd Earl has been granted a medal for his services in this connection. There is also a formal invitation to a dinner at the Mansion House on 21 March 1850 to meet the Prince Consort, and a letter of 1852 to the 3rd Earl from the Prince Consort.
17	1832: 1849–56	Very miscellaneous correspondence of the 3rd Earl, one of the letters from his youngest brother, the Hon. Laurence Parsons, one about the 3rd Earl's sitting for his portrait to H.W. Pickersgill, others about subscriptions to various things, including, apparently, the erection of a statue to the Prince Consort, and others claiming kinship or discussing Parsons family history. Belonging to this sub-section is an outsize, coloured pedigree of the Earls of Rosse down to 1854, now (1984) framed and hanging in the Muniment Room.
18	1852–3: 1857 1862	Correspondence of the 3rd Earl with the War Office and the Board of Ordnance concerning guns, ammunition, the education of the Prussian army and other matters in which the 3rd Earl was either an official or an unofficial consultant; the principal correspondent is Field Marshal Viscount Hardinge.
19	1834: 1836: 1852–3: 1864–6	Letters to Mary Field, Countess of Rosse, one of them from Queen Victoria, and 7 from or about her uncle, Colonel Richard Wharton Myddleton [the great fortifier – see also O/32–4], who in one of these letters encloses a sampler, 'the first piece of work of my dearest sister, Ann, now half a century old' (this sampler is preserved in Lady Rosse's cabinet in bedroom No. 3 in Birr Castle). Other topics covered in Wharton Myddleton's and the other letters in the sub-section are: travels and jaunts, social engagements, photography (of which art Lady Rosse was an early, indeed pioneer, exponent – see Section P), the design for new Birr Castle gates [see 0/30], admission to the British Museum, the death of the 3rd Earl, etc; together with photocopies of archives and printed matter relating to Lady Rosse's photographic prowess, 1856 and 1859, and letters and bills to her from Walpole Geoghegan, Suffolk Street, Dublin, relating to table linen, 1864–6. Also present is a copy of her marriage certificate, 14 April 1836, signed by the 2nd Earl and Alice Countess of Rosse, John Wilmer Field (Mary's father) and Jane Knox (the 2nd Earl's daughter).*

* For other papers concerning Mary Rosse (in addition to O/30 and P), see E/39, G/14, 16, 19 and 62, O/41–4 and W/17/4.

J/20   N.D.: 1853:   Formal invitations, and letters conveying invitations, to the 3rd
              1859: 1865   Earl from sundry notable persons, among them the Duke of Argyll
                               and Frances Anne, Marchioness of Londonderry, including two
                               letters written by the Prince Consort's secretary requesting that
                               Lord Oxmantown (the future 4th Earl) and one of his brothers
                               come to play with the royal children.

21   1854: 1865:   Two sets of copies (one of them MS., the other damp-cloth) of the
              1906–7   3rd Earl's letters to the naval and military authorities during the
                               Crimean War (the Duke of Newcastle (Secretary of State for War,
                               1854–5), Sir Howard Douglas, Sir John Burgoyne and Sir Baldwin
                               Walker) advocating – for the first time – the building of 'ironclad'
                               ships, a daring and revolutionary proposal which was not acted
                               upon. The second half of the sub–section consists of
                               correspondence of the 4th Earl about the publication of these
                               letters in the *Bulletin of the Institute of Naval Architects*. [They were
                               later reprinted in Sir Charles Parsons (ed.), *The Scientific Papers of
                               the 3rd Earl of Rosse* (London, 1926), pp 207–21.]

22   N.D. [*c.* 1855] Letters to the 3rd Earl (and Lady Rosse) from Nassau Senior, some
                               of them referring, after the event, to a visit to Birr [see J/6].

23/1–3   1848–67   Three volumes, two quarto and the other folio, containing
                               damp-cloth copies of letters and draft addresses or articles by the
                               3rd Earl on miscellaneous topics, including landlord-tenant
                               relations, drainage, astronomy, the Russian gun presented to Birr
                               [J/7], etc.

24   1856–65   Original bundle of correspondence and valuations concerning the
                               acquisition of parts of Ballindarra, Crinkle, etc, from the 3rd Earl
                               to complete the line of the Parsonstown-Portumna Bridge Railway.
                               [See also O/46.]

25   1863: 1865:   Yachting papers of the 3rd Earl, including journals of cruises
              1977: 1981–4   undertaken in 1863 and 1865, written partly by him, but mainly
                               by the future 4th Earl – for the 4th Earl's yachting and tour
                               papers, see M/4 and M/8; the journals also include information
                               about photographs taken by Lady Rosse. Also included in the sub-
                               section is correspondence of 1977 and 1981–4 giving extensive
                               information about the 3rd Earl's yacht, 'Titania', and contemporary
                               drawings of the Titania's sails, Oct. 1863 [see also L/4/4].

26   1863: 1867   Letters to the 3rd Earl as Chancellor of Dublin University,
                               mainly about his appointment of Sir Joseph Napier as his Vice-
                               Chancellor, the installation of the 3rd Earl as Chancellor, Henry
                               Fawcett's bill concerning TCD, etc; the correspondents include
                               Lords Carlisle, the Lord Lieutenant and Derby the Prime Minister
                               [– see also K/8]. Also present are an ode on the 3rd Earl's
                               installation by John Francis Waller, LLD, January 1863, a choral
                               hymn, or ode, composed and set to music to mark the occasion,

J/26 *contd.*		and re-used in November 1999 as part of the celebration of the 500th concert season of the University of Dublin Choral Society, of which the 3rd Earl served as patron, and a printed copy of the programme for the 500th concert season.
27	1866–8: 1983: 1997	Two disbound volumes containing cuttings, with some MS. Comments and draft public letters by the 3rd Earl, on Irish land reform, the disestablishment of the Church of Ireland, other political and economic issues of the day, 'the Rosse Monument' erected in memory of him in Birr, and miscellaneous biographical and obituary material about him; together with later correspondence of the 7th Earl, 1983 and 1997, about the 3rd Earl's death and memorials to him.
28	[*c.* 1840– *c.* 1867]	Half tin box of 61 small (some of them very small) pocket-size notebooks in which the 3rd Earl has scribbled, often in pencil, drafts of letters, addresses and articles on all manner of subjects, often more than one disparate subject in the one little book; the letters are to correspondents who feature in section K as well as the present section, and the topics include matters astronomical, as well as matters which are appropriate to J; the latter include landlord-tenant relations, the abolition of the office of Lord Lieutenant, presidential addresses to the Royal Society, etc.
29	1853–80	Half tin box containing original bundles of letters, vouchers, rentals and other papers concerning the estates in King's County, Co. Wexford and Co. Tipperary settled on the Hon. Laurence Parsons, third son of the 2nd Earl. [For particulars of these estates, see 0/37. The King's County and Tipperary part, which now constitutes the Birr Castle home farm, was ultimately reacquired by the main branch of the family.]
30	1829: 1837: 1840: [*c.* 1875]: 1900–01: 1934: 1981–3: 1985–7: 1993: 2003	Artificial sub-section of letters and papers concerning the 3rd Earl's sister, Alicia, and brother-in-law, Sir Edward Conroy, (2nd Bt, son of the Duchess of Kent's favourite, Sir John Conroy), who madea runaway marriage with the 3rd Earl's sister, Lady Alicia Parsons,in 1837, as follows: small quarto volume containing water-colour sketches by Lady Alicia, 1829; typescript extracts from Conroy's journal for May 1837 recording his elopement to Gretna Green with Lady Alicia, made by Mrs Katherine Jessel, 1981; letter from Conroy to the 3rd Earl (then Lord Oxmantown) about the investment of £10,000 of Lady Alicia's fortune of £16,000, 1840; photographs of Sir John Conroy, (3rd Bt, Lady Alicia's son), a fellow of Balliol College, Oxford, *c.* 1875, and of his grave, 1901; letters to the 4th Earl of Rosse about Conroy memorabilia, some from Kensington Palace, sent from Oxford to Birr Castle, 1901; a quotation from a letter in the Killadoon Papers, NLI, from Lord Clements, House of Commons, to Lady Leitrim, 4 July 1836, stating that Sir John Conroy looked so

J/30 *contd.*   charming at the Duchess of Kent's that '… at royal dinner parties
                          in the next reign, we expect to be obliged to toast Sir John Conroy
                          and the rest of the Conroyal family …'; and letters about the
                          Conroys, a copy of a list of the Conroy Papers in Balliol College
                          Library and a copy of a Conroy pedigree, all sent by Mrs Jessel,
                          1981–3 and 1985–7.

31   1857   Marriage settlement of Arthur Edward Knox of Castlerea, Co.
                          Mayo, son of the 3rd Earl's and Lady Alicia's sister, Lady Jane, who
                          had married Arthur Edward Knox in 1835. [Chewed by a rodent.]

K/	DATE	DESCRIPTION
1–40	1840–1909: 1913–14: 1938: 1964–81	Correspondence of the 3rd and 4th Earls of Rosse with fellow-astronomers or about the Birr and other observatories, including correspondence of the 5th and 6th Earls about the Birr Observatory.*

Excluded from this section are copies of letters preserved in miscellaneous letter-books or notebooks (J/23 and J/28). The loose correspondence of which the section is composed was found scattered all over the house and all through the archive, and was initially sorted roughly by P.R.O.N.I. into 'correspondent' bundles. The contents of these bundles were subsequently described in greater detail by J.A. Bennett and Michael Hoskin of Cambridge University, whose list (and introductory remarks), published in the *Journal for the History of Astronomy*), xii (1981), pp. 216–29, is transcribed below. Subsequently (1982) the contents of this section and the succeeding section (L) were transferred temporarily to the Whipple Museum of the History of Science, Cambridge, for conservation and microfilming – the latter with a view to making more widely available material which is undoubtedly of international interest. The originals are now (1986) back at Birr Castle, and copies of the microfilm may be purchased from MAB Services Ltd, Eagle House, Spoon Lane, Smethwick, Warley, W. Midlands B66 1PA.

'The "Leviathan of Parsonstown," the giant reflector with 6ft mirrors erected by the 3rd Earl of Rosse in 1845 in the grounds of Birr Castle in central Ireland, is among the most famous telescopes of all time. Yet its history, and the history of the observatory which was in use from the 1820s until the early years of the present century, has never been studied in detail. A volume of *The Scientific Papers of William Parsons, 3rd Earl of Rosse, 1800–1867*, was assembled by Sir Charles Parsons (London, 1926), but this adds nothing to the existing printed record. Patrick Moore gave a lecture at Birr in 1968 at the centenary exhibition to commemorate the third 3rd Earl and later developed this into a little book, *The Astronomy of Birr Castle*, which has just been reissued at Birr as a paperback, but this is no more than an eighty-page outline. Meanwhile, although the tube and wall supports of the great reflector were by then on display at Birr along with a few other items, little was known of the surviving instruments and papers or of the light they would shed on the history of the astronomical work of the 3rd and 4th Earls.

In 1980, Professor Sir Bernard Lovell told us of the eagerness of the 7th Earl, who had recently succeeded to the title, to care for the surviving instruments and papers and to mount an extensive exhibition for visitors to the castle grounds. One of us (M.A.H.)

---

* Available on microfilm in PRONI – see MIC 512.

K *contd.*   visited the castle late in 1980 to assess the scale   of the task, and a
research grant from the Royal Society enabled us both to spend
several days at the castle the following spring, when we prepared a
listing of the papers that had then come to light. … In dealing with
the papers we were greatly helped by the earlier work of Dr Anthony
Malcomson of the Northern Ireland Public Record Office, who had
sorted the entire Birr archive.

CORRESPONDENCE

K/1   6 letters to the 3rd Earl from Sir James South: 24 Oct. 1840, 11 Nov. 1840, 23
Nov. 1840, 24 Dec. 1840, 16 Sep. 1845, 14 Nov. 1862.

In addition: a copy of South's printed advertisement, 'Observatory, Campden Hill,
Kensington. To Shy-cock Toy Makers – Smoke Jack Makers – …'

2   12 letters to the 3rd Earl from Sir John Frederick William Herschel: 17 July 1843,
9 Mar. 1845, 9 Nov. 1853, 26 May 1854, 8 Jan. 1855, 24 June 1858 (?), 16 Aug.
1860 (a reprint of Herschel, 'On Atoms'), 23 June (?) 1862, 25 Dec. 1862,
27 Jan. 1863, 23 July 1867, 1 undated.

In addition: the original of a letter from Herschel to the 3rd Earl, 9 July 1843 [not
included in the microfilm copy] and a copy of a letter from Herschel to Sir Edward
Sabine, 10 Dec. 1862.

2A   Envelope of photocopies of correspondence in the Herschel Papers, Royal
Astronomical Society, 12/1.2, concerning the 3rd Earl's contribution to Herschel's
General Catalogue of Nebulae, 1847–63.

3   10 letters to the 3rd and 4th Earls from Sir George Biddell Airy: 10 Sep. 1843, 22
Sep. 1847, 19 Dec. 1849, 28 Nov. 1853, 24 Oct. 1855, 15 Aug. 1863, 28 Mar.
1873. 18 Apr. 1874, 24 Apr. 1874, 9 May 1879, plus 4 letters from Airy to
Colonel Sabine, R.A., concerning the plans for mounting the telescope mirror, 12
Aug. 1853, 26 Aug. 1853, 1 Sep. 1853, 21 Oct. 1853.

In addition: an incomplete letter from Airy, and copy of part of a letter of 16 Oct.
1848 from Mrs Airy to Lady Herschel about her husband's recent visit to Birr to see
the operation of the telescope, which is suitably commented on. [See also K/40.]

4   A handwritten treatise, submitted to the 3rd Earl, 16 Sep. 1844, by Francis
Rauchmuller, Chief Building Director of the Kingdom of Hungary.

5   50 letters to 3rd and 4th Earls from Thomas Romney Robinson: 1 Dec. 1840, 26
Jan. 1841, 7 Apr. 1841, 15 Dec. 1841, 19 Nov. 1845, 2 Jan. 1846, 30 Jan. 1846, 6
Nov. 1847, 19 July 1850, 16 Aug. 1850, 27 Feb. 1851, 30 Aug. 1853, 13 Dec.
1856, 12 Sep. 1857, 23 Oct. 1865, 9 Dec. 1865, 2 Jan. 1866, 6 Jan. 1866, 12 June
1866, 16 June 1866, 1 Nov. 1866, 27 Dec. 1867, 28 Dec. 1867, 1 Jan. 1868, 8 Jan.
1868, 13 Jan. 1868, 15 Jan. 1868, 15 Jan. 1868, 21 Jan. 1868, 24 Jan. 1868, 27 Jan.
1868, 24 Feb. 1868, 27 Feb. 1868, 2 Mar. 1868,' 3 Mar. 1868, 11 Mar. 1868, 17
Mar. 1868, 19 Mar. 1868, 24 Nov. 1870, 13 May 1872, 11 Nov. 1873, 16 Jan.
1874, 11 Apr. 1874, 12 Mar. 1876, 25 Mar. 1876, 7 Apr. 1876, 8 Apr. 1878.

In addition: some 22 letters from Robinson that are either incomplete or bear no year; a letter from the 4th Earl to Robinson, 14 Jan. 1868; a copy of another of around this date, and a few miscellaneous related papers.

K/6　11 letters to the 3rd and 4th Earls from Sir Edward Sabine: 8 July 1848, 19 Mar. 1849, 28 Apr. 1849, 7 Nov. 1849, Mar (?) 1850, 31 May [1850] (accompanied by a copy of part of a letter or report by Airy commenting on an application from T.R. Robinson for a Royal Society grant to publish a volume of observations), 18 June 1850, 22 Sep. 1850, 6 Jan. 1871 13 Jan. 1871, 20 Jan. 1871.

In addition: a letter to Sabine from James Nasmyth, 22 Aug. 1853, and a draft letter to Sabine from the 4th Earl.

7　10 letters to the 3rd Earl from John Russell Hind: 23 Apr. 1850, 22 Apr. 1851, 25 Apr. 1851, 19 May 1851, 8 May 1852, 16 June 1852 (accompanied by a list of Hind's astronomical discoveries), 17 June 1852, 25 June 1852, 28 June 1852, 23 Aug. 1852.

8　6 letters to the 3rd and 4th Earls from Humphrey Lloyd: 6 Mar. 1865, 9 Jan. 1866, 8 Feb. 1866, 22 Nov. 1873 9 June 1876.

In addition: 1 undated, with related notes by the 4th Earl concerning meteorological observations.

9　6 letters to the 3rd Earl from Henry Fox Talbot: 24 June 1852, 30 July 1852, 30 July 1852, 27 May 1853, 5 Feb. 1854, 11 Feb. 1854, one of them declaring his intention of releasing his photographic technique from the restrictions of patent; together with photocopies, provided by the Fox Talbot Museum at Laycock, Wiltshire, of the 3rd Earl's letters to Fox Talbot.

10　3 letters to the 3rd and 4th Earls from William Lassell: 6 May 1852, 7 Dec. 1852, 10 June 1875.

11　2 letters to the 3rd Earl from Robert Fitzalan: 9 Mar. 1861, 7 Feb. 1863.

In addition: a few papers concerning meteorology sent by Fitzalan.

12　18 letters to the 3rd and 4th Earls from George Johnstone Stoney: 15 Dec. 1861, 1 Jan. 1863, 3 Feb. 1866, 18 Nov. 1866, 20 Mar. 1868, 1 Oct. 1869, 23 Dec. 1870, 29 Jan. 1871, 10 May 1872, 13 June 1873, 2 Oct. 1873, 22 Nov. 1873, 8 Dec. 1873, 23 Feb. 1873, 1 July 1878, 3 Oct. 1878, 10 Feb. 1889, 11 Feb. 1889.

In addition: an incomplete letter from Stoney: a letter from him to Lady Rosse, 10 May 1872: a copy of a letter from him (?) to an unknown correspondent, 21 Jan. 1886: and a MS. Paper on spectroscopy by Stoney dated 6 July 1885.

13　11 letters of thanks, all c. 1862, to the 3rd Earl for presentation copies of his paper *On the Construction of Specula of Six-foot Aperture*. Includes letters from G.J. Stoney, J. Challis, E. Cooper, C. Piazzi Smyth and G.G. Stokes.

14　(a)　28 letters to the 3rd and 4th Earls from Thomas Grubb: 12 Dec. 1862, 19 Dec. 1864, 27 Oct. 1865, 3 Nov. 1865, 6/7 Nov. 1865, 8 Nov. 1865, 2 Dec. 1865, 12 Dec. 1865, 1 Jan. 1866, 10 Jan. 1866, 15 Jan. 1866, 18 Jan. 1866, 17 Mar. 1866, 20 Mar. 1866, 29 Oct. 1866, 31 Oct. 1866, 29 Jan. 1867, 30 Dec. 1867, 2 Jan. 1868, 11 Jan. 1868, 16 Jan. 1868, 22 Jan. 1868, 27 Jan. 1868, 13 Feb. 1868, 2 Oct. 1871, 16 Apr. 1872.

In addition: copies of letters from W. De La Rue to E. Sabine, 20 Nov. 1865, and from T. Grubb to E. Sabine, 27 Nov. 1865.

K/14 (b) 10 letters to the 4th Earl from Howard Grubb: 16 Dec. 1874, 12 Mar. 1875, 23 June 1875, 9 Aug. 1876, 22 Oct. 1877, 29 Oct. 1877, 13 Sep. 1878, 6 Dec. 1878, 19 Oct. 1883, 3 Nov. 1884.

In addition: among other related papers is correspondence related to Grubb's refractor for the Vienna Observatory, and an undated copy of a letter from the 4th Earl to H. Grubb.

15   1 letter (28 June 1864) from George Gabriel Stokes to the 3rd Earl, and 26 to the 4th Earl: 12 June 1866, 20 July 1867 (accompanied by a copy of a letter by W. Lassell), 31 Aug. 1867, 5 Sep. 1867, 18 Sep. 1867, 10 Dec. 1867, 13 Dec. 1867, 26 Dec. 1867, 18 Jan. 1868, 1 Feb. 1868, 27 Feb. 1868, 29 July 1870, 22 Apr. 1870, 6 Aug. 1870, 8 Sep. 1870, 7 Oct. 1870, 20 June 1873, 11 July 1873, 27 Oct. 1873, 27 Oct. 1873, 19 Jan. 1874, 27 Jan. 1874, 2 Jan. 1877, 22 Jan. 1877, 19 July 1877, 2 July 1879.

In addition: related papers include an incomplete letter from Stokes, 2 undated copies of letters from the 4th Earl to Stokes, and a copy of a letter to Stokes from W.H. Miller, 3 Sep. 1867.

16   3 letters to the 4th Earl from William Huggins: 29 June 1866, 11 May 1872, 11 Feb. 1878.

17   Miscellaneous astronomical correspondence to the 3rd Earl. Includes letters from: L.A.J. Quetelet (16 Nov. 1850, 12 June 1851, 14 July 1851); D. Brewster (22 Aug. 1849, 2 July 1850); J.F. Tennant (10 Feb. 1863); F.W.H.A. von Humboldt (no date); W. De La Rue (13 June 1854); J.H. Madler (9 July 1858); A. Cayley (no year); J. Challis (26 Nov. 1850); J.C. Adams (8 Oct. 1852); J.P. Gassiot (21 Oct. 1853); W.R. Birt (25 Jan. 1865), 31 July 1867); Mary Somerville (11 Nov. 1843); D.F.J. Arago (17 Sep. 1849); W. Whewell (3 Sep. 1853); J. Nasmyth (30 Dec. 1852).

18   9 letters to the 3rd and 4th Earls from Warren De La Rue: 6 Jan. 1867, 4 Oct 1867, 9 Oct. 1867, 7 Jan. 1868, 11 Jan. 1868, 19 Jan. 1868, 27 Mar. 1868, 28 Feb. 1874, 28 July 1874.

In addition: a draft letter from the 4th Earl to De La Rue, no date.

19   4 letters to the 4th Earl from Franz Friedrich Ernst Brunnow: 27 Nov. 1868, 27 Oct. 1873, 18 Dec. 1873, 27 Feb. 1874.

20   4 letters to the 4th Earl from E.S. Butler: 17 Mar. 1869, 1 Apr. 1869, 9 Apr. 1869 (?), 1 Jan. 1870.

21   28 letters to the 4th Earl from Ralph Copeland: 25 Oct. 1870, 11 Nov. 1870, 26 Nov. 1870, 5 Mar. 1872, 8 Apr. 1872, 7 May 1872, 26 Mar. 1873, 15 Apr. 1873, 10 May 1873, 15 May 1873, 20 May 1873, 23 July 1873, 20 Jan. 1874, 10 June 1874, 13 June 1874, 17 Oct. 1874, 10 Dec. 1874, 20 May 1875, 15 Oct. 1879, 24 July 1880, 3 Aug. 1880, 17 Aug. 1880, 7 Sep. 1883.

In addition: other related papers include one undated letter from Copeland (the first he wrote to the 4th Earl), one incomplete letter from him, and a draft letter from the 4th Earl to Copeland.

K/22   4 letters to the 4th Earl from R.H. Scott, Meteorological Office, London.

23   A large collection of letters and documents, 1872–76, relating to building the
equatorial mount for the 3ft reflector: mostly correspondence with W.G. Strype of
James's Gate Brewery, subsequently of Custom House Mill, Dublin, and William
Spence of Cork Street Foundry and Engineering Works, Dublin.

24   12 letters to the 4th Earl from Bindon B. Stoney: 21 Feb. 1872, 30 Mar. 1872, 21
Apr. 1872, 26 Aug. 1872, 1 Apr. 1873, 6 Apr. 1873, 21 Nov. 1873, 16 Apr. 1877,
10 Oct. 1899, 13 Oct. 1899, 2 Apr. 1901, 17 Dec. 1907.

In addition: 1 incomplete letter from Stoney.

25   4 letters to the 4th Earl from Albert Marth: 28 Jan. 1874, 18 Feb. 1874, 14 Mar.
1874, 14 Apr. 1874.

In addition: 2 pages of astronomical data initialled by Marth.

26   14 letters to the 4th Earl from John Louis Emile Dreyer: 4 May 1874, 19 May
1875, 9 June 1875, 12 June 1875, 6 Jan. 1876, 5 June 1876, 30 Apr. 1877, 17 Sep.
1877, 7 Dec. 1878, 1 Jan. 1879, 5 Sep. 1879, 16 Oct. 1879, 27 Oct. 1879, 2 Aug.
1880.

In addition: a manuscript in Dreyer's hand, headed 'Observatory, Birr Castle.
Report on work done in 1877', and biographical notes on Dreyer's time at Birr,
2002.

27   3 letters to the 4th Earl from Edward Singleton Holden: 25 Apr. 1874, 24 July
1877. 1 undated.

28   3 letters to the 4th Earl from Otto Boeddicker: 5 Aug. 1880, 26 Aug. 1880, 18 July
1898.

In addition: a letter from the 4th Earl to Boeddicker, 28 Jan. 1905.

29   Correspondence between the 4th Earl and Messrs Longman concerning publication
of Boeddicker's drawings of *The Milky Way*.

30   Miscellaneous letters to the 4th Earl related to various publications.

31   Letters to the 4th Earl from instrument makers including John Browning (12 Nov.
1870, 17 Jan. 1871) and Adam Hilger (11 Oct. 1879, 22 July 1885, 6 Aug. 1885,
9 Oct. 1890).

32   Letters to the 4th Earl from individuals about visiting Birr to see the observatory.
Correspondents include H. Helmholtz (19 Mar. 1881, 3 Aug. 1881). R. Grant (18
June 1873, 20 Aug. 1873). I. Roberts (31 May 1892).

33   Letters, 1880, relating to unsuccessful applications to the 4th Earl for the post of
assistant astronomer at Birr.

34   Letters and papers of the 4th Earl concerning rainfall.

35   Large collection of letters and papers, 1892–99, concerning the appeal to raise a
fund for the Magnetic Observatory on Valentia Island, in order to pay the
meteorological observer to take the magnetic readings. The appeal was sponsored
by the 4th Earl and George Francis Fitzgerald. Correspondents include R.S. Ball,

K/35　　A.A. Rambaut, Lord Kelvin, E. Cooper, G.J. Stoney, A.W. Rucker and Lord
contd.　　Dunraven.

36　　Miscellaneous astronomical correspondence of the 4th Earl. Includes letters from
O.W. Struve (14 Apr. 1880, 13 July 1880), T.E. Espin (undated), A.A. Common
(11 Apr. 1900), E.E. Barnard (30 July 1893), H.L. d'Arrest (2 Apr. 1874), C.
Wheatstone (16 July 1873), C.V. Boys (6 May, no year given), Lord Lindsay (24
Nov. 1879), Lord Adare (9 Dec. 1874?, one undated), I. Roberts, (16 Dec. 1888),
S. Newcomb (31 Oct. 1875).'

36A　　1844: 1852–3:　1880 Seven further letters from O.W. Struve of Pulkova
Observatory [additional to the 2 in K/36)], all but one of them to
the 3rd Earl. [These turned up after the sorting and listing of K,
but not too late to be included in the microfilm.]

36B　　1837: 1844–6:　Miscellaneous letters and papers of and about the 3rd and 4th
　　　　　1848: 1850:　Earls, which came to light too late for inclusion in the microfilm
　　　　　N.D. 1867:　and which overlap with material so included, including letters
　　　　　1873–4: ?　from William Keleher, Thomas Romney Robinson [irretrievably
　　　　　1878–80:　damaged], G.G. Stokes, Edward B. ?Knobell, Ralph Copeland
　　　　　1891: 1895–6:　[?S.W.] Burnham (of the Lick Observatory, University of
　　　　　1899–1900:　California), Otto Boeddicker, etc; also included are typescript
　　　　　1905: 1910–12:　copies of letters from the 3rd Earl and Lady Rosse to Sir William
　　　　　1935: 1937　Rowan Hamilton, 1837 and 1846–50 (the originals of which are
in the Hamilton-O'Regan Papers, TCD MSS 5123–33),
'Directions for fitting up the astronomical clock', *c.* 1855, a
photocopy of Robert Ball's printed testimonials written in support
of his candidature for the Andrews Professorship of Astronomy at
T.C.D., 1874, a photocopy of a note from the 4th Earl to Mr
Dancer about an object glass, 1874 (supplied by the University of
Texas at Austin, where the original is), and a photocopy of a letter
from the 4th Earl to Capt. Toynbee about meteorological records,
1874.

37　　1909: 1913–14　Letters and papers of the 5th Earl of Rosse about the presentation
of the six-foot speculum to the Science Museum, Kensington, with
copies of photographs of its arrival there, supervised by the Hon.
Clere Parsons, a younger brother of the 4th Earl, and an uncle of
the 5th.

38　　1938: 1964–77　File, letters, newspaper cuttings and papers of the 6th Earl of Rosse
about the astronomical achievements of the 3rd and 4th Earls, the
3rd Earl's correspondence with Sir John Herschel, the Birr
centenary celebrations of 1968, etc, including many newspaper
cuttings, drafts and proofs of Patrick Moore's *The Astronomy of
Birr Castle* (London, 1971), a letter from Eamon de Valera [see
also T/63] joking about the distinction between Birr and
Parsonstown, etc, etc.

K/39   1977   Letters and papers of the 6th Earl about the opening of the
                         telescope museum at Birr.

40   1980–81   Printed matter concerning the 3rd Earl's cousin and collaborator,
                         the Hon. Mrs Ward *nee* King of Ballylin, King's County, 'artist,
                         naturalist, astronomer and Ireland's first lady of the microscope'
                         [see also W/17/7], together with other papers of the 7th Earl
                         relating to a commemorative plaque to Mary Ward at her family
                         home, Ballylin, Ferbane, and to the 3rd Earl.

L/	DATE	DESCRIPTION
	[pre-1828–1908]	Journals containing astronomical observations, drawings of nebula, drafts for articles and speeches on astronomy, and other papers (excluding correspondence) of the 3rd and 4th Earls of Rosse on the subject of astronomy.*

[The following list was made by Bennett and Hoskin (see Section K) and is transcribed verbatim:]

PAPERS

L/1 OBSERVATION JOURNALS

1. Small notebook "Journal of Observations 1848 January 4 to 1848 June 19" (this original having been "recopied May 1874").
2. Small notebook of observations "July 1848 to Mar. 22 1849" (this original having been "recopied May 1874").
3. Small notebook of observations "1861 July 26 to 1862 Dec. 31".
4. Small notebook of observations "1863 Jan. 2 to 1864 May 7".
5. Small notebook of "General Notes and Observations. 1872, Jan. 7 to 1874, Feb 21".
6. Small notebook of "Original Observations. Aug. 1874–Dec. 1875. Nebulae – 6ft".
7. Small notebook of "Original Observations of Nebulae, 1876, 6ft", but including a few observations of the stars and the Moon in 1877.
8. Folio volume entitled "Lord Rosse's Diary of Astronomical Observances 1883–1894" and containing a fair copy of observations from 6 Apr. 1883 to 28 Mar. 1894, when the entries cease.

L/2 SYSTEMATIC RECORDS OF OBSERVATIONS OF NEBULAE

1. Folio volume entitled "Astronomical Diary" *c.* 1849–1857". Despite this title, the volume contains observations of nebulae listed in order of John Herschel's 1833 catalogue. Where the space allowed proves insufficient, the notes continue at the end of the volume. A few pages also contain observations of the solar system. Pasted in at the back are two letters from Otto Struve (10 Dec. 1850 and 6 Feb. 1851) on Liapunov's observations of stars in the Orion Nebula, and reporting Liapunov's belief "that the nebula has undergone several remarkable changes since the drawing of Sir John" Herschel.
2. Folio volume entitled "Astronomical Diary *c.* 1850–1867", A fair copy of the preceding volume, but with additional material on both nebulae and the solar system.
3. Folio volume entitled "Nebulae" with cuttings from the 3rd Earl's 1861 *Philosophical Transactions* paper systematically pasted in as headings and supplemented by manuscript notes mostly in the form of abbreviated descriptions.
4. Quarto volume entitled "Nebulae Observations – 3rd Earl of Rosse" but blank except for trigonometrical calculations.

---

* Available on microfilm in PRONI – see MIC 512.

L/2
contd.

5. Quarto volume, untitled and almost wholly blank except for a page of nebular observations dated 2 Oct. 1840 and a page of observations of Uranus dated Nov (?1840).

6. Small notebook, *c.* 1840–*c.* 1852, systematically listing nebulae (cf. 1 and 2 above) with notes of observations.

7. Small notebook, fair copy of 6 above.

8. Small notebook, "Nebulae, 1866 (17 Feb. 9 Nov.)", with reference numbers taken from John Herschel's *General Catalogue* and pencil notes of observations.

9. Small notebook, "Orion", with observations of Orion Nebula *c.* 1865–67.

10. Small notebook, undated, with on each page the position of a nebula and the reference number from John Herschel's *General Catalogue*. In a very few cases there is a note of the type of spectrum observed by Huggins, followed by notes of observations made at Birr.

11. Sewn pages, "Catalogue of Objects to be observed from 0^H to 11^H both inclusive – March 11, 1848", listing positions of nebulae and their reference numbers according to John Herschel's 1833 catalogue, with abbreviated descriptions.

12. Manuscript drafts, 1867, for the *Philosophical Transactions* paper. "An account of the observations on the Great Nebula in Orion".

L/3 DRAWINGS OF NEBULAE AND OBJECTS OF THE SOLAR SYSTEM

1. Large folio scrapbook entitled "Astronomical Photographs and drawings – Most Vital drawings –Important", but containing only printed or photographed drawings of the Great Reflector and of nebulae planets and lunar features published by the Rosses and by other observers.

2. Large folio scrapbook entitled "Astronomical Drawings of Lord Rosse" and containing numerous original sketches of nebulae and planets, several of them later published. Included is a drawing of M51 "sketched 1845, carefully compared with original on different nights, but no micrometer employed. Handed round the section at the Cambridge meeting".

3. Similar volume with same title, containing original sketches of lunar features, many dated to the period 1860–64.

4. Large folder entitled "Original Sketches Made with the Great Telescope 1848–66". There are manuscript sketches of 31 nebulae, some drawn more than once, together with a few printed drawings. The sketches mostly have a contemporary caption (*c.* 1853) and were apparently prepared for a display. In most cases they seem to be derived from earlier sketches such as those in 2 above.

5. Original sketches and proofs of plates for 1878 paper of 4th Earl on the polarization of light from the Moon and Venus in *Scientific Proceedings of the Royal Dublin Society.*

6. Sheet (framed) showing 25 sketches of Jupiter drawn by 0. Boeddicker in 1882 and 1883.

7 Sheet (framed) showing 9 sketches of Mars drawn by 0. Boeddicker in 1881 and 1882.

L/3   8.   Sheet (framed) showing 20 sketches of Mars drawn in 1872 and 1873.
contd.   Similar to above but not signed.

           9.   Manuscript notes, undated (*c.* 1865) written to accompany photographs of
                 drawings of lunar features and describing the observing methods.

          10.   Descriptions of appearance of Jupiter, 1860–61, 2 pp.

L/4   NOTEBOOKS AND PAPERS RELATING WHOLLY OR PARTLY TO THE CASTING OF
           MIRRORS AND RELATED TOPICS

           1.   Small notebook of the 3rd Earl, *c.* 1838, with notes and drafts on a variety of
                 topics, including notes on the casting and polishing of specula in 1838 with a
                 view to a paper to the Royal Society on the subject.

           2.   Quarto volume, *c.* 1840, entitled "Notebook of 3rd Earl of Rosse". The
                 scientific content comprises a draft for the 1840 *Philosophical Transactions*
                 paper, "An account of experiments on the reflecting telescope".

          3.1   Quarto volume, *c.* 1840, with drafts for the same *Philosophical Transactions*
                 paper.

          3.2   Quarto volume, *c.* 1840, with a further draft for the same paper.

           4.   Bundle of drafts entitled "Materials for a Manual on the Construction of
                 Reflecting Telescopes collected by the [3rd] Earl of Rosse during part of the
                 years 1866 and 1867".

           5.   Notebook *c.* 1866, with notes of experiments on telescope mirrors and of a
                 device for measuring the speed of the yacht Titania.

           6.   Notebook, "1863. Silvering glass – description of process – Results of
                 experiments in sil[verin]g glass & removing silver film – Data of various kinds
                 relating to yacht Titania" [see J/25].

           7.   "Notes on some points in the polishing of specula for telescopes", 4 pp., post–
                 1875, by the 4th Earl.

L/5   PAPERS RELATING TO THE MOON

           1.   Bundle of papers marked "Lunar Heat" and containing manuscript and
                 printed materials including a 37-page manuscript of lecture by the 4th Earl to
                 the Royal Institution, 31 May 1895, on "The radiant heat from the Moon
                 during the progress of an eclipse", and a letter from Boeddicker dated 10 May
                 1895 promising slides for the lecture.
                 Papers in the bundle unrelated to lunar heat include letters to the 4th Earl
                 from G.G. Stokes (1 Aug. 1867) on the publication of the paper on the
                 Orion Nebula; from F. Terby (1 May 1874) on Jupiter; and from O. Struve
                 (18 Apr. 1880) on the time of a conjunction of Saturn with the Sun; also
                 notes by the 4th Earl for lectures on the history of the telescope, and a
                 few pages of draft for the 1880 paper on nebulae and clusters in *Scientific
                 Transactions of the Royal Dublin Society*.

           2.   A roll of papers on "Polarization of Moon's light".

           3.   A small notebook *c.* 1872 containing astronomical tables and observations of
                 the Moon.

           4.   A (framed) chart entitled "Lunar radiant heat", with graphs of phase curve
                 and extinction curve.

5. A (framed) chart entitled "Lunar radiant heat during a total eclipse" showing graphs for the eclipses of 4 Oct. 1884 and 28 Jan. 1888.

L/6   MISCELLANEOUS ASTRONOMICAL PAPERS

1. Thick folio volume, "Astronomical Scrapbook, 3rd and 4th Earl of Rosse", with many blank pages but containing papers both pasted-in and loose, many of Parsonstown, with the great telescope [3ft] 1840" by T.R. Robinson and an account by Robinson of the very first observations with the 6ft; sketches of nebulae, some dated between 1840 and 1846; copy of a letter from James Nasmyth to Robinson, 11 Oct. 1849, on the casting and polishing of mirrors; a letter from Otto Struve, 28 July 1869, thanking Rosse for the memoir on the Orion Nebula but suggesting that rather than speaking of resolvability one should say "there is a tendency of the nebulous matter to form itself in separate knots sometimes in this, sometimes in an other direction"; extensive notes on polishing a 6ft speculum in 1863; letters relating to the advantages and disadvantages of equatorial mountings (from 1863); notes of experiments on silvering glass for optical purposes (1859); very extensive notes on polishing 3ft and 6ft specula; an account of the casting (Mar. 1845) of the 6ft speculum; and a "Copy of Sir J. Herschel's report on Ld. Oxmantown's Paper", July 1840.

    Includes letters from T.W. Webb (24 Dec. 1865). J Challis (21 July 1843). G.B. Airy (30 Aug. 1848, another of the same date, 26 Jan. 1850, 5 Nov. 1857, 25 May 1861, 17 Oct. 1868). J. Nasmyth (11 Oct. 1849 – copy; 15 Dec. 1852 – copy). O.W. Struve (28 July 1869). H. Lloyd (8 Jan. 1866). S. Hunter (27 July. 1868). B.B. Stoney (27 July 1868, 25 Sep. 1868). J.F.W. Herschel (22 Feb. 1863) – copy of letter to E. Sabine; 12 Aug. 1868). W. De La Rue (15 Feb. 1863) –copy of letter to E. Sabine; 9 Dec. 1867; 24 Feb. 1868); T.R. Robinson (5 Mar. 1863), 28 Mar. 1863, 23 Dec. 1868, 8 Jan. 1869, 28 Feb. 1871, 3 Mar. 1871). R.S. Ball (1 Jan 1869, 5 Mar. 1874), W.R. Birt (6 June 1864, 2 July 1864), J. South (9 Feb. 1856).

2. Quarto volume entitled "Book of Visitors to Telescope 1850–1911" and containing signatures of visitors from 9 Sep. 1850 to 21 Feb. 1912 (and from 9 Sep. 1977).

3. Quarto volume entitled "Notebook" and including notes on theoretical astronomy together with six pages of a diary of a holiday in 1859.

4. Small quarto, volume, c. 1878. "A Catalogue of the Books and Pamphlets on Astronomy, Mathematics, Physics and Chemistry in the Library at Birr Castle".

5. Quarto volume entitled "Meteorological Papers", mainly blank but with certificates of examination of a barometer (1872) and thermometer (1878).

6. Small notebook, c. 1865, with miscellaneous jottings including a few visual observations of nebulae and also spectroscopic observations of nebulae by Huggins and at Birr.

7. Small notebook, undated, labelled "Rosse", with miscellaneous jottings on many subjects including photometry.

8. Quarto volume, undated, entitled "Scientific Formulae – Glass Silvering – Photography". Mainly blank, but includes notes and letters related to glass

L/6   **8.**   silvering processes (with manuscript of "A method of silvering a glass mirror
contd.   face upwards" by Edward Crossley and a covering letter from Crossley (14
May 1902) asking Rosse "to keep the enclosed process strictly private and
only communicate it for scientific purposes"); also manuscript of "Directions
for keeping the telescopes in order" and unsigned typescript note (16 Dec.
1907) re. sale of Admiralty searchlight reflectors to Lord Rosse.

    9.   Quarto volume *c.* 1908, containing short bibliographies on astronomical
topics.

    10.   File of documents relating to the equatorial mounting of the 3ft, including
detailed drawings, and drafts for a paper describing the mounting.

    11.   A miscellaneous file, mostly of minor and unconnected documents, but
including brief reports on the work of the observatory in 1881 and 1883;
meteorological records; "Notes on an electric control for an equatorial clock-
movement" (5 pp., no date) by the 4th Earl; and a list of astronomical
instruments at Birtr (post-1880).

    12.   "Directions for using Ramsden's telescope", 5 pp., with engraved drawing, no
date.

    13.   Octavo volume of notes on theoretical (Newtonian) astronomy, ?pre-1828,
apparently in the handwriting of the Hon. John C. Parsons, younger brother
of the future 3rd Earl.

M/	DATE	DESCRIPTION
1–42	[1860]–1956	Correspondence and other papers of the 4th and 5th Earls of Rosse on subjects other than astronomy, including estate and other King's County affairs, the 4th Earl's contributions to public life as a representative peer, Chancellor of Dublin University, etc, etc.
1	[1860–63?]	T.C.D. exercise book of the 4th Earl? on ancient and British history, with related printed papers, and the 4th Earl's degree in Physics.
2	1864: 1868	King's County and Co. Tipperary commissions of the peace for Lord Oxmantown, subsequently the 4th Earl.
3/1–16	1867–9	Letters to the 4th Earl from the Chief Secretary, Lord Mayo, and others about representative peerage elections, including that of the 4th Earl himself.*
4	1868: N.D.: 1895	Correspondence of the 4th Earl about yachting, Cowes, etc. [See also J/25 and O/8.]
5/1–35	1868–70: 1872 1875–1910	Letters and papers of the 4th Earl about Parsonstown/Birr: the Castle – his youthful recollections of it, extensions to it 1867–72 [see also M/25], a magazine portrait of his way of life there, 1898, and magazine obituaries of him, 1908; an incident which took place on the road between Banagher and Parsonstown and in which the 4th Earl and his party were stopped and temporarily put in gaol by a drunken R.I.C. man, 1868; the Parsonstown Barracks, 1869, 1899 and N.D.; the Parsonstown Town Commission and Commissioners, 1870 and 1885; admissions to the demesne of privileged locals, 1876–1910; and one of the bridges in the Birr Castle demesne, and the Rivers Brosna and Camcor, 1880 and 1896. The correspondents include Gladstone, W.E. Forster and Lords Strathnairn and Roberts. The sub-section also includes a small account book recording local subscriptions to the Parsonstown Defence Association, the Property Defence Association, the legal fund of the Irish Land Committee, and the Field and Rossmore Testimonials, *c.* 1882.
6	1869: 1872–4: 1880–81: 1885: 1896: 1898– 1900–01: 1906–7: 1911	General political and patronage correspondence of the 4th and 5th Earls, including letters (and an outsize volume of newspaper cuttings, all 1869) about Disestablishment, Poor Law reform, Orangeism, Conservative registration, Home Rule, the Irish Land question, etc.
7	1870–99	Letters and papers of the 4th Earl reflecting his membership of learned bodies – the Royal Irish Academy, the Royal Institute, the Royal Society, the Institute of Naval Architects, etc; the correspondents include W. Burne Jones and [the 1st Marquess of] Dufferin and Ava.

* See detailed calendar.

M/8	1871–2: 1884: 1890–1: 1897–8	Diaries of the 4th Earl (including a largely empty diary for 1872 of his wife, Cassandra) recording a tour in England, 1871, tours in the United States, 1884 and 1891, a visit to Jamaica, 1891, and a tour of India, 1897–8: together with two of his passports, 1890 and 1897.
9	1873: 1892	Papers of the 4th Earl about his eldest son, Lord Oxmantown: two copies of Lord Oxmantown's birth certificate, and a letter from Dr Benjamin Jowett about his admission to Balliol College, Oxford.
10	1874: 1897: 1902: 1911	Formal invitations to the 4th and 5th Earls – to civic functions in Belfast, and to Edward VII's and George V's coronations.
11	1868	Original bundle of applications/ recommendations for the post of head gardener at Birr (Andrew Hume being the successful applicant).
12	1879: 1885	Correspondence and maps concerning Lisheen military rifle range, beside the 4th Earl's property at Clonoghill, on the outskirts of Birr.
13	1878: 1880: 1892: 1895: 1897–1924	Box containing six miscellaneous letters and papers of or about junior branches of the Parsons family, all of them probably the children of the Hon. Laurence Parsons, youngest brother of the 3rd Earl [see J/29], including an epitome of the settlement made on the marriage of one of the Hon. Laurence Parsons's daughters, 1878; together with numerous case papers and court orders concerning the lunacy of the Hon. Laurence Parson's eldest son, Capt. Laurence Hardress Hector Parsons (d. 1924), 1897–1924.
14	1882–3: 1886–8	Letters to the 4th Earl from Arthur Kavanagh of Borris House, Co. Carlow about the work of the Irish Land Corporation.
15	1883–1909	Tin deed box containing tradesmen's accounts to the 4th Earl, mostly in original bundles.
16	1885	Correspondence of the 4th Earl with Sir Henry Hervey Bruce and others about misrepresentations of the 4th Earl in evidence before the select committee on Irish industries.
17	1885: 1888: 1897: 1903	Letters and papers of the 4th Earl as Chancellor of T.C.D., including his patent of appointment, 1885.
18	1870 onwards	Quarto recipe book kept by Miss Edith A. Cramer of Loughborough, housekeeper at Birr Castle, 1873–1919. [This book is kept in the small library in Birr Castle. For other recipes/recipe books, see A/17, E/13A and G/20, and for Miss Cramer, Q/383, 1/11/1 and T/157.]
19/1–2	c. 1886–1903: [c. 1880?]	Largely empty, quarto volume into which the 4th Earl has stuck 'puzzles' and other jokes, one of the jokes being a characteristically illegible letter to him from Lord Ashbourne Lord Chancellor of Ireland, c. 1886–1903; and largely empty folio volume, dated

		1823, but containing a child's? MS. Copy of parts of the Book of Survey and Distribution for Co. Galway, *c.* 1880s?
M/20	1886: N.D.: 1905–14	Letters and papers, mostly of the 4th and 5th Earls and Dr Otto Boeddicker, concerning Parsons family history and genealogy, including information about the Oxmantown/Phoenix Park property, sold by the elder branch of the Parsons family to the crown in 1672. Of particular interest is a paper entitled 'How the Parsons, Earls of Rosse, got the titles of Baron and Viscount of Oxmantown'.
21	1893–1919	Seven bank books of Lord Oxmantown, from 1908 the 5th Earl of Rosse. [Not in chronological order.]
22	1894	Original bundle of letters and papers of the 4th Earl concerning a bill to prevent rabies by muzzling dogs, including numerous answers to a circular which, clearly, he had addressed to Poor Law Unions all over Ireland seeking information about the incidence of rabies within their respective localities. [Not in chronological order.]
23	1894–1908: 1911: 1915: 1918	Personal and military papers of Major Lord Oxmantown, from 1908 the 5th Earl of Rosse], including commissions, illuminated addresses from the Heaton and Shipley tenants on his coming-of-age, 1894, and from the Birr Parish Vestry on his marriage, 1905 [both framed and hanging on the main bedroom floor of Birr Castle], a fairly savage attack on him in *The Midland Tribune* at the time of his return from the Boer War in 1900, letters from him to Toler R. Garvey Senior during the Boer War and the first World War, a page recording the signatures of Lord Oxmantown and other Irish notabilities who attended a shoot at Ashford, Cong, Co. Mayo, during a visit by the Prince of Wales, 1905, the 5th Earl's London address book, 1911, etc, etc.
24	1897: 1899	Amalgamation of two original bundles of applications/recommendations for the posts of blacksmith and forester at Birr.
25	1891: 1900–18	Letters, tradesmen's accounts, inventories of plate, specifications, tender and other papers of the 4th and 5th Earls, all concerning the contents of Birr Castle or improvements and alterations to Birr Castle and demesne and to houses and cottages owned by the estate – the installation of motors and turbines, plumbing, lighting, heating, redecorating, 'hacking off' plaster-work, etc. [Not in chronological order. For other inventories of plate, etc, see H/8 and T/83.]
26	1901–4: 1908	Original bundle of letters and papers concerning the 4th Earl's patents for a machine which he had invented for removing leaves and other matter from turbines, 1901–4; together with notes on his experiments with electro-plating, 1908. [Not in chronological order.]

M/27   1901–4: 1907   Original bundle of letters and papers of the 4th Earl about sewage disposal at Birr, by turbine and sundry other methods; the correspondents include Bindon B. Stoney [see K/24. Not in chronological order.]

28   1900–31   Papers about Birr Church of Ireland church and parish, including historical compilations of the rev. Dr Samuel Hemphill, Rector of Birr, covering the period 1612–1903. The compilations consist of a small quarto notebook containing MS. copies of 1642 depositions concerning the neighbourhood of Birr; another containing a history of Birr Church of Ireland church (taken from vestry books, parish registers, etc), 1760–1903; and two succession lists of Birr incumbents, 1612–1912. The sub-section also includes a series of printed annual reports on the parish and on the diocese of Killaloe and Kilfenora, 1900–10.

29   1905–11   Letters and papers of Lord Oxmantown, subsequently 5th Earl of Rosse, as a trustee of the marriage settlement of the 5th Earl of Malmesbury. [Not in chronological order.]

30   1906–11: 1929: 1951   Letters and papers, mainly of the 4th and 5th Earls, concerning the marriage settlement (1906) of Lady Muriel Parsons/Grenfell, daughter of the 4th Earl, with subsequent, related papers. [Not in chronological order. See also H/114.]

31   1908–9: 1912   Patents appointing the 5th Earl Lieutenant and Custos rotulorum of King's County in succession to his late father, including two letters from the Lord Lieutenant, Lord Aberdeen, on the subject (one of them making unsubtle reference to the necessity for the 5th Earl to commit himself to political support of the government of the day), letters to the 5th Earl giving confidential opinions as to the suitability of various people for appointment as J.P.s, and a tradesman's account for supplying a Lieutenant's flag for Birr Castle. [Not in chronological order.]

32   1899: 1901: 1907–9: 1914–56   Family, and family history, correspondence of the Hon. Geoffrey L. Parsons, including: a letter from his father, the 4th Earl, just before the latter's death; letters from his brother, the 5th Earl, who writes from the Front during the First World War, and a letter reporting that the 5th Earl has been seriously wounded; letters from Anthony de Brie, a portrait-painter, about his portraits of the 4th Earl and of Parsons's wife; letters from Dr Otto Boeddicker offering items of antique furniture for sale; and an envelope of newspaper cuttings and other material concerning the family collected by Geoffrey Parsons, c. 1915–55. [For letters to Geoffrey Parsons from his uncle, Sir Charles Parsons, see Section R.]

33/1   1908–16   Letters and tradesmen's accounts to the 5th Earl relating to seeds, shrubs, trees and planting, including 3 letters from Augustine Henry, botanist renowned for his flora-collecting explorations in

M/32 *contd.*		central and western China. [see also S/13], 1908–10. One of Henry's letters, dated 26 July 1909, is about Chinese? plant specimens at Birr; it has been photocopied by PRONI, T/3498/4.
33/2	1913–16	Printed price lists from Irish, British and French nurseries, including Lissadell, Co. Sligo.
34	1910–12	Letters and papers of the 5th Earl in connection with the trust set up under the will of Lady Rosse's relation, the late Mrs A.A. Hope of The Deepdene, Surrey ('the Hope Trust') [see also N/8. Not in chronological order.]
35	1910–30	Four envelopes of tradesmen's accounts to the 5th Earl, including a few to Lady Rosse, from London, Dublin and Birr tradesmen (primarily the first) for all manner of goods (among them a pendant brooch supplied by C. Fabergé, 1910), but excluding accounts for major items connected with Birr Castle and gardens [for which see M/25 and 33 respectively], 1910–18; together with 7 volumes of Birr Castle house-keeping books kept by Lady Rosse/de Vesci and (in one case) her sister, Countess de la Feld, 1910–30. [See also T/30. Not in chronological order.]
36	1912–14	Letters and papers of the 5th Earl concerning his shares in the San Sebastian Development Syndicate and the International Nitrogen and Power Company Ltd; part of the operations of the latter involved a process for cutting peat, and there are a number of letters to the 5th Earl and Sir Charles Parsons? on this subject.
37	1915–16	Two fat envelopes of post-cards and letter of thanks to Lady Rosse from prisoners of war in Germany belonging to Irish regiments, mainly the Irish Guards, for the Red Cross parcels sent to them by the organisation she set up at Birr Castle for that purpose.
38	1868: 1870	Small bundle of family settlements, the deeds of 1868 being a sequel to the 3rd Earl's marriage settlement of 1836 [see E/39], the deeds of 1870 together constituting the settlement made on the marriage of the 4th Earl to the Hon. Frances Cassandra Hawke [see H/114].
39	1898: 1909: 1920–21: 1932–3	Bundle of deeds and copy deeds constituting a re-settlement of the Rosse estate by the 4th and 5th Earls (1898), with sequel releases and appointments of new trustees of the settlement.
40	1905: 1932–3	The same in respect of the settlement made on the marriage of the 5th Earl to Frances Lois Lister Kaye.
41	1908–56	Vast bundle of deeds, letters, succession duty and other accounts, etc, etc, all concerning the will (1903) of the 4th Earl (d.1908) and the trust established under it, mainly for the benefit of his younger brothers, Rev. Randal, Richard Clere and Sir Charles Algernon Parsons.

M/42   1918–28:   Probate (1919) of the will (1918) of the 5th Earl, together with
            2005–6   legal papers and costs in connection with the will, later accounts
                                  relating to the cost of repairing his memorial in St Brendan's
                                  Church in Birr, and much later (2005–6) correspondence and
                                  accounts about having the memorial photographed in connection
                                  with the War Memorial Project.

[For further estate letters and papers of the 4th and 5th Earls, see Section Q. For one bundle of astronomical correspondence of the 5th Earl, see K/37. For letters to the 5th Earl's widow, Frances Lois, Lady Rosse/ de Vesci, from her second son, Desmond, see U/1.]

N/	DATE	DESCRIPTION
1–46	1739–1995 (mainly 1876–1973)	Letters and papers of the Lister Kaye family, of Denby Grange, near Wakefield, Yorkshire, one of whom, Frances Lois, second daughter of Sir Cecil Edmund Lister Kaye, 4th Bt, married in 1905 the 5th Earl of Rosse [see M/40].
1	1739: 1752: 1761: N.D.: 1806: 1812–13: 1824: [c. 1910]	Letters, pedigrees and other papers concerning the Listers, Kayes and related families, including: 'An account of Mr Roberts['s] family', 1739; a letter concerning the death of Sir John Lister Kaye, 1752;' a memorandum regarding cedar seeds, 1761; various 18th and early 19th century pedigrees and exemplifications of arms; letters from Sir Isaac Heard, Garter King of Arms, Office of Arms, London, on the same subject, 1812–13; and correspondence about a portrait of Shakespeare, 1824.
2	1732: 1770: 1791: 1796	Printed matter, as follows: one issue of *The General Evening Post* (recording the death of Sir John Lister Kaye), 1752, five issues of *The St James's Chronicle*, 1770, one of *The York Herald*, 1791, and a playbill, printed on silk, for the Old Theatre, Drury Lane, Newcastle-upon-Tyne, 1796.
3	1825: 1846: [pre–1855]: 1856	Four letters and papers of Lister Lister Kaye and his wife, Lady Caroline Lister Kaye, including one letter of 1825 to her mother, then Mrs Charles Pepys, later Countess of Cottenham. Lister Lister Kaye died young, and in the lifetime of his father, Sir Lister Lister Kaye, 2nd Bt; when the 2nd Baronet died in 1871, he was succeeded by Lister Lister Kaye's elder son, John Pepys Lister Kaye, who was in turn succeeded in 1924 by Lister Lister Kaye's second son, Cecil Edmund Lister Kaye, father of Frances Lois, Countess of Rosse.
4	[c. 1860]; 1882–6: 1896: 1911: 1923: 1928	Further letters and papers about the Listers and the Kayes and related families, such as the Bowers and the Staffords. The writer of the letters about the last-named family, James Stafford, appears to be a headcase, whose letters charge the Jerningham family with misappropriating the ancient barony of Stafford.
5	1876–8: 1880: 1887: 1889–91: 1895	Half-yearly rentals of the Denby Grange and Dalton estates, Yorkshire, the property of Sir John Pepys Lister Kaye, 3rd Bt.
6	1872: 1878–9: 1908–10: 1917–19: 1924: 1980: 1989	Letters and papers of Sir John Pepys Lister Kaye about personal, official and business matters: the family settlements, 1878–9; his Court appointment as Groom of the Household to Edward VII, 1908–10; the Chinese government's reneguing on the mining concession in the Anhui Province formerly granted to him, 1909; his bankruptcy in 1914 and the purchase of Denby Grange by his brother, Cecil (who succeeded him in the baronetcy in 1924); his First World War work organising the London Motor Transport [ie. Ambulance] Volunteers, 1917 and 1919; and obituaries of him, one of them headed 'The Happy Warrior', 1924.

N/7   1905: N.D.   Correspondence of Sir John's wife/widow, Natica, about life in 1915: 1917–19 1924: 1929: 1937   Peking, whither she presumably went with Sir John in pursuance of his mining concessions, c. 1905?; her fund-raising among fellow-Americans in New York, Washington and elsewhere for the London Motor Transport Volunteers, 1917–19; her attendance at American Presidential inaugurations, 1929 and 1937, etc, etc. Three of the letters are written on behalf of or by Queen Mary, 1917 and 1924. [Only in rough chronological order.]

8   1866–1928   Box of letters and papers concerning the 6th Duke of Newcastle and his wife, Henrietta, daughter and heiress of Henry Thomas Hope of The Deepdene, Surrey, present among the Lister Kaye Papers because one of their daughters, Lady Beatrice Adeline, married Cecil Edmund Lister Kaye, subsequently 4th Bt.

The letters and papers are arranged as follows:

8/1   [c. 1866?]   Small envelope of letters and newspaper cuttings concerning the scandal over the Duchess of Newcastle's affair with an operatic tenor from Gloucestershire called Thomas Theobald Hohler, whom she married in 1880, a year after the death of the Duke. The sub-section includes newspaper cuttings alluding in not-very-veiled language to the affair, an anonymous letter to Mrs Hope, the Duchess's mother, warning her of what was going on, a letter to Hohler from someone who was obviously acting as his go-between or second in an impending duel over the Duchess's good name, and 3 sweetly reasonably letters from the Duke (one of them a copy in the Duchess's hand), protesting that he has not been persecuting or spying upon her. [Not in chronological order.]

8/2–4   [1866–73?]   Three envelopes of love letters from Hohler, who writes from innumerable places in England, Scotland and Ireland where presumably he was performing in operas, to the Duchess, some of them referring to the duel and to the Duke, but most discussing ailments, lovers' tiffs, assignations and arrangements, etc, etc. Very few of the letters are dated, but the few that are fall within the period 1866–73. The first envelope (8/2) contains letters in which Hohler addresses the Duchess as 'Dear Duchess' or 'My dear Duchess', and which presumably fall within the early days of their relationship. The letters in 8/3 and 8/4 begin with much more imaginative endearments, which sometimes however include the adjective 'old' – an insensitive reminder of the disparity in years between the Duchess and the tenor.

8/5   [1866–73?]   Letters from the Duchess to Hohler, similar in character to the foregoing, although for the most part found in their original envelopes which have date stamps on them. [Not in chronological order.]

8/6   1879–1928: 1980   Letters, newspaper cuttings and other papers of Cecil Edmund Lister Kaye, subsequently 4th Bt, and his wife, Lady Adeline

N/8/6 *contd.*   Beatrice, about her father, the 6th Duke of Newcastle, and brothers, the 7th and 8th Dukes. The papers refer to: family rows; the attempt by Lord Francis Hope, later 8th Duke of Newcastle to sell pictures which had been designated as heirlooms, 1892, and the seizure of these or other heirlooms by bailiffs, 1902; the affairs of 'the Hope Trust' [see also M/34]; the coming-out of 'Miss Lister Kaye', one of Cecil Edmund Lister Kaye's three daughters, which was held at the Newcastle seat, Clumber; etc, etc. Also included are correspondence and a family tree of 1980 deriving from Anne Countess of Rosse's interest in 'the Hope Diamond', also inherited and apparently sold by Lord Francis Hope, 8th Duke of Newcastle. [Not in chronological order.]

9   1882–1927   Letters and papers of Sir Cecil Lister Kaye about his marriage settlement trust, the provision for his daughters, heirlooms inherited by him from his aunt, Miss Emma Lister Kaye of Overton, etc. [Not in chronological order.]

10   [*c.* 1894–1924]   Family and personal letters to Sir Cecil and Lady Adeline Beatrice Lister Kaye, in the following combinations and permutations: from Lady Adeline Beatrice to her husband, and from their daughters, Frances Lois (Countess of Rosse) and Adeline (Countess de la Feld) to them and to each other.

[A confusing factor in segregating these letters is that mother and daughters all address Sir Cecil as 'Pup' and mother as well as the appropriate daughter seems to subscribe herself 'Adeline' – though Lady Adeline Beatrice had been known as 'Beatrice', or simply 'B', in the Newcastle family. The principal correspondent is probably 'Adeline the younger', who did not marry Count de la Feld until comparatively late in life, in 1920, and up to that point spent much time in Russia, particularly Kiev, and among other things was responsible for the first (and probably still the best) translation of Chekhov into English; her letters contain a number of references to her work on Chekhov, as well as to such things as a production of *Pelléas et Melisande* at Covent Garden. Other letters from her, and many of those from her mother, are written from the Palazzo Doria, Rome, the house of Lady Adeline Beatrice's sister, Emily, who was married to Prince Doria. References to London and, less frequently, Dublin society are common, particularly to the Prince of Wales (the future George V) and other members of the royal family. One amusing letter of *c.* 1905 describes a visit to the Viceregal Lodge, Dublin, where were encountered '… Lord and Lady Pirrie, Mayor and Mayoress of Belfast, harmless, but quite middle-class …'. [Not in chronological order.]

11   1898–1914   Letters to Cecil Lister Kaye from his elder brother, Sir John, the earliest from the British Legation, Peking, and elsewhere in China,

N/11 *contd.*		the latest about Sir John's bankruptcy in 1914, mitigated (in the eyes of the Carlton Club, which did not expel him, as it did on principle other bankrupts) by his 'patriotic' refusal to bail himself out of his difficulties by selling the Denby Grange colliery to either the German or the Austrian government. [Not in chronological order.]
12	1902: N.D.	Personal letters to Cecil Lister Kaye from his mother and aunt, Miss Emma Lister Kaye. [Not in chronological order.]
13	1902–21	Letters and papers of Cecil Lister Kaye as a trustee of Princess Doria's marriage settlement. [Not in chronological order.]
14	1903: 1911: 1916–18: 1922	Letters and pedigrees of Cecil Lister Kaye about the Arbuthnot family and the related family of Gordon of Letterfourie (the wife of Sir Lister Lister Kaye, 2nd Bt, had been an Arbuthnot, of the same family as the Rt Hon. Charles Arbuthnot and the Duke of Wellington's Mrs Arbuthnot); Cecil Lister Kaye's principal correspondent is Mrs P.S. Arbuthnot of Harley House, Regent's Park, London, 1916–18. [Not in chronological order.]
15	1906–8	Letters to Cecil Lister Kaye about the marriage of his third daughter, Florence, to Major Charles Vaughan of Courtfield, Ross-on-Wye, Herefordshire, of which Cecil Lister Kaye disapproved, partly on religious grounds, and partly because he claimed that the Dowager Duchess of Newcastle had arranged the match behind his back. [Not in chronological order.]
16	1907: 1916–78	Letters and papers of Cecil Lister Kaye, subsequently 4th Bt, about the Denby Grange Colliery, including valuations of it, correspondence about the resettlement of it effected in 1919 whereby three-eighths of it was to pass to Cecil Lister Kaye on Sir John's death and in spite of Sir John's bankruptcy in 1918. [Not in chronological order.]
17	1913–15: N.D.	Letters to Cecil Lister Kaye from his sister-in-law, Natica, the wife of Sir John, mainly about Sir John's debts and disgrace. [Not in chronological order.]
18	1913–26	Agent's letters to Sir Cecil Lister Kaye from Percy Greave, the manager of the Denby Grange colliery. [Not in chronological order.]
19	1913–29	Denby Grange estate and colliery accounts of Sir Cecil Lister Kaye. [Not in chronological order.]
20	[*c.* 1915–20]	Small quarto volume containing political jottings of Sir Cecil Lister Kaye, including references to Home Rule, Lord Haldane at the War Office, the evacuation of Warsaw, Lloyd George, the League of Nations, etc.

N/21	1920	Letters to Sir Cecil Lister Kaye about the settlement on his daughter, Adeline's, marriage to Count de la Feld. [Not in chronological order.]
22	1925–6	Correspondence of Sir Cecil Lister Kaye about coal-owning politics, the General Strike, etc. [Not in chronological order.]
23	1927–8	Letters and papers of Sir Cecil Lister Kaye as a trustee of Lord Sherborne's family trust. [Not in chronological orders.]
24	1924–63: 1976	Huge bundle and 1 box file of letters and papers of Sir Kenelm Lister Kaye, 5th Bt, only son and successor of Sir Cecil Lister Kaye, who died in 1931, about his estate and colliery interests – Denby Grange Collieries Ltd, Terry Greaves & Lister Kaye Ltd, trusts established under the marriage settlement of Sir Cecil and Lady Adeline Beatrice Lister Kaye (Sir Kenelm's parents), the settlement trust set up by Sir John and as a result of his bankruptcy, the property in the Irish Free State, Mearescourt, Mullingar, Co. Westmeath, which Sir Kenelm acquired after he had sold Denby Grange, the winding-up of Sir Kenelm's estate after his death in 1962, and heritage items left by Jean, Lady Lister Kaye (Sir Kenelm's widow), to the 6th Earl of Rosse, 1976. [Not in chronological order.]
25	1931–46	Letters and papers of Sir Kenelm Lister Kaye concerning the Rosse family trusts and estates, and particularly the jointure interest which his sister, Frances Lois, Countess of Rosse, who married the 5th Viscount de Vesci after the death of the 5th Earl of Rosse, in 1918. The papers principally concern a jointure trust established for Lady Rosse/de Vesci, and the Bradford and Womersley estate trusts [for these Yorkshire estates of the Parsons family, see Sections G and H. Not in chronological order.]
26	1935–50	Letters and papers of Sir Kenelm Lister Kaye as a trustee under the will of his late aunt, Lady Florence Pelham Clinton his mother's unmarried sister, who died in 1935, principally her Harefield estate, Middlesex. [Not in chronological order. See also N/35.]
27	1943–54	Annual accounts for the property and shares included in the late 'Sir John Lister Kaye's settlement'. [Not in chronological order.]
28	1944–55	Annual accounts of Sir Kenelm Lister Kaye's income, annual trading accounts of Denby Grange Collieries Ltd, etc. [Not in chronological order.]
29	1946–52	Accounts and correspondence of Sir Kenelm Lister Kaye concerning the trusts and affairs of his mother's late brother, the 7th Duke of Newcastle, including the affairs of a company operated by the Newcastle family, called the London and Fort George Land Company Ltd. [Not in chronological order.]

N/30	1951–3	Letters and papers of Sir Kenelm Lister Kaye as a trustee for Capt. R.A. Grosvenor's marriage settlement trust. [Not in chronological order.]
31	1918	Commission of Sir Kenelm Lister Kaye as a lieutenant in the Royal Air Force.
32/1–44	1897–1940	Two boxes of letters and papers of Adeline Lister-Kaye, later (1920) Countess de la Feld, mainly dating from before the First World War, as follows:
32/1	1902–40	Fat bundle of letters and postcards to Adeline Lister-Kaye from her grand Roman relations, the Dorias, with whom she lived for long periods prior to the First World War. The connection derived from the marriage of her mother's sister, Lady Emily Pelham-Clinton, to Prince Alfonso Doria Pamphili in 1882. The correspondents include Princess Emily, her son, Filippo, and her daughter, Orietta, etc. [For the post-war continuation of the Doria correspondence, see N/36.]
32/2	1903–5	Letters and postcards to Adeline Lister-Kaye from her uncle, Sir John Pepys Lister-Kaye, mostly from foreign parts, especially Peking.
32/3	1903–4	Letters to Adeline Lister-Kaye from Lady Beatrice Child-Villiers, daughter of the 7th Earl of Jersey, who m. (1904) the 18th Lord Dunsany, Middleton Park, Bicester.
32/4	1905–8	Letters and postcards to Adeline Lister-Kaye from Count? Guido Pasolini, Villa Ponti, Varese, Lombardy.
32/5	1905–[c. 1908]	Letters to Adeline Lister-Kaye from Jean, wife of the Hon. Sir John Hubert Ward, second son of the 1st Earl of Dudley, and daughter of the American Ambassador to London, Whitelaw Reid, Wrest Park, Ampthill, Bedfordshire; Cap Ferrat; Dudley House, Park Lane; and Dorchester House, Park Lane.
32/6	1905–13	Letters to Adeline Lister-Kaye from Alfred Henry Tarleton, Breakspears, Uxbridge. He describes himself as her much older cousin, and writes about literary and antiquarian matters in an irritatingly facetious style.
32/7	1905–14	Letters and postcards to Adeline Lister-Kaye from Princess, Marchioness or Countess? Rufina ?Granidli, Rome and Portici (Naples).
32/8	1906–58	Letters and postcards to Adeline Lister-Kaye from her sister, Lois, Countess of Rosse, later (1920) Viscountess de Vesci, together with one or two from her second husband, the 5th Viscount de Vesci.
32/9	1907	Letters to Adeline Lister-Kaye from Lord Bury afterwards 9th Earl of Albemarle, then ADC to the Governor-General of India and

N/32/9 *contd.*		later in the year to the Governor of the Orange River Colony, writing from Peshawar, Bloemfontein, etc.
32/10	1907	Letters to Adeline Lister-Kaye from John Corbier, University Club, New York, writing in interesting vein about their mutual interest in literary matters.
32/11	1907: N.D.	Letters and postcards to Adeline Lister-Kaye from Mabel [Gerry? – name taken from the endorsed caption to a snapshot in N/32/42], 2 East 61st Street, New York.
32/12	1908–14	Fat bundle of letters and postcards to Adeline Lister-Kaye from 'Bill', Betu Tiga, Selangor, and Salak North, Perak, both in the Federation of Malay States; the Customs Office, Taiping, Perak; the Government Monopolies Department of the Chinese Protectorate of Malacca; Quala Lumpur, Malaya, etc. His letters are long and detailed, and discuss his work, local customs, philology, etc.
32/13	1909–19	Medical prescriptions for Adeline Lister-Kaye.
32/14	1910–17	Extremely fat bundle of letters to Adeline Lister-Kaye from Princess Vera Demidoff, Korsoun, Russia, one of them referring to a pre-war ball in St Petersburg given by the nobility to the Tsar and Tsarina.
32/15	1910–12	Letters to Adeline Lister-Kaye from Princesses Olga and Lepouphine Demidoff, Korsoun. [They presumably were sisters of Princess Vera?]
32/16	N.D.: [*c.* 1910]	Four letters to Adeline Lister-Kaye from a male friend nicknamed 'Spinach', Hove; 61 Grosvenor Street, London; Badminton, R.S.O. Gloucestershire; and Coker Court, Yeovil. The letters are flirtatious in tone.
32/17	[*c.* 1910]	Letters and a telegram to Adeline Lister-Kaye from M.A. Grinchu [who seems also, however improbably, to be called Viola Marowety?], Metropolitan Club, Paris, etc.
32/18	[*c.* 1910–20]	Letters to Adeline Lister-Kaye from M. de ?Priseri, Lisbon and 20 Connaught Square, London. [The writer seems to be a woman, and 'M.' is her initial rather than an abbreviation of 'Monsieur'; the letters are in French.]
32/19	[*c.* 1910?]–1927	Letters to Adeline Lister-Kaye from 'Cis.', alias 'C.M.', who writes from two successive addresses in Chelsea and from a series of hotels and rented country houses all over England and Scotland. The writer appears to be married to one Edmund. Her letters are intelligent, sensible and affectionate. In one of them she offers to finance the private publication of short stories by Adeline Lister-Kaye.
32/20	1911–12	Letters to Adeline Lister-Kaye from Home Peel (private secretary to E.S. Montagu as Under-Secretary of State for India), India

N/32/20 *contd.*   Office; 51 Jermyn Street, St James's; and Sunninghill, Ascot. The
                                  letters are light and humorous in tone, but the writer seems to be
                                  romantically attached to her.

32/21   1911–14   Letters to Adeline Lister-Kaye from Teneral Landon, 83
                                  Charlwood Street, London SW, and Delhi. He addresses her as
                                  'My dearest'.

32/22   1911: 1918:   Letters and telegrams to Adeline Lister-Kaye from the children of
            1926: N.D.:   her sister, Lois – the 6th Earl of Rosse, his brother, Desmond, and
            1937   his sister, Lady Bridget. The last item is a telegram from Lord
                                  Rosse announcing the death of Desmond Parsons. [For post-
                                  Second World War letters from Lord Rosse and Lady Bridget, see
                                  N/34 and 35.]

32/23   1912–29   Letters to Adeline Lister-Kaye from Charles Allsopp, 3rd Lord
                                  Hindlip (then a Conservative Whip in the House of Lords), 22
                                  South Street, Park Lane; Hotel Ritz, Place Vendome, Paris;
                                  Carlton Club, Pall Mall; Turf Club, Piccadilly; and Cannizard,
                                  Wimbledon. (Lord Hindlip was a married man with four children,
                                  but it is hard not to interpret the letters of *c.* 1912 as love-letters.)
                                  Most of the letters are about arrangements for meetings, or rather
                                  assignations, but there are occasional references to politics, e.g.:
                                  'poor Granard was well roasted [in a House of Lords debate of *c.*
                                  1912]. As one of his own side said, it won't hurt him!'

32/24   1913–20   Letters to Adeline Lister-Kaye from 'Linny' [her uncle, the 7th
                                  Duke of Newcastle, formerly Earl of Lincoln], Berkeley House,
                                  Hay Hill, London; Forest Farm, Windsor Forest, etc. He was
                                  clearly very fond of his niece, and his letters are full of fun and
                                  vivid description – the latter including an account of an air-raid
                                  warning during a performance at the Garrick Theatre which he
                                  attended with 'the impious one' [a lady friend?].

32/25   N.D.: 1914–18   Letters to Adeline Lister-Kaye from her parents, Sir Cecil and
                                  Lady Beatrice Lister-Kaye, writing mainly from Denby Grange.

32/26   1914–20:   Box of letters to Adeline Lister-Kaye from Count Gugliemo de la
            1925–7   Feld (an Italian who probably came from the north of the then
                                  kingdom of Italy), whom she married in 1920; together with a few
                                  letters from her to him, an envelope of newspaper cuttings about
                                  their marriage, an envelope of letters of condolence to her on his
                                  death in 1927, and papers about his grave and funeral monument
                                  at Hendon. As is apparent from these dates, Adeline Lister-Kaye
                                  had known the Count for some six years before she finally married
                                  him. He writes to her from London, Paris, Rouen, Naples and
                                  Rome. In 1916 he arrived in London to work for an Italian Red
                                  Cross committee set up to look after the UK-based families of
                                  Italian service-men. His other postings were also in connection
                                  with the Italian Red Cross. Their letters to each other are written

N/32/26 *contd.*		in Italian. He was much older than she was and, although by the time she married him she was almost forty, it was still a match which was regarded as hardly suitable by her friends [see N/32/37].
32/27	1915[–16?]	Three letters to Adeline Lister-Kaye from 'Frankie' (Francis de Tuyll), writing from the Western Front.
32/28	1915–27	Letters to Adeline Lister-Kaye from Edward Scawen Wyndham (b.1883) of Edmonthorpe Hall, Oakham, mostly about the last year of the First World War, in which he was fighting.
32/29	1915–16: 1939	Letters and a telegram to Adeline Lister-Kaye from her friend, Ethel Frothingham, who writes from hotels in St Andrews, Paris and Monte Carlo.
32/30	1915–19: 1958	Passports of Adeline Lister-Kaye, together with a copy (1958) of her birth certificate (1881).
32/31	[*c.* 1915–18]	Letters to Adeline Lister-Kaye from 'Lottie' [Charlotte] Ismay, who m. (1915) Capt. Bryan Fairfax of [?Derry]thorpe, Yorkshire, writing from various addresses which do not seem to be her own. She refers to their war work together, the 1918 general election in which her husband stood (unsuccessfully) as a candidate for some part of Yorkshire, etc.
32/32	1915: 1949: 1952	Letters to Adeline Lister-Kaye from her sister, Florence Vaughan, and brother-in-law, Capt. Charles J. Vaughan of Courtfield, Herefordshire, writing from 21 Alexandra Court, London, SW7, etc.
32/33	1916–18	Letters to Adeline Lister-Kaye from her brother, Kenelm, later 5th Bt, Denby Grange; 10th West Yorkshire Regiment, BEF; 3rd West Yorkshire Regiment, Eansdon, Northumberland; 84 Squadron RFC, BEF, etc.
32/34	1918	Two letters to Adeline Lister-Kaye from Thomas Ashby, British Military Mission, Italy.
32/35	1918: N.D.	Letters to Adeline Lister-Kaye from L. Leclerc, Paris. The letters are written in French.
32/36	1918: N.D.: 1930	Letters to Adeline Lister-Kaye from Air Commodore John D. Boyle, writing in 1918 from H.Q. No. 3 Group, Royal Air Force, Cambridge, and in 1930 from H.Q., Royal Air Force, Hillingdon House, Uxbridge. Most of the letters are undated, and it is possible that all but two can be assigned to 1918.
32/37	1919–20	Four long letters to Adeline Lister-Kaye from Isabel Clarke, Rome and Florence. The first two are about the last illness and death of Adeline Lister-Kaye's aunt, Princess Doria. The last comments significantly on the marriage to Count de la Feld: 'You are right – I am both interested and disappointed in hearing your news. I had hoped – as you know – something very different for you, and

N/32/37 *contd.*		please forgive my saying so, as everyone knows their own business best in this world, but your letter has left the impression upon me that you are not making the kind of marriage you ought to make. I am sure he must be devoted to you, and there is no doubt that he's a very lucky man, but you say he is old and hasn't much money, so I don't quite see where you come in. But if you really feel happy about it, then I congratulate you on having secured that, and wish you all the blessings possible. I suppose he is not a Catholic as you are to be married at Clumber? I hope you will not think me "churlish" for writing like this, but I feel you ought to make a very good marriage if you make one at all. If you had told me of your engagement to your cousin [Prince Filippo Doria?] or to de Salis (who always had a weakness for you), I should have had nothing but congratulations to offer! Another blow for poor little Ashby. ...'
32/38	1919–28	Tradesmen's accounts to Adeline Lister-Kaye, Countess de la Feld, mainly from London tradesmen and almost all for luxury items and services.
32/39	1925	Letters to Adeline Countess de la Feld from the Hon. Mrs Muriel Yorke, wife of General Ralph Maximilian Yorke, 1 Southwick Crescent, London W2, and The Commander-in-Chief's House, British Army of the Rhine.
32/40	1925	Three letters to 'Adeline my dear' from 'Russell', writing from no stated address.
32/41	1897–1925	Fat bundle of letters to Adeline Lister-Kaye, Countess de la Feld, from miscellaneous correspondents about personal matters and the First World War. Included is a letter of September 1919 from the Naval Intelligence Department of the Admiralty thanking her for her services to the geographical section of the department during the war.
32/42	1905[–*c.* 1920]	Fat bundle of photographs deriving from Adeline Lister-Kaye, Countess de la Feld, and some of them with endorsements throwing light on the identity of correspondents in N/32/1–41.
32/43	1905[–*c.* 1920]	Drawings and doodles.
32/44	1911–39	Miscellaneous printed matter. [For Adeline Countess de la Feld's writings, 1915–50, see N/44.]
33/1–3	1940–78	Post-Second World War letters and papers of Adeline Countess de la Feld about mainly financial matters, as follows:
33/1	N.D.: 1941–58: 1967	Inventories/valuations and a 1967 Christie's sale catalogue, all relating to Countess de la Feld's jewellery, and of interest because some of this jewellery once formed part of 'The Hope Collection', together with letters to her from Lloyds' Bank, London, and from solicitors, etc, about Lister Kaye family trusts, other financial

matters, and her own will (which, again, makes mention of jewellery).

N/33/2 1949: 1953–78 Business letters to Adeline Countess de la Feld as a trustee of the Lady Florence Institute, set up under the will of Lady Florence Pelham Clinton, and correspondence and accounts of her nephew, the 6th Earl of Rosse, in the same capacity.

33/3 1940: 1948: 1972–4 Letters and papers of Adeline Countess de la Feld about churches and charities, particularly in the diocese of Wakefield.

34–40 1945–73 Post-Second World War family and personal correspondence of Adeline Countess de la Feld, as follows:

34 1945–72 Fat bundle of letters to Adeline Countess de la Feld from her nephew, the 6th Earl of Rosse, including a few from Anne, Countess of Rosse, many of them correcting false impressions she had been given (by Lady Bridget) of recent Parsons family affairs; the 6th Earl tactfully attributes the Countess's susceptibility to these to her remoteness from the British Isles. (The Countess spent most of her time, post–1945, in Edmonton and Victoria, Canada, and died there in 1975.)

35 1951–69 Fat bundle of letters to Adeline Countess de la Feld from her niece, Lady Bridget Parsons.

36 1952–4 Letters to Adeline Countess de la Feld from the Dorias, mainly Prince Filippo, his sister, Orietta, and brother?, Alfonso. Included is a newspaper obituary of Prince Filippo, who died c. 1955, of which the following are extracts: 'Prince Filippo Andrea Doria-Pamphili-Landi died in Rome on Tuesday ..., [aged] 71. Prince Filippo was the last male descendant of one of the oldest Genoese noble families, with a history going back as far as the twelfth century. His health had been indifferent since the war, when the combined persecution of Fascist and Nazi police, interspersed with brief terms of imprisonment, undermined his not too strong constitution. His mother, who before her marriage to his father, Prince Alfonso, was Lady Emily Augusta Mary, daughter of the 6th Duke of Newcastle, died in 1919. Two years later Prince Filippo married in England an English [sic – Scottish] girl, Miss Gesine Mary Dykes. During the Ethiopian war, the Prince became an active and violent anti-Fascist. The Rome palace of the Doria-Pamphili was raided then by a black-shirted mob. The resolute and dignified intervention of the Princess succeeded in turning the mob away and preventing damage to the Doria-Pamphili art treasures, which are considered to be some of the most valuable in private ownership in the world. ... [During the Second World War, Prince Filippo] was in deep water when it was discovered that he contributed financially to the underground organisation which took care of and sheltered escaped Allied prisoners of war. At the

N/36 *contd.*		end of the war, the Allied military authorities appointed him as the first mayor of Rome. His inaugural speech to Romans was the shortest on record. He said to them in Roman dialect: "Let us love one another". The late Prince is survived by an only daughter, Princess Orietta Doria-Pamphili-Landi, who was born in London in 1922.' [She married a Mr Pogson and died in 2000. For letters from her and from other members of the Doria family to the 6th Earl of Rosse, see T/8.]
37	1953–4: 1962–71	Fat bundle of letters to Adeline Countess de la Feld from her great-nephew, Lord Oxmantown, later 7th Earl of Rosse, many of them describing his work for the United Nations, and obviously generating lengthy replies from her because of her own interest in such causes as famine relief in the Third World, foreign missions, etc, etc.
38	1953: 1958–9	Three letters to Adeline Countess de la Feld from her younger great-nephew, the Hon. Martin Parsons.
39	1949–58: 1985–6	Letters to Adeline Countess de la Feld from her 'godson' (in the sense that she stood sponsor for him when he was received into the Russian Orthodox Church), Robin Bryan of Brighton and London. The later items, of 1985–6, consist of letters from Bryan to the 7th Earl of Rosse (Countess de la Feld's great-nephew) giving fascinating information about the Countess's early life and about recent Parsons family history, particularly in relation to Lady Bridget Parsons.
40/1	1958: N.D.	Personal letters to Adeline Countess de la Feld from Mrs N.Y. Herzberg of Victoria, British Columbia.
40/2	1950–73	Personal letters to Adeline Countess de la Feld from miscellaneous post-Second World War friends, many of them from British Columbia.
41–44	1918–58	Writings of Adeline Countess de la Feld (including very little about her translations of Chekhov, the work for which she is best-known and regarded), arranged as follows:
41	1937: 1944	Bundle consisting of a 2-volume rough draft, a 2-volume final typescript (both written in 1937) and a 1-volume abbreviated version (written in 1944) of Adeline Countess de la Feld's life of her late mother, Lady Beatrice Lister Kaye (d.1935). Although the main emphasis is spiritual (eg. the chapter about her birth and early days is entitled 'Genesis'), the work does contain some information about the history of the Hope and Newcastle families, *c.* 1800–1875.
42	1953–8	Bundle of jottings and papers of a still more religious complexion, titled 'Journals, diaries and records, 1953–1958'.
43/1–10	1918–53	Series of tied-up parcels containing a diary kept by Adeline Countess de la Feld, as follows:

N/43/1	N.D.–1917	Volume missing.
43/2	Jan. 1918– May 1921	Vol. 2 of the diary.
43/3	May 1921– Mar. 1922	Vol. 3 of the diary.
43/4	Apr. 1922– May 1924	Volume missing.
43/5	June 1924– Sep. 1927	Vol. 5 of the diary.
43/6	Sep. 1931– Dec. 1936	Vol. 6 of the diary.
43/7	May 1937– Mar. 1939	Vol. 7 of the diary.
43/8	Mar. 1939– Dec. 1945	Vol. 8 of the diary.
43/9	Sep. 1947– June 1953	Vol. 9 of the diary.
43/10	1951–3	'New Zealand diary, 1951–3.'
43/11/ 1–6	1924: 1926: 1942: 1946: 1949: 1950	Six volumes of a smaller, pocket-size engagement diary.
44	1910–55	Box of miscellaneous writings of Adeline Countess de la Feld on religious, historical and philological subjects, including 'Fantasies, monologues, musings on many topics, 1919–1934', letters from Heinemann's and Jonathan Cape about her translations of Chekhov, *c.* 1915–25, a letter from the Earl of Ronaldshay about her comments on his book on India, 1925, etc.
45	1888–95	Volume of press-cuttings of uncertain provenance, but at least appropriate in date to this section of the Rosse Papers, kept by Mrs Clifford Cory, nee Lethbridge, a member of a junior branch of the Lethbridge family, baronets, of Sandhill Park, Taunton, Somerset, and a sister of Julia, the wife of Lord Carew of Castleborough, Enniscorthy, Co. Wexford. The cuttings all concern Court and social events in London and Dublin.
46	1975	Letter to Anne Countess of Rosse from Sir John Lister-Kaye, 7th Bt, with a list of Lister-Kaye plate which he had been successful in buying at auction in Dublin and had been sold (according to Lady Rosse's endorsement) by 'bloody Nora'.

O/	DATE	DESCRIPTION
1–66	*c.* 1610: 1638: [*c.* 1690]: *c.* 1745–1970	Maps, plans and drawings, mainly of a size which makes it physically convenient to form them into a separate section, and either framed and hanging in the Muniment Room in Birr Castle, kept flat in the horizontal drawers of an old vestment chest in that room, or rolled in the left-hand compartment of that chest or in the cupboard to the right of it. [For other maps, plans and drawings, see A/17 and 24, B/8/7, E/4, E/39, G/64 and L. For leases with integral maps, see under Q/1–15 and 17–90.]
1A	*c.* 1610	Photocopy of map of the barony of Eglish, found by Rolf Loeber in The National Archives, Kew.
1	1638	Coloured map of John Crewe's park in Siffin Wood, Parsonstown, by Francis Morley. [Damaged and incomplete.]
2	[pre–2 Apr. 1691]	Photostats of a plan of Birr Castle and its defences, by Michael Richards; the original is among the papers of George Clarke, Wiliam III's Secretary-at-War, in Worcester College, Oxford, of a letter from Richards of 2 April 1691 referring to this plan, and of a memo. By the historian, C.H. Firth, on the Clarke papers and maps, N.D. [A coloured print of the plan is framed and hanging in the Muniment Room.]
2A	1730	Rolled, coloured map of the lordship of Upper He[l]msley, Yorkshire, belonging to John Wilmer, Gent., surveyed by Robert Bowlay. [See G/32.]
3	1745–6	Architectural drawings by Samuel Chearnley, a native of Co. Tipperary, resident in Birr, who was a cousin and protégé of Sir Laurence Parsons, 3rd Bt, but who died too young to make much mark in his profession, as follows: volume containing *c.* 80 'Miscellanea structura curiosa, or [a] collection of different designs, inventions and edifices, as ruins, grottoes, surprises, cascades, fountains, … triumphal arches, … plans and elevations, by Samuel Chearnley, October the 24th 1745' [but actually 1745–6], several of these often fantastic wash drawings dedicated to Sir Laurence Parsons; ground plan, with on the verso a front elevation, by Chearnley for a Classical mansion house to the specification of Parsons, N.D.; and a drawing, of similar type and period, for a temple-style folly, N.D. [The volume of 'Miscellanea structura curiosa' is currently bound in *c.* 1923 purple half calf, but as the drawings are interleaved with paper marked 1829, it was probably first bound by the 2nd Earl of Rosse. It is not kept along with the other maps, plans and drawings, but in the Library in Birr Castle. For modern papers about its interpretation and publication (in 2005), see W/27.]

O/4	1763	Plan, on parchment, by Nicholas Moran of the route from Dublin Barracks to Tullamore, King's County. [Damaged and incomplete.]
5	1769	Plan, by John Carry, of the road from Birr to Cloghan.
6	1781	Plan, also by Carry, of the road from Birr to Portumna.
7	1784	'Plan and section designed for strengthening the market house of Birr.' [Damaged and incomplete.]
8	1786	Map, by John Carry, of the lands of Drinagh, barony of Eglish, King's County, part of the estate of Sir William Parsons, 4th Bt. [Damaged and incomplete.]
9	[1780s?]	Map of Derrinlough, between Birr and Cloghan. [Damaged and incomplete.]
10	[late 18th century]	Design for the former ceiling in the library in Birr Castle, reproduced in Part 1 of Mark Girouard's 1965 *Country Life* article on Birr Castle. Girouard comments: 'This room used to have what must have been an impressive, coffered ceiling, but although the original design for this survives, the ceiling itself was unfortunately destroyed by fire in 1919. The design, incidentally, was copied very closely from one of the coffered burial chambers in a mausoleum at Palmyra, taken from Robert Wood's *Ruins of Palmyra* (1753), a much-used source for detail in the later 18th century.'
11	[early 1790s]	Folding printed copy of Alexander Taylor's 'new map of Ireland', with MS. Markings made in May 1826 to denote mail coach roads, mail cart roads and riding posts, [and, obviously, deriving from the 2nd Earl of Rosse's position as Joint Post Master General for Ireland.
12	1796	Folding printed copy of John Gary's map of England and Wales with part of Scotland, dedicated by permission to the Post Masters General of Great Britain.
13	[1790?]	Folding printed map of the north of France.
14	[c. 1790s–c. 1810s]	Bundle of 23 MS. or printed drawings of facades of buildings, mainly castles and churches, interior features such as doors and windows, etc, etc, probably collected by Sir Laurence Parsons, 5th Bt, later 2nd Earl of Rosse, with an eye to his own architectural alterations to Birr Castle.
15	[1790s]	Bundle of 22 ground plans, elevations, and other drawings, with measurements and other details written in the same or a similar hand, and all in a robust, not to say coarse, style; one of them signed, 'E. Johnston, 1793'. Possibly plans for Birr Castle, and by the father or some other relation of the John Johnston whom shortly afterwards the 2nd Earl was to employ as his architect.

O/16   [*c.* 1801–2]   Notebook containing sketches, in the 2nd Earl's handwriting,
                          from which John Johnston worked. This documents is described
                          in Part 2 of Girouard's *Country Life* article as: '... full of little
                          sketches of projects for the new work – for castellating the
                          entrance front, for building a grand Gothic staircase at the end of
                          the hall, for a new Gothic entrance gate from the town, and so on.
                          The entrance was never executed, though a grand Gothic saloon or
                          drawing-room was built along the river; the front was gothicised
                          with a new facing of smooth, grey limestone, and there was further
                          gothicising at the back. The new front was based on the simpler of
                          the sketches, without, for instance, the great central turret shown,
                          in one of them, rising from behind the battlements of the central
                          porch. This porch, with its giant recessed arch, is now the
                          dominant feature of the front ... . It is a skilfully conceived
                          feature, for its striking form diverts attention from the fact that the
                          front of the house is only approximately symmetrical. In fact, the
                          wall to the right of the porch is set considerably farther forward
                          than that to the left; and the windows and the two sides by no
                          means match each other.'

17   [*c.* 1801–2]   Bundle of 26 ground plans, all apparently in the handwriting of
                          the 2nd Earl, for his alterations to Birr Castle, and showing, in
                          particular, what Girouard describes as his '... most memorable
                          creation there, the Gothic saloon. A number of plans and designs
                          for this survive, one of them on paper water-marked 1801. It is
                          built out over an undercroft on the south side of the house, and its
                          three Gothic windows look straight down into the river. It is fitted
                          between the main block of the house and the yellow drawing-room,
                          one half of which is in the old south flanker, probably originally a
                          free-standing tower, and set diagonally to the rest of the house. The
                          need to fit one end of the room between the main block and the
                          diagonal wall of the flanker suggested the idea of ending it with a
                          half-hexagon; in the interests of symmetry, the other end was
                          finished in the same way; and the result was the extended octagonal
                          shape that is one of the principal charms of the room.'

18   [*c.* 1801–4]   Folder of 8 designs, some in the handwriting of the 2nd Earl, for
                          the ceiling of the Gothic saloon, and for other internal features of
                          the saloon and the new entrance hall, some of them paper-marked
                          1801, one paper-marked 1804. Girouard Comments: 'Slim white
                          and gold Gothic columns support a Gothic plaster vault, also of
                          white and gold, and resembling a light and elegant Gothic tent.
                          There is no elaborate ornament; but the tracery of the three large
                          windows has the delicate absurdity of Georgian Gothic at its best.'

19   [*c.* 1803]   Bundle of 14 drawings for the entrance front and central porch at
                          Birr Castle, one of them signed by John Johnston, dated April
                          1803, and showing the porch almost as it was built, some of them

O/19 *contd.*		probably representing sketches of what other castles looked like rather than serious suggestions for Birr; included in the bundle is an engraving of the entrance front at Birr Castle, *c.* 1840, by which time it had undergone alterations described by Girouard after a fire in 1832.
20	1803	'A map of the demesne of Parsonstown, taken in the rough from the original, May 7th, 1803, … [by] Patt. McNevin, land surveyor, etc.' [Now framed and hanging on the wall in the Muniment Room of Birr Castle.]
21	1809	'A map of the old road leading from Birr to Cloghan …, by William Horocan, land surveyor.' [Damaged and incomplete.]
22	1816	'A map of that part of the lands of Parsonstown [on the Mountmellick road] now in the possession of Patrick Nevin …, [by] Patrick Nevin.' [Damaged and incomplete]
23A	[pre–1818]	Rolled, printed map, by John Taylor, of the environs of Dublin, dedicated to the Lord Lieutenant, Viscount Whitworth, and the Postmasters General, the 2nd Earl of Rosse and Earl O'Neill.
23B	1821	Printed, hand-coloured map of Dublin, by J. Cooke, architect and surveyor.
24	[*c.* 1820]	Front elevation (pen and wash) for an unexecuted 'Chinois' design for Tullynisky Park, Birr, together with a contemporary drawing of Birr Castle by George Petrie. The architectural design was acquired by Thomas Pakenham among a collection of such drawings, and was presented by him to the Birr Castle Muniment Room. Originally, it was found among drawings signed by Bernard Mullins, the architect of a number of buildings in Birr in the period *c.* 1810–1820. It is unsigned, but may conceivably be attributable to Mullins. For leases of Tullanisky, see Q/56.]
25	[*c.* 1820]	Bundle of 4 designs for fireplaces, one of them paper-marked 1821.
26	1822	Non-contemporary, *c.* 1880s?, coloured copy of an 1822 map of Parsonstown, the original possibly drawn by Thomas L. Cooke, whose name is mentioned in the description in the margin. [Framed in the Muniment Room in Birr Castle, and not kept with the other maps, plans and drawings.]
27	1823	'Tracing from map on lease to Robert Robinson (of passage to water wheel), dated 29 September 1823, but not executed.' [Damaged and incomplete.]
28	[*c.* 1828]	Front and side elevations (2 versions of each) for 'John's Hall' (the memorial building in Birr to the Hon. John Clere Parsons, second son of the 2nd Earl), with 'A design from the temple at Ilissus …, selected by the Rt Hon. The Earl of Rosse'; all apparently (some actually signed) by Bernard Mullins probably of Henry & Mullins, Talbot Street, Dublin. [see E/23].

O/29   1834   Printed sale rental of certain lands in the barony of Athlone,
                        Co. Roscommon, belonging to one Ignatius Keogh, to be sold
                        under a decree of the Court of Chancery.

30   [c. 1840–45]   Twelve designs by Mary Countess of Rosse and/or Colonel
                        Wharton Myddleton [see J/19] for a 'bell ceiling' for the hall of
                        Birr Castle], for the mock-Gothic structure housing the Great
                        Telescope, for the iron gates set into the keep gate-house at Birr
                        Castle, together with a ground plan and a pen and ink and
                        watercolour design for the keep gate, showing the drawbridge with
                        soldiers on guard.

31   Blank in the sequence.

32–4   [c. 1850]   Series of 3 outsize, rolled coloured plans for an intricate, formal
                        garden immediately in front of Birr Castle, the first two in the
                        handwriting of Colonel Wharton Myddleton [see J/19], the third
                        not in the same handwriting but apparently related to these
                        unexecuted plans. [Two of the 3 have been framed and are
                        hanging in or near the Muniment Room in Birr Castle.]

35   [c. 1850?]   Sketches for a stove.

36   [c. 1850?]   Engraving of the interior of St Brendan's Church, Birr.

37   1852   Volume of 'Maps of the estates of the Hon. Laurence Parsons
                        [third son of the 2nd Earl], situate in the King's County and county
                        of Wexford'. These estates total 3,666 statute acres, 2,000 of which
                        are in Wexford, and consist of the lands of Bloomfield, Ballinapierce,
                        Ballyduff, Howell's Land, Knockmarshal, etc. [see B/12].

37A   1853   Outsize, rolled map of Birr, with the houses and holdings
                        coloured red and the street numbers marked on them. " [Kept in
                        the cupboard to the left of the vestment chest.]

38   1853–6   Outsize volume of 'Maps of the estates of the Rt Hon. William,
                        Earl of Rosse, in the King's County and county of Tipperary …;
                        [surveyed by] John Logan, Dublin, 1853, 1854, 1855, 1856'; these
                        are fine coloured maps, with survey particulars given on the page
                        facing each. They appear to cover all the agricultural land in the
                        Rosse estate, together with the Birr Castle demesne, but omit the
                        town of Birr. The total comes to 16,914 Irish acres, of which 1,139
                        are in the barony of Lower Ormond, Co. Tipperary, and the rest in
                        the baronies of Ballybritt, Eglish, Garrycastle and Coolestown,
                        King's County. [Kept flat on top of the vestment chest.]

39   post–1855   Tracing from a map of part of Birr Castle demesne. [Damaged
                        and incomplete.]

39B   [c. 1850s?]   Tracing from a map of the lands of Bunraven, the property of Sir
                        Robert Blosse Lynch, Bt, which lie between the Hon. Laurence
                        Parson's townlands of Clondallow and Dovegrove.

O/40	1859	'Plan of proposed new road from Parsonstown to Banagher between the three roads at Annaghanerrig and three Roads in Clonrah at Derrinsallagh [sic – Derrinsallow] Mills', by John Hill, Tullamore.
41–4	c. 1860	Four, rolled, coloured ground plans for Mary, Countess of Rosse's extension to Birr Castle, one of them endorsed, 'A. Salvin's plans for new kitchen …'.
45	[c. 1860]	Rolled, coloured elevation for an unexecuted extension beyond the dining-room, on the town side of Birr Castle.
46	1861–3	Original bundle of tracings, valuations, correspondence, etc., concerning parts of the townlands of Corraduff and Kileen needed in connection with the Parsonstown-Portumna Bridge Railway. [Not in chronological order. See also J/24.]
47	1863	Four rough maps of parts of Shinrone, the joint estate of the 3rd Earl of Rosse and John Lloyd, by James Kennedy, Parsonstown, together with a photocopy of a deed of partition dividing the estate between the 3rd Earl and Lloyd. (The original of this deed is in the possession of Mrs Trevor Lloyd, formerly of Gloster. For an earlier deed of partition, see E/38.)
47A	1865	Large, long tin case containing plans of the townships of Heaton and Shipley (Mary, Countess of Rosse's estate at Bradford, Yorkshire), with a related statutory declaration by one Timothy Stocks. [Kept in the left-hand cupboard in the Muniment Room. See also G/64.]
48	1866	Outsize, rolled, printed map of the English Channel and the south coast of Ireland, possibly present because of the 3rd and 4th Earls' enthusiasm for yachting. [see J/25 and M/4.]
49	1867	Outsize, rolled, coloured drainage map for the Parsonstown district, by William Fraser, C.E.
50	1869	Tracing of a map of Ballincloghan, near Frankford, King's County?.
51	[1860s?]	Sketch map of Boolinarrig drainage district.
52	1879	Drawings of Cappaneal cottages, built 1874–8, with reference.
53	1885	Sketch for reredos?, 'Birr Parish, agreed by S[elect] V[estry], Dec. 9 1885'.
54	[c1885]	Two small albums of watercolours and other sketches by Lord Oxmantown, later the 5th Earl of Rosse.
55	[c. 1885?]	Tracing, probably from a much earlier plan, of the layout of Birr Castle and demesne.
56	1904	Letter and specification from Sir Thomas Drew, together with coloured and uncoloured drawings by him, for the new reredos for St Brendan's Church, Birr.

O/57	[c. 1890s?]	Clutch of coloured ground plans for the Royal Dublin Society's premises in Leinster House, Dublin.
57A	1898	Map of Killeen, near Roscrea, with subsequent sketch marking Leap Castle. [This is a different Killeen from the Birr Castle home farm, and the map is endorsed, 'Darby v Drought. This suggests that it may derive from the Droughts of Whigsborough, King's County – see V/11.]
57B	1900	Tracing for an enlargement of Clonoghill Cemetery, Birr.
57C	1909	Ordnance Survey map of Birr. [See also O/60–61.]
57D	[c. 1914–18]	Three tracings for a forge and farm buildings at Birr Castle?, by Thompson Bros., contractors, Wexford.
58	[c. 1915–18]	Printed maps of the Balkans, Egypt, France and Germany, one of the maps of Germany dated 1877, but all presumably related to the 5th Earl's service in the First World War?.
58A	[c. 1915]	'Map of Mrs Mary Ann Clary's premises at Mill Street [Birr]'.
59	1919	Tracing of Kemmis's estate in Tara [near Durrow. For the significance of this document, see V/16.]
60–61	[late 19th-mid 20th century]	c. 60 rolled or folded sheets of Ordnance Survey maps, some of them with MS. markings, together with c. 25 loose, rolled maps of King's County and other parts of Ireland and the world. [These maps are kept in the left-hand cupboard in the Muniment Room.]
62	1920	Coloured street plan of Birr.
63	1921	Outsize, rolled map of the Birr Castle demesne, by H. Browne.
64	[c. 1939?]	Crude tracing of the Boora Bog, Co. Offaly, acquired by Bord na Mona.
65	1957	Roll of designs for alterations to the yellow drawing room, Birr Castle. [See also T/39.]
66A	1965	'Proposed alterations and additions to houses in Rosse Row [Birr].'
66	1970	Offaly County Council plans for an old people's home in Birr.

P/   DATE   DESCRIPTION

c. 1870–*c.* 1975 Twelve photograph albums, ranging in size from folio to small octavo, 5 bundles of loose photographs, and other material yet to be examined, deriving from the Earls of Rosse and the Lister Kaye family.

The earliest of the photographs are of Lister Kaye provenance, and consist of one humorous and one not-so-humorous album of group and individual portraits, *c.* 1870 onwards; a subsequent Lister Kaye album shows Frances Lois Lister Kaye, the future Countess of Rosse, and her sisters skating or otherwise actively employed.

The earliest Rosse album is dated, in whole or in part, 1882, and consists of a collection of photographs of eminent contemporaries mainly in the scientific field, made by the 4th Earl; loose in the fly-leaves are a couple of letters from scientists enclosing photographs at the 4th Earl's request. The Rosse albums of the period *c.* 1890–*c.* 1910 record a number of foreign tours, notably in Holland, France, Italy and India, the last of 1898 and made by the 4th Earl. Nearer home, they record the external appearances of numerous county houses, not only the Rosse houses of Heaton and Womersley, both in Yorkshire, but many other stately homes in England, Scotland and Ireland, such as Longleat, Wiltshire, and Lough Cutra, Co. Galway. An album of 1906–12 is devoted to shots of the 2nd Battalion of the Lincolnshire Regiment, mainly of its officers, at Aldershot and, later, serving in Canada; this album presumably derives from the 5th Earl. There are one album and numerous loose photographs for the 1930s and 1940s, most of them depicting Birr Castle gardens, with a few shots of the interior, together with a box of photographs relating to Anne Countess of Rosse, the Messel family and Nymans, Sussex, [see also S/7], *c.* 1900–60.

One loose, but mounted photograph, shows Cumberland Square, Birr, with the Duke of Cumberland still on top of his column, *c.* 1875 [see B/4]. Another bundle of loose photographs, sent to the 6th Earl in 1928, is devoted to shots of plasterwork in, and interiors of, houses some of which have since been destroyed; the houses include Belvedere House (Dublin?), Castle Ward, Dowth Hall, Florence Court, Flatten, 4 Rutland Square (Dublin), Summerhill, etc.

The Rosse archive is of great importance to the historian of photography, because of the activity of Mary, Countess of Rosse, wife of the 3rd Earl, as a pioneer photographer. In 1985 an exhibition was mounted at Birr Castle entitled 'Impressions of an Irish Countess: Centenary Exhibition of the photographic

P *contd.*

Heritage of Mary Rosse, 1811–1885' [see J/19/2 and W/17/4]. The following is an extract from the catalogue:

'Mary Rosse's darkroom … is in one of Birr Castle's remotest towers and remained unknown since the Countess' death. What has been preserved is a photographer's treasure trove: a darkroom as set up a hundred and thirty years ago with boxes of glass plates showing the *impressions* of the times and cupboards full of the chemicals used.

This exhibition shows for the first time the essential contents of this darkroom with other items portraying the life and work of Mary Rosse in photography and other fields: the models she made for the Keep and the Main Entrance, the great heraldic gates she made in the turf-fired foundry, as well as fascinating early photographs of her family and friends in the 1850s.

The exhibition starts with the Countess' childhood in Yorkshire and her marriage to the future 3rd Earl of Rosse. He was the astronomer famous for building the largest telescope in the world and her first pictures were of it. On show is the actual correspondence exchanged between her husband and William Henry Fox Talbot describing her first attempts at photography. In 1856 Mary is believed to have become the first lady member of the Dublin Photographic Society and won their magnificent silver medal "For the Best Paper Negative". This is on display, as are some of the cameras used by Mary Rosse, many contemporary journals and booklets on the early processes by the pioneers like Gustave Le Gray and Fox Talbot.

There are examples featuring Mary's groups, landscapes, the castle and even the building now serving as exhibition gallery. We can thus see Birr and its environs as it was a hundred and thirty years ago. Also to be seen is something of the part played by this Victorian lady as wife and mother. Her money paid not only for the construction of the telescope, but she also had the moats and fortifications rebuilt as famine relief. As a mother, she was no less remarkable, giving birth to eleven children and raising those that survived to emulate their parents. Their youngest child, Charles, shown in the exhibition as a boy in a perambulator, went on to invent the steam turbine.

Also featured are photographs of Birr and other views of Ireland taken in the nineteenth century by the 4th Earl and other amateurs.'

Q/	DATE	DESCRIPTION
1–395	1604: 1662: 1668: 1673: 1675: 1679: 1685–2006	Papers transferred from the former Birr Estate Office, opposite the main gates of the Castle, to the Muniment Room, mainly dating from *c.* 1850, but including 26 boxes of leases some of which date back to the 17th century. The material is arranged as follows: leases and leasebooks (1–99); rentals and rent accounts (100–250); other accounts (251–314); miscellaneous, including Irish Land Commission papers (315–326); and letter-books and correspondence (327–395).

Q/1–15 LEASES OF PROPERTY OUTSIDE KING'S COUNTY

1/1–3	1604: 1662	Original lease (1604) and 2 non-contemporary copy leases of 'The Myrtle House', Youghal, former home of Sir Walter Ralegh, held by the Parsonses of Parsonstown under a lease from the 1st and Great Earl of Cork.
2	1736: 1760: 1790–91: 1809: 1830	Envelope of leases of premises in Dublin City and County, principally the Stephen's Green house of the 1st Earl of Rosse (1736 and 1760), the lease of which was assigned by his widow to the 2nd Earl in 1809; and the 2nd Earl's own house (when Sir Laurence Parsons, 5th Bt) in Rathmines Road (1790–91). [See also E/5.]
3/1	1793	Lease to the 2nd Earl, when Sir Laurence Parsons, of a house in Newtown Pery, Limerick, presumably occupied by him when the King's County Militia was stationed in Limerick.
4	1675: 1698: 1700: 1725: 1728: 1732: 1736: 1739: 1749: 1752: 1759: 1761–2: 1770: 1776: 1780–81	*c.* 25 leases of lands in the manor of Parsonstown, Co. Wexford, which reverted to the Parsonses of Parsonstown, King's County, between 1708 and 1711, and seems to have been settled by them on a younger son, Piggott Parsons, brother of Sir Laurence Parsons, 3rd Bt, on the failure of whose issue it seems to have reverted to the King's County Parsonses, only to be used again as an appanage in the mid-19th century. Some of the lands mentioned are Cullentrough, barony of Gorey; Ballyduff, Mangan, Killenagh, Howell's Land and Glascarrig, barony of Ballaghkeen; and parts of the manor of St John's (Tomnegranoge, Knockmarshal, etc), barony of Bantry. [The documents are in date order and are ready for numbering, or rather re-numbering, as each has an obsolete number written on it.]
5/1–16	1793–5: 1799: 1802: 1808–9: 1814: 1827: 1831: 1833: 1837: 1840	Wexford estate leases granted by Sir Laurence Parsons, 5th Bt, 2nd Earl of Rosse. [In date order.]

Q/6/1–3	1851: 1864: 1875	Wexford. Estate leases granted by the Hon. Laurence Parsons, third son of the 2nd Earl, on whom the Wexford estate was settled [see 0/37].
7	1783: 1802: 1805: 1815–16: 1819–20: 1824: N.D: 1895: 1943: 1978	Envelope of Co. Tipperary estate leases: Ballyloughnane, alias Riverstown, barony of Lower Ormond. The leases up to and including 1820 are granted by Lord Dunalley, as this and a couple of other townlands forming part of his Sopwell Hall estate, near Cloughjordan, Co. Tipperary, were purchased from him for £20,000 in that year (see E/38). The envelope also includes papers relating to the sale of the premises to George Kennedy. In date order. [For leasebooks which include the Tipperary estate, see Q/16.]
8	1789: 1795: 1801–2: 1865: 1867: 1922–3: 1926–7: 1935: 1937: 1945: 1958–9: 1974: 1976–8: 1981: 1991	Envelope of Co. Tipperary leases: Croghan, barony of Lower Ormond, also part of the Dunalley estate. The leases of 1795 and 1802 are to Sir Laurence Parsons, 5th Bt, who held parts of Croghan as a tenant or sub-tenant prior to his acquisition of the fee in 1820. [In date order, but with obsolete Q/8 piece numbers on them, and some unnumbered.] Also included are papers relating to the sale of the premises to Louis McCormack.
9/1	1783	Lease of Corraghduff, part of the Dunalley estate in the barony of Lower Ormond, Co. Tipperary.
10	1844: 1847: 1849: 1855: 1882–1902: 1920: 1936: 1941: 1947: 1954: 1958–9: 1972: 1993	Two large envelopes containing a few leases, but mostly tenants' wills and case papers, all relating to Derrinsallagh, barony of Lower Ormond, Co. Tipperary, (which may or may not have been part of the Dunalley estate, but probably was a much later acquisition of the Earls of Rosse.) This section also includes Irish Land Commission sale papers relating to the 'Derrinsallow' property of John Pilkington.
11	1829: 1874: 1891: 1896–7	Envelope of leases of Drangan (and Newtown), barony of Middlethird, Co. Tipperary, not part of the Dunalley estate. [In date order.]
12	1801–2: 1813: 1819: 1821: 1866: 1879: 1889: 1922: 1933: 1937: 1941–2: 1947–8: 1959: 1973: 1976	Envelope of leases of Killeen, barony of Lower Ormond, Co. Tipperary, part of the Dunalley estate; including the will of one of the tenants, William Burke of Killeen, 1821. [In date order.]
13/1–4	1830: 1839: 1867: 1874	Leases of Killenaule, barony of Lower Ormond, Co. Tipperary, which may or may not have been part of the Dunalley estate. [In date order.]

Q/14/1–3 1873: 1881: Three leases, and a deed merging tithe rent-charge, in respect of
1902: 1909 two further townlands in the barony of Lower Ormond,
Carrigagowan and Clonmona.

15/1–3 1718: 1739: Three singleton leases of lands in Co. Tipperary with baronial
1786 location not specified: Lelagh (1718), Lissballyard and
Rathmakeena (1739), and Kilgrogane (1786). The first 2 leases
were granted by Sir William Parsons, 2nd Bt; the last does not
have a Parsons as a party.

16/1–3 c. 1710–1965 Three large folio leasebooks [see also Q/249–50], the first started
c. 1820 but containing details of leases back to c. 1710 and
continued up to c. 1850; the second and third started c. 1850,
containing details back to c. 1775 and continued almost up to the
present day. The second and third are still in the Estate Office, so
only the first has been examined. It contains few entries later than
1840, but this possibly reflects the fact that few leases were granted
after the 1830s, rather than that the book ceased to be maintained.
It is arranged in 2 sequences: first, King's County property; second
'the Killeen estate' (ie Tipperary property, principally of Dunalley
provenance). The leases are arranged alphabetically according to
the initial letter of each tenant's name, although within each letter
of the alphabet no order is observed. The book is thus a ready-
made finding aid for genealogical inquiries, which are likely to be
strong on surname but weak on location. With its aid, it is
probable that further refining could be made of the arrangement
of the individual King's County leases which follows, as the
leasebook sometimes (particularly in the case of renewals) contains
details of location which the individual lease or renewal does not.
Nevertheless, this is a slow business, and time did not permit
much research along these lines. [Q/16/1 has been copied by
PRONI – see MIC.564.]

16/4 c. 1705–1864 Smaller folio leasebook recording, c. 1865, details of leases back to
c. 1705 on the estate of the Hon. Laurence Parsons in King's
County and Cos Tipperary and Wexford [see 0/37 and Q/6.
Q/16/4 is also on MIC564].

17–56 KING'S COUNTY LEASES, OTHER THAN BIRR TOWN, ARRANGED IN ROUGH ALPHABETICAL ORDER BY TOWNLAND

17 1747–1898 Box of leases of Ballindarra, barony of Ballybritt, on the outskirts
of Birr. (Sometimes these, in common with other leases of
suburban or rural townlands in King's County, include in the same
lease premises in the town of Birr. There is therefore a good deal of
inevitable overlap between the King's County and Birr runs of
leases. Within each townland or denomination there is also a good
deal of duplication, because when renewable leases expired, the
tenant's original was returned to the Estate Office and often
survived there along with the Estate Office counterpart.)

Q/18   1746: 1796:   Envelope of leases of Ballindown, barony of Eglish. [In date order.]
        1802: 1816:   The envelope also includes two documents relating to the transfer
        1831–2: 1866: of parts of Ballindown from the Birr Estates Company to Erin Peat
        1969–70   Products Ltd. [For this and other transactions relating to bogs on
                       the estate, see also Q/326A.]

19   1726: 1728:   Envelope of leases of Ballinree, barony of Ballybritt, adjoining Birr
        1747: 1778:   and Crinkle. [In date order.]
        1783: 1794:
        1796: 1799:
        1831: 1903:
        1921–3: 1943:
        1948

20   1707: 1719:   Envelope of leases of Ballyduff, barony of Ballybritt. [In date
        1758: 1776:   order.]
        1802: 1814:
        1817: 1832

21/1–4 1804: 1831:   Leases of Ballykealy (and Ardgoga), barony of Eglish. [For further
        1862   leases of Ardgoga, either on its own or in conjunction with other
                       townlands, see Q/25. In date order.]

22   1787: 1793:   Envelope of leases and deeds of conveyance of Ballywilliam,
        1816: 1821:   barony of Ballybritt, near Birr. [In date order.] The envelope also
        1881: 1897:   includes modern papers about the sale of Rangers Lodge in
        1921–2:   Ballywilliam to Bridget and James Callaghan.
        1975–7

23/1–2 1803: 1823   Lease and surrender of premises in the town of Banagher
                       apparently unconnected with the Earls of Rosse.

24   1658–9: 1668: Envelope of leases of Boolanarrig, barony of Eglish, the lease of
        1673: 1797–9: 1801 being of a part of Boolanarrig called Clonmelin. [In date
        1801–2: 1815: order.]
        1817: 1825:
        1831: 1834

25   1774: 1807:   Envelope of leases and deed of conveyance of Bruckera,
        1810: 1817:   Brockerybeg, Cushnavanlagh, Gortgreen and Ardgoga [see Q/21.
        1831   In date order.]

26   1769: 1771:   Two envelopes of leases of Cappaneal, including Cows Bawn,
        1773: 1795–6: barony of Ballybritt, on the outskirts of Birr. [In date order.] The
        1801: 1816:   sub-section also includes papers relating to the sale of properties
        1830: 1833:   in Cappaneale to Tony Kelly and various other purchasers.
        1903: 1975–77:
        1985: 1989:
        1991–93:
        1994: 1996–8:
        2001

Q/27/1	1815	Lease of Cloghan, barony of Garrycastle. [For leases of Clonbaniff, see Q/44.]
28	1816–17: 1832: 1858: 1865: 1872: 1892: 1909	Envelope of leases of Clonbrone, barony of Ballybritt. [In date order.]
29	1796: 1800: 1817: 1824–5: 1860: 1865: 1872: 1932: 1941–2: 1956: 1965: 1977: 1986–9: 1990–91: 1997	Envelope of leases of Clondalla, alias Clondallow, alias Clondallagh, barony of Eglish, adjoining Boolanarrig. [In date order.] The leases, up to and including 1825, are from members of the Berry family of Dovegrove, an adjoining townland; Clondalla, Dovegrove and Clonahane were held by them under a perpetuity from the Viscounts Loftus/ Marquesses of Drogheda. In or about the 1830s, the 2nd Earl of Rosse must have acquired the Berry interest, which was tantamount to outright ownership, in these townlands, subject to continued Berry occupation of and residence in part of Dovegrove. These townlands were then subsequently settled on the 2nd Earl's third son, the Hon. Laurence Parsons, who is a party to the leases of 1860, 1865 and 1872 in this sub-section. The sub-section also includes papers relating to the sale of Clondallow to Daniel J. Earley, and deeds and documents relating to the (re)purchase of 'Finnegan's field' in 1997.
30	1694: 1794: 1802	Envelope of leases of Clonivoe and other parts of the Sprigge estate in the barony of Coolestown. [In date order.]
31	1726: 1736: 1792: 1796: 1818	Envelope of leases of Clonlagga, barony of Ballybritt, a bog adjoining Birr. [In date order.]
32	1668: 1673: 1832	Envelope of leases of Clonlyon, barony of Garrycastle. [In date order.]
33/1	1787	Lease of Cowspark, barony of Eglish (probably near Birr).
34	1741–1946: 1985–9: 2006	Box of leases of Clonoghill, barony of Ballybritt, on the outskirts of Birr, and adjoining Newbridge, to which some of the leases refer [see Q/84]. Also mentioned are the 2 substantial houses situated in the townland of Clonoghill, Elmgrove and Syngefield. A number of papers, ending in 1946, relate to the former property. Because of Clonoghill's proximity to Birr, an unusually high proportion of the leases also include holdings in the town. One interesting component of the box is the probate of a local land surveyor, Maurice Downer, 1786, whose estate included part of the lands of Clonoghill; this will is of interest as giving some indication of the degree of affluence enjoyed by a member of his profession. The box also includes papers relating to grants of Elmgrove bridge and Clonoghill cemetery to the local councils, 1989 and 2006.

Q/35	1763–1946: 1980–90: 1993	Box of leases of Crinkle, alias Crinkhill, barony of Ballybritt, on the outskirts of Birr, and many of them therefore including holdings in the town. The Crinkle leases also contain an above-average number of integral maps, some of them rather handsome. Included under Crinkle are the sub-denominations of Whiteford and Birr View, the latter of which is described in a lease of 1797 as 'the spot of ground whereon the viewing-house for the quality is placed to see the races of Birr'. Crinkle was also the site of the Birr Military Barracks, and a lease of 1831 is from the 2nd Earl of Rosse to the Ordnance Department. A number of the leases are dated 1763 (the earliest date in the box), which would suggest that a substantial middleman's lease, perhaps of the whole townland, fell in in that year. The box also includes papers relating to the sale of a fee farm grant of the Military Road (purchased by Michael O'Dwyer) and to the sale of the Old Schoolhouse (purchased by John and Sophia Hogan).
36	1735: 1747: 1767: 1773–4: 1797: 1815: 1831: 1838: 1875	Envelope of leases of Derrinduff, baronies of Ballybritt and Clonlisk. [In date order.]
37	1791: 1794–6: 1822: 1827: 1829: 1831–2: 1841: 1864: 1959–60	Envelope of leases of Derrinlough, barony of Eglish. [In date order. See also Q/47.] The envelope also includes a deed of conveyance of Derrinlough from the 6th Earl to the Birr Estates Company.
37A	1831	Lease of Derryadd, barony of Eglish.
38	1771: 1810: 1822: 1831	Envelope of leases of Derrymullen and Carrigeen, alias Corrageen, barony of Eglish. [In date order.]
39	1800: 1855: 1864: 1881: 1893: 1916: 1939: 1948–9: 1953: 1958: 1972	Envelope of leases of Dovegrove, barony of Eglish. [See also Q/29 and 47. In date order.] The envelope also includes an agreement with John Boland to fell timber at Dovegrove, a Land Registry certificate, and the conveyance of a Dovegrove fee farm grant to Mrs. Emily C. Mitchell.
40	1740–42: 1763: 1792: 1801: 1807–8: 1813: 1816: 1819: 1824–5: 1830: 1834: 1861: 1888: 1898	Large envelope of leases of Drumbane, barony of Eglish, on the outskirts of Birr. [In date order.]
41/1	1794	Lease of Drynagh, barony of Eglish.

Q/42	1733: 1796– 1830: 1906: 1939: 1992–3: 1996: 2002–3	Half-box of leases of Eden and New Eden, barony of Ballybritt, on the outskirts of Birr. The box also includes papers relating to the sale of property at 6, 7, and 8 Eden Road to Assumpta Molloy and other purchasers.
43	1746: 1764: 1781: 1796: 1809: 1815: 1836: 1894	Envelope of leases of Feddens, Feddenmore and Feddenbeg, barony of Garrycastle. [In date order.]
44	1701: 1784: 1794: 1802: 1804: 1807: 1824: 1832: 1933–5: 1942: 1945: 1973: 1976–8: 1981–2: 1985: 1988	Envelope of leases of Lisclooney and Clonbaniff, barony of Garrycastle. The earliest lease, of 1701, was granted by William Sprigge of Clonivoe, so these townlands, together with Clonivoe itself [see Q/30] and probably all the lands in the barony of Garrycastle, must have formed all or part of the Parsons family's inheritance from the Sprigges. [In date order.] The envelope also includes papers relating to the sale of Lisclooney Cottage to Oliver Claffey.
45	1747: 1759: 1763: 1780: 1797: 1816	Envelope or leases of Loretto, barony of Ballybritt. [In date order.]
46	1823: 1831: 1864: 1872: 1885	Envelope of leases of Lumpcloon, alias Lumploon, alias Lumcloon, barony of Garrycastle. [In date order.]
47	1757: 1794: 1802: 1815–17: 1831: 1857: 1886: 1920	Envelope of leases of Newtown, barony of Ballybritt, the lease of 1757 (which is long and complicated, and which makes reference to the debts of Sir William Parsons, 4th Bt) also comprising parts of Derrinlough and Dovegrove [see Q/37 and 39. In date order.]
48	1815–17: 1841	Envelope of leases of Parkmore, barony of Eglish. [In date order.]
49	1815–17: 1831: 1921	Envelope of leases of Powlduff, barony of Ballybritt. [In date order.]
50	1805: 1808: 1815: 1817	Envelope of leases of Rathbeg, barony of Clonlisk. [In date order.]
51	1794: 1828: 1844: 1859: 1873: 1912: 1926: 1936: 1942: 1994:	Envelope of leases of Rossacareen, alias Rossecareen, alias Ross Wood, barony of Eglish, which contains a limestone quarry. [In date order.]
52	1734: 1790: 1793: 1801: 1808: 1814: 1824: 1831: 1844: 1898: 1930: 1967: 1983–93	Envelope of leases of Scurragh, barony of Ballybritt, on the outskirts of Birr. The lease of 1912 describes Scurragh as being part of the Townparks of Birr, and the subsequent leases are of 'Townparks' and do not specifically mention Scurragh. The envelope also includes papers relating to the sale of properties in Scurragh to the Birr Urban District Council and other purchasers.

Q/53	1775: 1818: 1832	Envelope of leases of the Shinrone estate (Shinrone, Cloughmoyle, Manure, etc) owned jointly by the 2nd Earl of Rosse and the Lloyd family of Gloster. Leases of this property seem to have continued to be made jointly, in spite of the partition effected in 1806 [see E/37. In date order.]
54/1	1779	Renewal of an unspecified King's County property.
55	1710–1942: 1973–75: 1988–93	Box of leases of Siffin, alias Seffin, barony of Ballybritt, situated on the outskirts of Birr towards Roscrea. The box also includes papers relating to the sale of properties and fee farm grants in Seffin to Edward Dooley and other purchasers.
56	1778–1835: 1894: 1921: 1936: 1946–7: 1954: 1957: 1959: 1963: 1972: 1989–2000	Box of leases of Tullynisky, alias Tullaneskeagh, etc, etc, Woodfield and Woodville, barony of Eglish. (The present house on this townland, Tullynisky Park, was built by and for the two bachelor brothers of the 2nd Earl of Rosse, Rev. William Parsons and Thomas C. Parsons, *c.* 1820; but in the first half of the 18th century the heir apparent to the baronetcy seems to have lived in an earlier house situated in this townland. From *c.* 1860 it was the residence of the three generations of the Garvey family who acted as Rosse agent, up to at least the 1890s being called 'Thornvale' (an English translation of the Irish, Tullaneskeagh) – see V/27. Woodfield and Woodville are sub-denominations, not townlands in their own right.) The box also includes papers relating to a 10-year lease of Tullynisky Park to George Gossip, together with maps of the premises, an agreement to surrender, and a 1997 licence to extract sand and gravel from Kiltemony Quarry, beside Tullynisky.
56A	20th century	Box of files and deeds relating to the selling of the fee of numerous properties. [To be sorted and distributed round Q/17–90.]

57–90 LEASES OF BIRR TOWN, ARRANGED WITH SOME REGARD TO GEOGRAPHY

57	1747–1849: 1859: 1862: 1975–93	Box of leases of The Green and The Upper Green. [Some of the earliest leases of Cumberland Street (see Q/58) state that it was built on The Green, so it is probable that, as building progressed, leases of The Green change names to leases ofsundry streets.] The box also includes papers relating to the sale of properties and fee farm grants in Green Street to the Birr Urban District Council and other purchasers.
57A	2005	Draft index to Birr town leases, prepared in 2005 by Margaret Hogan. Properties are arranged by street and ordered chronologically within each street. The index (copies of which are included on a CD and diskette) also gives the name, occupation, and other particulars about the lessees.

Q/58 1760–1835: Half-box of leases of premises in Cumberland/Duke Street and
1889 Square. This section also includes an original fee farm grant of the
premises, offered to Mrs E.M. Quigley.

59/1–5 1749: 1801: Leases of and a conveyance of premises in Church Lane. [In date
1829: 1831: order.] This section also includes papers relating to the sale of a
1834: 1993 Church Lane fee farm grant to Patrick Daly.

60 1791: 1801: Envelope of leases of premises in Connaught Street. [In date
1816: 1824: order.] The envelope also includes papers relating to the sale of the
1827–9: 1832: pub in Connaught Street to Thomas and Ann Rohan.
1834: 1840:
1845: 1880:
1945: 1999

61 1856–7: 1868: Leases of premises in Wilmer Road and Wilmer Terrace. This
1891: 1930–77: sub-section also includes papers relating to the sale of properties
1986–93 in Wilmer Terrace to Ann Ritchie and other purchasers.

62 1710–1886: Half-box of leases of premises in or near Main Street, also called
1896–7: 'the street of Birr' or 'the town street'. This sub-section also
1997–2000 includes papers relating to the sale of fee farm grants of Bowes'
Shop (purchased by Mary McLoughlin) and Griffin's Bakery
(purchased by John and Arthur Joyce), both on Main Street.

63 1721: 1762: Envelope of leases of 'Samuel Abbott's holding' between Main
1773: 1783: Street and Back Lane, together with fields and parks on the
1803: 1843 outskirts of Birr. [In date order.]

64 1733: 1739: Envelope of leases of premises in Back Lane. [In date order.]
1767: 1780:
1787: 1795:
1801: 1803:
1822: 1824:
1826: 1828:
1838: 1840: 1914

65 1780–1824 Envelope of leases of premises in Langton's Lane and other
premises bearing the name Langton, which seem to have been in
the vicinity of Chapel Lane and Back Lane. The Langton who was
extant in the 1790s was a Philip Langton of Trinidad, but clearly
the family were major Birr tenants of the Parsonses, some of whose
leases were probably reacquired by the 2nd Earl of Rosse, who
seems to have been active in buying out long and perpetuity leases
in the town – presumably in connection with his building plans.

66 1782: 1794: Envelope of leases of premises in Chapel Lane or described as 'near
1799: 1802: the Chapel'. [In date order.]
1810: 1824:
1834: 1838:
1865: 1899:
1944

Q/67	1868: 1900: 1902: 1908–9: 1919–20: 1928: 1937: 1943: 1961–2: 1964–5: 1967: 1972–83	Envelope of leases of premises in Brendan Street, formerly Kennedy's Lane, and Market Square. The envelope also includes papers relating to the sale of properties in Brendan Street and Market Square to the Electricity Supply Board and various other purchasers.
68	1710–1809: 1843	Envelope of leases of the tuck mill of Birr and premises nearby.
69	1710–1847: c. 1920: 1966–91	Envelope of leases of premises in or near Mill Lane. The envelope also includes papers relating to the sale of a Mill Lane fee farm grant to John Harte.
71	1719: 1724: 1728: 1772: 1779: 1804–6: 1808–9: 1812: 1816: 1834: 1855: 1857: 1860: 1937	Leases of premises in Graveyard Street, which in the lease of 1857 is described as having been re-named 'High Street', though this name did not stick. [In date order.]
72	1740–41: 1792: 1833: 1976–8	Envelope of leases of premises in Moore Park or Moorpark Street. [In date order.] The envelope also includes a file relating to the sale of property in Moorpark Street to Mary Dunne.
73	1752: 1793: 1796: 1843	Envelope of leases of premises in Mount Sally. [In date order.]
74	1709: 1719–20: 1727: 1737: 1796: 1799: 1809: 1829: 1859: 1876–7: 1941: 1956: 1973–8	Envelope of leases of premises which are described as being near the old bridge, near the old gaol (alias 'house of correction') or in Old Bridge Street. [In date order.] The envelope also includes papers relating to the sale of property in Bridge Street to Mary Dunne.
75	1685–1912 (with many gaps): 1943: 1987–8: 1991: 1999–2000	Box of leases of premises in Castle Street, including a lease and counterpart lease of 'Crotty's Church', 1837 [see E/11], and papers relating to the sale of a Castle Street fee farm grant to the personal representatives of Claude Corcoran. The box also includes a large folder of correspondence about the Birr Trustee Company's proposed purchase of Spinner's Bistro in Castle Street, which was eventually bought by another party.
76	1818–1949: 1951–8: 1964: 1971–2: 1974–80: 1982–9: 1997–9: 2002	Three folders of leases of premises in Oxmantown Mall/Place, together with 14 files of more recent papers relating to the sale of properties and fee farm grants in the same location to various purchasers.

Q/77	1824: 1899: 1946: 1950– 2001	Envelope of leases of premises in Mellsop Street, the last of them stating that it is now known as Townsend Street. [In date order.] The envelope also includes papers relating to the sale of Townsend Street fee farm grants to Michael Kearns and Gerard and Evelyn Bell.
78	1804: 1822: 1919: 1946: 1950	Leases of premises in Townsend Street.
79/1–3	1866: 1883: 1942	Leases of premises in Pound Street.
80/1–5	1818: 1832: 1949: 1976–7	Leases of premises in Walcot Avenue off William Street and in William Street itself. This sub-section also includes papers relating to the sale of 187 William Street to John Sherlock.
81/1–3	1809: 1819: 1831: 1978	Leases of premises in Rosse Row/Street.
82	1766: 1783: 1808: 1855: 1952	Miscellaneous leases, which seem to have it in common that they are of premises and fields near the Birr Castle demesne. [In date order.]
83	1728–1842	Envelope of leases of premises and fields in Clonahane or on the outskirts of Birr in the direction of Clonahane. [For the background to Clonahane, see Q/29.]
84	1735–1862: 1889: 1937	Half-box of leases of premises in Newbridge, Newbridge Street and Newbridge Lane [see also Q/34].
85	1839–49: 1859: 1861: 1873: 1887: 1890: 1892: 1896–7: 1913: 1920: 1944: 1947: 1959: 1963–4: 1979–2000	Large envelope of leases and fee farm grants of premises in John's Place/Mall. (The short time-span (1839–49) of the original lettings is a reminder that this street was laid out in memory of the adored second son of the 2nd Earl of Rosse.) The envelope also includes papers relating to the sale of properties in John's Mall to various purchasers.
86	1719: 1741– 1860: 1891: 1921: 1946	Half-box of leases of premises in Burkeshill.
87	1742: 1792: 1803: 1807	Envelope of leases of premises which are all described as being on the road to Burkeshill or as adjoining Burkeshill, and have no other intelligible indication of location. [In date order.]
88/1–2	1764: 1830	Leases of premises in Love Lane.
89	1769–1878	Half-box of leases of 'the Fair Green', 'the Factory Field' and other premises and parks described as being bounded on one side by 'the new road from Parsonstown to Frankford'.

Q/90	1679: 1715– 1864: 1896: 1994	Box of leases of premises in or near Birr which, even with the aid of Q/16/1, it has not proved possible to pin precisely or even approximately. [See also Q/56A.]
91–9	1870–1951	Series of original bundles of tenants' proposals or agreements for and surrenders of conacre, grazing, weekly, monthly, yearly and caretaker lettings most of them relating to King's County and Birr, but some of them quite possibly relating to the Tipperary estate. Ideally these papers should be integrated with Q/17–90, but as the labour involved in so doing would be considerable, and as they are distinguished from the earlier leases by their temporary nature, they have been left in their original state, except that they have been reduced to rough chronological order, as follows:
91	1870–79	Box of conacre, grazing, weekly, monthly, yearly or caretaker proposals/agreements.
92	1880–96	" " "
93	1897–1905	" " "
94	1905–12	" " "
95	1913–21	" " "
96	1922–32	" " "
97	1933–79	Half-box "
98	1879–1907	Lease-book titled 'R[osse] agreements, No. 1', recording details of such lettings as the above.
99	1908–50	The same, titled 'R[osse] agreements, No. 3', [and continuous as far as dates are concerned, although No. 2 appears to be missing?].
100–231		**SLIM, FOLIO VOLUMES OF RENTALS, WITH AGENT'S ACCOUNTS INCORPORATED**
100A	1848: 1931: 1988	Rental of the 'Outer estate', which includes the Sprigge lands of Lisclooney, Clonivoe and Lumpcloon, and has a half-yearly rental of £6,500. Papers about the sale of Lisclooney to one Oliver Claffey can be found in the black tin Estate Office box in the right-hand corner of the Muniment Room.]
100B	1848	Rental of the 'Inner estate' (Parsonstown and the immediately outlying townlands), with a half-yearly rental of £4,500.
[101–5]	1849–52	Volumes missing.
106A–B	1853	Rental and account.
107	1854	Rental and account.
108	1855	" [Also on MIC564]

Q/109	1856	Rental and account.
110	1857	"
111	1858	"
112	1859	"
113	1860	"
114	1861	"
115	1862	"
116	1863	"
117	1864	"
118	1865	"
119	1866	"
120	1867	"
121	1868	"
122	1869	"
123	1870	"
124	1871	"
125	1872	"
126	1873	"
127	1874	"
128	1875	" [Also on MIC564]
129	1876	"
130	1877	"
131	1878	"
132	1879	"
133	1880	"
134	1881	"
135	1882	"
136	1883	"
137	1884	"
138	1885	"
139	1886	"
140	1887	"
141	1888	"

Q/142	1889	Rental and account.
143	1890	"
144	1891	"
145	1892	"
146	1893	"
147	1894	"
148	1895	" [Also on MIC564]
149	1896	"
150	1897	"
151	1898	"
152	1899	"
153	1900	"
154	1901	"
155	1902	"
156	1903	"
157	1904	"
158	1905	"
159	1906	"
160A	May 1907	"
160B	Nov. 1907	"
161	1908	"
162	1909	"
163	1910	"
164	1911	"
165	1912	"
166	1913	"
167	1914	"
168	1915	"
169	1916	"
170	1917	"
171	1918	"
172	1919	"
173	1920	"

Q/174	1921	Rental and account.
175	1922	"
176	1923	"
177	1924	"
178	1925	"
179	1926	"
180	1927	"
181	1928	"
182	1929	"
183	1930	"
184	1931	"
185A	1932	"
185B	1933	"
186	1934	"
187	1935	"
188	1936	"
189	1937	"
190	1938	"
191	1939	"
192	1940	"
193	1941	"
194	1942	"
195	1943	"
196	1944	"
197	1945	"
198	1946	"
199	1947	"
200	1948	"
201	1949	"
202	1950	"
203	1951	"
204	1952	"
205	1953	"

Q/206	1954	Rental and account.
207	1955	"
208	1956	"
209	1957	"
210	1958	"
211	1959	"
212	1960	"
213	1961	"
214	1962	"
215	1963	"
216	1964	"
217	1965	"
218	1966	"
219	1967	"
220	1968	"
221	1969	"
222	1970	"
223	1971	"
224	1972	"
[225]	1973	Missing.
226	1974	Rental and account.
227	1975	" [In respect of the 'Oxmantown Trust']
228	1976	" "
229	1977	Rental and account for the Birr Estates Company [ie *not* the Oxmantown Trust]
230	1978	"
231	1979	"

232–5	1900–67	**RENT LEDGERS FOR WEEKLY TENANTS**
232	1900–16	Weekly tenants' rent ledger.
233	1917–32	"
[234]	1933–51	Volume missing.
235	1952–67	Weekly tenants' rent ledger.

Q/236–8 1852–1926	**RENT BOOKS FOR HON. LAURENCE PARSONS'S ESTATES**

236	1852–76	'Tenants' accounts' for the estates of the Hon. Laurence Parsons in King's County and Cos Tipperary and Wexford [see 0/36 and Q/6 and 16/4].
237	1876–1926	"
238	1890–1920	'L.P. ledger, No. 2.'

239–48 1834–7: 1844–6	**RENT ACCOUNT BOOKS**

239	1834–7	Quarto account book in which the agent, Dr George Heenan, has kept his rent accounts with the 2nd Earl for the entire Rosse estate in King's County and Tipperary. [Also on MIC564]
[240–42]	1838–43	Volumes missing.
243	1844	Heenan's rent account book for the half year to April.
[244]	1844	Volume missing.
[245]	1845	"
246	1845	Heenan's rent account book for the half year to October.
[247]	1846	Volume missing.
248	1846	Heenan's rent account book for the half year from July to October.

249–50 1881–1924	**RENT RECEIPT LEDGERS**

249	1881–99	Thick folio volume titled 'Parsonstown (ie inner estate): tenants' accounts', including details of tenures and therefore possessing elements of a leasebook [see Q/16].
250	1899–1924	The same titled 'Outer estate: tenants' accounts'.

251A– 253	1875–1931	**'OUT-GOINGS' LEDGERS**

251A	1875–85	Battered folio ledger titled 'Out-goings, 2 [no sign of '1'], recording 'out-goings' on sundry people and for sundry purposes (drainage, interest, head rents, game and farm expenses, etc).
251B	1886–1903	Battered folio ledger, titled 'Out-goings, 3', recording 'out-goings' on sundry people and for sundry purposes (drainage, interest, head rents, game and farm expenses, etc).

Q/252	1904–16	'Out-goings, 4'.
253	1917–31	'Out-goings, 5.'
254–60	1904–42	**DAY BOOKS**
254	1904–8	Squat folio volume, titled 'Ledger, No. 10' [no trace of 1–9], recording estate, farm, demesne, forestry, garden, etc, receipts and out-goings on a day-by-day basis, and therefore in the nature of a day book rather than a ledger.
255	1908–12	'Ledger, No. 11.'
[256]	1913–16	Volume missing.
257	1917–20	'Ledger, No. 13.'
[258]	1921–6	Volume missing.
259	1926–33	'Ledger, No. 15.'
260	1933–42	'Ledger, No. 16.'
261–7	1894–1974	**FARM, FORESTRY, PERSONAL AND GARDEN LEDGERS**
261	1894–1955	Ledger for the home farms at Dovegrove, Killeen and Newtown.
262	1904–55	Forestry 'out-goings' ledger.
263	1909–13	'Forestry account ledger' [mostly empty].
264	1909–45	'Forestry account cash ledger', 1909–39, used simultaneously as a Birr Manor Sawmills account book, 1910–45.
264A	1929–32	'Forestry account timber sales ledger.'
265	1930–60	'Rt Hon. Earl of Rosse: private ledger.'
266	1961–74	Ledger: 'Earl of Rosse – personal account and Womersley Park'.
267	1949–55	Birr Castle gardens ledger.
268	1929–30: 1933: 1947	Box containing bundles of weekly returns of income and expenditure (mainly on labour) for Birr Castle, gardens, pleasure grounds, forestry, farm, etc, sampled from a vast quantity of similar material in order to show how the accounting system then in operation worked.
269	1917–19: 1922–36	Box containing annual sets of estate and farm accounts, audited by Stokes Bros. & Pirn of Dublin [see also Q/393].
270	1937–46: 1949–64: 1971: 1979–80	Box containing annual sets of estate and farm accounts, audited by Stokes Bros. & Pirn of Dublin [see also Q/393].

Q/271–314	1901–56:	**LABOURERS AND WORKMEN'S TIME BOOKS**
	1902–74	
271	1901	Slim, workmen's time book – miscellaneous farm, forestry and sawmills work. [Also on MIC564]
272	1901–3	Slim, workmen's time book – miscellaneous farm, forestry and sawmills work.
273	1903	Slim, workmen's time book – miscellaneous farm, forestry and sawmills work.
274	1904–5	"
275	1907–8	Same format – sawmills only.
[276]	1908–10	Volume missing.
277	1910–11	Slim, workmen's time book for the sawmills.
278	1911–12	"
279	1912–13	"
280	1913–14	"
281	1914–15	"
282	1916–17	"
283	1918–19	"
284	1919–20	"
285	1920–21	"
286	1921–2	"
287	1922	"
[288–9]	1923–5	Volumes missing.
290	1926–8	Slim, workmen's time book for the sawmills.
291	1928–31	"
292	1931–5	"
293	1935–8	"
294	1938–9	"
295	1939–40	Slim, workmen's time book for the sawmills.
296	1911–12	Slim, daily labour book (woods).
297	1913–14	"
298	1915–17	"
299	1917–18	"

Q/[300]	1919–20	Volume missing.
301	1921–4	Daily labour book (woods).
302	1924–7	"
303	1927–30	"
304	1930–32	"
[305]	1933–4	Volume missing.
306	1935–7	Daily labour book (woods).
307	1937–9	Daily labour book (woods).
308	1939–43	Thicker, folio volume recording workmen's time and accounts (forestry, sawmills, garden, farm, etc).
309	1943–5	"
310	1946–9	"
311	1950–53	"
312	1953–5	"
313	1956	Softback, quarto wages and time book for forestry workers.
314	1972–4	"
314A	*c.* 1950–1998	Six garden books kept by the head gardener, Michael Hogan.
314B		" "
314C		" "
314D		" "
314E		" "
314F		" "
315–23	1854–1967	**MISCELLANEOUS VOLUMES RECORDING STOCK, GAME, VALUATIONS, ETC.**
315	1854	Printed *Griffith's Valuation* of the Union of Parsonstown.
316	[*c.* 1850s?]	Octavo volume recording, by townland and then alphabetically by tenants, houses and offices on the 'outer estate'. [Q/316 is also on MIC564.]
317	1876–82	Large folio stud book.
318	1889	Printed Blue Book on market rights and tolls in Ireland (p. 383 et seq. consisting of evidence from Toler R. Garvey Senior about Birr.).
319–21	1896–1918	Three chronologically overlapping game books.

Q/322 1931–3 Octavo bank book of the 6th Earl of Rosse recording, among other things, investments.

323 1950–67 Small folio volume recording turf-cuttings on the bogs of the Rosse estate.

324 1884–*c.* 1935 Large cardboard box and small tin deed box containing Land Court case papers and Irish Land Commission sale papers, including lists of tenants, of court cases to be heard, some correspondence [but see Q/388], a small quarto volume of *c.* 1900 recording valuations of holdings, either for land purchase purposes or in connection with appeals against judicial rents, etc, etc, all in connection with the Rosse estate in King's County and Co. Tipperary.

325 1874–*c.* 1910 Five envelopes containing miscellaneous estate accounts and financial and estate correspondence of the Birr Estate Office, much of it about arterial drainage (including printed matter back to 1869), one account of 1874 mentioning the cost of labour on the mounting for the three-foot telescope, and other long runs of accounts relating to the Dovegrove, Killeen and Newtown farms and stock, and to the manor saw mill, 1886–1912. [Not in chronological order.]

326 1928: 1933: Envelope of legal papers about the estate, including non-
1935: 1944: contemporary copies of deeds back to 1909, and counsel's
1947: 1954: opinions on cases concerning repairs to tenanted houses, rates on
1957: 1960: such houses, the claims of J. Laurie, a dismissed steward [see
1966: 1970: Q/389], etc, etc.
1974

326A 1957–73 Envelope of papers about the bogs on the estate. [See also Q/18.]

327 1940–42 Carbon out-letter book of the sawmill manager, W.Y. Chisholm [see Q/383].

328–82 1879–1951 **AGENTS' COPY OUT-LETTERS**

328–82 1879–92: 52 quarto volumes of damp press, copy out-letters from Toler R.
1899–1900: Garvey Senior and Junior and Capt. Alec Drought, successive
1903–26: agents for the Rosse estate, writing from the Birr Estate Office.
1928–51 [The bindings of some are in a shocking state of repair, so a progressive operation of conservation is under way. When the volumes currently with the binders are back at Birr Castle, it will be possible to provide a chronological breakdown for each volume and to ascertain which volumes are missing and which were with the binders.]

Q/383–394		**1910–51 IN-LETTERS TO AGENTS** Series of original bundles of in-letters to the successive Rosse agents, Toler R. Garvey Junior and Capt. Alec Drought, alphabetically arranged by correspondent (with all the usual inconsistencies which such a system produces) by Garvey and Drought, and now boxed in alphabetical order, except where strict adherence to the alphabet would have meant an uneconomical use of the boxes. The principal problem with the in-letters to Garvey (which constitute the lion's share) is that he ran other agencies besides the Rosse from the Birr Estate Office and used the one alphabetical system for his correspondence, regardless of agency or estate. The result is that at least half the letters to him rightfully belong in Section V (the section devoted to the other agencies of Garvey, his father and grandfather). To divide up the correspondence by agency and estate would take an inordinate amount of time, would probably not be wholly practicable, would dismantle an original filing-system and in any case would give an unnaturally 'cut-and-dried' appearance to Garvey's daily office routine. No such attempt has therefore been made. Instead, the correspondence has been arranged, exactly in the bundles as it was found, as follows:
383	1910–51	Box of in-letters from correspondents whose names begin with 'A' and 'C', including correspondence about Sir Nesbitt Armstrong's trusts, and letters from James Callaghan (a thatcher employed by the Rosse estate), from the 'Chief of Staff, January 1923' about the occupation of Birr Castle by the Free State Army, from W. Y. Chisholm (manager of the Rosse sawmill [see Q/327]), from Miss Edith A. Cramer, [see M/18], from Messrs Coutts & Co., etc, etc.
384	1910–51	'B' – principally Richard F. Barry & Son, solicitors, Birr.
385–6	1910–51	Two boxes of letters from 'D' -principally Darley, Orpen & McGillycuddy/Synnot, solicitors, Dublin, who write mainly in their capacity as solicitors to the Rosse estate, but who also acted for other employers of Garvey as well.
387	1910–51	'E', 'F' and 'G' – principally Evans, Barraclough & Co., Bayswater, London (solicitors to the Hon. Richard Clere Parsons), French & French, solicitors, Dublin (who acted for Mrs Manning Robertson of Drumbane House, Birr, another of Garvey's employers), the General Accident Assurance Corporation and the Guardian Assurance Company, both of Dublin (who write about Birr Castle and the Rosse estate), etc, etc.
388	1910–51	'H', 'I' and 'J' – principally the Irish Land Commission [see also Q/324] and Inspectors of Taxes in Dublin and various Irish provincial out-posts.

Q/389   1910–51   'K' and 'L' – a very miscellaneous lot, but including Colonels Kingscote and Lodwick (two more of Garvey's employers -[see Section V/21–2]).

390   1910–51   'M' – an over-full box, including letters from Allen H. Morgan, solicitor, of Thurles, Co. Tipperary (who writes about the Bennett/Ryan estate [see V/3–6]), Montgomery & Chaytor, solicitors, of Dublin (who write about the Eyre estate [see V/10]), A. Meldon & Co., solicitors, of Dublin (who write about the Banon estate [see V/2]), etc, etc.

391   1910–51   'N' and 'O'.

392   1910–51   'P', 'Q', 'R' and 'T' – including the Hon. Geoffrey L. Parsons, members of the Pigott family [see V/24], Mrs Manning Robertson, the 5th and 6th Earls of Rosse, J.H. Tyler (the Womersley agent [see H/117]), etc, etc.

393   1910–51   'S' – principally Stokes Bros. & Pirn of Dublin (the Rosse accountants [see Q/269–70]), E. & G. Stapleton, solicitors, of Dublin (who write about the Barrett estate [see V/7]), etc, etc.

394   1910–51   'W' and 'J' – principally Edward Walsh (town clerk of Birr, who writes about all manner of local government matters), Harold J. Wiley & Co., insurance brokers of Dublin (who write about Birr Castle insurance), Mrs F. White Spunner of Milltown Park, Shinrone, King's County (whose estate Garvey managed although, apart from these letters, no other record of this agency survives in the archive at Birr Castle), etc, etc.

395   1958–65   Original box of Birr Estate Office in-letters to the then Rosse agent, A.E. Telford, many of them from the 6th Earl and Anne Countess of Rosse. Lord and Lady Rosse's letters do not confine themselves to estate business, but include arrangements for house parties at Birr Castle. [For the other side of the correspondence with Lord and Lady Rosse, see T/34].

R/	DATE	DESCRIPTION
1–16	1856–2006	Artificial collection of letters, obituary and biographical notices, printed orders for memorial services, photographs, etc, received or assembled by the 4th, 6th and 7th Earls of Rosse, the Hon. Geoffrey L. Parsons and Mr Laurence Parsons, all concerning the inventor of the turbine, Sir Charles Parsons, a younger brother of the 4th Earl. The material has been arranged as follows:
1	1856–*c.* 1910	Miscellaneous photographs, original and copy, all featuring Sir Charles Parsons and the steam turbine.
2	1884: 1898: 1918: 1932	Formal documents relating to Sir Charles and Lady Parsons, including a photocopy of a patent of 1884, an original letter of 1898 announcing Sir Charles's election as a Fellow of the Royal Society, a letter concerning a presentation to Lady Parsons by the Order of St John of Jerusalem in recognition of her First World War work; a draft of a licence to manufacture and sell turbines; and a copy of court proceedings relating to the well-known 1932 patent case, Parsons v. United States.
3	1896–1909	Photocopies of letters from Sir Charles to 'My dear Simpson', clearly a business associate, about the 'screw propeller question' (1896), the results of 'some runs on the Tyne today' (1897), scientific evidence being given to the Privy Council (1898), the need 'to wait until we have a destroyer going and a success' (1899), Mr Street's 'methods of calculating the age of the earth by radium' (1909), etc, etc.
4	1896–1932: 1944: 1949	Two envelopes of miscellaneous letters and papers, mainly printed matter, collected by the Hon. Geoffrey L. Parsons, about the work of Sir Charles and about inventions and engineering generally. The envelopes include what appears to be a rough, working drawing by Sir Charles, his report on vessel propulsion published for a 1905 navigation congress, and a letter to the Hon. Geoffrey L. Parsons from a University College (Dublin) professor describing Sir Charles as a 'superb embodiment of handcraft and redecraft (the power of extracting from books the knowledge we seek for, the ability to ponder over it and to digest it) in action, working hand in hand to guide a great engineer to wonderful achievement.'
5	1907–34	Highly artificial bundle of letters from Sir Charles and Lady Parsons to other members of the Parsons family, mainly the Hon. Geoffrey L. Parsons, Mr Laurence Parsons and the 6th Earl of Rosse.
6	1931–8: 1950	Mainly printed obituary and memorial material about Sir Charles and Lady Parsons, including a letter from Eamon de Valera to the 6th Earl, 1950, observing, 'It was a bad lapse on my part not to have known that Parsons of the steam turbine was of your Family.

R/6 *contd.* I am delighted that Ireland has to her credit so distinguished a scientist and inventor'; and articles on the dedication of a Sir Charles memorial window in Westminster Abbey (1950).

7 1941–2: 1944: 1948: 1950: 1954 Four published Sir Charles Parsons Memorial Lectures, collected by the Hon. Geoffrey L. Parsons, as well as letters to G. L. Parsons from one Stanley Goodall regarding the research and writing of Goodall's 1942 Parsons Memorial Lecture.

8 1933–55 Correspondence and papers of the Hon. Geoffrey L. Parsons, mainly about the editing and publication of the *Scientific Papers and Addresses* of Sir Charles (Cambridge, 1934), together with a few miscellaneous letters, including one from a Mrs Kathleen Consdale regarding the late Sir Charles's interest in the x-ray analysis of artificial diamonds.

9 1942: 1952–55 Correspondence and papers of the Hon. Geoffrey L. Parsons, mainly relating to shares in and the management of the Parsons Marine Steam Turbine Company, Limited.

10 1954 Cuttings from newspapers and periodicals, and other printed matter, relating to the career of Sir Charles, published to mark the centenary of his birth.

11 1956–2002 Correspondence of the 6th and 7th Earls of Rosse about Sir Charles's only child, Rachel Parsons, whose executor the 6th Earl was. The 6th Earl's letters and papers about her include: a copy of a page from a photograph album at Ray showing a coarse-shooting party (with the signatures of each participant, including Rachel Parsons, captioned below) and in the background a view of the gardens in summer; a biographical note on Rachel Parsons from Newnham College, Cambridge; photographs of her inkstand; a 6-paragraph appreciation of her by Anne Countess of Rosse, 1956; numerous press-cuttings about Rachel Parsons and her death, and a copy of an undated letter of protest from the 6th Earl to the editor of some periodical which had printed an article misrepresenting as 'wicked' and devilish Miss Parsons's 'eccentric habits'. (Rachel Parsons had been eccentric for most of her life and died violently at the hands of a stable boy. Because she died intestate, her considerable estate was divided among her relations, the 6th Earl's share (of *c.* £10,000) financing the creation and decoration of the Yellow Drawing Room at Birr Castle (see T/39).) The 7th Earl's letters and papers about Rachel Parsons include his correspondence, 2000–01, with Edward Raphael Baldrusski, who was hoping to publish a piece about her and who raises the question of how the Women's Engineering Society began and developed; it had been founded on Lady Parsons's initiative, and had Rachel Parsons as its first president.

R/12   1955: 1957:   Letters to the 6th Earl of Rosse from his cousin, Norman Parsons,
           1962: 1966–7:   head of C.A. Parsons & Co. Ltd., and other members of the
           1971: 1974–8   Newcastle-upon-Tyne branch of the family.

13   1964–9   Miscellaneous printed matter collected by the 6th Earl and Lord
                              Oxmantown about Sir Charles, together with a letter from G.M.
                              Sisson to the 6th Earl, 1969, enclosing and commenting on a
                              lecture by Sisson on Sir Charles's contribution to astronomy and
                              referring to Sir Charles's adventures with the Russians in 1925
                              which, according to Sisson, 'make most amusing reading.'

14   1984: 1988:   Letters and papers of Lord Oxmantown, now 7th Earl of Rosse,
           2000–02   and his mother, Anne Countess of Rosse, about the Sir Charles
                              Parsons Centenary Exhibition in Newcastle, 1984 (including 2
                              letters on this subject from Prince Philip, Duke of Edinburgh, who
                              writes to Anne, Countess of Rosse, '…I am glad that his many and
                              varied achievements have been so aptly commemorated'); about
                              the First and Second Parsons International Turbine Conferences,
                              held at T.C.D., 26–8 June 1984 and 1988 (to the first of which
                              Norman Parsons contributed a paper entitled 'Parsons – the man',
                              a 4-page copy of which is present), papers on subsequent Sir
                              Charles Parsons Lectures, memorial events, etc, which were
                              attended by the 7th Earl, and correspondence of the 7th Earl
                              about his purchase in May-July 2000 of a model of Sir Charles's
                              experimental vessel, the 'Turbinia'.

15–16 1981–91: 2006   Two envelopes of original and photocopied printed matter, all
                              collected by the 7th Earl and relating to Sir Charles Parsons. [See
                              also W/17/1.]

S/	DATE	DESCRIPTION

1–17   1802: 1809?:   Letters and papers of the Linley, Sambourne and Messel families,
1826: 1873–   the ancestors of Anne (nee Messel), Countess of Rosse, wife of the
2005   6th Earl. These include: bills of 1802 to Thomas Sambourne and
an inventory of 1809?; a letter of 1826 to Edward Mott
Sambourne of Easton, Pennsylvania; letters, newspaper cuttings,
pedigrees, etc, of his son, Edward Linley Sambourne of 18 Stafford
Terrace, Kensington (cartoonist-in-chief to Punch), and daughter-
in-law, Marion, daughter of Spencer Herapath, all concerning
family history and genealogy, the wedding of the Edward Linley
Sambournes in 1874, etc, etc, and letters to the 6th Earl and
Countess of Rosse about 18 Stafford Terrace, [1960], 1969, 1972,
1977–8 and 1981 [see also T/38].

There is a great deal more Linley and Sambourne material in the
former family home in Stafford Terrace, which is now a museum
administered by the Victorian Society. This includes material on
slave-ownership in the West Indies, and possibly on the early
Linleys, including the celebrated Elizabeth, wife of Richard
Brinsley Sheridan. This Linley connection is commemorated today
by the viscountcy of Linley, the courtesy title of the Earl of
Snowdon [see T/169], who is the son of Anne, Countess of Rosse,
by her previous marriage to Ronald Owen Armstrong-Jones.
Shirley Nicholson, author of a book on the Herapaths and
Sambournes of Stafford Terrace, published in 1988 under the title,
Victorian Household, listed the material which has subsequently
been formed into S/1/1–7 during a visit to Birr Castle in May
1989, as follows:

1/1   'Letters from Linley Sambourne to Marion Herapath, April to July 1874, including
his proposal of marriage dated 21 May 1874. (Two other letters from this period
are at 18 Stafford Terrace).

1/2   Letters from Marion Herapath to Linley Sambourne, April to July 1874.

1/3   Letters from Marion Sambourne to her husband, September 1875. He was in
Scotland with Arthur a'Beckett, making drawings for the book they published
together called "Our Holiday in the Scottish Highlands". Marion was staying with
her parents at Westwood Lodge, in Kent, after the birth of their first child, Maud.
(Letters from Linley to Marion covering this period are at Nymans, Sussex but have
not yet (1995) come to light among the papers of Anne Countess of Rosse, who
died in June 1992.) Also two letters from Marion's brother, Spencer Herapath, and
one from her mother, to Linley.

1/4   Letters concerning the Sambourne American connection – not very informative.
(More of these at 18 Stafford Terrace).

1/5   Three packets of letters and genealogical notes, put together by Marion Sambourne,
concerning the Sambourne, Herapath and Moore families. (More of these at 18
Stafford Terrace).

S/1/6 Letters and bills (1802–1809) concerning Thomas Sambourne. Bill for funeral of James Wheat Sambourne, 1843. Letter from a friend in America to Edward Mott Sambourne. (All contained in envelope inscribed by Linley Sambourne, but inscription and contents do not match).

1/7 Letters from Gilbert Wheat, descendant of Thomas Wheat, the grandfather of Thomas Sambourne, about the said Thomas Sambourne (1981–4). Letter and genealogical information from Annie Gray, descendant of Thomas Sambourne and his wife Elizabeth Linley. Various letters *circa* 1978 ..., [1981 and 1986].'

2 *c.* 1888–92 Run of letters to Marion Sambourne ('Polly') from her husband, Edward Linley Sambourne ('Dickie'), some of them including rough cartoons. They are personal letters, but they range over all manner of topics and are not without relevance to Linley Sambourne's career. They include a thoughtful parody of Southey's poem on the Battle of Blenheim.

3 1888–92 Letters to the Sambournes from their children, Maud and Roy, from Marion Sambourne's mother, and from various people about business matters and Edward Linley Sambourne's work.

3A/1 1993 Thesis prepared by Mary Anne Roberts for the Royal College of Art, on Edward Linley Sambourne and photography, 1993.

3A/2 2001 Correspondence and materials about the Linley Sambourne exhibition called 'Public Artist: Private Passions', which was opened by the 7th Earl at Leighton House in 2001, and whose detailed 60-page programme, with a foreword by Lord Snowdon, is here included.

4 1899–1904 Bills and receipts to Roy Sambourne from tailors and other tradesmen, tutors, clubs, hotels (frequently the Randolph in Oxford), charities, etc, mainly in Eton, Oxford and London. Some of the bill-heads are of interest in their own right.

5 1903–4 Letters to Roy Sambourne from his parents, Edward Linley and Marion Sambourne, his sister, Maud (Mrs Leonard Messel), 'Aunt Gabby' at Pyt House, Tisbury, Wiltshire, and all manner of friends, 'dates' and the mothers of the young ladies concerned. Generally, these letters recreate the life-style of an amiable, if somewhat dissipated (and, from the point of view of the young ladies' mothers, evasive) young man-about-town. Discordant notes are struck (a) on the subject of Roy Sambourne's fondness for drink, and (b) on the subject of his neglect of his military duties in Leonard Messel's regiment. Also included are a few printed ephemera, among them invitations, programmes for dances (with names of partners inserted in pencil), Christmas cards, etc.

6 1901–15 Box of family and personal letters to Maud Messel, daughter of
(mainly Edward Linley and Marion Sambourne, and wife of Colonel
1901–4) L.C.R. (Leonard) Messel, then of Balcombe House, Balcombe, Sussex, later of Nymans, Handcross, Sussex.

S/7	1906: *c.* 1910–50	Registration paper and photographs relating to Ludwig Messel's motor car, 1906; water-colour of the garden at 25 Eaton Terrace, 1930, and photograph of the front of the house, N.D., the latter endorsed by Anne Countess of Rosse, 'The home that my father gave up on [my] marriage to Mr A.-Jones in 1925'; and miscellaneous Messel family photographs *c.* 1910–50, including youthful photographs of Anne and Oliver, *c.* 1910. [N.B. These latter photographs should ultimately be incorporated in Section P, but since this is the most physically dispersed and imprecisely described section of the archive, they have been left here for the moment, for ease of retrieval.]
8	1908	Diary-cum-address book of Mrs Leonard Messel, with some loose, later enclosures, 1908–25.
9	*c.* 1910–50	Recipé book and loose recipes kept by Mrs Leonard Messel.
10	[*c.* 1930]: 1942: 1947: 1949: 1971: 1984	Letters and papers of Colonel Leonard Messel and his daughter, Anne Countess of Rosse, about the firm of Ludwig Messel & Co., stockbrokers – a list of the partners since 1871, some correspondence about its activities in the 1940s, a printed catalogue of 'The Messel Collection' of recent paintings purchased by it in 1984, letters of the same year from the then senior partner, David Lloyd, to Anne Countess of Rosse about the firm's 'alliance' with Shearson Lehman American Express, etc.
11	1934–59 (mainly 1951–9)	Box of letters and papers of Mrs Leonard Messel, Nymans and (from 1947) Holmstead Manor, Cuckfield, Sussex, from family (including Anne Countess of Rosse and Oliver Messel), friends, tradesmen, etc, and also including letters and printed matter about the death of Colonel Leonard Messel in 1953. The most important 'tradesmen' are Maggs Bros. Ltd., who write in 1947 offering an autograph letter embellished with 2 sketches by her father, Linley Sambourne, to 'My dear Birch', which concerns a decorative design he has to do for an in-coming Lord Mayor and asks Birch if he knows of a male model, Garrick Club, 1888 (together with that autograph letter, which Mrs Messel obviously purchased), and Henry Sotheran Ltd, who write in 1951 offering Mrs Messel '... a fine run of *Punch's Pocket Books* from 1845 to 1881 ...' and various other items. Also included in the box is a fairly youthful letter from 'Maudie', writing from 18 Stafford Terrace, to '*My own darling Nana*', and illustrating her letter with charming pen sketches.
12	1947–9	Box of letters and papers of Colonel Leonard Messel and Anne Countess of Rosse about the fire which in 1947 destroyed most of the house at Nymans and the bulk of the collections which it contained [see T/25], the ensuing insurance claims, Colonel Messel's purchase of and move to nearby Holmstead Manor, Cuckfield, the compiling of inventories of his surviving collections

S/12 *contd.*

both there and in London, the work of Michael Tapper, FRIBA, in converting the stump of Nymans into a habitable house, the trust set up by Colonel Messel to provide for his grandchildren (and also, presumably, to endow the garden at Nymans, which he had decided to leave to the National Trust at his death. Clive Aslet, in *The Last Country Houses* (New Haven, 1982), p.166, describes Nymans as '... a traditional-looking manor house ..., evolved out of an unsatisfactory Regency building ... which Lt-Colonel Leonard Messel ... inherited in 1915. The Messels had an attachment to the house, which had been Leonard Messel's boyhood home, but required a building that would set off Mrs Messel's oak furniture. Consequently, Norman Evill built a "Tudor" front and Walter Tapper a mock 14th-century great hall. Christopher Hussey entered into the spirit of the thing and wrote a spoof topographical history for *Country Life* [in 1932]. ...' The habitable stump of the house became one of the homes of Anne Countess of Rosse and the 6th Earl.])

13   1937–54   Letters and papers of Colonel Leonard Messel about the Nymans garden [see also T/24–5], including letters from Professor Hen Hsu-Hu, Director of the Fan Memorial Institute of Biology, Peking [see T/16 and 18], and the Directors and other officials of the Royal Botanic Gardens at Kew and Edinburgh, letters and other papers about plant-hunting expeditions to China and Mexico, letters of appreciation from visitors to the garden at Nymans, and newspaper cuttings about its opening as a National Trust property in 1954. To this sub-section have been added photocopies of 8 letters, 1924–5, to Colonel Messel from Augustine Henry [see M/33/1], Professor of Forestry at the College of Science for Ireland, Upper Merrion Street, Dublin, asking about *Glyptostrobus heterophylla*, sending seeds or seedlings of Polish Larch, crab apple, Widdringtonias, Athrotaxis selginoids and Telopea truncata, and enquiring about the leaf-fall of certain trees; the originals are in the National Trust-administered archive at Nymans, and the photocopies were sent to the 7th Earl of Rosse by Ms Rebecca Graham, House Steward at Nymans, in July 2006, along with a 2-page list of the letters, etc, in the archive relating to the garden at Nymans.

14   1947–50: 1953   Five diaries kept by Colonel Messel.

15   1945–9   Letters to Colonel Messel from miscellaneous correspondents about the Second World War and about personal and minor artistic and literary matters.

16   1946–52   Letters to Colonel Messel about miscellaneous matters of business (other than those already covered) -the insurance claim following a burglary at Nymans in 1946, wills and deceased estates, building work on 104 Lancaster Gate and 18 Stafford Terrace, etc.

S/17 1961–3:
1966–70:
1972–4:
1976–93:
1998–2005

Box of letters and papers of Anne Countess of Rosse, the 6th Earl and their son, the 7th Earl, about the Messel family and Lady Rosse's share of the Messel artistic inheritance. Included are a copy of the National Trust's list of the 'Nymans family archive', 1863–1997, (which includes many things which rightfully belong in the archive at Birr Castle), 1998; inventories of Stafford Terrace and letters and papers about its being made over to the Victorian Society via financial support from the GLC, 1978–9, letters about the Herapath family, 1966 and 1980?, letter from Sir Nikolaus Pevsner, 1976, and other papers about the architect, Alfred Messel (1853–1909), letter and newspaper cutting about Anne Countess of Rosse's work on the Linleys, 1970, letters to her about the collection of fans formed by her grandfather, Ludwig Messel of Darmstadt, and her father, Colonel Messel, 1963 and 1969, letters and papers about her collection of her own and her mother's dresses and accessories (some of them by the designer, Charles James), the loan of some James items to the Brooklyn Museum, New York, and the placing of the whole collection in the Royal Pavilion Gallery and Museum, Brighton, 1981–3, and letters and papers of the 7th Earl and her about the sale of the fan collection to the Fitzwilliam Museum, Cambridge, and the opening of the first display of it there, 1984–6, principally correspondence with the Museum's Director, Professor Michael Jaffé [see also T/60/6]. Also included is a copy of Anne Countess of Rosse's 2-page typescript biography of her father entitled 'Leonard Messel, the Collector and the Man, 1872–1953', 1985, letter with enclosures to the 7th Earl from Shirley Nicholson [see S/1/1–7] discussing the Messel family and her research visit to Birr Castle, 1989, correspondence about the restoration of the Sambourne family tomb, and the original of the diploma in natural sciences conferred on Rudolph Messel of Darmstadt, Anne Countess of Rosse's great-uncle, by the University of Tübingen, Wurttemberg, in 1870. [The papers about the fan collection, which are the biggest component of the subsection, have been grouped in one large folder. For personal and family letters to Anne Countess of Rosse from her Messel relations, see T/165–7.]

T/	DATE	DESCRIPTION
1–173	1914–2002	Letters and papers of the 6th Earl and Anne, Countess of Rosse.

FAMILY HISTORY

T/1	1918: 1923: 1926: 1935–8: 1940–42: 1945: 1947: 1950: 1952–3: 1956: 1961: 1965: 1967–71: 1983	Letters to the 6th Earl and Anne Countess of Rosse, some of them from Thomas U. Sadleir of the Office of Arms, Dublin Castle, and papers (many of them inherited from the 6th Earl's uncle, the Hon. Geoffrey L. Parsons [see T/10]), about Parsons, Boleyn, Savage and Sprigge genealogy and family history, including: a typescript copy of the well-known letter written by Francis Johnston in 1820 in which Johnston itemises his architectural opera to date (and excludes Birr Castle from the list); extracts from Gilbert's *History of Dublin* concerning the raffish life of the 1st Earl of Rosse (of the first creation) in Dublin in the 1730s and his patronage of the portrait painter, James Worsdale; an MS. copy of a poem by Sir Laurence Parsons, 5th Bt, *c.* 1793, on the decadence of the Irish parliament taken from Wolfe Tone's *Life*, by his son; the loss or destruction of the papers of the Lloyd family of Gloster, near Birr; etc, etc. Also included are correspondence and papers about the 6th Earl's being placed on the roll of baronets, 1918, and establishing his right to vote in Irish representative peerage elections, 1936–7.

T/2–12		**LETTERS FROM MEMBERS OF THE 6TH EARL'S FAMILY**
2	1914	Two post-cards to the 6th Earl, then Lord Oxmantown, from his father, the 5th Earl, in Berlin, one of them showing and commenting upon a Zeppelin.
3	*c.* 1920–1979	Three boxes of letters to the 6th Earl, including some to Anne Countess of Rosse, from his mother, the Dowager Countess of Rosse who in 1920 married the 5th Viscount de Vesci, whose letters to the 6th Earl will be found at T/12.
4	1922–39	Two envelopes of letters to the 6th Earl from his younger brother, the Hon. Desmond Parsons, including letters about Desmond's whereabouts and health, numerous letters of condolence on Desmond's early death in 1937 and several obituary notices. [See also Section U.]
5	1923–72: 1997 onwards	Large envelope of letters to the 6th Earl (including a few to Anne, Countess of Rosse) from his sister, Lady Bridget Parsons. Also included is an original bundle of letters of condolence on her death, 1972, and correspondence of the 7th Earl with John Jamieson of Michigan, who was/is interested in writing her *Life*, 1997 onwards.

T/6/1–4	1920–38	Letters to the 6th Earl from his maternal grandparents, Sir Cecil and Lady Beatrice Lister Kaye, and his great-aunts/uncles on the Lister Kaye side of the family [see Section N], as follows:
6/1	1924–35	Envelope of letters from Sir Cecil and Lady Beatrice Lister Kaye.
6/2	1920–24: 1946: 1957	Envelope of letters from 'Linny' (Lady Beatrice's brother, the 7th Duke of Newcastle), 1920–24, together with one from her nephew, the 9th Duke, 1946, and a letter accompanying a photograph of a portrait of Adrian Hope of Amsterdam (1709–81), 1957.
6/3	1935: 1946: 1949–50: 1952	Three letters from 'Aunt Kathleen Newcastle' (Lady Beatrice's sister-in-law, widow of the 7th Duke), together with one written on her behalf.
6/4	1928: 1938	Three letters from Natica Lister Kaye (widow of Sir Cecil's brother, Sir John Lister Kaye, 3rd Bt).
7/1–3	1924–72	Letters to the 6th Earl from his mother's brother and sisters, as follows:
7/1	1927–56	Envelope of letters from Sir Kenelm Lister Kaye, 5th Bt son and successor of Sir Cecil, and his wife, Jean.
7/2	1924–53	Envelope of letters from Florence Vaughan daughter of Sir Cecil and other members of the Vaughan family of Courtfield, Ross-on-Wye, Herefordshire.
7/3	1926–75	Two envelopes of letters from Adeline, Countess de la Feld (another of Sir Cecil's daughters).
8	1925–68: 2000	Envelope of letters to the 6th Earl from the Countess Orietta Borromeo d'Adda, daughter of Lady Beatrice Lister Kaye's sister, Emily, Princess Doria, and from Countess Orietta's son, Carlo, and other members of the Borromeo and Doria families; including an obituary of the last Princess Orietta (Pogson) Doria-Pamphili, 2000. [For the Dorias, see also N/32/1 and N/36.]
9	1922–36	Envelope of letters to the 6th Earl from his great-uncle, the Hon. and Rev. Canon Randal Parsons.
10	1927–56	Envelope of letters to the 6th Earl from his uncle, the Hon. Geoffrey L. Parsons of The Manor House, Froyle, Alton, Hampshire, and box file of papers and correspondence concerning the winding-up of his estate after his death, 1956–7. [See also T/36.]
11/1–3	1910: 1921–77	Letters to the 6th Earl from other Parsons relations, as follows:
11/1	1910: 1920–21	Three letters from his grandmother, Cassandra, Countess of Rosse *nee* Hawke, the first of them to Miss Edith A. Cramer [see T/157].

T/11/2 1936: 1958:   Envelope of letters from John and Alice Parsons of Little Grillions,
          1967–9: 1971   Croxley Green, Hertfordshire.

11/3   1947–77: 1986   Envelope of letters from miscellaneous Parsonses, including Rev.
                           Desmond, Canon Edward, Christopher and 'Cousin Lawrie'. [For
                           letters from yet another branch of the family, see Section R.]

T/12–29 HORTICULTURAL AND BOTANICAL CORRESPONDENCE

12   1924–52: 1957   Letters to the 6th Earl from the 5th Viscount de Vesci (his step-
                           father, who had married the widow of the 5th Earl in 1920), about
                           family affairs, de Vesci manorial rights in Rotherham, Yorkshire,
                           the difficulty of obtaining insurance on Irish property because of
                           the fears in the City of civil commotion in Ireland (mainly 1932),
                           and seeds, trees and gardening. Although Lord de Vesci owned
                           nearby Abbeyleix, these letters are almost all written from London
                           (where he had a house at 1 Hyde Park Street) or his country house,
                           Monk Hopton, Shropshire. Also included are letters from Lord de
                           Vesci's younger brothers, Osbert and Thomas Vesey, and from
                           Evelyn, Viscountess de Vesci (widow of the 4th Viscount), 1922–
                           30 and 1951. [For letters from the 5th Viscount's nephew and
                           successor, see T/170.]

13   1920–21:   Three envelopes of bills to the 6th Earl from sundry nurserymen
          1925: 1927–78   and seedsmen (all British and Irish), and also from booksellers
                           specialising in horticultural materials; [in continuation of M/33.
                           The first envelope contains all the booksellers' bills and most of
                           the significant seedsmen's: envelopes 2–3 consist mainly of
                           seedsmen's bills from Drummonds and Rowans, both of Dublin,
                           and from Watsons of Killiney, Co. Dublin.]

14   1929–38   Quotations to the 6th Earl – some of them involving detailed
                           horticultural explanations – from all manner of nurserymen and
                           seedsmen, principally Hilliers of Winchester, and two firms
                           quoting for wrought-iron garden arches and a gate.

15   1933–5: 1952:   Letters and papers of the 6th Earl about plant-hunting expeditions
          1962: 1985   led by Frank Kingdon Ward, Joseph F. Rock and James C.
                           Archibald, including an offprint of a *Country Life* article on the
                           subject by William and Mary Webb, 1985.

16   1933–8   Communications to the 6th Earl from the Royal Horticultural
                           Society, London, about his appointment to its council, Professor
                           H.H. Hu's Chinese expedition, etc.

17   1934 onwards   Designs by Anne, Countess of Rosse, for the Birr Castle gardens
                           – some executed, others not [for earlier garden designs, see O/32–
                           4]; together with instructions written by her on the planting of
                           borders, on taking chrysanthemum cuttings, etc, notes of talks she
                           gave overseas on the gardens of Birr Castle, and cards sent from
                           some of the other gardens (like Bel Oeil) which most inspired her.

T/18	1933–42	Letters, bills and printed catalogues to the 6th Earl from botanists and horticulturists in Hong Kong and China -Professor Geoffrey Herklets of Hong Kong, and R.C. Ching, Sohstu G. King and Professor Hen Hsu-Hu [see also S/13 and T/25/1], all three of them associated with the Fan Memorial Institute of Biology, Peking, and the Lu-Shan Aboretum and Botanical Garden, Ruling, Kiukiang, China. Professor Hu's 3 letters, 1935–7, are mainly about the possibility of a seed-collecting expedition going to north-west Yunnan and south-east Tibet, and there is another letter from Hu to Sohstu G. King about sending a plant specimen to the 6th Earl [all 4 of them have been photocopied by PRONI, T/3498/6]. Of particular interest is a detailed price list of Chinese tree seeds, 1935. Also included is a letter from Schwerin, Germany, proposing an expedition to China, 1933, a letter from the plant hunter, J.F. Rock, about funding for the publication of a 'Plant Geography of West China', and a bill for plant seeds bought by the 6th Earl from the Lu-Shan Arboretum, 1938 (PRONI, T/3498/7).
19	1932: 1937–43	Letters to the 6th Earl from Sir Charles Barrington of Fairthorne Manor, Botley, Southampton [a former trustee of the Rosse estates – see H/117], about gardening.
20	1938–9	Letters to the 6th Earl from horticulturists and botanists in America (North and South), principally Dr B.P. Reko of Tacubaya, Mexico, T.H. Everett of the New York Botanical Gardens, P.J. le Clair of the Soil Conservation Service, Chapel Hill, North Carolina, and Professor M. Martinez of Mexico City.
21	1938–40	Letters to the 6th Earl from F.W. Chaundy and Lady Beatrix Stanley about *The New Flora and Silva*, an illustrated, quarterly horticultural journal, published by a company of which the 6th Earl was chairman.
22	1924–39: 1943	Mainly pre-war letters to the 6th Earl from miscellaneous British and Irish horticulturists and botanists, including representatives of the Royal Botanic Gardens at Kew, Glasnevin and Edinburgh, the 2nd Lord Aberconway President of the Royal Horticultural Society, 1931–53, Peter Coats, Manning Robertson, Wilfrid ?Fox, Lords Dunalley and Headfort, etc.
23	1938–47	Letters to the 6th Earl from the successive head gardeners at Birr Castle, James Armit and Thomas Fenton.
24	1938: 1940: 1944: 1947–8: N.D.: 1970: 1984: 1992	Letters to the 6th Earl and Anne Countess of Rosse from James Comber, head gardener at Nymans, Handcross, Sussex, together with a letter from J.D. Boles, Director-General of the National Trust, and a copy of a letter to Lord Gibson, Chairman of the Trust [see T/61/5], about the Nymans garden, 1978 and 1984 respectively, letters from the 3rd Lord Aberconway, President of

T/24 *contd.*   the RHS, 1961–84, and others about a RHS visit to Nymans,
                                     1984, and other papers and photographs about Nymans. [See also
                                     S/12–13.]

25/1   1945–84: 1994   Large bundle of post-war letters to the 6th Earl and Anne
                         Countess of Rosse from miscellaneous horticulturists, botanists,
                         and garden enthusiasts. These include Professor Hu [see also S/13
                         and T/18], Jules Delacroix and Lucie Delacroix (in whose house at
                         Tirlemont the 6th Earl had been billetted during the war), Lady
                         Lovell (writing on behalf of 'the Congleton horticulturists',
                         Cheshire), Sir George Taylor (Director of the Royal Botanic
                         Gardens, Kew), Harold Fletcher (Regius Keeper of the Royal
                         Botanic Gardens, Edinburgh), Patrick Bowe, Peter Coats, Brian O.
                         Mulligan (Director of the University of Washington Arboretum),
                         Richard Evans Schultes (Director of the Botanical Museum of
                         Harvard University), R.B. Walpole (of Mount Ussher, Ashford,
                         Co. Wicklow), John Fowler, the 5th Marquess of Dufferin and Ava
                         and his wife, Lindy, David Webb [see also T/51–2], and Mrs K.N.
                         Sanecki and Mrs Mavis Batey (successive Hon. Secretaries to the
                         Garden History Society, of which the 6th Earl was Vice-President).
                         Some of the letters discuss particular gardens (Claremont, Surrey,
                         Levens Park, Westmorland, etc [see also T/61/6]), many praise and
                         comment on the gardens at Birr Castle and Nymans, many discuss
                         particular plant species, many reflect the fraught politics of the
                         Northern Horticultural Society in the period 1952–3, and many
                         refer in general terms to matters which cannot be pinned to any
                         particular botanical organisation with which the 6th Earl was
                         connected. The last items, of 1994, relate to the planting of a tree
                         at Birr Castle in David Webb's memory.

25/2   1950–73   The same, except that the letters are from the 7th Lord Talbot de
                         Malahide ('Milo') and a few from his sister, Rosie Talbot, although
                         not all of them are about horticulture. Lord Talbot's letters, in
                         particular, are many of them written from his overseas postings (eg
                         Laos and Paris) in the British diplomatic service.

25/3   1964–75   The same, except that all the letters are from the 4th Duke of
                         Abercorn, writing mainly in his capacity as President of the
                         International Dendrology Union/Society, of which the 6th Earl
                         was Chairman.

25/4   1964–78   The same, except that all the letters are from the Duke's successor
                         as President, the Vicomte de Noailles.

25/5   1965–79   Loose letters and papers of the 6th Earl as Chairman and, in 1979,
                         President of the I.D.S., including letters from its successive
                         Secretaries, and from Sir George Taylor [see also T/25/11], Harold
                         Fletcher, Lulu de Vilmorin, Avenue Foch, Paris, etc, etc.

T/25/6	1971–8	File titled 'International Dendronology Society', and sub-divided into ' AGMs, Council, Finance, Year-book, Tours, Correspondence, General correspondence'. [N.B. The distinction between the contents of this file and of T/25/5 is not clear and probably nonexistent.]
25/7	1976–8	Loose letters and papers of the 6th Earl about I.C.O.M.O.S. – the International Council on Monuments and Sites and, in particular, its International Committee on Historical Gardens and Landscapes. [See also T/61/10.]
25/8	1977–8	File titled 'I.C.O.M.O.S.', and subdivided into 'U.K. Committee, I.F.L.A. (Paris), I.F.L.A. (correspondence), U.K. Historic Gardens Committee – formation, minutes, correspondence'. The correspondents include René Pechere, Rue du Chatelain, Brussels, Paul Miles and J.D. Sales of the National Trust [see T/61], Dorothy Stroud of Sir John Soane's Museum, etc, etc.
25/9	1965–8: 1970: 1972: 1979	Letters to the 6th Earl from Robert de Belder of the Kalmthout Arboretum, Belgium, mainly but not exclusively about the affairs of the I.D.U./I.D.S.
25/10	1961–82	Letters to the 6th Earl from Lanning Roper, who describes himself as 'Garden Consultant' and is endorsed by Anne Countess of Rosse as 'Darling Lanning', about the I.D.U./I.D.S., I.C.O.M.O.S. and horticultural matters generally.
25/11	1969–70: 1971–2: 1975: 1978: 1985	Letters to the 6th Earl from Patrick Synge, sometime Secretary to the I.D.U./I.D.S. and Chairman of its Conservation Committee, Byworth Edge, Petworth, Sussex, about the affairs of that organisation and about horticultural and botanical matters generally.
26	1948–9	Letters and papers of the 6th Earl about garden statuary.
27	c. 1950–69	Disintegrating folio notebook containing rough garden designs and horticultural notes of Lady Rosse and, loosely inserted, some seedsmen's bills and quotations to her.
28	1949–69	Large bundle of letters and papers of the 6th Earl in connection with the Royal Horticultural Society of Ireland: the silver medal won by him for his collection of hippeastrums, and his minutes and correspondence as President of the Society, most of the correspondence being letters supporting him and regretting his resignation over the royal toast incident in 1969. One major correspondent is Phyllis Moore of Willbrook House, Rathfarnham, Co. Dublin, one of whose letters is endorsed by Anne Countess of Rosse '... widow of the great Sir Frederick'; this might be thought to be satirical, except that another letter is endorsed 'Dear Lady Moore'.

T/29   1959: 1975   Original bundles of correspondence, photographs and newspaper
                      cuttings, all relating to the I.D.U.'s/I.D.S.'s [see T/25/2–11] Irish
                      tours and visits to Birr Castle gardens.

[For other correspondence about horticulture, see T/61, 79, 81, 107, 114 and 148.]

T/30–41 AGENT'S AND OTHER LETTERS ABOUT BIRR CASTLE, TOWN AND ESTATE

30   1916–17   Original bundle of accounts to the 6th Earl and his mother,
                         Frances Lois Countess of Rosse, from Birr tradesmen. [See also
                         M/35.]

31   1921–37   Letters to the Dowager Countess, now Viscountess de Vesci, to her
                         brother-in law, the Hon. Geoffrey L. Parsons, and to the agent for
                         the Rosse estates, Toler R. Garvey Junior, (the only person
                         permanently on the spot at Birr during the minority of the 6th
                         Earl), concerning the Civil War as it affected Birr Castle and other
                         places; including a letter from the Countess of Bandon about the
                         destruction of Castle Bernard, Co. Cork, and the kidnapping of
                         her husband, Lord Bandon, 1921. The principal topic, however, is
                         the Free State government's responsibility to the Rosse family for
                         loss and damage incurred as a result of the Free State army's
                         occupation of Birr Castle from 1922 to 1924, which the shrewd
                         and resourceful Garvey construes as extending to the cost of Lord
                         and Lady de Vesci's London house, No. 1 Hyde Park Street (!).
                         Included in the bundle is a copy of a letter from Garvey to the
                         Irish Land Commission [see Q/324 and 388] arguing that
                         compulsory acquisition of any more of the home farm at Birr
                         would serve as a major disincentive to the 6th Earl's taking up
                         residence and therefore giving widespread employment there on
                         his coming-of-age, 1926. Also present are long-subsequent papers
                         of 2003 about the execution by Free State government forces of
                         three young Republicans condemned by court martial for raiding
                         homes in Tullamore, the executions, which took place on 26
                         January 1923, were commemorated by a plaque set into the wall
                         of the gateway into Birr Castle (where they took place) on the
                         eighthieth anniversary of the event).

32   1928–46: 1948 Two bulging envelopes of letters to the 6th Earl from or about
                         Toler R. Garvey Junior, including letters of condolence and
                         appreciation at the time of his death in April 1946 (which show
                         the importance which the 6th Earl and Anne Countess of Rosse
                         and their close friends attached to Garvey's services). [For letters
                         from the 6th Earl to Garvey, see Q/392.]

33   1946–57   Bulging envelope of letters to the 6th Earl from Garvey's successor,
                         Capt. Alec Drought.

T/34	1957–9: 1961–78	Envelope of letters to the 6th Earl from Drought's successor, A.E. Telford. [See Q/395.]
35	1932–53: 1957–76: 1979–80: 1984: 1986	Letters and papers of the 6th Earl and Anne Countess of Rosse and printed histories, all relating to the Roman Catholic and Church of Ireland churches and communities in Birr; the correspondents include Monsignor J. Ryan, Rev. Dr Edwin Owen (later Bishop of Killaloe and Limerick [see also T/53]) and Mrs Owen ('Peggy'), and Monsignor Patrick J. Hamell.
36	1930–32 1936: 1947–9: 1956–7: 1977	Letters and papers of the 6th Earl about the re-modelling of the morning room in Birr Castle, 1930–32, and about the 'garage bath room', 1936, new churchyard gates designed by Anne Countess of Rosse in memory of her brother-in-law, the Hon. Desmond Parsons, 1939, 'central heating', 1947, 'dining room and own bedrooms', 1948–9, 'inscription on statue to the 3rd Earl of Rosse: Michael Briggs', 1956, 'Uncle Geoffrey L. Parsons's memorial: new chancel steps', 1957 [see T/10], and 'roof repairs to Birr Castle', 1977.
37	1928–60: 1966: 1969: 1976: 1987: 1995: 2002	Bills and correspondence concerning the purchase/restoration/ identification/sale of furniture, pictures, objets d'art, flags, etc, for 25 Eaton Terrace or Birr Castle, including: a bill to the 6th Earl for £15 in respect of a William Kent side table, 1934; letters about the purchase by him of alleged Parsons family portraits, 1936; letters from E.J. Gwynn about the 6th Earl's purchase of a set of Voltaire's Works for the Birr Castle library, 1939; and a letter from a retiring railway official in Dublin sending him a plaque of the defunct Dundalk, Greenore & Newry Railway Company (formerly hanging in the television room at Birr Castle, but sold in 2002), 1952; and a bill to Anne Countess of Rosse for 3 Chippendale settees and 10 armchairs purchased by her for the Birr Castle saloon in 1935 at the sale of the contents of the Marquess of Zetland's town house in Arlington Street, together with a photograph of Chippendale's bill to Lord Zetland's ancestor, Sir Laurence Dundas, 1766, and later correspondence about the suite, 1987 and 1995. [It was subsequently (1988) sold and is now at Charleville, Bray, Co. Wicklow.]
38	c. 1958–65: 1973–7: 1980	Inventories of jewellery, plate and pictures at Birr Castle, in the bank, etc. [For other such inventories, see H/8 and 117, M/25 and S/17.]
39	1945–59	Disintegrating volume in which Anne Countess of Rosse has written or inserted designs and notes for decorative schemes for the Yellow Drawing Room and other rooms in Birr Castle, and inserted magazine illustrations, tradesmen's quotations, etc, 1945–59; together with a correspondence file on the same subject, 1957. [See also O/65.]

T/40	1954–7	Correspondence of the 6th Earl, together with legal papers, concerning the unsatisfactory performance of a turbine installed in the Birr Castle demesne in 1947 [see also M/26–7].
41A	1926–79: 1988–9	Miscellaneous letters, papers and photographs of the 6th Earl and Anne Countess of Rosse concerning Birr Castle, town, gardens and estate: the commissioning of a locally famous and still extant 'Birr Castle dairy' van or cart, with its name written in both English and Irish, by the 6th Earl in 1926; congratulations from Birr Urban District Council on his marriage, 1936; the Irish Girl Guides' rally at Birr Castle, 1939; letters and papers about his efforts to promote industry and employment in Birr, 1940–52; Birr Hospital, 1947–9; the visit of the International Castles Society to Birr, 1961; the Birr Branch of the Women's British Legion, 1963–9; Mark Girouard's *Country Life* article on Birr, 1964–5; valuations made of Birr Castle, the home farm, timber, etc. 1970–74; papers about the Birr Castle woodlands and pleasure grounds, 1977–8; papers about the Birr Community School, 1978–9; papers about the general financial situation of the Birr estate and the Rosse family trusts, 1977–9 [for the continuation of this, see T/66B and W/5]; etc, etc.

[For further papers of the 6th Earl on Birr, see K/38–9.]

41B	1933–70	Correspondence, account books, minute books, etc, of Anne Countess of Rosse and Mrs K.M. Doolan of Oxmantown Mall, Birr, concerning the Birr Jubilee Nursing Association, of which Lady Rosse was Patron and Mrs Doolan Hon. Treasurer.
41C	1962: 1987–78	Minute books of Birr Branch of the Irish Society for the Prevention of Cruelty to Children, of which Anne Countess of Rosse was chairman.

42–64   CORRESPONDENCE AND PAPERS CONCERNING THE 6TH EARL'S CONTRIBUTION TO PUBLIC AND CULTURAL LIFE

42	1936–44: 1947–52	Loose letters, and overlapping file of letters, to the 6th Earl about an architectural advisory committee established at his suggestion to record by means of drawings buildings of merit in Dublin; the principal correspondents are Professors R.J. Best and R.M. Butler, T.U. Sadleir [see also T/1], George Furlong (Director of the National Gallery of Ireland), Gordon Sutton Kelly, Sir Shane Leslie, 3rd Bt [see also T/136], etc.
43	1937–40: 1944	Letters and papers of the 6th Earl about European Federal Union; the letters are from R.R. Figgis, the 3rd Lord Derwent and others.
44/1	1937–45	Letters to the 6th Earl, a founder, subsequently Chairman and ultimately (1969) President, of the Georgian Group, a conservation body formed in 1937 by Robert Byron [see T/182]

T/43 *contd.*   and him with the object of preserving Georgian buildings, from another of the Group's founder-members, Lord Derwent, who writes from Hackness Hall, Scarborough, and from various places in France and Switzerland about the early years of the Group (one of them a 'confidential' letter of 1946 about the future of Osterley Park Isleworth, Middlesex).

44/2   1948–68   Letters to the 6th Earl from the 5th Marquess of Salisbury, President of the Georgian Group, mainly about his annual, Presidential address to the Group and about other Georgian conservation affairs, but including references to Standing Commission [see T/55–60] and National Trust [see T/61] business.

44/3   1947–62   Letters to the 6th Earl from the 3rd Viscount Esher, Chairman of the Society for the Preservation of Ancient Buildings about the work of the Georgian Group and about National Trust business and conservation generally.

44/4   1938–9: 1947: 1960–64: 1967: [*c.* 1970]: 1983   Letters and papers of the 6th Earl about the Georgian Group's campaign to save Georgian buildings in London, to limit the height of new buildings, etc, etc. Some of the buildings particularly referred to are Chiswick Villa, St John's, Smith Square [see also T/61/13], St John's, Westminster, the Regent's Park Terraces, the Euston Arch or Portico (ie the entrance to Euston Station) – a campaign in which the Georgian Group co-operated with the Victorian Society, Wimborne House, Cumberland Terrace, various developments in Bloomsbury, Little Venice, etc, etc.

44/5   1945–50: 1952–4: 1959–66   Letters and papers of the 6th Earl about the work of the York Georgian Society and the preservation of Georgian buildings in Yorkshire – the Richmond Theatre, Heath Hall, Hickleton Hall, Holy Trinity Church, Leeds, Flixby Orangery, near Huddersfield, etc, etc. [Presumably Yorkshire is disproportionately represented among the 6th Earl's Georgian Group papers because he was himself a Yorkshire resident and landowner. See also H/118.]

44/6   1939–40: 1942: 1948: 1950–53: 1960–65: 1967–8   Letters and papers of the 6th Earl about Georgian Group activity elsewhere in England than London and Yorkshire – the Oxford and Cambridge colleges; the Pittville Pump Room, Cheltenham; and Georgian houses in that town; the Lancaster Music Room, Staunton Harold, near Ashby-de-la-Zouch (threatened by open-cast mining); St George's Church, Great Yarmouth; Raynham Hall, Norfolk; Seaton Delaval, Northumberland, etc, etc. [See also T/96/1.]

44/7   1949   Folder containing an original run of letters and papers of the 6th Earl about the Georgian Group's visit to Dublin.

T/44/8 1937–40:   Letters to the 6th Earl and Anne Countess of Rosse from
       1945–7: 1951:   miscellaneous correspondents, and some miscellaneous papers of
       1954–74: 1985   his, all relating to the Georgian Group. Some of the letters straddle
                        the divisions between previous sub-sections of T/44, (i.e., they
                        may relate to buildings in London *and* elsewhere in England.
                        Many relate to general matters of Georgian Group policy and
                        administration (including the hiring and firing of secretarial staff),
                        to fund-raising events such as balls and dinners, and to attempts to
                        induce individuals to join and subscribe. Among the subscribers
                        are Evelyn Waugh [see also T/96/2] and Violet, Lady Leconfield
                        (whose letter is endorsed by Anne Countess of Rosse: '... the mad
                        Violet Leconfield, who got into the lift naked at Claridges ...' – the
                        rest of the endorsement is illegible, but concerns 'the poor little
                        liftboy's nose'). Other correspondents are Angus Ackworth, Cosmo
                        Russell (who writes about Moor Park, Hertfordshire), Sir Albert
                        Richardson, Sir John Summerson and Sir Anthony Wagner. [For
                        John Betjeman's contribution to Georgian Group affairs, see
                        T/148.]

45   1939–48:   Letters and papers of the 6th Earl about the Second World War:
       1984: 2000   his personal role in it as an intelligence officer attached to the
                        Guards Armoured Division (including numerous 'newsy' letters
                        from brother-officers), his scheme to prevent the bombing of
                        cultural landmarks (with a letter from the Grand Duke of
                        Luxembourg to the 7th Earl on this subject, 1984), the 6th Earl's
                        top-secret personal notes on Operation Overlord, 1944, as well as
                        a map and a diary of troop movements and casualties, etc, together
                        with correspondence of the 7th Earl about the Centenary of the
                        Irish Guards in 2000. This section also includes many wartime
                        photographs taken by the 6th Earl.

46–8   1951–6   Two box files of correspondence and proofs and 1 large tin box
                        (equivalent in size to 4 ordinary boxes) of loose drafts and proofs,
                        all concerning the 6th Earl's and Colonel E.R. Hill's *Story of the
                        Guards Armoured Division, 1941–1945* (London, 1956), including
                        correspondence over a row with Collins, the publishers.

49   1946–69:   Fat bundle of minutes and correspondence of the 6th Earl
       1977–9   concerning An Taisce, the National Trust for Ireland, of which he
                        was a founder-member (in 1948), including a letter from L.D.
                        Trant of Dovea, Co. Tipperary, offering the proposed body a
                        portrait of the 1st Earl of Clare, letters from Brian and Henry
                        Fitzgerald about the Castletown obelisk, 1946, letters from Mary
                        Princess Royal and Countess of Harewood and the 3rd Lord
                        Killanin about Portumna Castle and Dominican friary, Co.
                        Galway, 1948, letter from Lord Kildare about the future of
                        Carton, Maynooth, Co. Kildare, 1949, letters from the Duke of
                        Wellington about the Wellington column at Trim, Co. Meath,
                        1953, letters from Lord Pembroke about the E.S.B.'s intention to

T/49 *contd.*		acquire and demolish good buildings on the Fitzwilliam of Merrion estate in Dublin, 1963, correspondence about the 6th Earl's proposal that the bogs of Ballywilliam and Clonoghill, Co. Offaly, be vested in An Taisce in order to ensure their permanent preservation, 1970–71, letters and minutes about An Taisce's Heritage Gardens Committee, 1977–9, etc, etc. [This sub-section provides case histories of a number of major Irish buildings.]
50	1951–75	Correspondence of, and annually (1954–73) sampled minutes kept by, the 6th Earl as a government-nominated member of the Arts Council of Ireland, 1951–73; together with 3 letters to him about the Gulbenkian-funded report on the arts in Ireland, 1975.
51	1950–77	File and miscellaneous correspondence of the 6th Earl as Vice-Chancellor of Dublin University, particularly concerning his successful fund-raising in the British Isles and the U.S.A. for the library extension and the New Arts Building, and including 2 photographs of him in Vice-Chancellor's robes. The correspondents include the 2nd Earl of Iveagh (Chancellor of the University), Provost Henry Alton and his wife/widow, John Sparrow, Warden of All Souls, Oxford, and David Webb [see also T/25/1].
52	1963	T.C.D. correspondence of the 6th Earl for that year alone, particularly concerning the election of a Chancellor vice Lord Iveagh.
53	1939: 1941: 1943: 1951: 1953–7: 1965–71: 1976	Mainly 'personal' or 'confidential' letters to the 6th Earl, as a leading Church of Ireland layman in the diocese of Killaloe, concerning the filling of that bishopric and other diocesan affairs.
54	1956: 1965–6	Letters to Anne Countess of Rosse about the Arts and Crafts Society of Ireland.
55/1	1964–78	Letters to the 6th Earl as Chairman of the Standing Commission on Museums and Galleries (his most important cultural role), 1956–78, from successive Secretaries to the Commission, Miss Armide Oppé, Mrs Barbara Granger-Taylor and Arthur Heskett; Heskett's letters, in particular, range over all manner of policy issues and personalities connected with the work of the Commission.
55/2	1962–6	Letters to the 6th Earl, as Chairman, from the 7th Earl Spencer, a member of the Standing Commission.
55/3	1964–7: 1969: 1972–3	Letters to the 6th Earl, as Chairman, from Sir Colin Anderson, Chairman of the Royal Fine Art Commission and Vice-Chairman of the Trustees of the Tate Gallery, London, about Tate Gallery and wider Standing Commission affairs; one of these letters is endorsed by Anne Countess of Rosse with a note that the 6th Earl owed his K.B.E. to Anderson's recommendation.

T/55/4 1964–5: 1972: Letters to the 6th Earl, as Chairman of the Standing Commission,
      1976: 1978   from Field-Marshal Sir Gerald Templer, Chairman of the
Executive Committee of the National Army Museum, about the
affairs of that museum; the item of 1978 is an envelope of
photographs of a N.A.M. banquet.

55/5   1958–78   Letters to the 6th Earl, as Chairman of the Standing Commission,
from miscellaneous correspondents including Lords Anglesey,
Ilchester and Trenchard, the Duke of Wellington, Dennis Farr
(Director of the City Museums and Art Gallery, Birmingham), Sir
William Hayter, Dr John Tanner of the R.A.F. Museum, Robin
Fedden of the National Trust [see T/61], John Letts of National
Heritage (about the 'Museum of the Year Award' scheme), Brian
Morris (Professor of English Literature at Sheffield University, who
writes an important letter about the future of the Commission,
1976), etc, etc.

56/1   1956: 1963–5: The same, except that all the letters relate to the appointment and
      1966–8:   re-appointment of the 6th Earl as Chairman and of other people
      1970–75:   as members, and partly consist of letters from the Prime Minister
      1977–8   or the Prime Minister's Office; although the Prime Ministerial
communications are fairly pro-forma in content, the sub-section
includes a number of private and confidential letters about the
suitability or otherwise of various individuals for service on the
Commission, among them letters from the individuals concerned
expressing their reasons for wishing to continue or to retire. [There
is no logical distinction between the contents of this bundle and of
the folder on the same subject (T/56/2).]

56/2   1970–78   Folder of letters and papers about the Standing Commission,
marked 'Personal', and mainly relating to the 6th Earl's
appointment and re-appointment as Chairman.

56/3   1978   Letters to the 6th Earl from members of the Commission, heads
of leading museums, etc, etc, all paying tribute to his work and
regretting the necessity for his retirement on grounds of age, and
some of them providing insights into his skills as a chairman; the
correspondents include the Prime Minister, James Callaghan, and
the 6th Earl's successor as Chairman, Sir Arthur Drew.

57   c. 1956–75   Exercise book containing speech-notes in the 6th Earl's
handwriting, and the text of numerous other lectures and speeches
made by him, mainly in connection with the work of the Standing
Commission.

58/1   1958–9:   Letters and papers of the 6th Earl relating to the Standing
      1963–78   Commission's intermediary role with government in the matter
of tax incentives to prevent the sale and dispersal of works of art,
in co-ordinating the acquisitions policies of the major national
institutions, etc, etc. This sub-section in fact represents a merger of

T/58/1 *contd.*   loose papers, an untitled original folder about the Land Fund, and three original folders respectively titled 'Purchase grants' and 'Works of art in lieu of Estate Duty'. The correspondents include the 3rd Earl of Halsbury, Denis Mahon, Mrs later Dame Jennifer Jenkins (Chairman of the Historic Buildings Council for England), 'Bobby' Gower of the National Trust [see T/61], Peter Thornton (Keeper of Furniture at the Victoria and Albert Museum), Patrick Cormack, M.P., Ronald Adams of the Treasury, J.C. Stormonth Darling (Director of the National Trust for Scotland, who writes about the house and contents of Lennoxlove and other houses and contents owned by the Duke of Hamilton), etc, etc.

58/2   1964–79   Correspondence between the 6th Earl, as Chairman of the Standing Commission, and sundry Ministers and officials about funding for the building and acquisitions programmes of the various museums, tax incentives to help secure privately owned works of art, responsibility as between different Ministers and Departments for museums and the arts, planning difficulties impeding the expansion of the National Gallery, the National Portrait Gallery and the Museum of London, etc, etc. The correspondents include the Prime Minister (notably Harold Wilson and Edward Heath), the Paymaster General (notably Viscount Eccles [see also T/61/1]), the Secretary of State for Education and Science (notably Shirley Williams), Ministers of State and Ministers for the Arts within the Department of Education and Science (notably Jennie Lee and Lord Donaldson), and the Chief Secretary to the Treasury and other Treasury Ministers and officials.

58/3   1977   Folder of letters and papers of the 6th Earl, marked 'Personal', about the appeal to save the Cornbury Park Bellini.

59   1966–9:   Folder, to which a number of related papers (found loose) have
        1972–7   been added, about 'Conservation', particularly proposals, notably from the Gulbenkian Foundation, to set up a centralised conservation institution which would fulfil the requirements of the various museums, the self-interested response which this evoked in some quarters, etc, etc; the correspondents include Sir Robin Darwin of the Royal College of Art, Lord Kilmaine (Secretary to the Pilgrim Trust), Sir Charles Whishaw of the Gulbenkian Foundation, etc, etc.

60/5   1965–71   Folder of correspondence of the 6th Earl, as Chairman of the Standing Commission, titled 'Transport Museums', and mainly relating to the creation of a specialised Transport Museum in York, to which the relevant holdings of other institutions, particularly the Science Museum in London, were to be transferred.

60/6   1965–78   Letters to the 6th Earl, as Chairman of the Standing Commission, from and about university museums, particularly the Fitzwilliam

T/60/6 *contd.*   Museum, Cambridge, the Ashmolean and Pitt Rivers Museums,
                              Oxford, various museums connected with the University of
                              Newcastle, and the Manchester Museum. The correspondents
                              include Sir Arthur Armitage, Michael Jaffé [see also S/17], David
                              Piper and Sir Kenneth Wheare.

60/7   1959–60:   Letters and papers of the 6th Earl, as Chairman of the Standing
         1965: 1970:   Commission, about English museums other than those already
         1978   covered in T/60/1–6: the Museum of London, the National
                              Maritime Museum, Greenwich, the Royal Air Force Museum,
                              Hendon, the Dulwich Picture Gallery, the Iveagh Bequest,
                              Kenwood, the Walker Art Gallery, Liverpool, the Beamish North
                              of England Open Air Museum, the Cooper Art Gallery, Barnsley,
                              and the Bagshaw Museum, Batley, Yorkshire.

60/8   1962–7: 1972:   Letters and papers of the 6th Earl, as Chairman of the Standing
         1977–8   Commission, about museums in Scotland, Wales and Northern
                              Ireland, principally a site near Glasgow for the Burrell Collection,
                              1962, '... the proposal for a building on the Chambers Street site
                              in Edinburgh to be used by both the National Museum of
                              Antiquities of Scotland and the Royal Scottish Museum', 1964,
                              the National Museum and National Library of Wales, 1964, the
                              National Library of Wales (again), 1977, and the National
                              Museum of Antiquities of Scotland (again), 1978. The letters and
                              papers relating to Northern Ireland include some important
                              correspondence about a report by the Standing Commission on
                              the funding of the Northern Ireland museums, 1965–6. A letter of
                              the early 1970s discusses the 'pretty dim' situation of the Ulster
                              Museum (and also raises a 'staff in confidence' matter about that
                              institution), and a partly confidential letter from Paul Channon,
                              Minister of State at the Northern Ireland Office, discusses future
                              responsibility for the Armagh Museum, 1972.

61/1   1939: 1943:   Miscellaneous letters and papers of the 6th Earl in relation to the
         1946: 1951–2:   National Trust, and mainly reflecting his important roles within
         1955: 1957:   the Trust as its Vice-Chairman and the Chairman of its
         1959–60:   Properties Committee. The correspondents include Sir John Beith,
         1968–77   J.D. Boles, Viscount Eccles [see also T/58/1], Lord Fairhaven,
                              Robin Fedden, 'Bobby' Gower [see also T/58/1], Eardley Knowles,
                              Duncan Sandys, the Duke of Wellington, etc, etc, and some of the
                              properties mentioned are Clumber (Nottinghamshire), Cragside
                              (Northumberland), Nostell Priory (Yorkshire), Runnymede and
                              Waddesdon (Buckinghamshire). [N.B. a number of these
                              correspondents recur elsewhere in T/61, but in sub-sections where
                              their letters have been arranged by subject.]

61/2   1936–88   Long run of letters to the 6th Earl and Anne Countess of Rosse
                              from James Lees-Milne, mainly but (as he was a close personal
                              friend) not exclusively about the National Trust. Lees-Milne was,

T/61/2 *contd.*

from 1936, the first Secretary to the Trust's Historic Buildings Committee, of which the 6th Earl subsequently became Chairman.

61/3 1946–77

Fat bundle of letters to the 6th Earl from the 28th Earl of Crawford and Balcarres about the National Trust, of which he was Chairman, and also about the Standing Commission [see T/55–60], of which he was a member.

61/4 1938: 1940: 1949–71: 1973: 1975: 1977

Letters to the 6th Earl from Lord Crawford's successor as Chairman of the National Trust, the Earl of Antrim, [who was also an old friend via Lady Antrim, a member of the Sykes family – see T/96], one of them (dated 2 April 1971) commenting on the future of Waringstown [Co. Armagh], as follows: '... although it is not important architecturally, it is of considerable local interest, as it is almost certainly 17th century, was built during the Plantation and, with Springhill, gives a fair idea of what the local undertakers, as they were known, were able to build. I think one must look at it with entirely different eyes from its counterpart in England ... . Undoubtedly ... we should have to ask for an endowment from the Ulster Land Fund which will be far bigger than anything we have had from that source up to date. ...'

61/5 1971: 1975–9: 1983–4

Letters to the 6th Earl from Lord Antrim's successor, Lord Gibson, including letters to Anne Countess of Rosse from Lady Gibson. [See also T/24].

61/6 1968–82: 1991–2

Letters to the 6th Earl and Anne Countess of Rosse from John Cornforth, mainly about the National Trust, but including some more general discussion of incentives to private owners of heritage objects, etc, etc. Among the National Trust topics discussed are rows over the Bath Assembly Rooms [see also T/61/9 and 12–13], over the gardens at Levens Park, Westmorland [see also T/25/1], and over the re-decoration of Sudbury Hall, Yorkshire, recently acquired from Lord Vernon (who started the row).

61/7 1946–51: 1967–72

Letters to 6th Earl from various private owners about negotiations (successful or otherwise) with the National Trust over the acquisition of their properties, the terms of the endowment, etc, etc. The properties, apart from a couple of unspecified ones, are Attingham Park, Shrewsbury; Carlton Towers, Coole, Yorkshire; Clifton Hall, Nottingham; Dunham Massey, Altrincham, Cheshire [see also T/79]; Bramham Park, Boston Spa, Yorkshire; Holkham Hall, Norfolk; Kedleston, Derbyshire; the West Markham Mausoleum (to be uplifted to Clumber), Nottinghamshire; and Wood Hall, Norton, Worcester. The correspondents include Teresa Lady Berwick (one of whose letters is dated 1937), the 4th Baron Howard of Glossop, later 17th Duke of Norfolk, and the 10th Earl of Stamford.

T/61/8	1949: 1959: 1962: 1969: 1971	Correspondence of the 6th Earl about the Northern Ireland Region of the National Trust, principally about Primate Robinson's Chapel in the grounds of The Palace, Armagh. The correspondents include Hugh Armitage Moore of Rowallane, Saintfield, Co. Down, Lady Bangor of Castle Ward, John Lewis-Crosby (Secretary to the National Trust Committee for Northern Ireland) and Archbishops McCann and Simms. There is also correspondence about the National Trust's only Irish property outside Northern Ireland, Kanturk Castle, Co. Cork.
61/9	1950: 1952: 1954: 1961: 1974	Letters and papers of the 6th Earl about Bath Assembly Rooms [see also T/61/6 and 12–13], particularly about a row with the Bath City Council over the design of a bar, 1974. Correspondents include Viscount Head, Chairman of the National Trust Committee for the Wessex Region, and John Fowler.
61/10	1948–9: 1952: 1961: 1965: 1970–78	Letters and papers of the 6th Earl about National Trust gardens, the National Gardens Scheme of the Queen's Institute of District Nursing, I.C.O.M.O.S. and other schemes for listing gardens [see also T/25 17–8], the future of Westonbirt Arboretum, (Gloucestershire) (1952), and the gardens at Clumber (Nottinghamshire), Erdigg (North Wales), Felbrigg (Norfolk), Mottesfont (Hampshire), and Stourhead (Wiltshire) [see also T/61/12]. The correspondents include J.D. Boles, Robin Fedden, Ivan Hill (the Trust's Chief Agent), the Earl of Euston, Lady Heald, etc, etc.
61/11	1954: 1961–2: 1967–79	Letters and papers of the 6th Earl about National Trust personnel, paid and unpaid. Some of the letters and papers take the form of tributes, obituary or otherwise, to staff and committee members (Robin Fedden, the 6th Earl himself, etc), but others are of a 'staff in confidence' nature, and some throw revealing light on clashes and antagonisms at a senior level within the National Trust.
61/12	1958–68	File containing an original arrangement of letters and papers of the 6th Earl relating to the National Trust – the Bath Assembly Rooms [see also T/61/6, 9 and 13], Stonehenge, the Stourhead grotto [see also T/61/10], etc – including letters from correspondents such as James Lees-Milne who feature elsewhere in T/61.
61/13	1959–63	Similar file titled 'Special cases', which are: St John's, Smith Square (also a concern of the Georgian Group -see T/44/4); Avebury; Bath Assembly Rooms, Cusworth; Woolbeding fountain; and Conway Suspension bridge. The same overlap of previous correspondents applies.
61/14	1969	Letters and papers of the 6th Earl about a promotional tour of Denmark which Anne Countess of Rosse and he made on behalf of National Trust.

T/61/15	1973–4	Letters and papers of the 6th Earl about the Trust's archaeological and industrial-archaeological sites and the special responsibilities which these entail.
61/16	1977–8	Letters and papers of the 6th Earl about the Trust's acquisition of Speke Hall, Liverpool.
62	1945–7: 1949–52: 1964–5: 1976: 1985	Formal documents and related papers and correspondence about some of the honours and honorary degrees conferred on the 6th Earl (and, in one instance, Anne Countess of Rosse): his M.B.E., 1945 and 1949, his doctorate of laws at Queen's University, Belfast, 1964, etc. [For a separate and original bundle of correspondence about his K.B.E., 1974, see T/164. This latter was conferred in recognition of his contribution to public and cultural life, while the M.B.E. of 1945 was primarily for military services.]
63	1945–51: 1959: 1963 1966–7: 1969: 1972–5	Letters, mainly of thanks and compliment, to the 6th Earl and Anne Countess of Rosse from various diplomatic and political 'notabilities' – Lord Rugby (British representative in Eire), Mr and Mrs George Garrett (the first American Ambassador to Dublin), Eamon de Valera [see also K/38], Erskine Childers, Jack Lynch, Freddie Boland, the French Ambassador to Dublin, Terence O'Neill, etc. [For another diplomat, Reginald Ross-Williamson, see T/150.]
64	1939–40: 1945–50: 1956–7: 1964: 1967: 1972–9: 1989–91	File and miscellaneous correspondence of the 6th Earl concerning cultural and charitable activity in Ireland – the Friends of the National Collections of Ireland (of which he was President), the Moyne Institute in T.C.D., 1950, the 'Rosc' exhibition of modern painting in 1967, the National Monuments Advisory Council, the future Irish Architectural Archive, the Irish Landowners Convention Ltd (and in particular its Historic Properties Sub-Committee), the Edgeworth Society, a proposed Irish Victorian Society, 1974, the Adelaide Hospital, etc; including correspondence of 1989–90 about planting a tree to commemorate the 6th Earl's chairmanship of the Adelaide Hospital.
65	1934: 1936: 1940: 1942–6: 1950–56: 1965–78	Miscellaneous correspondence of the 6th Earl concerning cultural activity in the U.K. – the Bath Preservation Trust, the Boston (Lincolnshire) Preservation Trust, the research and publications of Haio Ch'ien of the School of Oriental Studies, London University (1942–3), Glyndebourne, the Ancient Monuments Society (of which the 6th Earl was President), the Society of Dilettanti, the London Society, the National Monuments Record (with particular reference to its obtaining from the 6th Earl photographs of Denby Grange [see N/24]), the Furniture History Society (numerous letters, mainly from the Chairman, Francis Watson of The Wallace Collection), the Victorian Society (Nikolaus Pevsner's knighthood for services to it in 1969), the Buildings of England Group, the

T/65 *contd.*		Historic Houses Association, and unspecified addresses, meetings, etc.
66A	1979–85	Box containing obituary and memorial material about the 6th Earl, mainly reflecting his various contributions to public and cultural life, but including letters and papers of Anne Countess of Rosse about Simon Verity's wall monuments to him in Birr and Womersley parish churches, and also including a file kept by her, 1980–81, as one of the executors to his will, and drafts and copies of her own wills, codicils and 'wishes' [see also W/1].
66B	1979–94	Box containing 10 folders and a bundle of accounts with Coutts & Co., all deriving from the 6th Earl's other, and active, executor, Alistair J. Buchanan of Hillbarn House, Great Bedwyn, Marlborough, Wiltshire. These papers range over all manner of issues – the tax liability on the 6th Earl's estate, mineral rights at Womersley [see H/119], putting the management of the legal and financial affairs of the family's Irish estate into new hands, minimising the tax liability on the estate of Anne Countess of Rosse, the family's right of residence at Nymans after her death in 1992, etc.

[For other correspondence reflecting the 6th Earl's contribution to public and cultural life, see T/69–70, 80, 82, 125, 130 and 137–156.]

T/67–85 LETTERS FROM 'THE RAILWAY CLUB', 'THE AESTHETES' AND OTHER OXFORD FRIENDS

67	*c.* 1924–43	Letters to the 6th Earl and Anne Countess of Rosse from William Acton.
68		Blank in the sequence.
69	1929–79	Fat bundle of letters to the 6th Earl from Harold Acton, written mainly from Acton's Villa, La Pietra, situated between Florence and Bologna, where the 6th Earl and Anne Countess of Rosse frequently stayed with him. The letters of 1937–8 are written from Peking and relate to the shipping home of the late Desmond Parsons's effects (Harold Acton having been his executor) – see U/51.
70	1940–89	Box of letters to Anne Countess of Rosse from Harold Acton. In 1939 Acton entrusted to Anne Countess of Rosse a considerable volume of his own papers prior to that date, which were at Womersley until 2005 and whose future location is currently (2005) under discussion.
71	1924–7: 1936	Letters to the 6th Earl from the Hon. Hugh Lygon, younger son of the 7th Earl Beauchamp, of Madresfield Court, Malvern, Worcestershire, and, probably, from Hugh's elder brother,

T/71 *contd.*		Viscount Elmley; including letters from other members of the Lygon family about Hugh's early death in 1936. [For other letters from Hugh Lygon's sisters, see T/88–9].
72	1924–36	Letters to the 6th Earl from Berkeley Villiers, many of them written from India.
73	1925–32	Letters to the 6th Earl from Romney Summers, who accompanied him on his travels in Eastern Europe in the late 1920s.
74	1925–7	Letters to the 6th Earl from Bryan Howard.
75	1925–36: 1941	Letters to the 6th Earl and Anne Countess of Rosse from David Plunket Green (with sympathetic and affectionate endorsements by Anne Countess of Rosse, whose endorsements on letters are frequently of a contrary description).
76	1925–67	Letters to the 6th Earl from Mark Ogilvie Grant, whose post-war letters are written from Greece.
77	1926–32	Letters to the 6th Earl from Johnny Drury Lowe of Locko Park, Derby, and his fiancee/wife, Ronnie *nee* Hope-Vere.
78	1926–59	Letters to the 6th Earl from 'Harry Stavordale', later 7th Earl of Ilchester. For a letter from the 6th Earl of Ilchester, see T/55/5.
79	1926–76	Letters to the 6th Earl and Anne Countess of Rosse from and about Colonel Charles Brocklehurst of Hare Hall, Macclesfield, Cheshire, many of them relating to horticulture, some to his hopes of being appointed National Trust curator of Osterley in 1946, one to the Georgian Group, 1955, one to negotiations over the National Trust's acquisition of Dunham Massey from the then 'fragile' Lord Stamford [see also T/61/7], 1969, and several to the desirability of obtaining an honour for him when he retires from the chairmanship of the Trustees of the Wallace Collection after four years in that office and 21 years as a Trustee, 1976.
80	1928–83	Letters to the 6th Earl and Anne Countess of Rosse from John Sutro, including an envelope of letters and papers, 1929–33, about 'The Railway Club' of which he was the founder and of which the 6th Earl was a member, and letters to John Sutro from Major Algy Sladen [J/145] about their travels with the 6th Earl in Central Europe in 1930. John Sutro (1904–85), film producer and brilliant mimic, was a lifelong friend of the 6th Earl.
81	1929–38	Letters to the 6th Earl from the Hon. John Fox-Strangways, youngest brother of Lord Stavordale.
82	1930–46	Letters to the 6th Earl from Robert Byron and his mother Margaret.
83	1930–40: 1946: 1952	Letters to the 6th Earl from Patrick Balfour, from 1939 3rd Lord Kinross the well-known journalist, who was press officer to the

T/83 *contd.*		R.A.F. during the Second World War, the last of them containing an amusing reference to 'Sexy Rexy' [Rex Beaumont].
84A	1930–66	Letters to the 6th Earl and Anne Countess of Rosse from Sir Roy Harrod of Holt, Norfolk, Fellow of Christ Church College, Oxford, editor of *The Economic Journal,* and pupil and biographer of John Maynard Keynes.
84B	1927–36	Letters from the 6th Earl to Sir Roy Harrod (returned by Lady Harrod in 1982).
84C	1928	Letters from [?El Cayle] to Sir Roy Harrod giving the 6th Earl's final results at Oxford.
85	1931–58: 1974	Letters to the 6th Earl from 'Henry Weymouth', later 6th Marquess of Bath and his first wife, Daphne *nee* Vivian, subsequently Daphne Fielding. The last 2 letters, of 1974, are entertaining and characteristically brusque responses to requests that Lord Bath give talks on Longleat.

[For other letters from Oxford friends see T/106–9, 124 and 127.]

T/86–105 LETTERS FROM VARIOUS 'BRIGHT YOUNG THINGS' OF THE TWENTIES AND THIRTIES

86	[*c.* 1925]: 1938: 1965	Four letters to the 6th Earl from Princess Indira of Cooch Bihar.
87	1925–31: 1944	Letters to the 6th Earl from Eddie Tatham, who worked for Messrs Justerini & Brooks, wine merchants of London.
88	1924–7: 1933	Letters to the 6th Earl from the Ladies Dorothy and Lettice Lygon and from their mother Lady Beauchamp. (These and various other ladies are described, in a series of amusing endorsements by Anne Countess of Rosse, as 'idiotic', 'dotty', 'adoring', etc, etc.) [See also T/71.]
89	1926	Letters to the 6th Earl from another of the Lygon sisters, Lady Sibell. [See also T/71.]
90	1926–9: 1937	Letters to the 6th Earl from Lady Mary Ashley Cooper daughter of the 9th Earl of Shaftesbury and of her husband, Napier Sturt, 3rd Lord Alington.
91	1926–7	Letters to the 6th Earl from Francis Stoner, whose identity has been ascertained from the appropriate volume of the Birr Castle visitors' book, an invaluable source for this purpose.
92	1927	Letters to the 6th Earl from Henry Douglas-Home.
93	1927–33	Letters to the 6th Earl from the Hon. Mrs Georgie Ward.
94	1927–30	Letters to the 6th Earl from a so-far-unidentified 'Kit' (who is

T/94 *contd.*		neither Christopher Sykes nor another friend of the 6th Earl, Kit Dunn, daughter of the Canadian financier and art-collector, Sir James Dunn, and later Mrs Robert Adeane).
95	1927–52	Letters to the 6th Earl from one Alice Preston.
96/1	1927–71	Letters to the 6th Earl from Sir Richard Sykes, 7th Bt, of Sledmere, Malton, Yorkshire, including two letters of 1947 about the restoration of Liverpool Town Hall, and one letter from Sykes's younger brother, Christopher, the biographer of Robert Byron (see T/82) and of Evelyn Waugh. The latter was an Oxford contemporary but not a particular friend of the 6th Earl.
96/2	1946–7	Two letters to the 6th Earl from Evelyn Waugh about Waugh's wish to buy Charleville, Tullamore, Co. Offaly or some other 'habitable castle' in Ireland for *c.* £15,000. [See also T/44/8.]
97	1927–32	Letters to the 6th Earl from Diana Fellowes, subsequently Diana Broughton, together with a letter from her husband thanking him for his condolences on her early death.
98	1928–35	Letters to the 6th Earl from 'Baby' Youngman.
99	1929–31: 1951	Letters to the 6th Earl from Geoffrey Allen of David Allen & Sons. [N.B. There may be more than one Geoffrey in the bundle, so they may not all be from Geoffrey Allen.]
100	1929–32: 1955: 1967: N.D.: 1980	Letters to the 6th Earl from Lady Diana Bridgman, subsequently Lady Diana Abdy (it is difficult to distinguish this Diana from Diana Fellowes, and the attempt which has been made may not be wholly successful), and from her husband, Sir Robert Abdy.
101	1929–38	Letters to the 6th Earl from Cedric [Alexander].
102	1929–41: 1946: 1951	Letters to the 6th Earl from Gavin Henderson of Buscot Park, Berkshire, later 2nd Lord Faringdon, who accompanied the 6th Earl on his travels in India and later gave Buscot to the National Trust; together with a letter to Faringdon from Oliver Messel, pre-1937, tearing strips off him.
103	1930–34: 1938: 1940	Letters to the 6th Earl from David (later Sir David) Barran, who writes on Burmah Shell writing paper from Calcutta and Bombay and makes frequent reference to 'Robert Byron'. He appears in the Birr Castle visitors' book in May 1932, but his signature there is illegible.
104	1930–39	Letters to the 6th Earl from the Hon. Sir Gerald ('Timmie') Chichester, younger son of the 3rd Lord Templemore and private secretary to Queen Mary, including a letter from Lady Templemore about Sir Gerald's premature death in 1939.
105	1931–7	Letters to the 6th Earl from Lord Charles Cavendish of Lismore Castle, Co. Waterford younger brother of the 10th Duke of Devonshire, and his wife Adele, sister of Fred Astaire].

T/106–115		**LETTERS FROM AMERICAN FRIENDS**

106 1925–67: 1976: 1986

Huge bundle of letters to the 6th Earl from Robert Coe ('Bob'), sometime U.S. Ambassador to Dublin, but a close friend of the 6th Earl from Oxford days, and one of the godparents of the 7th Earl; including 3 letters from Coe's sister, Natalie, and correspondence of 1986 between the 7th Earl and Coe's executors concerning Coe's legacy to his godson.

107 1927–78

Two envelopes of letters to the 6th Earl from Benjamin Kittredge, another American at Oxford, and also a kindred spirit because of their shared interest in horticulture, including letters from Kittredge's successive wives, Carola and Daphne.

108 1931–75

Letters to the 6th Earl and Anne Countess of Rosse from Eugene Reynal, the third American friend from Oxford days and a fine art publisher, and Reynal's wife, Kay.

109 1927–34

Letters to the 6th Earl from Heyrick Pease, an acquaintance and contemporary at Oxford([though not a friend in the sense that the foregoing three were friends).

110A 1927–9: 1937

Letters and invitations to the 6th Earl from Laura Corrigan, the famous American hostess, philanthropist and Mrs Malaprop.

110B 1927–32

Letters to the 6th Earl from Mabel Drury (endorsed by Anne Countess of Rosse, 'great American hostess') and other members of the Drury family.

111 1939: 1945–6

Three letters to the 6th Earl and Anne Countess of Rosse from 'Emerald', Lady Cunard, another great American hostess, whose biography was written by the 6th Earl's friend, Daphne Fielding, sometime Marchioness of Bath (T/85)], together with a letter from Sir Thomas Beecham written on Lady Cunard's instructions.

112 1929

Letters to the 6th Earl from Walter B. Ryan Jr of Pine Street, New York.

113 1931–65

Letters to the 6th Earl and Anne Countess of Rosse from Schuyler L. Parsons (endorsed by Anne Countess of Rosse, 'our very dear bogus relation').

114 1951–77: 1985–6

Letters to the 6th Earl from Henry McIlhenny of Glenveagh Castle, Churchill, Co. Donegal, containing disappointingly few references to horticulture.

115 1959–61: 1968: 1984

Letters to the 6th Earl and Anne Countess of Rosse from Ved Mehta of 'the New Yorker', a friend of the future 7th Earl at Oxford], and described in an endorsement by Lady Rosse as a 'Totally blind Indian boy and a wonderful personality and writer'.

[For letters from Mr and Mrs George Garrett, two other American friends, see T/63.]

T/116–120		**LETTERS FROM CONTINENTAL FRIENDS**
116	1924–36	Letters to the 6th Earl from Germaine de Noirmont, who has escaped endorsing by Anne Countess of Rosse, but was a major correspondent of the 6th Earl prior to his marriage.
117	1927–75	Large bundle of letters to the 6th Earl and Anne Countess of Rosse from Prince Henry Lubomirski of Cracow, Poland.
118	1930–32	Letters to the 6th Earl from the Prince Lonyay of Oroszvar, Hungary, and from his steward, mainly about the 6th Earl's purchase of Tockay.
119	1930–33	Letters to the 6th Earl from Hanna ?Wickes, a Hungarian or Rumanian lady who seems to have been friendly with the Londonderrys as well as with the 6th Earl.
120	1930–39: 1945: 1947: 1952	Letters to the 6th Earl and Anne Countess of Rosse from Count Giovanni Gregorini. [For letters from other Continental friends, see mainly T/25.]
T/121–136		**LETTERS FROM MEMBERS OF THE GUINNESS FAMILY AND OTHER IRISH FRIENDS**
121	1925–32	Letters to the 6th Earl from Tanis Guinness, later Montague, who belonged to the English banking side of the family, and therefore is not particularly Irish.
122	1925–31: 1943	Letters to the 6th Earl from the sisters Maureen and Aileen Guinness, daughters of the Hon. Arthur Ernest Guinness of Glenmaroon, Chapelizod, Co. Dublin, and Luggala, Roundwood, Co. Wicklow – the latter of which houses features prominently as a meeting place for the 6th Earl's circle; Maureen and Aileen Guinness subsequently became Marchioness of Dufferin and Ava and Mrs Brinsley Plunket respectively.
123	1928–33	Letters to the 6th Earl from Ladies Honor and Evelyn Guinness and Henry ('Chips') Channon, subsequently husband of Lady Honor.
124	1925–78	Large bundle of letters to the 6th Earl from Bryan Guinness, subsequently 2nd Lord Moyne, and his successive wives, Diana (*nee* Mitford, subsequently Lady Mosley), and Elizabeth; Lord Moyne's letters of the 1930s and 1950s-70s include references to Georgian Group, National Trust and other conservation affairs. Lord Moyne could be classified as an Oxford as well as an Irish friend of the 6th Earl.
125	1954–71: 1976: 1978	Letters to the 6th Earl from the Hon. Desmond Guinness, second son of Lord Moyne, and the 6th Earl's godson, including one from his first wife, Mariga, some of them about conservation matters. One of Desmond Guinness's letters, and the only letter from

T/125 *contd.*   Mariga Guinness, express thanks for hospitality received on the
                                  occasion of Princess Margaret and Lord Snowdon's visit to Birr
                                  Castle in 1965, and Mariga Guinness's letter (which makes
                                  entertaining comments on the security arrangements) goes on to
                                  refer to the alterations to the hall at Belvedere, Mullingar, recently
                                  made by Rex Beaumont.

126   1975: 1977   Two letters to the 6th Earl from the Hon. Jonathan Guinness,
                                  Lord Moyne's eldest son, mainly about investments but with some
                                  reference to the wealth tax in the Irish Republic.

127   1924–39:   Letters to the 6th Earl from 'Billy' Clonmore, later 8th Earl of
             1946–50   Wicklow, an Oxford as well as an Irish friend of the 6th Earl.

128   1925–35:   Letters to the 6th Earl from the 4th Marquess of Headfort, Lady
             1943: 1947–8:   Headfort and their second son, Lord William Taylor. [For letters
             1949   from Lord Headfort about horticulture, see T/22.]

129   1927: 1932   Two letters to the 6th Earl from 'Tom' Ponsonby of Kilcooly
                                  Abbey, Co. Tipperary, a sometime trustee of the Rosse estates.

130   1927–52: 1977   Letters to the 6th Earl from Sir Alfred Beit 2nd Bt and Lady Beit,
                                  one of Sir Alfred's letters discussing his purchase of Russborough,
                                  Blessington, Co. Wicklow, as a fitting setting for his picture
                                  collection, the letter from Lady Beit (of 1977) discussing the
                                  opening of Russborough to the public. One of Sir Alfred's earlier
                                  letters is endorsed by Anne Countess of Rosse, 'a cheque from
                                  Alfred Beit!'.

131   1935–8: 1945:   Letters to the 6th Earl from Colonel Charles Howard Bury of
             1949–50: 1962   Belvedere, Mullingar, Co. Westmeath.

132   1936–40   Letters to the 6th Earl from the 8th Earl of Granard, Master of the
                                  Horse, 1924–36, and subsequently H.M.'s Comptroller at Ascot.

133   1938–79:   Letters to the 6th Earl and Anne Countess of Rosse from and
             1990: 1992   about Roderic More O'Ferrall of Kildanagan, Monasterevan, Co.
                                  Kildare, one of the earlier ones relating to advice given him by the
                                  6th Earl about alterations to Kildangan. The last item is a letter to
                                  the 7th Earl about planting a tree in memory of O'Ferrall.

133A   1946: 1950   Letters to the 6th Earl and Anne Countess of Rosse from the 28th
                                  Lord Dunboyne about escorting 'William' the future 7th Earl by
                                  boat and train to London, about the future of Dunboyne Castle
                                  and about Lord Dunboyne's marriage in 1950.

134   1960-87   Letters to the 6th Earl and Anne Countess of Rosse from Derek
                                  Hill of Churchill, Co. Donegal. They are mostly about social trivia
                                  rather than artistic matters, but include letters about an exhibition
                                  of Hill's pictures at the Wexford Opera Festival in 1965. Also
                                  included is correspondence of 1987 between the Office of Public
                                  Works and the 7th Earl of Rosse about the loan of Hill's pictures

T/134 *contd.*		of Birr for an exhibition marking the 70th birthday of the artist, together with a catalogue of this exhibition, which opened at the Glebe Gallery, Churchill, and then moved to Kilkenny and to the Royal Hospital, Kilmainham. To this sub-section has been added a photocopy of A.P.W. Malcomson's List of D/4400/C/10/44–6 of the Derek Hill archive, now deposited in PRONI, which covers Derek Hill's letters to the 6th Earl and Anne Countess of Rosse and the 7th Earl and Alison Countess of Rosse over the period 1958–99.
135	1963	Three letters to the 6th Earl from Micheal Mac Liammoir.
136	1961–85	Letters to Anne Countess of Rosse from Anita Leslie King, née Leslie of Castle Leslie, Glaslough, Co. Monaghan, the authoress, who writes mainly from Oranmore Castle, Co. Galway, including two letters of 1950–51 from her brother, John Leslie later 4th Bt, letters from her father, Sir Shane Leslie, 3rd Bt (see also T/42)], 1956, and letters of 1967 and *c.* 1975 to the 6th Earl from 'Bill' King, her husband. One of Sir Shane Leslie's letters refers to a visit from American book-dealers to whom he gave the entree to private Irish libraries, including 'Mr [John] Fleming ([A.S.W.] Rosenbach's heir)', who '... are most knowledgeable and are to distribute information as well as largesse. Everybody wants to know what are masterpieces and what are not.'
T/137–156		**LETTERS FROM MISCELLANEOUS CORRESPONDENTS, MAINLY LITERARY OR ARTISTIC**
137	1925: 1929–39: 1952: 1959: 1971	Letters to the 6th Earl from Nancy Mitford and her brother, Tom Mitford, children of the 2nd Lord Redesdale.
138	1930	Three letters to the 6th Earl from one Harry Thomas of 9 York Gate, Regent's Park, London.
139	1930–69	Letters to the 6th Earl from Lord Herbert, subsequently 16th Earl of Pembroke, and other members of the Herbert family of Wilton, Salisbury, Wiltshire. [See also T/49.]
140	1932: 1946	Two letters to the 6th Earl from Peter Quennell.
141	1932–40: 1948: 1954: 1967: 1969	Letters to the 6th Earl from Adeline Genée/Isitt, endorsed by Anne Countess of Rosse, 'the famous ballerina'.
142	1933: 197[?6]	Letters to the 6th Earl and Anne Countess of Rosse from Sir Cecil Beaton.
143	1933–7	Four delightful letters to the 6th Earl from Rosa Lewis of 'The Cavendish'.

T/144	1934–77	Letters to the 6th Earl from Sacheverell and other Sitwells, one of them (of 1947) referring to 'the other and much more beautiful Castletown' (ie Castletown Cox, Co. Kilkenny).
145	1934–8: 1946	Letters to the 6th Earl from Major Algy Sladen of The Travel Club of Great Britain and Ireland. With his wife, Freddie, Algy Sladen had earlier toured Central Europe, where the Sladens had many contacts, with Robert Byron and John Sutro in 1928 and with the 6th Earl and John Sutro in 1930. [See also T/80.]
146	1937: N.D.	Letters to the 6th Earl and Anne Countess of Rosse from Osy Darell, who according to Anne Countess of Rosse's endorsement doped and drank himself to death.
147	1938: 1952	Letters to the 6th Earl from Sir Owen O'Malley, British Ambassador to Mexico at the time the 6th Earl and Anne Countess of Rosse visited it in 1938, together with 2 letters from his wife, Mary, whom Lady Rosse identifies as '... Anne Bridge, the authoress'.
148	1930–72: 1975: 1978–9: 1984	Letters to the 6th Earl and Anne Countess of Rosse from Sir John Betjeman, mainly about Georgian Group [see T/44] and other conservation matters (and including unflattering references to Nikolaus Pevsner); also included is an unpublished poem about Birr Castle, and a moving and informative letter to Anne Countess of Rosse written shortly after the 6th Earl's death in 1979.
149	1940: 1946: 970	Letter to the 6th Earl and Anne Countess of Rosse from Dame Una Pope-Hennessy and her son, James Pope-Hennesy (who writes about his biographies of Lord Houghton and Anthony Trollope).
149A	1945–52	Letters, of a purely social and personal nature, to the 6th Earl from 'Tom' (identified by the 7th Earl as Thomas Calderwood Dundas, later 7th Bt, a Director of Barclay's Bank), who writes from various addresses in Sussex.
150	1946–64	Letters to the 6th Earl from Reginald Ross Williamson (sometime British Representative in the Irish Republic) and his wife, Eileen.
151	1945–50: 1963–5	Letters to the 6th Earl from Jocelyn Pereira, one of them about the 6th Earl's criticisms of Pereira's book, *A distant Drum*, 1947.
152	1947–50: 1953: 1956	Letters to the 6th Earl and Anne Countess of Rosse, endorsed by Lady Rosse 'Oggie Lynn, the singer.'
152A	1949–50	Letters to the 6th Earl from 'Kitty', Viscountess Mersey, née Lady Katherine Petty-Fitzmaurice, Baroness Nairne, who writes from Bowood, Calne, Wiltshire, about the possibility of a re-arrangement of the family property whereby she would acquire Derreen, Co. Kerry.
152B	1952: 1955: 1961: 1972: 1986	Letters to Anne Countess of Rosse from Emlyn Williams, the actor.

T/153	1962: 1967–8	Letters to the 6th Earl from Sir Desmond Cochrane, 3rd Bt, Consul General of Ireland to the Republics of Syria and Lebanon.
154	1965–6: 1975: 1977	Letters to the 6th Earl from Kobina Kessie, a prominent Ghanaian from Ashanti.
154A	1967–71: 1982	Letters to the 6th Earl from John Barr of the Metallgesellschaft, Frankfurt-am-Main, mainly written from Melbourne, about the career and prospects of the 6th Earl's second son, Martin, who was then working in Australia. [See T/172.]
155	1964–5: 1968	Two letters to the 6th Earl from Harold Nicolson about Nicolson's Illness in 1964, and two from Nigel Nicolson congratulating the 6th Earl on Lord Oxmantown's work for the U.N. in Ghana and acknowledging condolences on Harold Nicolson's death.
155A	1972	Two letters to the 6th Earl from Diana Holman-Hunt, the writer.
155B	1967: 1975–84	Letters to Anne Countess of Rosse from Jane Abdy, Lady Abdy [third wife of Sir Robert Abdy, 5th Bt (T/100); antique-dealer and society figure], who writes mainly about literary and artistic matters and with some telling comments (1980) on the writings of Anita Leslie (T/136).
156	1939: 1957: N.D.: 1959: 1961: 1969: 1971: N.D.: 1977: 1983	Letters to the 6th Earl and Anne Countess of Rosse from miscellaneous 'celebrities', including Henry Yorke (the writer, Henry Green), 1936; Gerald Berners, 1939; Dame Margot Fonteyn, 1957 and N.D.; Sir John Glubb, 1959; Sir Compton Mackenzie (mentioning the Wexford Opera Festival), 1961; Elizabeth Bowen, 1969; Peter Sellers, 1971 and N.D.; and Lady Diana Cooper, N.D.; her son, John Julius, (2nd Lord Norwich), 1977; Lady Longford, 1983; and Sir Hugh Casson, *c.* 1983.

T/157–159		**LETTERS FROM NANNIES**
157	1929–42	Letters to the 6th Earl from 'Gran Nannie' (Miss Edith A. Cramer of Loughborough, the former housekeeper at Birr Castle, who died at a very advanced age in 1941 – see also M/18 and T/11/1), including two much earlier letters *to* her from the 5th Earl, then Lord Oxmantown.
158	*c.* 1926–31	Letters to the 6th Earl from 'Nannie', Mrs Harvey, who really had been his nannie.
159	1921–38	Letters to the 6th Earl from Kathleen H. Grant, writing mainly from Barbados, whose affectionate mode of address has drawn down numerous irate endorsements from Anne Countess of Rosse, but who was – according to a letter included in this sub-section – the former nannie of the Hon. Desmond and Lady Bridget Parsons].

T/160–164		**PERSONAL LETTERS ARRANGED OTHER THAN BY CORRESPONDENT**
160	1917–24	Early personal letters to Miss Anne Messel from her nanny, various friends and some officers on active service in the First World War; together with a series of pocket diaries of the same period kept by the future Anne Countess of Rosse, recording not only engagements and events but her reactions and impressions of things.
160A	1940–45	Box-file and fat bundle, the former endorsed by Anne Countess of Rosse, 'War-time letters from dear friends to Womersley [where she lived for most of the war, while the 6th Earl was away on active service] – so many dead ...'. The box-file contains a largely original arrangement of the letters she received from miscellaneous correspondents during that period, including Capt. John Pelham, 8th Earl of Chichester of the Scots Guards, who was killed in a car crash near Womersley, Capt. George Godfrey Faussett of the Welsh Guards, John Schiff of the U.S. Navy, sundry 'poor Air Force splendid lads – all killed', Field-Marshal Alexander (whose letter or letters Anne Countess of Rosse notes that she 'burned', and none of which survive), etc. etc. [N.B. The only respects in which this arrangement has been disturbed is that the fat bundle has been added and that letters of some content from lifelong correspondents of the 6th Earl and Anne Countess of Rosse, such as James Lees-Milne and Harold Acton, have been removed and united to the sub-sections devoted to these individuals.]
160B	1921–90	Fat bundle of miscellaneous personal letters to the 6th Earl and Anne Countess of Rosse, either too few in number or unimportant in content to merit a separate sub-section for the writer concerned.
161	1928–32	Letters to the 6th Earl from miscellaneous correspondents concerning his travels in Russia, India, China, etc.; the correspondents are mainly British and foreign diplomats and colonial governors who write about visas, social engagements, etc., etc.
162	1935–8: 1940: 1962: 1976	Miscellaneous newspaper cuttings and pro forma material concerning the 6th Earl, Anne Countess of Rosse and their circle; the pro forma material consists of summonses to the coronations of Edward VIII and George VI.
163	1935	Large bundle of letters of congratulation to the 6th Earl and Anne Countess of Rosse on their engagement/marriage, with other papers about the wedding.
163A	1968: 1970: 1984–5	Letters to Anne Countess of Rosse about her contributions to various books, from Barbara Cartland's *We Danced all Night* (1970) to Derry Moore and Michael Pick's *The English Room*

T/163 *contd.*		(1984); the correspondents include Christina Foyle of W. & G. Foyle Ltd, Lord Weidenfeld of Weidenfeld & Nicholson and Merlin Waterson of the National Trust.
164	1974	Box of letters of congratulation to the 6th Earl on his receiving the K.B.E. [The patent conferring this honour and signed by the Queen and Prince Philip, is framed and hangs in Lord Rosse's dressing room in Birr Castle. For some of the 6th Earl's other honours and decorations, see T/62.]
T/165–172		**CORRESPONDENCE BETWEEN THE 6TH EARL AND ANNE COUNTESS OF ROSSE, AND LETTERS TO THEM FROM THE MESSELS, LADY ROSSE'S CHILDREN AND THEIR OWN CHILDREN**
165	1914–57	Box and a half of letters to Miss Anne Messel/Mrs. Ronald Armstrong-Jones/the Countess of Rosse and to her second husband, the 6th Earl, from her parents, Leonard and Maud Messel, including a few letters from grandmothers and aunts and 4 letters from Mrs Messel's brother, Roy Sambourne, 1918 and 1943–5.
166	1919: 1936–8: 1947: 1951: 1982–3	Letters to the 6th Earl and Anne Countess of Rosse from her brother, Linley Messel, his first wife, Anne, and his son (by his second wife), Thomas, etc.
167	*c.* 1914–1983	Box of letters to the 6th Earl and Anne Countess of Rosse from and about her brother, Oliver Messel, the artist and designer, including numerous letters of condolence on his death in 1978. This section includes one drawing and two paintings which Oliver Messel did of lilies and wildflowers at Birr Castle.
168	1934–79	Outsize, black, tin deed box of correspondence between the 6th Earl and Anne Countess of Rosse, including her account of the coronation of Queen Elizabeth II. The letters of 1937 mainly relate to the illness and death of the Hon. Desmond Parsons.
169	1938–91	Box of letters to the 6th Earl and Anne Countess of Rosse from and about her son, Anthony Armstrong-Jones, subsequently created 1st Earl of Snowdon, and from members of the royal family; the other correspondents include her ex-husband, Ronald Owen Armstrong-Jones and his second wife; Princess Margaret; Queen Elizabeth II; Queen Elizabeth the Queen Mother; Sir David Bowes-Lyon, etc., etc.
170	1935–87	Letters to the 6th Earl and Anne Countess of Rosse from her daughter, Susan Armstrong-Jones, her daughter's husband, John, 6th Viscount de Vesci, and their children. [For previous de Vesci correspondence, see T/12].

T/171   1936–90   Two boxes of letters to the 6th Earl and Anne Countess of Rosse
                       from their elder son, Lord Oxmantown, subsequently 7th Earl, his
                       wife, Alison [see Section W], and their children, including letters
                       from others about Lord Oxmantown's health and education in
                       early life. The later letters, from 1963 onwards, are of much more
                       than family and personal interest, because they document the 7th
                       Earl's career as a Principal Officer of the United Nations
                       Development Programme, and include significant comment on
                       the countries in which he served in the following capacities:
                       Reports Officer, Ghana, 1963–5; Assistant Resident
                       Representative, Dhomey, 1965–8; Area Officer for Mid-West
                       Africa, UN Headquarters, New York, 1968–70; Assistant Resident
                       Representative, Iran, Representative of UNESCO and Field
                       Director, United Nations Volunteers, 1970–75; Deputy Resident
                       Representative, Bangladesh, 1975–8; and Deputy Resident
                       Representative and Acting Resident Representative, Algeria, 1978–
                       80. From 1980 on, the letters mainly relate to the 7th Earl's plans
                       to put family finances back on a sound footing and develop the
                       heritage and tourist potential of Birr Castle and gardens.

172   1951–91   Box of letters to the 6th Earl and Anne Countess of Rosse from
                       and about their second son, Martin, and his wife, Aline. [A
                       considerable quantity of personal letters *to* the Hon. Martin
                       Parsons, mainly while at Eton, 1951–6, will be found in the
                       bottom drawer of the left-hand, matching chest of drawers in no.
                       12 ('The Boys' Dormitory') on the top floor of Birr Castle. See
                       also T/154A.]

173   1992   Letters of condolence to the 7th Earl and Alison Countess of
                       Rosse, together with printed obituaries, appreciations and orders
                       of service, all relating to the death of Anne Countess of Rosse.

U/	DATE	DESCRIPTION
1–52	1920–38	Letters and papers of the Hon. Desmond Parsons, younger brother of the 6th Earl of Rosse [originally kept in a suitcase and a large red trunk in his former bedroom (No. 3) in Birr Castle], and including travel journals and other writings of Desmond Parsons, letters to him from his brother, the 6th Earl, his sister, Lady Bridget, his aunt, Countess de la Feld, and miscellaneous British and Chinese correspondents, including Robert Byron (who was in love with him), John Sparrow, the future Warden of All Souls College, Oxford, etc. etc.

New light on Desmond Parsons has been shed by James Knox's recent *Robert Byron* (London, 2003). A few basic facts and dates may be found in the following contemporary obituary notice of 1937 (T/4): 'At Zurich, on 4th July, Desmond Parsons died after suffering for two years from an illness which seemed to have been the outcome of hardships while travelling in China. Though aged only 26, he had made active advances in the study of Chinese civilization which was his chosen work. Having visited places of archaeological moment in the provinces of Honan and Shensi, he made a journey to Tunhuang in difficult circumstances, examining the geographical features of the ancient highway to the West along the Kansu corridor. Some misunderstanding by the local authorities led to his arrest, and he was released at Lanchou only after diplomatic intervention. Before that he had managed to take over 120 photographs in the famous Buddhist cave-shrines at Tunhuang, including certain wall-paintings which had not yet been recorded. Copies are preserved in the Courtauld Institute, and in the collections of Harvard University and several American museums. Possessed of an unusual capacity for observation and of a fine scholarly instinct, he would doubtless have contributed ably to the Chinese studies he loved. His charming personality and transparent honesty of purpose claimed the admiration of all who knew him.'

Desmond Parsons's best-known correspondents (ie those who are likely to be studied in their own right) also feature prominently and over a far longer period in the correspondence of the 6th Earl and Anne Countess of Rosse—eg James Lees-Milne (T/61/2), William and Harold Acton (T/67–8) and Robert Byron (T/82B).

U/1–5 FAMILY CORRESPONDENCE OF THE HON. DESMOND PARSONS

1	1923–37	Correspondence between the Hon. Desmond Parsons and his mother, Lady de Vesci. [See also T/3.]
2	1924–37	Letters to Desmond Parsons from his brother, the 6th Earl, along with one letter from Anne, Countess of Rosse.

U/3	N.D.: 1937	Letters to Desmond Parsons from his sister, Lady Bridget Parsons. [See also T/5.]
4	1926: 1929	Letters to Desmond Parsons from his grandfather Sir Cecil Lister Kaye.
5	*c.* 1934	Letters to Desmond Parsons from his aunt Adeline, Countess de la Feld. [See also N/32–40 and T/7/3.]

U/6–41 LETTERS TO DESMOND PARSONS FROM FRIENDS AND ASSOCIATES

6	[*c.* 1928–9]	Letters to Desmond Parsons from Robert Byron. [See also T/82.]
7	1929–37	Letters to Desmond Parsons from John Sutro. [See also T/80.]
8	1930–38	Letters to Desmond Parsons from William Acton. [See also T/67.]
9	1931–4	Letters to Desmond Parsons from miscellaneous German correspondents.
10	1931–6	Letters to Desmond Parsons from Harold Acton. [See also T/69.]
11	1930–34	Letters to Desmond Parsons from Count Stephanie Vichlitz-Amade, Böös, Hungary.
12	*c.* 1930	Letters to Desmond Parsons from Mark Ogilvie Grant. [See also T/76.]
13	*c.* 1932	Letters to Desmond Parsons from Axel Viale, Barcelona, etc.
14	1932–33	Letters to Desmond Parsons from Dame Una Pope-Hennessy. [See also T/149.]
15	1932–33	Letters to Desmond Parsons from Frances Dakyns, 5 Devonshire Place, London W.1 and Pulborough, Sussex.
16	1932: 1936	Letters to Desmond Parsons from Piet Meyer, endorsed by Anne, Countess of Rosse as a 'very dear friend of Desmond.'
17	1932–5: 1937	Letters to Desmond Parsons from Roy Harrod. [See also T/84A.]
18	1933	Letters to Desmond Parsons from Mrs. Vera Bryce later the first wife of Randall Plunket, 19th Lord Dunsany.
19	1933	Letters to Desmond Parsons from Dr T.H. Rosenheim, Berlin, all written in German.
20	1934	Letters to Desmond Parsons from Shelley Lee, Peking.
21	1934	Letters (3 from each) to Desmond Parsons from 'Mushvag', who writes from Thatta Gurmani, Muzzaffargarh District, Punjab (and seems to be a lover), and from 'Anijadi,' Ashiana, Lahore (who is a mutual friend). There are references to a trip to Afghanistan which Anijadi's father, an official of the Indian government, was arranging for Anijadi, Mushvag and Desmond Parsons to make.

U/22	1934	Letters to Desmond Parsons from David Barran. [See also T/103.]
23	1935	Letters to Desmond Parsons from J. Chang, Western City, Peking.
24	1936	Letters to Desmond Parsons from John Hope-Johnstone, Peking City.
25	1936	Letters to Desmond Parsons from Larry Luckman, endorsed by Anne Countess of Rosse as 'The Great Orientalist.'
26	*c.* 1936–7	Letters to Desmond Parsons from Gabriel Herbert, together with three letters from her mother, Mary, née Vesey, only child of the 4th Viscount de Vesci.
27	1936–7	Letters to Desmond Parsons from his servant, Chou Feng Lin, Peking.
28	1936–7	Letters to Desmond Parsons from Dr Otto Burchard, 20 To Fu Hsiang, Peking, East City.
29	1936–7	Letters to Desmond Parsons from the Hon. Stephen Tennent of Wilsford Manor, Salisbury.
30	1937	Letters to Desmond Parsons from 'Dig' [?], 58 Rutland Gate, London S.W. 7.
31	1937	Letters to Desmond Parsons from James Lees-Milne. [See also T/61/2.]
32	1937	Letters to Desmond Parsons from Cecil Beaton. [See also T/142.]
33	*c.* 1937	Letters to Desmond Parsons from Peter Quennell. [See also T/140.]
34	1937	Letters to Desmond Parsons from 'Freddie' [Ashton?], 9 Guilford Place, London W.C. 1. [The writer is a ballet-dancer; hence the tentative attribution to Sir Frederick Ashton.]
35	1937	Letters to Desmond Parsons from John Sparrow, future Warden of All Souls College, Oxford. [See also T/51.]
36	N.D.	Letters to Desmond Parsons from Osy Darrell. [See also T/146.]
37	N.D.	Letters to Desmond Parsons from Hamish Erskine, Bangor, North Wales; Coolham, Sussex; and New College, Oxford.
38	N.D.	Letters to Desmond Parsons from Georgia Sitwell.
39	N.D.: 1935	Letters from Desmond Parsons to Sir Alexander (probably the British diplomat who secured his release from prison at Lanchou (see U/45)) and to 'Eddie', together with a letter of introduction given to Desmond Parsons to give to a senior official in Sarawak whose first name seems to be 'Vyner'.
40	1932–3: 1935–6	Scholarly correspondence of Desmond Parsons from miscellaneous British and Chinese correspondents, who write from the University of London Courtauld Institute of Art, the University of

U/40 *contd.*		London School of Oriental Studies and the National University of Peking.
41	1924: 1933: 1935–6	Personal letters to Desmond Parsons from miscellaneous correspondents of British, Irish, Indian and Chinese origin.

U/42–45 PHOTOGRAPHS AND WRITINGS OF THE HON. DESMOND PARSONS

42	N.D.	Photographic prints and negatives taken by or for Desmond Parsons, featuring various scenes from his foreign travels, stored in two oriental-patterned boxes.
43	1930–35	Box of travel journals, notebooks and diaries belonging to Desmond Parsons, with writings on topics as diverse as 'Chinese Radicals,' European history, and Rainier Maria Rilke. This section also includes an account of Desmond Parsons's voyage to Bali in 1935. Written in French, German, and Chinese, the notebooks illustrate his breadth of knowledge.
44	1935	First-person accounts of daily life in the Far East, written or typed by Desmond Parsons. Several of the papers in this envelope describe in detail his arrest following a photographic expedition to Dunhuang. Suffering from dysentery, Desmond Parsons was unfairly jailed and detained until the British authorities were able to obtain orders for his release from the Governor.
45/1–6	1936–7	Letters and papers pertaining to the publication of *Chinese Fairy Tales and Folk Tales,* translated and edited by Desmond Parsons and Dr W. Eberhard, as follows:
45/1	*c.* 1936	Three black notebooks containing drafts of various Chinese fairy tales, written or copied by Desmond Parsons.
45/2	1936–7	Correspondence of Desmond Parsons concerning the publication of *Chinese Fairy Tales and Folk Tales* from Dr W Eberhard, much of it in German, including editing suggestions; contract letters from the publishing company Routledge and Sons, Ltd.; book reviews from various newspapers; and one letter from Dr. W. Eberhard to the 6th Earl of Rosse explaining the royalties agreement following the death of the Hon. Desmond Parsons.
45/3	1937	Handwritten manuscript for *Chinese Fairy Tales and Folk Tales,* written in English by Dr W. Eberhard.
45/4	1937	Typed manuscript for *Chinese Fairy Tales and Folk Tales,* written in German by Dr W. Eberhard.
45/5	1937	Handwritten manuscript for *Chinese Fairy Tales and Folk Tales,* written in English by Desmond Parsons.
45/6	1937	Typed manuscript for *Chinese Fairy Tales and Folk Tales,* written in English by Desmond Parsons.

U/46–52 BUSINESS AND MISCELLANEOUS PAPERS OF DESMOND PARSONS

46	1920–23: 1923–28	Half- and end-of-term school reports on the Hon. Desmond Parsons from his days at Winton House, Winchester; and Eton College, Windsor, together with a small collection of evaluative letters sent to Parsons' mother, Lady de Vesci, from the Eton House Tutors.
47	1931–35	Receipts and subscriptions for various purchases and services, together with Desmond Parsons's bank book for 1932–3.
48	1932–3	Medical reports on Desmond Parsons, accompanied by x-ray photographs, by Dr. J. Tugendreich, Derfflingerstrasse, 21 Berlin W 35.
49	1932–35	Correspondence and papers from the Berkeley Property & Investment Co. Ltd. and the Provincial Garden Cities Co. Ltd. regarding Desmond Parsons's mortgage plans and financial engagements.
50	1934–6	Various travel brochures and guidebooks collected by Desmond Parsons, several of which suggest itineraries for voyages to places as exotic as Bali and Sumatra.
51	1937–8	Formal estate and legal papers of Desmond Parsons, drawn up following his death on 4 July 1937, including a will, an executorship account, and a schedule of personal articles and effects. The envelope also includes papers pertaining to the shipment of his personal articles from Peking to Birr, all of which was arranged and executed by Harold Acton [see T/69] and the 6th Earl of Rosse.
52	1924: 1933–6	Two envelopes of miscellaneous printed matter collected by Desmond Parsons and apparently found among his effects after his death.

V/	DATE	DESCRIPTION
1–27	1840–1945	Letters and papers of the successive Rosse agents, George and Toler R. Garvey Senior and Junior in their capacity as agents for other estates, mainly in King's County and Tipperary. The papers have been arranged in rough alphabetical order, by landlord's/employer's name; strict alphabetical order has been departed from when it would have been uneconomical of boxes.
1	1840: 1854: 1868–1910	Box of letters, leases, agreements, proposals, Land Court case papers, Irish Land Commission sale papers, etc, etc, relating to the estates of Charles B. Baldwin, M.P., of Totness, Devon, who was succeeded by his son-in-law, the Rev. Hans Hamilton (he was also resident in England), at Bovean, Kilkerran, Kilcoleman, Lisduff, etc, King's County, and near Clonakilty, Co. Cork, including 2 leases granted by Baldwin, 1840 and 1854, and a rent receipt book, 1868–79.
2	1886–1935	Box containing a ledger, a rent receipt book, letting agreements, etc, all relating to Broughall, King's County, the estate of Christopher J. B. Banon (d. 1919) and, after his death, of his widow.
3–6	1852–1946	One outsize volume and 3 boxes relating to the estate of Francis Valentine Bennett of Thomastown Park, Birr, and Upper Sackville Street, Dublin (d.1890), Frederick Philip Bennett of Thomastown Park (d. 1905), and their successor, Valentine J. E. Ryan of Thomastown Park, at Thomastown, Boolanarrig Little, Coagh, Lisheen, Raheenglass (where the home farm was), etc, baronies of Eglish and Garrycastle, King's County and now appropriately located in Birr Castle because the property was very much intermixed with the Rosse estate, as follows:
3	1852–66	Outsize rent receipt book for the Bennett estate.
4	1859–1945	Box of proposals and agreements, Land Court and Irish Land Commission papers, correspondence, valuations and miscellaneous papers, 1859–c. 1925, together with Thomastown Park garden and forestry accounts and Raheenglass farm accounts, 1925–45.
5	1866–87: 1930–46	Box containing a rent receipt book, 1866–87, and estate and farm ledgers, 1911–30 and 1930–46.
6	1871–9	Box containing original bundles of vouchers for the Bennett estate.
7	1921–4	Envelope of Court Orders, accounts, letters and letting agreements, all relating to the estate of J. S. P. Malone Barrett [see Q/393], a minor, at Temora, King's County.
8	1893–8	Ledger recording receipts of rent and out-goings of various kinds in respect of the estate of L. Biddulph at Fortal, Coolinariney, etc, King's County.

V/9	1895–6	Envelope containing papers about the tithe rent charges due to the Marquess of Downshire out of estates in King's County [this probably reflects Toler R. Garvey Senior's agency for the Rosse estate rather than for that of Lord Downshire?].
10	1914–32	Envelope of correspondence, Irish Land Commission papers, etc, relating to the estate of G. Briscoe Eyre of Eyrecourt, Co. Galway [see Q/390], and his widow Mary.
11	1860–84	Box of rentals, accounts and vouchers deriving from the Garveys (George and, from 1879, Toler R. Senior) agency for the estate of the Drought family of Whigsborough. [By coincidence, the last Drought to live at Whigsborough was the Rosse agent, Capt. Alec Drought – see Q/328–95 and T/33. For a related? map, see O/57A.]
12	1872–1906	Box of papers relating to the estate of Major Richard Galbraith of Cappard House, Loughrea, Co. Galway, consisting of the lands of Cappard, Doonally, etc, and of property near Gort as well as Loughrea. The papers principally consist of a rent receipt book, 1872–86, a ledger, 1898–1903, and letting agreements, 1898–1906.
13	1863–78	Box of original bundles of vouchers, together with a couple of leases, relating to the affairs of Colonel Simpson Hackett of Moore Park, Birr, including labour accounts for turf- cutting on Clonkelly Bog. These papers have been preserved, not because Colonel Hackett was a significant landowner (which he was not), but because they may be of interest as throwing light on the life-style and level of affluence of a gentleman residing in a provincial Irish town.
14	1907–47	Ledger relating to the estate of Edward Hanks in and around Birr.
15	1892: 1895	Two case papers relating to the estate of the Head family at Derrylahen, King's County.
16	c. 1900–1910	Tenants' account book and Irish Land Commission papers relating to the estate of A. H. N. Kemmis of Croydon, Surrey, at Loughaun, Doory, Coolnahely, etc, King's County. [See also O/59.]
17	1891: 1911: 1926–50	Box of collectors' books, account books, correspondence, printed matter, etc, all relating to the King's County Protestant Orphan Society, and apparently deriving, not from Toler R. Garvey Junior, but from the clerk in the Birr Estate Office, T. F. Ovington, who was Hon. Secretary to the Society.
18–19	1860–82	Two boxes of rentals, accounts and vouchers kept by George Garvey as agent for the estate of Bassett W. Holmes at Moneygall, King's County (with a rental of c. £925 in 1870), and Nenagh, Co. Tipperary (c. £1540), including a few leases of those estates. The rentals and accounts run from 1860 to 1879, and the vouchers from 1865 to 1882 (with gaps).

V/20	1920–31	Envelope containing a power of attorney to Toler R. Garvey Junior and 2 bank books, all relating to the estate of the King family of Ballylin, Ferbane, King's County.
21	1908–9: 1916	Envelope containing a 'Waste book', 1908–9, and a deed of receivership, 1916, both relating to the estate of Colonel Randolph A. F. Kingscote of Newport, Co. Tipperary [see Q/389], at Drumbawn, Farneigh, etc, barony of Owney and Arra, Co. Tipperary.
22	1885–1920	Envelope of letting agreements and other estate papers relating to the property of Colonel and Mrs Blanche F. Lodwick [see Q/389] at Lisheen [not the King's County Lisheen, near Birr], Middlewalk, etc, Co. Tipperary.
23	1866–78	Bundles of vouchers deriving from George Garvey's agency for Robert J. E. Mooney of The Doon, King's County.
24	1854–1922	Box of papers relating to the estate of William J. Pigott of Dundrum, Co. Down (fl. *c.* 1900), at Tincurry, near Cahir, Co. Tipperary, and at Shragh, King's County, including some papers about the Dames Longworth family, who (as well as being landlords in their right) were tenants of Shragh. [N.B. Pigott really did live at Dundrum, *Co. Down*, not Dundrum, Co. Tipperary. See also Q/392.]
25	1872: 1897–1940	Ledger, 1897–1940, and letting agreements, 1872 and 1897–1903, relating to the estate of John Purser of Queen's College, Belfast (the owner in the late 19th century) at Arborhill and Clonmona, Co. Tipperary.
26	1870	Three tenants' proposals to the Hon. Otway Toler, second son of the 2nd Earl of Norbury in respect of Acanthue, Nenagh, etc, Co. Tipperary. These papers are of interest, in the context of the Birr Castle archive, as a reminder that it was through the Toler family that the Garveys came to be employed as Rosse agents, the connection being that Otway Toler's sister married the Hon. Laurence Parsons, third son of the 2nd Earl of Rosse. George Garvey's father had been agent for Lord Norbury, and had been murdered in that capacity at the Norbury seat, Durrow Abbey, King's County, in 1838. The Christian name, Toler, which two generations of the Garvey family bore, derived (obviously) from the Norburys.
27	1858–1940	Box and outsize volume consisting of miscellaneous agency papers of the Garveys: Thornvale [ie Tullanisky Park – see Q/56] workmen's and labourers' accounts, 1870–78; miscellaneous bank books, 1858–1940; agents' fee book, 1909–40; ledger, 1906–19; etc, etc.

[One other major estate for which the Garveys were agents was that of Trinity College, Dublin, at Ballycahill (Templemore), Co. Tipperary, Rathcoursey, Queen's County, and elsewhere. Papers deriving from this agency have been transferred, as they have come to light (1976 and 1987) to the Manuscripts Department, TCD, where they bear reference MUN V/82/27, MUN P/23/1852–99, MUN P/26/159–62, etc, etc.]

W/	DATE	DESCRIPTION
1–36	1955–2005	Letters and papers of the 7th Earl of Rosse and his wife, Alison.

W/1–8 PERSONAL AND BUSINESS PAPERS

1	1951–2000	Box of deeds, correspondence and other papers about family settlements, trusts, estate companies, etc, with much duplication of deeds. Almost everything relates to the post-1979 period, following the succession of the 7th Earl.
2	1957–8	File of letters and papers about Lord Oxmantown's coming-of-age and the associated celebrations.
3	1955: 1961	University degrees (Grenoble and Oxford) of Lord Oxmantown, subsequently 7th Earl of Rosse.
4	1961–2001	Fat envelope of letters and papers of the 7th Earl as an underwriting member of Lloyds of London, from which he extricated himself in 2001. The papers also relate to his life insurance policies which, originally intended to provide him with an income during his father's lifetime and pay school fees, were later used to cover Lloyds losses.
5	1963: 1966	Very small bundle of correspondence about Lord Oxmantown's marriage to Alison Cooke-Hurle.
6	c. 1985–6: 1991	Envelope of papers, mostly of earlier date, assembled by Alison Countess of Rosse, and relating to her own (Cooke-Hurle) family, formerly of Kilve Court, Somerset and now of Startforth Hall, Barnard's Castle, and to other branches of it, including the Scottish and Irish Forbeses.
7	1998–2004	The same in relation to the history of the Parsons and related families. The most significant component of this sub-section are papers of 1998 about the 7th Earl's baronetcy and subsequent correspondence with the Standing Council of the Baronetage about meetings and events. [The papers about the baronetcy are currently missing.]
8	1991–4	Correspondence of the 7th Earl with Manorial Auctioneers Partnership, London, and others about the sale of his baronies of Clonlisk, Eglish and Garrycastle, Co. Offaly; together with later correspondence with Frank O'Donnell, and a draft of O'Donnell's book entitled 'L'Esprit de titre' which is about the preservation of what the author calls intangible cultural heritage, of which territorial baronies are one example.

[A considerable quantity of personal correspondence of the 7th Earl, c. 1955–91, much of it written to him while he was serving overseas with the UN (see T/171), will be found on two shelves of a cupboard in his office in Birr Castle.]

W/9–14 PAPERS ABOUT OVERSEAS DEVELOPMENT AND IRISH PUBLIC LIFE

9	1963–2005	File of typescript, printed and newspaper articles by Lord Oxmantown on subjects which include: the Dublin Hellfire Club (with correspondence up to 2005 about a film on the Hellfire Club made by David Ryan); letters in the archive about the '98; the design and decimalization of coinage; Afghanistan; and the UN programmes in the various countries in which Lord Oxmantown served. [See also W/34.]
10	1963: 1968	Newspaper articles by Lord Oxmantown on 'Our Modern Coinage', etc, and copies of letters and a memo from him to the Irish Minister of Finance about the design of the decimal currency to be introduced into Ireland.
11	1980–89	File of papers of the 7th Earl about 'Concern', an overseasdevelopment programme of the Irish government, including a copy of his government-commissioned 'Evaluation of Concern's Sudan Programme, March-April 1989'.
12	1981–90	Letters and papers of the 7th Earl as a nominee of the Irish government on the Agency for Personal Service Overseas.
13	1985–8	Half-box of similar papers of the 7th Earl as a nominee of the Irish government on the Advisory Council on Development Co-operation.
14	1989–2005	Formal documents and correspondence relating to the honours conferred on the 7th Earl, including his Hon. LL.D. at TCD, 2005.

W/15–22 PAPERS ABOUT BIRR CASTLE AND EXHIBITIONS AND OTHER EVENTS HELD THERE OR DERIVING FROM ITS HERITAGE CONTENTS

15	1980–91	Folder of letters and papers of the 7th Earl as a Board Member of the Historic Irish Tourist Houses and Gardens Association ('HITHA'.)
16	1981–5	Fat envelope of letters, newspaper cuttings and other papers about the Irish Driving Championships, held annually at Birr Castle from 1981. [N.B. Papers from 1985 to *c.* 2005 exist, but have yet to be added to this bundle.]
17	1981–2005	Series of files and envelopes relating to the annual exhibitions at Birr Castle, as follows:
17/1	1981–2	File of correspondence and printed matter about the 1981/2 exhibition, 'The Scientific Achievements of Sir Charles Parsons' [see Section R].
17/2	1982–3	Two files of correspondence and printed matter about the 1983 exhibition, 'Speaking from the Past'.

W/17/3	1983–4: 1988: 1994	Three files of similar papers about the 1984 exhibition, 'The Making of the Gardens', together with a file of papers on the re-staging of the same exhibition in 1994.
17/4	1983–6	Two large envelopes of letters, papers and newspaper cuttings about the 1985 exhibition, 'Impressions of an Irish Countess … Mary Rosse, 1813–1885' and its subsequent moves to other locations in Ireland, the UK, Germany, etc. [For other papers concerning Mary Rosse, see E/39, G/14, 16, 19 and 62, O/30, O/41–4 and P.]
17/5	1983–6	Envelope of letters and papers about the 1986 exhibition, 'Out of the Cupboard: the Things they Wore'.
17/6	1987–9	Envelope of letters and papers about the 1987 exhibition, 'At Work and at Play: Three Centuries of Childhood', which was subsequently set up again in Atlanta, Georgia, in 1988.
17/7	1987–9: 2003	Envelope of letters and papers about the 1988 exhibition, 'The Wonderful World of Mary Ward,' and subsequent correspondence and articles about Mary Ward. [See also K/40.]
17/8	1989–91	Envelope of correspondence and printed matter about the 1991 exhibition, 'William and Mary: Kings County Cousins'.
17/9	1990–1	Envelope of correspondence and printed matter about an additional 1991 exhibition, 'Seeing Stars'.
17/10	1991–2	Envelope of letters and papers about the 1992 exhibition, 'Irish Tri-Colour, Colour Photography—A Dublin Discovery'.
17/11	1991–2	Envelope of letters and papers about the 1992 Easter exhibition, 'Let There Be Light.'
17/12	1993	Envelope of letters and papers about the 1993 exhibition, 'Sugar and Spice: Castle Cooking Down the Ages,' together with photographs of the display.
17/13	1994–2000: 2005	Envelope of letters and papers about the 1995 exhibition, 'Dressed for the Occasion,' together with two files of correspondence on similar fashion exhibitions staged at the Ulster Museum in Belfast. The two Ulster exhibitions, 'Irish Fashion since 1950' and 'Genius of Line' opened in 1994 and 1999 respectively, and displayed gowns on loan from Birr Castle.
17/14	1996	Correspondence on the 1996 exhibition, 'Demesne of Discovery.'
		[The files on subsequent exhibitions have still to be transferred to the Muniment Room.]
18	1985–90	Envelope of correspondence about proposed (but so far unmounted) exhibitions. Most of the papers relate to a proposed exhibition to mark the 150th anniversary of the invention of photography.

W/19/1–3 1980–2004 Three large envelopes of correspondence about visits to Birr Castle made by various cultural, horticultural, historic and scientific groups. Included are invitations relating to the official opening of Oxmantown Hall by President Mary McAleese on her visit to Birr on 29 June 2004.

20 1988–2004 Large folder of letters and papers about concerts held in Birr Castle, either as part of the Festival of Music in Great Irish Houses, or as events specially arranged for Birr Castle by the 7th Earl.

21 1983–90 Envelope of printed and typed matter relating to the 7th Earl and Alison Countess of Rosse and to Birr and Birr Castle.

22 1989 File of papers about the 7th Earl's tour of the USA to lecture on 'Gardens of Ireland'.

W/23–32 **PAPERS ABOUT BIRR CASTLE AND ITS HERITAGE CONTENTS**

23 1970–91 Folder of letters and papers of the 7th Earl and Alison Countess of Rosse about tapestries and other textiles in Birr Castle, their conservation, loan for exhibition, etc.

24 1978–2005 Three folders of letters and papers about pictures at Birr Castle (both sales and purchases). [For one particular picture, Walter Sickert's 'The Gardener's Daughter', see W/29].

25 1980–83 Folder of letters and papers, including a printed catalogue, about the sale of selected heritage contents of Birr Castle in 1980.

26 1980–2005 Folder of letters and papers about books in Birr Castle (both sales and purchases), including the purchase of Dorothy Parsons's 1668 recipe book [A/17.]

27 1980–2005 Folder of letters and papers about Samuel Chearnley's 'Miscelanea Structura Curiosa' [O/3], research into the provenance and creator of the drawings, articles based in whole or in part upon them, and the publication of an edited facsimile of them in 2005.

28 1982–93 Envelope of correspondence of the 7th Earl about the Dowris Hoard, its loan for exhibition to various institutions, etc.

29 1985–2002 Folder of letters and papers about the attempted sale of Sickert's 'The Gardener's Daughter'.

30 1986–9 Folder of letters and papers about 'The Drumsallagh Torc' (dating from the 13th century BC), a Parsons family possession restored to Birr Castle by the 7th Earl.

31 1988–2003 Folder of letters and papers about the restoration of the 1620s plaster frieze in the Muniment Room in Birr Castle.

| W/32 | 2000 | Folder of papers about the Birr Castle roof, principally plans, estimates and a photographic survey by Christopher Southgate & Associates, Cork. |

W/33–36 MISCELLANEOUS

33	1870: 1931: 1955–2005	Folder of letters and papers (including original certificates of ownership dating from 1870) relating to the 7th Earl's box (No. 14) at the Albert Hall, London which Sir Charles Parsons had inherited from the 4th Earl and which the 6th Earl had acquired from Lady Parsons after Sir Charles's death.
34	*c.* 1961–91	Envelope of miscellaneous newspaper and typescript articles by the 7th Earl, with associated correspondence, on subjects as diverse as Birr Castle, Nepal and Russia. [See also W/9.]
35	1994–8	Small envelope of letters and papers about minor cultural and heritage developments in the town of Birr.
36	1997–2001	Folder of letters and papers of the 7th Earl as a director of the Quest Campus Foundation, Charleville Castle, Tullamore, Co. Offaly.

[For other letters and papers of the 7th Earl, see D/7, H/119–121, K/39–40, R/11 and 13–16, S/17 and T/1, 45, 64, 106 and 134. His letters and papers about the Birr Scientific Heritage Foundation and Ireland's Historic Science Museum are held elsewhere at Birr Castle, in the office of the Foundation. Some very current business files of the 7th Earl on other subjects, most of them not intended for transfer to the Muniment Room, are held in his office in Birr Castle. His and Lady Rosse's search correspondence about the archive is filed in a wooden filing-cabinet deriving from the 5th Earl and now placed in the Muniment Room; where the correspondence relates to a particular section of the archive, it has been placed in a folder bearing the alphabetical reference letter for that section – eg 'R' for correspondence about Sir Charles Parsons.]

DETAILED CALENDAR

of

PARTS OF SECTIONS

A–F, J, M, R AND T

A/4

DATE	DESCRIPTION

1612–94:
1912:
1940

Tattered vellum-bound volume covering the period 1612–94, microfilmed by the National Library (n.5483: p.5650), and containing, according to the *Hayes* description: memoranda about Star Chamber procedure, with notes of cases heard *c.* 1612–16; official letters relating to the plantations of Co. Longford and King's County, 1619–26; orders for the preservation of royal rents and revenues in Ireland, 1623, 1623; instructions to officers of the Exchequer as to their duties, 1623; instructions of Sir L. Parsons for his plantation at Birr and for markets in and the government of the town, 1626–7; rentals of the estates of the Parsonses of Parsonstown, mostly in King's County, 1629–94; and medical and kitchen recipes, 1645–52; together with (and not covered by the microfilm) a lease of 1912 and legal papers of 1940 relating to the tolls, fairs and markets of Birr and reciting earlier grants back to the 1620s.*

Some of the contents of this volume are described in the second edition of Cooke's *Picture of Parsonstown*, which was published in 1875 under the title *The Early History of the Town of Birr or Parsonstown ...*, pp. 48–49 and 383–7, as follows:

PAGE	DESCRIPTION

p.38

'... The Order for giving Sir Laurence possession of Birr is dated the 22nd of June 1620; and by the letters patent, dated 26th of the same month, it appears that Birr must have been then looked on as of considerably military importance: for it is there described as the castle and fort village and land of Birr. It was by the same letters patent erected into the manor of Parsonstown; and on the 7th of July following, the High Sheriff, Captain Francis Acland, removed the former proprietors, and put Sir Laurence Parsons into possession, in presence, as his return states, of Hobert Dillon, Teige McDough O'Carroll of Rathmore, Phillip O'Dwiggan, John Dalton, who was Sub-Sheriff, Gregory O'Dullahan, John Maynaghan, Cullogh Fitzpatrick, Richard Evans, William Dalton, John Taylor, and John Forde. In these letters patent are also included the lands of Ballindarragh and Bealaneale, otherwise Cappineale, with several other lands, including the castle, town, and lands of Clonoughill, but excepting the castle and bawn and a portion of the lands of Ballindarragh.

Almost immediately after getting the possession of Birr, Sir Laurence Parsons commenced to build and make other improvements there, at considerable expense. On the 23rd of November 1620, he obtained a grant of a Tuesday-market, and two fairs to be held in Birr on the festivals of St Mark and St Andrew; and afterwards, on the 27th of April 1627, he obtained a grant from the Crown of a Saturday-market and two additional fairs to be held on the 1st

p.39

of February and 15th of August, which two last-mentioned fairs, owing to the change of the style, now fall upon the 11th of February and 25th of August. The other two fairs are now held on the 6th of May and 10th of December. ...

A/4 *contd.*

p.40   Shortly after Sir Laurence had been put into possession of Birr, Teige McCallagh O'Carroll, the representative of the ancient proprietors, petitioned the King, setting forth that Birr belonged to him, and praying to be re-instated. However, this and a second memorial to the same purpose not having produced the wished for effect, he a third time petitioned, referring to his former memorials, and stating tht he was seized of this place, and that it was enjoyed by his ancestors for upwards of one thousand years; and praying that it might be peremptorily referred to the Master of Requests to re-instate him in Birr, which he called his chief seat. Thereupon the King had the petition transmitted on the 16th of July 1622, to Lord Viscount Falkland, then Lord Deputy of Ireland; and it was by him referred to his Majesty's Surveyor General of Lands in Ireland (Sir William Parsons), who, on the 17th of October following, reported thereon, setting forth the title of the Baron of Galtrim, and of the Earl of Ormond, as already mentioned; and he ultimately decided against the pretensions of O'Carroll as unfounded. The Surveyor General also stated in his report, that Sir Laurence Parsons had then built on the premises at a very great expense.

p.41   Whether the claim then made by him was well founded or not, it is in no way strange that this Teige McCallagh O'Carroll did not succeed in his petition against Sir Laurence Parsons, when such success depended upon the report of the Surveyor General, Sir William Parsons, the brother of the person complained against. …

p.46   It appears that so early as 1626 there was a Free School in Birr, and that Sir Laurence Parsons, on his petition, obtained for a while, a grant of 200 acres for the use of the schoolmaster. The petition was a follows:- "To the Right Honorable the Lord Deputy, the humble petition of Sir Laurence Parsons – declaring that when there was allotted upon the divisions of Fercall, 200 acres for a Free-school to be erected in that plantation, which lieth still in His Majesty's gift. The premises considered, and forasmuch as there is a schoolmaster in your petitioner's town of Birr, who teacheth the youth of that country to the great good thereof, your suppliant therefore humbly prays that your Lordship will be pleased to grant him a Custodium of the said land for the use of the said schoolmaster, until such time as your Lordship shall otherwise dispose thereof, and your suppliant shall pray – 8th July 1626." On the foregoing petition, an order, signed by Lord Deputy Falkland and the Council, was made as follows:- "The land allotted for the Free-school in the King's County being yet undisposed of, we are pleased to grant the same unto the petitioner to the use of the Schoolmaster residing at Birr, and the Sheriff of the King's County, is to put him in possession, to continue for and until such time as we shall otherwise

p.47 dispose thereof." The Birr schoolmaster did not long enjoy his 200 acres, however, for in two years afterwards it was granted to Banagher school, to which it still continues attached. It is creditable to modern Birr that a schoolmaster is now by no means such a rara avis there, as the one referred to in the petition of Sir Laurence appears to have been, in 1626.

    From time to time, after getting possession of Birr, Sir Laurence made several curious, and – as some of them would appear at the present time -very arbitrary

A/4 *contd.*   ordinances for the regulation of the town in various ways. Those are the more remarkable as having been made by a Baron of the Court of Exchequer, which Sir Laurence then was. Thus in August 1626, he made an order for the paving and cleaning of the town, "as well beyond the bridge as within the town," which might form a precedent for some modern town councils. In these times all beyond the old bridge was considered to be outside the town.

Again, in December of the same year, he passed an ordinance for the regulation of drinking-houses in Birr, which might also rival modern legislation on the subject; and by it he directed – for reasons not very flattering to the gentler sex -that no single woman should supply drink, on pain of being put in the stocks for three market days; and in 1627, he made a by-law to compel the inhabitants to build chimneys, or in default to be banished from the town. The reader will find some of these curious ordinances (Nos. 5, 6 & 7) in the

p.48   Appendix. Most of the fines were to be applied to the repairs of the Parish Church, and of "the Market Cross;" but it does not now appear where this cross was, or what has become of it. This same year (1627), Sir Laurence, with the assistnce of the Rev. Robert Sheeply, the then Vicar, published regulations for burials in the Church-yard, now the old Church-yard of Birr. It appears by these regulations, dated 4th October 1627, that the Churchwardens were to be paid for burials in the body of the Church, and the money arising therefrom was to be applied towards the repairs of the Church, and other things necessary for it. The sum to be paid for such interment was six shillings and eightpence for a parishioner, and thirteen and fourpence for a stranger; and the burial of a stranger in the Church-yard was to be agreed for with the minister and churchwardens, and the money to be applied to the same use as the former. The burial of parishioners in the Church-yard was free, except the payment of one shilling to the minister, fourpence to the parish clerk, and fourpence to the sexton, who was to make the grave. On the interment of foreigners or strangers, the minister, clerk, and sexton were to be entitled to double fees. ...

p.49   The tolls payable in Birr in 1626 were as follows: a horse, threepence; a cow, threepence, twopence of which went to the book-keeper; a pig, one penny; a sheep, one halfpenny, and if ten sold to pay one penny, and if twenty, twopence; woollen cloth, every piece of, containing twenty yards, one half-penny; bag of brogues, one penny; every hide above three years old, one penny; ditto under, one halfpenny; every seven pounds of butter, one farthing.

p.383   **APPENDIX**

NAMES OF THE "UNDERTAKERS" WHO OBTAINED GRANTS OF LAND, IN 1619, ON THE "PLANTATION" OF ELY O'CARROLL, AND THE COUNTY OF LONGFORD; WITH THE QUANTITY ALLOTTED TO EACH.

Sir Thomas Button; Sir Wm. Sinclair, of Rosling; Sir James Younge; Mr Laurence Parsons; James Gibb, of Carrybor; and Charles Dutton, son of Sir Thomas Dutton; one thousand acres each.

A/4 *contd.*   Robert Gordon, son of Sir Robert Gordon; Captain Arthur Blundell; John
Knock [*sic* – Knox], Lord of Ranferly [*sic* – Ranfurly]; Walter Leckye; Captain
Henry Stradford; Robert Glendoning; George Blundell, the younger; William
Drummond of Rathorden; and Captain Arthur Forbes; six hundred acres each.

William Carr; Robert Lindsay, son to Bernard Lindsay; James Irwing, son to Sir
William Irwing; Lieut. Nicholas Fitton; John Beere, "our late servant's son;"
Lieut. Clarke; James Alexander; William Alexander; Henry Stanes; Edmond
Medhopp; – Conrey, of Kelwood; and Daniel Gookinge; five hundred acres each.

Captain John Pikeman; Lieut. William Hamden; Claude Hamilton; Thomas
Dalzell; Lieut. Henry Fisher; Lieut. Brent Moore; and James Forrett; four
hundred acres each.

Francis Edgeworth; Patrick Hannal; Nynian Herune; James Phelp; "Sergeant"
Hodges; and Joseph Rodgers; three hundred acres each.

p.384   Ensign Thomas Prescott; Robert Hannae; William Ferror; William Lermouth;
James Lermouth; Thomas Deepupp; John Marsh; Bryan M'Connel, "footman to
out son;" and Henty Piers, "soldier;" two hundred acres each.

p.385   No. 5.

ORDINANCE BY SIR LAURENCE PARSONS, FOR THE PAVING AND CLEANING OF BIRR, IN THE YEAR 1626.

"Since I am at great charges in digginge and bringinge of stones, wch I intend to
have layed in the middest of the streete onely to serve for comon passage,
Therefore it is the least that the inhabitants can doe to pave xii foote broade a
well before theire houses as alsoe so longe and as farr as theire houses yards
gardens or plotts doe reach and touch upon the streete, still carryinge the
pavemt. twelve foote broade. This to bee done at the tennts charge both for
stones gravell and workmanshipp. But the prent under-tennte is to beare the
charge thereof soe farr as his pte of the plott extends (if he bee able) by the
judgment of the steward and constable, otherwise the chief tennte of the plott is
to beare the whole charge and such chief tennte is to pave the wast land of his
plott howsoever; This worke to bee done by Whitsuntide next at the farthest as
well beyond the bridge as whin the towne, and whosoever shall make default of
his pte herein, shall be psented in the Court leete for the same and shall have a
heavye amciamt imposed upon him to bee leavyed of his goods by way of distres,
and to bee imployed for the publige good of the towne according the discretion
of the constables and church-wardens; And if any take the stones provided by
mee for the middle of the streete the constable or any of the surveyors may take
his distresse for xiid. ster. for evy such default, to bee imployed to the publique
use of the towne: And if any pson cast any dunge rubbidge filth or sweepings
into the forestreete and doe not cleanse the same and carry it cleane away evy
Saturday, then the constable may distreyne every pson soe makinge default and
leavy foure pence ster. upon him for evy such default and double the same
weekly till the same bee cleansed. "Aug. 1626."

A/4 *contd.*

No. 6.

ORDINANCE FOR THE REGULATION OF DRINKING HOUSES, ETC., IN BIRR, IN THE YEAR 1626.

After reciting the evils caused by having young women to "draw ale and beare" in Birr, this ordinance directs as follows:

"Therefore I doe ordayne that henceforwards noe single woman other than hired servants for meate drinke and wages or clothes shall draw any ale or beare, or keepe vittling in this towne, uppon payne to bee sett in the stocks by the constable for 3 whole m'kett dayes, one after another, and those wch retaine suche in their houses to paie xxd. str. for each default, to bee levyed by the constable and Serjant Lewis Jones for repayring the church and bridg of this towne, and they are allso to banishe anny single woman out this towne that nowe or hereafter shalbe found wth childe (first setting such in stocks for xij houres for the terror and example of others). And if any tennte in this towne
p. 387   shall hereafter receive any inmate or undertennte wthout the allowance of the constable or of my steward who are therein to take the advice of M'Calloughe FitzPatricke or Robt. Tewe, or Robt. Sweetman, or Phillipp Tradye, such receiver shall forfett xxd. ster. for each default to bee levyed and imployed as aforesaid. "Laur. Parsons. "xvij Decembris 1626."

No. 7.

ORDINANCE FOR THE ERECTION OF CHIMNEYS IN BIRR, IN THE YEAR 1627.

"A Byelawe for dwelling houses in Birr without chimneys.

"Ffor as much as it is seene by fearefull experience that many townes and villages have binn consumed by fire in divers pts of this realme and especially occasioned thorowe fires made without chimneys; Therefore I doe ordeyne that if any tennte or under-tennte in my towne of Birr shall after Alhallowtide next kepe any fire whatsoevr eyther in dwellinge house or smithes forge or otherwise without having a stone chimney (if they bee tyed thereto by the tenor of theire leases[)], or els a forrest chimney wherein to make theire fires. And whosoevr makes default herein shall bee banished from the towne whereof they are to take this notice and forewarninge at their pills. "7 Augusti 1627.""

A/5

DATE   DESCRIPTION

1617–94   Folio volume similar to A/1 and described in other sub-sections of A as 'Mss 1',
           containing 94 very miscellaneous documents. This volume has been microfilmed
           by the National Library (n.527: p.795), and is described in *Hayes* as 'A volume
           (marked vol. ii [*sic* – i] of papers relating to the Parsons family of Birr, dealing
           with private and public affairs, covering the period 1617–1692 [*sic*], ... but
           mostly dated 1640–49'. In the appendix to the *First Report of the Royal
           Commission on Historical Manuscripts* (London, 1870), p.127, it is described (by
           Sir John Gilbert) as 'A volume in large folio containing about 90 original letters
           and documents connected with the affairs of Ireland from 1626 [*sic*] to 1694,
           and having special reference to the transactions in the King's County and its
           vicinage'. In the appendix to the *Second Report* of the H.M.C. (London, 1874),
           pp 217–23, a full description is given:

PAGE   DESCRIPTION

p.217   'COLLECTION OF THE EARL OF ROSSE, BIRR CASTLE,
           PARSONSTOWN. [SECOND REPORT.]

           The documents referred to in my first report* on this collection, as comprised in
           the volume there designated No. 2, include many unique papers elucidating
           affairs from 1641 to 1690. Amongst them are letters from some of the Irish
           leaders of 1641; memoranda of daily transactions of Captain William Parsons in
           London, 1644–5; one of the rare original debentures under the Act of
           Settlement, 1663; papers connected with the surrenders of Birr Castle in 1642
           and 1688, and with the trial, condemnation, and respite of Sir Lawrence Parsons
           under the government of James II.

           The contents of the volume are as follow, in order of date:-

           1610, May 15. Order of James I. to Deputy and Chancellor of Ireland, to
           confirm grants to Sir Richard Hardinge in Ireland.

           1611. King's letter to Sir Arthur Chichester, directing grant to John Wakeman of
           Mary's Abbey near Dublin.

           1620. Agreement between Richard Roche Fitz David and Sir Lawrence Parsons,
           for lands of Shinanagh in county of Cork.

           1625, October 23. Acquittance from Ri. Smith & John Knollis to Laurence
           Parsons, for eighty-four pounds English for the redemption of two plowlands in
           White's Island, which Captain Tent lately sold. 23 October 1625.

           1626, July 3. – Dublin. Order by Lord Deputy Falkland and Council on
           platation of barony of Eglish in the King's county, and assignment there of lands
           to John MacFarroll, as a native.

           1636, January 14. Indenture between Lady Anne Parsons of Parsonstown, alias
           Birr, and Donogh O'Kenedy of Tirreglasse, in the county Tipperary, and

---

*   See *First Report of Royal Commission on Historical MSS.*, 1870, p.127.

A/5 *contd.*   Edmond O'Kenedy of Portlaghan, in said county, his son and heir, with respect to town and land of Lackenboy in Lower Ormond.

1636, April 4. – Dublin. Order on composition between William Parsons and Commissioners, on defective titles. Signed by Adam Cusacke and James Ware.

1636. Order to William Parsons for Birr and other lands in the King's county. Signed Ri. Bolton, dated Trinity term, 1636.

1636. Certificate signed Ri. Bolton, with respect to lands of Ballindowne and Ballywilliam in the teritory of Fercall.

1636. Chancery order to William Parsons, for Newtown and other land sin King's county.

1638. A schedule of the lands and hereditaments for which William Parsons, Esq., compounded with Commissioners for remedying of defective titles, with order thereon, and autographs of Wentworth, Adam Loftus, Gerrard Lowther, Ri. Bolton, Christopher Wandesforde, Rob. Meredith, James Ware, and Adam Cusak. Dublin Castle, 15 June 1638.

1639, November 13. – Dublin. Order by Lords Justices and Council to Captain William Beisly and William Parsons, for the searching of the house of John O'Carrol of Clounlish.

1639, December 16. Examination of Hugh Gilhane, Mr. John O'Carrol's footman.

1640, March 25. Acquittance from Donnell MacCahirr O'Molloy to the Lady Anne Parsons, for one hundred pounds in redemption of mortgage by Arthur Coghlan.

1641, July 12. Statement of payment of the second subsidy of the four entire subsidies within the King's county.

1641, November 12 – Dublin. Commission from the Lords Justices and Council to William Parsons, for raising footmen and forstmen within the country of Ely O'Carroll, giving him the command in chief of all the said forces.

p.218   1641. Letter addressed "For William Parsons, Esquire, "at Birre – These be delivered":-

"Mr. Parsons,

"I intercepted yor lettere before it came to my Colonell's hands, wch when I perused I beganne to be jealous for your partiality, offeringe yor protection to the head and excludeinge ye members from the winge of yor mercy. You write to my Colonell forthwth to repare unto you and to helpe you in suppressing those that have offended his Matie, but who are the offendors, the English or Irish? I say wthout any partiall regard of either nation that they are partely of the Irish and for ye most parte ye English officers and governors who, contrary to his Maties gratious intention, opposed ye poore subjects, wch bred a greate scandall to the King's dignity and crowne. If you ioyne wth them Mr Parsons wee cannot in conscience ioyne in an unlawfull matter wth you or wth any body of yt

A/5 *contd.* faction or any faction els'. Contrarywise, if you be a true subjecte or if God (that I may use yor owne words) hath yett some share in yor recanteinge yor former life wch yoll have lived this 3 moneths last past. I promise you in my Colonells name his Maties protection promising you have faithfully my best endeavors for the preservation of yor self, yor wife, children, and yor good mother, whom wee held hitherto to be goode neighbors with all assureinge you that the good opinion wch wee conceaved of you and yr mother was ye onely cause yt wee behaved ourselves so mild and tender hearted towards you, wch thinge yor brother-in-law [Chidley Coote] will try by experience to be true if hee be too forwarde, especially against ye poorer sorte, whom as I am informed he hangs and kills wthout remorse of conscience, wch is no signe of manhoode or civill Christianity. If you be pleased therefore to accept of this motion you shall have it to the more security of your life, wch is exposed to farre greater dangers at the castle of Birre then where wee are, or if you bee pleased to convey yorselfe elsewhere you shall have our free passe, otherwise if you iogne with Coote be not offended wth us if wee doe our best against you all for or owne safety, if you come you shall understande yt first of all you are to subscribe to our oath of allegiance consistinge in 4 points; ffirst, yt you will endeavour to maintaine the King's prerogative; secondly, to finde a redress for ye abuse done to ye Queene; thirdly, to use all meanes in oppressinge ye oppressors of ye common wealle; ffourthly and lastly, to assist yc Catholicke army against the puritants, and thus much for yt.

"As for my Colonell's heade wch you write in yo lre yt it will not stick longe to his shoulders, you may peradventure say it not out of yor owne mynd but by ye perswasion of others who by pollicie of state use all meanes to encurrage you promiseinge what will never be performed and blindeinge others to keep theme in theire confederacy untill at length they feele the smarte, but suppose an army come out of Englande to succour you wee are stronge enogh God be thanked against you all if you bee not too many, for wee have in Irelande 100,000 men in armes and God as or guide wch is the chiefest thinge, but that I may returne to my Colonell's head, I will doe this if you please, I will picke out 60 men and fight against 100 of yor choise men if yoll doe but pitch yor campe one mile out of yor towne, and then if you have ye victory you may threaten my Colonell, otherwise doe not reckon ye chickens before they be hatched. Thus I wrote to you out of a certaine affection I bore you presenteinge wth all my keinde offer unto you, desireinge you if you be wise to take hold of it. And so concludeth, expecteing yor answere.

"Your friend if you will,
"PHELEM MOLLOY."

Eglish, dated at the Catholique Campe ye 17th of March 1641.

1642, April 1 – Dublin. Order by Lords Justices and Council for twenty-five horse for Captain William Parsons and one hundred foot for Captain Chidley Coote, for keeping of the castle of Parsonstown and defence of said town and country thereabouts.

A/5 *contd.*   1642. Letter addressed "To my respected (contd) friend Mr. "William Parsons at Parsonstown – These present:-

"Mr. Parsons,

"I have receaved yor letters whereof I understood that you are desirous to know my minde. My minde is always goode towards those that deserves it; as for shootinge to yor moors I gave no direction till poore men this side were shooted by you contrarie to your aleadged order. As for peace, whereof you speake, wee love it to with all our hearts, knowinge it to be the end of warres. You wrote to Colonell Richard Butler, as I heare, that you was desirousto comme and speake to him privately; if yor meaneing was to knowe the generall's resolution in giveinge of quarters and due convoyance or anie other termes or condicions of yeldinge I knowe and am acquainted with both generalls in Linster and Mounster, and Generall Moore is in the borders of Ely about this tyme, and if you please I would be a means to bringe you and him to some agreemt, as for hindringe yor markett itt is not my dooinges, but the general consent of the armies, wch I cannot forgoe without further direction from my superiors; as for sheddinge of blood, specially of poore sillie people, women, and children, wee hate it to our verie hearts, and as you were the first soe wee wish you to be the last actors of such inhumanitie if they be not occasioners themselves; as for not killinge of men when they cann be taken prisoners, I see no reason to the contrarie, though by experience I know wee are thought [*sic*] from you contrary to the lawes of armes all in nations; and Mr. Parsons, indeede I wish you well, and would you had beene better advised both for your owne and the countryes welfare wherein you may conceave how truely I am desirous of yor welfare though unacquainted; as for the provision you speake of I cann doe nothing of meselfe without special direction from my generall wherein (if yoll please) I will be solicitous in yor behalfe. As for newes I believe that you have heard of the arrivall of Owen Roe O'Neill in the north wth Spanish assistance, and Collonell Preston att Wexford wth 7 shippes loaden with armes and amunition, Towmgranie was battred by the artillerie of Limricke last Thursday, and the rest of the English in Tuomond are to be served if not alreddie in the same kind. Thus in hast I rest from our garrison, 28th of July 1642.

"Yours if you please as above,
'FARELL O'KENNEDY."

1642. Letter addressed "To my much honored and "highly esteemed the Lady Ann Parsons – these be "presented":-

"Much honored Lady,

'I receaved yor letter wch might easily move me to doe yor ladyship any lawfull service or courtisy wch I have allwayes coveted to do unto all such of yor condicion, vertue and worth; and muche the rather for that I find all the gentry and neighbours of these parts to much honor, esteeme, and love you, and in that degree, that one would thinke you are of their blood* and flesh, and there detained against their wills+ ... to their great greefe. Butt, good madam, it pleased God by his will or sufferaunce that this great alteration and sepperacion of many freinds should happen, wch hath reduced us to that condicion that

---

*   She was daughter of Sir George Shirley, Chief Justice of King's Bench in Ireland.
+   Obliterations denoted thus. ...

A/5 *contd.* those who weare a little while since loveing freinds, are now bourneing, killing, and destroyeing one another. And for yor parte, yett are you the support and maintayner of that place, and those that are wth you being known, as I heare, to be malitious, will take any thing you have to help their designes, as they have used those horses you writt off, and by liklyhood would doe againe, soe that, if I should gett them restored, I should arme or help my enemy against my selfe, in wch case (if you weare a judge yor selfe) you would condemne me as ... any. But if I weare assured noe such use should be made of them, I hould butt a poore courtisy and nothing to what I should find my selfe willing to doe yor ... same way. I would write a little more that might rather tend to yor good then otherwise, butt that I will not imitate some who stuffe their letteres bragging, flawnting, and invent ... newes, butt onely I wish with all my hart that yor ladyship weare out of ye danger that some think you are in, for I heare you wish well to all honest people. And soe I take leave & remaine yor ladyship's friend and servant in what I may.

"RO: MOORE."

Dated the 5th of 7ber 1642.

Endorsed "The 5th of September 1642. From O'Moore "to my mother about her coach horses."

1642. September 9. Order by the Council of War respecting the taking away of horses belonging to the troops and carriages of his Majesty's army under divers pretexts. Signed John Borlase, George Kildare, Ch. Lambart, Fra. Willoughby. - Copy certified by Maurice Pue.

1642. October 29. Receipt of Chidley Coote, J. Williams, and Simon Tench, for money received from William Parsons, Commander-in-Chief of Eli O'Caroll, **p.219** and borders thereof.

1642. "A note of what moneys hath beene laid out by me, William Parsons, to the souldiers under the comand of Capt. Carroll, and of other moneys layd out for the use of the garrisons lying at Parsonstowne alias Byre, Ballyndarrow, and Cloynakill, from the 26th of November 1641 untill ye 20th of January 1642."

1642. Surrender of Birr Castle* to the Irish: "Articles of agreement made and concluded upon, by, and betwixt the Right Hoble the Lord Generall of Leinster of the one parte and William Parsons, Governour of Birr, of the other parte, dated this 20th of January 1642.

"1. In primis, it is agreed upon that the said governour is to have six horses armed, besides his officers to attend himselfe, and all his horsse with their saddles and swordes.

---

* "He [Preston] came before it [Birr Castle] on Jan. 13, viewed the ground, raised a battery, and tried to undermine the place. At last on the 18th, being instructed by a mason who had been employed in the building of the castle they hit upon the right ground, a green clayish bank on the west side of the castle. The mouth of the mine was not above four yards distant from the very foundation of the walls. The garrion hearing the sap, fired some shot and rolled great stones down the bank upon the enemy; but by break of day they were got under the ground and out of all danger ... . They beat a parley on the 19th and capitulated to march out the next day." *Life of James, Duke of Ormonde*, by T. Carte, ii, 384, Oxford, 1851.

A/5 *contd.* "2. Item, six of his owne muskets to be put into my Lord Conwayes land, and at his departure from the convoy to be surrendered unto him.

"3. Item, the said governour is to have the one halfe of his owne and his mother's mony and plate to be left with them, and the one halfe of his brother Cootes mony and plate to be left to himselfe, and soe all men and women in the house to have the one halfe of their monyes and plate to themselves, and the ladies and the governour and his wife and captaine and his wife havinge their owne halfe wayed out to them to pass with it unsearched, and if any other person that hath his halfe allotted to him shall be found with any more, he shall loose the benefitt of his quarter.

"4. It is agreed that the liutenant of his horsse and captaine Coots ensigne of the foote shalbe left with the Lord Generall as pledges, and that they shall all have a safe conway with Sir Robert Talbott and som horss and foote to Maryborough, and from thence 2 pledges shall goe with them to the Naase, to witt, Captain Oliver Darcy and Liutenant James Malone, whoe are to be safely conveyed from the Naase to Ballysonan, and then their 2 pledges are to be safely sent to the Naase.

"5. Item, it is agreed that the governour and all the rest of the people shall have all their horsses to their owne use, and the generall will issue his warrants to the contry for the furnishings of the governour with 20 housses more to ayde them in their cariadges.

Item, it is agreed that the Lady Phillips and the Lady Parsons* shall have to each of them 2 paire of sheetes, and the governour's lady and Captaine Cootes lady shall have each of them 2 paire of sheetes, and the governour's children 2 paire of sheetes, and to each paire of sheetes a paire of pillowbeers, and all theire clothes of lynen and wollen with their truncks and chests to carry them in, and two fether bedds for his children, and the redd bedd that is laced with willow collour lace, with its furniture, that the soulddiers and all other of their people shall carry away [with] them all their wearinge apparrell both lynen and wollen and their swords by their sides.

"Item, I the said Lord Generall doe bynd my selfe to the true and honorable performance of all theis articles, and the governour is to give up the armes this night, savinge those that the governour is to have by vertue of his former articles, and to morrow morninge the governour is to deliver up the keies of the gates toe his Majesty's use to his lordshipp as he marcheth out of the gate having taken out with him such things as are contayned in the former articles, and noe comon soulddiers shall dare to com within the doores to frighten the ladies untill they and the carriadges be gon out.

"Item, it is agreed that the governour and every other man shall have free liberty to carry away with them all their writtings, evidence, bookes, papers, and manuscripts that they have.

"Item, it is agreed that the governour and all others shall have free liberty to carry with them such provision of meate and drinks as shall serve them in the journey.

---

* Dorothy, wife of Sir William Parsons, was daughter of Sir Thomas Philips, of Limavady, county of Derry. Her sister, Alice Philips, married Chidley Coote.

A/5 *contd.* Item, it is agreed tht Sir Robert Talbott shall see the devision of the plate and mony and the rest of the things contained in the articles, and that noe souldier nor other person shall dare to goe into the governour's howse this night upon paine of being shott.

"Item, it is agreed that the governour shll freely have 2 draught of oxen to draw his cariadges, and his coatch and horsses with their ladies shall goe freely unfrightened and unsearched. Given at the campe this 20th of January 1642.

T. PRESTON."

"I doe heerby promise my Lord Generall to use all my best endeavours that I can to the Lords Justices and Councell that they will discharge the bodies of Nicholas Ogann [Wogan] of Rathcoffy and Katherin Preston, his wife, with her sister a relegeous wooman, the hopes of which inlargement have incouradged his lordship to give me soe faire and honorable quarter. Given at the campe this 20th of Janu. 1642.

WILLIAM PARSONS."*

"Forasmuch as Captayne Oliver Darsy by reaon of indisposition in his body beinge not able to travill, being formerly appointed one of the pledges for the safe conveying of the governour to the Naase, I am most willing to accept of Captayne Dardis as a pledge in his place. Witnesse my hand, Willi. Parsons."

Copy of preceding paper, but with omissions of the two appended articles, and ending as follows:- "This is a true coppie of the original which remained with Mr. William Parsons, examined this xiijth of December 1652. Gilles Phillips, Matthew Lock, Jos. Paine, Dorothy Parsons." Endorsed: "The articles that my brother Parsons made with Preston at the Burr."

[1642.] "By the Lords Justices and "Councell.

"Wm Parsons. Jo Borlasse.

"Whereas Captaine Wm Parsons with thirty-five horsemen under his comand, and Captaine Chidley Coote with one hundred ffoote under his command (both raised and armed by the said Parsons and Coote) have since the beginning of this rebellion maintained the Castle of Byre in the King's county against the rebbells, though often besedged by armyes of them, and preserved therein the lives of many hundreds of his Majesties good Subjects, British and Protestants, who had bin otherwise destroyed by the rebbells, and by that strength of horse and foote did kill and destroy many of the rebbells, and so continued preserving that place and his Majesties good subjects there untill the 20th of January last, at which time (being noe longer able to hold out against a powerful army of the rebbells that then besedged them and undermined the said castle) they after seaven dayes seege were constrayned to give it up to the rebbells on quarter, and brought the said horse troope and ffoote company, or most of them, with them hither to Dublin to serve his Majesty here as they should be appointed. And whereas the said Capt. Wm Parsons having direction from this board for maynetayninge the forces there, did in his zeale to the publique services, and in confidence to be repayed by his Majesty pay the said thirty-five horse and one hundred ffoote besides theire officers (the captaines meanes excepted in parte) from the 20th of

---

* Carte does not mention this article in his enumeration of the terms of capitulation referred to above.

A/5 *contd.*   November 1641 to the said 20th of January 1642 out of his owne purse to his exceeding great charge. And albeit those 35 horse and one hundred ffoot were soe maintained by him and employed in continuall service as aforesaid, yet by reason of the great distance between this place and that, and the multitude of rebbells which were continualy in the way, hindring accesse from hence thither there could be no commission sent him for putting the said horse or ffoote in pay. And fforasmuch as it is not fitt that soe great a burthen and charge concerning the publique service should be layd on the said Captaine William Parsons, who hath already lost his estate to a great value by this rebellion, and is now reduced to very great extreamity and want, as is also the said Capt. Coote who hath in like manner lost all his estate of good value by this rebellion, and for that he and the said Captaine Coote have for the publique service since this rebellion began often hazarded theire owne persons and (for their services) merited well from his Majesty and this state. Wee therefore thinke fitt and so doe order that our very good Lord the Lord Marques of Ormond, Lievtenant-Generall of the army doe issue several commissions to the said several persons (vizt.) to the said Capt. William Parsons to be captaine of the said horse troope of thirty-five, besides these officers (vizt.) Phelix Wilson as Leivtenant, Thomas Proctor as cornett, John Hodgson as quartermaster, and Anthony Stockdale as corporall and a trumphetter, which persons have hitherto discharged the dutyes of

p.220   those places and endured besieging severall times in the said castle. And the said Capt. Chidley Coote to be captaine of the saide ffoote company of one hundred besides usuall officers. And that the said Lord Marques doe give warrant that the said severall captains, officers, and souldiers, as well horse as ffoote be lysted in his Majesties army, for and from the said 20th of November 1641 at the like entertainments and pay as other such captaines, officers, horse troopes, and foote companyes in his Majesties pay in this kingdome are and shall be allowed. And that soe much of the pay of the said ffoote company as hath beene already disbursed by the saide Captaine Parsons be repayed to him. Given at his Majesties Castle of Dublin xvi February 1642.

	Ormond.
"La[ncelot Archbishop of] Dublin.	Adam Loftus.
Cha. Lambart.	Edw. Brabazon.
Gerrard Lowther.	Tho. Temple.
Fra. Willoughby.	Tho. Lucas.
	Robt.Meridith."

1642. April. "An accompte of such sommes as have bin disbursed by me, Captn William Parsons, in readie moneyes by virtue of directions from the Right Honorble the Lords Justices and Councell, towards the payment of the troope and ffoot company garrisons att Birre alias Parsonstowne in the Kinges countie, from the twentieth day of November, Anno Domini 1641, untill the twentieth day of Januarye Anno Domini 1642."

1643. May 23. – Dublin. Order by the Lords Justices and Council for the repayment to Captn William Parsons of his disbursements for officers and company of Captn Chidley Coote, &c.

A/5 *contd.*   1643. June 3. – Dublin. Order from Ormonde to Capt. Wm Parsons to march with his troop to Jobs town.

1643. June 20. – Dublin. Order from Ormonde to same to march to Monasterevan.

1643. July 5. Order signed by Ormonde, Lieutenant General to Captn William Parsons or the officer commmanding his horse troop in chief, to march to Kilgobbane, county of Dublin.

1643. "By the Lords Justices and Councill.

"Jo. Borlase Hen. Tichborne.

"Wee are pleased heereby to declare that all ffarmers, plowmen, and others of that condition usually accustomed to keepe plowing and tillage wthin three miles of Monasterevan, in the countie of Kildare (other then such persons of those conditions as are free boulders that are or have beene or shalbee in rebellion, and other then such as have beene comanders or officers amongst the rebells), and all gardeners may, wthout interruption, plowe, manure, and sow theire grounds, fields, lands, and gardens, and to that end use horses, garrans, oxen, cowes, sheepe, swine, and poultry, and keepe and preserve meddowes and pastures for hay and grasse wthin the said limitts, and wth such condicions and limiticions as in the proclamations dated the ninth of February 1642, and sixth of March, 1642 are expressed, and that as beneficially as if the said Monasterevan were particularly named in the said proclamacions. Given at his Maties Castle of Dublin, 25th August 1643.

"Ormonde.
"Cha. Lambart.

"Edw. Brabazon.
"Fr. Willoughby.

"Tho. Lucas.
"Ja. Ware."

1643. October 14. – Dublin. Order from Ormonde to Captn Parsons to march with his troop from Naas to Dublin garrison.

1643. March 8. – Dublin. Order by Lord Lieutanant and Council on disbandment of horse troop of Captain William Parsons.

1643. Petition of Captain William Parsons for delivery of arms and ammunition received out of the King's store by John Gifford, with order of Lord Lieutenant thereon.

1644. May. His Majesty's answer at Oxford to the Commissioners from the Irish.

1644. Memoranda of Captain William Parsons:

"Occurraunces from the 25 of Maye 1644 –

"25. Saturdaye to [*sic*] 25th of Maye. I came out of Oxford to Mr. Parsons his house at Milltoune.

A/5 *contd.*   "27. Mundaye the 27th of Maye some of the Parliament troopers tooke me awaye prisoner to one Capten Duke and sent me to my Lord Generall who commanded me to wayght on the Parliament.

"28. Tewsday the 28th. I sent Gunn to Oxford.

"29. Wednesdaye, I came to Alesbarry in Buckinghamshire.

"30. Thursdaye, I came to London.

"31. Fredaye, I visited my friends.

"1. Saturdaye the 1 of June 1644, I was by the meanes to my Lord Lyle and Mr. Renolds brought to the House of Commons, where the Speaker asked me many questions, that he understood that I was commanded by my Lord General to wayght on the House, & how wee were received at Oxford, and who weare buy when wee weare first presented to the King, to the which I answered that there was only his Matie and Secretarie Nicholas and those that came out of Ireland. The Speaker asked me what answer the King gave us, I told him that he gave us a very gratious answer which comforted us mightilie, which was that he knew the contents of our petitions to be trew, but his Matie said that the Irish tooke it uppon there salvatiouus to him that the Pale was forced out by the governours, and that he was well assured that those Collonells that should have you into frayme weare well affected to his service, and would neaver have prejudiced him. Then they asked me what Lords at Court did countenance us. I told them that wee received little favour from any saving my Lord Lycester who came twice to see us, and very civell respect wee had from my Lord Duke of Lenox. He asked me to what Comittee wee weare referred, and I told him. He asked me weather my Lord Digby should say that the greatest favour he could doe was˙ ... our propositions the pr ... of madd me ... that he might not accompt us Councillors. I answered that we weare told noe such thing to our face, but some thing to that purpose was told; they asked me by whome, I answered by Lievetenant Collonell Sellenger.

"3 of June. I wayted on Sir John Clotworthy, Mr Renold and Mr. Jepson, where they putt me many questions, and wished me to draw the whole story into writing.

5 of June, being Wednesdaye, I wayted on Sir John Clotworthy and Mr. Renolds, and shewed them how far I had done, where I hard strange stories from them, and advised the forbarance of a declaracion for a time, untill my fellow agents came heather.

"12 of June, wee weare with the Committee of both kingdoms by order of the House of Commons.

"The 28th of June 1644. The Comittee of House of Commons came to our lodging, and there wee gave them a narrative of the proceedings of the Protestant agents.

"The 1 of July. The Comittee came to us agayne, and advised about drawing up a declartion upon the narrative.

"The 2 of July, Mr. Ridgwaye and my selfe dined with the Lord Maior of London."

1644. Acknowledgement of Joane, Countess of Kildare, for money owed to her cousin Mrs. Dorothy Parsons.

---

*   Obliterations indicated thus ...

A/5 *contd.*   1645. September 13. Extract from proceedings of Committee of Lords and
Commons for Ireland on petition and demands of Captain William Parsons.

1645. Memoranda of Captain William Parsons -much decayed:

"Memo. of proceedings about m ... since the 8th of August 164 ... the 10th of
August 1645 wee presented y ... propositions to the Comittee for Ireland for ...
for the souldiers.

"The [blank] of Septem. 1645, wee received warra ... for 6,000l. for the
souldiers.

"The 27th of Septem. 1645, wee attended ... Grosers hall with a letter to borrow
the m ...

"The 30th of Septem. wee attended againe ... could gett noe answer.

"The 14th and 15th of Octo. 1645, wee attended ... Common Counsell and
they satt ...

"The 16th of Octo. 1645, wee attended the Co ... Councell againe by order of
the House of Com'ons with 4 members, and had to answer that they had
appointed a Committee ... to meet the Com'ittee of Grosers ... which was to
raise that ...

"The 20th of Octo, 1645 wee attended a ... Hall for an answer where the Comi
... met saving 2 or 3, and putt it off till ne ...

"Wednesday the 20th of Octo. we attended againe, and they wanted the
Ordinarie ... the coppy of the warrants, and did noth[ing] butt putt us off till
Saturdaye following, then they promised an answer.

"The 23rd of Octo. wee mett, and Mr. Davis ... house with Sir John Clotworthy,
and there, after debate, Mr. Davis promised to lend 1,000l. unto Co ... Jepson
to carry awaye his horse upon the C ... of the warrant of 4.000l.

"The 25th of Octo. 1645 wee attended againe ... sers Hall for an answer till 12
a'clocke but no answer by raylings at Mr. Davis."

p.221   1646. September 29. – Cork. Letter from Robert Southwell on lands in South of
Ireland.

1646. October 27. Order, signed by Salisbury and others, that the troop of horse
raised by Captain William Parsons, should proceed to Chester for shipping.

1646. November 17. Order by Committee of Lords and Commons for Ireland to
hasten payment to Captain William Parsons of amount due on his contract with
the Committee for raising, arming, and transporting a troop of 70 men and
horses to Ireland.

1646. March 18. Proceedings of Committee of Lords and Commons for Ireland
on Petition Captain William Parsons.

1647. May 13. Order by Committee of Lords and Commons for Ireland for
payment of troops of Captaine Parsons and Meredith at Chester.

1647. June 11. – Kinsale. Letter of Robert Southwell to Captain William
Parsons, St. Martin's Lane, London, concerning lands of Barryoge, and other
lands about Kinsale.

A/5 *contd.*   1648. August 2. Extract from Journal of House of Lords, concerning order for payment to Captain Parsons and others, 2 August 1648.

1648. August 3. Order by Parliament for payment of money disbursed by Sir William Parsons, 3 August 1648.

1648. Draft of "Capt. William Parsons, his humble desires."

1652. August 26. Order with reference to Commissioners for compounding to examine, and pay out of Treasury of Goldsmiths' Hall amount due to Captn William Parsons, by ten pounds a week.

1652 September 2. Order by the Commissioners for compounding, &c., on case of Captn William Parsons, 2 Septr 1652.

1652. September 30. Extract from will of Fenton Parsons, proved at London, 30 September 1652.

1652. Copy of preceding, concluding "This is a true coppie of the originall, wch remained with Mr William Parsons, examined this xiiith of December 1652." Signed, Gilles Phillips, Matthew Lock, Jos. Paine, Dorothy Parsons.

1652. February 14. An Abstract drawn out of the original "specialties," with the names of the debtors and several sums of money due to the dowager Lady Parsons.

1654. February 13. letter from Jone Countess of Kildare, to the Lady Philips and Mrs. Dorothy Parsons at London, at the Lady Philip's house in Orchard Street, near Westminster. Dublin, 13th of February 1654.

1659. The Commonwealth survey of the barony of Eglish.

Draft of petition of William Parsons to his Excellency Lord General Cromwell. – Much injured.

1663. Debentures under Act of Settlement:*

"By his Majesties Commissioners   )
appointed to execute the Act, entituled An Act   )
for the better execution of His Majesties   )
Gracious Declaration for the Settlement of   )

˙His Kingdom of Ireland, and satisfaction of   )
the several Interests of Adventurers, Souldiers,   )
and other His Subjects there. "Upon   )
examining and stating the accompt of the   )
Arrears of Pay, claimed for the service of   )
William Parsons from the 21st of November   )
1641, to the 14th September 1643, as Capt. of a   )
Troope of Horse.

"There appears to be due to the said   )
William Parsons, out of the several securities   )
appointed by the said Act for satisfaction of   )
such Commissioned Officers who served his   )

* The portions in manuscript in the original printed form are indicated by italics.

A/5 *contd.* Majesty or his Royal Father of Blessed)
memory in Ireland, before the fifth day of June)
1649, the sum of *one thousand one hundred*) ll. s. d.
and twelve shillings & seven pence to be) 1,112 10 07
satisfied to the said *William Parsons*, his heirs)
executors and administrators or assigns, in such)
manner order and proportions as by the said)
Act is limited, and appointed, and subject to)
such deductions and defalcations as are)
warranted by the same. Given under our)
hands and seals at the King's Inns Dublin, this)
tenth day of *March 1663 (339).*)

Exd Tho. Taylor.	*Edwarde Smythe*	(seal).
Exd Thomas Symes.	*Edward Bering*	(seal).
Jo. Burmston.	*Edward Cooke*	(seal).
Ow. Silver.		
"No. 39 7."		

1663. "Instructions to bee observed by the Commissioners apponted for the assessing & ordering of the fifth, sixth, seaventh, and eighth subsidies of eight entire subsidies of ye temporality granted by an Act of this present Parliament."

1665. July 15. Receipt from Edmund Coghlan for part of purchase money for lands of Fedan Lower and Fedanbeg.

1666. September 26. Particulars of thirty-sixth lot of the debt which was drawn the eightieth lot of the credit. Jo. Burmston, Jo. Buckridge.

1667. Constat from Court of Chancery of grant of Castle and lands of Clonlyon, King's County, to Robert Bowyer.

1668. February 13. Memorandum on sale by Thomas Buckridge, of town, castle and lands of Clonlyon and Glean, in King's County, to Wm. Hamilton.

1668. Certificate from Rolls Office, Dublin, of grant from Charles 2 to Elizabeth Hanwell of part of Clonlyon, in barony of Garrycastle, King's County.

1668. Exchequer order concerning Laurence Parsons.

1680. January 4. Acknowledgement by Sir Wm. Parsons, of Langley, in the county of Bucks, for 300l. from his uncle Sir Lawrence Parsons, and sent unto his Aunt Parsons in England.

1680. Account of Sir Richard Parsons with Michael Cole for silk, satin, gauze, &c.

1688. Feb. 14. Warrant sealed and signed by Owen Carroll, directing the keeper of His Majesty's goale for the King's County to receive and keep in custody till delivered by due course of law, John Clay of Birre, yeoman, "one of the persons that continue assembled in the Castle of Birr in contempt of his Majesties lawes and government, and contrary to the late proclamation," as appears by his own confession and by information taken on oath.

A/5 *contd.*   1688. Captain Oxburgh's order to Town Watch at Birr:

"Orders for the Toune Watch, being 12 men:-

"First, lett 3 men watch att the sconce neere Nethercote's house.

2dly, let 3 men watch towards the castle about Coghlan, the smyth's, house.

"Lett 3 men watch beyond the water, as the Capt of the gard there shall direct them. Dat., 15th Febr. [16]88. He[nry] Oxburgh. To Darby Ryan, Heigh Constble, these."

1688. Surrender of Birr Castle to Jacobites: "Articles of agreement made and agreed upon by & between Coll. Howard Oxburg and Lifnt Coll. Robert Grace for and on his Majesties behalfe on ye one part, & Sir Lawrence Parsons Barnt, as well on his owne behalfe, as on ye behalfe of those other persons now wth him in ye castle of Birr, for and touching surrendering ye sd Castle to his Majest's use this 20th day of Feb. 1688:"

"Imprimis. It is agreed upon by and betweene ye sd parties yt ye sd Sir Lawrence Parsons shall & will imediately after perfectn heareof, disperce & send home to thear respective houses & habitations all ye sd persons soe with him in ye Castle of Birr, & keepe none thearin but his one private family, and alsoe receive into ye sd Castle such number of men to be garrisoned thearin for his Majty as ye sd Coll. Howard Oxburgh & Liftnt Coll. Robert Grace shall think fitt, & ye same to continue thearin till his Exlciy comands ye contrary.

"2ly Itm. It is further agreed upon between ye sd parties, yt all ye sd persons now in ye Castle of Birr shall and may carry away & make use of all the goods & chatties wch they have now in the sd Castle excepting only thear horses, amunition, & armes wch

are to be disposed of to his Majesties use, & for his service and excepting alsoe the provision & victualls they have now in ye sd Castle wch is intended for ye use of ye King's garrison if ye Lord Deputy will not before ye last day of this month thinke fitt to order ye same to be restored to ye right owner.

"3dly Itm. It is alsoe agreed:upon by & between ye sd parties yt all ye sd persons, soe now in ye sd Castle of Birr wth ye sd Sir Lawrence Parsons shall have the full protection and benefitt of ye laws, as well to protect thear persons from any violence as to preserve & secure thear goods to ym whilest they shall peacably demeane ymselves towards ye King, his lawes & Govent, & yt all ye sd persons shall be bound one for another before the sd Coll. Howard Oxburgh to apeer next asizes, wch recogs the sd Howard Oxburgh is to keep in his one hands, & not returne to ye asizes if the Lord Deputy will soe order it, & yt till his Exes plesure be knowne touching ye sd provision & Victualls, the gd Coll.

p.222   How.Ox[burgh] is to give the owners of ye sd provisions and victualls, the one moiety thearof for thear subsistance. In witness whearof ye sd parties have to these presents interchangable sett thear hands and seales, the dale and yeare first above written.*

---

*   A copy of these articles with the following letter addressed to Bishop King, is among the correspondence of the latter, noticed in my Report to this Commission for the present year:-

"My Lord

"Mr. Bonell tells me your Lordship desires an act of my triall, and to know whether I was not condemned for articleing wth King James. In order to your Lorsps satisfaction, I under wright a copie of ye articles, and doe further sertefie your lordship ye cheef evidence against me was ye articles wch Sir

A/5 *contd.*   Sighned, sealed & delivered in ye presence of us. -
           Owen Carroll.   How. Oxburgh
           Mathew Moony.   Rob. Grace.
           P. Moore."   Law. Parson.

1689. Colonel Garret Moore's certificate to the Duke of Tyrconnell:-

"These are to certifie that his Grace the Duke of Tyrconnell, being Lord Deputy
of his Majts kingdome of Ireland, being informed that Sr Lawrence Parsons was
fortefieing & makeing a garrison of his house att Birr, commanded mee to go
thither and enquire further, and accordingly I did go to his said house and tould
him what information was giuen agt him. His answere to mee was that he shut
upp his foregate and kept his back gate open for any that would have pleased to
come to see him, and haveing treated further with him, tould him that hee
received many armed men into his said house, his answere was that some of his
neighbours and tents intreated him to give them roome in his house, wch he said
he could not in charety deny them, haveing beene plundred of their goods, and
pretended to be affraid of their lives, and tould mee hee would bring them all
before mee in the castle yard, wch he accordingly did, and did obserue there
were more or as many women & children among them as men. I tould

Henry Linch, my judg, caled for and declared thear was noe neede of any
farther evidence, for articling wth the King was high treason; besides this twas
proved I bilt a stone wall and made spike holds in it, and yt some of my men
threw stones at ye Kings souldiers, & yt I kept men wthin my house, and
exsersized daily, all wch he declared was high treason. To all wch when I offerd to
speake for my selfe he fell in passion and railing bitterly at me would not heer
me but wthout more cerremony, after ye pickd jury had deliverd thear vardict,
sentenced me & two more to be hangd, drawne and quarterd. This and many
other sircumstances too long to trouble your Lordship wth, I am able and redy
to justifie when ever I shall be thearto required. For ye saving my life I procured
five severall repreeves, wch I have by me. I was in close prison from ye date of
these articles till ye route at ye Boine. I am my Lord,

"Your Lordships faithfull, hum. sert,
"LAW. PARSONS."

"Dub: Mar. 18th 1691/2.

"I intend for England soone, whearr I shall be glad to receive yr Lordsps
recomenditory letters wch I humbly begg yr Lorsp will be pleasd to send me
hither.

My Lord. Coll. Oxburgh was my fathers sert, and my tent & Sert this 30 yrs,
and had ye managt of my estate at this time, who owed 4,000l in my debt, and
would have hangd me. He had 100l per ann' for receiving my rents, and was to
allow me 500l yearly, and pay my debts with ye rest, but pd nothing, and wth
my mony raised a regmt for King James; this acct in breef I presume tohim that
hee must disperse them, or that his Grace would not bee satisfied, who declared
hee would burn or garrison the said house if hee had not; and the said Sr
Lawrence asked the people whether hee sent for any of them to his house or
detained any of them agt their wills, who answered hee did not, on wch I said

A/5 *contd.*   that will not serve, but you ought to disperse them; his answere was, hee could not well command them away considering the fear they pretended to bee in of their lives, but he ordered that all the arms in the house were putt upp and lockt in one roome least any of the people would committ any act of hostilitie, and brought mee to the rome where the arms were, and assured mee hee would not suffer any acts of hostilitie to be committed, and wuld suffer any of his neighbours to come into him and go out as they pleased; and this treaty wth him was about foure days before hee gave upp his house to Coll. Oxburgh, and I'm credibly informed that hee did not suffer one shott to be made in a hostile, mannr dureing the time hee had the said people in his house, and do further certefie that he'es an aged and gouty person, all wch I thought fitt to certifie this 8th day of March 1689.

"GARRETT MOORE."

1689. Reprieves for Sir Lawrence Parsons, etc.: James R.

"Whereas Sr Lawrence Parsons of Birr, Barrnt, James Roscoe of the same, skinner, and Jonothan Darby of the Leap, all in our county, were lately indicted at Phillipstowne in our said county for rebellion against us and our royall authority, and have received sentence of death thereupon, which they are to undergoe except wee be gratiously pleased to interpose. Wee being resolved to reclaim our subjects by mercy, and to shew that wee delight rather to forgive then punish, doe hereby strictly charge and command you to forbeare the execution of the said sentance given against the said Sr Lawrence Parsons, James Roscoe, and Jonothan Darby, for the spce of two months from the expiration of theire last reprieve, for which this shall be your warrant, and hereof you are not to faile at your perill. Given at our Court at Dublin Castle, the 22d day of May 1689, and in the fifth yeare of our regne.

"By his Maties command.
"MELFORT."

give yr Lordship, heering yr Lordship is wrighting the late transactions, in wch I pray yr Lordship will be pleased to particularise my great sufferings." The case of Sir L. Parsons is referred to by King in the *State of the Protestants in Ireland,* London, 1692, p.104.

"To our trusty and welbeloved
Francis Coghlan, Esq., High
Sheriff of our County."

"James R.

"Whereas Sr Lawrence Parsons, of Birr, Barront, and James Rascoe of the same, skinner, were lately indicted at Phillipstone in our King's Countie for rebellion against us and our royall authority, and have received sentence of death thereupon, which they are to undergoe except wee are gratiously pleased to interpose, wee being resolved to reclayme our subjects by mercy and to shew that wee delight rather to forgive then punish, doe hereby strightly charge and command you to forbeare the execution of the said sentence given against the said Sr Lawrence Parsons and James Rascoe for the space of six moneths from

A/5 *contd.* the expiration of their last reprieve, for wch this shal be your warrant, and hereof you are not to faile at your perill. Given at our Courte at Dublin Castle, the seaventh day of August 1689, and in the fifth yeare of our reigne.

"By his Maties command.
"MELFORT."

"To our trusty and well beloved Francis
Coghlan, Esqr, High Sherriff of our
county aforesaid, and to his successors
sherriffs of the said county."

"James R.,

"Our will and pleasure is, tht you suspend for the space of three months the execution of Sr Lawwrens. Persons, Baront, and James Rosko, now prisonrs in yr custody, and for soe doing this shall be yr sufficient warrant. Given at our Court at our Castle of Dublin, this eight day of March 1689, and in the fifth yeare of our reigne.

"By his Majties comand.

"MARQUIS D'ALBYVILLE."

"To our trusty and well beloved our
High Sheriff of our county, ye
King's county."

1690, Aug. 5. Petition of John Weaver to Commissioners for management of Forfeited Estates, concerning claim on Col. Oxburgh, and lands in Clonkelly, in King's County, with order thereon. Copy certified by J. Weaver and others.

1690, August 28. Bond for returning sheep if it appear that they are the property of Col. Oxburgh or any forfeiting person.

1690. September. Petition of Sir Lawrence Parsons, Bart., to Commissioners for management of Forfeited Estates, and order thereon, dated September 1690.

1691–2. February 27. – Dublin. Order from Lord Justices to Governor and Deputy Governor of Kings County, at Birr, to restrain injuries and oppressions by officers and soldiers of the militia in taking stock and household goods under pretence of late proclamation for disarming. Autographs of Charles Porter and Thomas Coningsby.

1694. October 12. – Hague. Order of William III, concerning allowances to foot and dragoons in the Low Countries.

Undated Papers

Letter signed by Wm. Colley, Wm. Usher, Wm. Plunket, and others, addressed to Captain McWilliam Ridgway, Sir Chas. Coote, Sir Fras. Hamilton and Capt. Wm. Parsons, with reference to the application of the agents sent over to Charles I. from the confederate Roman Catholics of Ireland for the recommitment of the four privy councillors, by his Majesty's direction, enlarged from restraint.

A/5 *contd.* "A remonstrance humbly presented to the honble counsell of State for the speedy raising of mony in an ancient way by subsidy and without partiality; and that some greivances of the people may be eased that they may pay the more cheerfully."

p.223 Letter to Sir John Croke and His Majesty's Solicitor General on suit of Henry Lea concerning writings connected with his lands in Ireland, in custody of Sir Robert Gardiner, knt.

Two letters signed W. Parsons. – Much injured and dates lost.

Letter from Joan Countess of Kildare to her cousin Parsons, "this Friday night."

Letter from same to "Good Cousin Parsons." "this Sunday night." Endorsed "for Captaine Parsons."

Draft of King's letter for manor of Birr and lands in King's County.

Petition of Capt. William Parsons to Parliament for reimbursement for his expenditure towards the support of the army, &c.

Will of Dame Anne Parsons (copy).

Constat from Rolls Office, Dublin, of grant of James I., in 1621, of monastery of Lurcho, Tipperary, to William Dongon.

A/8

DATE   DESCRIPTION

1620–40:   Clutch of papers, crudely bound with a parchment cover,
1660–66   microfilmed by the National Library (n.5485: p.5650), and described in *Hayes*
           as 'Abstracts of leases of holdings in Parsonstown Manor made by Sir L. Parsons,
           1620–40; [and details of] births and baptisms of the children of [Sir] Laurence
           Parsons [1st Bt] and Frances Savage, his wife, 1660–66.' The volume was turned
           upside down and used by the first Sir Laurence Parsons to record accounts for
           the period 1627–8. These last have been transcribed (1983) by Miss Frances
           Wilson, and the MS. and typescript of her transcript are included with the
           volume.
               The contents of this volume (minus the accounts) are described in the second
           edition of Cooke's Picture of Parsonstown, which was published in 1875 under
           the title *The Early History of the Town of Birr or Parsonstown ...*, pp.41–50, 384
           and 68–9, as follows:

PAGE   DESCRIPTION

p.41   'Very soon after the grant of Birr to Sir Laurence Parsons in 1620, several
             persons took leases from him. In the Appendix (No. 4) will be found a list of
             these tenants taken from a Rental in the handwriting of Sir Laurence Parsons.
             This list is interesting, as it gives the names of some sixty persons who had leases
             in Birr about 250 years ago. These names are neither all Irish, as those of the
             'freeholders,' given in the copy currender of Ely O Carroll in 1576, nor are they
             all English, as the 'undertakers,' to whom land in Ely O'Carroll was granted on
             the 'plantation.' The Birr lessees appear to have been mixed, many having old
             Irish names, and others being clearly English. As far as can be judged by names,
             there are not in Birr in late years many descendants of these original lessees,
             either Irish or English.
                 It appears from an entry in the same rental that on the 9th of October 1623,
             Sir Laurence Parsons made a lease to Abraham Bigo, of the 'castle, town and part
             of the plow-land of Clonoghill; with a proviso that the tenant was 'not to set up
p.42   any glass house or glass work on any other land, or buy wood of any other for
             his glass work, but only of said Laurence Parsons.' This lease also contained a
             covenant that said Bigo should within a year build a stone or brick chimney to
             the castle, from which it appears that Clonoghill castle had no chimney previous
             to that time.
                 The Bigo family were Huguenots who had fled from Lorraine. ... These glass-
             works appear to have been carried on from 1623 to Easter 1627, when the lease
             was surrendered. The remains of an ancient glass-house, with part of crucibles
             and fragments of glass, were discovered some years ago at Clonbrone, adjoining
             Clonoghill, and not far from Birr, and which seems to have been the glass-house
             alluded to. Clonoghill Castle was burned in the year 1642 by the Irish, and the
             ruins are yet to be seen in Syngefield demesne, about half-a-mile from Birr.

A/8 *contd.*   There also appears to have been a fishing weir, of some importance in these early times, on the Little Brusna river, close to Birr, at the part of Cappaneal called Tircoragh, meaning, 'the district of the weir,' or 'the weir district,' from tir, a district, and cora, a weir. It appears from the rental already alluded to that this fishing weir was leased by Sir Laurence Parsons, the 4th of June 1621, to Thomas Teigh and Philip Trady, for six years. It also appears, however, that this weir was subsequently 'plucked down by a presentment of the Grand Jury and order of the Lord Justices, at Lent Assizes 1623.'

About this time there were likewise two grist mills at Birr, for there appears to have been a lease of them, made to Francis Morley the 18th of July 1623; and in the inquisition post mortem on Sir Laurence Parsons, who died in 1628, it is stated that at this period there were five water mills at Birr. One of these was distinguished even then, as 'the Old Mill;' and in these times the part of the present Chapel Lane, adjoining the river, and near the mill-pond and mill, went by the name of Lough-cora, which means, the lough at the weir.

p.49   ... In after years there was a market house erected in the market square of Birr, which was used at times for holding the County Assizes in, and many people were there sentenced to death, by court-martial or otherwise. This market house was also at times used as a military position, by either party, during the contentions which took place for the possession of the castle and town of Birr. The following entry in respect to this market house appears in the handwriting of a later Sir Laurence Parsons in the old Rental before referred to:- 'Mem. Darby Mulrean hath taken from me ye markett place of Birr whear he is to bild as good a house as is bilt in Roscrea, and to alowe a roome for ye come and measures to him yt takes ye markett customs, and his leace of seven years is expired and he is to shingle the hole house within twelve years of his terme ye Leace is to commence ye first of May next for twenty one years at three pounds rent per annum.

p.50   Dat, July 2nd 1671. ...

p.384   No.4.
NAMES OF THE BIRR TENANTS WHO TOOK LEASES FROM SIR LAURENCE PARSONS IN 1620. FROM A RENTAL IN THE HANDWRITING OF SIR LAURENCE.

Sir Francis Ackland, knight, Robert Aharan, Francis Beaty, John Burras, William Beetenson, Clement Benfield, James Blundell, Patrick Condon, Hugh O'Crokeran, Brian M'Hugh Coghlan, William Carrotters, Donnell M'Farshees Carroll, Gilchrist O'Carroll, Rory O'Dulhunty, Rory Ogle O'Dulhunty, Daniel Ogle O'Dulhunty, Joseph Evans, Edmund Fitzsymonds, Dermot Gavan, Denis Gothfirth, James Green assigned to Henry Evens, Philip O'Glessame, Teige P'Hogan, Dermot O'Hogan, Teige O'Herin, William O'Haghtir, John Hogan, Edward Hustler, Edward Hamsell, Oliver Humphry, Henry Hart, Richard Irwin, Robert Irwin, Jeremiah O'Kennedy, John Langton, Patrick Larre, Thomas Molly, Dermot M'Teige O'Magher, Francis Morley, John Murroghoe assigned to Alexander Prin, Stephen mabbot, Brian O'Naughten, George Percy, Richard

A/8 *contd.*   Rose, Michael Raghtor, William Rice, Richard Roose, Thomas Roch, Philip
Ridgeway, William Stockdale, Robert Sweetman, Simon Simonson, Robert
Sheeply clerke, James Saul, Thomas Teigh and Philip Trady, Richard Taylor,
Robert Trieve, John Trieve, William Walter, and Richard Williams. ...

p.68   ... The following is copied from entries made by Mr Laurence Parsons, from
1660 to 1663, in the old rental before referred to, and if not otherwise
interesting, is at least curious, as affording information as to the manners of
these long past times.

"The names of Laurence Parsons, his children, theare godfathers and god
mothers, and ye time when he married his wife.

"August 14th, 1660, I married my wife. Her name was Frances Savage, daughter
to Will: Savage of Castle Rebban, in ye County of Kildare, Esqr. We were
married in Sheep Street, in Dublin, at Cap: Sankie his house, who is married to
another sister.

"The 8th of June (1661) my son William was borne in my castle of
Parsonstowne about (12) a clocke at noone, being Saturday, and ye Wednesday
after was christened by Mr Well in ye church of Parsonstowne. His godfathers
weare my wife's father-in-law, Sr. Will: Fflower, and my brother-in-law, Sr. Will:
Parsons of Langly parke, in England, in Buckinghamshire, but neither of ym.
beingheare, my brother Blunt and my cousen Will: Parsons stood for ym. My
sister Sankie was his godmother.

"The 29th of June (1662) my sone Savage was borne in my castle of
Parsonstowne about (5) of ye clocke in ye afternoone, being Sonday, and ye
Wednesday after was christened in my wife's chamber, being weake.

p.69   His godfathers weare my cousen Rawsenand Cap: Peasly of Roskreagh. His
godmother was my mother Fflower. Ye (23) of Novr. after, he died and was
buried in ye church of Parsonstowne, neere my aunt Lowther.

"The 13th of August (1663) my daughter Dorothy was borne in my castle of
Parsonstowne. Her god mothers weare Mrs Cearle of Eglish, and Mrs Bullin of
Roskreagh. Her godfather was Bishop Worth, Bishop of Killalooe. Lau:
Parsons." '

A/8A

DATE   DESCRIPTION

1620–21   Volume, not at present to be found in Birr Castle and probably missing since the period 1826–75, described in the second edition of Cooke's *Picture of Parsonstown*, which was published in the latter year under the title *The Early History of the Town of Birr or Parsonstown* ..., as an account book kept by Sir Laurence Parson's steward, Francis Morley, and recording among other things the '... prices of provisions, work and materials for building in Birr in the end of 1620 and beginning of 1621 ...'.

The following is a transcript of the entire description given of it in the second edition, pp. 39–40:

PAGE   DESCRIPTION

p.39   'In the same month of November 1620, Sir Laurence sent his steward, Francis Morley, afterwards clerk of the subsidies, to put the castle at Birr in fit order for his reception, and the country was then so wild and uncivilized, that Morley was obliged to employ a guide to conduct him to the neighbouring village of Portumna, for which, and his own expenses on the journey, he charged Sir Laurence five shillings and eightpence of the then currency, as appeared by his account took, which in 1826 was still in the possession of the then Earl of Rosse.
    The prices of provisions, work, and materials for building in Birr, in the end of 1620, and beginning of 1621, were, according to this account book, as follows: A labourer received from sixpence to eightpence a day; a man and horse, one shilling a day; a mason, one and fourpence; mason work by the perch, two shillings and sixpence; ditto, finding materials, six shillings and eightpence; plastering, three farthings per yard; hewing stones for coins and corbels, twopence halfpenny per foot; wainscoting, one shilling and threepence a yard, and two shillings and sixpence the border; iron, two shillings a stone; shoeing a horse, fourpence a shoe; gunpowder, one shilling and sixpence per pound;

p.40   a mutton, three shillings and fourpence; a quarter of beef, four shillings and sixpence; butter, threepence halfpenny a pound; oats, three shillings and fourpence the barrel; hops, one shilling a pound; a quart of sack wine, one shilling; a quart of claret, sixpence; a quart of aqua vitae, one shilling and fourpence.'

A/9

DATE   DESCRIPTION

18 Oct.   [Capt. William Parsons's?] diary of the siege of Birr Castle in 1643 and other
1641–20   military events during the early years of the wars of the 1640s, re-bound in half
Jan. 1642   calf in the early 19th century, and some pages of its detached with a view,
[/3]   apparently, to conservation, but without having so far been conserved (these
                  pages have been placed loose between the front end-papers). The diary has been
                  photostated by the National Library (MS. 13667). The rest of the volume
                  consists of 44 pages of copies of deeds relating to the Savage family of
                  Cottenhoe, Buckinghamshire, [possibly relations of Frances Savage, wife of
                  Parsons's son, Sir Laurence, 1st Bt? – see T/1], 1609–35.

                  The Early History of the Town of Birr or Parsonstown ... contains the following
                  summary:

PAGE   DESCRIPTION

p.57   'The following account of occurrences at Birr in the early part of 1643 is taken
                  partly from Carte's Ormond and other writers, and partly from a MS. Journal
                  which was in the possession of the late Laurence, Earl of Rosse, in 1826. This
                  Journal purported to have been kept at Birr castle during the occurrences
                  mentioned in it had every appearance of being written at the time.

p.58   The writer of the present history, without wishing to be responsible for either the
                  accuracy or impartiality of this Journal thinks it better to give such information
                  from it, as in the mean [*sic*] facts, is corroborated by other authorities.
                      Birr Castle was again attacked early in the year 1643. Preston, the general
                  commanding the confederate army of Leinster, an officer of great experience,
                  having collected about 2,500 foot and some troops of horse, invested the castle of
                  Burris, which surrendered to him on the 30th of December 1642. From thence he
                  marched to Birr, having intelligence that the garrison had not powder to stand two
                  hours' assualt. On the 15th of January 1643, the forces in the castle received
                  information that he was approaching with great pieces of artilley; and on the same
                  evening about dusk, the governor's scouts saw about 200 of the enemy at Cree,
                  and Crinkle, or Crinkill, both near Birr. The following day, Sunday, General
                  Preston appeared with 100 horse and 200 foot, on Drumbawn Hill over the town.
                  From thence he reconnoitred the town and castle, and after firing some shots, he
                  encamped in the neighbouring woods; and from this time continued a close siege
                  until the place surrendered on the 20th. The enemy again showed themselves on
                  the 16th, with cavalry and infantry and waggon train, to the number of about
                  2,000, and fired several shots at the castle, to which they sent a drummer in the
                  afternoon with a paper containing the following words:- "A memorandum
p.59   for the drummer that desires that the governor, Mr. Parsons do send a safe
                  conduct for a gentleman, the Lord Governor of Leinster doth intend to send to
                  him." In reply to this the Governor stated, that any gentleman that came to
                  speak to him should have free egress and regress; and soon after, a person styling

A/9 *contd.*   himself Mr. Oliver Darcy, of Flatten, came from General Preston. Mr. Darcy required to know whether the Governor held the place for the King or for the Parliament, and desired that he should allow the Lord General to place a garrison there for His Majesty's use. To this the governor answered, that he had no intelligence either from His Majesty or the Parliament, concerning any difference between them but he held his castle and land by royal patent granted to his father, and then vested in him, and that he was by His Majesty's Commission, dated about twelve months before, appointed commander-in-chief of the territory of Ely O'Carroll and the borders thereof.

Preston, dissatisfied with his reply, pitched his tents in the fields adjoining the town, and in the course of the night drew a trench across the Governor's orchard, and another from the sessions house to the town. The confederate forces played their artillery the entire of next day upon the walls of the castle, and killed one man in the town; the remaining houses in which the Governor caused to be set on fire to prevent the enemy from taking shelter in them; and in the afternoon seven cannon shot were fired against the castle. The ensuing night, the enemy – having been instructed by a mason who had been employed

p.60   in building the castle – approached withineight feet of the walls, and having hit upon a green, clayish bank, on the west side of the building, they undermined it in two places. The mouth of the mine was not more than four yeards from the walls. The garrison hearing the sap, fired some shot, and rolled great stones down the bank upon the beseigers; but by break of day they were got under ground, and out of all danger. In the morning the beseiged discovered a barrel of gunpowder, which was left at the mouth of the mine, those who brought it having been obliged to desist, during the day-time, by the fire kept up from the castle. On the 18th, Preston's troops discharged eleven great shot at the castle, which the General declared his determination to beat down about the Governor's ears; and they succeeded in demolishing a great part of the wall in one of the flankers. Some of the balls were found in the building, and weighed nine pounds each. By this time a party which the Governor had placed in a mill, were strongly assaulted, and had killed from twenty to thirty of their assailants. However, their ammunition was exhausted, and the mill set on fire over their heads. To relieve this brave little corps, the Governor – although he knew the request would not be complied with -sent a message to Preston, desiring that his cattle might be allowed to graze abroad, which the latter refused to permit, but pending the negociation, the troops in the mill were withdrawn.

p.61   The garrison having bravely held out for two days after a mine was prepared beneath them, was obliged to beat a parley on the 19th. On the 20th, pledges were sent in for the Governor's safe return from the camp, to which he accordingly went, and after a long debate capitulated that the garrison should march out the next day, horse and foot, with arms, half their plate and money, their clothes, and as much provisions as they could carry.'

A/15
DATE   DESCRIPTION

[1666?]   Volume of near-contemporary copies of State Papers, etc, concerning the terms
of the Acts of Settlement and Explanation, briefly described in the *First Report* of
the H.M.C. as 'A folio volume of 90 pages containing copies of concerning Irish
matters, from 1651–1666', and calendared as follows by J.T. Gilbert in the
documents Second Report:

PAGE   DESCRIPTION

p.223   'The volume designated No. 3, in my first report on this collection, is bound in
vellum and endorsed in an old hand "My grandfather's acts in 1641, &c." Its
contents, as follow, mostly undated, were transcribed apparently in the time to
which they relate:

"To the King's most Ext Matie. The humble peticion of yor true and faithfull
Catholique subjects of your kingdome of Ireland."

"To ye King's most Ext Maty. The humble petic'on of Sr Robert Talbot and
Coll. Garrett Moore in behalfe of yor Maiesties Roman Catholique subiects of
Irelant."

"Answeares made to certaine exceptions against the clause and proviso tendered
in behaulfe of his Maiesties loyall subjects the Roman Catholiques of Ireland.
The clauses desired by the Irish papists to be added to the proviso (touching
Ireland) in the Act of Indempnitie and the exceptions thereunto."

"A brife narrative how things were carrid at the beginning of the troubles in the
years 1641 in Ireland, published in print in ye yeare 1660."

"A continuation of the Briefe narrative and of the sufferings of the Irish under
Cromwell. Printed in the yeare 1660."

"To the King's most Ext Matie. The humble petic'on of Sr Rob't Talbot, Bart,
and Collll Garret Mooree of the Roman Catholiques of Ireland."

"Answeares and reasons agt the clauses and motives urged to conclude those
whoe were forced to accept lands in Connaght."

"A briefe as well of certaine proposalls presented to his Matie in behalfe of the
English in relacion to the settlement of Ireland. As also of the severeall answeares
by the Irish Comrs given thereunto."

"Answeares at large to certaine proposalls offered in order to ye settlement of
Ireland."

"Reasons humbly offered to his Majesty in order to the settlemt of Ireland."

"A meadium or humble offers mde to his Maty in Order to the settlement of
Ireland."

An answeare to bitter exceptions agt ye medium."

To the King's Most Excellent Maiesty: The humble petic'on of Sr Robert Talbot,
Bart, and Collol Garret Moore in behalfe of the Roman Catholiques of Ireland."

A/15 *contd.* "Obversations on the declaracion humbly offered to your Majestves princely consideration."

"A coppy of a lettere sent into France to a certaine noblerman, and therein a petic'on to the Queene Dowager of England in behalfe of the Catholiques of Ireland by Sr Rob't Talbot, &c. London, July 1661."

"A coppy of the preamble of a bill transmitted out of Ireland for ye Royall assent: An Act for the better execution of his Majesty gracious declaration for the settlement of Ireland, and satisfaction of ye severall int'rests of Adventurers, Souldiers and other his Maiesties [subjects] there."

"To the King's Most ext Maty. The answeare to the annexed preamble presented by Sr Robt Talbot and Coll Garret Moore in behalfe of the Roman Catholiques of Ireland."

"The Answeare to the body of the Bill transmitted out of Ireland for the Royall assent."

"The answeare to the instructions. Sept. 24, 1661."

"The answeare to ye declaration and instructions."

A/23

DATE   **DESCRIPTION**

c. 1691   Volume, not now to be found in Birr Castle, described in the *First Report* of the
H.M.C. as 'A volume in small quarto, of 130 pages, written in a very minute
current hand about 1691, containing a narrative of the affairs of Sir Laurence
Parsons from April 1687 to 1691, detailing circumstances connected with the
wars of James and William in Ireland, the siege of Birr Castle by Jacobites in
1688, and of that castle and town in 1690'.

The Early History of the Town of Birr or Parsonstown ..., pp. 72–87, draws on the
narrative as follows:

PAGE   **DESCRIPTION**

p.72   'The following account of events connected with Birr, which occurred in 1688,
is taken principally from a "MS. Narrative of Sir L. Parsons, written in the time
of King William III." At this period the country about Birr was infested by
robbers and raparees, and particularly by one Fannin, with a strong party of
desperadoes, who kept the neighbourhood in perpetual alarm. In consequence of
this Sir laurnce Parsons received into Birr Castle at their request, about eighty of
his tenants and neighbours, with their wives and children, and ordered the gates
to be closed. Upon this Colonel, lately Captain Oxburgh, who had theretofore
acted as agent to Sir Laurence Parsons, but was now his enemy, and serving
under King James, reported to Lord Tyrconnell that Sir Laurence held a garrison
against the King, and had fifteen hundred men in arms within his castle, and
that he kept smiths there continually, manufacturing warlike implements. In
consequence of this, Oxburgh got an order, dated 3rd of January 1688, from the
Lord Lieutenant to place a garrison in Birr Castle, although Colonel Garrett
Moore, who had been sent by his lordship to make inquiries on the subject, had
reported that the charges against Sir Laurence were unfounded. In about a
month after getting the order, Oxburgh demanded possession of the castle, and
on Sir Laurence declining to comply until he should hear from the Lord
Lieutenant and Colonel Moore, Oxburgh and Colonel Grace besieged the castle,
with twenty-two companies of infantry, and a troop of dragoons. The siege was
closely kept up for several days and nights, so that no provision could be
obtained by the besieged, and the besiegers having commenced to undermine
the castle, terms of capitulation were finally agreed upon.

Upon the perfection of this treaty and consequent surrender of the castle, Sir
Laurence and five of his principal tenants were arrested, and all six kept closely
confined in the castle. In three days after the arrest of Sir Laurence, Mr.
Jonathan Darby, of Leap, and his brother John Darby, were put in the same
p.74   prison, charged with rescuing Captain Richard Coote; and Mr Thomas Roe
was imprisoned with them at same time.

On the 27th of March, the prisoners were sent to take their trial at
Philipstown Assizes, and were informed of the charges upon which they
were to

A/23 *contd.* be tried. These were as follows, viz: Sir Laurence Parsons and his tenants, John Philips, Philip Moore, Randal Knight, James Bury, and James Rascoe for high treason, in keeping the garrison of Parsonstown against the King; Jonathan and John Darby for high treason, in rescuing Captain Richard Coote; and Thomas Roe for high treason, for holding the house of Ballinmoney against his Majesty. Of these Philip Moore was never indicted.

The day of trial having arrived, and the evidence having closed, Sir Henry Lynch the Judge caused the articles of surrender to be read, and declared they were an overt act of high treason, and charged the jury to find all the prisoners guilty, and the jury soon agreed on a verdict against Sir Laurence, Johathan Darby, and James Rascoe, but acquitted the rest. The trial took place on the 30th of March 1689, and on the following Monday the convicts were brought up for judgement, and were sentenced to be hanged, drawn, and quartered. After reflection, however, the Judge reprieved Sir Laurence for a month, but refused to reprieve Darby, or Rascoe for more than ten days, and it was only

p.75   by sending a solicitor to Dublin, that they also received a reprieve for a month.

Upon the conviction of Sir Laurence, he was sent under escort to Birr, where he was imprisoned until the second of April 1690, during which period he was several times reprieved, and only escaped death, as King says, because it was not thought safe to execute him until the war was over. Sir Laurence was also attainted, as were likewise his son and brother, by the Parliament held in Dublin, under King James II, in 1689, and in which Colonel Oxburgh and Owen Carroll, already mentioned, sat as members for the King's County.

It appears from the same "MS. Narrative of Sir Laurence Parsons," that at this time Colonel Oxburgh's regiment consisted of twenty-two companies, two of which were quartered in the castle, and the other twenty companies in the town of Birr; as were likewise Captain John Oxburgh's troop of dragoons, and a company of infantry, under Lieutenant Colonel Robert Grace.

During these disasters, the Protestant minister of the parish, the Rev. Richard Crump, made away and deserted his flock; whereupon the profits of the living were seized upon for the King by his Majesty's Receiver, Garrett Trant, who set the Glebe to the Rev. Thomas Kennedy, the then Roman Catholic Priest of the parish. He also set the tythes of the whole parish to the same tenant. This seizure was the first of the kind made in the King's County, or probably in Ireland;

p.76   and in all likelihood would not have taken place, if the minister had kept his ground.

Soon after the Rev. Mr Crump's flight, viz., on the 28 of November 1689, Colonel Oxburgh's Officers went to the Clerk of the Parish, and with violent threats, demanded from him the key of the Church, which he was obliged to give them, and it was then handed over by them to the Rev. Mr Kennedy. Thereupon the Roman Catholic clergy were summoned, and attended in great numbers at the reconsecration, or reconcilement of Birr Church, which ceremony occupied several days. Mass was solemnized there on the 5th of December following, and so so, afterwards, continued to be until the Battle of the Boyne.

A/23 *contd.*   In April 1689, Lord Tyrconnell sent Colonel Sarsfield, with instructions to
review the army, and to disband as many as he thought proper; but so as to leave
in each regiment at least thirteen companies. Colonel Sarsfield was an
enlightened liberal man, above the prejudices of the day, and carried himself well
towards all parties, making no distinction between Protestant or Catholic, but
courteously treating all alike. Upon Sarsfield's arrival in Birr, Oxburgh's regiment
was drawn up on the Birr meadows, and several officers of distinction, and ladies
of the neighbourhood, attended the review. While the Colonel was inspecting
the troops, two soldiers threw down their appointments, and ran off from the
ranks, upon which Sarsfield put off his jackboots, and pursued

p.77   them. They were soon overtaken and brought back, and condemned to be shot;
but Colonel Oxburgh's wife and daughter being near at hand in great pomp in
their coach, threw themselves upon their knees, supplicating for mercy, and the
generous warrior Sarsfield, obliged to yield to their entreaties, forgave the
culprits. Sarsfield having disbanded nine companies of Oxburgh's regiment at
this review, went from thence to Portumna, where he disbanded forth-three
companies of Lord Galway's corps, the men of which being left without means
of support, were forced to become raparees and highwaymen. To make a slight
digression, it may be mentioned here that the "MS. Narrative of Sir Laurence
Parsons," states that the name "Raparee," so common in former times, comes
from a sort of half-pike, with which they used to be armed, and which the
"Narrative" says, was, in Irish, called rapparee. However, Mr O'Reilly, in his
Dictionary, says, that "Rapaire" signifies "a noisy fellow," and which appears to
be the more probable derivation of the word.

At this time, 1689, Colonel Oxburgh was appointed by the Government,
Provost Marshall of the King's County. He showed his authority by riding
through the country in great state, and causing gallows to be erected in several
places. Amongst the rest he had a gallows with three pegs, put up in the street of
Birr, which was then supposed to be intended for the execution of Sir Laurence
Parsons, Mr. Jonathan Darby and James Rascoe.

p.78   This gallows was erected on May-day 1689, and was, therefore, ever after called
Colonel Oxburgh's May-pole. At Shinrone, he also caused another gallows to be
erected, on which he hanged a poor man, because some mutton was found
hidden in his garden.

After Sir Laurence and the other convicts were brought from the Assizes, they
were confined in Birr Castle, but the noise and insults of Oxburgh's soldiers
there was so unsupportable, that they were obliged to have themselves removed
to the common gaol of Birr.

The fate of Oxburgh, according to the "Narrative" from which we have been
quoting, was as follows: The Colonel died, and his regiment was given to his son
Henry, but before his death, his wife (whose maiden name was Coghlan), and he
had a dispute, which ended in their parting beds. One of his daughters, then
about five-and-twenty years of age, and who was married to Lieutenant-Colonel
Carroll, died suddenly, of apoplexy, in the middle of the night. The other
daughter, who was married to Captain Pay, died of the small-pox, and two of
their sons were killed at the battle of Aughrim. The eldest son joined King

A/23 *contd.* William the Third's army after the siege of Limerick, but being soon after disbanded, spent the remainder of his life with his mother, in poverty and distress. This lady, who was present at the battles of Athlone, Galway, and Limerick, was, after the decline of her fortune, obliged to return to her house at Boveen, near Birr, where she afterwards resided in a poor condition, and was

p.79 forced to employ her coach in carrying firewood for sale into Birr, to maintain herself and family. A doleful example is this of the instability of human greatness.

Leaving for a while the "Narrative of Sir Laurence Parsons," we turn to some circumstances known from other sources concerning this Oxburgh family, so much mixed up in the history of Birr about this period. It appears by the old Rental of the Parsons family, before referred to, that Colonel Oxburgh held the lands of Crinkill, from Sir Laurence Parsons, in 1669, at £60 a-year, and the lands of Newtown, at £70 per annum. In a lease dated 11th December 1736, made by Mary Warren and others, to Thomas Dillon, of Kilcoleman, of the lands of Killenbrackan, not far from Birr, there is a recital that Henry Oxburgh, or, as he is there called, Oxbury (the Colonel's son), who was a life in the lease of these lands, was attainted and executed for high treason, a little subsequent to 1714. This deed states that by this Henry Oxburgh's attainder, these lands became vested in the crown. Oxburgh resided at Boveen, on the 28th of September 1707. Playfair's Irish Peerage states that Thomasina, daughter of "Heywood [*sic* – Heward] Oxburgh, of Bovine," was married to Thomas, son of Edward, son of Sir Thomas Loftus.

To resume from the "Narrative". In the end of 1689–90, an agreement was entered into between the English and Irish armies for an exchange of prisoners, and an order came from the King to Terence Coghlan, Esq., then High Sheriff

p.80 of the King's County, to bring up Sir Laurence Parsons, and Rascoe, to Dublin. On the 2nd of April 1690, they accordingly set out for Dublin, and on the first day went as far as Ballyboy, from whence they reached Edenderry on the second day, Leixlip on the third, and on the 5th of April, they arrived in Dublin. Thus, it required, in these times, four days to travel from Birr to Dublin, which can now be done in less than as many hours.

Sir Laurence having been kept a prisoner in Dublin some time, was liberated after the Battle of the Boyne, fought on the 1st of July 1690; and upon the establishment of King William's Government in Ireland, he was appointed High Sheriff of the King's County. The country was then very unsafe, being full of remains of the late King's army, and raparees, and it was the more unsafe to Sir Laurence, in consequence of there still being a large garrison of the Irish at Banagher, within a few miles of Birr. He was at this time also appointed a Commissioner of Array, the other Commissioners of Array for the King's County being, John Baldwin, jun., Daniel Gaghan, William Purefoy, Samuel Rolls, Hector Vaughan, John Weaver, sen., Jonathan Darby, Humphrey, Minchin, Archibald Adaire, Jeffery Lyons, John Reading, Richard Warburton, sen., and Richard Warburton, jun. Being thus authorized, Sir Laurence set out from Dublin for Birr, through a dangerous woody country full of raparees and strolling parties of the Irish solidery. He brought with him ammunition for the King's

A/23 *contd.*

p.81   County Militia, and on his way, swore in several Justices of the Peace, by virtue
of a dedimus given him by the Lord Commissioners.

The following is also chiefly taken from the "MS. Narrative of Sir Laurence
Parsons," already referred to.

On the 8th of August, Sir Laurence, accompanied by Captain Theobald Burke, a
younger son of the Earl of Castleconnell, and who was married to a kins-woman
of Sir Laurence, arrived at Birr. At this time the Castle of Birr was garrisoned by
the English, consisting of about eighty infantry, and a few dragoons, under the
command of Captain Curry, of Colonel Tiffan's regiment. The 11th of August
1690, information was received that a party of horse from Banagher was
approaching Birr, and had taken a great number of cattle, and part of the Birr
garrison having thereupon sallied out, a skirmish took place between them,
about ten o'clock in the morning. About twelve o'clock the same day, the Irish to
the number of about one thousand horse and foot, under the command of
Colonel Geoghegan, advanced to Burke's Hill, over Birr, and sent a summons to
the castle, but after some parley they retired.

Sir Laurence Parsons being then in Dublin, an Irish army consisting of seven
battalions of foot, six regiments of horse, and four of dragoons, with a train of
six pieces of artillery, and amounting in all, according to Harris's *Life of William
III.,* to ten thousand men, began, on the 16th of September 1690, to make their
p.82   appearance in the neighbourhood of Burke's Hill. Upon this a drum was beat to
recall the soldiers belonging to the castle, who were amusing themselves in the
town, and Ensign Ball, with twenty infantry, and a serjeant, was sent to occupy
the steeple of the church; and Lieutenant Newstead was sent with another party,
to observe the enemy's approach and clear the neighbouring hedges. An officer
with a few horses soon appeared, and informed him that Colonel Sarsfield,
the Duke of Berwick, and lord Galway, were advancing to attack the castle.
The main body of the Irish remained on Burke's Hill and a conisderable body
of cavalry was sent to Nicholson's Park near a place called Raelane, and
another party to the top of Drumbawn Hill. After sometime the infantry
marched towards the castle, with a twelve-pounder, a six-pounder, and a
three-pounder, and with colours flying, trumpets sounding, drums beating
and bagpipes playing. When they arrived at that part of the Green, where
Mr Cooke's house now stands, within musket shot of the castle, they planted
their battery against it.

In the commencement of the attack, the besieged hoisted a bloody flag on the
top of the castle, being determined to hold out. Seeing this Colonel Sarsfield
addressed his officers, and for reasons given by him, endeavoured to dissuade
them from the attack. Colonel Oxburgh, however, begged that the castle might
be laid in rubbish, so as to force the garrison to submit. Upon this the place was
again summonded to surrender, and Captain Curry having refused to yield,
p.83   the Irish Commanders, about two o'clock in the afternoon, began firing their
great guns. The first shot broke a hole in the roof of the castle, and made a noise.
At the commencement of the attack, the town's-people fled to the castle, and
the enemy entered and plundered the town. While approaching to form

A/23 *contd.* their battery, the Irish were greatly annoyed by the fire of small arms, and particularly by that from Ensign Ball's detachment in the top of the steeple of the Church, which was situated on an eminence, partly between the castle and the Irish. Sarsfield in the first place lined with infantry the hedges about the Green, Godsell's Park, and behind the Almshouse, which then stood between the Church and the Green. The fire from these was very annoying, although it did no execution, unless to kill the sergeant of Ensign Ball's party, who exposed himself too much above the battlements of the steeple. After the first fire from the artillery, the besiegers beat a parley, which had no good result, and the action re-commenced and continued until sunset, during which time the fire from the artillery, and of small arms from the hedges, which was briskly answered by sharp and thick vollies from the castle and steeple, resembled a continual roar of thunder. Lord Galway and several other officers got into the Market-house, which fronted the castle, and from thence they kept up a galling fire with fusees against the doors and windows, so that the besieged could not stir in any of the front rooms. The enemy's great guns being burst,

p.84 and their engineer killed at the setting of the sun, they drew off their cannon with some difficulty, and retired to Burke's Hill. The "Narrative of Sir Laurence Parsons," from which this is taken, adds that the besiegers lost sixty men, and the besieged only one man, and that the Irish broke up their camp, and marched away from Burke's Hill during the night. The writer of this work, however, does not vouch for the accuracy of the "Narrative".

In his *Life of William III.*, Harris states that upon the first news of the attack on Birr by Sarsfield, Sir John Lanier marched to dislodge him, but Sarsfield retired on his approach, the tidings of which occasioned Sir John to return to his former quarters; whereupon Sarsfield again invested the castle, as has been just described. At length Lieutenant-General Douglas, Major-General Kirk, and Sir John Lanier, with a strong body of forces, both horse and foot, advanced with a resolution not only of disturbing the siege, and throwing relief into the castle, but also with an intention to drive Sarsfield beyond the Shannon, and break down the bridge of Banagher, so as to prevent his incursions in future over that pass.

p.85 General Douglas arrived in Birr about three o'clock in the afternoon of the 18th, marched through the town, and encamped upon Burke's Hill. On the 19th he found Sarsfield very advantageously posted, about two miles beyond the town, amongst bogs and fastnesses, and was resolved to attack him, but Sarsfield retired to a place of more security beyond the Shannon. Although the principal design of this expedition was upon the bridge of Banagher, the attempt to break it down was found to be too hazardous, as the enemy was not only very strong on the Connaught bank of the river, but the bridge was defenced by a castle, and another work which protected it on two sides. The English army therefore returned to Birr, where they encamped for ten or twelve days, to countenance the people employed in fortifying with sodworks the town, which had previously been open and defenceless.

To resume from the "Narrative of Sir Laurence Parsons". The fortifications and trenches around Birr were commenced on Saturday, and twelve hundred men were employed at them on Sunday, and six or seven hundred men

A/23 *contd.* constantly afterwards for eight or ten days. Both gables of the Sessions-house were pulled down, and all the hedges, ditches and orchards within the works levelled, and the wood converted into fascines for the fortifications. On Major-General Kirk's arrival, his first act was to order all the Roman Catholics in the town to be seized, and imprisoned in the Market-house, where they remained confined for three or four days, until they became bound, one for another, for their good behaviour, and that they would not depart the town.

Kirk's next act was to order Lord Lisburn[e] to burn all the houses between the town and Racalier-bridge, to prevent the enemy from taking shelter in them. The town itself did not fare much better. Most of the houses without the fortifications were pulled down for fireing by the soldiery, although there

p.86 was turf enough upon the bogs near at hand. As to this Lord Lisburn, whose name was Adam Loftus, we learn from Crossley"s peerage that he was created Lord Viscount Lisburne, by James II., in 1685, and was killed on the 15th September 1691, by a cannon ball, in his tent before Limerick, at the siege, "for the tent stood too near the trenches". He is buried in St. Patrick's choir, Dublin, to the right of the communion table, joining the Earl of Cork's monument, and the cannon ball that killed him hangs up over his burial place. Thus Lord Lisburn was killed fighting against the King, to whom he was indebted for his title.

During their stay in Birr, King William's army not only burned the country round, but bread being scarce with them, they made that a pretext for stripping and robbing many of the Irish who had taken protection; which infamous practice, says Mr Harris, in the *Life of William III,* forced these people to go out upon their keeping, and turn raparees, and raised great numbers of enemies to King William, that would otherwise have remained quiet. This statement of Mr Haris as to the ill-conduct of King William's army, is confirmed by the fact of the Lord Justices having been at length obliged to issue orders for preventing such atrocites.

p.87 After the siege, the standing garrison of Birr consisted, according to the "Narrative" already mentioned, of three regiments of foot, under the command of Major Collier, who governed the castle. Sir Laurence's son, Captain William Parsons, commanded a troop of Militia cavalry in the town, and his brother was posted in Carolanty House. The Irish occasionally made sallies from their quarters at Banagher, and annoyed the town, but without doing any considerable damage. After the battle of Aughrim, the English army marched to besiege Limerick, and the Irish quitted the fort of Banagher, of which Major Collier immediately took possession, and stationed himself there; while Captain Parsons, with his troop, took Cloghan Castle, in which he left a garrison, under the command of Lieutenant Archibald Armstrong, and returned to Birr with the remainder of his men. The English army passed through Birr on their way to Limerick in 1691, and converted the castle into an hospital, leaving there four hundred sick and wounded men, who remained in it nearly two months.'

B/1	DATE	DESCRIPTION

1–13   1705: 1708:   Letters and papers of Sir William Parsons, 2nd Bt, including: a
        1714–16: 1721: copy of a letter from him to Ormonde, the Lord Lieutenant,
        [*c.* 1724]:   about the financial embarrassments of Parsons's kinsman, 'Mr
        1728–9: 1733:   Phillips', late of Limavady, Co. Londonderry, 1705; a badly
        1739: N.D.   damaged deed of settlement, 1708; a copy of a letter from the
                        Lords Justices of Ireland to Parsons, in the absence of the
                        Governor of King's County, Lord Shelburne, about the invasion
                        scare of January 1716; a division list recording the names of the
                        152 M.P.s (Parsons among them) who voted against the proposed
                        national bank for Ireland, and the 98 who voted for it, December
                        1721 [a different division list from the one in the Midleton Papers,
                        Surrey History Centre, Woking, MS. 1248/5, ff 105–6, although
                        both are on the same issue]; a copy of Parsons's will, 1733; and a
                        copy of Lady Parsons's (his second wife, *nee* Elizabeth St George of
                        Dunmore, Co. Galway) will, 1739.*
                        The sub-section includes:

6   9 Dec. 1721   Division list on the issue of a national bank.
                        'A list of those that voted against a bank in Ireland, December
                        9th 1721.

1. Mr Cross	23. Mr Coote
2. Mr John Eyre	24. Mr Corker
3. Mr James Caulfeild	25. Mr Busteed
4. Mr Clot[worthy] Upton, teller	26. Mr Tynte
5. Mr Spencer	27. Mr St Leger
6. Mr Henry	28. Mr Brabazon
7. Mr Skeffington	29. Mr Rogerson
8. Mr Dixon	30. Mr Ben[jamin] Burton
9. Mr Harrison	31. Mr Plunket[t]
10. Mr Wolseley	32. Mr Reading
11. Mr Weldon	33. Mr Miller
12. Mr Beauchamp	34. Mr Colvill
13. Mr Gilbert	35. Mr Rochfort
14. Mr St Jo[hn] Brodrick	36. Sir John Rawdon
15. Mr Hen[ry] Boyle	37. Mr Tighe, teller
16. Mr Hoar [*sic*]	38. Mr Campbell
17. Mr Hyde	39. Mr Hill
18. Mr Jephson	40. Mr John Cole
19. Mr William Brodrick	41. Mr Edward Ormsby
20. Mr Cox	42. Mr Trench
21. Mr Hen[ry]	43. Mr Shaw
22. Mr Bart[holomew] Purdon	44. Mr Blackney [*sic*]
	45. Mr Blennerhassett

B/1/6 *contd.*

46. Mr Brab[azon] Ponsonby
47. Mr Ja[mes] Barry
48. Mr Ri[chard] Warren
49. Mr Thomas Burgh
50. Mr Keating
51. Mr Flower
52. Mr Weymes [*sic*]
53. Mr Ed. Warren
54. Sir Robert Maude
55. Mr Bettesworth
56. Mr Ed. Deane
57. Mr Stephen Dean [*sic*]
58. Mr Agar
59. Mr Flood
60. Mr Edward Worth
61. Mr William Wall
62. Mr William Gore
63. Mr Theo[philus] Jones
64. Mr Gearing
65. Mr John King
66. Mr R. St George
67. Mr Oliver
68. Mr Foord [*sic*]
69. Mr Brazier
70. Mr Geo[rge] King
71. Mr Bury
72. Sir Rob[ert] Newcomen
73. Mr Parnell
74. Mr Pcppard
    Pennefather
75. Mr Harman
76. Mr Henry Edgewood
77. Mr Robert Edgeworth
78. Mr Rowley
79. Mr Norman
80. General Frcd[rick]
    Hamilton
81. Mr Ri[chard] Tisdall
82. Mr William Moore
83. Mr Mich[ael] Tisdall
84. Mr Brooke
85. Mr Ja[mes] Tisdall
86. Mr Townley
87. Mr Stannus
88. Mr Aston

89. Sir Art[hur] Gore
90. Mr Ludlow
91. Mr Percivall [*sic*]
92. Mr Carter
93. Mr Meredith [*sic* - Meredyth]
94. Mr St Lawrence
95. Sir Alexander Cairn[e]s
96. Sir William Parsons
97. Mr Cha[rles] Plunkett [*sic*]
98. Mr Lestrange
99. Mr Dawson
100. Mr Piggot
101. Mr Wall
102. Mr Warburton
103. Mr Short
104. Sir Edward Crofton
105. Mr Art[hur] French
106. Mr Crofton
107. Sir Hen[ry] King
108. Sir John French
109. Mr Thomas Caulfeild
110. Mr Sam[uel] Burton
111. Mr King[smill?]
     Pennefather
112. Mr Hamerton
113. Mr Buckworth
114. Mr Mat[hew]

115. Mr Guy Moore
116. Mr Step[hcn] Moore
117. Mr St George
118. Mr Thomas Ash
119. Mr Ed[ward] May
120. Mr Christmas
121. Mr Mason
122. Mr Rcd[mond] Barry
123. Mr Ja[mes] Barry
124. Sir Art[hur] Shaen
125. Mr Wood
126. Mr Handcock
127. Mr Hen[ry] St George
128. Mr William Jones
129. Mr Loftus

B/1/6 *contd.*

130. Mr Stopford
131. Mr Ed. Jones
132. Mr Cad[wallader] Edwards
133. Mr Thomas Meredith [*sic* -
     Meredyth]
134. Dr Worth
135. Mr Lehunt[e]
137. Mr Palliser
138. Mr Hen[ry] Ponsonby
139. Mr Abel Ram
140. Mr Boyle
141. Mr Houghton
142. Mr Doyne
143. Mr Saunders
136. Mr William Berry
144. Mr Percy
145. Mr Richard Edwards
146. Mr Sam[uel] Whitshed
147. Mr Edward Stratford
148. Mr John Stratford
149. Mr Sale
150. Mr John Jephson

A list of those that voted for the bank.

1. Mr Richardson
2. Mr Thomas Upton
3. Mr George Macartney
4. Mr George Macartney
   Junior
5. Mr Stevenson
6. Mr Lyndon
7. Mr Newborough [*sic*]
8. Mr Theo[philus]
   Clements
9. Mr Brins[ley] Butler
10. Mr I[e]vers
11. Mr Sam[uel] Burdon
12. Mr [?Knapp]
13. Mr Rugg
14. Mr Bernard
15. Mr William Boyle
16. Mr Coghill
17. Mr Monck
18. Sir Ralph Gore
19. Mr Gust[avus]
    Hamilton
20. Mr Topham
21. Mr Maxwell, teller
22. General Wynne
23. Mr Pearson
24. Mr Creighton
25. Mr Hen[ry] Singleton
[26. Missing]
[27. Missing]
28. Mr Ward, teller
29. Mr Medlicott [*sic* -
    Medlycott]
30. Mr Ross
31. Mr Robert Clements
32. Mr Hans Hamilton
33. Sir Gust[avus] Hume
34. Colonel Correy [*sic*]
35. Mr Agmon[disham] Vesey
[36. Missing]
37. Mr Thomas Crosby [*sic*]
38. Mr John Pratt
39. Mr William Crosby [*sic*]
40. Mr Rose
41. Mr Jos[hua] Allen
42. Mr Gra[y]don
43. Mr Mau[ricc] Cuffe
44. Mr Chaigneau
45. Mr John Cuffe
46. Mr Us[s]her
47. Mr Ja[mes] Macartney
48. Mr Folliott
49. Mr Fran[cis] Burton
50. Mr Manley
51. Mr Marlay
52. Mr Michael Cuffe
53. Mr John Bingham
54. Mr Hen[ry] Bingham

B/1/6 *contd.*

55. Mr John Preston
56. Mr Bligh
57. Mr Nat[haniel] Preston
58. Sir Thomas Taylor
59. Mr Taylor
60. Mr Trotter
61. Mr Lucas
62. Mr Willoughby
63. Mr Purefoy
64. Mr Forth
65. Mr Freeman
66. Mr Hen[ry] Sandford
67. Mr Robert Sandford

68. Mr William Ormsby
69. Mr Cooper
70. Mr Owen Wynne
71. Mr Andrew Mervyn
72. Mr Balfour
73. Mr Maynard
74. Mr Parry
75. Mr Lambert [*sic* – Lambart]
76. Mr Newcomen
77. Colonel Bellew
78. Mr Geo[rge] Ram
79. Mr Colclough
80. Mr Robert Allen

B/7	DATE	DESCRIPTION

1–6 | 1756–7: 1779: 1782 | Formal documents appointing Sir William Parsons to various local offices in King's County, 1756–7, 1779 and 1782, and as a J.P. for Co. Tipperary in 1779, together with a return of his King's County troop of dragoons, *c.* 1757.

The sub-section includes:

5 | 17 Dec., 19 George 3rd [1779] | Co. Tipperary commission of the peace for Sir William Parsons, naming the following previously appointed J.P.s:

The Mayor of the town of Clonmel	Michael Keating
The Mayor the city of Cashel	John Miles
Richard Lockwood	William Finch
John Cook	Anthony Parker the Younger
Richard Pennefather	William [?Bagwell]
Anthony Parker	John Briscoe
Richard Butler	Robert White
Cornelius Callaghan	Michael Head
Samuel Eyres	William Barker
Charles Langley	William Purefoy
John Bayley	James Massy Dawson
Rev. Michael Obins	Henry White
Rev. John Madder [*sic*]	Richard Cox
John Lloyd	Laurence Hickey
Rev. Edward Moore	Edmond English
John Firman	Gifford Campian
Francis Green Despard	Robert Waller
Henry Hunt	Christopher Kellet
Humphry Minchin	Robert Going
Richard Clutterbuck	John Watson
Thomas Hackett	Francis Mathew
Andrew Roe	Godfrey Taylor
William Barton	Rev. John Lord
John Minchin	Benjamin Lockwood
Thomas Otway	John Lidwell
John Lapp Judkins	Richard Butler of
James Ellard	Ballynehensy
Robert Bradshaw	John Head
Stephen Moore	John Willington
Peter Holmes	Francis Lodge
Mathew Bunbury	James Butler
John Bagwell	Hugh Massy of Pegsborough
Loftus Otway	William Baker
John Garden	Cook Otway
Daniel Gahan	George Pepper

B/7/5 *contd.*

Cornelius Callaghan the Younger
William Woodworth
John Cleburn
Samuel Alleyn
Jerrry Prendergast
Richard Bourke
Richard Gason of Killoshallow
Nathaniel Mitchell
James Thornhill
Rev. Thomas Sheppard
John Bloomfield
Thomas Newcomen
Thomas Mandeville
Thomas Lidwell the Younger
Solomon Cambie
Rowland Jackson
Richard Moore
Mark Lidwell
John Power
Henry Brittle
Henry Langley Junior
William Pennefather
John Toler

James Willington
Charles Walsh
William hayes
Richard Biggs
Alexander English
John Green
Wray Palliser
John Power of
Fourmilewater
Rev. Edward Baron
William Despard
William Percivall [*sic*]
John Kilpatrick
Vere Hunt of Cappagh
Christopher Lloyd
George Bennett
Edmond Doherty
Nicholas Mansergh
James Archer Butler
James Hastier
James Fogarty
Sir William Parsons, Bt

[Parsons was presumably made a J.P. of Tipperary in this year, not particularly because of his property in that county, but because he was sheriff of King's County, and might find it useful to be empowered to pursue offenders over the county boundary.]

B/8	DATE	DESCRIPTION
1–14	1761: 1768: N.D.: [1774]: 1780–81: 1784–6: 1790–91: 1912: 1963: [1983?]	Letters, poems and other papers of Sir William Parsons concerning personal, political and local administrative matters including: a letter from his namesake and cousin, William Parsons, elder son of the William Parsons (d.1771) described in B/5, giving an hilarious description of a fete champetre held by Lord Stanley at a house in Sussex in honour of his bride-to-be, Lady Betty Hamilton, 1774; an address of thanks and compliment from the King's County grand jury to the county M.P.s, Sir William Parsons and John Lloyd, September 1780, declining to impose on them any instructions from their constituents; a letter from Major Laurence Parsons, second son of the William who died in 1771, describing social life at Spa, 1781; a partly coloured 'Plan of the Volunteer army reviewed by General Sir William Parsons, 4th Bt, at Parsons Town, September 20th 1784'; and a letter from Laurence Parsons the future 5th Bt and 2nd Earl of Rosse about prospects for the King's County general election of 1790 at which Sir William Parsons, 4th Bt, was the successful but short-lived candidate.*

The sub-section includes:

| 10 | 20 Mar. [1789] | Laurence Parsons, [Parsonstown], to his father, Sir William Parsons, 98 Newman Street, Oxford Road, London. |

'My dear Sir, I am just returned from the assizes. Bowes Daly was there canvassing importunately, but I do not find he made much impression. Darby has not declared, nor do I think he intends to be a candidate, unless he should have a better opportunity than at present offered, for he had some hopes that Bury might have been so captivated with Italy as to have preferred remaining there to canvassing the King's County, which is not the case. Ed. Armstrong told me he should have no intention of offering himself [as] a candidate, if none appeared but you and Bury. But, if any third person did solicit, he should reserve to himself the liberty of being a candidate also. This, I think, could not injure, but serve, you. Daly also tells me that, if he should find that he should have no probability of succeeding, that [sic] he would not put you and the county to the trouble of poll.

O'Connor and Daly proposed resolutions approving of the conduct of parliament upon the subject of the regency, and they made every effort in their power to have them carried. They were opposed principally by Darby and me, who said, if he had been in parliament he should have voted exactly as I had done. We at last moved to refer the subject to a county meeting, and on a division there were but five on Daly's side, viz. himself, O'Connor, O'Moore, Armstrong of Clara, who is an active canvasser for Daly, and Purefoy. I think this will throw a damp upon Daly's canvass.

Dean Digby told me that he lately received a letter from Lord
Digby telling him that his interest in the King's County should go
to whatever candidates the Dean wished, and in consequence of
this, as Mr Bury is a young man and absent, he thought it right to
countenance *him* by an early declaration, and had made one in his
favour, and that the only objection he had to declare for you was
that he was afraid you would remain in England and not attend
your duty in parliament. This 1 obviated as far as I could by
assuring him you had no such intention. But I think you had
better mention to him in your letter your determination of
returning here very soon. Many pressed me on this subject, and I
told them all that about May, when the weather should be fine
enough for you to travel, that [*sic*] you proposed coming over. ...

I am sorry that the imperfect representation which the
newspaper conveyed to you of the conflict in the House of
Commons between G[ratta]n and me was not counteracted by a
private letter. I certainly ought to have written or made one of my
brothers write. I had not spoken a syllable at any time but was just
rising to speak, when the Speaker asked me good-humouredly, did
I rise to second his motion; upon which, G[ratta]n spring [*sic*] up,
and with most virulent tone and countenance said, "If I should
second it, he would withdraw it". An *insult* so unprovoked and so
unprincipled certainly drew from me some severe animadversions,
but I am sure I never delivered myself with greter calmness and
composure. This produced from him one of the most intemperate
ebullitions of prepared, commonplace scurrility that I believe was
ever vomited in a House of Commons or anywhere else. He was
quite beside himself with passion, and at last said that what I had
said was what the Freeman's Journal had said, and that what the
Freeman's Journal had said was a *lie*, that the author of it was a
liar, that it was not unparliamentary to say that *the author* of the
Freeman's Journal was a *liar* – a positive *liar*. He continued
repeating the last sentence five times, with such emphasis and
gestures, pointing at me, that at last I stepped towards him and
said "You are". Then the House was cleared, doors locked, etc. In
short, the insult is such that, if I had not noticed it in the House, I
must have assualted him the moment he left the House, or never
have showed my face in the country. You see, then, the justice of
those who would *kindly* attribute my retort, when first attacked,
not to the feelings of my own mind as a man of spirit, but to the
infusions of another person [Flood]. Would it not at least be as
just to suppose that the virulence of him, the agressor, proceeded
from my attachment to Flood? But while I continue to take an
active part in parliament, you must expect the partizans and
paragraphists to misrepresent me. For my own part, I give myself
no trouble about them, though they abuse me on one side for

B/8/10 *contd.*

voting *against* an unlimited regent, and on the other for voting for a limited pension list.

The Ambassadors are returned this day. Their incivility to you was very unwarrantable. I do not know what they really think of me, but individually they are all perfectly very courteous to me.

Harman [later 1st Earl of Rosse] and Lord Kingsborough have voted as I did, which has given me much additional weight. As to the M[arques]s of B[uc]k[ingha]m, he has been very civil to me since I took the part I did. But I assure you, a sentence on the subject before nor since, except in simple expressions of thanks, has not passed between us, neither immediately nor through the mediation of any person whatsoever. He does, however, consider himself, and I have some reason to think a higher personage does also, as personally obliged to me in a very considerable degree.

What measures will be taken towards this country by government, I do not however know. But this I know, that if they are not such as you and every honest a man can approve, that [*sic*] I shall not support them. Upon the late occasion, I did my duty to my King, when he was deserted by almost every servant of the crown here, and when his case was deemed desperate. If, in doing my duty to my country hereafter, I can co-operate with his government, I shall be glad of it: if not, I must oppose it as formerly.'

B/9	DATE	DESCRIPTION

1–4   N.D.: 1778–81:   Four notebooks of Sir William Parsons, all of them containing
       [1783]:   accounts of personal, household and demesne expenditure, and
       1785–90   three of them relating to other things as well: the earliest, and
                         undated, notebook contains a journal of a tour in England, with
                         architectural sketches of, and antiquarian observations on, Stourton,
                         Glastonbury, etc, and the 1783 notebook contains rough minutes of
                         the evidence heard by the committee of the House of Commons
                         appointed to try the Co. Sligo election petition of that year.

       The sub-section includes:

3   [1783]   Notebook containing some accounts for personal expenditure, and
                          rough minutes of the evidence heard before the Co. Sligo election
                          committee.

                         'Tuesday 17th, Foll[iott] W[ynne] [word illegible]. Lloyd had been
                         canvassing with Mr Crofton for votes for Co. Roscommon, and
                         had been down in that county among them.

                         Wednesday 18th. ... Knows Capt. J. Wynne, is his brother. Knows
                         John Moore of the town of Sligo. He is a reputable freeholder. He
                         was with Colonel and Capt. J.W. When Colonel W. applied to
                         Moore for his [vote] ... Capt. W. also applied to Moore, as he
                         supposes, for his vote. Does not know the conversation that passed
                         between them, but he knows Capt. W., from the answer he got,
                         flew in[to] a violent passion and damned him (Moore) for a rascal.
                         Upon this, walked off, and called Fol. Wynne after him, and said,
                         is not this pretty conduct in your brother. Desired witness to go
                         back and call Capt. J.W., which he did. Colonel W. seemed very
                         angry with him, and said, if this is your way of electioneering, I
                         desire you will ask no more votes for me, nor farther interfere in
                         my election. Nothing farther happened at that time. ...

                         Cross-examination. ... Cannot be positive, but believes Capt. J.W.
                         was present when Colonel W. came. Colonel W. solicited the
                         voters for their votes. Is pretty positive Capt. W. was in the room
                         part of the time Colonel W. was there, but not the whole time ...
                         Does not know that they were all Co. Roscommon voters. Is
                         positive some of them were not. ... Knows Daniel Gibson. Believes
                         he is a freeholder. Believes he voted for Sir B[ooth] G[ore] and
                         Ormsby. Was arrested by process out of his court just after he had
                         polled. Does not recollect any other process issuing out of his
                         court. Did not grant a process against Robert Taaffe. *Would have
                         done it, if applied to.* Considered the issuing a process pending an
                         election a matter of much consequence. He consulted eminent
                         counsel about it. Considered that, in obedience to his oath of
                         provost, he could not refuse issuing process when required. On
                         security being given Gibson was enlarged. ...Knew no place of

B/9/3 *contd.*

rendezvous for voters except two rooms in the courthouse. Did not know that Egan entertained until after the election. Was desired by Colonel W. to prevent any houses being opened, if he heard of any. Did not make any enquiry whether any were opened, as he could not suppose it. Does not know whether any voters paid for what they eat [*sic*] or drank. ...

Hugh O'Rourke ... . Cross-examination. Remembers Archibald Johnston, Robert Shanon [*sic*] and some more. Treated them to two bottles of claret at Plests. Believes W. Johnston would not perjure himself, as he swore he was bribed. That he did communicate to Mr Ormsby's friends that be believed Johnston was bribed, as he heard he never was at an election yet that he did not get a bribe. ... When witness went out, he believed he left Johnston and Capt. J.W. behind him. ...

Mr Gilmer. ... C[ross]-e[xamined]. Is a freeholder. Voted for Wy[nne] and Coop[er]. ... Has paid very small sums for Colonel W. since the election. Can't positively say what sums he has paid. Does not recollect to whom they were paid. ... Believes the publicans more cautious about entertaining and discovering who were to be their paymasters than on former elections. ...

Gilmer and Mrs McDonough [a publican] confronted. Cannot read or write. Got a note from C[apt.] J.W. ... Had expectations of being paid, as she had a gentleman's word, and would rather get it from one than collect it from nine. The freeholders had expectations, but were not certain of her getting the money, for they told her husband that he knew the bill, and [that] if he would not be paid by the gentleman that did promise (that is Capt. J.W., that promised her at that time), they would not see her at a loss. She can't tell anything whether those expectations made them call more freely. They called freely for liquor, but can't tell what expectations they had in their mind. ...

Shortly after the election, she went to Gilmer for her money, and had some, but very little, conversation with him in his office. She said the freeholders lived careful [*sic*] enough. ... The reason she did not get the money, she believed, was on account of a law. She thought there would be nothing hurtful after the election was over. ... She says she takes no part with either party, but came to speak the truth. ...

Rev. Dr Dodd (*not he that was hanged.*) Attended constantly the 3 first days, and mostly during whole time. Is and was then a justice of peace. Bribery oaths only administered by magistrates. Administered often by himself. ... Apprehends Johnston polled. ...'

[These minutes are more remarkable for the quality of Parsons's doodles, than for their sephological significance.]

C/1	DATE	DESCRIPTION

1–16   1765: [1769]:   Letters to Flood from miscellaneous correspondents, including
          1771: N.D.:   Edmund Burke [two previously unknown letters, recently
          1774: [1777]: published in *The English Historical Review*, no. 457 (June 1999)];
          1780: 1782–3 Edmond Sexten Pery, Speaker of the Irish House of Commons,
                      Denis Daly of Dunsandle, Co. Galway, M.P. for that county, the
                      1st Earl of Charlemont, etc, etc, about Irish (and British) political
                      affairs.

1   21 May,   Edmund Burke to 'My dear Flood.
        endorsed 1765 The last letter I wrote to you will naturally make you expect some
news. I wish to tell you some that may be depended upon, but I
cannot. All I can say is that all is in confusion.

The Secretaries of State have thought proper yesterday to insult the
crown in the House of Lords yesterday [*sic*], and, not indeed directly,
but with little management, to charge the late riots on the King, for
which they may meet their deserts. They made also a bold push to
have the D. of Bedford continued in the ministry, against the King's
will. In the evening of the same day, they sent a proposal in writing
to their master for a most extraordinary arrangement of the military,
which produced a resolution last night of appointing the D. of
Cumberland captain-general. Whether they will go through with the
measure, I cannot tell. But the fact is certain as to the determination.

For the present, the Duke has all in his hands. He went to Hayes
on Sunday with powers as large as could be given. But he [Pitt]
refused them. The assigned motive with regard to Lord Bute is
false. It might have been his secret reason, but was not his
ostensible one. This morning George Grenville and Lord Temple
had a meeting, but what the result was is not known. But it must
produce some effect.

I am in infinite hurry and not very sober. But my intelligence,
however unsatisfactory, is true. God be with you. If more turns up,
you shall have more. Adieu.'

2   18 July 1765 Burke to Flood.
'You may be assured it was not from the want of my taking a
very warm and sincere part in your affairs that you have not heard
from me much sooner. I felt for your uncertain situation probably
as much at least as you did yourself, and was very truly rejoiced
when I heard that you had got out of it with safety and honour.
The latter circumstance, indeed, could never have been doubtful.
Late as it is, however, I congratulate you upon it, and wish you the
same good forture in every event of your life. I had hoped, from
your letter, that as that affair had brought you to our side of the
water, you would not have returned to Ireland without letting us
see you in London. But a little reflection satisfied me that it could
not be.

C/1/2 *contd.*

You have heard, and I daresay without any sort of displeasure, of the late changes here, which have brought into power that set of people who had all along your good wishes. It is unlucky indeed that they can have no more of Mr Pitt with them than his name, his approbation and the assurance of his support, which, though very valuable things, do not thoroughly compensate, at least among foreign powers, his not actually coming into office. The uncertain state of his health in part, but principally the astonishing conduct of Lord Temple, has made him decline active employment, when it is certain he might have had what he would, and how he would. You will see, however, with pleasure that your friend, Chief Justice Pratt, is called to the House of Peers – a very proper and very popular act of the new administration.

It would be ridiculous in speaking of matters of such weight, to mention the advantage your two friends have had from the change, if your heart did not perhaps interest you as much in their concerns as your understanding does in the great line of things. Will. [Burke] is situated very reputably in point of office, and much to his satisfaction with regard to the person he serves. The person whom I serve [Lord Rockingham] is, I suppose, from the little I can yet know of him, one of the best in the world.

Do, when you have a little leisure, let us hear from you. Will. Burke desires to be remembered to you. ...

Remember me to Leland and Bowden. I shall soon write to them. Langrishe is, I suppose, in the country. Lord Charlemont is much better, and yet far from being completely re-established.'

3   31 Nov. [1768] Gervase Parker Bushe, Dublin, to Flood, St James's Coffee-house, London, asking for comments on a pamphlet of Bushe's (*The Case of Great Britain and America*), and particularly for his advice on a more suitable title.

'... There are some parts which, I fear, they will not like to print, but I should think that *Bingley would print anything.* If they won't [in London], I'll get it printed here. So I wait with impatience to hear from you. Direct it to Kilfane [Bushe's house in Co. Kilkenny].

I saw P[onsonby] today. He asked me who was to be our sheriff. I told him, I supposed Jack Hobson. He said he was a mighty proper person, and *if he had* interest, he would not oppose him. We talked about Lady Ann W[andesford']s match. He said, Langrishe, I hear I am to be turned out entirely [text defective] ... . to carry both members. I said, Yes, [text defective] ... . He said he had seen the [?returning – text defective] ... . He then talked of Callan, and of the little regard that was paid to A[gar]'s information at the Council, where he was present by *accident.* Shall I tell him the secret you know? I will not without hearing from you. Remember me to Griffiths [*sic*] ...

Lord Charlemont begs you will present his compliments to Lord
Rockingham. ...'

4   9 Dec. 1771   The 1st Duke of Leinster, Leinster House, Dublin, to Flood
                          sending '... him some papers relative to Ordnance accounts and
                          copies of his late and present Majesty's letters before passing them,
                          which he [the Duke] hopes may be of some use next Wednesday
                          when in such good hands as he has now the pleasure of putting
                          them into.'

5   11 Dec. 1771   Leinster, Leinster House, to Flood authorising Flood '... to make
                          use of his name, if it will be of any use. In regard to the papers, he
                          [the Duke] should wish none to be mentioned after the year *1765*,
                          as Lord Shannon was appointed to the Ordnance [in succession to
                          Leinster] in *1766*.'

6   26 Apr. [1774]   Edmond Sexten Pery, Speaker of the House of Commons, Dublin,
                          to Flood: 'I this morning received your favour of [?Saturday] and
                          am much concerned to hear of your indisposition, but hope it will
                          be of no consequence. The call of the defaulters is adjourned to
                          Tuesday. If it be necessary to make any excuse for you, I shall take
                          care to do it. Your Export Bill is returned unaltered, which gives
                          much satisfaction.'

7   26 Apr. 1774   Hercules Langrishe, Dublin, to Flood.
                          '... Mr Blaquiere moved that the [Export] Bill should be read the
                          first time. It has returned without any alteration, and when it was
                          read, I made a little flourish (not very uncivil to administration, as
                          you may guess) upon the importance of it, in which I was
                          succeeded by Sir L. O'Brien to the same effect. So everything went
                          on very gracious [*sic*]. Blaquiere did not move in it till he was
                          informed you would not come. The Castle is in high spirits on
                          obtaining this law, which they say, and I believe, met with much
                          opposition in England.
                             We had new heads of a bill brought in yesterday to obviate a
                          recent fraud. This new duty on port wine has tempted the
                          merchants to run it, for which purpose they have imported a great
                          deal in vessels so very small that it is evident their intention was
                          fraud, and indeed a great deal has been seized. We have therefore
                          brought in heads of a bill to oblige merchants to import wine (as
                          they must do spirits) in vessels of the usual size. Yet, I doubt
                          whether this will much delay the session, as the bill may get to
                          England tomorrow, and being short, may return with the last of
                          those already there.
                             Nothing is settled about the Judge's place vacant by Malone's
                          death. Some say Lill is to succeed to it, his wife to get a pension,
                          Dennis to be Solicitor and Scott Serjeant. Others say Scott will be
                          Solicitor and that Dennis waits to be made C. Baron on Forster's
                          [*sic*] resigning *cum pensione*. I hear nothing more of promotions,

C/1/7 *contd.* though I sometimes enquire out of *simple curiosity*. We see nothing like opposition in parliament. Hutchinson looks as if he lamented your absence! The Ely cause began yesterday. Malone got through half his state of the case for Rochfort – the other half, I suppose, today. It will take up the whole term.

The great cause on the will of Acheson Mo[o]re for £5,000 per annum, which he left from his daughters to a Mr Stuart, whom he supposed heir to the crown of England, was left undecided at 8 o'clock this morning (having consumed the day and night preceding) *by drawing a juror.*

Lady Ely is just on the point of death. Lady Staples is greatly recovered. Nobody is to be married that I know of ... .

Fourteen bills *in all* arrived. The rest expected. The session is not likely to be over before Monday fortnight.'

8   30 June 1774   Richard Griffith, London, to Flood, Kilkenny, about the terms of the will of Flood's sister, Isabella, which it seems that Flood wanted to set aside.

'... I am doing what I can to sell my employment, in order to secure something for my wife. A friend of mine has promised to apply to Lord Harcourt's private secretary, who is here now. ...'

9   27 Sep. 1774   List of the actors in a performance of 'She Stoops to Conquer' at Knocktopher, (Langrishe's house in Co. Kilkenny), on 27 September 1774, including Bushe, Flood, Edmund Malone and Grattan.

10   N.D.   Denis Daly, Cavendish Street, Dublin, to Flood, Dominick Street, Dublin.

'I am just come from Mr Malone, whose advice I asked with respect to our address. I could not prevail on on him to approve of anything of that kind without very deliberate consideration. He indeed seemed more disinclined to it than I had reason to expect. My opinion, however, remains pretty much the same, and I shall be very glad to add my voice to those who intend to support it. It would be very improper for me to move it, after asking his advice about it. I therefore leave it to one whose authority and abilities are best adapted to make it succeed.'

11   [5 June 1777]   The 1st Earl of Charlemont to 'My dearest Flood. ...

Adjoined I send you an account which I had yesterday from Lord Bruce. As it is certainly authentic, I take for granted you will be glad to see it, as well as surprised at its contents.

For my own part, I confess myself amazed and not a little vexed. Is it then impossible that this world can ever afford us any object of uniform admiration? Can you account for this conduct upon any principle consistent with the opinion you had formed of Lord Chatham? Is it that he feared to encourage the Americans by his silence to farther outrage? This is the best gloss that can be put

C/1/11 *contd.*   upon it. But is it not rather a preparation for his coming into the ministry and acting as other ministers do? ...

'Jack Beresford was last night married to his heart's content.'

12   6 Jan. 1780   Charles Jenkinson to Flood inviting him to '... Addiscombe Place [Kent] on Monday next, where he will meet the Attorney and Solicitor General ...'.

13   20 Jan. 1780   John Forbes, Dublin, to Flood, Nero[t]'s Hotel, King Street, St James's Square, London.

'Had anything occurred since my return to Ireland worthy of your attention, I should not have deferred so long what was equally a duty and gratification, the performance of my promise of writing to you.

The People of this county are not yet by any means satisfied. They seem to have constitutional objects in view of very great magnitude *indeed*, which must create much discussion and difficulty. If parliament does not [?show] more address than has hitherto characterised their conduct, there is too much reason to apprehend a disunion between the People and their representatives. I conceive that with some management the former could be restrained within the bounds of moderation, and the leading defects in our constitution remedied without producing any jealousy in Great Britain. But the Volunteer corps are daily increasing in numbers. I understand that his Excellency, the Lord Lieutenant, is canvassing in favour of Sir Edward Poynings. ...

I presume you have heard of the addresses obtained from the city of Dublin. It is apprehended that *successful applications* have been made to some of the city Patriots. However, the attempt failed, which was made, to procure Lords North and Hillsborough their freedom of the Guild of Merchants and to couple them with Grattan. Such heterogeneous qualities were found to prevail in these subjects, that it will be impossible to make them coalesce. ...

[He goes on to discuss the export of woollens from Ireland to Great Britain, but the letter is damaged and the text defective.] A good easy vent for this manufacture would afford immediate relief for the manufacturers in Dublin. ...'

14   12 Feb. 1780   William Jephson to Flood, St James's Coffee House, London.

'... The repeal of Poynings['s] Law is so vehemently called for here that I am convinced it will be effected. The most that can be done by the moderate party (my party) is to retain that part of it which gives the King and Council of England a power of altering, etc; but the other part, which relates to the interference of the Council of Ireland, will and ought to be destroyed. This, as I remember, was your plan in the days of Lord Chatham.

Now, what I want is that you should be the man to procure the repeal of this latter part with the good will of England. You will, if I [am] not much deceived, do much good and get much honour.

C/1/14 *contd.*

Both are objects. I wish also that it should be known that you have been the man to procure this improvement of the Irish constitution. Depend upon it, *the thing* must be done, and sure the Ministers had better do it at once, and with good grace, ... [text defective].

I am bursting with a pamphlet upon this subject, and the whole of the Irish constitution as it will stand when this is done. I think we are in a glorious way, and know that we are much indebted to you for it. ...'

15   11 Oct. 1782   Michael Jos[eph?] McCragh, Adjutant to the Galway Volunteers, Galway, 'To Colonel Flood.

Previous to the receipt of your very condescending and flattering letter of the 5th inst, the delegates of the Central Division of Connaught Volunteers held a meeting at Tuam, where, influenced by their feelings of the universal distress occasioned by the late violent weather, which, nearly destroying the harvest, has rendered the country a scene of desolation, and apprehensive that the intended review might interfere with the labours of the husbandman, which otherwise would be directed to prevent the threatening ruin, they determined to sacrifice their gratification to the general interest by rescinding the resolution which appointed a review for the 20th instant.

We lament exceedingly that, to the many calamities attendant on the late unfavourable season, should be added to [*sic*] the misfortune of being prevented from beholding the man to whom we look up as the great assertor of our rights ...', etc, etc.

I have the honour of enclosing you [not found] the resolutions of the Central Division.'

16   5 May 1783   Draft or rough copy of a letter from Flood to Edmund Malone.

'I have just received yours of the 24th of April and am equally concerned that we are not oftener together. I attempted your door last summer, when I was in London.

I have been a friend to Irish rights to the best of my poor power, it is true, and upon the fairest grounds. Some people said it was to recover my office, which I could have kept had that been an object. The late suspense with respect to one of those appointments revived this talk, and I never thought it worth my while to tell them what I said long since to Mr Eden, viz. that, if I were dismissed from the Vice-Treasurership, I never should resume it. I will keep my word. I am apt to do it. At the same time, I am sincerely disposed to English government. This you will readily believe, who know my principles and my situation, neither of which I will abandon. They are above vulgar ambition. I was suggested into office on higher motives. I embraced administration with an unsuspecting credulity. I felt it was their interest to act as they spoke. But I found myself deceived. I do not know the author

C/1/16 *contd.*   or the motive to [*sic*] this. You known the consequence.

I took your communication to be precisely such as you state. I have no immediate inducement to go to England, and if you have none to come to Ireland, let us at least correspond. I am perfectly assured of your good wishes and I flatter myself you are equally so of mine.'

C/2	DATE	DESCRIPTION

1–43 1767: 1771–80   Correspondence between Flood and Rev. Dr William Markham, his former tutor at Oxford, successively Bishop of Chester and Archbishop of York, consisting of originals of Markham's letters to Flood [only one other of which is in Add. MS. 22930] and drafts of Flood's letters to Markham, and concerning Anglo-Irish relations, Flood's complaints of ill-treatment and neglect in 1774 when he was passed over for the Provostship of Trinity in favour of John Hely-Hutchinson, his subsequent charges against the British government and justifications of himself, particularly in 1778–80, when Markham was endeavouring to restrain him and remind him of the paramount loyalty he owed to the British connection, etc, etc. [These letters are, even by the generally sorry standards of the 2nd Earl's papers, in urgent need of conservation.]

1   11 Oct. 1767   Markham, Bexley, near Maidstone, Kent, to Flood, endorsed 'About Lord Townshend going to Ireland as Lord Lieutenant'.

'... As to what regards yourself, my wish is that, without any sacrifice of duty or public esteem, you should have a reasonable attention to your own advantage. The times are not such as to afford many occasions for taking a side from conscientious motives, and as government now is, these motives should generally lead us to support it. ... I had some discourse with Lord Fred[erick] Campbell on your subject. He has a great personal regard for you, esteems your talents, and wishes to favour your pretensions. I can venture to assure you that you will find him an honourable, frank man, and that you need have no fear about committing yourself, especially as there is a disposition to accommodate those points for which you have pledged yourself to the public. I advise you, therefore, to be confidential with him. If he thinks your plan practicable, you will have his assistance: if not, you will have a plain answer and secrecy. ...'

2   25 Dec. [1769]   Flood to Markham.

'My prophecy with respect to Lord T-nd does not appear to have been without foundation. In truth, he is a very incapable person for the situation he is in. He had some difficulties to encounter, to be sure, but they were such as would have sunk before wisdom and temper. By him, they have been inflamed and strengthened, and the measures of *influence* which were the only resource of such a mind, instead of removing all other embarrassments, have been themselves the occasion of [text defective, but sense perfectly clear]. One of them, a scheme for five new Commissioners of Accounts, was attacked in the House of Commons, indirectly however, and so as that a defeat of our question should not be an explicit decision in favour of the measure. The Court had first 11,

C/2/2 *contd.*   then 8 and at last 5, majority; which last was composed of the five
gentlemen appointed by the patent. ...

Since this, the money bill came over altered, and was rejected by
a very great [majority – text defective] ... think as not to afford any
ground for difference between us and the ministry. Indeed, we
flatter ourselves that there are some among us who have prevented
private or party heat from taking the lead, as is too common, and
have confined opposition to such objects as are esteemed manly
here, and have preserved all decency and temper in the mode – at
least, so the wise and moderate here imagine, amongst the first Mr
Malone, whose propensities are all for the Court, but whom we
have had upon most of our great questions. ...'

3   Endorsed,   Markham, now Bishop of Chester to Flood.
             19 Feb. 1771   '... The D. of Grafton was tried on the subject of your views on
this side. I could never get an explicit answer. Have you any such
now? If you have, I shall be more in the way of [text defective] ... is
much more accessible as well as more attentive to the H. of
Commons that [*sic*] he was at that time. I have always wished that
your abilities had a better field. Do not be afraid of committing
yourself. I know the caution and delicacy with which such a
business ought to be treated, and I shall endeavour, if I cannot do
good, to avoid doing mischief.'

4   3 Mar. 1771   Flood to Markham.
'... There was a majority of 25 for paying the usual compliment
to the Lord Lieutenant on the first day of the session, when the
resolution for the address to the King was moved. ... The Court
say they will have 40 majority on the new election. I believe hardly
– that is to say on fair trials upon notice. I moved two questions
the other day, one of which passed unanimously, the other [of
which] was rejected by 21 majority only

I have no connection with the leaders or heads of interests here
that are in opposition. But Lord T-'s conduct to the public has
made me hitherto co-operate with them, or rather coincide. He is
a strange man and has acted most unaccountably and injudiciously
in many things. ...

The Lords have been warm. Half of the lay peers, wanting one,
opposed any address at all to the Lord Lieutenant, and have since
proposed that his protest made in their Journals against our
conduct as to the Council Money Bill may be expunged. They
have in both cases entered strong protests. You may judge from all
this that we are in a ferment.

As to what you are so kind as to [text defective] ... I am in the
same disposition as formerly. A change of that sort, however,
which takes a man from the management of his fortune, etc,
requires an adequate motive, and England is a much dearer
country than this. I need say no more at present, I believe.'

C/2/5   11 Mar. [1771] Flood to Markham.

'Since my last, a considerable revolution has happened. Mr Ponsonby has resigned the chair of the House of Commons rather than carry up an address of thanks to our present Viceroy, and Mr Pery has succeeded him. Mr Pery was set up by the Castle and carried it by four only, and even that by great mismanagement. Had he failed, Mr Brownlow, in consequence of a previous promise, would have been set up by the independents and [text defective] ... .

In this, as in everything respecting me, Lord Townshend has been governed by a little pique that misbecomes anything [*sic*] but a girl, and to which he has sacrificed even common justice. By the impatience and misconduct, however, of his principal adversary, he is at present victorious, and will a second time reap the laurels which he did not win. ...'

6   19 Oct. 1771 Flood to Markham.

'... I have been the busiest man in the world all the summer, both as a builder and as an improver of ground, or rather dresser of it strictly speaking.

The 8th of October, our day of meeting of parliament, has dragged me to this town. I will confess to you, I was surprised to see Lord Townshend address us once more from the throne. I thought he had merited his discharge in every sense, and that English government [text defective – had no sort?] of wish to give themselves unnecessary trouble or to embarrass those gentlemen of this country who wish as well to government as any men in the kingdom, but between whom and Lord Townshend there can be no co-operation. I sincerely believe that for English purposes he was as unadvisable a choice as could easily have been made. ...

I moved an amendment to the address prepared for the Commons in answer to the Speech ... . It was opposed by the servants of the crown strenuously, but in the course of the debate they found themselves deserted by many country gentlemen successively, till at length the whole fabric of their majority gave way. ...'

7   30 Nov.
     [endorsed]
     1771

Flood to Markham, Bloomsbury Square, London.
'... The large majority with which Lord Townshend completed the last session is so much diminished that he has been defeated on five or six material questions ... .

The conduct of opposition (I do not say so because I am generally one of that body) has been respectable. Two-thirds of the body are now not under the influence of any of the three great powers of this kingdom, as they have been called; nor could all those powers united disturb a sensible and gracious Governor, whose measures were unexceptionable. In the midst of great public distress, we have continued the augmentation of the army voted a

C/2/7 *contd.*

few years ago, and have provided for the increased expense of the army in another particular in consequence of a new arrangement of the companies: an instance of no small attention to the solid interests and wishes of the crown. To accomplish it, we have been obliged, after running considerably in debt the two last years, to empower government now to borrow £200,000 more, and not only this, but to grant for the internal improvements of the country and to our charitable foundations not half what we formerly granted. ...

We are more highly taxed in proportion to our ability, it is thought, than Great Britain herself. Our annual taxes are more than the current cash of the nation, and yet our Revenue is inferior to our expense in a sum of between £200,000 and £300,000 a session.

You will not wonder that we should not think this a time for the creation of new offices or for the introduction of new expense. We have therefore replied to Lord Townshend in such a manner as to express our disapprobation of such an idea. He has told us that he will refer our resolution to his Majesty. ...

In Lord Northumberland's government, the House of Commons had an assurance conveyed to them by Mr Tisdall, Attorney General and Secretary of State of this kingdom, that his Majesty had declared it to be his intention not to grant any more pensions for lives or years, except on extraordinary occasions. The first pension granted since, contrary to the idea conveyed to the Commons by this message, was a pension to Mr Dyson for three lives. This being the first and only infraction, the Commons have resolved this session not to provide for it, conceiving the crown to be deceived in its grant.

With respect to the partition of the Revenue Board, I have only to add that, as the law now stands, the Revenue could not possibly be collected if such an arrangement should take place, and that if the law were to be altered in the most advantageous manner for that purpose, the expense would be about £40,000 a session, according to the best estimate we can form, and the advantage nothing, for seven Commissioners can certainly do the business as well as twenty; and as to the business of government, I will venture to affirm that it can be transacted with success and dignity without such an addition of offices.

8   10 Jan. 1772   Markham, Bloomsbury Square, to Flood.

'... My opinion of Lord T., both as a man and a governor, agrees very much with yours. I believe him to be very reprehensible in both views, nor do I think it likely that he should be continued. But, whatever his character is, it can justify opposition only to a certain point ... [and should not] be aimed at the rights of the crown and the necessary dependence of a subordinate government.

C/2/8 *contd.*
I do not pretend to know the limits of powers which never have been defined, but as far as appears to me, though the withholding the supplies was in your power, you exceeded your line in challenging a particular pension. ... The principles which you avow in your letters are certainly generous and manly, and I think consistent with a subject's duty. ...'

9   15 Sep. 1772   Markham, Sion End, near Brentford, to Flood, endorsed, 'Observations on a translation of the opening of the Iliad'.

10   12 Nov. 1772   Markham, London, to Flood explaining that, because he '... knew that [Charles] Jenkinson was in [the new Lord Lieutenant, Lord Harcourt's] entire confidence ...', he has made an approach on Flood's behalf via Jenkinson to Lord Harcourt.

11   13 Nov. 1772   Markham to Flood.
'I saw Mr Jenkinson this morning, and have therefore given you a few lines in addition to my letter of last night. We both thought the business was in as good a train as possible, and that it depended upon yourself to have a larger share of the Lord Lieutenant's confidence than any of the King's servants.
Colonel Blaquiere (and no one person else) is acquainted with this transaction. Mr Jenkinson put it to him in such a light that he is very forward to promote the success of it. You must determine whether the negotiation is to be carried on by the party here or whether you will use the means you have of conducting it yourself. From what I know of Lord Harcourt's impression of you, and of your own good judgement, which will not desert you on this critical occasion, I cannot help considering the matter as already concluded. ... Lord H. would not be hampered with any of Lord Townshend's engagements, and till everything of that kind was settled, has been staying at Lord Vernon's. ...'

12   14 Jan. 1773   Markham, Bloomsbury Square, to Flood.
'... I told him [Jenkinson] the substance of your letter, said there had certainly been ill-management, which I could not ascribe to you, as I was far from wishing that you should do anything which might lower your consequence. He agreed with me, and read me a part of a letter from Lord H., in which he said that you had been received at the Castle with all the civility which he could show you; that he had expected you would have desired an audience, but that he had not heard from you, and was apprehensive you were gone into the country. ...'

13   20 Mar. 1773   Flood, Farmley, Co. Kilkenny, to Markham.
'I am just returned from Dublin, where I had the honour of a conversation with Lord Harcourt. I hope it was not unsatisfactory to his Lordship. He answered your description perfectly, to my mind. No man has more at heart the honour of his Prince than I have, and I feel the most sincere pleasure in hoping that the

C/2/13 *contd.*   welfare and satisfaction of the people will be promoted ... [text
                            defective] ...
                                 The administration that shall succeed in such an ardous attempt
                            will deserve well of their King and country. I sincerely hope Lord
                            Harcourt may. But it must be clear, I think, that, independent of a
                            sense of duty, the common inducements of office would not be
                            sufficient to incline a rational man to embark in such a voyage.'

14   3 Dec. [1773]   Flood to Markham.
                                 'I delayed writing till the session should take some decided turn.
                            The supply is now finished in effect, and a larger sum granted and
                            with more concord that [*sic*] Lord Harcourt could have expected.
                                 What I have formerly told your Lordship as to the parties of this
                            country has been most fully verified by experience. Nor is there
                            any danger of disturbance, unless [text defective] ... correctness or
                            of recollection shall expose administration to embarrassment. I
                            have supported them on the most liberal grounds and I believe
                            that the effect has not been less favourable than they expected. We
                            have voted £300,000 to be borrowed and near £100,000 a year of
                            taxes to be raised for the crown. This is the second time I have
                            been instrumental to the increase of the revenue of the crown and
                            the third administration I have supported without ever having
                            received a favour from his Majesty.
                                 The idea your Lordship stated in your letter is not in my mind
                            observed sufficiently. You know my idea, and the only one I can
                            entertain. Be so good as to give me your aid ...'.

15   30 Jan. 1774   Markham, Christ Church, Oxford, to Flood.
                                 'Your two letters of 20 and 21 have reached me today. I am
                            vexed and mortified at the accounts you give me. I am loath to
                            believe it possible that the principal can be so base or so silly as to
                            think of deceiving you. ...
                                 Your name has been mentioned in conversation for the
                            Provostship, and I was asked whether you looked towards it. I
                            could only say that I had never heard from you anything on the
                            subject, but that if the intention was that it should go in the
                            political line, no one would hold the place more ably and
                            honourably. I am really surprised at the designation which you
                            mentioned [Hely- Hutchinson?]. The persons whom I have heard
                            mentioned as likely to be thought of were yourself, upon one plan,
                            and Dr Leland, upon the other. ...'

16   31 Jan. [1774] Flood to Markham.
                                 '... Mr Blaquiere has thrown himself in appearance into the
                            hands of Mr Hutchinson, from the beginning of the session,
                            whose counsels are not generally thought to be of the wisest or
                            most salutary kind, but rather directed to personal profit. ...'

C/2/17 5 Feb. 1774 Markham, Bloomsbury, to Flood.

'... I have seen Jenkinson once, who was very full and explicit in doing justice to the very honourable and effectual part that you [had] taken, and ascribed the success and honour which had attended Lord Harcourt's administration to the frank and disinterested support that you had given, and seemed to have no doubt that your services would be remembered as honourably as they ought.

I likewise heard your conduct spoken of with approbation in various companies. At the same time, I cannot help apprehending that the conduct of the D. of Leinster and his friends, with the formal declaration which they have made to the Lord Lieutenant, may in some respects have taken off a part of the value which belongs to your services. It ought not to be so, but in the course of affairs, it cannot be avoided. ...'

18 13 Apr. 1774 Markham, Bloomsbury Square, to Flood making observations on an ode of Flood's.

19 4 June 1774 Flood to Markham.

'... I forgot to tell you that Lord Harcourt said he had written about the point I mentioned to you, but had not received an answer. If I were to relate the whole conduct of another person, it would surprise [you? – text defective] ...'.

20 20 June [1774] Flood to Markham.

'We have been grossly abused, both of us. Nothing can be more exceptionable than the conduct here in every instance. ...

[Lord Harcourt] has just offered me the Alnager's place in the room of the Prime Serjeant [Hely-Hutchinson], whom he recommends to be Provost. I refused it in civil terms to his messenger, but with no small contempt of mind.'

21 21 June [1774] Flood to Markham.

'... It never can be really wise in governors to destroy all sense of honourable confidence in those they employ. It is the thing of all others they ought to encourage. At least I am sure no man of sense and competency will have any connection with such governors beyond that of being a loyal subject. ...'

22 25 June [1774] Flood to Markham.

'... Without ... entering into the merits of the Provostship one way or the other, what could be more unexpected by your friend [Flood] than to have not that which had fallen, but a thing inferior, offered to him? He can consider this in no other light than that of offence and violation. ...

I expect any post to hear explicitly from you as to the object which has been formerly mentioned to you. I entreat you will not delay writing. ...'

C/2/23 6 Apr. 1775 Markham, Bloomsbury Square, to Flood, in reply to a huffy letter in which Flood has asked for the return of Flood's previous letters to Markham.

'... As to your affairs, I have heard no more than that Lord Harcourt is very earnest and pressing that you may be in some shape or other satisfied, and that Lord North is equally disposed. A negotiation with Hamilton [for the Chancellorship of the Irish Exchequer] has been renewed, but found to be impracticable. ...'

24 30 Oct. 1775 Markham, Sion End, to Flood referring to Flood's acceptance of one of the Vice-Treasurerships and to the coolness between them.

25 5 Jan. 1776 Markham, Bloomsbury Square, to Flood.

'... I had a conversation with one of the Ministers about your pretensions to a place in the [British] Privy Council. I found it had been taken up strongly as a thing new and unprecedented that a man who had no seat in the English parliament and even no property in England should be brought to that board, that it was a new thing to consider the place [of Vice-Treasurer] as giving pretensions, that Oswald's was the first instance, that there had been a facility in those appointments which wanted a regulation, and that a situation might happen which would make the present Privy Council dangerous to the state.

To all of which, I had only to answer that, without disputing the general propriety, your case should be attended to as being particular, that they were misinformed if they believed it had been asked by you, that it had been offered among other inducements before you had accepted the office, that the Lord Lieutenant might have been inadvised in offering it, but that as matters stood, it was a serious question whether they would refuse maintaining the faith of his engagement. The truth is that no one, I believe, aims at you, but there are some who are not his friends.

If the other point succeeds, as I think it must, this will follow of course. I am talking of a business which by this time may have taken a turn, but it is the last that I heard of it.'

26 [5–19 Jan. (1776?] Markham, Bloomsbury Square, to Flood.

'... Some time after we parted, I discovered that Lord North had never heard a syllable [text defective] .... When I found this, I went immediately to Mr Robinson, who is a fairer man, and more a man of business, than any of them. He agreed with me that Lord North ought to know it immediately, in justice to him as well as to you. He accordingly called upon me the next day with Lord North. ... [Lord North said] that he was well acquainted with your abilities, and with such talents, he did not wonder at your desire to get a seat in the English House and aiming at any honours or emoluments that this country could afford, but that you must consider [text defective] ... others who are in possession. I told him I had not discovered in you any aim of that kind, but that your

C/2/26 *contd.*   view to the seat [on the British Privy Council?] seemed to mean no more at present than your holding the office [of Vice-Treasurer] upon a better tenure. ...'

27   19 Jan. 1776   Markham, Bloomsbury Square, to Flood.
'... I began with the post of Privy Counsellor. I was glad to find that he [Lord North] spoke of [it] as a thing to which some, indeed, had raised objections, but what he always thought ought to be done, and that it either was done already or should be done immediately. The next topic was the seat in parliament, against which he had nothing to say but his engagements to several who had spent large sums and lost their election. After I had said everything that I thought was due to you, and much more than I can tell you, I think I left him in a disposition which, if helped so little from your side, must produce effect.
I am very glad to hear that the emoluments of your office are so much increased.'

28   25 June 1776   Markham, Sion End, to Flood, Kilkenny, discussing in great detail the circumstances under which the King has relieved Markham of his position as tutor to the Prince of Wales and the Duke of York.

29   10 Nov. 1777   Markham, now Archbishop of York, Bishopthorpe, Yorkshire, to Flood, endorsed, 'Respecting an attack on him in the House of Lords for the sermon he preached'; Markham describes the attack as having been '... concerted by the corps which met at Lord Buckingham's'.

30   9 Dec. 1777   Markham, Bloomsbury Square, to Flood.
'... I can easily conceive that little men should be jealous of your abilities, and that such a man as Hutchinson should find favour and trust with a jobbing administration. But I do not see so easily why you ought to be mortified, because I consider you as advanced to a higher line, and that though an attention to the public service may reasonably be expected from you, yet no men can expect more from you than belongs to the part which is assigned to you, and that it is of little consequence to you what part they assign. The rank which belongs to your office is a new thing in their system, and they possibly may themselves be cautious of seeming to expect more than you choose to give, especially if they think that you have not been explicit and hearty in offering it. They know very well that they are not your principals and that the administration which you look to must be that of this country, and this alone may beget a jealousy in that temper of mind which delights in cherishing its own creatures, and places its trust in those sordid motives by which itself is governed. ...
I have wished again and again that this was your theatre. Look towards it, and consider the pettish humours of those you are now amongst only as a cloudy day upon your journey.'

C/2/31 12 Dec. 1777   Markham, Bloomsbury Square, to Flood.
                        '... I have mentioned the business to several who are of
                        consequence, and am convinced that, whatever reasons may have
                        influenced the strange behaviour which you mention, they are not
                        in concert with any here, nor likely to find countenance. Every
                        step in the Lord Lieutenant's administration is disapproved, his
                        whole system condemned, not by Lord North only, but by higher
                        than him, warmly and strongly. Mr J[enkinson] told me you had
                        taken an honourable and manly part in doing justice to Lord
                        Harcourt's government, though he said he well knew you had
                        some grievances under it. Among others, I had a serious
                        conversation with my friend, Sir Ch[arles] Thompson, upon the
                        footing of a well-wisher to his brother-in-law [Lord
                        Buckinghamshire, the Lord Lieutenant], as well as to the general
                        cause of his Majesty's affairs. He was astonished at what I told
                        him, said he would write immediately, and asked me if he might
                        mention my name. I told him he might. ...'

32   10 Jan. 1778   Markham, Bloomsbury Square, to Flood.
                        '... I found by your last letter that a new face is given to the
                        business which has made the subject of your complaints, and that
                        you have been requiring the Lord Lieutenant to fulfil the
                        engagements of his predecessor. You will forgive me if, with the
                        freedom of a friend, I question the wisdom of such an application
                        at this time.
                          As the matter stood before, whoever hears the story will allow
                        that you had good reason to be dissatisfied with their want of
                        civility and attention, and that degree of respect which your rank
                        and abilities entitle you to. But I am afraid you have now given a
                        colour at least to lay it to ill-humour on your part for not being
                        gratified in demands which, in common opinion, the present
                        Governor will not be thought bound to answer, for it is certainly
                        true that, if he gave a life office in lieu of your present, he would
                        have nothing to [do] with the disposal of it; and you cannot
                        suppose that the plea of your services can have the same weight
                        with the present, as they had with the late, who was benefited by
                        them and had bound himself to reward them. I did not tell you
                        that in the judgement of many people, and those too who had no
                        ill-will towards you, the reward which you have got is thought, not
                        only unusual, but for any services in your line of politics excessive. I
                        believe it is right in prudential decisions to estimate the things by
                        the standard at which the world take them ...; and nothing in my
                        opinion disgraces a public man more than that fickleness of mind
                        of which Sir W. Meredith has just given us an example. I should be
                        sorry, too, that in such a moment as this, when this country is beset
                        with embarrassments, a war with France expected, and everything
                        around us so critical as to call for union and exertion, not only

C/2/32 *contd.*   among the King's servants, but among all honest men, any conduct
of yours should put it in the power of your enemies to say there is a
spot on that character which I am confident before had none.

Nothing is more unlikely than the change of administration
which you have heard of. It may be a doubt with what effect the
present set may be able to serve the public. But the others cannot
possibly do any good. They have put it out of their own power. ...'

33   26 Mar. 1778   Markham, Bloomsbury Square, to Flood about the gloomy state of
public affairs, with a further discussion of any possible ministerial
changes, and a reference to the American Commissioners.

34   9 Feb. 1779   Markham, Bloomsbury Square, to Flood, Farmley, Co. Kilkenny,
referring to the probable death of Markham's son at sea.

'... After telling you my griefs, what shall I say to yours? I will
make no comparison between them. As to me, the subject is
exhausted. If I could see your honour called upon to take such a step
as you have sometimes talked of, I should be the first to advise it.
But it is not so. The grievances you complain of are of too uncertain
and disputable a kind to bear you out in such a proceeding. Your
rank and your ability are both too high not to be attended with
some envy, and as you possess nothing which your services had not
earned, where can be the reason for parting with emoluments which
would only gratify those who have ill-will towards you, and, besides,
put it in their power to represent you as an impracticable man?

I have had some conversations with Sir R. Heron [the Chief
Secretary] upon this subject, and he assured me with solemn
protestation that both Lord B. and himself had never upon any
occasion the least idea of doing anything which could be offensive
to you, that they knew and valued your consequence, and should
deserve to be esteemed idiots if they had used a disobliging
carriage towards you; that however they might fail in their power
to gratify you in all your wishes, yet that they never had a thought
which was adverse to your interests. I will own to you that, when I
find declarations to be founded in commonsense, it goes a great
way towards making me believe them to be true. ...'

35   30 Oct. [1779]   Markham, Bloomsbury Square, to Flood expressing deep regret
that they have missed each other in London.

'... I know only rumours, and feel myself so agitated between
sorrow and indignation that I am really at a loss how to speak to a
[?friend] to whom I always opened my whole bosom. Can I
believe it possible that at such a moment as this the Protestants of
Ireland should threaten rebellion; and yet, if that is not the case, I
must disbelieve all I hear. I know perfectly the dispositions of men
in this country, and I am certain that by sobriety and moderation
Ireland may gain everything that its interests require. But if it has
sold itself to France, or what is much the same, if it means to lend
itself to a faction here, its demands will probably be of such a kind

C/2/35 *contd.*   as in their nature are impossible to be complied with.

They surely cannot expect an answer to so loose a demand as that of a Free Trade? England has no such trade. The trade of England is [?bound] in a hundred instances. Do they [?seek] the liberty to export their wool to France? If they do not, they ought to bring specific propositions; and even then, they ought not to come alone, for it is senseless to require a full share of the benefit without offering to take some share of the burthen with the benefit. It behoves you to consider what you are doing, for the pressure of the burthen will be immediate, and the benefit will come by slow degrees. ...'

36   16 Nov. 1779   Markham, Bloomsbury Square, to Flood.

'Your letter has been delivered to me and has in some points given me a ground of comfort which I had not found in any other account of Irish affairs. I have only to believe the views of these associations as innocent as you represent them, and yet I cannot help having fearful misgivings. ...

But my anxiety is not confined to the course of public events. I take a friend's part in everything which may affect your reputation or interest, and I will not dissemble with you that I find in your sentiments more traces of resentment than I think is justifiable at so awful a crisis. ... You cannot say more of his [Lord Buckinghamshire's] folly and imbecility than is imputed to him here by all mankind. It is a part of our calamity that among the men of high rank so few are to be found who are qualified for stations of business. That he must be displaced, I think unavoidable, but by whom is more than I can conjecture.

As to your conduct, I think, with the probity which I have always believed you to have, it is too plain to be missed. You are known to have your discontents: it would be honourable to forget them now. You may take the business out of the hands of the madmen and put it into a sober and temperate train. You will make men remember that the grievances are not of modern date, that established prejudices are not to [be] reversed in an instant without a violence that may be dangerous, that the Minister here has ill-humours in this country to look to as well as in Ireland. But what is most to be guarded against by those who wish the public welfare, is to preserve some respect to this country. There have been too many passionate words and too many threats. These are resented by all men, even by those who are most disposed to favour the pretensions of Ireland. I consider the six-months money bill as a very hostile measure, and think it foolish, sure that I am that Ireland may gain everything by gentle methods. I think, too, it was not candid to charge the King's answer with procrastination. They should ask themselves what other answer it was in his power to give. ...'

C/2/37 10 Dec. 1779 Markham, Bloomsbury Square, to Flood.

'The principal point to be answered in your last letters [C/2/42–3?] is your wishing to to know whether I had done anything concerning what you had said about waiting upon the King. Indeed, I have not. I did not think myself warranted by the terms of your letter, and if I had thought so, I should have had many reasons for wishing to be excused from meddling in such a business, and I will be free to own to you, one of them is that, if I should be questioned about my own opinions, I should not have had such an answer ready as a friend would wish to give. ...

You seem to take it for granted that you have enemies here. If there are any such, I do declare to you that I do not know them. But I cannot help saying that, if there are any, you have given them strong advantages. Another thing I will add, that from all that I can collect my belief is that you stand much better with administration than with the leaders of opposition. But, however all this may be, it is beside my view of the question.

You know already that it is intended to grant the Free Trade which has been asked, in the way that you expressed yourself when you said it would be absurd to require more than England shall enjoy. It is possible, however, there may be people among you who do not mean to be satisfied, and they will not be wanting men here to encourage them. If such a situation should arise, it will be a glorious opportunity for the men of virtue to make their stand. ...'

38 13 Dec. 1779 Markham to Flood:

'... We have a rumour that Sir Richard has retired from his office. So far well. A more unfit man he can hardly be replaced by. We never hear his name without an expressive epithet. ...'

39 28 Apr. 1780 Markham, Bloomsbury Square, to Flood.

'I have received your letter, and will be free to own to you that I am grieved. Ireland ought to be satisfied, and by all that I hear, without one rational motive, they are going to involve the country in distraction and ruin. You know very well that by my code of moral law, the men who move such questions are wicked citizens. ... I will now answer your question. I saw the gentleman, I think on the very day you left us. He reported from his principal [Lord North] that he was sorry for the ill-treatment that was complained of, when it was impossible it could be intended by him, and that he should have been happy to prevent it; that he was perfectly informed of your abilities and consequence, and would gladly have availed himself of them, particularly by a seat here; he remembered it had been agitated, but that by his accounts he understood that it would make a difference in your expenses of at least £1,000 a year, and you would expect it should be made up to you; but as he did not know when that might be in his power, it made a difficulty, especially as you had never explained yourself to him upon that

C/2/39 *contd.*   subject; that, however, he would see me if I pleased the next
morning. ... I ... declined the meeting. ... No man in his senses
would venture to negotiate in such circumstances. ...'

40   21 May 1780   Fragments of a draft of a letter from Flood to Markham in reply.
'... As to the other subject, the principal person was right as to
the fact of expense. Commonsense speaks it. But nothing could be
more explained than that your friend [Flood] did not solicit [text
defective]. ... .

My elections [in Ireland] are a point which a certain person
[Lord Buckinghamshire?] ought surely to decide in my favour
without delay. To a man that knows the world, difficulties in such
points prove nothing unless indisposition. A peerage to Mr George
Agar would free me from him in Callan, and the county [of
Kilkenny] could be settled for me with Lord Clifden and the
Archbishop of Cashel ... [text defective].'

41   21 May 1780   Markham, Bloomsbury Square, to Flood in reply.
'... He [Lord North?] lamented the unlucky circumstances
which he was afraid had alienated you in some degree from the
public service, or at least had abated the zeal which he should have
expected from your character. He appeared to have a general
knowledge of the county and borough dissensions, said he could
not tell why you should ever have a failure in [text defective – any
support?] which government ought to give, unless it was that your
opponents were before in possession and had preoccupied
engagements; ... that after the general election [in Great Britain] so
many of his friends had lost their elections or been thrown out by
petition, that he was in honour bound to take care of them first
... . The conversation ended with his saying that, as to the seat
here, he should be able in a short time to give me a more specific
answer. ...

What shall I say about your late proceedings? Surely foolish? I
hope not flagitious. I am willing to believe all you have said about
the honest views of those people [the Volunteers], but I sometimes
think you yourself are deceived. I love Ireland and am very sorry
that I find it impossible not to think hardly of it.'

42   [1779–80]   Tattered, incomplete draft of a letter from Flood to [Markham]
justifying Flood's conduct.
'... I have not resigned, because I think my office to be as fairly
mine for life as if it were so by patent.' [This appears to be one of
the letters to which C/2/37 is a frosty answer.]

43   [1779–80]   Smaller and even more tattered fragment to a similar purport:
possibly a more formal statement which Markham is expected to
lay before Lord North.

C/6

DATE   DESCRIPTION

1779–84   Reports of a number of Flood's major speeches in the Irish House of Commons, most of them corrected in his own hand.

The speeches concerned are those on the Short Money Bill, 24–5 November 1779?, on Grattan's Declaration of Right, 19 April 1780, on the Perpetual Mutiny Bill, 28 April 1780, on Flood's own conduct in retaining the Vice Treasurership while opposing the Irish administration, October 1781?, on Poyning's law, 11 December 1781 [one copy of this speech is corrected in Flood's hand, and there are two other and fairer copies, both entirely in Parsons's hand and both apparently incomplete], on Renunciation [this version consisting of a rough draft in Flood's hand for the latter part of the speech, and notes by him of mistakes made in the version printed in the first volume of the *Irish Parliamentary Register*, pp 407–14, 11 June 1782], on Flood's own conduct in response to Grattan's attack on him, and this version titled by Parsons, 'Second defence', that of 1781 being the 'First defence', October 1784 – in effect, a speech on parliamentary reform, in the wake of the rejection of the Volunteer plan. Several of these copies are prefaced by a summary of the 'Argument' in Parsons's hand, so that it looks as if he was preparing an edition of Flood's speeches. The later material in this sub-section is in dire need of conservation.

The following is Flood's 'Speech on the Short Money Bill', 24–5 November 1779?

'I will follow the Rt Hon. Gentleman through every part of his argument, convinced of his sincerity when he says that, if his arguments are fairly refuted, he will be ready to retract them.

First, he says that the present measure is not in itself an end [last two words supplied by Flood?], but a means only to that which is our end – viz. a free trade, in the rational sense of the word and in a reasonable limitation. As such, this measure is to be received or rejected, he says, according as [last two words supplied by Flood?] it is adapted to that end. Now, says he, that end is in part a matter of right and in part a matter of favour. This measure is a measure of coercion. As such, it is utterly inapplicable to the subject, as far as it is a matter of favour; for we are never [word inserted by Flood?] entitled to use force in order to obtain favour, though we may sometimes be entitled to use force to obtain a right [last four words supplied by Flood?]: that is to say when the right shall have been obstinately refused, but not till then. With respect even to that part of the subject which is matter of right, therefore, he thinks that this measure of coercion may be premature, and that with respect to the rest, it is wholly improper.

I answer that it is not premature, unless force is premature, unless force is premature whilst further solicitation is possible, and then it would be always premature, which is too absurd to mention. This right has been withheld injuriously for ages. It has been ... repeatedly denied. We have ... [text defective, as it is at the bottom of each page] ... even a verbal assurance of it, and the last [word supplied by Flood?] answer from the crown is less favourable than heretofore. Either, therefore, a strong or [three words supplied by Flood?], if you

C/6 *contd.*   will, a coercive measure is justifiable now, or it is never justifiable. But the Rt
Hon. Gentleman admits that that is sometimes justifiable, and therefore I
conclude we are justifiable in it now.

But, further, I admit that our object, viz. [words supplied by Flood?] a free
trade, is a mixed object, that is to say that it consists partly of right and partly of
favour. What follows? That this measure, which is a mixed measure also, partly
of grant and partly not of grant, is perfectly adapted to it. For, analyse [word
supplied by Flood?] this measure and what is it? It is in its first and only certain
operation a grant. In that, it is adapted to that part of the subject which is
favour, and by a preceding liberality invites the beneficence of the crown of
Great Britain. As to the future, it does not refuse; it only reserves a power of
refusing hereafter, in case that we are refused in the interim. In this, it is adapted
to that part of the subject which is of right, and which, if refused, will entitle us
to refuse. It is therefore for six months a grant unconditional and free. It is, for
the other 18 months, at most but an eventual and conditional refusal, which
event and condition can never take place but through the fault of Great Britain.

... [But the Rt Hon. Gentleman?] says that the subject is of less consequence than
is vulgarly [word supplied by Flood?] imagined, that we have already the most
valuable of our rights on this subject in possession, that all we ask is much inferior
[last two words supplied by Flood?] to what we have, that, [if] granted, it would be
long before we should [two of the last four words supplied by Flood?] feel it in its
most sensible operation, and that in half a century it should not add above a
million a year to our trade. Most part of this I will admit. But the slower its
operation, the sooner it ought to begin. Though not of so much consequence as all
that we possess, yet it is of great and mighty consequence. Though we may have
most of our natural [last three words supplied by Flood?] rights on this subject, yet
there is no reason we should not have the rest. Though it might take half a century
to mature its advantages, yet half a century to a state is nothing. Though the whole
of that period might elapse before the accession to our trade might arrive at its
completion, it would every day be improving, and for the greater part of that period
would produce the greater part of that accession in point of pocket. And, finally,
that if it did not in half a century produce more than a million, it would be great
object for that period and a much greater in futurity, because after it would
accumulate fast [last word supplied by Flood?]. Our revenue, which bears so great a
proportion to the wealth of the state, and which presses so hard upon the people,
our absentee drain, which exhausts [word supplied by Flood?] the land, are each
[last two words supplied by Flood?] of them about a million. Is that a contemptible
object that would equal the absentee drain or keep pace with the aggregate [last
word supplied by Flood?] of your revenue? And what would be the accession to
revenue in consequence of this accession of a million to your trade? Not less than
£150,000 a year or £300,000 in two years, a sum which would effectually equalise
your revenue and your expenses, which perhaps nothing else will. Such is the value
of the object even on the Hon. Gentleman's mitigated statement, which I am
authorised to apply against his argument, though not obliged [last word supplied by
Flood?] to adopt in my own.

For myself, I hold that it is impossible to reduce such objects as these within
the bounds of calculation [last five words supplied by Flood?] All that a wise and

C/6 *contd.* honest statesman can do is to give the virtue and industry of a nation free scope, and leave it to events to determine what shall be the stamp of their operation. Who can limit it? Looking at this country twenty years ago, who could have thought she would be what she is? Twelve months ago, who could have thought that this country could have placed herself in the state of defence in which she is, without the co-operation of government, or even with it? Who on speculation could think that this country, with her trade so restricted [last two words supplied by Flood?] as we complain, could have gained more ground within 70 years than Scotland has done with a trade perfectly free? And yet there is not an article by which you can estimate the prosperity of a nation, in which she has not. She has increased more in population, in revenue, in specie, in agriculture [last word supplied by Flood?], in manufactures, in everything. Who could have thought that the Swiss Cantons could have broke loose from the imperial diadem? That the United Provinces [last two words supplied by Flood?], a country the territorial produce [of which] does not more than pay the repairing of her dykes, could have braved [word supplied by Flood?] the power of Spain with the mines of Peru and Mexico to support her, and have become a potentate in Europe? Who could have thought 20 years ago that America could have been in her present strength, or who would have thought that Great Britain would have been in her present decline? The growth and the delcine of nations is not a subject of political arithmetic, nor is it reducible to the bounds of calculation [several words supplied by Flood?] That belongs to a more sublime science, the science of the high-minded and beneficent legislator, whose penetrating eye looks through the vicissitudes of time, and is sure that, whilst he encourages industry and virtue and valour, he can never fail. Oceans may [last two words supplied by Flood?] dry ... [text defective], but these can never cease to operate.

But the [Rt] Hon. Gentleman [words supplied by Flood?] says we can obtain our point without the coercion of this measure. Will the [Rt] Hon. Gentleman in the face of this country be surety that we shall? Will he stake his character, his property, his life on the event of his prediction and on the truth of his argument? But this is a matter too great for any man to be an hostage for it [four out of the last seven words supplied by Flood?]. And what is the dilemma? Either we can obtain it without the coercion, or we cannot. If we cannot, it is necessary, and if we can, it is at worst but superfluous. I admit with the [Rt] Hon. Gentleman that the crisis is favourable, but I conclude that it therefore ought not to be omitted. I feel the weakness of Great Britain, the disruption [last word supplied by Flood?] of America, the strength of the House of Bourbon, and the virtue and the valour of Ireland, a virtue and a valour which I admire as much as the [Rt] Hon. Gentleman though I cannot express it so emphatically. God forbid, however, that the virtue of our countrymen [last word supplied by Flood?] without doors should be a neceessary argument on this subject. I appeal to the virtue of our country[men] within doors, which I acknowledge to be great, and to that integrity of parliament, of which I doubt not we shall this day have a memorable example. ... [Text defective.]

But it is not only necessary that we should feel it ourselves, but that we should manifest it to Great Britain. The declaration of parliament on the first day of the session has been represented even [last two words supplied by Flood?] within

C/6 *contd.* these walls as unweighed and inconsiderate. The idea has sunk in this country only to rise in Great Britain. And where do you find it? Not merely with the ignorant manufacturer, with the interested merchant, with the misled member of parliament, with the misled or the misleading minister, but with the sovereign himself. Into his royal mind it has been insinuated. Witness the last answer from the throne which you have received: "His Majesty will do what appears to be best for the whole upon *mature deliberation.*" Are these words unemphatical [word corrected by Flood?]? Or do they not pronounce sentence on your supposed inconsideration and levity [word supplied by Flood?] even from the lips of Majesty? Is it not essential that you should dispel this error and that you should counteract this misrepresentation? And how can you do it so well as by your money bill? That is a subject [last two words supplied by Flood?] which goes through more forms and a longer and more mature deliberation. Committees on committees are charged with it in various shapes, and the House repeatedly ... [text defective] ... resumes it in the report of these committees. If indeliberation be imputed to you, this is the best method of refuting the imputation. And what so proper a vehicle for this national requisition as the money bill? The privilege of the Commons over the purse of [the] nation is the foundation of their power in Great Britain even. But here it is the only unimpeached authority of parliament. Make, then, this great national and uncontaminated [last word supplied by Flood?] privilege the vehicle of the purse of the nation, and let your desire of a free trade be carried to the throne through that privilege which is the foundation of all your freedom.

But the [Rt] Hon. Gentleman says [last word supplied by Flood?] that this is a measure of coercion in appearance only, that it only reserves a power, but does not execute it, and reserves a power which it will not and rationally speaking cannot exercise, that it is therefore an impotent menance [last three words supplied by Flood?] and holds out to ministers a threat which may exasperate but cannot terrify [last two words supplied by Flood?]. How consistent this objection is, I know not, but I admit it to be powerful. I admit also that the inconvenience of discharging these duties would be less felt in the first six months and more easily reparable than it would be before [last two words supplied by Flood?] the 18 months that followed, and that the session being at an end, the evil would become for so much irreparable. But I say it does not from thence follow that, because we grant now, we shall continue to grant six months hence. What do we say now to the British government? We do not believe you will do us justice, but we are not sure that you will not. A short period must decide. When parliament meets, if you [word supplied by Flood?] do us justice, we will strain [ditto] every nerve to supply you. If you hesitate, we will consider your hesitation as a negative, and then we will not supply you. What then do we do? We grant for six months, because we are too sober and too moderate to put either you or ourselves to any inconvenience, however small in comparison, that can be avoided. But we are also too determined not [to] suffer any inconveniencies [*sic*] rather than to make provision for your injustice and to reward your oppression. We acknowledge the evils of such a discontinuance of supply for the last 18 months will be much heavier than they would be in the first six months. But manly minds, though they will avoid every evil that they can, will meet any evil that is unavoidable. We feel all these evils in all

C/6 *contd.*   their aggravation. But who will be chargeable with them if they do happen? We for asking, or you for denying, justice? We admit the inconveniencies to be great, that our public securities, public charities and public works will fail, that the civil and military establishments will labour, if they shall not be overset, that our army in the midst of the war in which you have plunged us may be disbanded or mutinous [last two words supplied by Flood?] or reduced to live on free-quarters, or fall [last four words supplied by Flood?] a dead weight on your over-burdened exchequer. Neither can we be answerable for the commotion that the exasperated spirit of an incited nation may produce. We warn you of these evils, and we pray [last word supplied by Flood?] in a loud voice that you will be responsible for them to your king, your country and your god. Is this a trivial [last word supplied by Flood?] language to hold to a minister? And this is the language of this measure.

But even if it should fail as a measure of coercion, it will survive as a measure of economy [last six words supplied by Flood?]. If your application fails, retrenchment alone [last two words supplied by Flood?] will be left to you to serve your country. And how can you retrench with effect except by means of your supply? If that remain in reserve, you [last four words supplied by Flood?] can refuse to regrant, or if you regrant, you can [four out of the last seven words supplied by Flood?] grant on such conditions of economy as, ratified by an act of parliament, cannot be frustrated. But, besides being a probable measure to coercion in the first instance, if ministers are not insane, besides being in the second instance a certain measure of economy, if you are not insane too -besides this, it is in the last instance, if you are wise, a certain measure of control [last two words supplied by Flood?] also on all the measures of the session which, if I mistake not, are likely to be such as to involve in them the perpetual salvation or final ruin of the state.

The time is big with danger. The state of Britain and the councils of her ministers are desperate. What has the speech from the throne implicated [last word supplied by Flood?]? That your dearest interests should not disturb your unanimity [most of this sentence supplied by Flood?]. What, then, are our dearest interests at stake? Is it avowed in the speech from the throne, the words of which, especially when [?abstruse], have not been unemphatical? And when our dearest interests are at stake, is it a time to let slip idly the last stake and the great controlling power of parliament in the dispensation of supply? Who knows from what ruin this reservation may save us? Who knows whether our Volunteer corps may not ... [text defective – be disbanded? Whether the papist may not be] armed? Whether troops from abroad may not be sent to garrison us [several words supplied by Flood?]? Whether an attack on our tillage laws may not be meditated [last word supplied by Flood?] Whether attacks upon our lands may not be in agitation [last two words supplied by Flood?]? Who knows whether the annihilation of our legislature and our extinction as a nation may not, in the madness of the times and in the profligacy and the despair of our councils, be amongst the measures that are to harrass and afflict us? Will the Rt Hon. Gentleman tell us, even at this hour of the session, what are his measures? Or if the parliament of Ireland [word supplied by Flood?] have not weight enough to command or to induce such communication, will he release us from our fears by telling us at least what are not [word supplied by Flood?] his measures?

C/6 *contd.*   For my part, I will confess that the mystery of our councils alarms me. I fear that some fatality will creep upon us in this night in which we are involved. I would keep the supply, as the lamp of the constitution, to light us through this darkness. I would turn it on the face of the minister to detect his councils and would hang it up in our high places, if necessary, as a beacon [word supplied by Flood?] to alarm and assemble the people to oppose their ruin. Witness for me that in the hour of opposition [word supplied by Flood?], when in the most ardent pursuit of those manly councils in which only I embarked [word supplied by Flood?], I never once professed this measure, nor should I concur in [last two words supplied by Flood?] it, if I did not think the time required the last exertions. It appeared to me to be a measure which nothing but extremity could justify, and I now see that that extremity is come upon us. Believe me, my countrymen, it is not for a trifle I would speak thus. I hazard [word supplied by Flood?] more than any of you. Perhaps I do not see less. I have nothing to gain and I have much to lose by this conduct. If, however, I have power of discerning [word supplied by Flood?] our whole is at this moment at stake. Every inferior consideration must give way. Neither will the wisdom or the resolution of one man, or of a few, be sufficient to save [word supplied by Flood?] you. We must all unite. Here in the face of our country let us then unite. Let us gather round the altar of constitution. Let us call upon the genius [word supplied by Flood?] of the land. Let us prostrate our hearts before the God of truth, of liberty and of the world, and implore that, as he has long preserved us through all vicissitudes [word supplied by Flood?], he may give us strength and virtue to bear us through our present calamities and to leave behind us the name of men [word supplied by Flood?] who knew the blessings of law and liberty, who had fortitude to preserve them to ourselves ... [text defective – and virtue to deliver them down to posterity?].'

The following are extracts from Flood's speech on Grattan's Declaration of Rights, 19 April 1780: the extracts are disjointed because the top quarter of the page is wellnigh obliterated by damp:

'... That is to say as far as any general constitution prevailed in a time unsettled, all these authorities, from the highest to the lowest, were elective as to the individual and hereditary as to the family. Such was the case with regard to all the kings of Europe for many of the earlier centuries. Such is the case in Tartary, India and other countries very nearly to this day. The principal kings were almost wholly independent of the national king. His pre-eminence was rather honorary [word supplied by Flood?] and nominal than real. If ever he possessed more influence, it was owing to the strength of his own province and of his personal character [rather] than to constitution. Dermod, Provincial King of Leinster, and Roderick O'Connor, King of Ireland, were deadly enemies. The latter flew to Wales and England for succour. H[enry] II was to much occupied to take a part in the busines, but gave the necessary licence to some of his feudal followers to adventure with the King of Leinster. They did so. They established him and got some settlement, partly by ... [text defective]. Henry's character and power recommended him. The princes of Ireland had little attachment ever to the national king, and less than usual to Roderick, who did not deserve any [several words in the last sentence corrected by Flood?]. Their pride, and possibly

C/6 *contd.* they were persuaded their power, would be less hurt by a nominal superior at a distance that would seldom if ever trouble them, than by an ogre, one of themselves, whose superiority was the more odious. Henry came. It does not seem that any prince but the National King thought him a rival or opposed him in arms, nor was there anything like a conquest, though there was a superiority sufficient to intimidate Roderick. Henry, to conciliate, not to conquer, gave an option of the English laws and constitution of parliament to all the Irish nation. But the Irish nation in general never thought of accepting it. They retained their own laws and customs in everything ... [text defective].

In truth, till Queen Elizabeth's time, there was nothing like even a nominal adoption of the English government, nor was it ever real until the reign of James the first [word supplied by Flood?], in whose time, by instituting new shires and boroughs, and calling representatives from those parts which had never before accepted the English constitution, the first parliament was called in Ireland that could justly be called a national parliament. The same expedient was always used as fast as any territory was acquired or persuaded to accept of English government. [Text defective] ... . I feel, therefore, that though the English laws and parliamentary [word supplied by Flood?] constitution were offered very wisely by Henry [ditto] to the Irish, yet [ditto] the Irish nation, wedded as is usual [ditto] with men to their own customs, never thought of accepting them. But the English settlers did accept [ditto] them, and Henry did give them, as it were, livery and seizin of their constitution by holding a parliament at Dublin. A law passed in that parliament is recited in an Irish statute of Richard the third. Many parliaments in these early days were held in Ireland. Some were also called to England. Now, when called to England, either they did sit with the English parliament or they did not. If the former, it is a complete acknowledgement that the English parliament alone could not make laws even for the English settlement in Ireland. If they did not sit at the English parliament, but sat alone, then is it a complete acknowledgement that they alone were competent to legislate for themselves ... [text defective].

Bacon, born but a few years after the death of Henry the 7th, writing the history of that monarch [word supplied by Flood?] and speaking of Poyning's government in Ireland, particularly says that Sir Edward, having failed in his military progress, to make amends for the meagreness of his exploits in the war, called a parliament and passed that famous law, as he calls it, whereby he adds all the English statutes of a general and public import antecedent to that time do bind Ireland. But those made after (he expressly says) do not. He does not think the other law of Poynings worth mentioning, considering it to be, as it was, a domestic regulation for the satisfaction of the English settlers in Ireland, and not, "as it has since been corruptly construed, a total change of the" [whole passage supplied by Flood?] constitution. ... [Text defective.] Lord Coke's authority goes still further. He speaks of the holding of a parliament in Ireland under that law which by distinction we call the law of Poynings, but never speaks of it as having changed the constitution or as having transferred the legislative power from parliament to council. It is impossible these two greatest of all lawyers could have been ignorant of the change, if true; and they had every reason to promulgate and dwell upon such a revolution, if they had so

C/6 *contd.*   considered it [last three words supplied by Flood?]. But, to come back to the present subject, besides the clear implication and acknowledgement that the English parliament is not a legislature for Ireland, in adopting, re-enacting and giving force to such antecedent statutes in the tenth year of Henry 7th, let us never forget the positive assertion and decision of the great Lord Bacon that, in consequence of that statute, the antecedent acts of England did bind in Ireland, but that the subsequent do not. ... [Text defective.]

But the unfortunate divisions and weakness of this country, and the ignorance and corruption of her ministers, undid us, and we showed so little knowledge, sense or love of our constitution, that we tempted that parliament of England which had begun with such just ideas of our rights, to inflict the deepest wound upon our constitution that ever was given to it. ... All the Henrys, the Edwards, the Tudors and even the Stuarts have given proofs of your constitutional authority. The two conquerors of France depose for you. The politic tyrant, Henry 7th, the wild tyrant, Henry 8th, counselled by the despotic Wolsey, the wise but authoritative, Elizabeth, assisted by a Cecil, a Walsingham, a Coke, a Bacon, the cold but despotic Charles 1st in the arbitrary administration [word corrected by Flood?] of Strafford, the usurping parliament of 1641, the dominating soul of Cromwell – all of them acknowledge your legislative authority. God and nature declare for you; and shall an infant usurpation, begun in the scandalous reign of Charles 2nd, taken up in the first aspirings of the English parliament and in the total destitution of Ireland at the ... [text defective]. Shall a perfect legislature be offered to her [North America's] assemblies, not parliaments, and shall it be refused to your parliament, which was established between 400 and 500 years before an American colony was heard of? Shall it be refused to you? And by whom? By these men? By the very men who went across the Atlantic to make that offer to America – to mendicate her acceptance of it – and who returned rejected, without ever being suffered to enter into the land? Away with such meanness. The living exhort [last two words supplied by Flood?] – the dead will rise from their graves to chide you into manhood [last two words supplied by Flood?]. Look abroad. While England, who under pretence of protecting, claims a right to enslave, you – while an army, the expense of which has ruined you in fighting battles ... [text defective.]

Shall the individuals of the nation be incorrupt and noble, and shall the trustees and chosen representatives only be the contrary? If you have not native, have so much adopted, virtue as not to betray them in parliament who have preserved you out of it. You have a tenfold cause to do so. When they found that expressing their sentiments on political points was not plesing to you, they became silent. They had looked upon your virtue in the last session. They trusted it remained. They thought it a treason to your honour to doubt it without a cause. In this confidence, they went on in silence, practising every virtue of the citizen, amidst [word supplied by Flood?] every exertion of the soldier. And will you defraud [ditto] their confidence? Will you belie [ditto] their hopes of you?'

C/8	DATE	DESCRIPTION
1–85	1784–91	Correspondence between Flood and Parsons, consisting of original letters on both sides, but only a couple of them from Parsons to Flood. A large portion of the letters relate to Flood's chequered pursuit of seats in the British House of Commons, in which he was assisted by or associated with Parsons. The letters supplement those in Add. MS. 22930 concerning Flood's bitter and protracted dispute with the Duke of Chandos over the return for Winchester in 1784, and break new ground by documenting Flood's and Parsons's ultimately unsuccessful bid to be returned for Seaford, Sussex, their mustering of witnesses and marshalling of evidence for production before an election committee, etc, 1784–7. There are some references to Irish parliamentary affairs, including a number of cutting comments by Flood about Grattan, and a discussion of Parsons's attack on Grattan in the aftermath of the regency crisis in 1789, as a man who had already been paid too much for selling his country short and now over the regency had blundered yet again. The concluding letters relate to the hunt for seats, both for Flood and for Parsons, in the Irish parliament of 1790, which was unsuccessful in Flood's case, because his death occurred before a seat could be found. Conservation is, again, an urgent priority.
1	16 Jan. [1784]	Flood, writing under the pseudonym of J. St Clair, 43 Suffolk Street, London?, to Parsons. 'I have just got use enough of the forefinger of my right hand to tell you that I received yours of the 8th January, and that the same views and intentions remain here that existed when you left this, only rather more confirmed. Lord Ra[wdo]n is certainly mistaken in his present intelligence, but that person [the Duke of Rutland?] will, if I mistake not, see your side of the water as soon as the first burst here is over, which can't be unimportant. What can the other young Lord [Northington] mean by so strange a conduct? He must be warily dealt with. A narrow basis that can be depended on is better than a broader that cannot. If foundations are not firm, they are nothing.'
2–3	[c. Apr.? 1784]	Copies of notes from Flood to the Duke of Chandos claiming a return for Winchester, at Flood's expense, until the Duke can procure an alternative seat for Flood.
4	4 May [1784] onwards	Memorandum by Parsons about the progress of his negotiation on Flood's behalf for an alternative seat.
5	19 May 1784	Letter from Flood, Cleveland Row, London, to Parsons: an obviously ostensible letter, preparatory to Flood's challenging the Duke to a duel.
6		Blank in the sequence.

C/8/7	1 June 1784	Draft or rough copy of a note from Parsons to the Duke of Chandos: '... Mr Parsons wishes to apprise the Duke that a Mr Alves of Harley Street is said to have engaged eight votes, which Mr Parsons understands can give him no chance of success. If the Duke can prevail on Mr Alves to resign them to Mr Flood's election for Seaford on the present vacancy.'
8	12 June 1784 onwards	Memorandum by Parsons of the use made of C/8/7 and the Duke's response to it.
9	18 June 1784	Letter from Flood to Parsons. 'If the second vacancy should happen at Seaford before I return, I request that you will be so good as to see Mr Pelham in my name. He told me he would vote for me against [Lord] Mountmorres and in preference to any but his own candidate. If, therefore, his candidate cannot succeed, I confide that he will support me. If there should be two vacancies, there is no doubt that we should both succeed by a junction. My interest is so much stronger, however, that he cannot expect such a junction without paying attention to our friend, Mr Oldfield.'
10	27 July 1784	Flood, Farmley, near Kilkenny, to Parsons. '... By your two letters, I find that no further impression has been made on the rated voters [of Seaford] than that of which O[ldfiel]d's first letter gave an account. As to the offer of a junction from P[elha]m, it does not appear to me that that would give certainty of success as to the rated voters ... . By your last letter, it should seem that P[elha]m has gained ground. He had not five [votes] when I left England. ... I had the pleasure to see your good father both coming and going. The reviews of Galway and of Sligo were more numerous than ever they had been before. The people showed great spirit. ... You don't mention your ever having seen Hatsell [Clerk to the British House of Commons], or whether it is certain or not that no writ was issued this session. ...'
11	5 Sep. 1784	Flood, post-marked Kilkenny, to Parsons, Buckingham Gate, London: more about Seaford.
12	14 Sep. 1784	Flood, post-marked Kilkenny, to Parsons, Buxton, Derbyshire: '... I doubt the wisest way will be to push at rating as many of our club as possible. With respect to the non-parishioners, or certificated housekeepers (Oldfield speaks of them as synonymous, I think), I don't understand their situation or pretensions at all, and cannot therefore give the smallest opinion about them. ...'
13	29 Sep. 1784	Flood, post-marked Kilkenny, to Parsons, Seaford, Lewes: 'I have but a line to write, wishing ardently that you may have seen and settled with Mr Simpson, that you may be at Seaford, and that you may succeed in our appeal. ...'

C/8/14 26 Oct. 1784   Flood, [Dublin], to Parsons, Buckingham Gate, London.
'I am just returned from the second day's meeting of delegates for promoting the reform. The Catholic Question, joined to every other misrepresentation, made the meeting thin. We have therefore only vindicated ourselves and the people in a few resolutions, and without entering into new matter, I understand it is proposed to adjourn to the 28th of January, exhorting those counties who have not sent delegates to repair the omission by that time. I leave town by necessity tomorrow early. The Catholic Question has not yet been agitated, and possibly may not. ...'

The rest of the letter is about Seaford.

15   30 Oct. 1784   Flood, post-marked Kilkenny, to Parsons, Buckingham Gate, London.
'I have just heard from our friend Oldfield. I don't know what to judge from the strange and contradictory motions of certain people. All it convinces me of is that, if they do not immediately decide with me, I must, however unwillingly, consider the decision to be against me, and therefore without delay request an immediate junction with the other side – as far as the *next election* goes, and no further. ... I will hesitate no longer. It is a state of mind I detest and despise.

I hinted to you that the Catholic Question would go off unmentioned. I had the title of Congress altered to that of the Assembly of Delegates for promoting a Parliamentary Reform, lest the most ignorant people in England might have false conceptions with respect to our intentions, because I will confess that I have met with the most plebeian ignorance as to Ireland in very high places. ...'

16   31 Oct. [1784] Flood, post-marked Kilkenny, to Parsons, Buckingham Gate, London, referring again to Seaford.

17   5 Nov. 1784   Flood to Parsons:
'... At all events, we will have a battle at Seaford, and if we can have a double victory, we will sing Io [?Paen], and if none, we will be content and at any rate be superior to scoundrels, whether low or high, here or in England. On the whole, I think Jebb is decided as to the coalition.'

18   25 Nov. 1784   Flood, post-marked Kilkenny, to Parsons, 2 Canterbury Buildings, Lambeth, London.
'... You are right in thinking I cannot absent myself (as things now stand) from our first meeting of parliament in Ireland. I know how little you or I or the public can wish for your absence. I hope, therefore, that fortune may so far favour the right as that we may meet at the College Green next January.

As to P[elha]m's petition, it is clear to me that we ought not to depend entirely on that. Who knows by what negotiation that petition may be made to vanish? ...'

C/8/19 8 Dec. 1784   Flood to Parsons about Seaford, and asking him to '... see the Duke of Ch – s and tell him that I shall publish our correspondence with observations, but before I do so, will give him the satisfaction of arms, wherever he pleases. ...'

20   21 Dec. 1784   Flood to Parsons.

'I have received yours of the 13th instant, by which I found that mine of the 5th had not reached you. In that I have expressed my deliberate and final conviction as to my chance at Seaford. I would not have you lose a moment of the Irish session on such a bootless pursuit. I know *them* too well to expect fair play, and I owe it to your kindness and friendship to me to advise you to attend the parliament here in a session that must be marked.

I am happy that you spoke of the Society and have heard an account of it from other papers that pleases me much ... I am glad you gave my acknowledgement to Lee, but though I cannot decline his friendship at the Bar, and though I wish to engage his attention to my petition in parliament, yet I wish if possible to get him to act for me in the King's Bench in the usual way, and by fee, and at all events will employ Peckham or some other as good person as a feed lawyer, if Lee will not act on fee.

Though I am no partizan, I shall be ready to wear the livery of it; but not till then. You can't escape my meaning. ...

I long to know what his Grace will say. As to the other Duke [of Portland?], I think he will be governed by the hostile P[elham?].'

21   30 Dec. 1784   Flood to Parsons:

'... I laugh at the most puissant Prince [Chandos?]. Make a coalition, if you can, before you leave London – but for the *seat* only, you know. For, my parliamentary freedom I will not compromise. ...'

22   [Early? 1785?]   Flood to Parsons, apparently about Seaford.

23   24 [Jan. or   Flood to Parsons: the same.
          Feb.? 1785?]

24   26 Feb. [1785?] Flood, [Dublin], to Parsons, Trinity College.

'I received on getting home a lette from oracle Oldfield, and like an oracle, it is very doubtful. I missed of [*sic*] you in my leaving the House. At 3 today some friends meet in the House to *revive* my intended motion. In the meantime, to you *only* I communicate it, for suddenness is everything in such a case. "Resolved that the practice of attachment for contempt of court stands on the same ground of law in both kingdoms and ought not be extended further in Ireland than in England." This does not single out the King's Bench. It does not deny, whilst it does not express or defy, the legality of the power. It does not command the courts here to go as far, but it requires them not to go further. Don't mention it to Martin till we meet.'

C/8/25 18 Apr. [1785] Flood to Parsons, mainly about Seaford.

'... I am still exceedingly doubtful whether anything we can do in the King's Bench will avail. For my own part, I am almost convinced that, if the plain word "populacy" aided by the monstrous misconduct of the government interest in Seaford respecting the rates, will not gain us a favourable decision, nothing we can ask and obtain from King's Bench is likely to answer; and if what we ask is refused, it is best considering whether that would not hurt more than serve. ... Pelham stands between two fires. This, and his future views as to Seaford, may perhaps in the end produce in him no disinclination to forego the present election and assist us on such terms as are hinted to you here in conversation. To any friend of his, it will at present be sufficient and right to say that he cannot succeed on the rated against the Treasury, nor on the unrated against me, and that therefore his interest is at any event (respecting his future views) to join me in ousting the Treasury ... .

On this day, you will doubtless hear Pitt on the Report. I trust you will send me an account of it. ...'

26   30 Apr. [1785] Flood to Parsons about Seaford.

'... I do not see any ground or likelihood of coalition. But by your last conversation with Mountmorres, I am to suppose that Pitt and he are on good terms. If so, to whom does he impute that manoeuvre and duplicity he insinuated on the hustings at Seaford?

...

What do the Reformers say to Pitt's idea?'

27   25 May [1785] Flood, post-marked Ireland, to Parsons, St Albans Street, London, partly about Seaford.

'I thank you for your last, but though I admit the excellence of Woodfall, I wish you would have given me your opinion as to the manner and the occasional and specific superiority of the great actors in the parliamentary drama. It is certainly a subject of liberal curiosity and will not be unuseful to yourself or to your own exertions. ...

In the brief of the Reform Bill, there is an error. It is so that every man must be registered in the barony wherein he shall be resident. It ought to be, wherein he hath his freehold.'

28   5 June [1785] Flood, post-marked Kilkenny, to Parsons, St Albans Street, London.

'I have just received yours mentioning the result of the Reform meeting. I request you to obtain as full and accurate an account of Dr Jebb's objections to Pitt's plan as you can from himself in conversation (I had his printed letter). I wish to see the subject in every possible light, and I know nobody whose sentiments on it I wish to have more than his. I wish also much to have his free thoughts on the *deficiencies* of my sketch for, by the words *as far as*

C/8/28 *contd.*   *it goes*, I see he thinks it insufficient, and I am far from holding
that it is not. But I hope, if he will communicate his ideas freely to
me (which I doubt not he will, from his sincerity), that I shall be
able to meet his idea with an amendment, or to show that the
defect is owing to something irremedial in the state of *this* country,
of which there is no pretence in England. For instance, in England
populous town can everywhere be had to put in the place of the
depopulated. Here, there is no such resource. Our good cities and
counties are our only fund, and the majority of the people by far
being Roman Catholics, lays us under difficulties here, and in
every part of the system, to which the English Reformer is not
liable. In England, in short, it cannot fail, except from a want of
power in the sincere, or for a want of sincerity in the powerful.

Again, registry is essentially necessary here, on account of the
majority of Catholics. It was confined to the 40-shilling freeholder,
because the upper rank of the people were generally Protestant,
and because deception among persons of better property was less
to be expected and less practicable. But the last general election
did particularly prove the necessity of universal registry. I do not
know that in England it might not be useful, but this I am certain
that residence ought in both reforms to be required. Nothing can
so effectually curb expense, uncertainty and confusion.

I have enclosed two printed sketches of the Irish Reform Bill to
Mr Martin, one for himself and the other for Dr Jebb, hoping that
you will extract from them in conversation their free thoughts as
to such amendments as strike them to be most wanting. This will
give you an opportunity, which I request you will not lose, of
explaining to them the circumstances of this country and of
receiving from them all their ideas, as also in establishing a
confidence and communication with them in general, which will
be of great use and cannot possibly hurt. ...

As to Seaford, Ross's idea must be amended. I cannot myself see
why a man may not appeal against a rate in his own behalf as well
as in that of others. ... As to Mountmorres, I flatter myself you
believe that I never conceived that much good could arise from
any communication with him. I only meant it as one, and the
weakest, means of trying the faith of parties, amongst a thousand
which ought to be attempted – certainly, the more the better. ...

Mountmorres's publications must be unprinted. It is a pity that
more efficient men are not as apt to be usefully laborious as he is
to be uselessly so.'

29   23 July [1785]   Flood to Parsons:
'I have just received your favour and am sorry that
administration are so minded. When we meet, I will talk over the
Seaford business. In the meantime, I do not conceive that the
King's Bench is likely to interfere. ...'

C/8/30 30 Aug. [1785] Flood to Parsons, mainly about Seaford.

      '... If you don't go to England, I wish that you would be so good as to spend what time you can with me at Farmley, and that you would prevail on Burrowes to be of the party ...; and as to your French studies, you may prosecute them here, and we will talk bad French together as much as you please. ...

      Four votes to a county member [*sic*] would force government to corrupt every county member and per fas aut nefas to master every county election, and would therefore end in the destruction of the only good part of our representation. Such is my opinion. But I hold it with great respect to Dr Emmet.'

31   1 May 1786 Receipt from [?J.H.] Burley Oldfield to Flood for £50 'in full for half a year's expenses in and concerning Seaford ...'.

32   30 Aug. 1786 Flood, Farmley, to Parsons, Tours, Touraine, France.

      '... I leave this the 30 September, purpose to be in London the middle of October, and hope to see you there early in November, about which time it is probable that parliament may meet.

      I shall forget my French when I see you, but I will chatter what I can to you – as King George II said at Dettingen, I will expose myself, I will expose myself.

      We have got rightboys instead of whiteboys, and there is a great rout about them. Earls Sh[annon] and Ty[rone] are to be English peers. [Text defective] ... the parliament drovers are to be accommodated at St Stephens that they may the less object to sending their College Green cattle to Smithfield. No news.'

33   [Spring? 1787] Parsons to Flood about an unexpected claim put in by Oldfield.

      '... As to his demand of salary as an agent, he has no claim to it whatsoever, and if he had, for every day he has been really employed in your business he has been more than ten times paid. But the fact is, he represented himself to me from the first in a different character, as a friend to the reform of parliament, and, as such, wished to be introduced to you and to assist you in a canvass for Seaford, if you would undertake it. ...'

34   [Spring? 1787] Statement about Oldfield's connection with Flood and Flood's attempt to open the borough of Seaford, [in Parsons handwriting?].

35   [Spring? 1787] Flood to Parsons about the question of submitting Oldfield's claim to a reference.

36   [Spring? 1787] Peter Burrowes, post-marked Isle of Wight, to Parsons, Hot Baths, Bristol, about Seaford and Oldfield.

      '... I heard from Griffith, who informed me that Flood is surprisingly recovered and entirely out of danger. ...' [For the rest of Burrowes's letters to Parsons, see D/2.]

C/8/37 Post-marked   Flood to Parsons, Hot Wells, Bristol: the same.
        10 [?July] 1787

38   24 July 1787   Flood, post-marked Ireland, to Parsons, Hot Wells, Bristol.
                            '... The reference has had all the ill-effect I prognosticated. ...
                        As to the point of Ol – d's being an *agent* to me, I cannot admit it
                        with truth, nor in my mind with prudence. The fact you know to
                        be that he came to me as being himself a public character, wishing
                        me, as a public character, to be in parliament; that in that light,
                        expressly and only, he was stated by Dr Jebb; that Old – d stated
                        that in the popular elections in which he had taken part, the
                        candidates were put to no expense; that he himself had acted for
                        Fox and Shelburne and had been paid by neither ...'.

39   25 July 1787   Flood, post-marked Ireland, to Parsons, Hot Wells, Bristol: the
                        same.

40   14 Feb. 1788   Flood, London, to Parsons, Trinity College, Dublin.
                            'I have received yours containing the abstract of accounts. I am
                        sorry you have such difficulties to encounter. It is the rough brake
                        which virtue must go through. Be not discouraged. There are
                        winds and tides which we must all bow to, but which some time
                        or other will favour the man who is always in readiness to seize
                        them and who has firmness enough to rely on conscious rectitude.
                            There is nearly as much deadness here at this moment. The only
                        think vital, and that is not animated, is the impeachment of
                        Hastings and Impey. I went yesterday to see the spectacle, and a
                        more noble one cannot be conceived. But the whole day was
                        consumed (and so will this day be) in reading the charges and
                        answers. As soon as the meeting is over, Burke opens the whole
                        impeachment, and his speech is expected to occupy two entire
                        days. Then Fox commences the charge as manager for the first
                        article, which will probably decide the state of the impeachments
                        very nearly or fully. Thurlow addressed the prisoner in a few
                        words, but they were pithy, solemn and rhadamanthine. ...'

41   24 Feb.,   Flood to Parsons, Trinity College, Dublin, discussing the early
        post-marked   symptoms of the King's derangement.
        1788

42   13 Mar. 1788   Flood to Parsons.
                            '... I did not know but that the House or the public might hear
                        with patience and attention that which equally exposed the India
                        Bills [Fox's of 1783 as well as the current one of Pitt],and therefore
                        I stated yesterday a few ideas to justify my vote, which was the first
                        I had given on the subject. Heaven and earth had been moved by
                        government to draw in succours from the country, and some
                        clauses and some rant on the part of the Minister, with other
                        considerations, damped the House, and I think it was much hurt
                        in its spirit by a premature attempt in Fox's friends to construe

C/8/42 *contd.*   Pitt's bill as an argument in favour of their bill, to interpret the
shake amongst the country gentlemen into a degree of conversion
towards him and his bill, whereas in truth it was an indignation at
the dissimulated approach of his bill to that which they had
proposed. Yesterday it went so far as to a formal defence of Fox's
bill, which produced a formal attack on it. Thus they gave the
attack to Pitt instead of keeping it to themselves, and Pitt's bill
appeared less exceptionable from the juxtaposition of the other. I
don't suppose that these circumstances affected numbers greatly,
but it damped the spirit of the business, and spirit is strength.
There will be another division on Friday, viz. tomorrow. But I fear
that the increase of the ministerial division and the diminuation of
the free, will make it even worse than the last. My argument could
not be unpleasing to the Company, but could not be otherwise to
the two parties. It was a most awkward and distresing situation.

I thought it likely that the bill for the reduction of interest [in
Ireland – See F/3] would fail. On what public symptons the
measure was supported, I know not. But it is obvious that the
value of money is not wholly at the discretion of the legislature. I
wish the evidence as to the police may be printed. If it is, send it to
me, together with the publication of the Irish Academy. ...

Gr[attan] has assumed the ideas and fastuousness [*sic*] of an
Aristocrats [*sic*]. He can't forgive the people for having ever
differed with him.

I expect that Woodfall will mangle me. He is well-inclined. ...

To show to demonstration that so exceptional a declaration as
was proposed was wholly unnecessary, even for the measure of the
four regiments, if that were persisted in, I proposed this idea, that
the question of their being to be paid by the Company should be
left to a court of justice, and that a conditional provision for them
should be made by parliament before the session concluded; so
that, if the question should be decided in favour of the Company,
no inconvenience should happen. To this I don't see a possible
objection, but power is hardly ever content to do anything that it
can do without power. Strange infatuation!'

[For a draft or MS. copy of Flood's speech on the India Bill, see C/7.]

43   4 May [1788?]   Flood to Parsons about Seaford and Oldfield.

44   12 May [1788?] Flood to Parsons: the same.

45   [May–July?   Small quarto volume containing, among other things, copies of
        1788?]   letters from Parsons to Flood.

'We have had nothing like business in our House lately, except
the charge against B[aro]n Hamilton for illegally breaking off the
trial of a record at Limerick after one party had disclosed evidence,
by withdrawing a juror without consent of either party; and a new
speech from G[rattan]n upon tithes [on 14 February 1788].

As to the first, even if it had been legal it was unjust and arbitrary. But the fact is, there is not a case upon record of a judge in a civil case withdrawing a juror but by the consent of both parties. The only excuse suggested by his friends was the fullness of the goal, and that was not true in fact nor attempted to be proved so by evidence. He adjourned the civil court at 5 o'clock upon pretence of proceeding to business in the criminal court, without having a jury ready, or even detaining the jury he had in the civil, and then upon pretence of not been able to obtain one, he went to the Mayor's feast, where he spent the remainder of the evening.

The conduct of the lawyers in our House was very shameful. From the very beginning, before the first witness had finished his examination, they acted like mercenary advocates for the Baron. The House being almost to a man canvassed beforehand, relying on his numbers he had not even the decency to attempt any defence or produce a witness on his part, though those produced by the petitioners substantiated the charge without exhibiting a fact to palliate it. The laws, however, were all applied to declare his conduct was illegal, and he also acknowledged it to be so, by his prolocutor upon the occasion, M[arcus] Beresford. I should have spoken, only I thought the members seemed to be too much actuated by the same feelings which the Baron was accused of having suffered to triumph over his justice. Others, indeed, supposed that it was not so much his appetite for the Mayor's feast as for the attorneys' briefs for his son; for, I must inform you that one of the parties was an attorney and likely to have been the losing one if the suit had been heard out. It appeared in evidence that the influence of this attorney with the bar was such that not a lawyer of the Munster circuit would be employed against him, though he had made a most unfounded attack upon the property of the poor plaintiff who was therefore obliged to bring lawyers from Dublin at the cost of all the money he was worth, and notwithstanding was in the manner I have mentioned precluded a verdict.

As to Grattan's speech on tithes, it was the worst rhapsody I ever heard from him. It was illustrated with a variety of quotations from the old and new testament, introduced I thought unaptly and irreverently. The House was thin, and he was neither able to excite himself nor anyone else, which occasioned his prepared strains of enthusiasm to go off very ill. He seemed sensible himself that they were untimely, and his spirit drooped in the delivery of them. However, he persisted, and the whole was rendered palatable by the sarcasms that were sprinkled through it against the bishops, and which, by the way, were very indiscreet and many of them unfair and indecent. The clergy all foam against him, his old friend Kearney virulently.

There was a rumour that he intended to be a candidate for the College next election, and he has been working under cover, I

C/8/45 *contd.*

believe, with some of the young men, among whom he is popular. But this late abuse of the clergy has rendered him too obnoxious to the Fellows to have any chance of success. In 1782 his picture was voted by the Board for the new theatre, and about a month ago it was sent home by the painter. What will be done with it, I do not know. The Board will not suffer it to be hung up in the theatre. I have offered it to the Provost, and he has refused it.

Curran exposed an act of Chatterton's upon circuit similar to Hamilton's. He was sent auxiliary judge to Clonmel and Cork on account of the extraordinary fullness of the prisons. It was in a criminal case, and he connived at a juror withdrawing himself after the jury had been shut up a whole night and could not agree in verdict. Chatterton has been much disgraced by it. His conduct in the House of Commons was mean and equivocating, and he appeared no more gentleman than lawyer. Many senior King's Counsel were passed over in nominating him for the circuit. The scheme of government was, and I believe still is, to have estblished a kind of Kilmainham at Cork, and but for this blunder, to have made him the John Toler of it. In short, to erect the Co. Cork into a kind of palatinate for Lord Shannon.'

'Yesterday I attended the trial of Griffith, Hatton and Sir J. Freke before Lord Earlsfort. The D. of Leinster and many members of the Commons were present. A[lderma]n Exshaw, the principal witness against them, said very little more in substance than was contained in his affidavit, which I showed you at Farmley, viz. that he was walking in Merrion Square on Sunday evening, 13th of last May, and saw a great number of people there leaping, wrestling, shouting, etc, and that Archd[eaco]n Hastings suggesting to him that a profanation of the Sabbath was a disgrace to his district he went home for a party of the police; that he provided himself with ball cartridge for his men, made them fix their bayonets, and then advanced hastily on the crowd in order to disperse them and, if he could, take some of them prisoners; ... that Griffith, Hatton and Freke then came up to him, and some of the men having their arms presented, Griffith desired Exshaw "to consider what he was about to do; that he had no right to order his men to fire without reading the Riot Act, and that if they fired, they must kill many innocent persons". These words, Exshaw said, encouraged the mob, and they immediately attacked the police with stones, and wounded him and some of his men; that Hatton joined Griffith in the expostulation, and that Sir J. Freke looked as if he assented to the same.

It appeared on the cross-examination of Exshaw that he did not see any of the crowd rioting before he routed them with the police ... . He acknowledged that some of his men were drunk, but not so much so, he said, as to render them incapable of doing their duty;

that it was with great difficulty he prevented them from firing
upon the mob; ... that Griffith's wife and daughter were walking in
the square and exposed to danger, as was Lady A[nn] Hatton and
Lady C[atherine] Freke, and that his men were loaded and actually
presenting their firelocks at the time Griffith interposed; that
Griffith did not say one word exhorting the mob to violence, but
only advised Exshaw to prevent his men from firing, as it would be
illegal, and to march them quietly home. ...

Lord Earlsfort's charge was such as might be expected from a
man who waded to the bench through every sink of corruption. It
was not law, it was not justice, it was not truth; but a cunning,
insidious, perplexed suppression of every fact that was in Griffith's
favour, and an exaggeration of whatever was likely to make against
him. However, notwithstanding this charge, you will be astonished
when I tell you that a jury, deemed a respectable one, found him
guilty. I had strong suspicions that some of them at least, though
men of situation and character not to be directly tampered with,
were however come at by oblique ways. Kilty is FitzG[ibbon]'s
wine merchant, Ward a friend of Parnell's, and Cross[th]wait[e] of
Beresford's – Patrick, who showed his bias from the beginning, a
government contractor. Hat. and F. were acquitted. What Griff's
sentence will be is not yet guessed at.

This town is really in a sad state: the power of government
irresible, and the use that was made of it, especially by FitzGib.,
most severe and arbitrary. Had the drunken police fired, I think he
might have hanged Griffith.

Duquery and Curran were Griffith's principal counsel. The first
began eloquently and concluded weakly. The other was rather
indifferent about his client, but anxious about himself. He did not
attend in court during the greater part of the examination of the
witnesses, and collected his facts principally from the lawyers,
notwithstanding he was more eloquent than I ever heard him
before, or I think any lawyer anywhere. But his eloquence was
employed on those topics that favoured more his own display than
his client's cause, and of that kind that was fitter to gild a bad case
than throw light on a good one. His arguments, too, though often
strong and forcibly put, were lost and consumed in the blaze of his
imagination. In short, I have seldom heard more beautiful or more
animated eloquence, and seldom have heard so little persuasion.
What a pity that such talents were not fated to clothe a mind of
stern probity and patriotism.

FitzG. was as usual dry, shrewd and arrogant; and little Hewitt
closed with a feeble address to the jury, representing Griffith as a
demagogue, Lord Earlsfort a Patriot, and Alderman Exshaw a
primitive Christian. ...

The 24th of May I walked up Grafton Street and saw several
guards of police with fixed bayonets and cartouche boxes ready for

C/8/45 *contd.*

action. I went down Duke Street and saw another guard there. The same in Dawson Street, Molesworth [Street], and this is in the middle of the day. I began to be a little alarmed ..., [but] they told me Alderman Warren was to review the [sedan] chairs. ... This excited my curiosity further to see this great military alderman and his procession upon this occasion, for whose reception that formidable preparation had been made. ... Some may wonder what was really the meaning of all this; for, who can believe that it was merely to reconnoitre the sedan chairs that such military preparations were made ...'.

Also included in the volume is a character sketch of F[itzGibbon]:

F. may have much black-letter erudition, he may be a judicious and shrewd litigator, he may be able to confound truth and give an overbearing front to fallacy. But for talents as a legislator I have never seen an example of them, except the talent of doing mischief. Wherever he has meddled with the law, he has deformed it. The bill restricting the press gives unprecedented power to magistrates. By his doctrine of attachments he would invest the King's Bench with the illegal jurisdiction of the Star Chamber and despoil the subject of trialby jury – the most precious privilege of the Great Charter. By the Police Bill he has infused into our constitution the poison of a French prerogative; and the Riot Act of England, that intemperate effervescence of rebellion, in times of peace and loyalty he has inflicted on the people of Ireland. He is continually hovering over the law, and like the harpy, wherever he touches he taints its sound and salutory principles.'

46   [July? 1788?]   Flood to Parsons [in reply].
'I longed to hear from you, and find by two letters of yours that I have just received from Phillimore's that I ought to have had one sooner. I thank you for your full and satisfactory account of the last scene of your session, and for the picture of Irish criminal justice. It puts me into good humour with some things here that I was disrelishing ... [text defective], [including] Impey's case ... . I attended it, but to my great surprise I found Fox and all the managers receded from the strong point, the total illegality of the whole proceeding. ...

I see that this session will afford nothing, but it has prepared a good deal for the next. ...

I bought G – n's first speech here. Bring his second with you to Farmley.'

47   18 Nov. 1788   Flood to Parsons.
'I have stripped my hand of flannel to write in pain a line. I shall leave this the first instant I can. Let me hear from you often, I request. This is an unlucky crisis. When I went last from Waterford, I wrote to Charlemont; but, not receiving an answer, I

C/8/47 *contd.*

believe he never got mine. I therefore request you will be so good as to deliver this to him yourself. I need not say that the more you converse with him, the better. Amongst other things, take any lucky opportunity that offers of stating the possibility of my being out of parliament, and in Ireland what a solecism it would be. If he says anything, carry on the conversation till you make the most of it. In my letter, I request him to speak for me to Lord Longford, whose borough I once represented, and should wish to do so again on the usual terms. That or any other, in short. ...

Is it possible that the K – should last any time?'

48   20 Nov. 1788   Flood, post-marked Kilkenny, to Parsons, Trinity College, Dublin, about Parsons's canvass for T.C.D.

'... Lady Desart thinks that Brown's [*sic*] first tie is to Lord Donoughmore, but she hopes that she will get one voice for you. I don't know her enough to know the value of this promise. I will apply to Lord Altamont in England, before which I hope to leave this next Tuesday. ...'

49   26 Nov. 1788   Flood, post-marked Kilkenny, to Parsons, Trinity College, Dublin.

'Tomorrow I leave this for Waterford, hoping to be in London to [*sic*] the call of the House. ...

Lanigan's answer is that he will not engage till the King's death. His suffrage decays in June.'

50   16 Dec., post-   Flood, [London], to Parsons, Trinity College, Dublin.
       marked 1788
'I won't run mad, though after great example ... . I can't attend on this great day. To be lifted into a chair and thence into the House; to be silent or to desire to speak sitting, which would be laughed at and disliked; and then to speak as languidly as from weakness I must do, and not to be able to stay (to give even a silent vote) to late in the morning – all this would be to put life into one scale and dishonour only in the other, which would be too much. ...'

51   11 Jan., post-   Flood to Parsons, Trinity College, Dublin: more about the regency
       marked 1789   crisis.

'... This business is strangely delayed by the party spirit which mingles in every interrogatory ... . You will see, therefore, that, considering the manner in which it is likely to be fought, you will meet in parliament about the time that the Lords will be agitating our resolutions, after which a bill on those resolutions will be to be brought in. I think it is likely that the Marquess [of Buckingham, the Lord Lieutenant] will desire an adjournment. I have had a lette from Ch[arlemon]t such as you would expect. The *right*, however, of the Prince is completely given up, and that of parliament so established, that I doubt [text defective] ... . If Gr[attan] be going over [back to Ireland] a perfect Foxite, as is said, perhaps he will resume his doctrine of *inherent* right. That will be a glorious field for you. Pitt took prodigious advantage of it.'

C/8/52 14 [?Jan. 1789] Flood to Parsons.

'Our business is still further deferred till Friday, so that it is now certain that we shall have finished nothing so as to reach you by the time of your meeting. I request that you will give me as exact an account as possible of men's minds, of what government proposes, and of the likelihood of that's taking place or of being overruled, which to be sure it will not be, unless from advice and encouragement here, as we all know from every day's experience. Above all, let me know what you yourself have done and mean to do, and everything about you.'

53   Post-marked   Damaged fragment of a letter from Flood to Parsons, Trinity
          8 Feb. [1789]   College, Dublin.

'... Such meetings as you mention are terrible things. They are hard to avoid and embarrassing to attend. The few independent men that attend them are dragged into the vortex of those who are not so.

Since I have been able to stir out, no good occasion has occurred, and in my situation it would be absurd to attempt to force one, especially at such a time. ...'

54   8–12 Feb., post-   Flood to Parsons, Trinity College, Dublin.
          marked 1789   'I went yesterday to the House to vote against an attack which I hear Mr Rolle intended to make on the Prince of Wales; but it came to nothing. The House was not as full as usual, but nothing could be more tumultuary. In short, the subject had been so exhausted in passing the resolutions, and was considered as so far concluded by the acceptance of the Queen and Prince, that they would not listen to anything but short sparrings of the moment.

Burke screeched half a dozen speeches and seemed stunned almost to madness at their clamorous inattention. Grey, who is very warm, charged Pitt with insincerity in his pretended civility to the Prince. This inflamed Pitt to the highest degree you can conceive, so that, while Grey was speaking, Pitt shook a roll of paper he had in his hand at Grey, just in the action and with the countenance of a man going to strike another. It was a scene of disorder. Not one word on the great points of the question was spoken, and I saw that I might as well read the psalms and lessons to them as argue the point, and I felt little of, and could so little partake in, the outrage around me, that it even disgusted me, as a sober man is disgusted with a drunken company. ...

I have this moment received two letters from you. I am sorry you should have so much reason to lament the degradation of that body [the Irish parliament]. I forethought it. I never knew it otherwise almost. There is no dignity, no reserve, no prudence. This *stamps* 50,000 [Grattan] with the character of a tool of faction. Neither House here would receive the examination before the [Privy] Council, nor the Commons even from the Lords,

C/8/54 *contd.*   though the physicians were sworn before the Lords and could not
be so by the Commons. And why? Because it would be to recede
from a part of their independence. Yet, what is Independent
Ireland about to do? It is like the tribute for protection. It is
impossible for me to get to Ireland in time. In Ireland, that party
(Pitt's) has been absurd, and it was absurd to meet the parliament
in such weakness. They had been five years making their enemies
strong and putting them into the strongholds of government, and
they see the consequence. They are rooted up like a weed after
rain.

I think you must have felt that the rumoured letter from me to
the Marquess could not have contained such an universal
sentiment. You should have known it, if I had written. But I never
wrote a line, nor gave a sentiment in casual discourse. I feel the
importance of the moment more than some of our countrymen.
When my friends hear of me, they shall hear from me, and I hope
not to their dissatisfaction. I beg you will remember me in the best
manner to Sandy Montgomery. I respect and love him. As to
D[uquer?]y you don't say anything. Did he run [?garrah]?

Next week, I suppose there will be a general change of ministry.
Pitt will be strong in the Commons and Thurlow stronger in the
Lords, notwithstanding dismission.

Are there no records in Ireland? Is she too independent to
consult her own records? ...

Thursday, February 12th. I was too late for the post last night.
This day the Regency Bill concludes with us. After the new
ministry are re-elected, a new scene will rise. Fox is not determined
enough to return here. ...

You don't say whether you found yourself more at ease and more
master of the House. Tell me all about it. Was O'Brien in the
House?'

55   20 Feb. [1789]   Flood to Parsons, Trinity College, Dublin.
'... The Irish addresses will come to no effect at present ... . Fate
seems determined to make a certain person's [Grattan] measures
always stultify themselves. Simple Repeal,
Poynings and the Judges Bill were all blunders. We voted 20,000
seamen to England, though we had no seamen, but because we
have landsmen. Yet, of the latter, we could raise but a few
thousand ..., and those few thousand were no gain to England, for
they would have been got equally and with less expense by the
common recruiting service. The Irish propositions were at first
supported, and he burdened the public with £140,000, to pay for
what he did not understand, and to secure an economy which he
has not in [text defective] ... . On the contrary, he opposed a
resolve in favour of economy after, and opposed my motion either
to resume the taxes or to insist on some recompense for them.

C/8/55 *contd.* What was his conduct on the Press Bill, the Riot Act, the Police, and the resolve against the liberty of speech or writing? The post is going.'

56 5 Mar. [1789] Flood to Parsons, Trinity College, Dublin.
'... I have read your speech with much pleasure. You are right as to my motion in 1782 relative to Poynings['s] Law. I never attempted to do two things under pretence of doing one: first, because it is not fair; and next, because it usually creates a jumble that leaves both imperfect. I don't legislate by addresses, resolutions or etceteras. I therefore in a repeal of Poyning did not think myself called [text defective] ... .

There is nothing more clear than what government can and ought to do. But either ignorance or inattention or insolence prevents everything that is right. It has done so, at least, and I fear it will do. The moment I can give you any information, I will.'

57 7 Mar. 1789 Flood to Parsons, Trinity College, Dublin.
'... I shall be impatient to hear the results of Tuesday. I think, after the shake your letter mentioned among independent men, that the motion will fail. A very little time at least will show the faction [text defective – the folly?] as well as ignorance of the man. The round-robin (which is a circular signature used by sailors when they mutiny, that no ringleader may appear) is one of the most vulgar, nauseous and unconstitutional ideas that was ever thought of. ... There is an insobriety in every step. He ought to be sent to Dr Willis. Still, however, it must be confessed that the Irish servants of the crown whom he now tramples on, and the government itself, deserve in some degree the punishment they meet for having so long and so unworthily as well as absurdly fostered the faction which now is employed against them. Neither am I at all sure whether even this will induce them to establish a firm and rational system. ...'

58 9 Mar. 1789 Flood to Parsons, Trinity College, Dublin.
'... Hold up your head and go on. I am glad the Marquess had the decorum to send to you. If he and Pitt had a little more of that address, it would do them no hurt. As high-minded men we ought to feel that there are other high-minded too; and after repulsive conduct, they owe something to the feelings of honourable men. That Gr[attan] has arrogance enough to undo a dozen better men than himself. Yet his mercenary allies are suffered to remain in office, they [text defective] ... every day, and if they are dismissed, both they and their captain may be beat out of the field, if there be *wisdom*. Had there been wisdom in time, the crisis could not have happened. ...'

C/8/59 10 Mar., post-   Flood to Parsons, Trinity College, Dublin.
marked 1789   'I am just returned from the Houses. A speech from the King
was read by permission ... . The King's restoration is distinctly
stated. ... It is said that Lord Lothian is already removed ... . If this
be true, it marks a strong feeling, and if it extends to Ireland, will
be inconvenient to many *Patriots*.'

60   9 May 1789   Flood to Parsons, Castle, Birr.
'... I guessed your situation to be what you state. I hope soon to
see you in Berners Street. It seems to be that the most important
business is yet to do here, or that this must be a long one. The
Slave Trade question, the East Indian Budget, new taxes and a
probable Regency Bill, are still on hand.'

61   post-marked   The 2nd Earl of Aldborough, Belan, Co. Kildare, to Parsons,
4 July 1789   Dublin.
'I have had the communication with Mr Flood you desired,
previous to my leaving England, and everything settled, I returned
to Ireland last Friday, and on Monday at our corporation did my
borough [of Baltinglass, Co. Wicklow] the compliment of electing
you and Mr Flood corporators. It need be attended with no
inconvenience to either, but if at any time it suits either of your
inclinations to be sworn in, the charter days are the Monday after
St John the Baptist and the Monday after Michaelmas, and I shall
esteem it a favour if at those times you do me the favour of
making Belan your headquarters. At any rate, it will afford me an
opportunity of proposing your friend for the seat you wished him,
but I beg, till the time, that this may remain a secret in your
bosom.
Next session promises to be a warm one, from the late removals.
I think you will have been ungratefully served if left out in their
replacing, as no one laboured more successfully in the ministerial
vineyard. The new peerages are hitherto withheld, as I hear, till
those they are intended for give security to bring in each two
friends to government in the approaching new parliament, and that
£3,000 have [*sic*] been offered and refused for a seat on that score.'

62   10 Oct. 1789   Flood, post-marked Kilkenny, to Parsons, Trinity College, Dublin,
advising him to get to London before 31 October, lest delay '...
may give your enemies [at Seaford?] a second triumph.'

63   5 Mar. 1790   Flood to Parsons.
'I made my motion yesterday. Pains had been taken to prejudice
all minds and to treat it with disregard and ridicule, and the House
was evidently adverse. This, together with the weight of the subject
and my not having anybody to consult, oppressed me, as you may
guess. On the whole, however, at the end of the debate the House
got round, and I am told today that my conduct is approved. As to
my plan [of parliamentary reform], it had more good luck than I

C/8/63 *contd.*   expected. Several members, Fox, Sawbridge, etc, etc, said it was the best plan of any that had yet been offered, which includes the Duke of Richmond's, Lord Chatham's and Mr Pitt's; and Mr Duncomb[e], member for Yorkshire, who had seconded Pitt's last reform motion, thanked me, and hoped in another session to second me in a similar proposition to that which I had made.

Pitt professed his adherence to the principle, said he would have moved on it, had he thought it a good time, and therefore, as he could not vote against, nor for it, moved an adjournment. One of the members for the county of Suffolk seconded me. We intended to divide, but by a mistake, the Speaker did not hear us, and left the Chair. This was no great matter, as we should have divided weakly, and to expose some of the majority was no object to yours truly. H.F.'

[For corrected copies of Flood's speech on the occasion, see C/7.]

64   12 Apr. 1790   Flood to Parsons, Trinity College, Dublin, reporting that Dr Marsh has refused to vote for Parsons, and sending compliments to Lord and Lady Aldborough.

65   16 Apr. 1790   Flood to Parsons, Trinity College, Dublin.

'I have this instant received yours of the 8th and Lord Aldborough's of the same date. Enclosed [not found] I send the bond for you to keep, and also a draft on Latouche for you to keep. The economy of the business is a question only for me to consider [sense?], nor shall I ever force myself on any government. These, however, are considerations that are not at all within our bargain. If you find trifling, you must make it a point with [text defective – him? to] deliver a *peremptory message*, which [text defective] ... by going on the return of the post to Ireland. I hope you will have a majority to secure a return. I am *peremptory* not to relinquish the seat. ...'

66   17 Apr. 1790   Flood to Parsons, Trinity College, Dublin: more about the Irish general election.

'... It is impossible for me to leave this, having my seat here to look after. You have not said a word about Armstrong. If I succeed elsewhere, could you compass that which he spoke of? By something your brother said, it seems possible that, if you succeed at the college, you might with the assistance of Mr H[arma]n. ...

Your brother and I received your letters not till the 16th, by which time possibly your election was over. But, had there been more time, Holmes would not go.'

67   3 May 1790   Lord Aldborough, Belan, to Parsons annexing a copy of a letter he has written to Flood explaining why he has been unable to bring Flood in for Baltinglass.

'... Several of my corporators, yourself [Flood] of the number, were in England, six more prevented from attending by

C/8/67 *contd.*

indisposition, and several by other elections in which they were more interested. So many could not be spared from so few voters, especially as most of them were my own family and tenantry, and seemed extremely adverse to my bringing in aliens, and had drawn up a remonstrance, signed by fourteen corporators, beseeching me not to reject my own family, who pledged themselves on all *other occasions* to support my interests. From the expression scratched under [ie. underlined], I had the justest reasons to suppose that, availing themselves of the absentees, a most violent opposition would have been the consequence, if I persisted in rejecting them, and had my doubts of some of my tenants, who had run much in debt on [*sic*] the hopes of wiping it off on this occasion, and who might have gone against me, had my brothers chosen to discharge it. I showed all these matters clearly to Mr Parsons, whose exertions and arguments manifested the warmest zeal, and that to risk a defeat and the patronage of my borough and family was vey unadvisable, when he was not like to be benefited.

On my first coming to the country, I thought to have compromised the matter. But the evening of that day undeceived me, and occasioned a second letter to Mr Parsons by express to do away the purport of the former one. I also received excuses from Dean Walsh, Sir Allen Johnston [*sic* – Johnson], General Walsh, Mr Champigne [*sic* – Champagné] and others. Under these circumstances, I trust your candour will view matters in their proper light. My family told me last year they did not wish to come into parliament. The change of their sentiments, grounded on the request of so many corporators, friends to the family, hath occasioned this disappointment. We are all on the look-out for a seat for you, and shall readily contribute towards it, if you desire it; or I am ready to discharge the principal and interest of the bond whenever and to whomever you please to appoint. We are desirous to make any retribution in our power.

I told you your presence might turn the scale and be of a lasting importance, unless, as Mr J. Latouche has good-naturedly done, who is equally disappointed, you chose to yield your pretensions for the peace and accommodation of a family. I cannot compel electors to attend, if they do not choose, or if prevented ...'.

He also annexes a copy of a letter from his brothers to himself: 'We cordially congratulate your Lordship and ourselves on the event of this day, which forever conciliates our love and respect for you, besides the heartbroken joy of family peace and concord, and regarding you always as our head and ourselves as your support, you will derive that consequence to yourself which you once transferred to others, and [we] hope Mr Flood will by our united efforts e'er [*sic*] long join in our political career.'

C/8/68   4 May 1790   Flood to Parsons, Trinity College, Dublin.

'I need not say how much I am surprised and mortified at the perfidy of that scoundrel and of the other tyrant, if your conjecture be right, which we shall soon see. I can make one of them *feel* me, and if I can, I will both. Frame matters so as that you may be able to get to Farmley as soon as possible. ...

I cannot write to W[arden] Fl – d, so do you say what is necessary, and not more. I am confounded.'

69   11 May 1790   Flood to Parsons, Trinity College, Dublin.

'... If J[ohn] Str[atfor]d succeeds in Wicklow, the specific execution of the promise must be demanded: if he does not, some substitute. The ultima ratio must be used, and you must let me know for certain when parliament in Ireland meets, that I may be there in time.

You know the brothers promised that he [*sic* – each] should contribute to a certain amount, and that he should so write to me. He writes £200 himself, and the brothers £400. I mention this for two reasons: first, to show the concord and concurrence of the brothers (who are said to be at dire enmity) in their engaging thus for each other; and, secondly, to show you that nothing verbal, or that is not written, and that too by the person who is to perform, ought to satisfy you in dealing with men whom even writing does so imperfectly bind. At the same time, it may not be prudent to tell the brothers what the peer has said – at least till after they have been got to engage themselves as explicitly as possible for the peer's performance. ...

In the meanwhile, no other opportunity should be lost, and the matter should be talked of freely, that they may see the necessity of repairing the breach.

Thorp was here the other day and said that Lord Granard had two [seats]. We must try this, and everything. I will not be wanting, whatever the people of Ireland may.'

70   [pre 13 May 1790]   Copy in Flood's handwriting of a letter from Lord Aldborough to 'Dear Flood.

I have seen and conversed with Mr Hobart. Trim is not saleable, but I have some hopes he will, if possible, procure one for you that is. I shall see him again on Tuesday, when I hope for more certain tidings. If not as favourable as I wish, Mr Parsons heard my brother [John Stratford] say, as well as me, that on the success of his petition, you certainly should succeed him. ...

I told Mr Parsons I was ready, when you pleased, to discharge the £800 bond and interest.'

71   13 May 1790   Flood to Parsons, Trinity College, Dublin: further abuse of, and instructions concerning, 'the peerless peer'.

'... Theo. Jones will probably make a borough vacancy – General Cuningham[e] and the Westenras can give an account of it. I fear

C/8/71 *contd.*   Lord Kingston would not sell. I should think Charlem – t would
                        assist. Try everything. The same power will attempt the same here,
                        and with greater probability of success, which makes me unwilling
                        to leave this [London] just now.'

72   14 May 1790   Flood to Parsons, Trinity College, Dublin.
                        'In looking over a copy of the words I mentioned yesterday to be
                        delivered, I found that Seaford was omitted. This requires a slight
                        alteration, and it will run thus: "The *marked* conduct of the Mr
                        Hennikers, connected with that of the late Duke of *Chandos* at
                        Winchester, the circumstances of Seaford election, and the
                        notoriety of Mr Flood's being to be returned for Baltinglass, make
                        Mr Flood feel that, if administration does not furnish to Lord
                        Aldborough an *opportunity* for fulfilling his engagement, he (Mr
                        Flood) must consider it as a decisive proof of repeated and
                        unmerited hositility, on which ground no motive will induce him
                        to be the friend of an administration capable of so acting.". ...'

73   15 May 1790   Flood to Parsons, Trinity College, Dublin: the same.
                        '... With regard to H – rt, you see my object is a distinct
                        eclaircissement. They have waged smothered war. It is necessary to
                        uncover it, and therefore I entreat that you will not cease till you
                        bring it to a point, let the consequence be what it may. It would be
                        better it had been done much sooner, but it required a crisis. This
                        is one, and I must seize it.
                            Lord Bective will have a vacancy. If parliament does not meet so
                        soon as the 20th, I shall be there. Lady Frances leaves this
                        tomorrow. I follow in a fortnight.'

74   17 May 1790   Flood to Parsons, Trinity College, Dublin.
                        '... I request you will summon my relations, all of them that are
                        in parliament and who wish to befriend me will have a right [*sic*]
                        to make common cause with me (at least this once), and to say to
                        the Major [Hobart] that they will consider it as a family cause, if I
                        should by any manoeuvre be excluded. ...'.

75   19 May 1790   Flood to Parsons, Trinity College, Dublin:
                        'By the prorogation, it will be possible for me to be at the meeting
                        in Ireland. But a dissolution is hourly expected about that time here,
                        and it is essential for me not to be absent at such a moment. I
                        entreat, therefore, that you will leave no human means untried
                        where you are, that I may attend to the essential business here ...'.

76   31 May, post-   Flood to Parsons, Trinity College, Dublin: the same.
        marked 1790

77   1 June [1790]   Flood to Parsons, Trinity College, Dublin.
                        'I just received yours of the 25th of May. I wish you joy of your
                        father's estate. ... Clonmel is vacant. Lord Granard had two
                        vacancies. You write unsatisfactorily short [*sic*]. ...

C/8/77 *contd.*		Lord Mount Cashell [patron of Clonmel] was married to Lord Rawdon's sister. You will find whether Lord Rawdon has written on the subject. ... Lord Mayo's death, or any death, will produce a vacancy. Consider – as well as a double return. You are not as good an electioneerer [*sic*] as [Denis Bowes?] Daly. ...
78	2 July 1793	Formal statement by Flood of what he expects of Lord Aldborough by way of restitution.
79	4 July [1790]	Flood to Parsons, Trinity College, Dublin. '... I was mortified that I could not stay to see my excellent friend, Sandy Montgomery, and entreat that you will acquaint him with my situation and feelings. The Duke of Leinster's civility in the business of Baltinglass requires my acknowledgement, and I wish that Charlemont may know that nothing but my ill-health would have prevented me from finding him, whether in town or country.
		have had a very polite letter about Clonmel. If saleable, I should have had it.'
80–81	[May-July 1790]	Two undated fragments of letters from Flood to Parsons about the hunt to get a seat, but adding nothing to the foregoing.
82	5 Aug. [1790?]	Flood, post-marked Kilkenny, to Parsons, Trinity College, Dublin: 'I hope soon to hear from your concerning your visitation of the College?. But I would much rather hear from you respecting your visit. When shall we see you? I am over head and ears in mortar.'
83	22 Aug. 1790	Flood, post-marked Kilkenny, to Parsons, Trinity College, Dublin, renewing his invitation to Farmley.
84	19 May 1791	Flood, post-marked Kilkenny, to Parsons, now Sir Laurence Parsons, 5th Bt, in succession to his father, who had died earlier in the month, Birr. 'I cannot express the satisfaction your letter gave me, and I thank you for the details. It was a glorious victory [for Parsons at the King's County by-election], and with your good care and conduct, will secure your family establishment [*sic*]. It was perhaps lucky that you were ill-used on your petition [for T.C.D.], for the case might have been different, had you been to contend in any other name than your own, under such circumstances and with so much indisposition in certain places. The meeting at Cloghan seems to be calculated to enable a certain person to declare against you without odium. Certainly, to level you with your opponent (however respectable he is) was not friendly. It was endeavouring to deprive you of the propensity of the county to an old family interest. What a turn is Burke's political carer about to take! He has too much talent and too much enthusiasm not to have defenders in such a country as England. But the anti-American, anti-Gallican

C/8/84 *contd.*   and anti-Philosophic ideas he maintains will be too heavy for him.
.   Boswell in his colloquy with Johnson on Burke says that Burke is
                             an hawk, always falling and in rapid pursuit of his object. But he is
                             a hawk that never catches anything, says Johnson. In his climateric
                             years he has attempted to choose a stormy and isolated summit
                             which he never dared to occupy when in his vigour. ...

                             What a perpetually lucky man is Pitt, to see his adversaries
                             engaged in a contest where one is likely to run on the wrong side
                             of the post for the country, and the other for the King's plate.
                             What an even hand of degradation he held towards them both, as
                             far as he could – indeed, he avoided any compliment to Burke
                             with such caution that one might suppose that he thought Burke
                             might mean to pave his way to Court. Yet, I believe it to be mere
                             jealousy of Sheridan working upon original prejudices as to public
                             principles.

                             To come home – the end of all things – when shall I see you at
                             Farmley? Will it not be as well to be away from Birr for a space
                             after the election is over. If so, I hope you will try my new cook.'

85   23 Sep. [1791]   Flood, post-marked Kilkenny, to Parsons, Trinity College, Dublin.
                             'I wish you joy of being so successful a farmer, and hope you
                             remember that after Birr Races I have reason to think that you will
                             give me an opportunity of showing you that I am an active
                             builder. I expect early in October to have finished all but the attic
                             storey, as far as the shell goes. ...'

C/12	DATE	DESCRIPTION

1   [Paper-marked   Small octavo volume, not quite full, containing an account in
     1813]   Parsons's, now 2nd Earl of Rosse, hand of the life of Flood up to
                    1778, including some unique background information about the
                    Flood family in relation to the parliamentary borough of Callan
                    over which Flood fought a fatal duel in 1769. This account,
                    though obviously incomplete, seems to be too short to be intended
                    as a publication in its own right: possibly it was intended as an
                    introduction to an edition of Flood's speeches or to the 2nd Earl's
                    work identifying Flood as the author of the *Letters of Junius*.

'As Mr Flood possessed abilities which, both by nature and
cultivation, surpassed I think almost every man I have been
acquainted with, it seems to me to be worthwhile to give an account
of such circumstances of his life as are within my recollection.

He was born about the [year] 1730. His father was Lord Chief
Justice of the King's Bench in Ireland. His mother was an English
lady why had lived in the neighbourhood of Chester. Soon after
his father had been called to the Irish bar, he met this lady at
Finglas, near Dublin, where she was on a visit with some friends,
and possessing singular beauty as well as great dignity and grace of
manners, he soon became enamoured with [*sic*] her and,
despairing of obtaining his father's consent, who had some higher
connection in view for him, and she had but a small fortune, he
married her privately and, still dreading his father's displeasure,
who wished to unite him with Miss Agar, afterwards Countess of
Brandon, being the daughter of a gentleman in his neighbourhood
in the county of Kilkenny, the marriage was kept secret till the
Chief Justice's [*sic*] death, which happened not very long
afterwards. In this interval Henry Flood, of whom I write, was
born; and hence, when the county of Kilkenny was afterwards
divided by contested elections into hostile factions prone to
calumniate each other, a whisper was spread that he was
illegitimate. But this I believe to be unfounded. His mother was
always respected as a woman of strict virtue and propriety of
conduct. Among others the late Lord Clare in a court of justice
bore this testimony to her character. He said that his mother, who
[was] peculiarly delicate in the choice of her acquaintance, had
been very intimate with Mrs Flood, which he was certain she
would not have been, had there been any blemish in her character.
Besides, calumny never insinuated that her younger children were
illegitimate, though there never was even a report of a marriage
subsequent to the birth of Mr H. Flood. But he, being actively
engaged in these election contests, and being a most formidable
antagonist, there were many ready to assert anything which they
thought might disparage him.

Mr Flood was educated at some Irish school, where he was but imperfectly taught the learned languages. He afterwards entered Trinity College, Dublin, where notwithstanding this deficiency, he soon improved himself and was adjudged a premium at the quarterly examinations ..., which in that university was a great criterion of juvenile merit. ... His person, which was rather above the middle size, was very strong and well made, and his face, as his contemporaries have told me, particularly the Rev. Doctor Dobbin, who is still alive, surpassed in beauty every young man of his time; so much so that, when he went to London, he attracted as many eyes, as a man, as the Miss Gunnings, who afterwards were the Duchess of Hamilton and Lady Coventry, did as women. From Dublin College he went early to Oxford, where he was admitted ad eundem. Doctor Markham, afterwards Archbishop of York, was his tutor there. He soon discoverd the great abilities of his young pupil, and was assiduous in cultivating them. He introduced him into a small literary club there, consisting of about twelve members. ... Markham was not only one of the best scholars of his time, but a man of refined taste and an incomparable critic. Flood immediately perceived that his attainments were far inferior to those of the rest of the society, and therefore he resolved not to open his lips there on any literary subject for the space of one year, but to read intensely during that time, in order to put himself on a par with the other members. ...

Chief Justice Flood having a great partiality for the bar, which is usual in gentlemen who have been successful in that profession, sent his son from Oxford to the Temple, though he had sufficient landed property for every reasonable object which a gentleman could desire. Here he read law occasionally, but mathematics were his favourite study, and wishing to draw his knowledge from the original source, he read Euclid and Apollonius in the Greek. While he was at the Temple, he had a most unfortunate bout of illness which greatly changed his appearance, and destroyed all that beauty of face by which he had been so eminently distinguished. ... His voice was ... so much injured by his sickness that at this time he with difficulty made himself audible across the small chamber which was his lodging. Instead, however, of being discouraged by this defect, he persevered with extraordinary ardour in his pursuit, it being the cast of his mind to love struggling with difficulties, by which he was always excited, not dismayed. ...

In the year [1759] Mr Flood was chosen a member of parliament for the county of Kilkenny. He attended the House diligently every day, but resolved not to speak there during that entire session, wishing to observe the manner and powers of the members, and to become perfectly familiar with the forms and orders of proceedings in the House. For the latter purpose, he

C/12/1 *contd.*

studied the Journals indefatigably till he became a perfect master of parliamentary order. At the same time, to embellish his style, he read Shakespeare with uncommon diligence, and from each play he may [*sic*] short extracts of all phrases which he thought deserved particularly to be remembered ... . But Demosthenes became his favourite author. He had many of the orations nearly by heart ... . At what period he gave this preference to Demosthenes, I do not know, as he was nearly fifty years old before I was acquainted with him. ...

Mr Flood likewise practised speaking prepared and extempore speeches. His brother, Jocelyn Flood, who was also a young man of talents, and he used to practise speaking extempore together. But Jocelyn died when he was but twenty years of age.

The Irish parliament at this time met but every second year, and after the interval of this long recess Mr Flood thought himself sufficiently qualified to commence speaking in public, and did so with such great success as to be esteemed before any of the speakers in the House of Commons. He had overcome by great application the deficiency of his voice, for though it still continued deep and a little too nasal, it had surprising flexibility and uncommon strength and energy. His modulation, when he declaimed, was exquisitely beautiful and captivating, and by such delicate strokes as our great actors are distinguished by, he used to produce extraordinary effects. He was then very rapid, and Mr Grattan told me that, when he went to the Temple, having been used previously to hear Flood continually in the Irish House of Commons, he and the other young men of his acquaintance were much disappointed when they heard the English speakers, thinking Flood very superior to them ...

But the first speaker that seems to have roused Mr Flood's ambition most at this time, and gave him the highest idea of the power of eloquence, was Mr Gerard Hamilton. ... Hamilton made a speech that produced an astonishing sensation in the Irish House, as he had made one with similar success some time before in the English House. ... [He] prepared the few speeches he made verbally and with great care. His own expression was that he prepared to a dot over an "i", though he has said at times that he thought the best speech was that which was partly prepared and the parts well puttied together with extempore passages. He was a great master of tones and much of the effect he produced resulted from these. He was a man of weak nerves, but the consequent agitation probably gave a more interesting and natural manner to his delivery. Mr Flood said he began on a very high pitch, that his voice was almost like an hysterical screech, yet he kept up to that with great vehemence and rapidity in a very unexpected manner. It is very remarkable that he spoke but once in the English House and three times in the Irish. ...

The Chief Justice was proprietor of half the borough of Callan in the county of Kilkenny and Mr Wemys of the other half, and he sold his interest to the Chief Justice, who thus became proprietor of the whole. But after the Chief Justice's death by some indirect means Mr Agar, who lived near Callan, obtained some interest in the borough, and contested the representation of it with Mr Flood. This in its consequences was one of the greatest misfortunes of his life. He could not quietly submit to be thus deprived of what was considered as his private property, and the endeavour to preserve it occupied a considerable portion of his time and his fortune, brought him into continued contact with several low, vulgar men, caused bitter animosity between him and his friends, on the one side, and the whole Agar party and their connections and friends, on the other side. The contest was carried on with so much warmth that each party used to go armed into the town of Callan on the days when there was to be an election for magistrates or representatives. Riots frequently ensued and lives were sometimes lost. ... Finally, there was a duel between Mr Flood and Mr Agar, and the latter was shot through the heart: an event which might have been anticipated from the remarkable coolness and steady intrepidity of Mr Flood. Neither could Mr Flood reproach himself with any misconduct in this transaction. He had endeavoured to settle the immediate cause of difference amicably, as I have always heard, and continued to do so to the last moment. But Agar, instead of showing any disposition to do so, insulted him on the ground with the foulest language.

This unfortunate affair, however, did not terminate the contests for Callan, which continued to be carried [on] at much trouble and expense for a number of years afterwards, but not with the same ferocity. Mr Flood used to have at this time some of the burgesses from year to year constantly living in his house at Farmley, and he could not let them outside his demesne lest they should be tampered with by the opposite party. One of the burgesses was a Mr Griffiths, a literary gentleman of great wealth and honour, but of so generous a disposition that by giving away [money] and becoming security for friends, he was soon involved in considerable pecuniary difficulties. ... Mr Flood had much difficulty often in conveying him to Callan at the time of elections in such a manner that he might escape from being arrested for debt. On one of these occasions, Griffith was brought into Callan by night and placed in a loft over the courthouse, in the ceiling of which a hole was cut, and when it was Griffith's turn to vote, he put down his head through the hole and gave his vote, the bailiffs looking up at him, but could not reach him. ...

[Mr Flood's marriage] ... produced a political party composed of him and Warden Flood, his cousin, and the Beresfords. But it was of short duration. The views of Mr Flood and Lord Tyrone were so

C/12/1 *contd.*

different on political subjects that such an union could not last, and as often happens in cases of family feuds, bitter animosities followed, and which were only terminated by the death of the parties. ...

Mr Charles Townshend had a similar cadence ... [to Flood]; so much so, that some persons thought that they had copied from each other. Mr Flood, when he argued, was uncommonly powerful. Some of [his] speeches which are extant, particularly the two on the Renunciation, are the closest and best specimens of the argumentative style in our language, or perhaps in any other. When he argued, his accent was provincial, but this disappeared when he declaimed; for then his tones were those of the best public speakers and tragedians. He was very fond of frequenting the theatre and studying the expressions and delivery of the best actors. His action also, when he declaimed, was peculiarly fine, simple and impressive. ... Chief Baron Burgh... was also a most elegant and eloquent man; but his eloquence consisted in long, flowing, harmonious Ciceronian periods ... . [His] manner resembled Mr Pitt's manner. But Mr Flood had that power which we observe on the stage, of touching by a word or two – an art in which Lord Chatham excelled all the English speakers. ...

When Lord Buckinghamshire was Lord Lieutenant of Ireland, he appointed Sir Richard Heron his Secretary. Sir Richard had been a solicitor of Lincoln's Inn, and was totally unacquainted with politics and parliament. Therefore, when he was suddenly appointed prime minister of Ireland, and to a busy scene in parliament, feeling his own incompetence he remained silent, though questions were repeatedly put to him by the opposition. He sat immoveable on the Treasury Bench and, wearing [a] particularly stiff-curled, powdered wig, the newswriters of the opposition called him wig-block. ...'

C/14	DATE	DESCRIPTION

1–5   [c. 1810–15]   Loose-leaf clutch of 300 pages of octavo, consisting of an
autograph MS. in the 2nd Earl's hand on the subject of Flood and
Junius; together with 4 small quarto volumes, the first 2
containing c. 200 pages and the fourth c. 100, being a fair, clerical
copy of the same work. The 300 pages of autograph are some of
them paper-marked 1809, while the paper-mark on the 4 volumes
is 1814. Since the 2nd Earl's object was, not only to prove that
Flood was Junius, but to repel the assertion that Junius was 'an
assassin', much of the material relates to Flood's devotion to the
cause of liberty, his attachment to the constitution, etc, etc, and in
effect turns into a political biography of, or apology for, Flood.

'... When he ceased [to write anonymous polemics], Lord
Townshend was still Chief Governor of Ireland, nor was there any
idea whatsoever of Mr Flood's becoming connected with the Irish
government.

The first step to this appears in a letter of the Bishop of Chester
to him, written the 12th November 1772 [C/2/11] – that is in
about six months after he had ceased to write. His friend, Dr
Markham, then Bishop of Chester, who was uneasy at the line of
opposition which Mr Flood had taken in the Irish parliament, and
who had often endeavoured by his advice to moderate it, thought
that the appointment of a new Chief Governor would afford a
good opportunity of forming a connection between Mr Flood and
the government. He therefore, through a common friend, who was
in close confidence with the Court, stressed to Lord Harcourt, the
new Lord Lieutenant, he being then in London, the advantage
which was likely to result from such a connection. This he did
without any previous communication with Mr Flood, who, as the
Bishop says, should never have heard about it, if his wishes to be of
use had failed. ...

It is certain ... that Mr Flood had a communication with the
Lord Lieutenant prior to the next meeting of the Irish parliament,
which took place on the 12th of October 1773, and that they each
explained their views as to the government of Ireland. Mr Flood
specifically and in writing stated the terms for the public on which
he would consent to support Lord Harcourt's administration.
These were: a reduction of expenses, and the establishment of a
system of economy, the principal feature of which was that the two
Revenue Boards should be again consolidated into one, and five of
the Commissioners, with the officers under them, reduced,
causing a great diminution of expense and a greater still of
unconstitutional influence; secondly, that there should be a militia
bill in Ireland as in England, as a counterpoise to the standing
army, being a measure which the former administrations in Ireland

C/14 *contd.*

had always opposed; and, thirdly, that the false construction which had been put upon the law of Poynings should in future be resisted by the rejection of every money bill which should be altered in the Privy Council; fourthly, that a tax should be laid upon the land of absentee proprietors, not as a penalty upon them for residing in England, nor inorder to prevent them from living anywhere they pleased, but upon the principle that, as their properties were protected in common with others by the Irish government at a great expense, they should also contribute in common with others to defray the charges of that protection. These were the principal measures which Mr Flood when in opposition had urged, and to the adoption of which Lord Harcourt now consented; and therefore Mr Flood consented to support administration; and in two years afterwards accepted the office of Vice-Treasurer, which was a superior ofice to any which any Irishman then held.

Thus, in uniting with the Irish government, he did not give up his opinions or principles, but made it the express condition of his support that the government should adopt those measures which he had antecedently recommended. It was not he that bent to the government, but the government which bent to him. Nor was it merely on these stipulated measures that he expected to command the influence of government; he had grounds for believing that he would have had the lead in the House of Commons, as the Bishop of Chester had given him reason to expect it; that, holding the first office, he would be the first in weight; and that his influence would extend to the general administration of Ireland, directing every measure of importance in the manner most consonant to its welfare and its liberties. However, therefore, Mr Flood disapproved of the English administration, yet, as Ireland was a distinct kingdom, having a legislature of its own, he thought, with the assurances he had received and the measures which were promised, that he might secure good government for that part of the Empire which was naturally the peculiar object of his regard and solicitude. ... There was no incompatibility between good government in Ireland and bad in England. ... In uniting with that government [the Irish], he separated from no party, for he had never been connected with any party in England or in Ireland. The opposition in Ireland was not like that of England, formed on a party system. It was composed of a number of independent gentlemen, who had no tie to each other, who always disclaimed the idea of party, who acted on every occasion each according to his own judgement, sometimes supporting, sometimes opposing, the administration, as the measures seemed to them laudable or censurable. Mr Flood once, when speaking in the House of Commons, called them the incoherent country gentlemen: an equivocal expression which gave at the time some offence.

While Mr Flood continued in office, he endeavoured strenuously
to have the country governed according to those principles which
he had previously maintained. Every measure of economy which he
thought practicable he continually urged. Among these was that of
restraining a great waste of public money under the head of
stationery, all the members of both Houses ordering at discretion
what quantity they chose for their own consumption and that of
their families. Mr Grattan, at a time that he wished to speak
slightingly of this saving, said that Mr Flood with the feather of
economy had brushed the pens and paper off the tables. Mr Flood
resisted in the Irish Council, and with success, the design of the
English Ministers to send 4,000 foreign troops to Ireland, as an
unconstitutional and dangerous precedent. He was often, however,
thwarted by the other members of the Irish Cabinet. His ideas of
frugal government did not suit their views, nor did they feel the
same jealousy on subjects connected with the liberties and
constitutional rights of the country. Mr Anthony Malone was the
only member of the Cabinet who uniformly concurred with him
on such occasions. In 1779, when Mr Grattan proposed a
declaration of rights, the purport of which was "That the King,
Lords and the Commons of Ireland were the only power competent
to make laws for Ireland", a motion which Mr Grattan introduced
with a speech of most impassioned and splendid eloquence, Mr
Flood, though in office, and ungracious as such a motion must be
to English Ministers, still however supported what he conceived to
be the rights of Ireland, in a very long, argumentative speech of
extraordinary knowledge, ingenuity and force of reasoning [see
C/6]. He previously told the Viceroy, Lord Buckinghamshire, that
he would do so. Lord Buckinghamshire remonstrated with him.
But Mr Flood told him that he came into office, not to relinquish
his opinions, but to enforce them with greater effect, and that if his
general support did not appear to be acceptable on such terms, his
office was at his Excellency's disposal. ...

At this time [1781] Mr Flood stood alone in the House of
Commons. The leading men in the opposition seemed to be
jealous of his great ablities. They said he was impracticable, and
that he would not bend to their opinions. And the leading men in
the government dreaded him – as he fearlessly exposed whatever
he felt wrong; and therefore they countenanced the other members
of the opposition, and gave a more favourable reception to
whatever they proposed. But he was ready to combat them all, and
the more they thwarted him, the greater his superiority appeared.
The Irish juries had ceased at this time to pay any respect to
English laws, and as many properties were held in Ireland under
English acts of parliament, Mr Flood proposed a bill to ratify these
English acts and quiet possession. This, however, was opposed, not
only by the government, but by all the leading men in the

opposition. Mr Flood said on that occasion: "When a man brings in a bill to quiet possessions, it is hard to say that he intends to inflame. It is also hard to say that, because something more is to be done, nothing shall be attempted. But the opposition is to the particular man. I am the object of these puny efforts. But they harm me not. I shake them off, *as falls the dewdrop from the lion's mane.*" Well I remember the dignified air and triumphant tone with which he pronounced these words, while those who were opposing him seemed to dwindle into an inferior order of beings. What he said was true, that the opposition was to the man; for, in three days after, Mr Yelverton, who was then in opposition, did in concurrence with Mr Grattan, Mr Burgh and Mr Fitzgibbon, who were also all leading men in the opposition, propose a bill "for confirming all statutes made in England *concerning property* and commerce, so far as the said statutes relate to Ireland"; and this bill was agreed to by the administration and passed into law. ...

Of Mr Flood, the new government [of the Duke of Portland] does not appear to have taken any notice in the consideration of the measures then adopted for satisfying the people of Ireland. He was merely offered to be reinstated in the Privy Council, a compliment which he declined. Mr Flood continued through the remainder of the session to stand almost single. ... He particularly objected to Mr Yelverton's bill for new-modelling Poynings['s] Law, and in one of his speeches against it, he concluded with these words: "If I have a feeling in the inmost pulse of my heart, it is that which tells me that this is a great and awful day. It is that which tells me that if, after twenty years' service, I should pass this question by negligently, I should be a base betrayer of my country. It is that which tells me that the whole earth does not contain a prize sufficient to make me trifle with the liberties of this land. But I do, therefore, wish to subscribe my name to what I now propose, to have them handed down together to posterity, that posterity may know there was at least *one man* who disapproved of the temporising bill now before the House, a bill that future parliaments, if they have power, will *reform*, if they have not, with tears will deplore." The same day, in reply on the same subject to Mr Burgh, he concluded by saying: "... I would not leave an atom of power in an arbitrary Council, either English or Irish. Legislation does not belong to them, nor can you ever have a safe constitution while they interfere. You cannot raise a structure of adamant on a foundation of sand." In this manner did Mr Flood support his own opinions and combat singly against all parties. ...

[He proceeds to discuss the Renunciation dispute and the slanging-match between Flood and Grattan, in a manner which throws no new light on either.]

If we follow Mr Flood into the English parliament, we there find the same unbending, uncompromising, uncoalescing spirit of independence. ... He consulted with no man. He advocated no opinion but his own. When he opposed Mr Pitt on the commercial treaty, he at the same time complimented him at the expense of Mr Fox, warring with the one by his vote and with the other by his language, indifferent to the smiles or frowns of either. The predilections of his mind, however, were all on the side of Mr Pitt. He venerated the abilities and the character of his father. He disapproved of many passages in the public and private conduct of Mr Fox. On the illness of the King, when the great question of the regency was first debated, he coincided in opinion with Mr Pitt. Though flattering overtures were at that time made to him by Mr Gerard Hamilton, tempting him to join the opposition, then on the eve, as it was supposed, of permanent power, these he politely but proudly rejected. Sickness prevented him from attending the discussions. ... No occasion afterwards occurred in which he wished to interfere. Disapproving generally of Mr Fox's opposition, he could not take a part against Mr Pitt; and standing as that Minister then did so strong in his own great abilities and in the support of an immense majority, to take a part for him would have been superfluous. Besides, nature seemed to have disqualified Mr Flood from being subordinate to any man.

At length, he seized a subject on which he could stand alone, and he proposed his measure independent of every party. He moved for leave to bring in a bill for amending the representation of the people in parliament. This was his last public effort. ... It is very remarkable that the plan of reform which he then proposed perfectly coincides with the principles of Junius on that subject, as developed in his letter to Mr Wilkes. (It will be recollected that these letters to Mr Wilkes were never published till near thirty years after Mr Flood's death.) Junius objects to annual parliaments, but he is strong for triennial. Second, he objects to disfranchising boroughs, but he warmly approves of Lord Chatham's plan of adding 100 knights. This is precisely the plan which Mr Flood proposed. He would have 100 knights added, only with this improvement, that they should be chosen, not by the freeholders, but by the householders, in each county, thereby giving a very numerous and respectable body of the people an influence on the House of Commons which they have not at present. ... "I question the power *de jure* of the legislature to disfranchise a number of boroughs upon the general ground of improving the constitution." "I would not give representatives to those great trading towns which have none at present. If the merchant and the manufacturer must be really represented, let them become freeholders by their industry, and let the representation of the county be increased."

The same coincidence of principle also appears on this subject between Junius and Mr Flood's plan of parliamentary reform in Ireland in the year 1784. Mr Flood varied his plan for Ireland, but

C/14 *contd.*

the principle on which he founded it was the same. No Irish borough was to be disfranchised, but the right of voting in the borough was to be extended to the leaseholders in the adjacent district. He wished to adhere as closely as he could to the example of England, and therefore he recommended to the Convention then assembled in Dublin for the purpose, not to make any change which had not been sanctioned by the example of England; and as England had done in the case of Shoreham, so to do with the decayed boroughs of Ireland, by extending the franchise to the adjacent districts, and to have triennial parliaments, as established in England at the Revolution. ...

How different is this from what appears in the opinions of other men to whom these letters [of Junius] have at times been attributed! For instance, Mr Burke, who disapproved always of making any alteration whatsoever in the existing state of parliamentary representation. This instance alone would be decisive against Mr Burke being the author of these letters ... .

Mr Flood's speech in the English House of Commons on introducing his plan of parliamentary reform was a grave, argumentative, unimpassioned appeal to reason. Many were disappointed who expected an animated display of eloquence. But that he said was not suited to the time or the occasion. The plan, however, was much approved. Mr Fox said it was the wisest that had been suggested, and Mr Flood in his reply delighted the House with the wit of his retorts, the elegance of his phraseology and the brilliancy of his imagination. [See C/7]. ...

Many persons were surprised to find that Mr Flood disappointed public expectation the first time that he spoke in the English House of Commons. The fact is simply this. Having travelled from Dublin to London with great rapidity, he was much fatigued, and it was his determination that day only to speak a few sentences. But the House expected from him an oration. This was the very thing he wished to avoid. He did not like the notion which had been propagated in the newspapers that he went into the English parliament as a declaiming orator. He preferred the reputation of a statesman and of a man of knowledge and business, and he wished in the first instance to make merely a few plain observations on the subject then depending, before he gave his vote. But the moment he arose, a great anxiety to hear him was manifested. The members crowded in from the coffee-houses, and there was so great a bustle, it was some minutes before he could proceed. He then apologised for the trouble he had given. He told them he was too much fatigued, in consequence of the long and rapid journey he had just made, to go at large into the subject, which he would take another opportunity of doing, and having really only a few observations on it, he sat down. Immediately, several members who were ready to seize the first opportunity to

C/14 *contd.*

disparage and decry him, attempted to turn him into ridicule. They said he came from Ireland to tell them in how few hours he could travel from Dublin to London, and with such stuff as this they amused the House, which was very well inclined to pull down the Irish orator. The most absurd representations of what he said were made and credited, and the people were persuaded that, as a speaker, he was even below mediocrity. The fact is that in those days a most illiberal spirit towards Ireland, and towards everyone who came from it, prevailed in England. At present, the English can brook without humiliation a Wellington to lead their armies and a Castlereagh to conduct their most difficult negotiations. The upper orders there are at length convinced that all the abilites and talents in the world are not confined to the southern moiety of Britain. It was not so at the time of Mr Flood. Besides, he became a member of the English House at a time when much jealously existed towards Ireland. ... Mr Flood, too, had been a leading and most conspicuous opponent in Ireland of the authority of that legislature. Added to this, he was an unconnected stranger, who at his outset disclaimed alliance with every party, and this at a time when the party system was more in fashion and reputation than ever.

As some persons, from the representations they heard of Mr Flood's first reception in the English House of Commons, have supposed him to be inferior in abilities to the author of Junius, I have mentioned these particulars. But his speech in the English House on the commercial treaty with France [see also C/7] is a refutation of such idle notions. That speech alone, I believe, is a better model for pure eloquence than any extant by any of the other public speakers of his time, and would be preferred as such by any man of taste and judgement who was acquainted with the best productions of the Grecian orators.'

C/15

DATE   DESCRIPTION

[*c.* 1820]   Small quarto, 20-page series of anecdotes, by the 2nd Earl, of Flood and other contemporary orators and parliamentarians.

'... Flood used to say of his speeches that the person who took notes of them for the newspapers preserved only the flowers, but left the root to wither. ...

Speaking of the effect of pecuniary distress on most men, in gradually destroying their principles, he said: "All the bright stars of the mind one by one go out."

The Irish parliament had been at one time dissolved immediately after passing the supplies, before other matters in which the public were interested were taken into consideration. Speaking of this afterwards in the House, he said: "Like the bee, we brought our honey to the hive of the throne, and were smothered." ...

Mr Pitt had a very powerful voice and was master of all the tragic tones. When he spoke, the benches behind him vibrated so sensibly that it was perceptible by lowering the hand on them. This, however, arose, not from the force but the music of his tones, which was the effect of art; for it is only musical tones which will produce, by sympathy, such vibrations. Mr Fox spoke as loud, or perhaps louder, but produced no such effect. Mr Fox's tones were those of ordinary discourse, and his cadence, or recitative, if I may so call it, that of an ordinary lawyer. In short, his manner was not above that of a common bar manner, except as the vehemence of his mind and the great comprehension of his ideas forced it into elevation. If he had cultivated his talents for speaking, as Mr Pitt had done, he would have been much more powerful – almost, perhaps, irresistible. But Pitt was bred an orator by his father from his cradle. ...

Mr Cornelius Bolton was one of the least men ever seen, but neatly made and well-proportioned. When a bill for regulating the corn trade, about which Mr Foster was much interested, was in its progress through the House of Commons, Bolton happened one day to be chairman on the committal of the bill. When Flood came into the House, he whispered, "Foster, take care of your corn laws ..., for a mouse has got into the chair of the committee." ...

Mr Pitt was entirely an extempore speaker, as was his great rival, Mr Fox. The consequence was that the style of both of them was too lax, and consequently their speeches too prolix. ... Flood and Grattan spoke remarkably well extempore, as is [in] their replies continually evinced. But all their great speeches, whenever the occasion would permit, were prepared and got by heart. Their practice of speaking in both ways rendered them more perfect in both. They delivered their prepared speeches with all the ardour and naturalness of tone of extempore speeches, and their extempore speeches partook much of the density and point of preparation. Their manner was more solemn, dignified and pompous than Fox's or Pitt's – so much so, that all the young men of my time who went to London to the Temple were disappointed when first they heard the English speakers. ...

Tisdall, who was Attorney General, was asked one time, when Flood was speaking and animadverting freely on the government, if he would not presently

C/15 *contd.*   observe upon Flood. No, says Tisdall, for if I did, he would take an
                             opportunity of observing upon me. ...'

D/1	DATE	DESCRIPTION

1–6   1791: 1794–5   Letters to Parsons from the 1st Marquess of Lansdowne (collateral descendant of the Lord Shelburne who was Governor of King's County in 1716 – see B/1) about the support given to Parsons by Lord Lansdowne's King's County freeholders in parliamentary elections, about county politics generally, about the Lord Lieutenancy of Earl Fitzwilliam, 1794–5, the war, the state of Ireland, etc.

1   19 May 1791   Lord Lansdowne, London, to Parsons.

'I am no stranger to your talents and to your principles, any more than I can possibly be to the antiquity of your family. I suppose, with such pretensions, you cannot fail of success [in his candidature for the King's County by-election] and you have full liberty to avail yourself of my good wishes in your favour in whatever manner you think proper. I am sure, from your character, that you will not bring my name forward improperly.

I would have answered your letter [E/31/26] instantly, but I have been under some difficulty about Mr Bury. Having given him my interest at the last election, I expected to have heard from him upon this occasion, and wished to have explained to him my opinion of your pretensions at the same time I wrote to you. But not hearing from him, I flatter myself that he will not think, if he does stand, the preference I am disposed to give to your pretensions can arise from any disregard to him.'

2   25 Feb. 1794   Lansdowne, London, to Parsons.

'I am much honoured by your letter of the 11th instant, and would have acknowledged it sooner, but I have been far from well.

I had thoughts of communicating it to the Ministers, but from the manner of their receiving some remonstrances here from quarters of very high consideration, I thought it would be only exposing your name unnecessarily. I did however take the liberty of showing it to one of great property here and of still greater in Ireland [Lord Fitzwilliam?], who from circumstances ought to have great weight with the present government, and in speaking I alluded to the defence of Ireland in a manner that I am sure Lord Grenville perfectly understood, for I took care the public should not.

Our superiority at sea is so very great that I do not conceive there is much to be apprehended from any plan of invasion. But considering all you say on the state of the interior, in which everybody agrees, the greatness of the stake, and the enterprising and eccentric enemy with whom we have to deal, too much care cannot be taken; and in proportion as Ministers are slack, it behoves all men of property to be active. The division appears to me to be no longer between Catholic and Protestant, but between

D/1/2 *contd.*   the rich and poor. Everything should be set at work, not so much
to captivate as to ameliorate essentially the condition of the latter,
for power has been lavished upon them without any care being
taken to bring forward a corresponding proportion of property
and instruction. I should have great pleasure in communicating to
you every idea which has occurred to me upon the government of
Ireland, if you do me the honour of passing some time with me in
Wiltshire. You will be sure to find me in the neighbourhood of
Bath from June till December, August excepted, and very proud
and happy to receive you.

Things here are far from quiet. The public opinion is evidently
turing against the war, and everybody is waiting with anxiety to
know the consequence of the impending invasion of West
Flanders.'

3   20 Feb. 1795   Lansdowne, London, to Parsons, Dublin, '... requesting him
[Parsons] to send him an abstract of the returns of the troops,
which appear by the papers to have been moved for by Mr
Conolly. If Sir L. Parsons wants any information from hence, Lord
Lansdowne will be very happy to obey his commands on any
occasion.'

4   6 Mar. 1795   Lansdowne, London, to Parsons, Dublin.
'I am much obliged to you for both your letters, by which I
found what I suspected to be true, that the numbers [of the Irish
militia?] are less than what has been asserted here, and much less
than they ought to be upon every consideration, external and
internal.

I am truly concerned for the changes which are impending, and
see the consequences you state in a very alarming point of view. I
was early in life strongly impressed with the truth of Mr Locke's
principles regarding toleration and government. I have in
consequence always wished well to the emancipation both of
Ireland and the Catholics, and have contributed as far as lay in my
power to both. But I own, I should have been for proceeding more
gradually: first, upon the principle which has been universally
acknowledged in all ages and all countries, of the danger attending
too sudden changes; next, to give time to spread instruction and
something like property among the poor of all descriptions, to
make them properly susceptible of such an influx of liberty. But
Ministers, for reasons best known to themselves, thought proper to
participate the measure, and having done so, in my opinion they
will find it impossible to retract. They may change the Chief
Governor, but they cannot recall their engagement to the
Catholics, and their [?misbeordiness] will only have the effect of
putting an end to the sense of obligation and the confidence which
was growing. What remains to be done, I conceive, is to promote
with all the vigour possible the improvement of the interior, by

D/1/4 *contd.*

large, comprehensive measures, which ought to have accompanied the first repeal. I will take the liberty of mentioning some which have been floating in my mind, persuaded that much better must occur to persons upon the spot, whose local knowledge and experience must enable them to judge much better [*sic*].

To lend every barony in the kingdom suppose £1,000 to be lent out in small sums at a low interest among the lower order of people, before which they should be responsible, upon the principle of frankpledge (which I am convinced contributed essentially to originate the English character), to the barony, and the barony to government. I see no reason why money should not be planted out and grow like wheat or any other commodity, and what better sinking fund could be adopted for Ireland?

To establish a Board of Agriculture in each county, with power to distribute a like sum in agricultural premiums, with an experimental farm annexed, where boys might be taught the best modes of farming; the Board to give a statistical account of each county every seven years to the Dublin Society.

To apply such a part of the Phoenix Park as is not wanting for the use and dignity of the Chief Governor, under the direction of four gentlemen, one from each province, to promote the best breed of all sorts of cattle, which should be purchased by the public and spread from thence over the kingdom.

To establish at once a good government school in each barony for children of all descriptions, without waiting for the slow recovery of estates which have been diverted to private uses, which might be left to go to the public when recovered.

To establish four geat schools or academies, one in each province, where modern learning and modern languages should be taught, as well as ancient, without any or at least very short vacations.

The University of Dublin wants nothing but to extend their examinations to modern history and languages, and to have a school for political economy, to make it preferable to Oxford and Cambridge, and equal to any upon the Continent.

If the expense of these measures was to be summed up, it would amount to no incredible sum, at least the interest of it, especially if compared to the great sums voted for useless armies and, if I am informed right, for useless bounties. But if superadded upon both, no one would hesitate contributing by any *equal* tax to such purposes, if the application was secured by the only sure mode, that of the public election of all those concerned in the execution of them.

I say equal tax, because I certainly object very strongly to the proposal of an absentee tax, which I see made by Doctor [*sic*] Dequery [*sic*], whose general principles, however unsupported he may be, entitle him to great respect and attention. I am aware of

D/1/4 *contd.*   the imputation I risk in being against it. But with liberal men, I
am under no apprehension. The public service has cost me a great
deal, and I never have nor never will gain by it, and if a few
thousand pounds could contribute to the satisfaction of the people
of Ireland or compensate in their opinion for my absence, it would
be very heartily at their service to be disposed of as they thought
proper, though I cannot say that I like the idea of contributing to a
war which I dislike as much as Doctor D. does, or to strengthen a
system of corruption which requires to be starved not fed. But my
objection to an absentee tax is founded on general principles of
justice; the regard due to the sacredness of property and to the
general landed interest, all of which would suffer more than a
hundred times the amount of the tax could compensate; besides
the odiousness and almost impossibility of carrying it into
execution; and what is worst of all, the acceleration of a separation,
which both kingdoms ought equally to deprecate. When I say so
much, I should add that I am sensible the absence of so many
landowners is a grievance, not in a pecuniary point of view, but
because improvements of every kind naturally follow from the
residence of men of large property, and that it can only be
balanced by a variety of great advantages derived from English
connection. But it is an evil which in the nature of things must
lessen every day, nor do I think it impossible to suggest means of
attaining the same end without striking at the fundamental
principles of justice and property.

Everything here continues in a state of great uncertainty. The
inclination of Ministers to continue the war is supposed to
continue the same, and I see no prospect of any timely
interposition upon the part of the public. It has been remarked
that the news from Ireland has created more sensation than the
loss of Holland or any of our defeats have done. The impossibility
of bringing Austria and Prussia to any cordial co-operation, I think
must soon put an end to the war upon the Continent, and then I
suppose peace must follow. ...

Lord Hardwicke is much talked of as successor to Lord
Fitzwilliam, in which case I suppose Mr Douglas will be his
Secretary. But ministry are by all accounts in a state of great division.'

5   9 Apr. [1795]   Copy of a letter from Lansdowne, Landsdowne House, [London],
to [Parsons].

'Returning from the House of Lords, I was seized with the gout,
both in my hand and knee. I have been and am confined with it
ever since, so as not to be able to hold a pen, which obliges me to
avail myself of that of a Westminster boy, and though I am unable
to dictate many sentences, I am unwilling to defer longer
acknowledging the honour of three very kind letters, by which I
feel myself particularly obliged.

D/1/5 *contd.*   The newspaper I take in is the Dublin Evening Post. If there is any other you think more likely to give me a just notice of the temper of the public, I shall be obliged to you for telling me, and I will change it in consequence.

I need not tell you that I am most excessively sorry for the removal of Lord Fitzwilliam, though I never had any connection with him, and I have known your present Lord Lieutenant from his infancy. But I own to you that it has always appeared to me a problem whether the public gain most by a popular or an unpopular administration. What but a popular administration could have obtained the large supplies you have lately voted! On the other hand, I cannot recollect any unpopular administration that has not been obliged to give way to every measure which has been proposed for the public good. The fault, here at least, of whatever has not been done, has lain uniformly with the want of earnestness or union in opposition. I have been long of opinion that Ireland can never go on, the question of emancipation and others being settled, without a steady government which shall apply itself entirely and for a length of time to the interior, and without making it an object of considerable expenditure, when jobs will gradually correct themselves [sense?]. But the notion which you mention as unfortunately forward in both parties, I consider as only worthy of a Council de Propaganda at Rome. One of your late Lord Lieutenants valued himself to me upon making it necessary for the Irish to come here for education, just as if the more they learned at home, it would not be more likely for them to come abroad for more [sense?]. I am determined to try immediately for my own satisfaction the experiment of *village* schools and village loans.

I am sorry that I can give you no good accounts of peace. ...

I have lately seen my agent from the King's County, and have directed him to let leases for lives for several lots in Ballyboy, instead of years, as he proposed, as the votes may possibly be of some use to you; and if you will take the trouble to suggest anything of the same kind, I will take care that every suggestion of yours shall be complied with.'

6   30 June 1797   Lansdowne, Bowood Park, [Calne, Wiltshire], to [Parsons] inviting Parsons and his wife to Bowood, and asking if Lady Parsons is not the grand-daughter of an old friend of Lansdowne's family.

D/2	DATE	DESCRIPTION

1–18   1792: 1796–7:   Letters to Parsons from Peter Burrowes, his friend and political
1800: 1804:   asociate, an Irish barrister and M.P., who as early as 1784 had
1808: 1812:   written a pamphlet advocating the restoration of the Irish Roman
1814: 1828   Catholics to the franchise on a £50 freehold franchise, as the only
means whereby Irish Protestants could secure parliamentary
reform. He writes about Catholic Relief and Emancipation, 1792;
Co. Dublin politics, 1796; the negotiation of 1797 between
Parsons and the Irish administration (which was conducted via
Burrowes and Richard Griffith of Millicent, Co. Kildare, and
which came to nothing because of the complaint brought against
Parsons as Colonel of the King's County Militia in 1798; the
Orangemen, and the consequnces of the Union as far as the future
government of Ireland and the future discussion of the Catholic
Question were concerned, 1800; and, in the period 1804–14,
Lady Frances Flood, the mystery over the authorship of Junius, Sir
Frederick Flood, and Caesar Colclough (who in 1814 returned
from poverty in France to find himself in possession of £6,500 a
year in Co. Wexford). [For an earlier letter from Burrowes about
Parsons's candidature for Seaford, Sussex, see C/8/36. The letters
up to 1800 have been photostated by the National Library (MS.
13840, part), and a second set of photostats has been placed
alongside the originals.]

1   [Summer/   Peter Burrowes to Parsons.
Autumn   'I enclose you [not found] Burke, which I request you will read
1792?]   – not that I think he is everywhere conclusive, or even generally
closely argumentative; but that his great information, experience
and ingenuity have on this subject, on which I think he has
manifestly taken the right side, suggested considerations which must
produce conviction on the main subject, if they be attended to.
I do not mean by this that every candid inquirer must be
convinced that he ought to press any measure favourable to the
Catholic condition immediately. When and how much, are always
considerations of expediency, and though knaves will use them as
pretences, wise men will not renounce them. Attached as I am to
the popular part of our constitution, and sensible as I am how
much it is degraded in Ireland, yet I can well conceive
circumstances which, if I were in parliament, would induce me to
resist ever the most moderate reform. At present, there is no
danger of mischievous innovation, but there is much danger of
enabling government – I mean the Chancellor, Lord Shannon,
Lees, Cooke, etc – to do what they please. To speak plainly, I think
there appears in the grand juries and some of the county meetings
a mobbish spirit, highly disgraceful, to the national character. It
would be impossible (perhaps the attempt would be unwise) to

D/2/1 *contd.*

stem this spirit; but to control its excesses would be both practicable and prudent. Surely, for example, men must be dead to all sense of justice and of prudence, to tell the Catholics, in conformity with Giffard's manifesto, they are a conquered people, and are therefore just subjects of perpetual political subjection? Should the Protestant teach England that doctrine? Should they inflame the Catholic with a passion to have that argument in their favour?

I think it equally odious and inflammatory to say they shall never be enfranchised to any degree. Such a resolution is at once to renounce the British constitution. It is vain to compare them with non-electors through want of a qualification which may be obtained. If I were of opinion that no man in the community should in prudence vote who was not worth £500 or something equivalent, as there would then be more non-electors, in that event I should the more contend for their enfranchisement on the very principle on which I desired a qualification, and an high one. If they exceed the Protestant in property, every rational principle of representation perishes, if they be excluded. If they fall short, they cannot outweigh the Protestant in parliamentary influence. But a Protestant monopolist will answer, in the former alternative, I would prefer the injury of the constitution to the chance of popish ascendancy. Perhaps it is because I have no property to hazard that I cannot feel that danger. But, admit there is some danger in the event of their superior wealth. Would it be entirely done away by keeping them totally out of the constitution? Perhaps it is a paradox, but I think it would be increased by their exclusion, because I think their increased disaffection would in that event operate more against, than their political subjection in favour of, Protestant safety. Richness will naturally, and consistently with rational freedom, control poverty and numbers, but the world has never furnished an instance in which the fewer governed a wealthier majority under any government not despotic. However the wealth will attract the power, or the power the wealth, or there will be an indiscriminate enjoyment of power.

The position I have above stated, perhaps obscurely, is apparently contradicted in every government; for the governors are fewer and strictly inferior in wealth to the whole governed. But I speak of a separation from the constitution, in a free state, of a majority in number, in which majority is contained more or as many wealthy men as in the governing body. You have formerly much lamented the evil of excluding a majority, and seemed to think this country could not be safe from the designs of England while the Catholic party continued in such numbers. 'Tis worth considering whether political separation or coalition be most likely to diminish them as a political party. In the present temper of the Protestants, if the Pope's [?claim] was abolished, if a new

D/2/1 *contd.*

revolution substituted a new religion with the consent of all mankind, there would be Irish Protestant bigots – I mean political bigots – and therefore an Irish Catholic party; and I am not clear, if all pretences growing out of religion were gone, as they nearly are, but that they would change their denominations to simple English and Irish, and that all those who were derived, or claimed to be derived, from the English, would discover wise reasons for excluding all others from the constitution. While the Catholics exist under a threat of eternal political separation, their political ambition will be immortal, their clubs will be in constant action unless you crush all popular liberty. Men of their party will be ashamed and afraid to apostasise from a powerful and incensed party, and their growing patronage, which resentment will render liberal, will tempt many designing demagogues of the Established Church to feed their resentment, and many of the honestest and ablest Protestants in the community will be with them from principle, together with the discontented, factious and innovating of every description.

I know some men think these effects would follow more strongly from concession. I don't say what would follow from pusillanimous concession, nor do I argue for anything this session. But I am persuaded a moderate franchise, given by the Protestants with hopes of future enlargement, would tend much more to tranquillise than agitate; that the party principle of political violence being assuaged, the principal Catholics having already almost entirely lost their religious principle of cohesion, would drop from them in multitudes; and that the decay of popery and enlargement of privileges would mutually accompany and assist each other. ...

'Tis generally believed that there is a coalition of parties in England. How do things stand? England prosperous beyond example – an able, artful and ambitious Minister – without opposition at home – the rival nation in ruins – one party in the appendant nation calling for assistance against the other. Let the wiseacre grand jurors look to it. Everything will depend on the Irish patriotism of an English Minister.'

2   2 Oct. 1796

Peter Burrowes to Alexander Hamilton about Co. Dublin politics and Catholic Emancipation.

'I do assure you, I omitted no opportunity of urging your claims upon such of the late Catholic Committee as I had an opportunity of conversing with. Though I spoke to them apart, they answered as if they had deliberated upon the subject, and it appears to be their unanimous sentiment not to interfere in the county of Dublin, or anywhere else. I therefore despair of procuring you their general support. When you determine to stand, I shall then solicit any individual who I think on the ground of friendship, would oblige me, but I fear my services in that way must of necessity be very limited.

D/2/2 *contd.*

My late intercourse with the Catholics of Dublin, though still confidential, has by no means strengthened my influence amongst them, or given me cheering anticipations for this country. They are to a man discontented. So prevalent is their feeling of real, exaggerated or imaginary injury and *insult* from government, that, uniform and unsuspected as my zeal for their total emancipation hitherto has been, they seem to consider me as little better than an apostate for urging them to offer their services to government to repel an invasion. They are blinded by resentment, and do not see their own interest, insomuch that I firmly believe many men of large property would be *at best* neutral if a French party landed here, and the rabble of the country were [*sic*] likely to seize upon all power and property. The spirit of union with the Protestants, which I know existed sincerely amongst them, daily diminishes, and though they have not those clamorous and numerous meetings they formerly had, yet they meet more frequently and perhaps more effectually. They are constantly communicating to each other instances of the illiberality of government or of individuals in power towards their body, and feeding each other's discontent. They have collected and detailed accounts of the severities exercised since the late Catholic Bill towards their body, many of them but too authentic, and though such narratives will probably sleep forever if the country be quiet, yet if a storm should arise, I dread the effect of such materials in inflaming the public mind.

It is much to be lamented that some statesmen who are extremely clear-sighted in seeing one evil, often overlook a greater flowing from the remedies to which they resort. The confederacy of the religionists upon principles of democratic union, was a temporary evil which certainly ought to have been guarded against, and for that the best remedy in my judgement was to ascertain the co-operation of all men of property in the common cause. Now it appears to me that the very reverse has been the practical policy of our government – at least such it must appear to plain men who are not in the secret. The Catholic Bill which passed gives power to the rabble: that which was refused could only give constitutional weight to the wealthy. John Keogh and Ned Byrne in parliament would be cyphers or placemen or impotent demagogues. The weight they and such men now have – indeed their power of doing mischief -is incalculable – far, I am persuaded, beyond any idea of it entertained at the Castle. Now it appears to me that the policy of the government (I do not mean by that the present Viceroy or Secretary, who I believe never would knowingly encourage such a system) has been to throw general odium and suspicion on the Catholic body or their most favourite leaders, to excite Protestant jealousy against them, to disunite the people and to prevent or delay the operation of the Catholic Bill.

Witness the report of the late secret committee, blemishing the character of the whole Catholic Committee, upon certainly unfounded suspicion. Witness capital prosecutions of opulent Catholics, unsupported by a [? ray] of evidence. Witness an anxious pursuit of evidence to affect others. Witness incessant attacks in the government prints upon the whole body. Witness their exclusion by men under known government influence from all co-operation, particularly from their freedom in the city of Dublin. Witness the magistracy conferred on scarce any of them, and not on an individual who did not resist the measures in which they succedded, and of course lost their favour. Against the enormities in Armagh they loudly and vehemently exclaim, and insist that they have been encouraged or connived at by government, and state serious instances of real information coming from their friends [being] slighted at the Castle, and of protection refused to wretches who were in danger of being butchered or exiled. I well know that their statements are exaggerated and their suspicions in many instances unfounded, but I am well satisfied that the Orange boys have been excited and encouraged by Protestant Ascendancy Men, that the true state of things has not been fairly laid before the Castle, and that an equal exertion has not been used to suppress outrages from every quarter.

If I were to lay this statment before certain friends of mine, they would infer from it that the policy of government would be to watch, distrust and exclude from every political situation, a set of men so disaffected. I infer quite differently. I think no Catholic Bill that ever was meditated could transfer the power of the country to them, which never can be done through the constitution, or by any means but a revolution. I think the Catholic Bill which Lord Fitzwilliam promised, would destroy the influence of the factions. I know that the most formidable of themselves think so, and that they do not in their hearts wish success to the measure. I know that the individuals of the late Catholic Committee, who have the strongest republican tendencies, and particularly such as were connected in Belfast, evidently wished that the Bill which was carried had failed, and I perceived many measures at the time proposed by such men whose manifest object and motive appeared to me to be, to occasion a total rejection of their bill, although such a motive was not *publicly* avowed by any of them. Such men have constantly appeared to me to consider every Catholic Bill that was passed to be a barrier thrown in the way of their republican designs, and on that subject in my opinion they formed a sounder judgement than the Chancellor and the Speaker.

If I am not much mistaken, you received declarations issuing from the Catholics of Dublin importing to unite the question of parliamentary reform with the enlargement of Catholic privileges

D/2/2 *contd.*

and the defence of Ireland. Perhaps other reforms may be asserted or insinuated. If government be reduced by such conduct to forego every measure they meditate in favour of the Catholics at large, they will act just as the authors of such declarations intend and expect they should – though certainly from very different motives.

I have unintentionally entered upon this subject. 'Tis of great consequence – far greater to any man of fortune or expectations than anything he can hope from [? the favour] of government.'

3   15 Oct. 1797   Burrowes to Parsons about the possibility of Parsons's going over to the government's side.

'I have had your commission to me constantly in my mind. If it be your opinion that opposition will be fruitless or pernicious, and that you are likely to give government a general, though not a uniform, support (upon which doubtless you have considered well and deeply), I think it would be silly romance not to suffer your brother to reap the usual fruits of such conduct, even when the motives are bad and the professions insincere. For my part, I believe I think worse of government than you do, and have less apprehension from a bold and spirited opposition. At the same time, if you think differently from me, and will act accordingly, I feel myself perfectly justified in endeavouring that some private good shall be derived from your public measures.

A far better mode of communication has occurred than we thought of. Griffith is perhaps as much in the esteem and confidence of Pelham as any man in Ireland; so much so, that there is scarce a public measure or a public man on which and whom he does not converse freely with Griffith. He passed a few days at Millicent in retirement. You might doubtless, if you wish it, have communications with him upon the public measures, perhaps at Millicent, and Griffith, who is a plain, open man, will not deceive or misrepresent. I have already spoken thus far to Griffith: I said I believed that you were rather inclined to think violent opposition would hurt both yourself and the public, that I knew you had no personal indisposition to Lord Camden and Mr Pelham, that I thought it would be prudent in government to confer some mark of favour upon you, and that a living to William appeared to me to be the most applicable and agreeable mode. Griffith naturally said that such a thing must be asked, if not by you, at least by your brother, and seemed very ready to interfere. Rely upon it that I not only did not say I acted so far in consequence of any comunication with you, but repeatedly assured him that it was entirely my own suggestion. In fact, Griffith might as well be considered as the mover of the conversation as myself. If you wish to communicate anything to government, a letter to me stating your sentiments will, through Griffith, find its way to Pelham, and his sentiment be easily learned. I might myself be

D/2/3 *contd.*   introduced very warmly to him, and if I felt upon public subjects
                          as you do, would gladly embrace the opportunity. ...
                              I fear I may have expressed myself in this letter as if I thought no
                          public benefit could be derived from your intercourse with
                          government. On the contrary, even if you could have but [*sic*]
                          influence upon a few subjects, much good might follow – perhaps
                          more than from any opposition you could give. But of this I doubt
                          exceedingly.'

4   'Tuesday'   Burrowes to Parsons enclosing [not found] a copy of a letter he
                          has written to Griffith, who has taken up the matter '... with an
                          eagerness even exceeding my expectations'.

5   20 Oct. 1797   Burrowes, Leeson Street, [Dublin], to Parsons annexing a copy of
                          [another letter ?] he has written to Griffith on the subject of
                          Parsons.

6   [post 20 Oct. Copy of a letter from Parsons to Burrowes in reply.
           1797]   'Griffith, who is well-acquainted with the habitual energy of
                          your expressions, may not perhaps put a greater value on any in
                          your letter than you intend, but others, I fear, will be very apt to
                          do so. Saying "that I deem it too hazardous patriotism to oppose
                          government at this crisis", is telling them that my lips are
                          completely sealed up from uttering anything against them, if they
                          believe me to be a man of principle, and this before their
                          dispositions or determinations are at all known by me. There are
                          some great subjects which I may think it imprudent for many
                          reasons to agitate in parliament at present. But there are many
                          others that necessarily come under the view of the House of
                          Commons, and may be canvassed with perfect safety. The
                          consideration, therefore, is whether on these latter I should do
                          more good by opposing government or by the influence I should
                          obtain by consenting in general to co-operate with it.
                          Circumstanced as parliament now is, deserted and abdicated by so
                          many, I certainly at present think the latter. Besides, I feel no great
                          inclination at this time to the trouble and exertion of the former
                          line, though I might be roused to it. But even if I thought all
                          opposition whatsoever to government ever so pernicious, I do not
                          think it prudent to tell them so, because what would they want
                          more than to be secured of my inertia, and if they were assured
                          that principle alone would effect that, they would not think it
                          necessary to give my any influence, and so I should obtain no
                          equivalent for the [? certainty] by my acquiescence. I therefore
                          think this expression in your letter should be corrected and
                          explained away, and that there should be left no hopes of my
                          silence, if I should find myself slighted or neglected, but the
                          contrary. This I take to be the only way of dealing with such men,
                          who have no candour or liberality, and who only laugh at the
                          weakness of those who would act candidly and liberally by them.

D/2/6 *contd.*

I think also the expression too strong that I would *gladly* confer with Mr Pelham, for the utmost I would do would be coldly to consent to such a conference. I fear it will be construed into an *eager overture* on my part, whereas I could not stoop to any overture at all. This, also, I would therefore wish to have explained away. ...

I think your intimation to G. of my disposition, is the utmost commencement on my part that I could consent to, and that they should know that any further advance certainly would not be made.'

7   26 Oct. 1797   Burrowes to Parsons, Parsonstown, explaining that there is no harm done.

'Griffith left Millicent before my letter reached him, so that he could not have made any use of it.

I believe I qualified the generality of your supposed support of the government, so as to let in every exception you may be inclinable to make. As to words importing eagerness on your part for an interview, recollect that the expressions appear to be, as the [*sic*] really were and must be reported to be, if any use be made of the letter, in answer to an overture on behalf of the other party; and as you truly state, the language of the communication must be taken to be mine exclusively.

I hope you may have conversed freely with Griffith. When I meet him, I will explain the doubtful passages in my note.'

8   30 Oct. 1797   Richard Griffith, Millicent, Co. Kildare, to Burrowes, Leeson Street, reporting his interview with Pelham.

'In consequence of your letter, which I found at Millicent on my return from Connaught, I called on Mr Pelham yesterday morning, and as I deemed the matter which I was about to communicate of a delicate nature, I thought the best mode of opening the subject was to detail to Mr Pelham the circumstances which led to it.

I therefore informed him that, having lately dined with you (with whom I was in habits of unreserved communication), I expressed a wish that our friend, Sir Laurence Parsons, could be prevailed upon to give his support to government in the present dangerous crisis; that after having discussed the matter some time, I understood from you that, as far as you had been able to collect the political sentiments of Sir Laurence in the present juncture, instead of wishing to embarrass government, he was rather disposed to aid and support its measures, if they were such as might allow him to do so with propriety; that you were inclined to think that, if government were to consult him on public measures and to give that weight to his sentiments which the station he held in the public mind justly merited, he would afford the administration of Lord Camden a liberal support, reserving

D/2/8 *contd.*   however to himself full liberty to dissent from such measures as he
could not approve; that I told you that I was perfectly convinced
that it would be extremely grateful to [text defective – ? Mr
Pelham to be] made acquainted with the dispositions of Sir
Laurence, and that, if you would write to him on the subject and
draw from him manfully and decidedly his sentiments, I should be
extremely happy to communicate them to Mr Pelham; that you
had in consequence written to Sir Laurence, and that you had
informed me by letter that the answer you had received confirmed
your former opinion, namely that Sir Laurence was disposed to
give a liberal support to government in all measures which he
approved, expecting however that he should be consulted and his
opinions treated with the respect they deserved.

This is as nearly as I can recollect the purport of what I said to
Mr Pelham before he made any reply, and you will observe that I
was extremely guarded, lest I should say a word that could be
considered as committing our friend in any way, as I know he is
extremely punctilious (and properly so) in all matters of this
nature. Mr Pelham expressed very great satisfaction at what I had
mentioned; he said he was fully sensible of the benefit which
government would derive from the support and assistance of Sir
Laurence, whose talents and character with the public rendered
him a most desirable ally; that in saying this, he assured me he also
expressed the sentiments of Lord Camden, who would be highly
gratified by his support; and that undoubtedly Sir Laurence would
be consulted and fully communicated with, and a proper attention
paid to his sentiments. I then told Mr Pelham that, as I had gone
so far, I would of my own accord [text defective] bring Sir
Laurence and him together at Millicent, which was a sort of half-
way house between the Castle and Parsonstown. He said he would
with great pleasure attend my summons.

And now, Sir, though I am not quite so tedious a negotiator as
Lord Malmesbury, I think I have brought my business nearer to a
happy conclusion. It remains with Parsons to say when he will take
a family dinner at Millicent, at which place the two great men may
put their heads together, while you and I go and shoot rabbits. ...'

9   31 Oct. 1797   Burrowes to Parsons, Parsonstown, enclosing the foregoing, and
adding to them.
'... Pelham in the course of the conversation said that Lord
Castlereagh was extremely anxious that you should be propitiated.
Griffith signified to me that he wished I would go to Millicent
also. ...'

10   9 Sep. 1800   Burrowes, Leeson Street, Dublin, to Parsons, Scarborough Post
Office, Yorkshire.
'The only circumstance respecting affairs here within my
knowledge and probably not within yours, is that the Orange

D/2/10 *contd.*

institutions are still spreading. New and extensive lodges have lately sprung up. Lord Cornwallis, I think, hates them and their principles. Yet I never have been able to discover the slightest effort on the part of government to suppress them or moderate their virulence. I presume the English Unionists exult at the tranquillity which prevails here, notwithstanding the Union. Be assured, no change of sentiments favourable to the measure has taken place. How far a system of lenient and liberal policy may succeed gradually in weaning the heart of this country from its darling independence and reconciling it to a condition of virtual subjection, I will not pretend to anticipate. ...'

11   23 Oct. 1800   Burrowes, Llangollen, to Parsons, York, about the consequences of the Union.

'... I have no fears that an English ministry, if left to themselves, will encourage Orange institutions. I am persuaded that imperial policy, as well as the common feelings of humanity, which I believe exist in Ministers as well as other men, must obviously suggest the suppression of principles which must infallibly allienate the population and much of the property and talents of Ireland from British connection, and consequently attach them to France by the most operative of all feelings, a desire of revenge for injuries and insults. I fear, however, that, as the government of Ireland must depend upon local information, and as that information will be taken from men who recently encourage [*sic*] Orange institutions from an union of hereditary and political prejudices, the Minister will not see what every candid man in Ireland sees until the evil becomes incurable.

No man who has not had a general and in some degree a confidential intercourse with the Catholics of Ireland, can imagine what a determined and desperate spirit of counteraction the Orange outrages, and principally those which have been tolerated since the suppression of the rebellion, have spread amongst that body and their friends of every description. Terror for the present silences all expression of resentment ... . [Text defective] The Catholic sentiment is at present undecided, but I must add, unfavourably inclined. Lord Cornwallis's temporising, undecisive system (though Orangemen call him a papist and a rebel) has been only sufficient to keep it in abeyance. If it shall at the commencement of the new arrangement settle against England, remember I tell you the connection will be as unstable as the winds and waves upon which it must depend.

I do not call for acts of violent agression against these pernicious institutions and their stolid and savage principles. But, on the other hand, I say that the arm of government must be *visibly* stretched forth in protection of the Irish Catholics, and that Orange clamour should be disregarded in proportion to its

D/2/11 *contd.*

impotence. The only good that ever I could see in the Union was that it would enable the English Minister to curb the Orange faction without the hazard of parliamentary reprisal. But if the misinformation or influence of leading men from Ireland shall produce the same effect as the predominance of the Orange principle in parliament, what sort of tranquillity will remain? ...

I think that those who persuade themselves that Catholic discontent or disaffection is informidable because there are so many instances of the physical force of the country being kept in galling subjection by a few, confound things totally dissimilar. In Ireland, the Catholic body form a part of the effective government itself. Can the same be said of the blacks in Jamaica? They have much of the floating property, that is of that property which is of most avail in civil war and least hazarded by it. They have much more the talents of Ireland than we Protestants are willing to allow them, and some of the Protestant property and much of the Protestant interest would act upon their side, whereas they would be almost as one man if things came to extremities. I know no [? case] of modern times which is more calculated to puzzle future statesmen than to account for the stability of Protestant Ascendancy in Ireland since the Revolution. To continue it after the Union would be infinitely more difficult. Now that, by a relaxation of the penal laws, they have been suffered to outgrow that bondage, and with republican France eager to avail itself of their discontents, and wanting only some cement to keep their friends together, is it possible that the Catholics of Ireland can be permanently alienated and the two countries permanently united? The principle, therefore, of governing Ireland by its religious divisions must in common sense be abandoned in future. If it be persevered in, policy must dictate to elevate the Catholic. The feelings, however, of the English Protestant would be outraged by such a system, and no wise Minister should, I think, attempt [? it, though it] appears to me to be much more practicable than Protectant Ascendancy in a popish country adjacent to France. The result is, there is but one party which Ministers ought to conciliate, and through which they ought to govern: that is, the men of property, knowledge and virture, be their religion what it may. At present, government should offer the most vigilant protection, and even confer some favours, upon the Catholic body, but in future they should hold an impartial hand between them, which I think would in half a century obliterate the popish superstition and its long train of evils from Ireland.

| 12 | 23 Feb. 1804 | Burrowes to Parsons, Parsonstown, about money matters, and with commonplace news of British party politics. |
| 13 | 1 July 1808 | Burrowes, Leeson Street, Dublin, to Parsons, now 2nd Earl of Rosse, Parsonstown, about money matters. |

D/2/14 15 Oct. 1812   Burrowes, Leeson Street, to Rosse, Parsonstown, referring to the
                        illness of John (Rosse's barrister brother) and to the clearing of
                        Burrowes's debts by the sale of his country house.

'... I stated the subject [of Junius] to Lady Frances Flood.

She received my communication nearly as you have described.
She said with some agitation that she did not like to speak upon
the subject. After an interval, she said you ought yourself to speak
to her. After a farther interval, she spoke of Malone, as if she
expected something would appear from his papers; and, finally, she
said that Flood was not Junius, or that she thought he was not
Junius. This last declaration was spoken as if to correct an
impression to the contrary which she might have made, and which
she thought she ought not to have made. Upon the whole of her
conversation, I would harbour a strong suspicion, at least, that
Flood was Junius, or at least acquainted with Junius and privy to
the publication at the time. The latter I would probably prefer as
the most probable, and I would ascribe the authorship to Malone,
if I considered him as capable of such a work. As to Flood, I not
only consider him as equal to the work, but really would doubt its
coming from him, from some bad rhetoric, weak observations and
inconsequential reasoning which I think I discern in the work.'

[For the whole question of Flood and Junius, see C/13–14.]

15   20 Sep. 1814   Burrowes, Tintern, post-marked Fethard, Co. Wexford, to Rosse,
                        Parsonstown.

'... I am detained here making arrangements with Caesar
Colclough, who has returned from France after an absence from
Ireland of 23 years. He fled his country about 1790, to avoid the
disgrace his father's folly and profligacy brought upon him, and
after many years spent in indigence, and more in captivity, he has
returned to the enjoyment of about £6,500 clear estates, with a
tenantry who all have most advantageous interests in their
holdings. He really is an object of great curiosity. He goes to bed at
9 and rises before 5 o'clock, unless when forced out of his regimen
by company, to which he submits with great reluctance. Though a
resident of the South of France, he has not drank [sic] a quart of
wine or spirits during the last 13 years. His animal spirits are
invariably high. He abounds with anecdotes relating to French
transactions, and Buonaparte in particular. He appears never to
have forgotten anything he ever read, saw or heard of. He is, I
believe to a most uncommon degree, cultivated in mechanics,
chemistry, botany and minerology – indeed in all physical and
practical sciences. I really believe, if necessary, he could earn a
competent livelihood by manual labour at thirty different trades.
He suggests solid improvements to every artist or mechanic he
meets. He was a prisoner for some months under Robertsbierre
[sic] and procured his enlargement by making, without any

D/2/15 *contd.*   assistance, a model in wood of a threshing machine and sending it
to a committee of science. This machine was not then known or
was not in practical use in France. He had seen it at work in the
county of Wexford, and recollected it so precisely that he did not
mistake one log in the model he framed.

Sir Frederick Flood is ready to resign the representation of the
county to him, but I believe he will not embark in politics. This is,
however, not to be stated. ...'

16   Post-marked   Burrowes to Rosse, Parsonstown, apparently about securing
        19 June 1820   Burrowes's various borrowings from Lord Rosse by one mortgage.

'... Young Grattan has just arrived and talks of changes of
ministry as likely to take place immediately. The Hutchinsons are
in daily consultation with the King, who is in a state of *furious*
exasperation with his Ministers.'

17   18 Aug. 1828   Burrowes to Rosse, Parsonstown, condoling with him on the
                         death of his son, [John C. Parsons – see E/23].

18   25 Oct. 1828   Burrowes, Killarney, to Rosse, Parsonstown: the same.

D/4	DATE	DESCRIPTION

1–14   1793: 1797–8:   Letters to Parsons from the Hon. Robert Stewart, Viscount
1804–5: 1807   Castlereagh, the earliest of them written as a backbench political
1817   associate of Parsons in the Irish House of Commons, those of
1797–8 as acting Chief Secretary or Chief Secretary to the Lord
Lieutenant, and the rest as a member, in various capacities, of the
British government: the topics include the political manoeuvrings
of the parliamentary session of 1793; the state of the barracks in
which the King's County Militia has been accommodated, 1798,
the fate of prisoners in Parsonstown Gaol who, in spite of having
surrendered within the terms of a government proclamation of
amnesty, have been arrested and incarcerated there, 1798; Parsons's
relations with the second Pitt administration and hopes of being
appointed to the Chancellorship of the Irish Exchequer under it,
1804–5, and more minor matters of patronage, 1807 and 1817.
[Some of these letters have been photostated by the National
Library (MS. 13840, part), and a second set of photostats has been
placed alongside the originals. The letter of 1805 is in particularly
urgent need of conservation.]

1   Endorsed 'May   The Hon. Robert Stewart to Parsons, Parsonstown.
1792': but 1793   'There seems at least a suspension of the political courtship
which was observable on a former night. One or other of the
parties are [*sic*] coy, but I fancy sooner or later it will be
consummated. The opposition maid is poor, and pride has little
chance, when opposed to poverty. Besides, I think I perceive Jack
Forbes suspects the fidelity of his wife and he is preparing his
brows for the horns which they are destined to wear. However, last
night the Police Bill gave rise either to a mock or real skirmish.
Grattan was angry, and Ponsonby by no means conciliated. I voted
against Grattan's bill, which appeared to me making bad worse.
Today Forbes brings on some motion relative to the powers of the
new Treasury Board, which I understand he has not
communicated even to G. Probably it is to bring his wife's virtue
to the test. I do not think there is any immediate necessity for your
coming to town, and in giving you this opinion, I am not
disinterested without a considerable effort, for at all times your
society is an object to me, and your advice a very great resource. If
I see anything critical, I will write to you instantly. Shannon's
people voted with government.'

2   Endorsed,   Stewart to Parsons, Parsonstown.
'May 1793'   'When I assure [you] that it is with regret I disobey your kind
summons, you will not doubt my sincerity, knowing as you do
that of all places I detest Dublin. At present, however, private
business which I have to transact for my father imprisons me, and
I shall be obliged to go to the North very shortly. It would make

D/4/2 *contd.*   me most happy to pass some time with you, and I trust that I may
                                  have it in my power before the year expires. ...

                                  I hope that we may be brought together upon [militia] service.
                                  If we could get our regiments into Dublin Barracks, it would be
                                  the best school for them and pleasantest quarters for us. Pray let
                                  me hear how you get on.

                                  There seems to be no longer any opposition. Hobart must
                                  repeat the miracle of the loaves and fishes, if he can feed all the ex-
                                  party with this new [Treasury] Board.'

3   11 July,   Stewart, Magherafelt, Co. Londonderry, to Parsons, Parsonstown.
           endorsed '1793'   'Here I am in the midst of my father's republican tenants,
                                  balloting for our militia. Upon the measure being fully explained
                                  to the people, they like it now as much as they detested it before. I
                                  am in great hopes that the regiment will be rapidly completed
                                  without difficulty.

                                  I left town as soon as the India question was disposed of. Had I
                                  foreseen that any debate was likely to have occurred on it, I should
                                  have availed myself of the permission you gave me to summon you
                                  up. A vote was not wanting, but the sanction of a person in your
                                  situation was important to convince the country that serious
                                  injustice was not done them. I have great hopes, from what passed
                                  in the last debate, that government have it seriously in
                                  contemplation to put the home trade between the two countries
                                  upon an equality – that is, to give us the propositions without the
                                  4th. If they do, I am sure you will agree with me that Ireland will
                                  no longer have any commercial ground of complaint.

                                  Pray let me hear from you direct to Magherafelt, and tell me
                                  how your regiment goes on.'

4   [3 Mar. 1798]   Rough draft of a letter from Parsons to Stewart, now Lord
                                  Castlereagh and acting Chief Secretary, refuting an allegation that
                                  the King's County Militia damaged a barracks in which they were
                                  quartered.

5   [10 July 1798]   Rough copy of a letter from Parsons to Lord Castlereagh pleading
                                  the cause of a number of King's County rebels who gave
                                  themselves up under the terms of a proclamation granting
                                  amnesty, under certain conditions, and who, in spite of coming
                                  within those conditions, have been incarcerated in Birr Gaol.

6   12 July [1798]   Lord Castlereagh, Dublin, to Parsons in reply.

7   22 July 1798   Rough copy of a letter from Parsons, Parsonstown, to Lord
                                  Castlereagh about the interpretation of the proclamation of amnesty.
                                  'I had the honour of receiving your letter of the 12th inst, and
                                  am induced to tell you once more of the situation of the prisoners
                                  in this and the neighbouring towns, lest, through any mistake,
                                  they might not receive the protection which by your letter is so
                                  liberally intended for them.

D/4/7 *contd.*   The proclamation of the 24th of May, I conceive, applies merely
to those who were in some manner *acting* in the rebellion, but I
find that the courts martial here consider [as included] any man
who was appointed captain, sergeant or secretary, however long
antecedent [to the rebellion] ... . Now, there has not been here, nor
anywhere within 20 miles of this town, any insurrection or
attempt at insurrection, from the commencement of the rebellion
to the present day. Most of the prisoners who have been tried by
the court martials not only went to their neighbouring magistrates
with their arms and pikes and gave them up, but such of them as
were captains, sergeants or secretaries acknowledged also that they
were so, expecting thereby to make atonement and obtain pardon,
and it was so generally understood here that those who did so
would be pardoned, that the magistrates everywhere let them
return to their homes, and it was not till several days or weeks
after, and without any new act on their part, that they were
apprehended anc confined.

The county of Tipperary is within a furlong of this town, and
though the people there have been guilty of exactly the same
crimes – that is, have been appointed captains, etc – yet there,
having acknowledged their offence in the same manner as the
people here, they have been allowed to remain at perfect liberty.

The prisoners, therefore, here, and their friends who are
continually petitioning me, think their case the more hard ...: by
the last proclamation, even rebels who had risen in arms and
fought his Majesty's troops are given an opportunity of obtaining
pardon; whereas those here, who neither themselves nor their
associates made any attempt to rise, are sentenced to various
punishments. I must also observe that they are all mere peasants;
that I do not believe any security was or is obtained by the
imprisonment of them, but the reverse, by causing irritation; for
the people, if they were disposed to rise, could from the meanness
of their ranks in an instant have appointed captains,etc, as good as
these, for I have not heard that one of them had ever even been a
soldier.

I have been the more induced to trouble you with this
statement, because during this rebellion I continually disseminated
among the people my opinion. ...' [Letter incomplete.]

8   26 [July 1798]   Lord Castlereagh, Dublin, to Parsons, Parsonstown, informing
him that the matter has been referred to General Dunne, who will
investigate it and make a report.

9   30 July [1804]   Lord Castlereagh, East Sheen, to Parsons (letter marked 'Private').
'I shall not fail to take the first favourable opportunity of
putting your letter into Mr Pitt's hands, in the mode which may
appear to me most likely to recommend it to his protection. I
conclude you either have or will communicate with Lord

D/4/9 *contd.*   Hardwicke and Sir E. Nepean [the Lord Lieutenant and Chief
                                  Secretary] on your views and wishes generally. Much must depend,
                                  in the decision of Irish questions of this nature, on the sentiments
                                  of those in charge of the government on the spot, and it would be
                                  doing injustice to your own claims to pass them by. I trust you will
                                  excuse this hint.'

10   28 May,   Lord Castlereagh, India Board, to Parsons.
        endorsed 1805   'As I mentioned, Monday next is the probable day on which our
                                  report would be considered. I think it right to apprise you that
                                  Thursday sennight is the day fixed by Mr Whitbread for that
                                  business, on which day it is of the utmost importance that we
                                  should have the largest possible attendance. We are much
                                  disappointed that one or two friends have left town for Ireland
                                  without being aware how much it was wished they should remain,
                                  and it has been thought absolutely necessary to write and press
                                  their return.'

11   [pre 12 July   Lord Castlereagh, London, to Parsons.
        1805]   'I did not fail to communicate with Mr Pitt on the subject of
                                  your letter. Before it arrived, Mr Foster had suspended if not
                                  waived his resignation, which rendered it unnecessary for Mr Pitt
                                  to provide a successor. I also apprised him of Sir T. Fetherstone's
                                  friendly dispositions, as expressed to you, and he desired me to
                                  assure you that he is fully sensible of your zealous [exertions?] to
                                  augment the number of the faithful. The late resignations must
                                  only operate to redouble our exertions. ...
                                      We hope to close the session in the middle of the week. The
                                  King is unable to read his Speech, from the rapid progress of the
                                  complaint in both his eyes. It will be some time before the
                                  operation can be attempted. He bears the inconvenience with
                                  great temper and fortitude.

12   18 Oct. 1807   Lord Castlereagh, Priory, Stanmore, Middlesex, to Parsons (letter
                                  marked 'Private') in reply to a letter from Parsons urging that
                                  Parson's brother, John C. Parsons, he appointed a judge in the
                                  event of the death of Judge Day.
                                      '... The opinion of the Chancellor will, I have every reason to
                                  believe, determine the Irish government in their choice of judges
                                  as decisively hereafter as that of the Chancellor of Great Britain
                                  has long done in this country, and with so much benefit and
                                  honour to the public service. I am sure it will gratify your brother's
                                  feelings much more to owe his elevation to a principle of strict
                                  profesional selection than to any political interference, which I
                                  persuaded neither the Duke of Richmond or [sic] Lord Manners
                                  [the Lord Lieutenant and Chancellor of Ireland respectively]
                                  would listen to, and I beg to assure you that it would afford me
                                  great personal satisfaction to find him advanced to the bench.'

D/4/13 14 May,   Lord Castlereagh to Lord Rosse (letter marked 'Private') promising
endorsed 1817   to recommend Mr Drought to the Bishop of Clogher.

14   1 Sep. 1817   Lord Castlereagh, Cray Farm, Kent, to Rosse (letter marked
'Private') about '... your Lordship's request of a vice-consulship for
your friend Lt P. Macartney ...'.

D/5	DATE	DESCRIPTION
1–62	1798: 1800–02: 1806: 1817: 1822: 1824–5	Letters to Parsons from his younger brother, Thomas Clere Parsons (the fourth son of their father, and Assistant Barrister for King's County, 1803–25), including a run of blow-by-blow accounts of the rebellion, May-July 1798, and discussion of the Union, family history, estate affairs, etc (Thomas C. Parsons appears to have acted as his brother's head agent up to 1803); also included are other letters and papers of Parsons, now 2nd Earl of Rosse, about the local furore arising out of complaints that Thomas C. Parsons had misconducted himself as Assistant Barrister, 1822, and letters of condolence to the 2nd Earl on, and a printed poem about, Thomas C. Parsons's death, which took place at Tullynisky Park, Birr, the house he shared with another brother, the Rev. William Parsons, in 1825. [The '98 Rebellion letters, with one exception, have been photostated by the National Library (MS. 13840, part), and a second set of photostats has been placed alongside the originals. Most of the original letters in the sub-section are in urgent need of conservation.] The sub-section includes:
2	6 Apr. 1798	Thomas C Parsons, Dublin, to Parsons, Parsonstown, inveighing against the excesses of the military, and concluding: '... I think you should resign the governorship of the King's County.
5	24 Apr. 1798	Thomas C. Parsons to Parsons, Parsonstown: political news. '... I hear from tolerable [*sic*] good authority that the laws in favour of the Roman Catholics which were recently enacted are to be repealed, and that they are once more to enter the land of bondage. It is said that the idea of a bill of attainder is for the present laid aside, that the measure was warmly debated in Council, and that notwithstanding Lord Camden resolutely opposed it, a majority of the members present decided in its favour. But, however, the minority was too numerous and respectable [to?] suffer the partisans of so important an act of government to conclude in its adoption. ... Conolly has certainly resigned. The reason which he has stated to the Lord Lieutenant for so doing is, I hear, his bad state of health. I fear the introduction of these foreign troops into this country is only intended as a precedent to send over a large body of them. But it can't be prevented. ...'
6	3 May 1798	Thomas C. Parsons, Parsons, about a petition from the Irish Whig Club.

D/5/6 *contd.*

'... I send you [not found] the petition of the Irish Whig Club, which is to be presented to the King by the Earl of Moira and Mr Fox, but until it is, it is not to be made public. I therefore beg you'll not show it to anyone but to Mr L[loyd?], John and William. I need not name to you the person who wrote it. He is one whom you know well [Grattan?], and almost every sentence gives you his portrait. In the narrative is to be found much of his obscurity, in the declamation much of his eloquence, in the satire his severity, and in some of the images that [? vivissik] pencilling which incarnates thought and deludes vision. I wish the facts had been stated more perspicuously, because it will probably continue an important state paper, because it is now a palliation for the excesses of the people, and resembles one of those manifestoes which antecedes a public rupture. ...'

9   15 May 1798

Thomas C. Parsons, Parsonstown, about the general military and political state of the country.

'... I see nothing to control the hands of the executive. The correcting influence of parliament is turned another way, and of the influential part of society, some survey what's going forward with delight, some with apathy, and but few, very few, with that interesting anxiety which becomes freemen. I hear people almost of all destcriptions speak of the proclaiming of this city and county with as much sang-froid as if it [were] the annunciation of a general fast or a birthday ball or something as inconsiderable. ...'

20   3 July 1800

Thomas C. Parsons to Parsons, Harrogate: '... The Clonivoe tenants have promised to pay their arrear at the assizes of Philipstown. ... Dr Heenan's daughter dead. ...'

21   8 Sep. 1800

Original of a letter from Parsons, Scarborough, to Thomas C. Parsons, Parsonstown, discussing at considerable length a portrait of Sir Laurence Parsons, 3rd Bt, of *c.* 1673, and then going on to give instructions about estate affairs.

'I have injured my tenants more than once, by letting them indulge their speculations, and miserable speculations they always are, for they have not one atom of knowledge to found a conjecture upon, and therefore their speculation always is a dream of good fortune, waiting to the last moment for an increase of price till the value of the commodity falls or the vermin destroy it. Indeed, at the price corn is now, any of them might well pay double the present rent ... .

As to the angle of the castle, I confess I have no apprehension about it, for the wall batters so that I believe, if it opened a foot wide, it would still be within the perpendicular, and consequently could not fall. You know a wall cannot fall out, unless it projects beyond its base, or unless it crumbles down from being badly cemented. As to the former case, when you look at it, you will be

D/5/21 *contd.*   satisfied that there is no danger of it; and as to the latter, I believe the cement of it is as hard as the stone itself, and that even if the wall projected beyond its base, the cement would not give way, and I am sure that it is much stronger than any new angle which could be now built up, as the mortar of the new would not acquire such [?derridity] for a century. The more I have considered it, the more satisfied I am that it is perfectly safe, and that nothing need be done till next April, when I shall have an architect there.

We shall remain here during the rest of this month, and then go to York to get William innoculated, and about the latter end of October we shall proceed to London. ... The Dames's of the King's County are here, and dine with us today. ...'

| 22 | 9 Sep. 1800 | Thomas C. Parsons, Parsonstown, to Parsons, Scarborough. |

'... D'Arcy is returned after buying the timber and glass for the hot-houses. ... Your trees of all descriptions are in the most most flourishing state. Those against the wall are making great strides to its summit, and the seedlings, particular the larch, are sitting up with vigour. ...'

| 23 | 27 Sep. 1800 | Thomas C. Parsons, post-marked Parsonstown, to Parsons, Scarborough. |

'... No races here this year – the Birr misses distracted at the disappointment. Mrs Walsh was collecting subscriptions for a lady's plate, but there were no horses prepared to run, as the notice was so short. ...'

| 24 | 24 Oct. 1800 | Thomas C. Parsons, Parsons, to Parsons, St James's Coffee-house, London. |

'... D'Arcy intends shortly to begin Lady P.'s garden at the back of the castle, according to a plan you sent him some time ago. Query: whether it would not be better to postpone doing it, until the work at the angle of the castle is finished, for I apprehend any ground improvement in that quarter would be spoiled by the persons and materials employed in doing the other? ... I examined this day the fissure in the angle of the castle, and I am confident it is increasing. In the room over the parlour, I can see light through it, and bits of mortar often fall from the edges of it. Large pieces of mortar have lately fallen in the cellar under the terrace, and have broken bottles. However, as the upper part of the wall does not project over the base, I suppose it's not in any danger of shortly falling. ...

John says he hears that Smith is to be Attorney-General. It is mortifying to see the enemies of the country fatten on her richest spoils and wear those honours which are due only to virtue.'

| 25 | 5 Nov. 1800 | Thomas C. Parsons, Parsonstown, to Parsons, St James's Coffee-house, London, about their Boleyn ancestors, and about the contents of some of the family papers. |

D/5/27 21 Nov. 1800 Thomas C. Parsons, Dublin, to Parsons, St James's Coffee-house, London, about the Clere pedigree and the will of the 2nd Earl of Rosse of the first creation – d.1764.

'... With respect to Lord Rosse's will, I think, after reading it, that the beneficial contingency it contains is of but little value to you. He devised his estates in the first instance to Lady Elizabeth Parsons in *strict settlement*; then to Hussey, now Lord Beaulieu; then to Lord B.'s brother; then to Lord Netterville; then to a person of the name of Blake; then to another of the same name; then to his *godson*, Boyd; and lastly to his own *right heirs*. These several remainders were all, as the first devise to his sister, in *strict* settlement; so that Lord B. has no power whatsoever over the property, save that of enjoying it during his life and making leases for three lives; nor can the remainders ever be barred; nor your remote interest destroyed, until one of the persons in remainder, after he comes into possession, suffers a common recovery together with his son of full age; and that among so many remainders such an opportunity will occur and will be taken advantage of, is hardly to be doubted. ...' [See also D/18.]

28 1 Dec. 1800 Thomas C. Parsons, Dublin, to Parsons, 21 Berkeley Square, London.

'The drawing for Irish members of parliament took place today. Harry Grady was the first drawn, which I think is ominous of the very low degradation this poor country is doomed to. George Ponsonby is candidate for the Co. Wicklow in the room of Westby, who is dead. Knox sits for the College. Browne is to be agent to the new Primate. The Chancellor has signified from the bench his intended departure from Ireland in a few days. He parts with all his servants. Sir Michael Smith is to sit for him, and *St George Daly* is to be the new Baron.

I think Dublin is beginning already to feel severely the effects of the Union, in the languour of trade and the desertion of her inhabitants. ... The finest of houses are reduced in many instances one-half, in general a third. What will they be next winter? I hear Mr Ponsonby intends selling his house in Henrietta Street. Tom Goold has bought Sir F. Flood's house for £920. A year ago it would have brought £1500. There's a magnificent house in Buckingham Street, a new street not far from Summerhill. The person who wishes to dispose of it will give anyone £500 to take it off his hands, though there was upwards of £4,000 laid out on it since it was built, and the rent is less than £150. ...' He goes on to make snobbish observations about how the lower orders will thus be enabled to purchase the former mansions of the great.

30 13 Dec. 1800 Thomas C. Parsons, Parsonstown, to Parsons, 21 Berkeley Square, London.

D/5/30 *contd.*

'... The hot-house is nearly finished – the frame and brickwork done. But the sashes are not yet glazed. D'Arcy is thickening all the clumps and planting where directed.

I suppose you have heard of Miss Bernard's marrying a Mr Poe contrary to her father's desire. Mr B has resolved never to see her or give her any fortune, and he is a man of a stern and pertinacious mind. ...'

31   19 Jan. 1801   Thomas C. Parsons, 22 Molesworth Street, Dublin, to Parsons, Berkeley Square, London.

'... The canal company have lately valued the ground for a new line between Tullamore and Banagher, by which Parsonstown is to be passed by with scorn, and as this line will be seventeen feet lower than the one which they formerly marked out, Parsonstown would ever continue excluded from the benefit of this navigation, if this latter cut was the one finally followed ... [text defective].'

34   24 Feb. 1801   Thomas C. Parsons, Molesworth Street, to Parsons, Berkeley Square, London.

'... Everyone here thinks that the new administration is the entire work of Mr Pitt and to be moved by his hand; that it has been formed solely for the purpose of making such a peace as Pitt could not have condescended to make; and that it is to be cashiered as soon as this object is obtained; and that the Catholic Question is nothing but an instrument of popularity to be made use of as occasion shall require. ... I fear Lord Cornwallis's departure will cause a revival of religious persecutions in this country and the system of fire and sword which are [*sic*] the inevitable consequences of them. ...'

35   28 Feb. 1801   Thomas C. Parsons to Parsons.

'... Major Parsons desires me to thank you for being so interested about him. He thinks he would have no chance of obtaining the new Lt-colonelcy from L'Estrange, as he's anxious to elevate Stepney and his brother; and he [Major Parsons] would rather get the paymastership than any rank in the militia.

Tom Bernard, Hackett and Kearney are going to set up a bank in Parsonstown. ...'

38   15 Mar. 1801   Thomas C. Parsons, Parsonstown, to Parsons, Berkeley Square, London, about hot-houses, vines and other plantings.

39   18 Mar. 1801   Thomas C. Parsons to Parsons, Berkeley Square, London.

'It occurs to me that you might without impropriety write to the Lord Lieutenant in favour of Williams, in consequence of his promise both to you and him, particularly as he's about to leave Ireland, and therefore has no future favours to court or reward, and has I presume by this time satisfied all the engagements which the Union gave occasion to. Besides, I think he's a man who would not wish to forget any promise he had made, particularly to you. ...'

D/5/41 1 Feb. 1802   Thomas C. Parsons to Parsons.

'I saw Lord Charlemont today and stated to him the substance of your letter. He said that he was almost certain that Mr Foster would not take the money that was subscribed for him, but that he would ascertain the fact beyond doubt in the course of an hour, and let me know by a note. I gave him my address, but have not heard from him since. When I do, I will communicate to you the information.

I told him what your intention was, if the subscription would not be accepted. He said he thought it exceedingly liberal and handsome, and that there would be great occasion for it, as there were several of the anti-Unionists much embarrassed by the pecuniary advances they either made or subjected themselves to for the public benefit when the Union was under discussion.

He instanced Tom Gould [*sic* – Goold], who was saddled with £1200 on account of that measure. Dick Dawson, he said, was in the same predicament, but did not look to be reimbursed, and that there were a few much distressed by their liberality at that time, and whom he thought it but justice to relieve, as they could not relieve themselves.

The Chancellor was buried yesterday. A vast number of carriages and of barristers attended the funeral. The crowd of populace was also very great, and the mode of indicating their feelings very expressive, for as soon as the body appeared, they burst forth into loud hisses and hooting, and in this manner followed the hearse to the grave, and when the last office of Christian piety was finished, they re-iterated in still louder strains the cry of reprehension and waved their hats in sign of triumph and joy. [Letter incomplete?]'

42   8 May 1806   Thomas C. Parsons to Parsons, Gloster, [King's County].

'... I hear Beresford may set at defiance the run on his bank, which to a certain degree still continues. It is said that the Irish Croesus [Luke White?] advanced him £50,000.

Ponsonby pronounced his first decree today, in the cause of Wheeler against D'Esterre, and by it reversed a decree made by Lord Clare. The cause had come before Lord Redesdale on a re-hearing, but he had not time to decide it. However, he expressed his disapprobation of the decree made by Lord Clare, and would most probably have done what Ponsonby did today, had he continued on the bench. Ponsonby in giving judgement was elegant and perspicuous, and his decision seems to meet the approbation of the bar. ...'

[The concluding items in the sub-section, E/5/46–62, are for the most part dated 1822 and 1825, and relate to the investigation into Thomas C. Parsons's alleged misconduct as Assistant Barrister for King's County, 1822, and his death and the testimonial to him, 1825. These events are fully described, and indeed the documents

D/5/42 *contd.*

themselves drawn upon, in Cooke's *Early History of Birr,* pp 114–121 and 395–6.]

p.114 'The first of the extraordinary scenes which at different times occurred in Birr Quarter Sessions Court, between the Assistant Barristers then presiding there, and a portion of the magistrates of the district, took place on the 27th of July 1822, when Thomas Clere Parsons, brother to the Earl of Rosse, and who had been appointed in 1803, was still Assistant Barrister for the King's County. The origin of this very remarkable and unusual proceeding, which was not concluded until October Sessions, 1822, was as follows:- On the 5th of July 1822, one Minton, an inhabitant of Birr, lodged a complaint before a magistrate who lived five or six miles from the town, against a widow named Kerley, another inhabitant of the town, for recovery of five shillings or so, claimed to be due for labour. Upon the hearing of the complaint, the defendant was adjudged to pay the money, and a warrant was granted to levy the sum "and charges," without specifying the amount, and the poor woman's cow having been seized under this warrant, she was advised to lodge an appeal, and which she accordingly did.

When this appeal came on at Quarter Sessions on the 27th of July, the Order appealed against had not been returned by the convicting Justice and the case having been then adjourned to thelast day of the Sessions it was then further adjourned to the following October Sessions, in consequence of the absence of the Order. Upon this adjournment of the case, eight of the Justices

p.115 attending the Court of Quarter Sessions retired to the magistrates' chamber, leaving the Assistant Barrister and the Justice who had taken the appeal, the only occupants of the bench. It appeared that these eight Justices were of opinion that no Justice should take an appeal to an Order, without a previous communication with the Justice by whom the Order had been made. As to this, the Justice who had taken the appeal in the present case differed with them, and the Assistant Barrister agreed in opinion with him. On retiring to the chamber, the eight Justices sent to request the Assistant Barrister to join them there, but he declined to do so, as he and the other Justice were then engaged in Court on the trial of a criminal case. Upon this, the eight Justices in chamber passed two resolutions condemning the conduct of their brother Justice in having taken the appeal, and they also resolved, "That we think it expedient to request the attendance of every magistrate on the first day of the Crown business at the next Sessions of Birr, for the purpose of appointing a chairman, and taking this subject into consideration, as well as other matters relating to magisterial duties." These eight Justices then also resolved, "That we direct the Clerk of the Peace to send a copy of these resolutions to every

D/5/42 *contd.*

magistrate in the Birr District."

Mr. Parsons, the chairman against whom these resolutions were principally directed, published, before the next Session, a long reply in the shape of an address to the magistrates of the King's County. To this address there appeared as a rejoinder, a pamphlet from "a freeholder of the King's County," addressed to

p.116 Mr. Parsons, and intended to prove "his legal incapacity to fill the situation of chairman of the King's County Quarter Sessions." The day for deciding the question at length arrived. The October Sessions of 1822 set in, and upon Thursday, the 10th of that month – the first day for disposing of criminal business – there assembled in Birr the most numerous meeting of magistrates that ever was seen in the King's County. It may be interesting, after a lapse of nearly fifty years, to peruse the names of about sixty magistrates who then assembled, and which will be found (No. 12) in the Appendix. The humble parties to the appeal having in the meantime settled their little difference between themselves, it became unnecessary to enter into the matter on their account. Never was better exemplified the truth of the adage, "Saepe scintilla parva magnum incendium excitavit." The business commenced by Colonel L'Estrange, one of the magistrates, adverting to the resolutions of the former Sessions, and to the chairman's published reply, and he called upon the eight Resolutionists to withdraw their resolutions. Upon this, one of these gentlemen agreed to have the resolutions withdrawn, in order, as he said, to avoid a division amongst the magistrates. It was then moved by Colonel L'Estrange, and seconded by Thomas Ryder Pepper, Esq., that the business should proceed as usual with the usual chairman; but after some discussion, it was proposed by Colonel Atkinson, and seconded by Mr. Palmer as an amendment,

p.117 that the Earl of Rosse should be appointed chairman. Finally, however, the original resolution to proceed with the usual chairman, was carried with the most enthusiastic applause perhaps ever heard in a Court of Justice, the peals of which, echoing round the Jury-rooms and different parts of the court, acquired new strength as they resounded through the town, the streets of which were crowded with persons of all ranks, anxious to show their joy at the result.'

'Mr. Parsons, the respected chairman of the King's County Quarter Sessions Court, died in August 1825, and on the 3rd of May 1827, the solemn and imposing ceremony of laying the first stone of a cenotaph to his memory took place in Birr. In some time after his death, a public meeting was held in Birr to offer a tribute to his memory, and it was there resolved, "That a handsome Memorial be erected by public subscription, to perpetuate at once the said Thomas Clere Parsons' memory, and

D/5/42 *contd.*

our regard for departed excellence." This meeting appointed a committee to carry out the object in view, and a subscription list was opened, the Rev. Mr. Adamson being treasurer. The subscribers after some time comprised not only all the gentry and respectable traders of the town and neighbourhood, but likewise many persons resident elsewhere, including the Earl of Charleville and Daniel O'Connell, M.P., afterwards "the Liberator." The amount of subscriptions having reached over £200, the committee, on their part, unanimously adopted the design of an obelisk, as furnished by Bernard Mullins, Esq., which was

p.118   intended to be about seventy feet high, and would resemble the Wellington Testimonial in the Phoenix Park, Dublin, but be smaller, and more beautiful. An appropriate site for this obelisk was selected at Scurragh, near the town, where, on a rising ground over the river, and visible from all sides, it was intended to be a lasting testimonial to departed virtue.

p.395   [APPENDIX]

NAMES OF THE MAGISTRATES WHO ASSEMBLED AT BIRR QUARTER SESSIONS, THE 10TH OF OCTOBER 1822.

Frederick Aldridge, Maunsel Andrews, John Armstrong, Samuel Armstrong, Thomas St. George Armstrong, Colonel J.W. Atkinson, Charles Baggot, Valentine Bennett, Thomas Bernard, William Berwick, W.H. Birch, Sir B. Bloomfield, Bart., W.N. Briscoe, J. Brownrig, Rev. J. Burdett, Shaw Cartland, E. Cox, James Cox, J.A. Drought, James Dunn, Robert Eraser, Abraham Fuller, J.E. Gamble, Richard Grattan, Rev. Skelton Gresson, Simpson Hackett, Rev. Thomas Hawkins, D.D., Thomas Hobbs,

p.396   G.A. Holmes, M. Kearney, Major Charles L'Estrange, Edmond L'Estrange, Colonel H.P. L'Estrange, Robert Lauder, William Minchin, John Molloy, R.J.E. Mooney, Sandford Palmer, Thomas R. Pepper, John Percy, Thomas Powell, Right Hon. Laurence Earl of Rosse, George Slator, Bernard Smith. Thomas Stannus, J.W. Tibeaudo, Frederick Thompson, Adam Tyrrell, H.P. Vaughan, Richard Warburton, B.B. Warburton, B. Warburton, William Wallace, John Wetherelt, Charles White, and Corker Wright.'

D/7	DATE	DESCRIPTION

7/1–173 1800: 1802–34: 1837–8: 1842; 1898: 1905: 1849–50: 1976: 1983: 1987–8: 1992

Letters to Parsons from his uncle, Laurence Harman (Parsons) of Newcastle, Ballymahon, Co. Longford, 1st Viscount Oxmantown and subsequently (1806) 1st Earl of Rosse, and, after the 1st Earl's death in April 1807, from his widow, Jane, Countess Dowager of Rosse. The letters concern all manner of family, political and financial affairs. At the time of writing, the 1st Earl and his widow were almost invariably in England, either in London or at their successive country houses in various parts of the country – mainly Stretton Hall, Wolverhampton, Staffordshire – where he lived 1806–7, and she, 1807–38), and Parsons almost invariably in Ireland. The 1st Earl's letters relate to the family's relations with the Addington, Pitt and Grenville administrations; complaints about Parsons's absence from parliament in 1806, on account of his wife's ill-health, when the government expected him, as a Lord of the Irish Treasury, to attend; Co. Longford and King's County elections, particularly in 1806, when the 1st Earl visited Newcastle for electioneering purposes; the 1st Earl's reluctant consent to apply for the earldom, but solely on condition that it was remaindered on Parsons, 1806; etc, etc. The letters from the Dowager Lady Rosse concern the 2nd Earl's taking possession of the 1st Earl's Dublin house in Stephen's Green, 1807; her nearly fatal accident while out driving in her carriage in the same year; King's County and Co. Longford politics and elections (with the 2nd Earl acting as the Dowager Lady Rosse's adviser and sometimes spokesman in respect of the latter); the Dowager Lady Rosse's relations with her nephew and son-in-law, the 1st Viscount) Lorton; the 2nd Earl's disappointment on discovering in 1818 that he was going to inherit none of the 1st Earl's Harman/Co. Longford property; the intimidation of the Dowager Lady Rosse by some deranged kinsman called William Parsons [see D/24]; etc, etc. Copies of some of the 2nd Earl's letters to the Dowager Lady Rosse are present in the sub-section, whereas only the other side of the correspondence between the 1st Earl and him survives. The papers of 1838 and 1842 (which are subsequent to her death) relate to the provisions of her will, 1838, and an estate bill initiated by Lord Lorton, 1842. The letters and papers of 1898, 1903, 1949–50, 1976, 1983 and 1987 respectively relate to the ruinous state of a monument to the 1st Earl in a cemetery off Hampstead Road, London, a portrait of him painted in 1809, King-Harman family portraits at Newcastle, a portrait of the Dowager Lady Rosse hanging in Rosse Hall, Kenyon College, Ohio, and the 7th Earl of Rosse's visit to Kenyon College in 1987, following which he received from the college photocopies of correspondence, 1824–7, relating to the Dowager Lady Rosse's benefaction to it.

The sub-section includes:

D/7/1 [Late June? 1800]

Lord Oxmantown, Teignmouth, Devon, to Parsons.

'Yours of the 17th inst has at last reached me. I wish you much joy of a son and hope it and Lady Parsons are as well as can be expected. I will with pleasure comply with your request of being its sponsor and as a little premium is always given to the nurse for particular care, will you permit me to request you will give ten guineas for me; and as I have a wretched memory I trouble you with a draft for it.

Lady O. joins me in compliments to Lady P.'

2   20 Aug. 1802

Oxmantown, Whitworth, Rochdale, Lancashire, to Parsons.

'By a letter I had lately from our friend Mr Clibborne I find Lady Parsons had gone to Dublin to lie in, which has given very sincere pleasure to Lady Oxmantown and me, who has commissioned me to renew the request she made to Mr William Parsons when he was leaving Newcastle, of being permitted to stand [sponsor] for the next little one, which we hope he did not forget to do, lest there might not now be a vacancy. I hope in your next you will be enabled to inform us that Lady Parsons and the little stranger are as well as can be expected and that my godson is very well, whom I take for granted you left at the castle.

The result of the King's County election gave me great pleasure, not that I know Mr B[ernard], nor that I have any personal dislike of Mr D[aly] nor objection to his representing Galway; but I cannot forget how he got into the former county. ...'

4   21 Sep. 1803

Oxmantown, Wrexham, to Parsons.

'Before I left town I spoke to Mr Wickham about your brother William for a living for him and he at *once* said he *had* his name down for one, so that I am in hopes he will soon get one.'

5   24 Nov. 1803

Oxmantown, Leeswood Hall, Mold, Flintshire, to Parsons.

'I am much obliged to you for your account of the political face of your country, and trust in God that those gentlemen who are so confident in the sudden (if at all) change of the R.C. sentiments may not have reason to change their opinions. If it has happened, and I don't doubt but to a certain degree it has, it has arisen from the cause you have so properly attributed it to. The wealthy R.C. fears for his property; if he joins the French and they are beat, it will be then forfeited and if they succeed he dreads he may be plundered. The great security of the country, next to the Almighty, is the great military force we have (in which I include the yeomanry) and which will be increased every day from this country, as the volunteer system here matures. Whatever hopes I may have from the R.C. laity I have none from their clergy. It is impossible but they knew of the business of the 23rd of July and yet all that time Doc. [Troy] was persuading the people at the

D/7/5 *contd.*

Castle that everything was perfectly quiet and they were foolish enough to believe him and perhaps do so now. It is impossible they could be ignorant of it, particularly those in Dublin. I was sorry to observe Judge Day compliment them so much in his Charge. It must have been the result of ignorance or (more probably) of crooked policy. ...'

6   9 Dec. 1803   Oxmantown, Leeswood Hall, to Parsons.

'I was extremely vexed when I read that part of your letter which mentioned government having given away a living lately to Mr Kellet instead of your brother, and that without any apology to you. However, upon considering the business I cooled a little, as it strikes me the matter is thus. On the worthy Bishop telling Mr P. that he must resign either his corps or his living, he or the Marquess [of Headfort?] waited on government to know if they would give it to their friend, Mr K., who I believe has some connections in the county of Meath that have been and may be useful in elections, as in that case he would resign it, if not, the corps, and as it was no great difference to them they complied with his wishes. If I am mistaken in this conjecture I will be very much displeased.

I am extremely sorry to find that government are so duped by the present professions of the R.C.s. I should have thought that it had had sufficient experience of their duplicity *never* to trust them, for I am as confident as I ever was or can be of anything, that ... they will turn against us. But the reason his Excellency gives for this confidence is the most absurd and ill-founded in my opinion, of any that could be urged. If the Pope has wrote this letter it must have been at the desire of Bonaparte.'

7   12 Jan. 1804   Oxmantown, Leeswood Hall, to Parsons.

'Finding that Mr Wickham was to resign his situation in February I thought there could be no harm in my writing to Mr Addington in your favour, not that I expect my writing will be attended with much good. However as I can say things of you that you would not of yourself, I determined upon it. Indeed if I had not done it I should have no peace at home for Jane urged me very strongly to it and that, though it might not be of service *now*, it might on some other occasion; and at all events I would have the consolation of thinking I had done all I could.

I stated to him the great necessity of having a man of talent and ability who knows the country, the objects and views of the different classes of inhabitants and is of mild and conciliatory manners, with a mind cautious, penetrating and firm; that you had paid the most sedulous attention to every subject that could occupy a statesman ever since you were first returned for our university, which was at a very early period; that you had manifested your attachment to the King and the unity of the

D/7/7 *contd.*

executive government of the two countries (this last point I added to do away anything [which] might arise from your opposing the Union) in a very conspicuous manner on the Regency.

I assured him I had no personal view in this for I assured him there was not that in the gift of his Majesty I would ask for, though assured it would be granted, and that if I was aware that any person equally qualified was likely to be found without taking him from a higher situation (this I said as possibly he might consult Lord Hobart or Castlereagh) I would not mention you to him at this time, as you had a most excellent private property and I was fully aware of the arduousness and the responsibility of the office; that there were but few men would follow his bright example and quit a most honourable and lucrative situation to uphold a sovereign sinking under anxiety and a country almost overwhelmed by the number and power of its enemies; yet it was the duty of every loyal man at so momentous a period, to endeavour to emulate such noble conduct and give up his ease, if his exertions could be of service to his country; [that] our influence in parliament was not inconsiderable, as there were three county members [who] thought in politics as you and I did.

I then observed how much I should be obliged etc, etc, and that my poor state of health had prevented my attendance [in] the two last sessions. ...'

8   24 Jan. 1804   Oxmantown, Leeswood Hall, to Parsons.
'I am truly happy that my fruitless effort has been pleasing to you, of which I was informed by yours of the 17th inst. On Sunday and yesterday I wrote again to Mr Addington stating as Mr W[ickham] was to retire that you might still be enabled to render great service to government if more "station and consequence" was added [to] the office which [to my mind meant] that the person holding it in future should be a Privy Counsellor; that such an arrangement seemed to arise out of the Union as the Secretary was obliged to attend parliament here, during which time his office was to a certain degree vacant by which very serious consequences may occur (I was near saying, had) ...'.

9   18 Feb. 1804   Oxmantown, Leeswood Hall, to Parsons.
'I have just had a civil letter from Mr H[iley] Addington saying his brother had received both my letters but being extremely [busy] had desired him to say that there neither was nor is there any likelihood of Mr W[ickham]'s office being vacated etc, etc, etc.'

10   27 Feb. 1804   Oxmantown, Leeswood Hall, to Parsons.
'I had the satisfaction of yours of the 18th as also of the 22nd and am glad to find you take our disappointment so well; in fact it is what we ought to do, for as you very properly and wisely remark we have a [cause] to serve here and a part to act here, on the

D/7/10 *contd.*

propriety of which will depend our future happiness; and not on
our success here, which often acts as a snare and leads to
distraction. ...'

He continues with remarks about the virtue of not locking
oneself up in cloisters and the necessity for making an effort to put
one's point of view clearly before the public.

11   31 July 1804   Oxmantown, Leeswood Hall, to Parsons.
'This day your letter of the 20th came here from Dublin where
Lady O. had sent it thinking I might be detained longer than I
intended. I am sorry I did not know of your intention of leaving
England so soon, as I would have renewed our wish to have the
pleasure of seeing you and Lady Parsons and my godson here; but
as you had not said anything of it I did not conceive you had it in
so immediate contemplation. I could easily have postponed my
trip to Dublin ...'.

The letter continues with thanks to Parsons for enquiries about
houses at Berwick, where Lord Oxmantown evidently wished to
reside for a time.

'... I am gratified by the motive that induced you to write about
the earldom. I am afraid I did not make myself understood on this
subject; for, if it was offered to me I should most certainly decline
it unless, as I ... [the letter is damaged at this point but it is clear
that Lord Oxmantown did not wish to apply for the earldom and
warned that, if Parsons wanted to include himself in the
application, presumably for the remainder, he should consider the
effects on his career]'.

12   20 Aug. 1804   Oxmantown, Leeswood Hall, to Parsons.
'Yesterday I had the pleasure of yours of the 17th and this day,
that of the 18th. I hope you perfectly understand that nothing can
induce me to accept of the earldom but your wish [?to my] title,
and being included in the patent. I am much obliged to you for
giving me so much of what passed between you and Sir E[van]
N[epean]; it helps one to form a judgement of present and future
matters. I agree with you in thinking that all the difficulty that is
thrown in the way is to make you [?relish] what they feel stands in
need of it. ... I suppose it is not intended that Sir E[van] N[epean]
is to continue Secretary: it really shows very little regard to the real
interest of Ireland to leave it without a Secretary and only a
nominal Lord Lieutenant.'

13   27 Aug. 1804   Oxmantown, Leeswood Hall, to Parsons.
'I sit down in a great hurry to acknowledge yours of the 23rd
inst, and to express my astonishment at the contents of it. I wished
you to accept the situation in the Treasury, though much less than
I thought would have been offered to you. Supposing the
sentiments of government to be friendly to us, as I know it ought,
I took it for granted that in the first opportunity you would get

D/7/13 *contd.*   some more suitable [post]. My surprise was of course much
increased to find any hesitation. I cannot conceive on what ground
it is; what competition can you have, who have served government
so successfully and so honourably and who can continue to do, as
we have and may? When I consider members, talent, property,
character and county representation, I say, none. I am therefore
convinced from Sir E[van] N[epean]'s general character and
particularly from what you have told me, that our situation has
been withheld from government or perhaps misrepresented. You
should set him right on this subject; he has too great a mind and is
much too good a politician not to see it in its true and proper
light. I have only time to say that you should lose no time in
undeceiving Sir E[van] N[epean] ...'.

14   7 Sep. 1804   Oxmantown, Leeswood Hall, to Parsons.
      'I agree most perfectly with you that the mode of proceeding of
some people is most disgusting and dishonourable. If the language
of my letters to you astonished him, probably it would have much
more so, had I been present, which I am glad I was not when he
talked of my influence. I shall not dispute his power to dispose of
his places, and I will not allow him to presume to limit my
influence. I have asserted it and no man can contradict it. I have it
under his [Sir Thomas Fetherston's?] hand, not indeed that I asked
for it, or ever should, but he wrote just after the election was over
to thank me for the very great expense I had gone to for him and
that he would be [always] happy to follow my advice in parliament
at all events. Sir E[van] N[epean]'s consideration must have been
taken up merely for the occasion or was founded on a most perfect
ignorance of the circumstances of the case; for how can he be
called an independent man in a parliamentary view who is
brought in for a county in which he has *not a freehold* and though
about £4,000 was expended on the election, it did not cost him
one guinea. Lord G.'s interest and my money brought him in so he
must surely belong to one of us. I am glad my letter seemed to
electrify him; it was of use, I am in great hopes, as probably it
made his blood run warmer towards you. ...
      Mr Pitt looks more to English than Irish influence. Lord
A[bercorn] spoke violently against Pitt in the House of Lords this
session (since he was Minister) and was on bad terms with him when
he went out. Sir E[van] N[epean] did not show much personal regard
when he countermanded Lord H[ardwicke]'s recommendation.'

18   24 Dec. 1804   Oxmantown, Leeswood Hall, to Parsons.
      '... What a number of livings his Excellency has given away since
he told you there was but one or two to be provided for before
your brother. However, I don't see how he can defer it any longer
and after what has happened I will never be certain of anything for
either of you until it is done. ...'

D/7/21 2 Apr. 1805   Oxmantown, Leeswood Hall, to Parsons congratulating him on his appointment as a Lord of the Irish Treasury and in particular because he had insisted that he would not take the situation unless he succeeded Mr C[orry?].

22   23 Apr. 1805   Oxmantown, Leeswood Hall, to Parsons.
    'The first indication I had of your being returned again [for King's County on 6 April 1805] was from your last letter, though I should have been happy to hear from you on other accounts. I had no anxiety about that, as from Lord Charleville's declaration, I was convinced there could not be even the shadow of opposition.'

27   [pre-8] July 1805   Oxmantown, Tiberton Court, Hereford, to Parsons.
    'I am sorry to find by the newspapers that your idea that Mr Foster would resign, is confirmed. He is the only man, in office, I ever saw that appeared to me to comprise, and in an extensive point of view, the real interest of Ireland, or who seemed [?pressingly] anxious to promote it. I own I could wish he had held it some time longer, by which time a proper successor would be in readiness to replace him and that the politics of the day might be more settled and, to appearance at least, more likely to continue in the same line. For if you were to succeed now and any great change to take place, you would most probably lose it, though, if you liked it, you might retain your present situation (and such a change seems to be considered likely, though I am rather inclined to think otherwise). However, you are on the spot and much better able to judge of those things than I am. Therefore do what you think best and make what use of me you please with his Excellency ...'.

28   8 July 1805   Oxmantown, Tiberton Court, to Parsons.
    'I have received yours of the 2nd inst, and yesterday wrote to Mr Pitt as you wished, though I think your having done so would have been [useful] as you could have stated your claims more stronger [sic] than me. However, it is a satisfaction to me to think that he has had an opportunity of knowing your pretensions by a criterion far superior to any statement. In my last I mentioned my opinion [that] you would do well to apply to Mr P[itt], as also to Lord H[ardwicke]: not that I think there can be much good in it, except that he might be offended if he was not spoke to on the subject. I don't see how Mr Pitt can reappoint Mr Corry to that situation and probably Lord Abercorn may think he has done enough for the K[noxes?]. I should think he [Abercorn] would be more likely to wish for Sir J. Stewart, who I believe has been active in the prosecution of Judge Fox, which is a measure he has much at heart.
    As I take for granted Lord Sydmouth [sic] is, or soon will be, out, I suppose we shall have a new Secretary. How is it possible for the affairs of Ireland ever to be understood or brought into a good state, if these rapid changes are forever to continue.'

D/7/30 11 July 1805   Oxmantown to Parsons.

    'Though I wrote to you the day before yesterday, yet I cannot avoid writing again to express the satisfaction I feel at the conduct of Lord Hardwicke towards you; and I think his having recommended your writing to Mr Pitt and *above* all his desiring you to make use of his name and proposing to send your letter with his, puts his sincerity above all doubt; and I am also inclined to gratify myself with the idea that both he and Mr M[arsden] are impressed with the idea that you stand well on this side of the water, and being likely to succeed, they would wish to be upon better terms with you than they were with Mr Foster; and I trust and believe you will, but not, however, by a mean or too supple a compliance with their wishes, for that is [as] disgraceful as is a dictatorial and forever opposing manner. ...'

32   27 July 1805   Oxmantown, Tiberton Court, to Parsons.

    '... Your conjecture that Mr Pitt had not given up any of his time [to] Mr F[oster]'s business must be well founded, or else he would have come [to] a decision long since. ...'

34   Sep. 1805   Oxmantown to Parsons.

    '... I wish they would leave Mr F[oster] where he is and appoint you joint Secretary. The more I think on that measure and the more I see of the manner in which the affairs of Ireland are managed or rather, not to say the worst, left undone, the more I am convinced of the benefit of it. ...'

35   16 Oct. 1805   Oxmantown, Tiberton Court, to Parsons.

    'I am sincerely sorry for the outcry that has been set up against Mr F[oster] but I am not at all surprised at it; it was only what he I dare say expected. He has attempted a reform in Revenue, which required it almost as much as the Naval Department did here, and has raised the hornet's nest against him as Lord St Vincent did, but he is not likely to be as well supported ... . You know I am no partizan of Mr F[oster] and have no kind of connection with him, but I own I wish him to continue in office because he is the only man I ever knew in a leading situation that possessed the same ability and manifested the same zeal to serve Ireland that he has always done, and I have no reason to hope that his successor would be the one I wish. ...'

38   7 Dec. 1805   Oxmantown to Parsons.

    'As I can see it would be very desirable to you to have the earldom fixed on you as soon as possible, I have consented to take it, if that was done, but not otherwise; in fact there is no political event, indeed none of any kind, except death of friends, [that] could be more disagreeable to me than the change. However, if you consider it as of advantage to you, that will in some measure reconcile me to it.'

D/7/39 [*c.* 7 Dec. 1805] Draft of a letter from Oxmantown to [Charles Long, the new Chief Secretary] stating that he wishes the earldom to be remaindered on Parsons so that the latter could succeed to the old title of his family.

41   14 Dec. 1805   Oxmantown, post-marked Hereford, to Parsons.

'I do not know when I received a letter that has distressed me so much as yours of the 9th inst which I have just got. When first you mentioned this subject I was very explicit in telling you that nothing could induce me to accept of it unless that you considered it would be to your advantage to be in remainder, and that you were so accordingly; and as you have not mentioned that you are to be in remainder or had applied for it, I must take for granted that it is not so and therefore I am sorry to have it to say that I feel much hurt at this transaction on many accounts. I did not think it possible for any man to be more [word illegible] explicit on any subject. I assure you that in consenting to take it on the conditions of your being in remainder, I made the greatest sacrifice of my feelings that can possibly be conceived. My only hope is that my letter may be in time to stop it. To Mr L[ong] and Lord H[ardwicke] I request you will have the goodness to make my best acknowledgements and to say that they will add very much indeed to my obligation on this occasion, if they can prevent their kind intentions being carried into effect, unless on the condition I mention in my letter to Mr L[ong].'

42   21 Dec. 1805   Oxmantown to Parsons.

'I have this moment the satisfaction of yours of the 17th inst and request you will conceive, for I have not words to express it, how much I am impressed with your very kind and most disinterested and honourable conduct in regard to the earldom. I see all has arisen from a mistake which was caused, allow me to say my dear Sir Laurence, by your not taking notice of my having mentioned anything relative to the remainder in answer to my letter on that subject; because if you had I should have dilated more upon it and the business; but as you said nothing I considered you was indifferent.'

43   8 Jan. 1806   Oxmantown, post-marked Hereford, to Parsons.

'In a letter I had lately from Sir Thomas he mentioned he hoped he would be soon able to come over if I wished it. He had not been well. I have wrote to him this day to recommend him *for his own sake*, not to be absent at the opening of the session. I have no doubt but he will attend.'

44   19 Jan. 1806   Oxmantown to Parsons referring to Lord Hawkesbury's request that he attend the opening of the session. He explains that he will probably not do so, as he has a cold and in addition a swollen cheek.

D/7/50 21 Mar. 1806   Lord Rosse as (Oxmantown had become), post-marked Hereford, to Parsons. He has written to the Duke of Bedford and Lord Grenville with reference to promotion in the law for John C. Parsons. He transcribes a reply from the Chief Secretary, William Elliot, who explains that the new administration wishes to rely on the advice of its senior law officers with regard to promotions.

51   3 Apr. 1806   Rosse to Parsons.
'... From what Mr Moffett tells me there is a likelihood of Mr H[?enry] Forbes being a candidate for our county [of Longford], and among the numerous reports in circulation, one which will surprise you. A particular friend of Lord G[ranard?] told a friend of mine that I had formed a junction for the next election; that the P[rince] of W[ales] had made it a request when I was in London that I would do so; many others also, but I think these are enough to astonish you. I need made no declaration on the business, as you know my sentiments fully on the subject of elections. On these occasions the best way generally is not to mind reports. Your hints, and most excellent they are, shall be attended to. I fear the registry is in a very irregular and probably in a very mutilated state. I will be most obliged to you to send me the last election act. Have you not a power to send and receive packages free of postage? However if you have not, you can easily get it done, as there are many in the Castle that can. There are [a] good many leases drawn and executed by the tenants who are in possession that want my signature to complete them. I had desired Mr Moffett to send them to you and that you would be so good as to forward them to me, and I hope I may be able to return them to you in the same manner. I am sure you will not forget the visits I wished you to pay and anticipate the result will be very successful.'

52   5 Apr. 1806   Rosse to Parsons.
'I have just had a letter from Mr Moffett to tell me he has sent to my house at the Green a parcel of leases to be forwarded to me, to be executed. I will be most obliged to you the first time you pass by to call for them and transmit them to me directly. I fear they will not be in time for the 15th inst, but probably they will, as it is likely the session will be kept sitting for some days or that a very short adjournment will take place. I hear Lord G[ranar]d is to register for 436 – that is doing business and what I could not do, so I think Sir W[illia]m [Gleadowe Newcomen] or I will be out.'

53   22 Apr. 1806   Rosse to Parsons.
'Many thanks to you for getting Mr Maconchy's interest. It has always been with me and it might be a good one. How will the second votes go? It would be very desirable to secure as many of them as possible. It can be done in a quiet way by asking what were their feelings. If you find as you could wish, to a certainty, leave it there; if otherwise, to keep them disengaged. I fear from

D/7/53 *contd.*

what I hear some of our friends are not attentive to that. That is wrong in every point of view in which it can be placed. As we may have occasion to talk of the different candidates that are talked of and as it is not pleasant to mention names, suppose we call Lord F[orbes] 'A', Mr H[enry] F[orbes], 'B', Mr N[ewcomen], 'C', Sir Thomas [Fetherston] 'D'. Unless Dr H[utchinson]'s tenants have changed, which I have no reason to think, they will go with me as usual. Eight is the number. His sister, Mrs West, always went with me. Crookshank, the late Judge, had an interest. Dr H. is one of the chaplains through Lady Downshire's interest. I have not yet heard how Mr E. or Mr William D. go. ...'

He refers with regret to the government's caution with regard to legal promotion for John C. Parsons.

54   29 May 1806   Rosse, Stretton Hall, Wolverhampton, to Parsons.

'I dare say Lord G[ranar]d will get many things to assist his interest [from government], but he knows so little of the county that he will be getting things for those who cannot serve him. Do you know whether he has secured the second votes of Mr E. and others? I wish I could find out those things; for, without being able to judge on what grounds others stand, I don't know where or to what extent to make exertions. Moffett is very anxious for me to go over and says if I don't, he will come and see me, which I know would be very inconvenient to him; and I feel great reluctance in leaving Lady Rosse as she is in too weak a state to enjoy the society of strangers ...'.

55   3 June 1806   Rosse, Stretton Hall, to Parsons.

'I think your excuse to Mr E[lliot?] was a very proper one. I am sorry you had so well-founded a one; at the same time I don't think Mr W[indham]'s bill such a measure as to make one very anxious to take a long and very inconvenient journey to support. However I see he has been obliged to give up some of his most absurd and [?ridiculous] ideas. Your observations on Mr E[lliot] pressing you and not going himself, nor pressing Sir Thomas, are very material and not very easily accounted for, unless they are looking for an excuse to break. If Mr E[lliot] thought that John would succeed the next [Judge] even, I think he would throw out a hope, but of that he steers quite clear. Sir Thomas was in town and not a word said to him. He however mentions in his last letter "that it was observed at the Castle a few days ago that I was in town and not going over, but a friend said I was, and only waiting for a fair wind; he is only just returned or he should have a letter, was the reply." These are Sir Thomas's words. The friend he alludes to is, I believe, dear W[illiam]: as the reply "he is only just returned etc, etc" was occasioned by their supposing he had only just come from England.

I did hear some time ago that Lord G[renville] and Mr F[ox]

D/7/55 *contd.*

had a great difference. If that was the case probably it was on Mr W[indham's] bill, and as Mr E[lliot] is attached to Lord G[renville] and not Mr F[ox], perhaps he was the less anxious about the measure ...'.

56   18 June 1806   Rosse, Stretton Hall, to Parsons.

'... The two conversations you have had lately with Mr E[lliot] will probably bring matters to an issue. I am rather disposed to hope and believe it will be a favourable one, and if your brother is not now appointed that there will be a positive and solemn assurance that he shall on the next vacancy. I like Mr E[lliot's] manner better in the last than in the former one and am very much pleased with the Duke [of Bedford]'s manner, who might possibly have contributed to the change, as I suppose, in Mr E[lliot's] manner.

I then mentioned [to the Duke of Bedford] that when Lady Rosse got a little better I proposed to go to Ireland in order to forward Mr Forbes's view towards the representation of the county of L[ongford]. I really cannot be blamed for not giving my proxy sooner, as it was never hinted to me before. As to Sir Thomas, you know it was his intention to go to town as soon as he fixed his daughters, but he has been very poorly with a nervous complaint which travelling in such very warm weather made much worse. In his last letter, the 14th inst, he mentions that even writing a short letter, as it really was, was very distressing to him. If you should think it necessary for him to go up, I know he will, if it be possible. At the same time, it, in all probability, will be very injurious to his health, which is of great consequence to so very large and motherless a family. It certainly has not been from design that we have not attended; no doubt a different conduct on the part of government might have made us more zealous.

I think I gave a strong proof of my wish to serve them when I agreed at the earnest solicitation of Lord M[oira] etc, etc, to support Mr Forbes. The Marquess of B[uckingham] and Lord G[renville] ought to feel it also. You know I had no reason to be partial to Lord G[ranar]d, for, though he could not hurt me, he manifested a strong disposition so to do; and you also know how and why the part I have taken is considered by my best and best informed friends. The G[ranar]ds are not popular and I am sorry for it; even among the R.C. though they have Dr Cruise and many others at their table continually. (His being [*sic –* Lord Granard was] very nearly put to death in Ballymahon by a mob from all parts of the county, all R.C. It was not even alleged that there was one Protestant among them. Dr C. was in his house the whole time and must have seen and heard what was going on, but never came out.) Perhaps it might be as well to let the Duke know that, agreeable to his intimation, I immediately wrote to Lord

D/7/56 *contd.*		G[renville] for a proxy, and you may mention any of the subsequent parts you may think proper. The Ballymahon business may be left out; I only mentioned it to show you that no reliance is to be placed on a subserviency to those people.'

57   22 Aug. 1806   Rosse, near Ballymahon, to Parsons. He records his gratitude to Dr Cleghorn for giving his interest to Sir Thomas Fetherston in Co. Longford. He also mentions that he has bought Ballinamuck from Fetherston and wishes to establish a weekly market and two fairs there. He seeks Parsons's advice on how to go about getting a patent for this.

58   [?Aug. 1806]   Rosse, near Ballymahon, to Parsons.
'As far as I can judge I think Sir [Thomas Fetherston] stands upon very sure ground. Mr N[ewcomen] I hear is anxious the second votes should not go to Lord F[orbes]; his friends have no doubt but he would succeed if I remain neuter.'

60   19 Sep. 1806   Rosse, near Ballymahon, to Parsons.
'I sit down merely to say that I propose to be in town [Dublin], please God, about five o'clock on Monday next and hope to be able to sail for England on Wednesday eve; and I hope I shall find Lady Parsons getting better, [and] you and the boys perfectly well.'

61   12 Oct. 1806   Rosse, Stretton Hall, to Parsons.
'You may remember I applied to Lord L[ongford] last spring in London for his support in favour of Sir Thomas, to which he wished to defer saying anything then. Of course I did not in the smallest degree press him. I have had a letter from him in which he mentioned that having two friends now candidates he cannot support mine. The letter is couched in the most polite and friendly terms, hoping that it may not in the smallest degree lessen that esteem and friendship that has so long subsisted between us and our families. I thought it right to apprise you of this, as something may occur that may make it desirable that you should know it. I am inclined to think he will not benefit either of his friends by the part he has taken. I must be the more attentive, lest he should.'

62   16 Oct. [1806]   Rosse to Parsons.
'I am much obliged to Drs Cleghorn and Clarke for their kind intentions towards me. As to Mr Maconchy having made the freeholders to [?serve] Mr N[ewcomen], I have not the smallest reason to believe [it], except that Mr [?M.] says so, and of course it must be true. If report is true, however, Mr M. declared, before his death, he would never vote for him. He certainly always supported me and Sir Thomas and you may remember on Mr [Caleb Barnes] Harman's election, he supported him, though Sir W[illiam Gleadowe Newcomen] was so strenuous against him.'

D/7/63 22 Oct. 1806   Rosse, Stretton Hall, to Parsons.

'I should have told you that I had wrote to Mr Moffett the moment I heard of the intended dissolution of parliament, to announce the connection with Lord Forbes and to concert measures with him as to the future. I wish I had mentioned it to you, as before you left town you could have told it to Dr Cleghorn and such others as had promised one vote and not engaged the second. If this should find you in town, which I am sure it will not, I would be obliged to you to see Surgeon McEvoy and also Mr Dec. [*sic*] for Mr Tyrrell. I wrote to the latter, but as I got no answer I take it for granted he did not receive my letter. Does Dr Hutchinson continue to decline interfering with his tenantry or to vote himself? There is also Mr [? Speer], the optition [*sic*], has an interest; his shop [is] in Capel Street, his hotel in Merrion Square. Mr Crookshank (late Judge) and Dr Hutchinson's sister, Mrs West, have also interests.'

64   31 Oct. [1806]   Rosse to Parsons.

'It gives me sincere satisfaction to find you will not have any contest in the King's County, for surely if any was intended you would have perceived symptons of it. I feel great satisfaction and delight, not only in the very powerful support Lord Charleville gives you, but the very handsome and friendly manner in which he gave it to you.

I am glad Lord G[ranard] feels the obligation he is under to me. I cannot think but if Mr G[reville] was *warmly* pressed [?he] would have voted for Sir Thomas, and I think he may be yet brought to it; and they stand for their own credit, as well as to show their gratitude, to effect it. For if they don't do that, all they bring us is the Bonds' that, between you and I, I am certain will not amount altogether to 50, and the Marquess of B[uckingham] and a very few (for they don't exceed 12 on the whole property) on the property of the late Bishop Marlay, now divided between Mr Grattan and Dr Lake. The latter is most strenuous with us. Lord G[ranard] may have 8 or 10. Had I joined Mr N[ewcomen] or even remained neuter, I would have saved the expense and trouble of a contest. I cannot well account why he did not get Mr White's second votes; he has 60 votes in Leitrim where Mr W[hite]'s son is a candidate. Mr W[hite] has not more than about 15 that he can be said to have any claim upon. For most of them and all the others Lord G. will be indebted. Now it really seems odd he did not stipulate for the second when he had 60 to give for 10 or 12. It is putting me under a very heavy obligation to ask those people to vote against their landlord. So I will let them vote for Mr N. Perhaps they want to have a majority over Sir Thomas; but I may be perfectly wrong and I most sincerely hope I am.'

D/7/65 3 Nov. 1806   Rosse to Parsons.

'I am much obliged to you for writing to Mr Tyrrell. If I had not been very stupid I would have recollected that [?he] has a property in the King's County, at least the family had. His father and uncle, both whose properties he has, always supported me, as indeed did he, to the best of my recollection. Certainly his connection with D[?aly] warped him latterly but I have reason to think against his inclinations. If he is not positively engaged I think your letter will secure one vote and that will be a great thing. This business of Mr G[reville] vexes Moffett and I very much, as we cannot conceive but he would have given the second as well as the first for the same consideration -or, at all events, for a very little more; and surely they ought to have done that for me, if it was not their *own* intention to have done it. If they had, or if they do, I think *there might* be no *contest*, or if there is, by having that interest for Sir Thomas I will be able to transfer a great many split votes to Lord F[orbes] that otherwise must go to Sir Thomas. Besides, though Mr G[reville] says they shall vote singly for Lord F., there is a great danger many may not, and then, by voting for Mr N., it defeats by so many the advantage expected from the interest. If Lord G[ranard] or Lord F. are in town I will be obliged to you to lay this matter before him, as you approve. Lord L[ongfor]d I hear is likely to be very hostile to Sir Thomas though he went to London last summer and stayed a month there in very dreadful hot weather, to attend Lord Wellesley's business. Lord L[ongfor]dd's sister is married to the General [Sir Arthur Wellesley]. I should suppose one word from government would prevent that. ...'

The letter continues with the request that Parsons will secures Mr Greville's interest.

66   5 Nov. 1806   Rosse to Parsons.

'I really am vexed at troubling you with so many letters, but this business of Mr G[reville] annoys me very much, and more since your last letter, as it mentioned Lord L[ongfor]d being very active for Mr N. Therefore I should not be at all surprised if many of Mr G.'s tenants were to vote for Mr N. Those people don't like to vote singly. They wish to lay as many as possible under obligations. Now their doing so must have a bad effect either as to Lord F. or Sir Thomas, or both. I am so ignorant of the state of the county and not being acustomed to run in couples, I certainly feel uneasy. For till I hear more I cannot conceive Mr G. would have made any difficulty in voting for Sir Thomas. If he had, I think there would not [be] a contest, or [it] would have enabled me to serve Lord F. essentially with split votes.

I should not trouble you again with all this but [to] tell you I wrote last night to Lord Moira upon this subject, and as he stated to us that he was sure Mr G[reville] would instantly join us on his

D/7/66 *contd.*   writing to him, I thought it a prudent if not a necessary measure
for him to adopt and I stated I considered it to be more so as I
found from several, and from you who were making every exertion
for Lord F., that Lord L[ongfor]d who is connected by blood and
intimacy was working hard for Mr N. It will be a great thing to
secure Mr [?Ball], though he has not, I am certain, ten votes
instead of twenty as Lord G. says, I mean such as can vote at this
election. Colonel Ahmuty has but very few indeed nor do I believe
he is registered, but I believe he can register at any time. Rev.
Dudley Bates, or Bates Dudley [*sic* – Rev. Sir Henry Bate Dudley]
has a vote by being Rector of Kilglees [*sic* – Kilglass]. The Bishop
of Limerick can tell you where he is. ...'

He concludes with the names of several other gentlemen who have
interests in Co. Longford.

70   20 Feb. 1807   Rosse, Stretton Hall, to Parsons.
'... The account of Lord Charleville's attachment and steadiness
gives me great pleasure and must undoubtedly ensure your perfect
tranquillity in your county which is a very pleasant circumstance.
...'

71   [Feb. 1807]   Rosse, Stretton Hall, to Parsons.
'I am not surprised that you should feel inexpressible satisfaction
that no one was hurt by the fall of the vaults [at Birr Castle] and
the more so when you reflected that the dear little dogs might have
been under it. No doubt you have had all the others properly
inspected, lest another crash might not be attended with such
favourable circumstances.
I am very glad to hear you are attending to the registry of your
freeholders; no one is so likely to maintain peace as he who is best
prepared for war. I have heard something more amiss about a great
personage's heart. I trust God will mend it.'

74   3 Apr. 1807   Rosse, Stretton Hall, to Parsons.
'As in your letter which I received last night you do not say
anything of your coming over I think it likely you will not, at all
events not till I return from town, where I propose to go on
Monday and be in town by dinner on Tuesday, easily, in order to
attend the debate on the M[arquess] of Stafford's motion which no
doubt will have an oblique censure on the King for dismissing his
ministers for wanting to swindle him out of his assent to their
measure. For their own minute of council proves that that was
their intention, otherwise they would have specifically mentioned
the particulars of the object they had in view, but which it does
not appear they over did. Lord G[renville] has my proxy so that if
I did not go I would be made to vote against my most decided
opinion. I am sorry at the same time they ever broached the
question. ...

D/7/74 *contd.*

I have just received a very polite letter from Lord Hawkesbury to request my attendance on Wednesday. It was dated the 28th ult.'

[This is the last letter from Rosse as he died on 20 April 1807.]

87   25 Sep. 1815   The Dowager Lady Rosse, Stretton Hall, to [Parsons, now 2nd] Earl of Rosse. She writes of the disturbances she has heard of in Ireland and mentions that she would like to find 'a respectable tenant' for Newcastle.

88   5 Sep. 1816   The Dowager Lady Rosse, Stretton Hall, to Rosse. She has decided not to let Newcastle to Mr [Luke?] White. She commiserates with Rosse on the damage which has been caused to the church at Birr, and reflects on the state of Ireland.

'... Certainly poor Ireland is a very savage country and the Union by taking the best people away has greatly contributed to make it as it now is. The love of legislating for other countries and taxing them has led England into sad errors and would do the same with Ireland (if it was more distant) as it did with America. I hope they are now convinced that it is overtaxed and [will] be more merciful in future; but that was the great object of the Union so they must [be loath to?] give it up, even though they must see how unproductive overtaxing is in the end. ...'

91   20 July 1818   The Dowager Lady Rosse, Stretton Hall, to Rosse.

'I cannot express, dear Lord Rosse, the satisfaction your last letter gave me. To know that all was concluded so well, after such preparation for a contest, was really pleasant. Mr Malone's friends, as they call themselves, were acting like bitter enemies to him. I am glad he had the courage to remove himself out of their hands before they quite ruined him. It will surely have the good effect you mention; this attempt having been made and failing, will promote future peace in the county, and your family have reason to rejoice for many years in the prudent management and wisdom with which you steered through the storm.'

92   31 July 1818   The Dowager Lady Rosse, Stretton Hall, to Rosse.

'I thank you for yours of the 18th from Dublin and am much pleased at what you tell me on election matters in the King's County, and that even those who were ungrateful to you are now desirous to be friends again. It is impossible to put much confidence in such persons, though perhaps from Christian motives you may not quite reject their advances at a reconciliation.

It is thought by some persons that elections in Ireland would be a less formidable business if freeholds were upon the same footing as in England, where none vote but out of their *own* property, little estates, instead of leases. I have a poor head for such things, but it seems to me as if it would cut up the power of the priests, by depriving those over whom they have such influence of their power to intimidate men of Protestant principles from standing

D/7/92 *contd.*   for counties. In a former election for Leitrim I heard there were
200 priests attending and forcing the poor, low freeholders to vote
against their landlords; but they failed. Now they have succeeded
by going [to] still greater lengths; and Mr White in the joy of his
heart sent ten barrels of ale to Longford to have his health drank
[*sic*] there and now declares he will be a candidate whenever Sir T.
Fetherston dies. Some friends have written to [have] me consider
in time who I would support in that case, but I hope it may be
some years first; and if your son John should be of age, then I
should be happy to support him if you approve. England is in
general fond of altering things in Ireland and putting [them] on
the same footing there as here; if they were to do it in elections
would it not be a great advantage? I should like greatly to know of
your opinion on the subject.

Sir Edward Littleton of this country admired greatly your
speeches on the popery business years ago, when you endeavoured
to limit the powers of voting to £20 and £10 freeholds. Happy
would it have been for the nation had you succeeded. He intended
writing only in the year before he died and desired to be informed
whenever you should come here.'

93   4 Aug. 1818   The Dowager Lady Rosse to Rosse.
'Since I wrote to you I received the enclosed [not found], by
which I find Sir Thomas Fetherston's health is thought to be worse
than I imagined and if so it will be necessary to consider the
subject more carefully than I was inclined to do. I wish to know
your opinion and how the peace of the county may best be
preserved. Lord F[orbes] has certainly been very active in the
county but I have seen things in the [word illegible] Freeman's
Journal that I did not like. However I have made a civil answer to
his letter saying that I shall be glad to see him when in England.
Perhaps before that time I may be able to judge what is best to do
and how people are inclined towards me. George Fetherston I
think would not be liked, being unpopular, and who would
support the Protestant cause in parliament I know not; but that I
ought not to support any other is clearly my sense of duty.'

94   31 Aug. 1818   The Dowager Lady Rosse to Rosse.
'Many thanks, dear Lord Rosse, for your kind letter of the 24th
inst and intimation of Longford news. I had not heard so much
before as you mention though I was told Mr Shuldham looked to
the county. The estate he has recovered there is but between
£3,000 and £4,000 a year and would not well bear a contest I
should think. He has however got some arrears of the rent that was
[?disputed] during the lawsuit. I wonder is he the person Lord
Forbes had in view when he wrote to me, and as their politics are
the same I think it possible. He said if I wished for it he would
give his honest opinion as to the best means of rendering

D/7/94 *contd.*

opposition vain. I did not ask the question in my answer, though curious to know who he meant, but when he comes here, he may perk up and be more open in speaking than in writing; and I must endeavour to be the more guarded, as his mother is no friend and wonderfully clever. [She] will stop at nothing to gain her point. I shall therefore be glad to have your advice on the subject before I see him and beg you will write freely and not scruple to give me such caution as may be necessary for one so unskilled in electioneering arts and indeed in any art, yet whose duty it is to act faithful to the trust confided to me by my regretted Lord. I still hope Sir T[homas] F[etherston] may hold his present place till your son John is of age, but as that is so uncertain, I wish to act wisely and therefore ask the advice of a wise man.

The personal interest of my dear Lord in the county *was very great* but that has dwindled away the more by Sir T.F. getting things more to please himself and even Lord G[ranard] than to serve the friends of N[ew]castle who supported him. Mr Moffett's head has failed, though his heart is true to me; indeed I am much distressed by his present state, for his son is not like him and I get unpleasant letters from the tenants. The Protestants are not pleased at my supporting Lord F[orbes] and therefore ought to have one member true to *them*; and they look to us for that, and I don't wish to shrink from the expense. How far expense without active friends can promote success I know not, but have my fears, though I don't express them to others.'

95 Sep. 1818

Copy of a letter from Rosse to the Dowager Lady Rosse in reply.

'I felt the same curiosity that you expressed to know who Lord F[orbes] meant. I have suspected that Mr Fox might have been the person, but he said nothing to that effect. How he is inclined on the Catholic subject I do not know; for though I was very well acquainted with him formerly, he having been in my class in college, I have not often met him since. Neither do I know, if he were put in, whether he would be willing afterwards, according to your kind intentions, to make way for John. I should think the safest way, in any interview with Lord Forbes, would be to express your willingness to hear his sentiments fully, and to listen to everything he has to suggest, and after he had done, to tell him that you would consider attentively what he recommended; and you could then take your own time for acting according to his suggestions or not, as on reflection you might deem best. Fox represented Shuldham as a vain, silly, empty man – fond of making speeches and speaking much nonsense. If you think that my going to Newcastle at any time would be a means of keeping up your interest in the county, I should do so with great pleasure. It would make no difference to me whether I spent a little time there or here, and it might in some degree help to keep up that

D/7/95 *contd.*   personal interest which you apprehend is declining. But I only
suggest this. You are a much better judge of the matter than I can
be. In short, anything I can do to assist in securing the county and
preventing contests and expense there, I should be very ungrateful
if I did not feel compelled to do by every possible consideration.'

96   22 Sep. 1818   The Dowager Lady Rosse, Stretton Hall, to Rosse.
'I cannot form a guess who Lord Forbes meant but no doubt it
must be someone of his own sentiments in politics, etc. Mr Fox is of
the same, like his uncle Edgeworth, and besides would never retire if
once he succeeded nor feel himself bound by any engagements to
me. Indeed there is great hazard in trusting to honour in such
matters. But to you I will acknowledge [that] my view is to preserve
the county in the family; and as your son John is by my will next in
remainder after Laurence King to the estate, it appears to me proper
that he should represent the county till Laurence is of age. This I am
the more anxious for, as I trust he would support the Protestant
cause as you did so ably at the time the elective franchise was so
foolishly granted, that now causes so much trouble and is so very
injurious to the peace and prosperity of poor Ireland.'

97   30 Sep. 1818   Copy of a letter from Rosse to the Dowager Lady Rosse.
'Until I received your last letter I was certainly in a great error as
to the disposition you intend to make of your estates. And as the
last injunction my late dear uncle laid on me was always in my
communications with you to be open and candid, I will state to
you exactly and without any reserve, how I feel the circumstance.
From what he said to me, and from what you said to me at
Nerot's Hotel, and also from what you mentioned to me at
different times since at Stretton Hall, that the money was for the
Lortons and the estate for me, I had not the slightest notion that
you would ever have changed your determination. I have been
eleven years in that persuasion, without the least apprehension to
the contrary. Though I have during all that interval lived with
great prudence, yet I have kept up my interest here at somewhat a
greater expense than I should have done under my present
impression. I consequently have not diminished the encumbrances
on my estate here as expeditiously as I had hoped. But I felt the
less uneasy about that, expecting a day would come, when my
family would have such a property as would make these
encumbrances light and at the same time enable them to support
their rank in life. I am now past sixty, and I cannot rationally look
forward to many years for the improvement of my affairs. Though
I have reduced the encumbrances on my estate, I must still add
again to make a provision for four younger children. And though I
mean to make this provision most moderate, for which I shall be
obliged immediately to make a new will, yet the whole of the
encumbrances that will be on my estate then, together with the

jointure, would leave it more heavily charged at my death even than it was at my father's death; while there would be a high rank to support, which I had not.

You may probably have thought that, by prudent management, my affairs were now in a better situation. But I got my estate with encumbrances heavy beyond all proportion to its extent. In addition to these I have had most expensive lawsuits, which consumed much of what I should have otherwise applied to reduce those debts. The suit with Stirling alone has been reported by the Commissioners on Fees in Courts of Law as the most expensive that had ever occurred in our Chancery. This was a business that burst upon me like a mine. I had heard nothing of it for fourteen years after my father's death, and until nine years ago I thought I should have nothing to pay on account of it. It originated in debts of my grandfather before I was born. The suit was unavoidable. I offered to pay £12,000 to compromise it, but the litigious attorney who is a party, refused. I afterwards paid by order of the Chancellor £4,000 on account of it, while I lived at Fulham, exclusive of the law expenses. It will be finally decided soon, when I suppose I shall have still to pay at least £12,000 more. But the money I have saved and placed in the funds for the purposes would nearly meet that sum. Thus will the savings of many years be all swept away by a single suit, and the old encumbrances will still exist.

During the last four years I have lived entirely here to avoid expense of journey, etc, but the tenants made so little during the time, of their lands, and my estate being in general let for about the value, they paid so badly, that together with the expenses of a threatened contest, I could save but little. I however paid last Christmas about £1,800 to Mr Deverell, being the residue then remaining due of that charge on my property. And I also paid while I have been here some other debts. These payments are slight compared with the great encumbrances remaining. I know your kindness would not allow any of these facts to transpire, for if I was not thought to be much richer than I am, I should be overborne in the county. By paying ready money for everything, and always taking care to have a little command of it, I get what I want on moderate terms and preserve the reputation of wealth. Paying also most punctully the interest of the debts, I am not put to any trouble or expense about them. My children are all most modest in their desires. They have no hounds or hunters or anything else that is expected. I endeavour to make a good appearance when anyone is with me; and when we are alone, which is generally the case, we are frugal in everything.

Notwithstanding what you said to me respecting your intentions, I have really never looked to the possibility of my possessing your estates. I had in truth no selfish wish about them, except as far as

D/7/97 *contd.*

self is concerned in the future comfort of my children. I never was
so unkind or so unwise as to calculate on my succeeding you in
becoming the proprietor of them. Indeed I hold all these
speculations and castle buildings on the property of another very
culpable, because they at last lead to coveting another person's
goods. Besides we are both about the same age. Still, I will frankly
own to you, that your letter was a great blow to me; reflecting on
the very inadequate income I must now leave to all my family, in
proportion to their rank in life. I really thought, from what you
said, that my family was as sure of those estates as if you had made
over to me the reversion of them by a deed. From the time that you
desired me to get a lawyer to draw your will in London, which you
were then so impatient to execute, lest the property by any delay
should go contrary to my uncle's intention, from that time I never
anticipated any occurrence which could change your intention, nor
had I ever an intimation of it, till I received your last letter. Had I
such a property as would enable me to leave my children as persons
in their sphere usually are, I should feel but little about it. But as
that is not the case, I certainly feel the disappointment acutely, and
it would be uncandid in me and dissembling from you that which I
think I ought not, if I concealed it. When you recollect therefore
eveything that has passed, I trust you will not deem my present
disappointment unreasonable, nor my reminding you of the
circumstances, which I wish most sincerely to do with great regard
and affection to yourself. ...

P.S. I am sure that John, who is most amenable in everything,
should you return him for the county of Longford, will act in
every respect according to your wishes.'

99   Received 15   The Dowager Lady Rosse to Rosse.
              Nov. 1818   'Your letter of the 30th of September gave me great concern as
                                 it showed me how greatly you had mistaken my intentions, for I
                                 have always been particularly guarded. When at Nerot's Hotel, I
                                 did wish to know more of your affairs and was near asking some
                                 questions, but instantly checked myself and resolved rather to
                                 remain ignorant than raise expectations. You too were quite
                                 reserved and, as I thought, far from friendly to me in regard to
                                 some letters. But as I thought my own death was then near at
                                 hand I certainly wished to make a will without delay, as I was
                                 greatly displeased with my daughter's behaviour to her father when
                                 he was last in Ireland and ill there. She never made the least
                                 enquiry after him and as soon as I discovered it I wrote her a very
                                 sharp letter on the subject, in answer to which she proposed
                                 coming over if he would receive her. I let him know it but he had
                                 not consented. I know not what he might hve said to you, but I
                                 can assure you in the most solemn manner he never said one word
                                 to me of his wishes or intentions towards you. I wish he had, for

then I might have the satisfaction of acting according to his wishes, which I have often regretted his not telling me; but I believe he had not come to any decision, or he would not have left me in the dark. The coolness which had subsisted between you at one time might have made him slow in deciding, yet I cannot think he would ever have overlooked a younger grandson. The eldest certainly will have enough, and could not leave that beautiful place [Rockingham] to reside at Newcastle; therefore I think myself justifiable in giving it to the younger.

The attorney I employed to make my first will was recommended to me by Mr Bainbridge and he took the opinions of lawyers on it, but I did not know you were acquainted with any of them. It was a hurried and ill-considered will which I determined to set aside if I lived to make a better; and my whole thoughts were lost upon the subject and nearly arranged when I met the accident that nearly occasioned my death, for the doctors gave me up the fourth day. However it pleased God to spare my life and I was raised up the fifth day so as to wish for Mr [Morgan] Crofton to come over with all speed to meet the attorney from London here, and my will was made according to the instructions given before the accident. I have however made others since, as time gave me opportunities of judging better, and I hope and believe I have acted justly. That you should have fallen into the mistake you mention hs given me much pain, and I am sure I never said anything in the different visits after my illness to deceive you. The last time I even said, when talking of John, that he would have five thousand, and I then thought you looked rather disappointed, and as if it had cleared off some mistake.

Every good father must feel as you do for your children – I cannot and do not take it ill – though I must truly regret the mistake continuing so long. I am now old and infirm though my memory and understanding are as good as ever, yet I have for some time resolved to make no more wills. Your second son is next in remainder to my own grandson and your third after him. I supposed your fortune sufficient for your eldest and I preferred your family to a nephew I greatly love and think amiable. John will have six thousand; Laurence three thousand; Lady Jane five. I think it right to mention these things as you talk of making another will.

A letter from Mr Crofton tells me Lord Forbes has been with him and the person he wishes me to support is Mr Fox (as I suspected). The Granard family would then have both members, though he says it would keep the county for us, as Mr Fox's eldest is a clergiman [*sic*].

If you wish John to stand he should have my support in every way, if living; but if you do not I shall probably take no part in the business. The plan was for Mr Fox to be called my M.P. and to pay his expenses and perhaps Lord F. would be so honourable as to let

D/7/99 *contd.*   him vote for the Protestant cause; but I don't expect Mr Fox would
                          do so for me – it would be contrary to his principles. I sent Lord F.
                          a civil answer and that I would consider the affair. In the
                          meantime [I] hope there will be no vacancy as Sir Thomas is in
                          better health than at the election. ... Our friend Mr Moffett is no
                          longer able to attend to the business and things go on badly, the
                          tenants desiring the abatements I made in bad times shall be made
                          permanent, or won't register. ...'

100   15 Nov. 1818   Draft of a letter from Rosse, Dublin, to the Dowager Lady Rosse.
                          He begins by assuring her that he does not believe she had any
                          intention to deceive him.
                              '... Certainly so long ago as when my uncle had me named in
                          remainder to his title, I and most people conceived that he had
                          further intentions towards me. Your most respected father at that
                          time told me "it indicated a great deal more". Thus early was the
                          expectation raised in me and in proportion to its duration, must
                          have been my disappointment. At the time Mr Deverell's* son was
                          born, which was I believe two years before my uncle's death, he
                          communicated to me when we were in London more explicitly
                          than he had done before, for he then feared that the birth of that
                          child would cause a suit about the property on his death. The year
                          following, when we were together at Nerot's Hotel, which was the
                          year before his death, he spoke to me quite freely about his affairs
                          and his intentions towards me and the property which I would
                          one day have. ... [The following nine lines are deleted and are of
                          no particular importance. The letter picks up again:]
                              Many expressions of your own to me must have faded in your
                          mind, but which confirmed me in the same expectation. At the
                          first interview after his death you pointed to your writing box,
                          which was on the table, and you said his will was in it. You gave
                          me the key to open it. You said that it had been made several years
                          before when there was a coolness between me and my uncle; that
                          if he had made one latterly it would have been in my favour; and
                          that whatever he intended you would do. The distress you were
                          then in may have obliterated these expressions from your mind,
                          but they were too important to me not to often and continually
                          recollect them. You afterwards desired me to get a lawyer to draw
                          your will immediately and I mentioned to you that perhaps the
                          best way would be for you to write a note to the Attorney General.
                          You objected to that and then I suggested your sending to your
                          banker to recommend a proper person, and you then made the
                          will in my favour when your recollection was most fresh of my
                          uncle's intentions. After I came to Ireland you sent me my uncle's
                          seal with the Harman arms, which I have used occasionally since.
                              Surely then, my dear Lady Rosse, you will not deem me
                          unreasonable in the expectations I had formed. If anything, however,

*   R.B. Deverell was the husband of Anne Harman, only child of the 1st Earl of Rosse's elder brother.

D/7/100 *contd.*

could make the expectations still more strong, it was what you mentioned to me one morning at Nerot's. You began by saying you were not superstitious, and then you told me of a very awful occurrence which I need not repeat, and the object of which you said was a call upon you to do justice to me. These really were your own words at that time. To remind you of them now is I think a duty which I owe both to you as well as to my own family. I know you will always do whatever you think right, and whatever that may be, you will find me in affection and regard unalterably attached to you. You have given too many proofs of your kind disposition to me and my family, even if we did differ upon any point, for me not always to feel the greatest gratitude towards you and the most anxious wish to act in whatever way I thought would be most agreeable to you. ...

Anything about the county of Longford that I can do I shall always feel a sincere pleasure in doing when at any time you let me know your wishes, and which I hope you will do freely. Your tenants are unreasonable in requiring the old abatements to be continued, for there never was a time more favourable for the farmers than the present, everything that the land produces bearing an extraordinary high price. Mr Crofton is not in town today, but is expected tomorrow. I will then try to see him and talk over the county of Longford politics with him, for the interests there must be much changed since I was there; and I will suggest anything that occurs to me for strengthening yours. It would be very gratifying to me that my son John should be your member for that county.

Do, my dear Lady Rosse, always write freely and openly to me, as I shall always do to you, for be assured you have no friend who can be more strongly attached to you than I am, and if any expression of mine should ever be disapproved by you, ascribe it to anything rather than an intention on my part to say anything that I could think would be unpleasing to you.'

101 24 Feb. 1819 The Dowager Lady Rosse, Stretton Hall, to Rosse.

'I am still undecided as to whom I shall support for the county of Longford. Mr White and his sons were here when I was very ill about Xmas time so I did not see him. I hear the most popular man in that county is John Fetherston, and who I am told would be supported by all parties except Lord Newcomen. I don't wish to fight the battle against Mr White but I know the Fetherstons could not do it themselves, and if it can be done at no greater expense than the bringing in of Sir Thomas I would not grudge it. There was a report of the nabob, Mr Blackall, who purchased the Nugent [?estate], and he is a loyal man and could fight for himself. Sir Thomas Fetherston is rather better in health but not able to attend parliament as yet and his life is a very precarious one. His eldest son George [is] a good young man but shy and not popular; his uncle John is very much so, and many wish me to support him. My poor friend Moffett died of the 20th stroke [*sic*]; I have hardly courage to attempt a contest

D/7/101 *contd.*   without such an active friend, and sincerely hope there will be no
                           vacancy for Mr White to set us all at variance.'

102   9 July 1819   The Dowager Lady Rosse, Stretton Hall, to Rosse.
                           'I have decided to give Sir George Fetherston the same support
                           as I gave his father and have informed Lord Forbes, who wrote
                           anxiously to know and offering every support in his power and
                           even to go to Ireland if I thought he could be of use. I answered
                           that I thought much might be done at this side [of] the water with
                           the absentees, perhap Grattan and others. He tells me in a letter
                           just received that the Longford estate is not Lord Nugent's but the
                           Marquess's [of Buckingham] and that he will do all he can, for I
                           named it to him. He requested his former letter should be
                           considered confidential; so don't mention his offer to go over for
                           he dreads the word coalition and I would be sorry to vex him as he
                           appears hitherto sincere. In the letter just received from him he
                           says he has just got one from his father in France desiring him to
                           assure me of his warmest support.
                               Sir George has met so much encouragement that I hope there will
                           be no contest. Lord Longford, Joseph O'Farrell, Mr Tuite and others
                           promise him, and Major Blackall. I have received from London a
                           letter from the heir to Sir James Hutchinson enclosing a letter to his
                           tenants desiring him to go with me as in his uncle's time. This I
                           suppose should be sent to Mr Crofton. Therefore I will trouble you
                           to free the enclosed to him, as I don't like to send a double letter.'

103   13 July 1819   The Dowager Lady Rosse, Stretton Hall, to Rosse.
                           'Some time ago Mr M[organ] Crofton mentioned your lawsuit
                           not going as you wished and occasioning very great expense, as
                           you told me some time before, and it occurred to me that the
                           £6,000 I intended *adding* to the legacies I mentioned to you,
                           would be more useful were you to receive it in my lifetime. I
                           therefore told Mr Crofton to get Latouche to advance me as a loan
                           whatever may be necessary to make up that sum with what is in
                           their hands and to hold it ready for you whenever you wish for it.
                           So you have only to write a line to Mr Crofton and he will pay it
                           whenever you desire him.'

104   19 July 1819   Draft of a letter from Rosse to the Dowager Lady Rosse thanking
                           her for /103 and adding with reference to his children:
                           '... They get up by their own desire before 5 every morning,
                           and except during breakfast do not quit their studies till one, when
                           they go out and exercise till dinner and they renew their studies in
                           the evening. ...'

105   14 Sep. 1819   Rosse, Parsonstown, to the Dowager Lady Rosse announcing that
                           Mr White has decided to stand for Longford and has engaged
                           agents for that purpose.
                           '... I can send, if you choose, one agent who will act without any
                           expense or reward, and who is a very clever man, the same who

D/7/105 *contd.*

receives my rent. He was sent for to the Queen's County by Mr
Pole when Mr Malone declined and he was employed there as one
of the principal agents during the whole of that contest; and
afterwards Mr Prettie [*sic*] sent for him to attend the Tipperary
election, which he did and where there was a great contest also.
Therefore as he has had so much and so recent experience, I think
he might be very useful to Sir George Featherston. ... The last time
I went to the county of Longford was in November 1806 to meet
my uncle. We then thought there would have been a contest and
every preparation was made; but a very few days before the
election, Mr Newcomen declined. ...'

107   22 Sep. 1819   The Dowager Lady Rosse, Stretton Hall, to Rosse.

'I return you many thanks for your kind letter of the 15th. It is
true that Mr White will contest the county and I don't feel quite as
secure as my friends, as to the result; but I feel no uneasiness, let it
go as it may. I think I am doing my duty in bearing the expense
and that is all I am anxious about – to do that properly. I am
rather at a loss what I should give M[organ] Crofton, who acts
both as friend and lawyer; perhaps you can give me some
information on this subject and I shall take it as a kindness. He has
fixed on a clever person to act as chief agent and there are many
others retaining by the Fetherstons. The one he recommends is to
have 100 guineas so that I shall not need to get the one you
mention, though I feel truly obliged to you for thinking of it, as
well as for your kind offer of going to Newcastle, which now you
are a peer might not be so proper as formerly, and for the reasons
you mentioned.

The contest will I fancy be a sharp one as Mr White will stop at
nothing to raise his family in the world, and I believe there is an
understanding between him and Mr Fox; but the Protestants are
all hearty for Sir George and many of the others profess much
goodwill. ...'

108   20 Oct. 1819   The Dowager Lady Rosse, Stretton Hall, to Rosse.

'You have heard before this of the termination of the contest in
Longford; it was as severe and expensive as Mr White could make
it, yet of upwards of two thousand freeholders he could obtain but
370 votes, so I hope he will let the county rest in peace for the
future. ... I think you will not disapprove of the part I took. I
believe it was the right one. In some cases one should not shrink
from expense and it was better that I who have no younger
children should fight the battle than those who come after, who
may have many. ... I understand Lord Forbes acted in the most
honourable and friendly manner all through the affair. ...'

109   17 Dec. 1819   The Dowager Lady Rosse, Stretton Hall, to Rosse.

'I wrote yesterday to M[organ] Crofton rather inclining to give
the agency to Mr Robinson if he has not already too many

D/7/109 *contd.*   agencies and mentioning my fears that Rev. James Moffett is too
old for it. Now it has just occurred to me that his brother, Colonel
Moffett, lives near you and is I believe a worthy man and having
made a fortune in India would be good security. Now if he wished
to undertake it and is calculated for such a business (of which I am
perfectly ignorant), he might perhaps serve the poor brother by
dividing the salary with him and let[ting] him recover the small
rents for him.'

110   2 Feb. 1820   The Dowager Lady Rosse, Stretton Hall, to Rosse. She has just
discovered that Colonel Moffett is still in the army and has
therefore decided to offer the agency to Mr Robinson as
mentioned in /109.
  '... One more unfit than the last unfortunate man could not be
found. He has left an arrear of £10,000 on the estate while I am
paying Latouche interest for the election money, and even in the
election he did not follow Mr Crofton's orders, but took more
houses than there was any occasion for and employed street agents,
and in short did everything to create expense, by which it is made
on the whole between seven and eight thousand pounds.'

112   17 Mar. 1820   The Dowager Lady Rosse, Stretton Hall, to Rosse.
  '... Sir George [Fetherston] was determined to act upon the hints
you dropped to him in London and having acquired experience,
he saw the folly of many things done last year.
  He is a much better landlord than his father and grown more
popular in the county than at first. Mr White has acted very wisely
and by resigning in Co. Longford secures himself in Leitrim, I
believe without a contest, as Sir Hugh Crofton's great interest that
was against him last time will now go with him and Clements.'

116   26 Dec. 1823   Draft of a letter from Rosse to the Dowager Lady Rosse reporting
that he has lost his salary as [Joint] Postmaster [General] and that
he is also suffering from a reduction in his rents. He therefore
wonders whether Lady Rosse would care to pay off some of his
encumbrances as she once offered to do.

117   1 Jan. 1824   The Dowager Lady Rosse, Stretton Hall, to Rosse expressing
willingness to assist him, but not stating how she will do this.

119   27 Na. 1824   The Dowager Lady Rosse, Stretton Hall, to Rosse stating that she
will call in debts and rents in order to have a good sum ready at
the time when Rosse's lawsuit comes to a conclusion.

120   29 Oct. 1824   The Dowager Lady Rosse, Stretton Hall, to Rosse.
  'I write in haste having just heard from Mr Crofton that your
lawsuit is soon to be settled. I regret that I cannot give so much
assistance in it as I wished, but if you will have the goodness to
send the enclosed to Mr Crofton he will get £2,000 ready against
your want [of] it. ...'

D/7/121 22 Aug. 1825   The Dowager Lady Rosse, Stretton Hall, to Rosse.
'I rejoice to find your lawsuit is at an end and have given Mr Crofton directions in the enclosed [not found] to pay £2,500 towards the arrangement.'

122   14 July 1826   The Dowager Lady Rosse, Stretton Hall, to Rosse.
'... I sincerely rejoice that there were so few contested elections there [in Ireland] this time. Mr Tuite has much to answer for in disturbing the County Westmeath and occasioning [?murder]. ...'

123   2 Nov. 1826   The Dowager Lady Rosse, Stretton Hall, to Rosse.. She is concerned to find that Rosse is financially embarrassed once again and promises to send him £1,000 with another £500 after Christmas.

124   24 Jan. 1828   The Dowager Lady Rosse, Stretton Hall, to Rosse. She advances him a further £500 to relieve his embarrassments.

134   [postpark 21 July 1832]   The Dowager Lady Rosse, Stretton Hall, to Rosse asking if he knows where the copy of her husband's will was placed.

136   13 Nov. 1832   The Dowager Lady Rosse, Stretton Hall, to Rosse. She requests that he will not be induced by James King and others to go to law with her son-in-law, Lord Lorton.

137   17 Nov. 1832   Copy of a letter from Rosse to the Dowager Lady Rosse. He states that he is aware of the lawsuit pending between James King and his father, on the one side, and Lord Lorton on the other, and assures her that he will take no part in it.

139   25 May [1837]   The Dowager Lady Rosse to Rosse.
'Having nothing entertaining to say I made no answer to yours of 3 March. Now I have to tell [you] that my grandson, your namesake, was married to a Miss Johnson [sic – Johnstone] at Genoa and will reside at Newcastle in future; but the house is not quite ready for him, Bussey and his drunken family having put it into great disorder.
I was glad to hear of Lady Elizabeth Parsons['s] safety, and hope Lady Oxmantown will soon bring a still more welcome grandson.
There is a debt due on Newcastle that I wish to pay off, and would wish to get £10,000 on a mortgage on *Mosstown*, if you know anyone that has such a sum to lend. The title is perfectly clear and safe; but, having willed it to another, I am desirous to load it.
My best wishes attend you and all your family, being with truth, affectionately, dear Lord Rosse ...'.

140   [1838]   'Abstract of the will and codicils of the late Jane, Countess Dowager of Rosse, so far as they relate to the Earl of Rosse and his family.'
Lord Rosse and his family are left a contingent interest in the Newcastle and Mosstown estates, should the cadet line of Lord

D/7/140 *contd.*   Lorton's family run out of issue male; in particular, Lord Rosse and
his family are preferred to anyone in possession of Lord Lorton's
estate. The immediate bequest to Lord Rosse's family is £6,000 to
each of the four children of the 2nd Earl. However, a codicil of
1837 cancels the £6,000 as far as Lord Oxmantown is concerned,
'... as he has now no occasion for it', [having married the Field
heiress].

142   [1842]   Remarks on Lord Lorton's estate bill, as it affects the contingent
interest of Lord Rosse's family in the estates.

'... The only suppositions that I can make under which the late
Lord Rosse's family could be entitled to inherit, would be either of
the following:

First, that Dean Harman by his will leaving the estate to his
sister's second son (the 1st Earl of Rosse) expressly entailed them
on his male issue, and in default of male issue on the issue of the
oldest son (Wentworth], and in default of male issue by him, then
on the issue male of Sir William Parsons ... .

Secondly, that on the creation of the title of Oxmantown in
1792, fresh settlement of the estates took the place by which they
had been made to follow the limitations of the title.

In either of these cases, the 1st Lord Rosse would only have been
tenant-for-life, and then would have had no right to devise the
estates to his Countess.

The only enquiries which I can suggest as likely to lead to any
discovery of any supposed settlement or other limitations in the
favour of the late Lord Rosse's family would be:

First, to examine the records of the suit in which Mrs Deverell
recovered the entailed estate [see E/42] now enjoyed by her
husband's widow, in which most likely the wills and family
settlements would be set out.

Secondly, a search of the proper registries in Ireland for the will
of Dean Harman and for any settlement made on the marriage of
his sister or at any subsequent period.

It is to be observed, however, that the rights of the late Lord
Rosse, should they have existed, would have accrued on the death
of the 1st Earl (1807), since which a period of 35 years has
elapsed; and if he were then entitled absolutely, there has been an
adverse possession in the late Countess of Rosse sufficient to bar
any claim by his family. ...'

D/10	DATE	DESCRIPTION

10/
1–14
May-June 1805
Nov. 1806
Letters from Parsons to Lady Parsons, with one of November 1806 from her to him, containing many reference to political and parliamentary matters at Westminster.

The sub-section includes:

1   30 May 1805   Parsons, Red Lion Inn, Wolverhampton, to Lady Parsons.

'My dearest life, I wrote to you from the packet just as we came into the bay at Hollyhead [*sic*], and put the letter myself into the post office. I trust therefore that you received it regularly. I wrote to you again this morning from Llangollen but finding afterwards that there is no direct post from thence to Ireland, I took the letter with me to Shrewsbury, and gave it to the waiter there to put into the office. Lest however he should not do so, I write now, and will put this into the office in the morning at Bermingham [*sic*], where I propose to breakfast.

I long to hear from you and to learn what you intend to do, though I feel very confident you will go to Gloster. I hope you, or someone from thence, will write to me continually, as the principal gratification I can have while you and our little ones are absent, is hearing that you are well. For myself, I should feel less dreary on any other road than this; for here, where we have travelled so often together, every inn, room waiter, etc, reminds me that you are absent; every hill that we have walked up together; every object that we have remarked and conversed upon. This you will say is the quintessence of dreariness. It is however the simple truth.

I hope if any symptom of illness, however slight, should appear at any time, in either of the little boys, you will immediately ask medical advice. For though they have been hitherto so healthy that I have little apprehension on this account, yet disorder makes such a rapid way, whenever it begins, in such little bodies, that often a momentary omission can never be repaired. I mention this more particularly as you have not any person, conversant in children, attending them at present; but I hope you will find Dolly, when you go to the country, able to resume her functions.

I met the little Doctor yesterday, near the slate-quarry, going to Ireland to negotiate with me about Syngefield, and much disappointed, when he saw me moving in the opposite direction. He wished to have remained a little longer at Magdalen, and to have brought Sir Edward home with him. And this afternoon I overtook Geo. Synge, etc, creeping along near Lord Berwick's in their old voiture drawn by their old garrawns. I stopped and spoke with them.

As I do not find by the papers that any business of consequence will come on in the House tomorrow, I will go to bed here, and take my rest as usual, instead of pursuing my journey by starlight.

D/10/1 *contd.*

It it was of any use I could however easily have proceeded so as to be in London in time tomorrow. Now I do not propose to be there until the day after.

There are 1800 volunteers now on permanent duty from Shrewsbury, and have been there these three weeks; and, in the opinion of the waiter, they are pretty well disciplined. The rooms we used to sit in, were all thrown into one, for the officers' mess.

Mrs Knowles asked very particularly for you. She looked very pale. In short I am as much at home on this road, and all the innkeepers and waiters salute me as familiarly by name, as between Birr and Edenderry.

I do not recollect anything more to mention to you, and it is time I should go to bed, having now sat up sufficiently after eating my chicken and asparagus and a gooseberry tart, besides a luncheon of cold veal, etc, which I took at Shrewsbury. But the exercise of this fast travelling requires support.'

3   1 June 1805   Parsons, Nerot's Hotel, London, to Lady Parsons.

'As the House did not sit, I was at a loss where to go and get a dinner; for at this hotel there is not at present any room unoccupied except one bed chamber in the garret, where I am now writing; and as I had assurances of better accommodation in a day or two, I did not think it worthwhile to seek an apartment elsewhere. So I wandered at length to the British Coffee House; but there I was told that no dinner was prepared unless bespoke. I then crossed over to the [?Canon] and dined very uncomfortably, feeling all the time as if I was out of my place, and hoping that no person was there or would drop in who might know me. So I eat [*sic*] my dinner as fast as I could and passed back again to the British, where I read newspapers and drank tea. This latter is a sufficiently creditable place, where I did not care who might see me. And now I have returned here to my garret to give you an account of myself which having done I will go read the life of Chaucer and leave the rest of the paper for occurrences between this and Monday's post.

The letter is then resumed on Monday morning as follows:

Yesterday I dined at Mr Foster's; no one there besides, but Mr Brook[e], the adventurer of Prosperous. Today I have moved into the appartment here which we occupied last winter, so I can take my dinner at home, for which I am very glad. I have just been paying a visit to the Mahons; Lady Anne is confined to her room by a sore throat, but it is not very bad. I also called on the Kenmares, who very civilly asked me to dine with them next Sunday, but I have been previously engaged to Lord Castlereagh. I am however to go to her party that evening. I have no apprehension of being detained here many days. It is supposed that Mr Pitt will resist the impeachment of Lord Melville, and

D/10/3 *contd.*

thus stop all further proceedings at the very threshold. Expresses have been sent after such of his Irish friends as have left town, and every effort is making to have a decisive majority on the day of trial which will be tomorrow sennight. After that we all expect to depart. The King stays here for the event. I suppose the debate will last two days and that I shall set out the day after, which will be Thursday the 13th.'

4	4 June 1805	Parsons, Nerot's Hotel, to Lady Parsons.

'Again I repeat it, you need not be afraid of my being detained here. It is with difficulty that Mr Pitt keeps many of his friends in town even for Mr Whitbread's motion. He will therefore put an expeditious termination to the business, as he could not keep them longer. If he was inclined to agree to the impeachment, then indeed a tedious process might follow; but as he is detemined to resist, the failure of Mr Whitbread's motion puts an end at once to the business. I wrote to you so fully yesterday on my daily occurrences that I have little to add today. I took my veal cutlet solitarily in our old drawing room here; then took a walk in St James's Park; returned and read Chaucer for a while and went to bed. Lord Dunall[e]y, etc, are in this hotel. Mr and Lady C. Latouche, Colonel Veriker [*sic*]. But I have not seen any of them but Latouche. Lord Dunall[e]y visited me yesterday as did Lord Charleville. ... Having taken a walk, just as I was returning to the hotel I met Lord Castlereagh walking from Court to his house at the end of this street, so I walked with him, and collected from him that the opinion of the Cabinet is that Lord Melville has already been punished sufficiently by parliament for his misconduct; [and] that, as nothing to make his misconduct any greater has appeared against him since the former votes of the House of Commons, that [*sic*] there is no reason for any greater punishment now than what has been already inflicted. Consequently they will oppose the impeachment; and the one vote ends the business.

Adieu, my ever dear and amiable wife. I am just going to order a mutton chop, and make another solitary dinner.

P.S. Lord Castlereagh's present house is very large and his principal rooms look in[to] St James's Square.'

5	6 June 1805	Parsons, London, to Lady Parsons.

'Bernard remains to return with me, and as impatient as possible to set out. I dined with him at his lodgings yesterday. We had only a company of six, but a most excellent and expensive dinner. Young O'Moore was one of the party. It is not true that Miss H. came to London; she went to Cork.'

D/10/6 7 June 1805   Parsons, Nerot's Hotel, to Lady Parsons.
                              'I dined yesterdy at the St Albans Tavern with D. Browne, Lords
                         De Blaquiere and Kirkwall and some others. Today I am to dine
                         with Browne in the House of Commons Coffee House. Tomorrow
                         I dine with the Nevilles [*sic* – Nevills], and next day with Lord
                         Castlereagh. So I am endeavouring to kill time until my time
                         becomes pleasure to me again by being with your.
                              If you wish for a little Court scandal, know then that Big Bess,
                         the chambermaid at Kew, has produced a fine boy.'

7   8 June 1805   Parsons, Nerot's Hotel, to Lady Parsons. He speculates that the
                         debates in the House of Commons on Lord Melville's business will
                         be over on Friday morning, and continues: '... my cage door will
                         then be thrown open, and I will not delay a moment taking
                         advantage of it. Bernard and I propose to have a carriage ready at
                         his lodging, which is near the House of Commons, and set out the
                         instant the debate is over.
                              I dined yesterday again with Bernard, as did Browne, Dawson,
                         Sir J. Stewart, and he is very hospitable. We returned to the House
                         in the evening and sat there until three o'clock on the Duke of
                         Atholl's business. Today I dine with the Nevilles and am to be at a
                         small musical party afterwards at Mrs G. Knox's. She was at the
                         Birthday, and fainted, and has not been perfectly well since.'

8   10 June 1805   Parsons, London, to Lady Parsons.
                              'I dined on Saturday with the Nevilles, and happened to sit
                         by Mr Canning with whom I had a good deal of conversation.
                         He continues to be the prime favourite and councillor of Mr
                         Pitt; on my other side was Miss Neville who was lively and
                         conversible. ... I went in the evening to Mrs G. Knox's where
                         Dean Allott and his two daughters and son sang divinely. But of
                         poor Mrs Knox I heard a most ludicrous account last night from [?
                         fatty] Malone and Lady Sunderlin who I met at Lady Kenmare's.
                         They told me that when she fainted at the Drawing Room her wig
                         fell off, for she had cut her hair quite short, it being red, and had
                         adopted tresses of a more agreeable colour. As with the best
                         advantages of dress her face is not very agreeable, what must have
                         been her appearance when when she was thus dismantled! I hope
                         she is ignorant of the accident. Yesterday I dined at Lord
                         Castlereagh's – our party was principally Irish – Lord De
                         Blaquiere, Foster, with Colonel Lascelles and Hawkins Browne.
                         I scarcely saw anyone in the evening that I knew at Lady
                         Kenmare's but the Sunderlins and Charlevilles. The party looked
                         just as usual. French and Irish, and a few of the English nobility –
                         and the noise as usual extravagant.'

9   11 June 1805   Parsons, House of Commons, to Lady Parsons.
                              'My dearest life, the House is now fuller than I ever saw it. The
                         Prince of Wales and most of the Princes of the Blood and principal

D/10/9 *contd.*

peers under the gallery to witness this extraordinary day. Lord Melville is to begin – then Mr Whitbread and then it is supposed Mr Pitt. The debate will continue till a late hour this night and then be resumed again tomorrow, so that we shall not divide till tomorrow night. It is uncertain how it will be decided. I snatched this moment to let you know what we are doing and to tell you while the multitude in the House are thinking with earnestness on the policital scene before them, my thoughts and all the emotions of my heart are buried about my treasury in Merrion Square.'

11   13 June 1805   Parsons, London, to Lady Parsons.
'I was in the House of Commons until six this morning. There was a majority of nine against Lord Melville; so he is to stand his trial in the Court of King's Bench. Tomorrow Mr Whitbread will move his resolutions against Mr Pitt, but these will be opposed by a large majority. Some think the resolutions against Mr Pitt may cause two days debate, but it is not likely. He appeared much chagrined this morning at his defeat, which might have been prevented by a little exertion among the Irish members; but Mr Vansittart, the Secretary, voted against him – a thing unexampled in political annals. It is not therefore surprising that he should not have attended to the Irish members. Tomorrow, however, all Aldington's party will support the Minister. Mr Foster's distillery bill was thrown out of the House of Lords yesterday by Lord Hawkesbury without his assigning a reason for doing so. These are strange doings. I have not seen Foster since, but I suppose he is much exasperated. It was by the desire of Lord Hardwicke and Lord Redesdale that this was done; so is the rumour. So much for political news. Ross Mahon is soon to be married to an English lady and £10,000. I have not heard her name. This is a secret.'

12   14 June 1805   Parsons, Nerot's Hotel, to Lady Parsons.
'It is uncertain whether our Secretary [Vansittart] will continue to hold his office. I am sure that it must be the wish as well as the interest of Mr Pitt to remove him after his conduct on the last divison: otherwise I might endeavour to settle the business with him. But since Sunday last, when the Addingtons decided to take the part they did, Vansittart has abstained from all Irish business. This however you may be assured of, that neither public nor private business shall keep me at the utmost above three or four days longer.'

13   17 June 1805   Parsons, Nerot's Hotel, to Lady Parsons.
'... Since I wrote the above I have settled with Bernard to set out as soon as Thursday's debate is over from his lodgings which are just near the House of Commons. Our servants are to set out by the stage coach the day before. He is to send in the morning tomorrow to take places for them. I will not let my intention be

D/10/13 *contd.*

known, lest there might be an application to remain here a little longer. My mind is quite light and cheerful at the prospect of being so soon with you.'

D/13	DATE	DESCRIPTION
13/ 1–53	1809: 1812: 1819–19: 1821: 1823: 1825: 1827–8: 1830	Letters to the 2nd Earl from Morgan Crofton, law agent for the Harman estate in Co. Longford, about the 1st Earl's former house in Stephen's Green, Longford politics and elections, promotion in the navy for Crofton's son (with letters from the 2nd Viscount Melville, First Lord of the Admiralty, to the 2nd Earl on that subject), and estate and financial business. The sub-section includes:
9	27 Sep. 1819	Morgan Crofton to Lord Rosse. 'I have received a letter from Sir George Fetherston, by which he mentioned the election being fixed for the 8th of October and that this Mr Fox *does not stand*, yet he will not decide how he will himself go. His not standing gives us both the Bonds' and Mr Edgeworth's interest, about 200 votes, but his and Mr Fox's are near 100. Mr White seems quite sure of success as I hear, but that may be only an *election manoeuvre*. At all events there will be a sharp contest. ... I go down next week to Longford to be of what assistance I can to Sir George Fetherston.'
10	29 Oct. 1819	Crofton to Rosse. 'Lady Rosse is much pleased with our success at Longford and I really think Mr W[hite] will not try his hand again there. I hear he has purchased in Roscommon and is purchasing there every day, so that it is supposed it is there he means to try at the general election for his sons, it being a very Catholic county and their interest being great there. The Protestant tenantry in Longford stood by their landlords and money would not [? do] them, although I hear it was tried to a *considerable extent*.'

D/14	DATE	DESCRIPTION
1–12	1809: 1817: 1822: 1824: 1828	Letters, together with a printed pamphlet on the state of Ireland in 1822, to the 2nd Earl from the author of the pamphlet, the Rt Hon. Denis Browne, younger brother of the 1st Marquess of Sligo, about the Irish representative peerage elections of 1809, at the second of which the 2nd Earl was the successful candidate, Lord Oxmantown's (the future 3rd Earl) prospects of political office in 1828, etc, etc.
1	12 Feb. 1809	Browne, Wigmore Street, London, to Lord (Rosse) about the current vacancy in the Irish representative peerage.

1   12 Feb. 1809

'... Be assured that I did not forget, without your commands, to urge your right to the representative peerage. I have gone so far as to say that I was confident you would resign if you did not get it, but I was assured you were satisfied that the present strange disposal was in consequence of a *promise of Mr Pitt*, but that you were *ensured* the next vacancy. I think you were wise in taking this compromise. There was nothing better for you to do. I *know* that the Duke of Richmond did everything that was possible to get this object *for you*, and also I know that Wellesley and Castlereagh threw into you as much as possibly they could. Lord Dillon, my colleague in Mayo, is greatly dissatisified about this.

You cannot conceive anything so unpleasant and disgraceful as the examination in the Commons [of] Mrs Clark[e] and her associates, and a Dr [?Kyn], an Irish accoucheur, bred up in France, is a great mover in this business. Capt. Dodd, Secretary to the Duke of Kent, is or appears to be also informed of the intention, and nothing but the undoubted credit of this illustrious Duke, who pledged his honour in the Lords that he was not concerned in the attack on the character of *his brother*, could have kept him free of strong suspicion. ...

There is no union between the Grenvilles and Foxites, and the Foxites are split into two parties. The government keep them together, as I believe. While the King lives, there is no prospect of change, and if things go on well, the successor will make no other material change than to bring in Moira. His Lord[ship] made a speech or declaration of disunion with the party with which he was supposed to act, and hinted that he was ready to take what he could get. I hear he is greatly distressed. I do not like extravagance and distress. I think it breaks down all principle [and] feeling, [and] carries gradually all before it. Lean men like Cassio [*sic*] are [not?] to be trusted.'

2   17 Feb. 1817   Browne, Dublin, to Rosse (letter marked 'Private') about Rosse's personal political situation.

'The Chief Baron having fixed 3rd of March for his circuit of Connaught, I am obliged most reluctantly to give up my intention

D/14/2 *contd.*

of visiting Birr Castle, particularly now, when I think my visit might
be of some use to you; but I will endeavour to explain my plans to
you in writing, being assured of your favourable reception of them,
whether you may approve of their policy or prudence or otherwise.

And, first, I am to observe that you have let far inferior
contemporaries get before you and your family in the honours of
the Empire. Look at those who have got the British peerage lately,
a permanent family advantage of the greatest value; and are they
equal to you in birth, are they equal to you in character, talents or
acquirements? Certainly, they are *all* your inferiors much in most
of those points, and how comes it *they have got before you*? I will
leave this to your own recollections, only hoping that you will
examine it fairly and not so far blind yourself or excuse yourself for
it as to prevent your now setting it right. [A] British peerage [is] an
inestimable object to your family. If your son has talents, it will
enable him to show them: if he has not, it will put him in [a]
situation of dignity and ease, where he can wait till he produces
perhaps some opening. [?Now] it is your business to put him in
security as to this object, not to leave him to spend half his life in
getting [the] representative peerage, when he might employ his
influence and time in providing for the number of brothers you
have provided for him.

How comes it that you have not got the blue ribband, got by
your inferiors; how is it that, embarking as you have done with
government, that [*sic*] you content yourself with the way you have
made, and have not rather sought for permanent benefits for your
family? This is another question for examination.

I now tell you that, if by any mischance you lost your hold of the
county, not only you would [*sic*] thereby be barred from getting
forward, but you would inevitably fall backward; and yet you are
not young enough to work up again. I know how delicately you are
circumstanced with Mr Lloyd, but you must now be determined
and bring this to a close. Know from him his determination
whether he will attend. If he does, of course you must so have it till
your son comes of age, but with a clear understanding that the seat
of course is to be for him vacated. He probably, as I hear, will say *he
will not*, in which case you should set up your *brother, John Parsons*.
All the difficulties in this are trifles to the advantage you would gain
by it. The government would see that the permanent power of that
county was in you, and they will be glad to attach to them a county
power so circumstanced. As to his profession, etc, etc, Plunket, etc,
etc, answers that best. If he went there a month in the year at
snatches, it would do for your member for four years, the interval
of your son's minority. Do not be diverted from this plan. I know
its value. Looking to great objects, you must overlook trifles.
Nothing secures your family for the present or to come but
returning your brother, John Parsons, who will acknowledge this

D/14/2 *contd.*   allegiance and will hold, as I held and hold, as trustee for his own
family. Do not think of starting independent gentlemen, who will
set up for themselves before you can look about you. I could show
you this disadvantage in a thousand shapes going beyond the limits
of a letter.

Nothing will get you the British peerage for your family but three
points: keeping the county by brother as trustee, attending the
House of Lords yourself every winter, and there showing your
abilities as a statesman, making such foundations of interest in the
King's County as will make all look to you; and this you may easily
do at very small expense by means of your town. I have already
proposed to you to send you an agent of my own without cost to
settle all this for you. The principal use he would be of would be
settling the derivative interests, which might appear a stumbling
block to you, but which in most cases is [*sic*] of little consequence;
for example A is your tenant in the town for a street, and he has set
to 100 different people: if you and A understand each other, why he
will add a life to those tenures, an old life or young life, as you may
arrange. Very trifling concessions will satisfy A, and still more trifling
concessions his under-tenants. This is the skill which my agent has,
and he will make every chimney in Birr produce you a vote.

How will you stand? What signifies what is called canvassing,
when by the nonsense of our franchise the vote of a cobbler can be
set against that of the first man in a county. Lord Charlevil[le] has
another town. Between you, all opposition can be quenched. A
town such as yours is worth half the county for such a purpose. I
will engage that my agent shall add 100 votes to your present
interest, so as to frighten from you all future opposition. My advice
on such a subject is of use, for its is founded on experience. ...'

3   1822   Printed pamphlet entitled *A Letter from the Rt Hon. Denis Browne,
M.P. for Kilkenny, to the Most Noble, the Marquess Wellesley, on the
Present State of Ireland* (London, 1822); this copy incribed to
Rosse, Dublin.

4   4 May 1824 Browne, London, to Rosse about Lord Oxmantown's maiden
speech.

'Though this is a day of serious bustle in the House of
Commons on [the] subject of linen bounties, I cannot deny myself
the pleasure of imparting to you and Lady Rosse part of the
satisfaction I felt yesterday in the House of Commons witnessing
there the first effort of Lord Oxmantown on that stage. It was
brilliant, solid, successful. It was talent, too, working on a sound
understanding and a well-informed mind. In this I do not give you
the partial opinion of friendship for you all, but I give you the
opinion of the whole Treasury Bench, of Mr Canning privately
expressed to me – if I can call that private which was stated in the
voice of surprise loud [enough] to be heard by all. ...

D/14/4 *contd.*

John Parsons [Rosse's second son, presumably] spends his time at the Bar of the House of Lords hearing the appeals, as my son tells me. In his profession I have no doubt of his success; and now it is strange that anything like a change of system should be necessary for those young men. But, still, I think there is such a change necessary, and that is [the] change from at home to the world for the next seven years. They will wrong themselves, and you will wrong them, if you do not insist on their being *men of research* in the world for [the] next five or six years. Their birth, talents, character, will work well in this realm [England], where those qualifications rule everything.'

5   10 Jan. 1828   Browne, Rutland Square, [Dublin], to Rosse, again about Rosse's personal political situation.

'I have acted as I thought best, as you desired me so to do. God knows, my power or influence is below par. I have advised direct communication with Lord Rosse himself. My power of doing you service is little, but my zealous regard and my highest esteem and opinion are ever with you and your family.

You never looked high enough for your own rate of character and of ability [and] knowledge. You went into retirement before your work was done. Oxmantown has also mistaken his part. You are both my superiors in every way, but in one way: you have not as much as I have of the devil in either or both of you. How this may end, I know not ...'.

6   13 Jan. 1828   Browne, Rutland Square, to Rosse (letter marked 'Private entirely'): the same.

'... Now, suppose it were asked me, do you think Lord Oxmantown would take office with us, that his father would come to London and take part with us in the Lords. Should I say it is possible, but if you wish it, ask him, Lord Rosse? The Whigs are off with the goodwill of England. They never will come in again. How all this will end, we know not, except that a very strong government will be formed: Melvill[e], Peel, Bathurst, Westmorland. Lord Dudley, I think, may stay in, and Huskisson. Lord Goderich may recover his health. A line will do in reply – yes or no.

I speak from *no authority whatever*, except that of my esteem and affection for you and your son. A Lord of the Treasury twelve months, with his foundations and application, would [make] him a statesman. If I were to write the history of my own times, I would put that Sir Laurence Parsons, from my recollections of his character and conduct, was perhaps the most respectable man of that assembly [the Irish parliament] for its last twenty years.'

7   14 Jan. 1828   Browne, Rutland Square, to Rosse: the same.

'... This is an interesting moment. I know the Duke of Wellington's opinion of you, and also the opinion of the world of the talents of your son. I know what a singular worth is his, and I

D/14/7 *contd.*   think of two things within your reach now: Oxmantown a Lord of
the Treasury – he can afford to vacate his seat. I know not why the
loss of the income of Post Master [General] should fall exclusively
on you. Lord O'Neill should change places with you, for the length
of time you have served without pay. I think you should put this
forward yourself to the Duke of Wellington, now [the] proud setter-
up and puller-down of ministries. If you do not like this, I am ready
to work for you, and be assured in the matter your blushes shall be
spared, and I will do things discreetly. You have only to tell me that,
if I do not let you alone and urge you to go again on the political
stage, you will apply to your friends, the Romans, to try me; and I
have done. It *is a shame for you* not to be a British peer, when so
many Irish blackguards have that distinction. It is all your fault.'

8   19 Jan. 1828   Browne, Dublin, to Rosse.
'... I conclude you will soon hear from headquarters, but hope
you will not think me impertinent for offering to you my opinion.
Do not make at first any proposition about the Post Office. They
are not strong enough to drive away two members in Lords and
Commons. My young friend in the situation I have long wished
for, everything else will follow. It is *just and right* that the
emolument should be shared one way or other between those who
do the duty. A memorial to the First Lord will do it in a moment –
I am supposing that you and my friend shall have done good
service in the winter.'

9   25 Jan. 1828   Browne, Dublin, to Rosse (letter marked 'Most private') among
other things describing Rosse as '... *the only* really honourable
gentleman I knew in that pandemonium called the Irish
parliament, without excepting another friend to whom I was very
partial, Mr Denis Browne, member for Mayo. *There is no doubt* of
Oxmantown being a Lord of the Treasury. Prepare everything for
his re-election. ...'

10   1 Feb. 1828   Browne, Dublin, to Rosse enclosing [/11] a copy of a frosty and
evasive answer from the Duke of Wellington on the subject of
making Lord Oxmantown a Lord of the Treasury, and apologising
to Rosse for having, as it seems, misled him.

11   22 Jan. 1828   Copy of a letter from Wellington, London, to Browne described
in /10.

12   2 Feb. 1828   Browne, Cavendish Row, Dublin, to Rosse waffling on at some
length about the desirability of Lord Oxmantown's acquiring a
thorough knowledge of French, the language of diplomacy, and
pointing out that Canning was greatly disadvantaged by having
only an imperfect knowledge of French.

D/20	DATE	DESCRIPTION

1–4   1822: 1827   Letters to the 2nd Earl from the 1st Lord Redesdale, Lord
Chancellor of Ireland, 1802–6] about the state of Ireland, with
photocopies of the originals, and a copy of PRONI's calendar, of
the other side of the correspondence, the 2nd Earl's letters to Lord
Redesdale in reply (Gloucestershire Record Office, Redesdale
Papers, C/34: PRONI, T/3030/13/1–7, printed in Malcomson
(ed.), *Eighteenth-Century Irish Official Papers in Great Britian:
Private Collections, vol ii* [Belfast, 1990], pp 459–68).

In the calendar which follows, the text of the Rosse-Redesdale
letters is given as well, since the Redesdale-Rosse letters do not
make much sense in isolation; the sub-numbers refer to the
Redesdale-Rosse letters only:

30 Mar. 1822   Rosse, Dublin, to Redesdale about agrarian secret societies.
'As I know you feel particularly interested about Ireland, I send
you the Limerick paper, to let you see how far our south-western
districts still are from being restored to a state of order,
notwithstanding that a great military force, a police, judicial
commissions and the Insurrection Act have been all operating
upon them. What would our situation have been if the
insurrection had been general? For now, almost our whole army is
in the districts at present disturbed. And why it was not general
cannot be easily accounted for, for the disposition and general
organisation are so.

The organisation has been formed for about five or six years. It
began, I know, in the King's County about that time. The
members of it are all the young men of the lower orders, who are
Catholics. I believe that no Protestant has been a member of the
Association, or has been concerned in any of the outrages
proceeding from it. They are all sworn to obey their own leaders
and regulations; and the manner in which they carry their
decisions into execution is by a party of the association coming
from a distance, perfect strangers to the party to be punished,
rendering detection very difficult, and these waylay, assassinate,
burn, etc., according to their orders, and instantly return.

You may understand it better, perhaps, from a few instances
within my knowledge. A little farmer offended by being an
evidence in some trivial affair. Six months afterwards, he went to
Tullamore, 20 miles distant, to sell his wheat. On the canal wharf
at Tullamore, at the edge of the town, in open day, six men, perfect
strangers, without any notice to him, knocked him down and beat
him with their heavy, oak walking sticks, till they nearly killed
them [*sic*]. He had some months before got notice of this, but
thought the matter forgotten. He was for some months very ill
after this, unable to follow his business. In the summer following,

he came to the races near my town and where all the principal persons of the county were assembled, and on the course, while they were all there, three strangers attacked him as before and beat him in the same cruel manner, then escaping among the crowd.

In winter one night the wool was torn of [*sic*] the sheep of a tenant of mine. He got a constable and search warrant, and found his wool, which are identified by part of the skin having adhered to it, and which exactly fitted the raw parts of the sheep. He was threatened as usual, if he prosecuted, but I advised him to do so; and the offender was sentenced at the quarter sessions to be whipped. The family of my tenant implored me to prevent the sentence from being executed, for if it was, they were sure that it would be severely revenged. However, the man was whipped, and in about three months after, as my tenant in open day was returning from market, three strangers jumped out from behind a hedge and beat him in the most shocking manner, leaving him as they supposed dead.

I will not trouble you with more instances. You will see how difficult it is to get laws executed, where such a system is in operation. Besides, there is no adequate punishment for these acts. For, if the sufferer does not die, it is only an assault; for though we are certain it proceeds from the conspiracty, we cannot prove that it does so. The punishment, therefore, even if the offenders are discovered, which is very rare, is but a few months' imprisonment, in a better house than they have been used to live in, where they are fed on white bread instead of potatoes, and from which they come out healthy, fatter and better than when they went in. It seemed so obvious that, if this organisation was suffered to continue, that [*sic*] its operations would not be restrained to such instances as I have mentioned among the lower orders, that besides it was rendering the people cruel and ferocious and was a great obstruction to the execution of the laws, that I repeatedly mentioned and urged the necessity of some vigorous system to conteract it to government, but I suppose no plan could be agreed upon. The lower orders are much more formidable now than they ever were in this island, from their great increase in numbers, from fewer gentlemen residing, from the extinction of the great farmers who were protestants and the descendants of the English, and from the habit of organisation and the taste they have got for it; also from the number of disbanded soldiers and militia.

Forty years ago, the lands of Ireland were let in farms of 500 or a [*sic*] 1,000 or 1,500 acres: now landlords, finding that they can get higher rents and have more voters, let them to catholics in portions of 20, 30 or 40 acres, and these, as they multiply fast, again sub-divide them among their sons and daughters, as they marry. Therefore, the old modes of preserving order and enforcing obedience to law will not do now. They are also a great deal more

D/20 *contd.*

cruel than they were formerly, and more treacherous. When I was young, they had a great horror of murder. I recollect sixteen years to pass in the King's County without one capital conviction. We had then a small house of about six or eight rooms for a gaol. Twenty years ago, we built a new gaol, which we thought an immense building. It was doubled three years ago, and now there are plans for making it more than twice as large as it now is. Last week ten men were sentenced there to death, and the criminal trials could not be concluded, and the assizes adjourned. Eight of the ten men acknowledged their guilt to their attorney and counsel, yet the priest made them deny it at their execution. He has £30 a year from the grand jury for *taking care* of the *souls* of the prisoners. His bishop has been written to by some of the grand jury, but Lord Norbury thought it better at this time not to irritate by taking public note of it. Such is the state of our county, which we consider a quiet one.

We are, however, for this tranquillity in a great measure indebted to an expensive police, under the Peace Preservation Act, the chief magistrate of which, whose authority only extends over about three-fourths of our county, costs £1,200 a year, that is £800 salary, £200 for a house and above £200 more for forage, etc. I believe that the Lord Lieutenant is forming a plan for a general police, on a less expensive scale. He is indefatigable. But as I look much to you for the perfection of any legislative measures which may be brought forward for our country, I have taken the liberty of thus mentioning such facts as at present occur to me, which might assist in giving you a true idea of our situation. I think it probable that disturbances will not now spread, for those who have influence on the lower orders seem to wish that they should not. It is better to owe the peace and preservation of our families to the courtesy of such leaders, than to be in a state of general disturbances; but this surely is not the kind of tenure upon which we should depend under a civilised government. In England they seem to think that our magistrates might do much to preserve our tranquillity; but we have not, at least in the part of the country with which I am best acquainted and which is one of the best inhabited, a sufficient number of resident gentlemen for that office. About thirty years ago there was a qualification of £300 a year required for justices of the peace, but the law was repealed: a sufficient number of persons so qualified could not be procured. The number of such is now much diminished. Our road law now requires a sessions to be held, at which there must be three magistrates at least of £500 a year property to approve of presentments for roads, before the grand jury at the assizes can grant them. These sessions are held in districts composed of three or four baronies each. But frequently the whole presentments of a district are stopped for a year, from the impracticability of getting

D/20 *contd.*   three magistrates so qualified. It happened this year in one district of the King's County, and was very near happening in my own, two of us waiting in court for several hours, sending expresses in various quarters, to get a third magistrate. Yet you know, there is nothing about which country gentlemen are more anxious than their roads. But if the English magistracy had such an organisation to contend with as we have, so much secrecy, so much intimidation of witnesses, I apprehend that they would find themselves much perplexed. *While* our assizes were going on last week, the witnesses against persons who set fire to a house were attacked as they were returning, within ten miles of the county town, at a village called Edenderry, and cruelly beaten, and not a house there would admit them, such is the influence of terror. They must have been killed, only some police rescued them. I fear than an English parliament may not be willing to establish such a power in this country as will be sufficient to keep the lower orders from rising occasionally, as they have done, or perhaps from rising universally. They object to the Insurrection Act as being contrary to Magna Charta; but we consider the Insurrection Act as our Magna Charta. It was in force in our county a few years ago, and restored tranquillity; but instead of its powers being acted on with rigour, we only sentenced one man to be transported, and recommended that he should be pardoned, and he was. The present Judge Jebb presided. I do not believe that this act has been at any time severely executed, but the reverse.

This letter has so far exceeded in length what I intended, that I am almost determined not to send it. Trusting, however, that you will excuse me, and in the hope that it may possibly be of some little us in helping you to form an idea of our real situation, I believe I had better send it.'

1   2 Apr. 1822   Redesdale, Harley Street, London, to Rosse in reply.
'I am much obliged to you for the very instructive letter which you have sent me. I have never had a doubt that the disturbances which have of late prevailed in Ireland were the effect of a well-organised conspiracy, and that they cannot be effectually suppressed except by the destruction of that conspiracy. I have not been able to frame in my mind any effectual measure for the purpose. The Insurrection Act cannot reach that conspiracy, and cannot prevent its effect, so far as it can act by means of strangers to the country where outrages are committed, spreading terror everywhere.

Whatever may be said to the contrary, I have no doubt that it is in its final object a conspiracy against the Protestants of the country, and that if it shall continue in force, it must operate the destruction of the Protestant Establishment and of Protestant property, and end in the expulsion of Protestantism from Ireland

D/20/1 *contd.*

and the separation of Ireland from Great Britain. My opinion has long been that such is the ultimate object of a large portion of those who clamour for Catholic Emancipation, and my opinion has also long been that Lord Fingal[l] and other Catholics of property have dreaded this effect and fear that they may themselves be victims as well as the Protestant proprietors, that they fear the situation in which the Duc de la Rochefoucauld and other great proprietors in France found themselves, when they had raised a ferment the effect of which they could not restrain. Perhaps most of the Catholic bishops and some of the Catholic clergy have the same feeling, and I doubt whether many of the clergy may not be *apprehensive* that they may finally experience the fate of the clergy of France, and may not tremble for themselves, and yet may not dare to endeavour in private to stop proceedings which they openly may be permitted to reprobate; for it must be the interest of the conspirators, that is of the directors of the conspiracy, to lead the country to imagine that religious opinions have no influence in promoting insurrection. The object of those directors seems to be to be to gain the Catholic part of the population by their religious prejudices as well as their personal feelings, and not to throw off to them the mask of religion until they have involved their followers so deep in crime that they may be willing to throw off all religious feeling and become, as the French population did become, without religion. Then, and not till then, will the Catholic clergy *feel* the consequences of the conspiracy, though many of them may *dread* them now – those at least who have sufficient penetration to see consequences at a distance, and have minds not blinded by religious zeal.

I think Ireland on the brink of a revolution involving religion as well as property in one common ruin, and raising up a power as furious and as cruel as that which desolated France. Such a conspiracy as that which I apprehend exists in Ireland, can only be effectually met by a combination of the property in Ireland to preserve itself. Property, with arms, has generally been found able to preserve itself, if allowed to act in its own defence. But if one party can wage war and the other can only go to law, as has been well observed, it is easy to foresee which will prevail. I begin, therefore, now to fear that the proclamation of martial law will be necessary in the disturbed districts; but that should be, if possible, avoided. Universal association of property for its own protection, with arms, and properly organised, will do much, and I should advise such associations of men of all religious persuasions in every part of the country. Perhaps I may be mistaken in including all religious persuasions, but I am inclined to think that there can be only few Catholics of property so blinded by religion as not to perceive their own danger, at least to be so far doubtful that they may be roused to a sense of their danger, if proper means were

D/20/1 *contd.*   taken for the purpose. I know not what may be the feeling of the
Irish government on this subject, and I know not what may be the
jealousy, perhaps the well-founded jealousy, of Protestants. But in
Protestant parts of the country, I should think there can be no
doubt of the advantage of a general association for the preservation
of property and peace. ...

I have for nearly twenty years considered the ultimate object of
the agitators of Ireland, that is of the leaders, to be the property of
individuals as well as the property of the Church. I have said so in
parliament and have forewarned the Marquess of Lansdowne that
the Fitzmaurices are considered only as fellows who came in with
Strongbow, and that the seizure of his property with that of every
other proprietor not of Irish name is looked to as the final reward
of insurrection, the abolition of tithes and the confiscation of
Church lands being probably either a preliminary step or a
necessary consequence. I once thought that the Church property
would have been transferred from the Protestant to the Catholic
Establishment, but I now think its destruction more probable. ...'

2   15 Apr. 1822   Redesdale, Harley Street, to Rosse [in reply to a letter which has
not survived among the Redesdale Papers].

'I am much obliged by the information which you have sent me
and shall be glad to see Pastorini. I have long suspected that the
disturbers throughout Europe were connected and that they have
been connected for many years. It appears to me extraordinary
that the real promoters of disturbance in this country have never
been discovered. At least I have always so suspected.

In the riots of 1780 in London, the actors were certainly not the
directors. Some of the persons executed acknowledged that they
were directed to particular houses by persons they did not know,
and who disappeared as soon as the mischief began. The police of
this town was [*sic*] then very ill-conducted, and the justices were so
terrified by the trial of Justice Gillam for murder that they all ran
away when the riots began. I have little doubt that the same
persons, or rather, persons of the same description, have been at
work ever since. When I was in France in 1776, a German tailor
predicted the French Revolution, and stated to me circumstances
which operated strongly on my mind when I visited that country
agin in 1787, and convinced me that a revolution was then
inevitable. Yet, I still found many of the higher orders incredulous,
perhaps unwilling to believe and unwilling to take the steps
necessary to prevent what happened, if it could have been then
prevented. Even in 1791, when I saw the effects of the revolution,
I met with many respectable men, particularly elderly men, whose
minds were still blinded, and thought all would soon be remedied.
It seems to me that in this country many people are so unwilling
to believe that any such conspiracy as I have suggested subsists,

D/20/2 *contd.*

that they are incredulous in spite of all that can be said to them on the subject. It so happened in this country in the reign of Charles I. If anything can save Ireland from serious evils, it must be by convincing a large portion of those who have property at stake that there exists such a conspiracy as I have supposed, and the existence of which your Lordship's relation seems to me to prove. The late Lord Kilwarden, in the last conversation I had with him, mentioned to me circumstances within his own knowledge which led him to believe that Catholic Emancipation was only a cry, used for the purpose of engaging persons in a conspiracy of which they knew not the real object. ...'

19 Apr. 1822

Rosse, Parsonstown, to Redesdale about subversive publications in circulation around the lower orders of the Catholics.

'I enclose Pastorini. You will see in the preface that the work is sanctioned by Dr Milner, which gives it additonal credibility in this country. The 8th chapter is the one which particularly applies to our people. I have been for two days this week at Mr King's [Ballylin], who is married to Lady Rosse's sister, about 12 miles from this. He told me that Pastorini has been in circulation among the lowest orders in that neighbourhood for three years, and that last year a small book, being an extract from it, has been in circulation among them. Mr Daly of Castle Daly, who was there, told me that, travelling some time go, he was at the inn at Loughrea, and having asked for a book to read, the waiter brought him Pastorini, supposing from his name that he was a Catholic; and that the 8th chapter was so much dirtied by reading that it was scarcely legible.

A few days ago, two men near Mr Daly's were so cruelly carded that one of them had [*sic*] been in convulsions continually, and his life is despaired of. Also, since my last letter to you, a Mr Nicholson, a respectable farmer and a kind of half-gentleman, was shot in the evening in his own avenue in this county. He lived just to say that it was Murphy of the island who shot him; but as there are four or five of the name, it cannot be ascertained which of them. Thus are we living in the midst of a population abounding with characters more wicked than most of those in Dante's Inferno.

The oath found on Egan has appeared in the newspapers and is precisely the same as all the people have taken who have become members of this general conspiracy. Mr Massy of the county of Limerick says he has had information of the oath from hundreds, and that it is the same. The priest of this town about three months ago remonstrated with the people against taking it, and told them from the altar that a man ought sooner submit to be shot than take such an oath. I have spoken to several Catholics, and none of them expressed the least doubt that the oath everywhere contains

D/20/2 *contd.*

the clause for murdering the Protestants, and that this is the object
of the conspiracy. And they say that they have remonstrated with
the people, and told them that, if they could succeed so far, they
would afterwards murder one another, and be destroyed by armies
from England. This is the way they speak, but never questioning
that such is the oath. They tell me that they do not think the
people here will rise. This, however, must be uncertain. No man
can be sure that they will not. If they should, this time will be as
memorable for the massacre of Protestants as 1641. Then the
Protestants lived in the castles which we see every one in ruins, and
therefore they could often protect themselves much better than
now. An old woman told my neighbour, Mr Drought, to take care
of himself, for these were bad times. He said he was not afraid. She
said they were coming on like the waves of the Shannon, wave
after wave, until they would overturn everything. Others say
among themselves that the Protestants will be green and
flourishing in the evening, but that before midday they will be cut
down and withered like thistles in the sun. In this kind of
figurative language they indicate what appears to got possession of
their minds. Still, I rather think that they will not rise here. Those
who ascribe the disturbances in the south to the present distress of
the lower orders, and deny that they are caused by religious
considerations, should explain why not a single Protestant has
been concerned in any of these outrages; for surely the poor
Protestant tenants have rents and tithes and taxes to pay also. Yet
they remain peaceable.

I will immediately form here such an association as you
recommend ...'

He transcribes a ballad which is typical of those which are
printed and circulated among the lower orders of the Catholics.
Such ballads, he thinks, '... speak more certainly ... their views
than any evidence we could get, except the oath itself.

I would go over and state all I know in the House of Lords, if an
adequate end was to be gained. But then I could scarcely live in
this country after doing so, and I should be fired at from behind
the bushes in my own pleasure grounds. I therefore think it more
prudent to say nothing but to those in whom I can reasonably
confide, except so far as to endeavour to convince the people of
the impracticability of their schemes.'

3   29 Apr. 1822   Redesdale, Batsford Park, Moreton-in-Marsh, Gloucestershire,
to Rosse in reply.
'I am well persuaded that the book which you have sent me
must have done much mischief amongst the Catholics of the lower
order and prepared them for the machinations of others who give
little credit to Pastorini. If you should not be coming to England,
you will probably wish to have the book sent to you; but as I hope

D/20/3 *contd.*

the exertions of the country will put down the spirit of insubordination, I shall hope to see you in parliament. I find there are doubts whether Canning's motion, mischievous as it is, will not be carried in the Commons.

I am glad you have determined to endeavour to form such an association as I have suggested. ...

The spirit of reform, as it is called, has received a check but it is continually at work. All the arguments for reform are founded on the supposition that making elections more popular would produce a better House of Commons. I consider that such a reform would produce a worse House of Commons. The election of members for that House of Commons which obtained the assent of Charles I to the Petition of Right, of that House of Commons which finally proceeded to wage war against him, and that House which deposed King James and framed the Bill of Rights, was in principle the same as the election of the present House of Commons, except that by change of circumstances elections have become more popular, and thus an opening has been made for bribery and corruption; and the more popular elections may become, the more of bribery and corruption [there] will be. But all the reasoning for popular elections is founded on false principles. The great object of society is property. Property, therefore, ought to have political power for its own protection. Such is the principle of the British Constitution. It is founded on property. To give a man possessing 40/- a year an equal share of political power with a man of £400 a year, is not only contrary to the spirit of the British constitution, but in itself unjust. If the legislature of the country was formed of all who possess 40/- a year, they would so overpower the rest of the proprietors that the property of the rest would be at the mercy of the 40/-a-year members of the assembly. Complaint is made of extravagance in expenditure, and taxes. But who have most interest to prevent extravagant expenditure and exorbitant taxes but those who must contribute most to both. ... If no one had a vote for a county who had not £40 a year, instead of 40/-, and if no one had a vote in city or borough who has not a correspondent property, elections would be of men of property, free from the influence of bribery and corruption. Every county election is a scene of bribery and corruption, because the voters are men of 40/- a year. Such men may not receive, directly, money for their votes, but their votes are gained by expense of the candidate more than by his merit. ...

To bring Ireland to a proper state, a resident magistracy, such as we have in England, composed of the men of property in every county is most essential. Whether that can be obtained in Ireland as fully as it has been obtained in England, may be doubtful. But much may be done if the gentlemen of Ireland will seriously exert themselves for the purpose.'

D/20/3 *contd.*

3 May 1822

Rosse, Parsonstown, to Redesdale about the Catholic vote in parliamentary elections in Ireland.

'I have no occasion for the book I sent you [Pastorini]: I have another copy, printed in 1810 in Dublin, being the 4th edition.

I am very glad to find my opinions about parliamentary reform fortified by your Lordship. When first I came into parliament, I was led into an approbation of that measure by the example of Mr Pitt. But when the French doctrines of the Revolution began to prevail, I changed my opinion, and wrote a pamphlet entitled, Thoughts on Libery and Equality [see D/3], the groundwork of which was the same as that contained in your letter.

We have, however, in this country something approaching very near to universal suffrage. The farms are so divided and sub-divided in consequence of our great population, and every man who has a rood of ground, by getting a lease for one life being considered a freeholder, that their numbers are tremendous. At present they vote with their landlords, who are generally Protestants. But if Catholics could sit in the House of Commons, I apprehend that at the desire of the priests they would vote for the Catholic candidates. Religious fury would exasperate the party spirit which is so violent often at elections, and if the Protestant candidates persevered, the country would be one scene of war and outrage. We had a slight shadow of this four years ago when my brother was a candidate for this county. His opponent was Mr Malone, whose mother was a Catholic: and though he was a Protestant and a peaceable gentleman, we were so threatened with mobs that the freeholders began to be afraid of venturing to the election, unless they voted for Mr Malone. Mr Fitzsimmons [*sic* – Fitzsimon], a Catholic and a magistrate, came to me, to endeavour to prevail on my brother to decline, from the danger to the peace of the country. The commanding officer of the district received such accounts, and evidence of the intention of the populace to disturb the peace, that he had his troops under orders and had directed military patrols along the roads. The sheriff also called on him for troops to protect him on the hustings. Mr Malone, however, declined the evening but one before the election [see E/17/3, 6, 7 and 11], and Mr Fitzsimmons told me that a principal inducement to him to decline was the preservation of the peace, for that the country would soon become a horrid scene of outrage if the election had proceeded. Mr Bernard, the other candidate, had engaged boats to convey his freeholders by the Grand Canal under escorts, not conceiving the roads safe or even passable for them. And my brother, who you know is a liberal, unsuspecting man, had been all his life friendly to every concession to the Catholics. But both his parents were Protestants. Now from this judge what would be the state of this island at the

D/20/3 *contd.*

time of a general election, if the Catholics were admissible to parliament -especially too as it would be a great object with the priests to return Catholic members, in the hopes by degrees of advantages for themselves, whose interests have never been included in any Emancipation Bill.

A few years ago, the agent who received for me all my rents in this county was a Catholic. I selected him as a man of more than ordinary capacity and great integrity, though he had but a poor education. He was a farmer on my estate. He had a brother a priest. No one could have known the middle and lower order of Catholics better. I asked him one day, if the Catholic bill passed, whether my tenants would vote for my brother-in-law, who then represented the county, or for a Catholic candidate. He said, certainly for the Catholic. I expressed a disbelief of this, that my tenants must come twice a year to pay their rents, that they were in general improvident and in arrear, that they had various applications to make to me for favour and indulgence. He said that all that was very true, that I could injure them in this world, but that they believed that the priest could injure them in the next; that they must also go twice a year to the priest to confession. Says he, "If I was going along the road, and a priest demanded my money, I would not give it to him; and if he endeavoured to take it from me by force, I would defend myself against him as well as I could. But if he was at the altar, in the exercise of his holy office, I must do what he desired me, for then it is the spirit of God which speaks through his lips." He often told me not to grant more power to the Catholics; that they had enough, and if they had more, that they would make a bad use of it. I never new [*sic*] an honester man or of more strict veracity, and he continued in my service to his death.

The Catholic bill of 1793 has very much contributed to the expulsion of the middlemen, who were in fact the yeomanry of this country, respectable farmers, Protestants, descendants of Englishmen and attached to the government. Numbers of these have latterly gone to America. In short, about thirty years have annihilated them. Were the Catholic bill now intended to pass, may it not drive away the upper classes of Protestants? If the representation becomes Catholic, will not the sheriffs, the grand juries, the officers of militia and of yeomanry corps, be in a few years Catholic? Will not the patronage of government flow in the same line necessarily? Will the upper class of Protestants brook this longer than until they can escape from it? Will they not, according as they can extricate their property from their family settlements, withdraw it and themselves from this country? I have no doubt that they will. And what security will England have after for the continuance of the connection? For a time, the Catholics will be very submissive. They will vote with government until they get as

D/20/3 *contd.* much as possible into place and power, but the first moment that England by war, foreign or domestic, is in difficulty and enfeebled, they will break the connection and set up their own church and a government for themselves. The connection of these islands probably would not last fifty years.

Mr friend, Lord Londonderry, says that before the Union the Catholic measure would have been unsafe, as the Catholics might have become the majority in parliament; but now the Irish representation makes so small a portion of the House of Commons that no danger is to be apprehend. It is true that now the Catholics could not by a vote disturb the constitution. Their object is not to be effected at once and by a coup de gras [*sic*]. But they would effect it gradually in this country in the manner I have mentioned. The power of the government to withhold places, etc., from Catholics would be only nominal. These would certainly follow the representation. Neither can I agree with some who think it immaterial to England whether the principal people here are Catholics or Protestants, or whether the whole nation was Catholic. For, though the maxim, divide and govern, has been often reprobated, it is nevertheless true that the division facilitates the governing of the country. It may be problematical whether the connection would be more secure if all the people here were Protestants; but it seems evident that it would not be secure if they were Catholics, for notions of aboriginal possession, which are very strong, as well as religion, would be and are always working in the minds of the Catholics against the connection.

I fear I tire you, but the subject is so momentous, I find it difficult to restrain my pen.'

7 May 1822 Rosse, Parsonstown, to Redesdale: more about the Catholics and the franchise.

'Since I wrote last to your Lordship, I happened to meet Mr Mooney [*sic* – Moony], a magistrate of this county, who was to have voted for Mr Malone at the last general election. He told me that he had received information a few days before that election, when it was known that Mr Bernard's freeholders were to proceed in boats by the canal to the election, that the people were determined to make breaches in the canal and burn the boats; that this was to be done by strangers; and that great numbers of the lower class from the neighbouring county were passing near his house for a day towards the canal, and afterwards when Mr Malone declined, he saw them returning. I mention this to show the state we should be in, from the hostility of the people, if there were Catholic candidates.

It has been said that the priests have not hitherto shown much influence over the Catholic electors. But the reason is obvious: they have not, except in a few instances, attempted it, and then

D/20/3 *contd.*

privily, and for this reason, that they fear that if they were to exert it now, they would open the eyes of the Protestants and of the government as to the consequences of the Catholic measure. It is obviously their policy to keep quiet till it is carried. If it were carried, I am firmly persuaded that, previous to a general election, the Catholic bishops would meet and determine on their proceedings to obtain a Catholic representation, and issue their orders to the priests accordingly. When it would be general, they would keep each other in countenance, and the object would be so great that they would exert every power which they possess. They will never be satisfied while Protestant clergymen are in possession of their churches, glebes and tithes, as they consider them, and while their mitres are excluded from the House of Lords. According to Dr Troy's note on the 73rd psalm, 20.v., "Mean and ignoble wretches have been enriched with their estates and possessions, which they have unjustly acquired." I have now before me his bible, published as approved by him, by Keating, Duke Street, Grosvenor Square, in 1816. There is scarcely a page of the new testament in which the word heretic does not occur in the notes, with some observation to make us hated and detested by the Catholics – and yet Protestants are accused of not being sufficiently conciliating towards them. What is there [*sic*] disposition of conciliation, when even the word of God is made the [?passport] for conveying abhorrence and antipathy towards us when our church is pronounced "not only unprofitable, but damnable" – note on 10 ch. of acts, 9th verse. I wish this bible was laid on the tables of the House of Lords and Commons.

At any time when it is really necessary, I will go over and do my best. But until then I wish to keep quiet, as I should involve myself in contests in this county, which it is prudent to avoid, except upon a real emergency. If anything I mention in my letters should appear to you to be worth communicating privately to any friend of yours, I have no objection. I write hastily to you, but the thoughts I have long revolved. ...

P.S. Some say that the notes in this bible are only the language of the priests; but in this country, the language of the Catholic priests forms the principles and opinions of the Catholic people.'

9 May 1822

Rosse, Parsonstown, to Redesdale about the Catholics and the franchise and about a religiously inspired atrocity in 1798.

'My long residence in this country gives me so many opportunities of knowing the people of all classes here and their sentiments and views, that I write to you with a confidence in my own opinions respecting them, which otherwise I would not presume to do. But what I principally wish is to communicate to you the opinions of others who have had a better opportunity of knowing the Catholics than I have had.

D/20/3 *contd.*

I think that I never had any illiberal prejudice against them. A great many years ago, in the Irish parliament, I spoke and voted for the removal of all their political disabilities. The day following, Lord Clare spoke to me on the subject. I remember his words accurately. He said, "My father was a popish recusant. He became a Protestant and was called to the bar, but he continued to live on terms of familiarity with his Roman Catholic relations and early friends, and he knew the Catholics well. He has repeatedly told me that, if ever they had the opportunity, they would overturn the established government and church, and resume the Protestant estates." I happened the same day to call on the Rev. Dean Kirwan, the celebrated preacher. I was very intimate with him. You know that but a few years before he had been a Catholic priest. He was, however, connected with many genteel families in the county of Galway. He was a friar. He had a newspaper lying before him on the table, and he began by saying, "Sir Laurence, I have been reading your speech. You do not know the Catholics. If ever you give them the power, they will pull you and every other Protestant down, and turn you out of your churches and your property. I say this in strict confidence to you. My relations are all Catholics, and as I have abstained from preaching against them, or on any controversial point, I have continued and wish to continue on amicable terms with them, particularly on account of my mother", etc. Two or three days after, I called on an old friend of mine, who was very intimate with the late Lord Dunboyne. My friend, who is still alive, said to me, "Lord Dunboyne wishes very much to have some conversation with you." I said I should see him at any time with great pleasure, but I expressed my surprise, as I could not imagine what he wanted with me, as I was utterly unacquainted with him. My friend said, "Why, he wants to speak to you respecting your speech in the House of Commons. He says, Sir Laurence Parsons does not know what he is about; that if the Catholics get the opportunity, they will overturn the government and every Protestant in the country." You know, I believe that Lord Dunboyne had been a Roman Catholic *bishop* for a great many years. He *must*, therefore, have known the Catholics to the *bottom* of their hearts, and all classes and degrees of them; for, from his rank and property, as well as from his episcopal station, he must have known the sentiments and views of the highest class of them, as well as the lowest. I had not afterwards the interview with him, for I was then just leaving town, and I thought more lightly of such subjects then, but my friend is a person of the strictest honour and veracity; besides, the proposal being for an interview with him puts all idea of deception out of the mind.

I was not long ago speaking on the same subject to a person in very high station in this country [Lord Kingston?]. He did not know my opinion, because if it was promulgated it might raise a

D/20/3 *contd.*

hurricane against my family in this county on the first election. I therefore only communicate it privately, unless a great exigency should make it useful to do otherwise. He said to me, "Surely you cannot wish that the Catholics should get into parliament? It would cause a revolution in this country, which would be fatal to you and all the descendants of the English. I might escape, because I am of an old Milesian family and am considered as the head of a clan. I cannot conceive greater folly than the Protestants supporting such a measure. If I had a servant who I knew would rob me, if he had an opportunity, would I lay a case of pistols primed and loaded on the sideboard there, in his way, to enable him to do it?" Now, the man who said this to me is a man of eminent abilities as well as station, and who [*sic*] is peculiarly gifted with a penetrating mind for searching into the sentiments and opinions of men, and who from his connections has had much opportunity of knowing the men of whom he was speaking. But my friend, Plunket, living always among briefs, and in or near Dublin, where civility and intercourse have taught men to mask their sentiments, is a very inferior authority, great as his abilities are, to any of those whose opinions I have mentioned. His father was a Presbyterian clergyman of wit and ability, who resided in Dublin. I believe it was my friend, Mr P. Burrowes, who gave the present bias to Plunket's mind, for a great intimacy subsists between them, and Plunket's influence made him lately a Commissioner of the Insolvent Court. Plunket is perfectly sincere on the subject. So is Burrowes, who has a most impressive manner in private of communicating his sentiments. He has always been an advocate for the Catholics. His mother was a Catholic, and though on all other subjects he is a man of sound understanding, yet on this (partly perhaps from some early impressions made on him in his childhood, partly from the unbounded benevolence of his disposition) his mind seems to be deeply diseased, and so much so that nothing which he could now hear or see would cure it.

If anything could, the conduct of the Catholics towards his own brother would have had that effect, and as an instance of confidence in the kindness of Catholics, I will mention it to you. His brother was a Protestant clergyman, and a man of most amiable, charitable, simple disposition. The morning of the day on the evening of which the rebellion began in 1798, this clergyman was residing in his glebe-house in the county of Wicklow, where he was rector of a small parish. The Catholic priest came to him and told him that he had reason to believe that there would be an insurrection that evening, and entreated him to set out instantly with all his family for Dublin. Mr Burrowes replied that he had always lived on terms of the greatest kindness with his Catholic parishioners, and that he was sure they would not injure him or his family; that he had never meddled in politics of any kind, but

D/20/3 *contd.*   confined himself entirely to his parochial duties. The priest
endeavoured in vain to prevail on him to proceed to Dublin. In
the evening, while Mr Burrowes and his family were drinking tea,
they saw a great multitude coming down the avenue, and several
with firebrands. Alarmed, they secured the lower windows of the
house, and Mr Burrowes addressed them from an upper window,
and endeavoured by conciliating speeches to persuade them to
leave him unmolested; but they attacked his house. He at length,
and his sons, defended themselves by firing several shots at the
people. At last they found that the people had burned the hall
door and set the lower part of the house in flames. The people
then called to them to come out, and that they should not be
injured. They did so, and as they went out, they were one after the
other deliberately piked. One son, who was run through the body,
survived. He lived for about a year, frequently in great torture. I
had these particulars both from him and from Mr P. Burrowes.
This is a specimen of what we have to expect from these people,
however kindly we may treat them.'

21 May 1822   Rosse, Parsonstown, to Redesdale giving him further information
about Dr Troy's bible and replying to questions which Redesdale
had clearly asked about the soundness of the authority of Lord
Clare, Dean Kirwam and Lord Dunboyne.

27 May 1822   Rosse, Parsonstown, to Redesdale about the power of the Catholic
priesthood over Catholic electors.
          'It is often said in debates on the Catholic bill, "Show us the
danger." English gentlemen are not aware of the subjections which
the Irish Catholics are under to their priests. The priests are
despotic. They sentence them to the most austere and degrading
penances. They refuse them the rights [*sic*] of their church until they
submit. They can excommunicate if necessary; but they [the
Catholic laity] rarely disobey. The priests too are in complete
subjection to their bishops, who can remove them from their livings
when they choose. A deputation from the principal Catholics here
came to me about two years ago, to let me know that their bishop
had ordered the old priest of this town to go to another living; that
they were sure that the old man would die with grief; and they
requested me, if the bishop spoke to me about it, to remonstrate. I
proposed to write at once to the bishop, but they said that, if I did,
that would decide him inflexibly for the removal, for he would not
submit to any lay interference; that it would be suggested to him to
apply to me; that the parish would unite in remonstrating with him,
only that the doing so would have the contrary effect. I do not
know how they managed it afterwards, but the old priest remains.
They said that the power of the bishop was perfectly arbitrary.
          If the Catholic clergy had no more influence than the Protestant
or Presbyterian clergy have, we might perhaps, as to elections, have

D/20/3 *contd.*

fair play. At present there are, I suppose, eight or ten Catholic freeholders to one Protestant freeholder. They are in general of the lowest class. They are consequently dependent on their landlords, and vote with him at the elections. So that, in effect, it is the landed proprietors, with an influence proportionate to their estates, who elect the members. But the Catholic bill would transfer that power from the landlords to the priests; that is, the priests do not think it prudent at present to exert their powers, lest they should thereby defeat their bill. It is the Catholic priesthood, under the orders of their bishops, that would then nominate the members for most of the counties and great towns. I think it would be painful to the priest and to most of the Catholics of this town to vote against my son. But I am sure that they dare not do otherwise, if there were Catholic candidates. The Catholics are now building a chapel here much larger and more beautiful than our church, which cost above £8,000. We all contributed most liberally to this chapel. My son laid the foundation stone, we all attending. Their band, which consists of 24 wind instruments besides the singers, performed te deum during the ceremony. When my son last year was elected for this county, they and their band, along with the Protestant inhabitants, met him on his return here, decorated with ribbons, banners, etc., and drew him through the town. They, together with my Protestant tenantry here, gave a dinner on the occasion, where we all dined, the Protestant rector sitting with a Catholic priest on each side of him. Nothing could be kinder or more affectionate than their whole demeanour. But if the Catholic bill passed, this would all change to wrath and hositility. I grieve to think of it.

I think that there would be above fifty Catholic members from Ireland if their bill passed – perhaps sixty. In electing these, the whole island would be in a state of fury and convulsion, almost amounting to civil war. The landlords would be exasperated against their tenants, but what could they do? To persecute them for rents and arrears and treat them hostiley would be too cruel: it would also excite great disturbances. Besides, the landlords could not afford to remove and put down their tenants. They must submit. This the tenants are sagacious enough to know, while they know that their priests, if they disobeyed them and voted contrary to their orders, would punish them with unrelenting severity. "The exalted dignity of the priesthood is far above our understanding and the power of speech. The remission of sins is not granted to mortals, but through the ministry of the priest" – Troy's Life of Christ, p. 303. ... [There follow further quotations from the same source.]

How can we be surprised that a poor, ignorant, superstitious population, in whom such opinions are inculcated, should be slaves to their priests? English gentlemen probably judge of our

D/20/3 *contd.*   Catholics by what they have seen of Catholics in England and in
France. But the mental state of ours is quite different. They submit
to be beaten by their priests with a heavy oak stick, which is often
done in the presence of the congregation on Sundays. They go,
when ordered as penance, from the door to the altar, all the way
on their knees. I have seen them on their knees, going round and
round an old chapel, saying prayers on their beads. I have seen
numbers of them, men and women, walking after each other
through the stream of a sacred spring, repeating their paters and
aves. They submit to any penance, however degrading. They have
scraped at the earth where the late priest of this town was buried,
to take a little of it home as a charm, till the grave looks as if rats
had been working at it. And yet, the people here are better
informed than in most parts of Ireland, and Irish is not spoken
here. These are the kind of persons who are to return, at the will of
their priests, the greater part of the Irish members. They say that a
priest could, if he pleased, melt a man into the earth. English
gentlemen, I suppose, think, from seeing so many Irish members
vote for the Catholic bill, that the statements against the Catholics
are unfounded; that otherwise the Irish members would not vote
for it. But it is the weighty influence of the Catholics in their
counties that compels them to do so, and they are ashamed to
acknowledge this in England. It rests on the House of Lords to
save, not only this country, but the Empire.

The present bill is only the point of the wedge, but is a wedge
which will rend these countries asunder. I do not meet a
gentleman here who thinks that this country would be long
habitable for Protestants, if it passed. The act which admitted
Catholics to all situations in the army and navy may be considered
as harmless, because the power of promotion, conferring high
command, is in the government. But if a large portion of our
representatives were Catholic, they would force the government to
give the Catholics promotion and command. In short, as far as
Ireland is concerned, the Catholics would force their way into
every situation of power, civil and military; for while the remaining
Protestants would be, as at present, divided between the parties,
the Catholics would be in one phalanx, on every question where
their body was concerned and on others also for the
accomplishment of the former. They must keep together, for the
great object of the Catholic priesthood would still be unattained.
Dr Troy says of us in his bible, "Their false services have shifted
into our churches, instead of God's true and only worship."* The
Catholic priests are bound by every consideration of religion as
well as interest to see this rectified. They must remove "the
prophane and detestable table of the heretics", as he calls it in the
same note. ... it is even stated that it is allowable to put us heretics
to death for our religion ...'.

*   [Rosse's foot-note] 'Note on 1st Cor[inthian]s, *c.* 10, v.21.'

D/20/4 8 Oct. 1827 Redesdale, Batsford Park, to Rosse.

'... I am very sorry that your kind intentions in favour of Mr Colles have been ineffectual, in consequence of regulations which I have no doubt have been prudently adopted. ...

Now in my eightieth year, I have found a long journey rather fatiguing, and apprehend I shall never be able again to see my desolate acres in Redesdale. The importation of foreign wool has ruined many of the farmers in that country and checked the progress of improvement there and in the adjoining parts of Scotland, and I fear the importation of foreign corn will be a check to the improvement of the agriculture of Ireland. At the same time, I am persuaded that manufacturers and trade will suffer from the depression of agriculture here much more than they will gain by the reduction of prices produced by foreign importations. A barren country never was a manufacturing or trading country.

I fear we are not to expect to see your Lordship in England, but if you should ever again leave Ireland, I hope you will recollect that Batsford is very little out of the way from Holyhead to London.'

D/22	DATE	DESCRIPTION

1–33 1826: 1830–31: Letters to the 2nd Earl from his elder son, Lord Oxmantown, M.P.
       1833   for King's County, who writes from London, where he was
                 attending parliament, to his father in semi-retirement at Birr,
                 about currency and corn, reform of the Irish Post Office, of which
                 the 2nd Earl was Joint Postmaster General [see E/14], general
                 politics, etc.

1   [?9] Feb. 1826   Oxmantown, London, to Rosse about priestly influence in Irish
                          county elections.
                          'I have just returned from paying a visit to Denis Browne, but
                          too late to write you more than a few lines.
                          He and the priests are as much at variance as ever. I fear the
                          contest in Mayo will be rather close. He has obtained a list of the
                          freeholders, and James Browne has not an immense majority over
                          the other candidates, though the list has been made out by his
                          friends, and no allowance has been made for the influence of the
                          priests.
                          D.B. intends to move in the House for returns of sums paid to
                          the witnesses in the Irish enquiry. It will probably expose the C.
                          Bishops, as it is said their charges for attendance were immense. ...'

2   13 Feb. 1826   Oxmantown, London, to Rosse about '... this most difficult
                        currency question. ...
                        It appears to me, though many are of a very different opinion,
                        that the late panic and present distress are not to be attributed to
                        the [text defective – evils?] of our currency. It is, however, certain
                        that the bad foundation of many country banks has contributed
                        much to diminish confidence.
                        Mr [?Tanke], whose pamphlet has been much praised, devotes
                        50 or 60 pages to prove that the over-issues of the country banks
                        raised the funds, or, which is the same thing, lowered the rate of
                        interest, and that the lower rate of interest gave rise to the absurd
                        speculation in joint stock companies, etc, from which no return
                        could possibly be expected. But I think he totally fails to prove
                        that the over-issues of the country banks raised the price of the
                        funds; and, indeed, it seems much more natural to suppose that
                        that effect prevailed from the operation of loans, the repeal of
                        taxes, and the consequent more rapid accumulation of the capital
                        of the country. Mr Baring proposed that silver should be made a
                        legal tender as well as gold. In France, that is the case, and the
                        relative value of gold and silver is adjusted by an axis somewhat
                        similar to the assize of bread in this country. How a regulation of
                        that kind would be relished here, I cannot tell; but without some
                        similar contrivance, I think that the coin would be alternatively
                        melted down, according as bullion was higher or lower than the
                        mint price.

D/22/2 *contd.*

Until I understand this subject more perfectly, I think it more prudent to be silent. I have not been able to procure a copy of your pamphlet on the currency in London. Have you one at home? Should you wish again to consider this question, I can send by post those back according as I read them, which appear to me to contain the best information, and which are most highly esteemed.'

3   [18] Feb. [1826] Oxmantown, London, to Rosse: the same, at greater length.

'... Now, it appears to me that the defects in our currency arise from the issues of the numerous country banks. Being at great distances from the money market, they are not for a length of time affected by any transactions which occur there, and as they are not *practically* liable to be run upon for gold, like the Bank of England, they have not the same restraint upon their issues. It is, I believe, besides an undoubted fact that the Bank of England is so [?opposed] by the country banks, that it frequently fails in affecting the exchanges so as [to] preserve the supply of gold. When it contracts its issues for that purpose, the country banks extend theirs, and thus the circulation continues redundant.

I think that at a future time, when it could be done with safety, it would be better to deprive the country bankers of the privilege of issuing notes at all, and then the Bank of England or any other single establishment should be made responsible for fluctuations in the currency, as indicated by the exchanges, which it would then have in its power, and which it would also be its interest, to prevent. ...'

4   21 Feb. 1826   Oxmantown, London, to Rosse: more on the same subject, and at even greater length.

'... The House of Commons is quite sick of currency and banks. Nothing will go down but facts, stated by efficient or practical men, aided by broad assertions.'

5   27 Feb. 1826   Oxmantown, London, to Rosse about the state of health of Oxmantown's younger brother, John.

6   29 Feb. 1826   Oxmantown, London, to Rosse about the suicide of Thomas Foster, the painter whose portrait of Rosse is discussed in E/35/8.

7   1 Mar. 1826   Oxmantown, London, to Rosse: more about currency.

'I perfectly agree with you that Lord Liverpool is in error if he meant that Bank of England one-pound notes must drive gold out of circulation. I heard his speech, but do not recollect precisely what he said. ...

It appears to me not difficult to explain how country bankers may over-issue, and depreciate for a certain time and to a certain extent the circulating medium of their neighbourhood. ... [He proceeds to do so, at considerable length].

To the sudden contraction of the issues of the Bank of England, I think we may attribute almost the whole of the present distress.

D/22/7 *contd.*   Practical men in the City, as far as I have been able to ascertain, are
all of that opinion, though they cannot give any explanation of it.
It is to them quite a mystery. They say that a scarcity of money was
the immediate consequence of it, and that it was that which
created the panic. ...

In another letter, I will endeavour to explain what obliged the
Bank to contract its issues, and also my opinions on the subject of
exchange, which is intimately connected with the present
question; and I will also state what in my opinion can alone rescue
the Bank from being under the necessity of again suddenly
contracting its issues.

I forgot to mention that, in a country like Ireland, where there is
no commerce and scarcely any manufacture, particularly in that
part of Ireland where Bernard's bank was established, it was
impossible in my opinion for a country bank to over-issue in any
perceptible degree, for the overplus would be exchanged for Bank
of Ireland notes to be sent up to Dublin to be [?let] to merchants
or invested in public securities. ...'

8	2 Mar. 1826	Oxmantown to Rosse: '... I hope to be able to call upon Plunket about the schools. Denis Browne has succeeded in obtaining leave for a large legacy of plate left to a chapel in Mayo to be imported duty-free. This ... [text defective] much to appease the priests. ...'
9	3 Mar. 1826	Oxmantown, London, to Rosse: more about Foster's suicide.
10	4 Mar. 1826	Oxmantown, London, to Rosse about 'craniology', and recounting a tale told him by [Thomas] Attwood about how '... the present Mr Baring acquired his immense property'.
11	[4–6 Mar. 1826?]	John C. Parsons, writing on behalf of Oxmantown, who has a cold, to Rosse giving news of Oxmantown, and discussing Oxmantown's and his views on the currency question.
12	[4–6 Mar. 1826?]	John C. Parsons, to Rosse: the same with gossip about 'Bochsa, the composer'.
13	post-marked 6 Mar. 1826	John C. Parsons to Rosse, Birr Castle, Parsonstown: the same.
14	6 Mar. 1826	Oxmantown, London, to Rosse: more about Foster.
15	14 Mar. [1826]	Extracts from sundry newspapers, in Oxmantown's handwriting?, relating to the need for reform in the Irish Post Office.
16	15 Mar. 1826	Oxmantown, London, to Rosse describing a dinner party at Sir Charles Cootes's, and referring to John's health.
17	20 Mar. 1826	Oxmantown, London, to Rosse reporting that he has '... received a letter from Mr Lushington offering the situation of a clerkship in the Stamp Office, with a salary of £90 a year, for Mr Warburton. ...'

D/22/18   24 Mar. 1826   Oxmantown, London, to Rosse, Parsonstown, referring to Lord
                         Nettervillo's will [see D/18], the King's and John's states of health,
                         the lull in public affairs, various minor matters of patronage, etc.
                         '... With diligence, I think I may have my essay on the currency
                         finished by the end of the recess. ...'

19   25 Mar. 1826   Oxmantown, London, to Rosse mentioning an application to the
                         Admiralty.

20   29 Mar. 1826   Oxmantown, London, to Rosse about social engagements, another
                         minor matter of patronage, and John's state of health.

21   3 Apr. 1826   Oxmantown, London, to Rosse enclosing D/22/15 and reporting
                         an interview he has had with Sir John Newport on the subject.
                         '... I intend to enquire from any members I may know who were
                         in the House at the time, what he really did say. He was extremely
                         courteous, and expressed himself as if he had been unaware that
                         you were connected with the Post Office.'

22   7 Apr. 1826   Oxmantown, London, to Rosse: the same.
                         'I have not been able to ascertain that Newport made any charge
                         against the P.O. McNaghten told me that he manifested some
                         impatience at the report of the commissioners not being yet out,
                         but he recollected nothing further. McNaghten seems to be an
                         intimate friend of Lord O'Neill's. He said that he had written to
                         him representing the indecency of Colonel O'Neill's absence when
                         there was a possibility of charges being brought against him, Lord
                         O., and the P.O.
                         I could not learn from him any particulars respecting the report
                         of the commissioners, except that it would probably be out some
                         time before the close of the session. ...'

23   10 Apr. 1826   Oxmantown, London, to Rosse, among other things reporting a
                         rumour that Henry Goulburn is canvassing Dublin.

24   11 Apr. 1826   Oxmantown, London, to Rosse, explaining that he has still been
                         unable to see Goulburn [about the Post Office business].

25   [Feb.–Mar.?   John C. Parsons to Rosse referring to 'young Warburton', and
          1826?]   describing 'an evening assembly at Sir Watkin Wynn's on Monday
                         last ...; William had also an invitation, but of course did not go.'

26   13 July, post- Oxmantown to Rosse, Stephen's Green, Dublin, enclosing
          marked and   [D/22/27] a copy of a letter he has written to Lord Grey.
          endorsed, 1831

27   13 [July 1831] Rough copy of a letter from Oxmantown to Lord Grey '... drawing
                         your attention to the case of two officers of the Irish Post Office,
                         Messrs Mills and [?Denitt], who had been dismissed by the Duke
                         of Richmond [Post Master General of the new, combined Post
                         Offices of the United Kingdom] some time previously. ...'

D/22/28	14 July 1831	Oxmantown to Rosse annexing a copy of Lord Grey's answer of the same date.
29	23 July 1831	Copy of a letter from Oxmantown, 46 Clarges Street, London, to Lord Grey in reply.
30	3 Aug. 1831	Oxmantown, Ramsgate, Kent, to Rosse, Parsonstown, referring to the same subject.
31	2 Sep., post-marked 1833	Oxmantown to Rosse, Brighton, returning '... several packets of your manuscript, which I have read with great care and believe to be quite correct. Possibly, in page 16, you might introduce something respecting the physical constitution of the Moon ...'.
32	N.D. [mid-1825]	Page of a letter from Oxmantown to Rosse referring to the currency question as one which he has not yet read up. '... Lord Carhampton told John that the government here supported Lord F[arnham?, in the Irish representative peerage election of 1825?], but I do not believe it. D[enis] B[rowne] told me tht he had heard that Lord O[Neill?]'s peculiar connection with a strong party in Ireland rendered the government here apprehensive of making a martyr of him. ...'
33	3 Nov. [1833?]	Oxmantown to Rosse discussing a '... passage respecting the disintegration of the continents'.

D/23	DATE	DESCRIPTION

1–13   1828–9: 1831   Letters to the 2nd Earl from Catherine-Maria, Countess of Charleville, wife of the 1st Earl of Charleville, who lived at Charleville Forest, Tullamore, King's County, and at this time was in alliance with the 2nd Earl in county politics, about the death of John C. Parsons, county politics and elections, the political activities and prospects of their respective sons and heirs, Lords Oxmantown and Tullamore, the Catholic and Reform Questions, etc.

The sub-section includes:

4   16 Nov. 1828   Lady Charleville to Lord Rosse exhorting him to turn his attention to politics, if only to distract himself from the recollection of the death of his son, John.
'... The present state of the country affords such a source of serious reflections that it cannot be an idle speculation for such a mind as yours to consider and advise in; and, when we see the violence and know the prejudices and obstructions and machinations of so many on both sides, we must conclude government require the counsels of clear-headed counsellors, interested in the fate of Ireland. ...
There is serious doubts [sic], from good authority, of the stability of H.M.'s life, and certain convictions of the Duke of Clarence's unsettled state of mind; which, together with all our own embroilments, form a chaotic prospect. ...'

5   [pre 6 Dec. 1828]   Lady Charleville to Rosse: spiritual reflections, and a request that he will extend his privilege of free postage to accept delivery of a deed which Lord Charleville's London solicitor is sending.
'... It is an acknowledge[ment] of £2,330 which my Lord was compelled to pay for a debt of Mr Prittie's – entre nous. Mention not this when you write.'

6   6 Dec. 1828   Lady Charleville, Charleville, Forest, Tullamore, King's County, to Rosse, Parsonstown, thanking him, on Lord Charleville's behalf, '... for transmitting the papers relative to the establishment of the daily post at Pallas Kenry [on Charleville's Co. Limerick estate], which I forwarded to Mr Waller, one of the principal gentlemen there, who sent me yesterday the proposal of the present post-master at Pallas Kenry, which I enclose [not found]. ...'

7   [early 1829?]   Lady Charleville to Rosse about 'John's Hall', Birr, and about Catholic Emancipation.
'... I like the idea of the school-house, having, as I suppose, a portico, which will be ornamental, and the Ionic seems to me the fittest order for a light structure sacred to youth, and its classic purity most appropriate. But we have not here Stuart's Athens, and I do not exactly recollect it. ...

D/23/7 *contd.*		I thank you for wishing Tullamoore [her son – more usually known as Tullamore] to persevere and succeed. He has great quickness and natural talent, and writes *well* and with a *comprehensive* view of his subject. But I think it an unlucky moment to join a vessel sinking under the weight of influence and perhaps expediency! I, however, am now 64, and I fancy my intellects are more obtus[e] than formerly! So I am well pleased better heads should determine this great question.

The speech was tolerably given in the Morning Chronicle and the Mirror, but still garbled. One of yours delivered in 1792 [*sic*] on the subject of the elective franchise seems positively prophetic, and able beyond all that has been since said on the subject. I read it with respect and admiration.

I can never believe the priests will suffer their penitents to shake off their political subserviency, or that Protestants shall ever meet with fair play from any real Catholic. Deists and philosophers may not act against us as religionists, but they will as a corps. However, better anything than bloodshed and a degraded population incensed continually by misrepresentation against us. ...'

| 8 |]7 June 1829 | Lady Charleville, Charleville Forest, to Rosse about his late son and about her own family. |

'... Louisa [Tisdall, her daughter by a previous marriage] and Colonel Marlay ... [are] here ... . He is a most sensitive, honourable man, whom, as her choice, I am satisfied with. The Chancellor has not yet determined upon making him any allowance, and Belvedere [Marlay's house in Co. Westmeath] without one is no acquisition. But while we live, their slender means are unimportant, and their family must be opulent. ...

As to politics, I do not feel easy while the manufacturing world is not so. I think we Irish should be a granary for England and to promote tillage all we could, that bread may be plenty [*sic*] there, for it is impossible that theories should satisfy hungry men. The Duke's is a master spirit, and I suppose he can manage best with military men. But old England did not bend to Marlborough, and sometimes I feel hurt the Commonwealth should have played a higher game then than at this day.'

| 11 | 5 Oct. 1829 | Copy of a letter from Rosse, Parsonstown, to Lady Charleville discussing 'the two old pictures of two young ladies [Anne Boleyn and her sister?] in the parlour' which she had remarked upon on a recent visit to Birr Castle. |

'... I have not yet found out anything respecting them, but I have received from Mr Cooke of this town the enclosed [no copy] paper relative to two other young ladies of ancient times, which appears to me very extraordinary and unaccountable. Mr Cooke is an attorney, but has given occasionally a good deal of his time to antiquarian pursuits.

D/23/11 *contd.*   Beneath, you have an impression from an ancient gold ring. It was Colonel *John Clere's*. It is his coat of arms. It was one of the trifles which was to have accompanied a small estate in the county of Tipperary which I derived from that family, and which was intended for him who is gone. The name is now extinct, as is any little gratification of vanity which I had annexed to it.'

12   27 Nov. 1829   Lady Charleville, London, to Rosse about matters of county patronage.

'... My Lord desires me to say that you will oblige him much by allowing John McDonald to succeed his father, our late post-master, who has died suddenly.

Mr [?Acres] will go security for him, so the public interest is secured; and the young man is so worthy of your protection that my Lord hopes you will give it him, and let Lord O'Neill know how interested he is for him.

The Ponsonby party make a [?quest], I find, about the court-house with government [ie that it should be located in Philipstown, not Tullamore]. But if you are consulted, I am sure Lord Oxmantown and your Lordship will express the same opinion of the propriety of the courthouse and goal being together, independent of your friendship and wish to serve us.'

13   Post-marked   Lady Charleville to Rosse, Parsonstown, about the Reform Bill.
       16 Nov. 1831   '... I heard *at the time* from a person belonging to the government all you fancy a *secret, concerning the transaction*, with only this variation, that you stood out for a peerage; in which I think you were right, for that might be a good for posterity, if in such times we may venture to look forward!!

I protest, in all honesty, I cannot think the late bill would produce a class of honester representatives than the present mode of returning members of parliament. I see in it nothing but a broader field for bribery and corruption, and the greater chance of blackguards being returned to the Commons. As to the borough proprietors, all *theory* is against them, and they should yield to the spirit of the times, I believe. But it certainly will lower the aristocracy of Britain, and perhaps they have deserved it by their yielding to the burdens imposed on the people and a sort of luxury which never fails to bring down empires in the end. This *history* tells us, but Lord Brougham calls it an old almanac, [?etc], so perhaps I should only talk of the young intellects of our sons, and, politics apart, yours seems to [?be] one example of great and solid acquirement in our class, which does him great honour, and which gives me real pleasure, for your sake and his also.

Adieu. I am going again to the Queen this evening. Her manners are very good, but the place is to me disagreeable. Lord Charleville is not well enough to give or take dinners, and there is nothing else doing.

D/23/13 *contd.*

I do not wonder they wished to secure you, and it shows more sense than has been always manifested in their councils.

Tullamoore is in Shropshire. His father has left him as free as you do Lord Oxmantown. I read his speech in the Mirror of Parliament, which seemed to be eloquent and gentlemanlike and true to his views of the question. But I don't speak with him often on those topics, for he is warm, and I have all my life thought more freely on politics than my Lord. Indeed, excepting my strong wish to support pure and simple Protestant religion in these *kingdoms*, we have seldom agreed on them in our equally sincere zeal for Ireland. ...'

E/2	DATE	DESCRIPTION

1–2   1792–4:
        1793–9:
        1802–8

Two small quarto account books, one kept on Parsons's behalf [by an agent or bailiff?], the other kept by Parsons himself, both recording household and demesne expenditure, and giving some information about rent receipts and rent; the second account book, Parsons's own, also gives information about interest money owed to and by him, King's County Militia expenses, etc.

E/2/2, the account book kept by Parsons himself, contains the following information.

In 1797, the gross rental of Parsons's estate, 'exclusive of Tipperary and Wexford rents and profit rent on Rathbeg', was £4,844, which was received by a Mr Melsop. From this had to be deducted nearly £400 in quit rents and head rents, and a total of £2,376 in interest payments and annuities (Parsons's capital debt, exclusive of the annuities, was £22,786). This meant that his disposable income, at least out of the rents in Melsop's receivership, was only *c.* £2,000.

The November 1799 'gale of Birr, Lisclooney, Clonlyn and Newtown' was £2,344, and this money was in the collection of Thomas C. Parsons.

'... 1793. Sum received for the purchase of the Glascarrig estate in the Co. Wexford, after paying Mrs Garstin's mortgage, £21,418.19.0. ... [ie. Parsons sold Glascarrig for this sum]'.

In 1791–4, Parsons sold the lands of Lawlesstown and Lismorta, Co. Tipperary, to Mr R. Sparrow for £10,645, of which £2,000 was left in Sparrow's hands to pay a debt of £2,000 from Parsons to the Bishop of Cork, secured on Lismorta. The sale price was calculated at 19 years' purchase on the net rental.

'... June 18th [1796]. I this day finally concluded the sale of Clonadd and Ballynamuddagh in the King's County to William Jackson. They are a lease forever from my father to Samuel Pearson, rent £205, renewal fine, £102.10.0. ... For this, Jackson paid me £3,900. My principal reason for selling this property was to pay Lord Oxmantown money he advanced to me in my father's lifetime for my election and petition for the College and other purposes. This amounted, with interest, to £3,704.18.7$^{1}/_{2}$.

July 5th, 1796. N.B. Lord O. refused to take the interest, so I sent him only the principal, being £1,946.17.4$^{1}/_{2}$. ...'

E/11	DATE	DESCRIPTION
1–70	1804–5: 1807–8: 1817–21: 1923–8: 1934: 1912: [*c.* 1975]	Letters and papers of Parsons concerning the town and immediate vicinity of Parsonstown/Birr: its Castle, barracks, canal, Protestant and Roman Catholic churches, Sunday school, streets, tolls, mill, etc, etc. Included in the section are 7 letters from the 1st Earl of Norbury, Lord Chief Justice of the Common Pleas, and a local landowner whose seat was at Durrow Abbey, King's County, and one from Sir Jonas Green, later Recorder of Dublin, about 'the Birr rebellion' of 1820, the popular name given to the scare engendered by the forgeries of Mrs Thomas Legg, wife of the local stationer, which for a while deluded the 2nd Earl and everyone else into believing that a repetition of the 1641 rising was about to take place at Birr; two letters of the same year from Thomas Lalor Cooke, a local solicitor and historian, whose *Picture of Parsonstown*, published in 1826, and republished by his son in 1875, drew on many original documents then and/or now in Birr Castle, about minor business matters, 1820; and letters and papers, one of the letters from William Conyngham Plunket, Lord Chief Justice of the Common Pleas, about disputes and skirmishes between the followers of the two rival parish priests at Birr, Revs. Patrick Kennedy (later Roman Catholic Bishop of Killaloe), and Michael Crotty, 1824–8 [see also F/21 and 23. For Crotty's subsequent career, see J/8.] Inserted in this sub-section [E/11/60], though not originally among the Rosse Papers, is Thomas L. Cooke's own copy of his *Picture of Parsonstown*, acquired by the 7th Earl of Rosse in 1981. This copy has many extra-illustrations and other printed and MS insertions, 1827– *c.* 1855, including glosses on ancient Irish place names in the locality, a plan of the battle of Culloden, a letter from Thomas C. Parsons to Cooke about the wording of the book's dedication to the 2nd Earl, and a letter from the 2nd Earl himself thanking Cooke for presenting him with a copy of the book, 26 January 1827. Also inserted in the sub-section is a typescript extract from the Hamwood Papers (at Hamwood, Dunboyne, Co. Meath) describing Birr in 1796, [*c.* 1975].

The second edition of Cooke, *The Early History of the Town of Birr or Parsonstown* ..., pp. 101–113, gives the following account of some of these events, part of it based on papers in this sub-section:

PAGE	DESCRIPTION
p.101	'... The building of Birr Barracks was commenced in 1809, and completed in three years. These barracks were intended to accommodate two regiments of infantry, and were built by Mr Bernard Mullins. The present Sessions House and Bridewell of Birr, were erected about the same time.

E/11 *contd.*

p.102　　In December 1812, a great meeting of "The protestant inhabitants of the King's County," convened by George Drought, Esq., the High Sheriff, was held in Birr, "to pronounce" on the claims for religious equality, which were then being made by the Roman Catholics of Ireland. This meeting, with other resolutions adverse to the Roman Catholics, passed the following:- "Resolved that as it has been asserted by our Roman Catholic fellow subjects, in various publications, that the majority of the Protestants of Ireland approve of an unqualified and unconditional repeal of all the laws which affect the Roman Catholic body, we deem it necessary to declare that this is not our sentiment, and we believe that but a very small portion of the Protestants of this Island are of that opinion." The meeting finally resolved that petitions be prepared for both Houses of Parliament, expressive of the sentiment contained in the resolutions. It is right to mention, that Messrs Maurice N. O'Connor, of Mount Pleasant; Armstrong, of Gallen; and Warburton of Garryhinch, with Colonel O'Moore, all attended this meeting and, on part of their Roman Catholic fellow countrymen, protested against and opposed the proceedings, but in vain. The *Parsonstown Gazette* newspaper, published in Birr at the time, by Mr. Joseph Bull, contained a full report of this remarkable, but illiberal, meeting.

　　The Protestant Church, now so great an ornament to Birr, was built in the year 1815. This very fine and handsome edifice, is said to have originally cost £8,000, and there have been several improvements made in and about it since. The Protestant Church of Birr has for many years been remarkable for the numerous and respectable congregation attending there. In it are several nice cenotaphs, amongst which is conspicuous, one commemorating Laurence, Earl of Rosse, who died in 1841. One of the Communion cups is old and very interesting, and bears the following inscription: "The Communion cup of the Parishe Churche of Parsonstowne, in the King's Countie, Anno Domini, 1636." The paten or cover is inscribed, "The cover of the Communion Cup of

p.103　　Parsonstowne, 1636." It has been seen (p.48), that Robert Sheeply was Vicar of Birr, in the year 1627, and, from an entry in the rental already referred to, there appears to have been a lease of 53 acres of land near Birr, made to him as "Robert Sheepley, Clarke", on the 8th of July 1626. The Rev. Marcus M'Causland is now, and for many years has been, the respected Rector of Birr.

　　In 1817, the present "Oxmantown Bridge" was erected at Birr, after the design of a bridge over the river Anio, in Italy, which design was selected by the then Earl of Rosse. The name it bears was given the new bridge in honour of Baron Oxmantown, the Earl's heir apparent. Mr. Michael Downey, mason, was the builder of this bridge originally, but the arches were lowered by Grand Jury presentment, in 1855. ...

p.104　　The foundation stone of the present very fine Roman Catholic Church of Birr, was laid on the 1st of August 1817. There were then several coins deposited in this foundation stone, as also a brass plate, with the following inscription: "On Friday the 1st of August 1817, the first stone of this chapel, named St. Brendan's Chapel, and dedicated to the worship of Almighty God, was laid by William, Lord Oxmantown, in presence of his father, the Right Hon. Laurence, Earl of

E/11 *contd.* Rosse, the Rev. Philip Meagher, P.P., the Committee appointed to superintend the building of it, and a large concourse of parishioners, who assembled on the occasion." The building of the Birr Roman Catholic Church was finished on the 1st of August 1824, just seven years after it was commenced, but in some years after it was considerably altered and remodel[l]ed, while the Very Rev. John Spain, V.G., was Parish Priest. To this very rev. gentleman, the parish is also indebted for the beautiful stained glass window behind the altar in this church, as also for the erection of the very elegant convent adjoining, and the great advantage to the town and neighbourhood, from the presence of the good and religious ladies who inhabit it. ...

p.108   In the commencement of 1820, the extraordinary occurrence commonly called the "Siege of Birr," and the "Birr Rebellion," took place there. About this time there were some disturbances in the neighbourhood of Birr, which, although not of much consequence, yet, owing to unfounded rumours of large parties of Ribbonmen having been seen, caused considerable anxiety to the authorities, and most of the inhabitants of the town. At length the alarm reached such a height that a meeting of "the magistrates and principal inhabitants of Parsonstown and its vicinity," was held on the 30th of December 1819, the Earl of Rosse in the chair, at which it was resolved that an association, consisting of "both horsemen and foot," be established, and that it be called "the Parsonstown Loyal Association." In some days after this, a document entitled "a Declaration made and subscribed on the 13th of January 1820, by the peaceable inhabitants of the Parish of Birr," was signed by a number of the people who thereby bound themselves to assist the authorities if necessary, and also to give up their arms for safe keeping if required. At this time there resided in Birr a printer and stationer named Thomas Legge, and while the public mind was in this very excited state, Mr. Legge's wife commenced to bring to Birr castle to the Earl of Rosse, a series of documents purporting to be threatening letters, which she stated had been brought or sent toher or her husband by a penitent amongst the Ribbonmen, by whom, as mentioned in these documents, his Lordship and many more of the people of the town were to be slaughtered.

p.109   Thus on the 28th of February 1820, she brought to Lord Rosse two documents purporting to be from this Ribbonman, and which were as follows:- "Mr. Legge, you are requested by a friend to deliver the inclosed letter to Lord Rosse's own hands yourself immediately, for if you don't, your life and the life of every Protestant in Birr will answer for it; so be quick, for there is no time to be lost." The "inclosed letter" ran thus:- "My Lord, As a sworn Ribbon Man I am bound to keep my oath, but conscience tells me as a Christian I ought to save the lives of my fellow brethren [*sic*] as far as I can without breaking that oath, so I have taken the earliest opportunity of informing your Lordship of the dangerous state you and your Town's Men stand in; I am informed your Castle and Town will positively be attacked on Wednesday night towards day if there be not something done to prevent it in time. Your life and Lord Oxmantown and the life of every man who has any power is particularly aimed at." Having delivered these documents to Lord Rosse on the 28th of February, Mrs. Legge again went to the castle on the following day with another letter directed to him, and which

E/11 *contd.* was as follows:- "My Lord, Has Mrs. Legge told you anything concerning your servants, ask her if she has not and I am sure she will tell you – for every information that is in my power to give you I certainly will but through no other person but her, my reason for it you shall know another time. Tell John Drought he has the greatest Rebel in town for a servant except what you

p.110 have got yourself – There was no less than Five hundred Armed Men within a mile of your town last night and were it not that I gave a false alarm there would have been some mischief done – It was one out of your own house that sent word of the town being prepared – I thought to have seen Mrs. Legge to-day but I am so watched I can't stir – You shall soon hear from me again – That is our crest." The "crest" alluded to was a kind of cross, with four letters within the arms, and which "crest" was at the commencement and end of the foregoing document.

With these and other somewhat similar productions, the fabricator went to Birr castle several times, and there generally kept her face covered to conceal herself from the servants, as she said, and so well did this self-commissioned envoy perform her part, that she appeared to faint from fright whilst relating the particulars of the intended massacre. Whether these fits were the effects of momentary excitement, or were only feigned, they certainly had great weight in giving the frightful story the semblance of truth. At all events, the Countess of Rosse, while these delusions continued, was in a dreadful state of suspense, expecting every moment to see her husband and children fall beneath the blows of some ruthless assassin. To provide against the threatened attack, most of the windows of the castle were then built up with stone and mortar by masons selected for the purpose, and from whom Roman Catholics were carefully excluded, as being more likely to be in league with the expected Ribbonmen. So

p.111 general was the alarm throughout the town, that an armed association was kept up the entire time, in which, although Protestants and Roman Catholics were united, it was with mutual feelings of suspicion and distrust. Two pieces of cannon, which had remained at Birr Castle since the memorable time of the Volunteers, were manned by such of the inhabitants as understood anything about the artillery service, and in compliance with the urgent request of the Earl of Rosse and the magistrates of the neighbourhood, Government ordered the 44th Regt. of Foot, then quartered at Templemore, to proceed by a forced march to the instant relief of Birr. "When arrived in Roscrea," said an officer of that gallant corps, "we expected to get some rest and refreshment, but to our great disappointment, we were ordered to proceed with unabated rapidity to Birr, which we reached in about four hours, after a march of nineteen miles. We there saw consternation depicted on every face. Most of the people had some kind of arms or other, and in the square were two pieces of artillery ready primed, and with lighted matches."

p.112 Such was the terror and confusion which then reigned in Birr, and to complete the business, one of the false letters recommended to get a few shots fired in the castle demesne, but fortunately this suggestion was not complied with, for these shots were intended as the signal for general destruction. The people of the town were to think them the commencement of an attack from the imaginary enemy,

E/11 *contd.* and thereupon Protestant and Roman Catholics, who had already been induced
to feel such mutual distrust of each other, were to be engaged in conflict. We
should not despair, however, even when things are at the worst, and in the
present instance, "a lucky chance which oft decides the fate of mighty
monarchs," led to the detection of this infamous contrivance. Mrs. Legge having
been pressed to discover the author of the letters, fortunately pitched upon an
industrious man of as good character as any person of the same means in the
country. This, added to some other fortunate circumstances, having created
suspicion, led to more minute inquiry. Then the talents of the performer were
again called forth, and more letters were written in an altered, angry tone,
denouncing all who should attempt an investigation. However, some account-
books were discovered, in which appeared the same remarkable handwriting as
in the letters, and upon this a public meeting was held, and a committee,
composed principally of magistrates, was appointed to inquire into the
transaction.

The principal members of this committee held several meetings in the bed-
chamber where the writer of this account of the occurrence was then confined
from the effects of an accident which he met with when travelling. In this
chamber the Earl of Rosse deposed upon oath to a long information detailing all
the facts, as far as he was concerned, and several others, including two or three
magistrates, also made sworn depositions on the subject. These depositions,
p.113   or copies of them, are in the writer's possession, but are too long to be set out in
full in this work. From them, however, sufficient evidence appeared upon oath
to show that the entire plot was the contrivance of the bearer of the letters, and
that an inferior tradesman in Birr was intrusted with some petty part in the
management. Sir Jonas Green, afterwards Recorder of Dublin, who was
consulted, gave his opinion, however, that the author of this nefarious plot could
not be prosecuted with a certainty of conviction, in consequence of a point of
law which bore upon the peculiar circumstances of the case; and this opinion
was the cause of the prosecution having been reluctantly abandoned. The
ultimate object of this plot still remains, and probably will for ever remain, a
secret; and lucky as was its early exposure, still some accidents were occasioned
by the hasty, armed preparations for defence, and the subsequent occurrences.
Thus ended this most audacious contrivance, commonly called "the Birr
Rebellion," and "the Siege of Birr," by which, in the nineteenth century, an
artful, designing woman duped and terrified for a time, not only a learned,
astute nobleman and politician, but likewise most of the inhabitants of the large
town of Birr.

In 1820, Wesley Chapel, in Cumberland Street, Birr, was erected, and this
date appears on a tablet in front. This very neat place of worship has been much
improved in late years, and is attended by a considerable congregation.'

E/14	DATE	DESCRIPTION
1–99	1808–31: 1833	Letters and papers (occupying two-thirds of a box) of the 2nd Earl about the Irish Post Office, of which he was Joint Postmaster General, 1809–30 [see the Introduction], including: papers about the alleged misconduct of the Secretary of the G.P.O., E.S. Lees, 1816 and 1822, among them a letter from Robert Peel, the Chief Secretary, on the subject; an undated note from Lees lamenting 'It is really too bad to have the Postmaster General's papers missent ...'; returns of balances in the hands of individual postmasters, 1817, 1824–5 and 1829; reports on proposals for contracts to carry the mail, among them a proposal of 1818 from Bianconi; memorials from the merchants and inhabitants of Castletownroche, Co. Cork, of Dublin, etc, mainly N.D.; correspondence about the 2nd Earl's dispute with the other Joint Postmaster General, Earl O'Neill, over a Post Office appointment at Limerick, 1828, and more amicable correspondence over O'Neill's wish for a marquessate in the same year; and correspondence about Post Office reform and the 2nd Earl's resignation on the fall of the Duke of Wellington's administration in 1830. [See also D/14, D/22 and 0/11.]

The sub-section includes:

| 15 | 12 Feb. 1816 | Peel, Irish Office, [London], to 'My dear Lord' Rosse (letter marked 'Private'). |

'I have lost no time in reading with great attention your Lordship's letter [rough draft present in this sub-section] to Lord Whitworth [the Lord Lieutenant], and all the papers which accompany it, and I have written to Lord Whitworth upon the subject.

I think that there are some charges preferred against Mr Lees which must without delay be immediately enquired into, but I have not recommended Mr Lee's suspension. I should be wanting in candour if I concealed from your Lordship the strong impression which the perusal of the letter and documents above referred to has left upon my mind, that it would have been of great advantage to the public service if Mr Lees had been confined to his proper sphere of duty, namely the execution of the orders of his superiors, and had been kept under that salutory control which can I fear be alone exercised by a personal superintendence on their part of the duties of the department.'

| 49 | 1822 | Rought draft of a private? memorandum submitted by Lord Rosse to the Lord Lieutenant, |

'In addition to a few observations which I had the honour of submitting to your Excellency respecting my situation in the P[ost] O[ffice] ... .

On the resignation of Lord C[lancarty] about the end of the year 1809 I was, without any aplication whatever on my part, transferred from the Treasury to the P.O. The D. of R[ichmond, the then Lord Lieutenant] was pleased to tell me at that time that, on considering of a proper person to undertake the management of that office, the government had selected me, and it was wished that I should adhere to the new arrangements made by Lord Clancarty for conducting the business of it. I found on my appointment that all these arrangements had proceeded from Lord C. alone, that Lord O['Neill] had taken no part either in framing them or in governing the office. I proceeded in the same manner as Lord C. had done. I began by establishing a system for the public accounts, as he had not time previous to his resignation to proceed to that branch of the business. From the establishment of the office in 1784 until my appointment, no account had ever been regularly settled and audited. ... I was at the Treasury when we had ordered the P.M.G. to have their accounts audited, and two attempts to audit [?past] years were then made, but the accounts were in such an improper state that it could not be effected. Giving up, therefore, the day to the usual duties of the P.O., I devoted every evening with the Accountant General to the formation of a new system of accounts, which I put into operation, and which the Commissioners of Accounts have pronounced to be complete and perfect, and which has enabled us to have our accounts regularly audited since.

In this and the various other regulations which I made at the time with respect to the administration of the office, Lord O. took no part whatsoever, nor did he express a wish to do so. Prior to my appointment, all orders for drawing money from the Bank were made merely on the initials of the Secretary, without any communication with the P.M.G. I made an order that the Receiver General should draw no money *whatsoever* on any account out of the Bank, except upon a bill signed by both the Secretary and the Accountant General, on which a warrant should be made signed by the P.M.G. This continued for about two years, but finding that Lord O. sometimes, when I was in England, signed the warrant, and apprehending that accounts might be submitted to him to which I might have objections, I proposed that in future no warrant should be isued but on the signature of both P.M.G. ... My only object in stating this circumstance of the double signature is lest it should be supposed from Lord O. also signing the warrants that the business was equally transacted between us. From the commencement of this new system, I examined the accounts with great care and attention, and corrected the charges which appeared to me to be improper, as the Commissioners of Accounts well know.

Immediately after my appointment, the Secretary proposed to

E/14/49 *contd.*

me, *as an experiment*, to have a second or midday mail coach to
Cork, in which I, being then but little acquainted with such
matters, acquiesced. But finding afterwards that the expense was
considerable, being about £34,000 a year, and the advantage
trifling, I told him it must be discontinued; when, to my
amazement, I found that Lord O. had, while I was in England,
signed a contract for it for 21 years. Mr An[derson] of Fermoy was
the contractor. However, as I saw no mode of undoing this, I only
made an order that in future no contract should be delivered to
the contractor until signed by both the P.M.G. In a few years
afterwards, a correspondence between Mr Anderson and another
of the contractors coming officially before me, it appeared to me
from thence that the contract for the Cork coach had been
fraudulently obtained by Mr A. About the same time also, Mr Lees
became very refractory about the mode I had established of having
the money issued from the Bank only on the warrants signed by
both P.M.G., and in various instances he trangressed this order.

On these and other accounts, however, I submitted to the [*sic*]
Lord Whitworth, then Lord Lieutenant, a statement of his
conduct, into which an enquiry was ordered, and the present
Judge Jebb and Mr Disney, a King's Counsel*, were appointed for
the purpose of investigating the charges against him. I
communicated the particulars of these charges and the grounds of
them to Lord O., and Mr Gregory, by Lord Whitworth's desire,
and afterwards Lord Whitworth himself told Lord O. that he
ought to join me in this enquiry and not throw all the invidious
burthen upon me. This Lord O. declined, and left town, and the
enquiry ended in the censure of Sir E. Lees.

It is unpleasant to me now to revert to these transactions, but I
do so merely to show that I was really the acting person, and that
all the burthen of duty of every kind rested upon me. ...'

---

*   William Disney, Assistant Barrister for Co. Kildare and actually not a K.C.

E/17	DATE	DESCRIPTION

1–21   Apr.-Aug. 1818   Letters to the 2nd Earl about the general election in King's
County, including:

1   11 Apr. 1818   The Rev. R. Drought, Trinity College, to Lord Rosse.
'Mr Drought of Droughtville was with me for a long time
yesterday. The approaching election was the subject of our
conversation. He mentioned that Bernard had gained ground
considerably, in consequence of having purchased Mr Daly's estate.
...' He continues by offering to secure Mr Drought's interest for
Rosse's brother, John C. Parsons.

2   Endorsed June   Richard Warburton, Garryhinch, King's County, to Rosse.
1818   'I am just this moment returned from dining at Lord
Portarlington's and found your messenger waiting for me. It
certainly never was my intention to support any person to the
prejudice of your interest. Nor would I on any consideration have
made the slightest promise to Malone, had I not conceived that
O'Moore and Bennett had promised their second votes to you.
What I can do consistent with the promise I have been led to
make, I certainly will do. You told me when I had the pleasure of
seeing you at Parsonstown, that your brother was safe and it did
not signify which of the other candidates I supported, which
induced me to promise Malone with a view of serving Pole. I shall
write immediately to Pole, and I hope I shall be able to prevail on
him to support your brother singly. If I can I shall be with you a
little after your messenger returns.'

3   Endorsed June   Draft of a letter from Rosse to Richard Malone
1818 [pre-21   'Since I have seen you, I have had a great deal of trouble in
June   making out a state of the county, even with the aid of the printed
registries; and without such books, I apprehend you must find still
more trouble in ascertaining it. As therefore your friend Dr Gold
suggested a comparison of our books, it has occurred to me that it
would be more satisfactory to you to have copies of those I have,
which you can with the assistance of your agents compare with
your own – and which, wherever they are incorrect or incomplete,
you can rectify.
I can only say that they are made out as accurately as I could
make them with the assistance of Mr Legg, who is well acquainted
with the county. The tenants are set down as voting with their
landlords, except in a few instances where I happen to know they
were independent, and would certainly vote otherwise. There are
of course instances in which some of them may be taken off from
their landlords, but these on trial would be found to be few, and
they would probably fall pretty equally for all the candidates.
There are also some whose leases since registering have expired –

E/17/3 *contd.*

particularly on Mr Armstrong's and Mr Drought's of Whigsborough's [*sic*], but as I did not know the exact instances, I have counted them with the rest. But your agent Mr Little must know them. Besides there are some similar instances among the tenants of some of your supporters, of which likewise I have taken no notice. All these are trivial when compared with the general state of the county, and would make little difference in the relative proportions of the candidates. As I did not notice such occurrences in other instances neither did I among my own tenants; a few and a very few of whom are similarly circumstanced, I think not more than ten, or at the utmost twelve. I mention this because between you and me there can be nothing but what is fair and candid. I have also put down all Lord Rossmore's, Mr Vaughan's, Mr Mooney's [*sic* – Moony] and Mr Geraghty's tenants as voting for you, notwithstanding what we have heard of their voting singly. Mr Mooney's son I put down for my brother, because he promised him, and is I am told very zealous for him. There must have been promises made to you that I do not know of. Others have promised my brother, of which I am likewise ignorant, as he has not been here to assist me. Mr Bernard may also have got some promises that I am unacquainted with. I have set down Mr Daly's late tenants as voting with their present master only. I hear they will do so – at least few of them will do otherwise. A pretty significant handbill has been served on them, letting them know to whom they are to pay their rents and arrears of rent in future. I have also set down the Tullamore people, except in a few instances that I happen to know the contrary, as voting singly for Mr Bernard. A letter I have just received from Lord Charleville would however add to my brother's numbers considerably in that town – but as the books were previously added up, I made no alteration to them. Mr Horner Mullock['s] and Mr Berry's will also support my brother, though noted singly for Mr Bernard. As to the people of this town, except the Mr Rackets and a few immediately under them, who will give Mr Bernard one vote, I do not know a man that is not entirely with my brother. I have therefore marked them accordingly.

Should you wish for any communication with me, I should be very happy to have the pleasure of your company here and any friends that may come with you – or I will wait upon you anywhere just as may be most convenient to you.'

6   21 June 1818   Richard Malone, Pallas Park, King's County, to Rosse.

'I am much obliged by the trouble you have taken and assure your Lordship I should by no means wish to give you or the county unnecessary trouble, and if I did not feel myself strong it would be my opinion to decline the contest and not to agitate the county by a contested election. I must however be entirely directed

E/17/6 *contd.*		by my friends, whom I shall consult as soon as I can compare the books you are so good to send me and shall afterwards have the honour of communicating to your Lordship on the subject. ...'
7	24 June 1818	Richard Malone, Pallas Park, to Rosse. He states that after consultation with his friends and inspection of the registration books he has decided to stand a contest.
11	27 June 1818	Richard Malone, Pallas Park, to Rosse.

'Since my friend Mr Fitzsimons [*sic* -Fitzsimon (see D/20/3)] communicated to your Lordship the determination of my friends that I should stand the election, some circumstances have appeared to change their opinion and induce me for the present to withdraw my pretensions even at this late period rather than disturb the county by a contest, the event of which appears doubtful, particularly from the very extraordinary and unexpected defection of Mr O'Moore which I only learned from him this day.

I hope it will appear plain to your Lordship that I was not at liberty to form an earlier determination, and I hope you will not attribute to me any intention of putting you or the county to unnecessary trouble, which I regret very much.'

E/25	DATE	DESCRIPTION

1–29 Oct.–Dec. 1832 Letters to the 2nd Earl and Lord Oxmantown, mainly the latter, about the King's County general election, at which Lord Oxmantown was one of the successful candidates.

1 4 Oct. 1832 Richard Warburton, Paris, to Oxmantown, Parsonstown.

'... As the Clerk of the Peace for the King's County is very old, and the appointment of his successor will either be at your disposition as Lieutenant or your father's as Custos Rotulorum of the King's County, I hope you will take into your consideration my son, George, a man of business, and who has some talent. ...

We shall remain at Dijon for some time, as it may be necessary for me to go over to Ireland for the elections. I understand Lord Tullamo[o]re is to be a candidate on the conservative interest. I have written to [?Tibeundo] to attend to the registries, and I have told him that I had no reason to vary from the line I followed at the last election, though I certainly think Lord T[ullamore] would be a very proper person to represent this county. ...'

2 11 Oct. 1832 George Palmer, Kilbeggan, Co. Westmeath, to Lord Rosse, Castle, Parsonstown.

'Previous to the last election, when I had the honour of seeing you in this town, you were kind enough to promise me that you would give directions to Mr Keenan, then your agent, about some land which I hold in [?Cloughlouge], near Eglish, on which there is [*sic*] some acres of it planted. At that period, your Lordship was kind enough to say that you would allow me the rent I pay for it. I now understand your Lordship has altered your mind, and that you will allow me to cut down the timber, instead of taking the land off my hands at the yearly rent which I pay for it, which is 18s. 5p per acre. Dr Heenan informed [me] of this today at Philipstown, where I have been registering my freehold. I was unfortunate in not having the honour of seeing you the last week, when in Birr, as you were so busy with some other persons.'

3 28 Oct. 1832 Richard Malone, Baronston, Co. Westmeath, to Oxmantown, Birr Castle, Parsonstown.

'The same reasons exist that prevented me on the last occasion from following my wishes by giving you any interest I had in the King's County, and therefore [I] am obliged under these circumstances to refuse at present making any promise. Indeed, my support will be of little consequence, as I do not believe my tenants are registered.'

4 28 Oct. 1832 George Drought, Athlone, Co. Westmeath, to Oxmantown.

'I am favoured with your letter requesting my support at the ensuing election, and assure you, my Lord, it gives me pain to withhold that support which I have been, as well [as] my family, in

E/25/4 *contd.*   the habit of giving yours for generations. But, were I to do so, I
should be going in opposition to the wishes of several branches of
my family as well as my nearest connections, who feel that you have
most pointedly slighted them, and as I cannot in candour but agree
with them, I am compelled, though with reluctance, to refuse.'

5   29 Oct., post-   Henry Prittie, ?Comillon, Roscrea, Co. Tipperary, to Oxmantown,
        marked 1832   Parsonstown.
                           'Circumstanced as I am with the candidates for the King's
County, I did not register my vote. Brother-in-law to Bernard,
uncle to Tullamo[o]re, and Lord Rosse having supported me for
25 years in Tipperary, I could not vote against him. I therefore
took that course. I believe some of my tenants at Loughan have
registered. You are welcome to try them, and I shall not be sorry,
be assured, to hear they vote for you. Under all my predicament, I
hope you will see I could do no more.'

6   10 Nov. 1832   Charles Bagot, Kilcoursey, King's County, to Oxmantown about
                           Bagot's missing freeholder's certificate.

7   11 Nov. 1832   John Darby, Marklye, Sussex, to Lord Rosse.
                           'I have this moment your letter of the 7th inst. I wrote you 20
October. The tenants waited a long time, and then told Horatio
that, as I had given no answer, they had promised Lord Tullamore.
I am yet in ignorance who is the fourth candidate. I write by this
post to say I shall be obliged to the tenants to vote for Lord
Oxmantown, and the enclosed [no longer enclosed] will be made
such use of as you see fit. George stands a good chance of success.'

8   12 Nov. 1832   The undersigned Protestant freeholders of the town of Edenderry,
                           Edenderry, to Oxmantown, Birr, requesting
                           '... your Lordship's presence here on Thursday next to investigate
the charge we have made against Major Crawford, Mr Newcomb
and the police under their command on the 5 of November inst,
as the magistrates will have an investigation on them privately in
the court-house in Edenderry, and if your Lordship does not
attend, let us know, and we will have another candidate that will.
But as your Lordship, being [sic] Lord Lieutenant of our county,
we prefer your Lordship to any other candidate.'

9   21 Nov. 1832   Viscount Tullamoore, Tullamore, to Oxmantown.
                           'I regret to have to report to your Lordship an attack on Sir
William Smith's house at three a.m. on Monday morning. They
broke with oak staves all the window panes in the drawing room
and dining rooms [sic], and with stones the upper windows ... .
                           Last night the police were attacked at [?Ballyrammon] Bridge
whilst escorting a canal boat (not one of Barry's) and fired on them
[sic]. They returned the fire, and have captured five prisoners. I
know none of the particulars, as Crawford is gone to that
neighbourhood to investigate.

E/25/9 *contd.*

I think it right to report these circumstances to your Lordship as the Lieutenant of this county, and to add that this district *is most disturbed* – five murders or attempts to murder within a fortnight.

Your Lordship has neglected sending me the commission as Deputy Lieutenant. If it is your desire I should act as such, you will oblige me by sending it to me.'

10   30 Nov. 1832   The 2nd Earl of Portarlington, Emo Park, Emo, Queen's County, to Lord Rosse.

'My interest is very small in the King's County. I have always supported Mr Bernard, and intend to do so on the present occasion. Should Lord Tullamore resign, who I likewise have promised to support, I shall have much pleasure in being of any use I can to Lord Oxmantown.'

11   3 Dec. 1832   Thomas Manifold, Cadamstown House, Kinnitty, King's County, to Oxmantown, Castle, Parsonstown, pointing out that his subscription to the King's County Hunt is overdue.

12   5 Dec. 1832   Gerald Dillon, Dunkin, post-marked Roscrea, to Oxmantown, Parsonstown, promising support.

13   5 Dec. 1832   Robert Gary, Portarlington, Queen's County, to Oxmantown explaining that Colonel Maude's and his votes have been incorrectly registered, but promising every other support in his power.

14   5 Dec. 1832   Francis Longworth Dames, Green Hill, Edenderry, to Oxmantown, Parsonstown, about the appointment of an assessor for the election.

'... If it should meet your Lordship's and the other candidates' wishes to have an assessor, and that my nomination should not be objected to, I would nominate a barrister going this circuit, but in no way connected with the county, viz. Walter Hussey Griffith. I have written to Colonel Bernard and Mr Fitzsimon on the subject, and shall feel obliged by an early answer from your Lordship.'

15   5 Dec. [1832]   Rev. John ?Hamiere, ?Amiabeark Glebe, Clonastee, to Oxmantown offering to canvass his parish.

16   5 Dec. 1832   George Warburton, Ballinas[?loe], to Oxmantown (letter marked 'Private') offering him the nomination to four vacancies in the ?police.

17   7 Dec. 1832   Hugh Armstrong Conahy, Frankford, King's County, to Oxmantown, Birr Castle, Parsonstown, promising support.

'... My ancestors, both paternal and maternal, for a great number of years always undeviatingly supported with their interest and votes your Lordship's most honourable, ancient and worthy family, and I hope and trust I shall always do the same whilst I live.'

E/25/18 8 Dec. 1832   Rev. William Higgin, Glebe House, Roscrea, to Oxmantown promising support.

19   8 Dec. 1832   John Howley to Oxmantown, Parsonstown (letter marked 'Private and confidential').
'I have this day heard from Frederick Ponsonby that he had a letter this morning from Colonel [Bernard] requesting from him *single* voices, as the contest would be between him and you. Ponsonby said that he would not accede to the request, but would support you as well as Bernard. I think it right to put you in possession of the above, that you may be on your guard against any attempt to deprive you of second voices. ...'

20   8 Dec. 1832   John Hussey Walsh, Kilduff, Tyrrellspass, Co. Westmeath, to Oxmantown, Parsonstown.
'In reply to your letter of the 2nd, which I received this day, I beg to state that, should your Lordship's views upon Irish questions be such as tend, in my opinion, to promote the general interests [of Ireland], you will have a claim upon my vote, which I shall very cheerfully acknowledge.'

21   9 Dec. 1832   ?Francis Enraght, Banagher, to Oxmantown, Birr Castle, mentioning that some unexplained obstacle prevents his supporting Oxmantown.

22   9 Dec. 1832   Frederick Ponsonby, Bishops Court, Co. Kildare, to Oxmantown, Parsonstown.
'I have just received your letter of the 7th. Your vote for my brother and that of Mr Parsons will be most thankfully received by both of us. He is determined to come to the poll, and will do so with a fair prospect of success.
I write to you by this post to Tullamore on the subject of your contest for our county, about which I am *very anxious* to hear from you. I hope my letter will catch you there, but lest it should not, I direct this to Parsonstown.'

23   9 Dec. 1832   W. Goode, Clare Mount, to Oxmantown, Castle, Parsonstown, explaining that Colonel Bernard is his first object.

24   10 Dec. 1832   W. Johnston (address illegible, postmarked Athlone), to Oxmantown, Parsonstown, promising support.

25   16 Dec. 1832   Printed address to the £10 freeholders of King's County, particularly the 'men of Birr, Banagher and Lusmagh', to throw off their chains and cast plumpers for Fitzsimon.

26   19 Dec. 1832   Charles Bagot, Kilcoursey, to Oxmantown, Parsonstown.
'... I think it right to inform you that I have received a letter through the post office threatening my life in case I do not vote for Mr Fitzsimon. My tenants who have registered, promised to give me one vote; but from what I hear, I am afraid I may not be able

E/25/26 *contd.*   to command even that. It is reported that all the Roman Catholics *must* give *plumpers* to Fitzsimon, and it is said that many of the Protestants won't go to the election. Your Lordship's not having waited on the electors in this barony (which the other two candidates have done) appears to have created a jealousy in the minds of some, but if your Lordship was to do so now, I am afraid you might not be well received by the mob, who have been I think a good deal excited here. ...'

27   20 Dec. 1832   William Williamson, Castle Street, Parsonstown, to Lord Rosse, Parsonstown, about Rosse's debts of £600 to him, and about the election.

28   31 Dec. 1832   Williamson, Castle Street, to Rosse reporting the result of his canvassing on behalf of Oxmanton.

29   [Jan. 1833?]   Bill, or possibly subscription list, for the cost '... of dressing a chair for Lord Oxmantown, with canopy, banners, flagstaffs, etc, etc, etc (printing excepted)'.

E/31	DATE	DESCRIPTION

1–28   1780–91   Miscellaneous political, personal and general correspondence of the 2nd Earl, then Sir Laurence Parsons, from miscellaneous correspondents, including Dr John Jebb, the English parliamentary reformer, the Hon. George Knox, a younger son of the 1st Viscount Northland, Lord Charlemont, etc. The topics include the split among the Patriots over the Simple Repeal of Poynings's Law, with which Grattan and his followers declared themselves satisfied, and the Renunciation on Britain's part of the right to legislate for Ireland, which Flood and *his* followers declared to be essential, 1783; parliamentary reform, 1784; the Commercial Propositions, 1785; the mode of drawing up the Irish public accounts, 1788; the regency crisis, 1788–9; and Trinity College, Dublin, and King's County politics and elections, particularly Parsons's failure to be re-elected for the former at the general election of 1790 and his election for the latter at a by-election in 1791. Also included is an undated, vituperative poem attacking the 1st Earl of Clonmell, *c.* 1790? One of the letters from Dr Jebb has been photostated by the National Library (MS.13840), and a second photostat copy has been placed alongside the original.

The sub-section includes:

2   20 July [1780]   James White, Bath, to Parsons, Trinity College, Dublin.
'... The House of Commons of Ireland have done wonders this season, to be sure. Yet, I cannot help agreeing with you that there has been a good deal of farce among the principal actors. *Apropos*, Yelverton I think threatens to make the ostensible Minister take a harlequin leap out of the theatre for his avowal of determined opposition to the Mutiny Bill. As for D[enis] Daly, he seems to have slid out of his own line of acting, to make his appearance in a new cast of characters. Hen[ry] Flood may be likened to those desperate Athenians, who having been branded with infamy for running away at Marathon, made one great bravado and died fighting at *Platea*.

Do you not congratulate the illustrious *Sir Freddy* [Flood] on his new dignity? It will suit him so smartly when he grows ripe for the bench; but he declares himself that the does not expect to be a *judge* these some years. No doubt he may support a wig and ermine as well as another. ...

Do you think Grattan will ever flinch, or that the spirit which has inspired the people of Ireland is likely to evaporate? I would have the real patriots cork it up in them to the utmost. I would have it sealed hermetically and the Journals of this session to be the label pointing out its use and application. ...

What is the poor Duke of Leinster doing? That man has been

E/31/2 *contd.*		obliged to play *Punch* to most of the political *showmen* for these some years, and be the step-ladder of ambition to the Prime Serjeant [Hussey Burgh]. By the way, how do you all reverence the new one? A hogshead of heavy ale, I dare say, after the smart, bottled beer that went before him. ...'
3	20 January [1782]	White, Bath, to Parsons. '... All our mutual acquaintances here agree in mentioning your intentions of offering yourself a candidate to represent the College at the next election. ... Your family have always been at the *right* side of the question, and you will not be the first to admit to be at the *wrong* one. The College will show its spirit of freedom by electing one bred up within its own walls and attached to it by friendships as well as regard for it as a body. I have no vote now. Emmet and your humble servant were disfranchised together. ... Believe me, if you wish to succeed with the independent part of the University, you must lay your shoulders heartily to the work, and show them that you are determined to obtain their confidence and approbation. ... By nature you are no *orator*. But ... remember *Flood* and *Grattan*, and never give up your pursuit. They have cultivated laboriously and have reaped plenteously. ...'
4	Apr. [1782]	John Lloyd, Gloster, [King's County], to [Parsons]. '... I suppose you are glad to take breath after the severe chase you have been engaged in. I never knew in my time opposition stick so firmly together. I think you may take credit, I am sure I give it to you, for the lottery of this year being so much more productive than the last. I will not say you have *robbed* certain people I could name of £40,000 or £50,000, but I think it certain you prevented them from putting such a sum into their pockets, by *shaming* them into throwing the matter into *open* market. I trust I shall see you at the assizes.'
5	post-marked 15 Sep., endorsed 1782	Dr John Jebb to Parsons, Birr. '... With respect to the great point now agitating in Ireland, I will candidly own that I thought Mr Flood to blame for moving anything further, after the people had so generally expressed their disposition to be satisfied with the repeal of the Declaratory Bill, and I am still of opinion that Mr Grattan has merited the highest honour for persevering in his demands for substantial rights, at a time when he was so little supported in parliament, and am persuaded that he has acted all through upon the most disinterested motives and the most perfect patriotism. I mentioned early to Mr Sheridan, late secretary to Mr Fox, my approbation of an idea once broached of a compact between the highest authorities in both nations. I now see from Lord Abingdon's proposal that England should speak still more decisively. Mr Flood's speeches are irresistible in point of argument. It is said he

E/31/5 *contd.*

should have made his objection sooner, but I enter not into the motives of man. I wish to attend to substantial facts. ...

I lament much the change of administration, particularly as I see a narrow policy is to be adopted respecting America, to the inhabitants of which, as assertors of the rights of men, I wish peace and independence and whatever else is good. ...

I am beyod measure alarmed at the institution of the fencible men. It certainly bodes no good. I look to Shelburne as the secret suggestor. The Duke of Portland and Colonel Fitzpatrick, of whose honour and good intentions I entertain the highest idea, either do not support it or do not see its very evident tendency. ...'

6   14 Feb. 1785   The Hon. George Knox, Lambeth, London, to Parsons, Trinity College, Dublin, referring among other things to the disputes over Seaford [see C/8].

'... Fox is rising a little in the popular opinion, or rather Pitt is declining. I still conjecture that the latter will not long retain his station. For God's sake recant what you said in your last respecting Flood's intention of giving up the English parliament. If he were to join Fox's party, he would soon be at the head of it. At any rate, he ought to rescue his character from the misrepresentations of ignorance and revenge. ...'

7   26 Feb. 1785   Dr John Jebb to Parsons, Dublin.

'I am grieved, I am astonished, at your report. I fear the evil has proceeded very far, and the infection sunk into the vitals of the nation, before such daring language could be used – "compel the Volunteers to lay down their arms". "Bring in a bill to *define* the rights of the people!" I tremble for the state of this country, which must submit to thraldom, if liberty be thus subdued in yours. I have remonstrated – I will remonstrate -against such open acts of despotism, for which no concessions of a commercial nature can atone.

I am ashamed of the illiberal spirit of too many of my countrymen, evident in their selfish opposition to what is no more, at the best, than a permission to avail yourselves of the advantages of your situation and other circumstances which the genius of the country and ancient habits have suggested. The principle is good. In the detail, there may be objections, but if it were not for the nefarious attempt that accompanies these propositions (more nefarious as [?moved] by such a character, who perhaps sees not the extent of his own principles but as the instrument of others [sense?]), I should really give some credit to the Minister, and the more so, as I hear he is to be powerfully if not successfully opposed.

As to our parliamentary reform, I think you will do wrong to wait for it. Your grievances, as you well explained the matter at our society dinner, are peculiar to yourselves. Reform them yourselves.

E/31/7 *contd.*   You will do better than if you wait for us.

I honour beyond expression Mr Flood for his manly language respecting the rights of the people. Does Orellana sleep? And is Lord Charlemont to review the Volunteers before the day on which you pile your arms? Is Dungannon the place appointed for that ceremony? ...'

9   25 Aug. 1785   Jebb, Parliament Street, [London], to Parsons, Dublin.

'I most cordially congratulate yourself, Mr Flood and your noble coadjutors on the distinguished stand you made against arbitrary power and the arts of corruption on the 12th inst, and on your complete victory upon the following Monday. ...

I have sent over the Public Advertiser of Monday the 22nd inst, in which is my letter signed Trebatius. After you have read it, will you send it with my compliments to Mr Ashenhurst. ...'

18   5 Feb. 1788   James Laffan, Kilkenny, to Parsons pointing out errors in the public accounts.

'... To a person not very conversant with the national accounts, there is a confusion and perplexity in the mode of keeping them which requires a good deal of time to unravel, and which I suppose is more owing to preserving old forms than a design to have them intricate. A consolidation of the additional duties and appropriations would very much sympathize them, and the expenses of managing the Revenue should not be intermixed with the premiums and drawbacks, but the gross sum of each distinctly marked, drawn so that at a view they may be distinguished.

As the national accounts are never returned until about nine months after the time in which they are made up, there should not be any return of arrears, unless in case of failure of collectors. ...'

19   [post 5 Feb.   Rough copy of a letter from Parsons to Laffan in reply.
       1788]
'... I am afraid that it is not merely for the sake of adhering to ancient forms, which in matters of this kind would be absurd, that the public accounts are kept so indistinct and involved, when they might be so easily rendered clear and intelligible. ...'

21   [1788–early   W. Cane, post-marked Tours, France, to Parsons, Trinity College,
       1789?]   Dublin.

'... I was solemnly assured the other day by an Irish family of the name Segrave, of Cabragh, near Dublin, that there was not a word of truth in the ... [received account of the 1641 rising]. I was then asked if I believed in the Powder Plot. I answered yes. You are wrong, said they; it was Cecil who trumped up the story, to estrange King James's affections from the Catholics, who had been fast friends to his mother. For the truth of this, they appealed to a Father Brady, who has strayed hither from the Co. Longford. He assured me that things were just so, and added that, now the Irish Catholics have a vicereine of the true religion [Lady Buckingham],

E/31/21 *contd.*   I should soon see and hear things that would surprise me. I think it not impossible but that the Parsons family may again inhabit the jail of their own building in their own town of Birr. ...

Gould said publicly here that his brother purposed proposing you for the University at the next election. ...'

22   26 Jan. 178[?9]   [The 1st Earl of] Charlemont, Dublin, to Parsons, St Albans Street, London.

'A thousand thanks to you for your very kind letters, which I only delayed to answer so that I could communicate their contents to Corry.

That gentleman desires me to assure you that he has for the present no idea of touching upon the business you wish to be avoided, nor does he mean to enter into it till it shall be forced on him, as it probably will be in the course of the session, by the other side of the House. At all events, he is entirely open to conviction, and will upon no occasion act in contradiction to the sentiments of his friends, among whom he is pleased to say that I hold the principal place.

But why, my dear Sir, is it only by a letter that we hear from you? Why are you not here at this imporant crisis? Believe me, the presence of every honest man is necessary at the present time, and when I have said so, I need not add that your attendance is ardently wished for.

If you should see Flood, tell him that I some time since wrote him a long letter directed *to him in London*, to which I have as yet had no answer. ...

Thank you for the pamphlet, which will be extremely useful.'

23   29 Jan. 1789   Lord Charlemont to Parsons.

'Some friends of yours and of mine having done me the honour to wish for a meeting at my house to discuss certain important business which will there be laid before them, I request the honour of your company on Saturday next at 1 o'clock. ...

I have not written to Sir William, as I believe he is not in town. If he should [be], bring him with you and make my excuses.'

24   9 Jan. 1790   Sir William Parsons, 4th Bt, Birr, to Parsons, Trinity College, Dublin, about Sir William's borrowings and debts.

'... Let me know something about politics. Will there be a short recess as usual? I would wish rather to defer going to town until I know what is expected, not wishing to embark early in a decisive measure.

When will John send that woman out of Ireland? I put it out of my power *to know him* until that event should take place. Whenever he does, he will always find me his affectionate father. ...'

25   4 Feb. 1790   Issue of *Faulkner's Dublin Journal* reporting a debate in the House of Commons in which Parsons took the lead in attacking the

E/31/25 *contd.*		government for adding two new Commissioners to the seven who had previously been found sufficient to manage the business of the Revenue, while at the same time professing himself to be of no party.
26	3 May 1791	Copy of a duplicated circular letter from Parsons to [the electors of King's County].

'As by the melancholy event of my father's death a vacancy has been made in the representation of the King's County, permit me to entreat your support and protection for the honour of representing it in parliament. I trust that the fidelity with which your late representative discharged that trust in six successive parliaments will be considered as some claim in favour of his son, and that the partiality which for such a long series of years has been shown by your county to my ancestors will not be discontinued to me, ambitious as I ever shall be of not being found less deserving. ...' [See D/1/1.]

27	19 May 1791	[Rev. Dr] M[atthew] Young, Trinity College, Dublin, to Parsons, Birr.

'You may well suppose your letter gave me much satisfaction, both for the intelligence it imparted to me [of Parsons's election for King's County] and the very striking instance it afforded of your friendship. In the midst of such complicated engagements, both of a private and public nature, I could not have expected that you should have thought of me, but your having done so leaves me under the greater obligation, and affords me the more sincere satisfaction. I have given your letter to your brother, and probably the Chancellor has received it this day. What the effect may be, I dare not guess, but whatever it may be, it can scarcely at the best give me greater pleasure than it has already. I congratulate the College on again having a second representative in parliament, and I almost now would rejoice at the past events, which at one time gave us so much concern. It must be a matter of great consequence to you already to have gained such firm footing in the county, and with all my partiality, I cannot avoid allowing your present return more honourable than any you could have had by us. ...'

28	[*c.* 1790?]	Poem attacking Lord Clonmell.

E/32	DATE	DESCRIPTION

32/1–   1794–1800   The same. In this continuation of E/31, the correspondents
37   include John Lloyd of Gloster (Parson's father-in-law), the 1st Earl
of Charlemont and his son and successor, the 2nd Earl, John
Foster (Speaker of the Irish House of Commons and, in effect,
leader of the opposition to the Union), Colonel E.B. Littlehales
(private secretary to the Lord Lieutenant, Marquess Cornwallis),
etc; and the topics include the recall of Lord Fitzwilliam in 1795,
the '98 Rebellion, King's County politics and law and order, the
Union, etc. Also included in the sub-section is a long, but
incomplete, MS. pamphlet, in the form of a letter to Parsons, *c.*
1797, and a special licence and a newspaper cutting relating to his
marriage to Alicia Lloyd of Gloster in May of that year [see E/38.
Several of these letters have been photostated by the National
Library (MS 13840) and a second set of photostats has been
placed alongside the originals. An envelope of papers including
and concerning the 7th Earl of Rosse's *Irish Times* article of 1963
on the '98 Rebellion has also been placed in this sub-section.]

The sub-section includes:

4   11 Feb. 1795   Dean W. Digby, Geashill, King's County, to Parsons, Parliament
House, Dublin, complaining of a want of attention from Parsons
over matters of patronage.

'... Recollect, I beg of you, the warm attachment I have shown
for these 20 years and more to the interests of you and your father
in this county. Ask you own heart, was the support you and he
have experienced from me of consequence or not.

I have never solicited any return from you, excepting *one*, of
which you cannot be ignorant. What efforts, or whether any, were
made by you to gratify my wishes, I cannot say. But of this you
must give me leave to throw you out now a friendly hint that if
you expect a continuance of my friendship, you cannot be
ignorant how to obtain it.

When you were arranging all your militia appointments, it was
natural for me to expect some little mark of attention would have
been shown me, although it would in fact of [*sic*] cost you
nothing, for I should not have availed myself of recommending
any friend whatever to you. The chaplaincy was the only thing
that would have suited my wishes in behalf of my nephew, but as
you had a brother in orders, it was very proper to prefer him.

Possibly, still, a chaplaincy or a church preferment of about even
that small amount, may in the course of this current year be
obtained somehow or other for him, and if you choose to wish for
my friendship, or shall deem it worthy of your desire, it is
probable you may be able to obtain such for him ...'.

E/32/4 *contd.*   Underneath is a copy of Parsons's reply.

'I acknowledge with very great gratitude the powerful support you have so often given to my family in parliament, and look forward with anxious expectation for [*sic*] the time when I may be able more strongly than by words to show my sense of it. But it has so happened hitherto that, without debasing myself by a parliamentary conduct which would have rendered me unworthy to claim your support on any future occasion, I could not obtain any influence with his Majesty's Ministers.

A more striking instance of this I cannot give you, than in my brother, to whom you allude, who, though he has been several years in the church, has not yet obtained the smallest church preferment, except the chaplaincy in the militia can be called one, and that expires on a peace. But he would rather live upon his very small income, and very small it is, than that I should stoop to any act derogatory from those principles which I and my ancestors have always acted upon. This is not only my sentiments, and his, but the sentiment of my other brothers also, who are alike utterly unprovided for, except by what their patrimony and their talents may produce to them. ...'

5   19 Mar. [1795]   Mrs Alice Hayes, Avondale, Co. Wicklow, to Lady Parsons? mainly about Lord Fitzwilliam's visit to Avondale.

'... The Grand Master was quite delighted with his dressing room, admires the chain of all things, and thinks the colour exactly the right tint, and has not yet done admiring the wild beasts, which would appear hid in obscurity, and approves much of the arrangement of all the prints. ...

The whole viceroyal [*sic*] suite were most attentive travellers. They went through all the rooms of this house, and I assure you, the new bed got its share of approbation. ... They left us before two. Mr Hayes attended them through the Flannel Hall and to the top of Rathdrum Hills. ... He [Lord Fitzwilliam] gave £20 to the poor of Rathdrum. There were about 200 miners drawn up at this gate, huzzaing and giving cheers as they passed. They wish to return to Ireland this summer, but don't mean to do it. He has given orders to build some additional rooms at Malton. He minutely inspected into all poor cabins in that neighbourhood and, notwithstanding the bad weather, went himself from cabin to cabin and conversed freely with the inhabitants and carried twenty guineas in his pocket, which he distributed among them. ...'

6   2 July 1795   General Charles Vallancey, Cove Fort, Cork, to Parsons, Colonel of the King's County Militia, Youghal, Co. Cork, about artillery, the defence of Cork, and an 'ammunition box' of which Vallancey annexes a drawing.

14   27 Mar. 1798   Copy of a letter from Parsons, Dublin, to Lord Camden, the Lord Lieutenant, resigning as Colonel of the King's County Militia, in consequence of the Commander-in-Chief's aspersions on the

E/32/14 *contd.*		'relaxed' discipline of the regiment. [For the background to this, see F/20.]
15	28 Mar. 1798	Lord Camden, Dublin Castle, to Parsons accepting his resignation, after observing that Parsons 'would easily have corrected' whatever want of discipline there was.
16	29 Mar. 1798	Thomas Conolly, Dundalk, to Parsons thanking him for sending Conolly copies of the correspondence over the King's County Militia.

'... The attack being personal, and I am certain unmerited, I can only lament the loss of the kingdom in these unprecedented times of so loyal a subject and so good a colonel, but you could do nothing but what you did.

I much fear our militia will turn out a rope of sand – instead of a national protection, will become a national grievance, by the uncommon folly or wickedness of our rulers. Observe these facts, and reason upon them. In January 1793, Lord Westmorland from the Throne was ordered to conciliate the goodwill and affections of *all descriptions* of his Majesty's subjects, Protestant, Dissenter, Catholic, in order to reconcile the latter, being by far the greater number, previous to the making of this war and forming a militia. The only objection to a militia in this kingdom *was* the difference of religions. This being got over by placing the Catholic nearly on the same footing as the Protestant, the militia was accordingly raised, and behaved as unanimously and as well as if the kingdom had possessed but one religion, till, unfortunately, the government, last year avowedly, and before clandestinely, took the Orangemen by the hand as a wise measure of government. This, and the great body of troops in Ulster, have kept that province in subjection. But the three others, being Catholic, will, for making these distinctions, retaliate, and the poor Protestants in them will be destroyed as Orangemen. This distinction, created in the community at large, has crept into the army and militia. Even in my regiment, very correctly attended to, I have been obliged to severely punish two soldiers of each persuasion for belonging to a Catholic society and an Orange club, contrary to a regimental order forbidding all such meetings. If, therefore, this unhappy spirit has got into mine, it must of course get into other regiments, and I much fear that this distinction in the militia will render it unfit to be trusted, and may be the occasion of mutiny or quarrels amongst a set of men upon whose unanimity and goodwill the whole security of this kingdom depends. ...

I have asked for leave to return to Castletown on this day sevennight. If I get it, I hope to see you with Lady Parsons there before you go to England, if you continue of that mind, which I suppose you will, as no man would live in this kingdom at present that could help it.'

E/32/17 [21 Apr. 1798] Rough copy of a letter from Parsons to the freeholders of King's County who had passed at the previous assizes resolutions '... in which you are pleased to express a disapprobation of my conduct in parliament.

I am therefore compelled to observe that, as I feel the gratifying consciousness of having always acted from the purest motives and of never having given a vote or uttered a sentiment with an interested view, I look back with perfect satisfaction to all my conduct in parliament, both recent and remote; nor shall any consideration induce me to depart from those principles of liberty and of humanity by which it has been ever directed.'

22   30 July 1798   Lord Charlemont, Dublin, to Parsons, Parsonstown, about the necessity for supporting the present Lord Lieutenant's policy of clemency.

'... [Richard] Martin's information is certainly not without ground, as an opposition to the Act of Grace may well be apprehended from a party who, from whatever cause, are undoubtedly discontented. Harrington, who is not Solicitor-General, has already opened the campaign by a preparatory speech, and if we may judge from private conversation and from gloomy countenances, much mischief is brewing.

I have, however, my doubts whether it will openly break forth, as a serious endeavour to counteract the measures of government must necessarily be alarming to those who have at all times fought under its banners, and as the spirit and calm perseverance of our present Governor afford no reason to suppose that either through persuasion or alarm he would be induced to recede from any measure on which his judgement has determined. I think, however, at all events, you ought not to be absent. Our friends, whose retreat I never approved, have again made their appearance in parliament, and will I believe, if necessary, support those measure for which they have hitherto vainly combated. Come to town as soon as you conveniently can.'

23   23 Aug. 1798   Capt. Herbert Taylor, Dublin Castle, to Parsons about the matter discussed more fully in D/4.

'... with respect ... to the prisoners of Birr, Capt. T. is directed to observe that they were tried, that they did not appear to have complied with the proclamation, and that the attention which Brig.-General Dunne appeared to have given to a minute investigation and report on their cases, was such as to merit his Excellency's approbation. ...'

24   16 Oct. 1798   Lord Charlemont, Dublin, to Parsons.

'On Sunday last, Lord Castlereagh and Mr Elliot called upon me, the former to communicate a letter just then received from his uncle, A. Stewart, who had seen the last engagement off the Isle of Tory from the heights of Horn Head.

After mutual congratulations on the probable importance of this action, the gentlemen were rising to depart, when I, unwilling to lose the opportunity, exclaimed that to me, indeed, the consolation of good news was absolutely necessary, as I was made miserable by the late report of an intended Union; adding that, sensible as I was of the impropriety of questioning him, I desired that he would say nothing on the subject, but would only suffer me to seize this occasion of assuring him that one principal cause of my anxiety was my certain conviction that the connection between the countries which had always been with me a dear object, would not outlive for ten years the execution of such a measure. To this, his Lordship, readily acquiescing with my request, answered nothing; but I, who viewed both him and his companion with a *Lavaterian* eye, thought I could perceive that the report was not absolutely groundless. I then went on to say that the rumour had gained the more credit, as it had been propagated by Lord B[uckingham]. At this he seemed surprised and, as I thought, in some degree offended; and I have since heard that the noble Marquess is not on good terms with the Castle.

This conversation, though of little importance, excepting to me, whose opinion has thus been communicated, I have here detailed in pursuance of my promise.

I called on Lord Pery, and had with him a long conversation. He appears adverse to the measure, and, considering his natural caution, was tolerably explicit. ...

How truly glorious are our naval successes, and what honour do they not reflect on Lord Spencer! Let our other Ministers be what they may, we most certainly never had a better First Lord of the Admiralty.'

Beneath is a copy of Parson's reply, dated Parsonstown, 21 October 1798.

'I am very glad that you had so good an opportunity of communicating your sentiments to Lord Castlereagh upon this fatal project, and that you availed yourself of it so freely.

I flatter myself that it is only in contemplation at present, and your decided tone must contribute much to dismay him from proceeding further. The more I resolve it in my mind, the more intolerable it appears to me. I am perused [*sic*] that it would engender such a mass of discontent that the English government could not keep the people in subjection but by ... means of a great military force and martial law ..., for a number of years at least, until their spirits should be completely broken down and destroyed. In this county, some of those gentlemen, I hear, who have been most zealous for government even in its most arbitrary paroxysms, say that they would prefer invasion to Union. I am happy, however, to inform you that I have had a letter from

E/32/24 *contd.*

Dublin which says that Lord Shannon is as hostile to it as ever, and I have authentic intelligence that the Speaker said a few days ago that it was utterly impracticable.

The country here is perfectly quiet. And those who had come into this town for protection have returned to their dwellings. Business of every kind goes on as usual, and the minds of all classes of the prople seem at length to be as much composed as ever.'

27   12 Jan. 1799   The 2nd Earl of Charlemont, Dublin, to Parsons.

'As nothing has ever affected me with more more painful astonishment than the shameful apathy and the consequent silence of the country at the present desperate crisis of our fate as a nation, so I have experienced few more real pleasures than in having found by the public papers that a meeting of your county, at least, has been called. ...'

28   16 Jan. 1799   The 2nd Duke of Leinster, Carton, to Parsons, Birr Castle, Parsonstown.

'A report having been most industriously propagated that I am to bring forward the question of Union, and as I find by a circular letter of Lord Castlereagh that the measure will be brought forward the first day of the session, I would wish those with whom I should wish to act on most occasions should know that the report is groundless, that I am decidedly against the measure. Though I had doubts as to taking my seat, I shall now attend to give the measure every opposition in my power.

I hope you will pardon the liberty I take, but [I] can assure [you] it arises from a wish to coincide with you upon this and other political subjects, for I have for some time past approved very much of the line of conduct you have pursued in parliament. I have only to lament that being disgusted with Irish politics, I was determined to withdraw myself totally, by which I am deprived of given [*sic*] the measure any opposition but my own vote in the House of Lords.'

29   27 Jan. 1799   Thomas Bernard Junior, Birr, to Parsons.

'I am first to congratulate you and rejoice with you on the prospect of maintaining our legislative independence.

You have at the other side a sketch of our resolutions, which you will see in the papers, and which I hope you will approve of. Though some may think them violent, they are more moderate than any that appeared at the meeting. I had put a few sentiments on paper, and though I did, I have with the advice of our friend, Mr Lloyd, preferred those, for moderation alone. We are to meet again on this day fortnight. I do not know who will be our next sheriff, but during my short time, we will constantly meet to oppose by every means within our power that measure so contrary to the wishes of the people, so inimical to the interest and honour

E/32/29 *contd.*   of our country. It is the only possible circumstance that could make me wish to remain an hour longer in office.

    The Minister, I think, should consider that the yeomen and people took arms for their country without bounty or reward, and that they would as soon turn them against him as the rebel, if he attempts to deprive them of their birthright. ...'

33   9 June [1800]   John Foster, Dublin, to Parsons, [Scarborough?, Yorkshire?].

    'I send you [not found] the address. The copying was done in a hurry and the printing in a greater. When the third reading came, many of our friends during debate talked of retiring from being witnesses to the final sentence - Lord Corry first and then Plunket. It took a sudden burst, and when Plunket sat down, all the anti-Unionists except aboutfourteen rushed out of the bar. The advantage was instantly taken to pronounce it a general secession, but there ws no such thing; for much remains to be watched.

    I hope you found Lady Parsons well; and much as we regret your going, I could not say a word to urge you otherwise, for I think I should have done the same in your situation. ...'

E/33	DATE	DESCRIPTION
33/1–47	1801–10	Miscellaneous political, personal and general correspondence of the 2nd Earl. The correspondents include Henry Addington (First Lord of the Treasury and Prime Minister), the Dowager Marchioness of Downshire (owner of the Blundell estate at Edenderry, King's County), John Lloyd, Arthur French of Frenchpark, Co. Roscommon (who complains of ill-treatment at the hands of the Pitt administration), Sir Thomas Fetherston of Ardagh, Co. Longford (who sat for that county on the electoral interest of the 1st Earl of Rosse), and the Dublin Castle powers-that-were, including the 3rd Earl of Hardwicke (Lord Lieutenant, 1801–6), William Wickham (Chief Secretary, 1802–4), and Alexander Marsden (Under-Secretary, 1807–9). The topics include both general politics and the local politics of King's County, Co. Longford, Co. Tipperary and Carlow borough, concerning the last of which the 2nd Earl is asked to act as a referee between the 1st Earl of Charleville, the patron of the borough, and Frederick John Robinson, to whom he had sold the seat; Lord Melville's trial; the 2nd Earl's initially unsuccessful aspirations to the Irish representative peerage, 1809; the charges against the Duke of York as Commander-in-Chief, 1809; and various minor patronage matters.

The sub-section includes:

1	26 Oct. 1801	Henry Addington to Sir Laurence Parsons thanking him for his letter and saying that he would be very obliged if Parsons would attend the debates in parliament.
2	28 Dec. 1802	The 2nd Earl of Glandore, Ardfert Abbey, Co. Kerry, to Parsons. 'From the manner in which my agent, Mr Blunden, has let my lands in the King's County, I fear but few of my tenants are freeholders. But if I have the disposal of any votes, they are all at your service. Mr Blunden, under a power of attorney from me, made leases of 31 years, instead of lives, contrary to my instructions to him. The term of these leases is more than half expired, and immediately after the last general election, I offered the tenants to give them freehold interest, instead of their present tenure, which they refused, as Mr Blunden informed me. ...' He continues with regrets that he could not contribute more effectively to support Parsons.
4	14 Jan. 1804	William Wickham, Phoenix Park, to Parsons thanking him for the support he has given to Lord Hardwicke's government during the time that Wickham has been Chief Secretary.
5	24 Apr. 1804	Lord Hardwicke, Dublin Castle, to Parsons acknowledging the support he has given to Addington's administration but regretting that he is unable to find a place for Parsons's brother on the Bench.

E/33/6 8 Dec. 1804   Sir Evan Nepean (Wickham's successor as Chief Secretary) Dublin Castle, to Parsons mentioning, among other things, that Parsons will receive a letter from Mr Pitt requesting his attendance at the House of Commons on 15 January 1805.

12   26 July 1805   Sir Thomas Fetherston, 2nd Bt, Ardagh, Co. Longford, to Parsons.
'I had the pleasure of your friendly letter yesterday and am much obliged for your anxiety on the occasion, for I am certain had you not taken it up as warmly as you did, I should have been laid aside until some very material business made them want a friend. Many such I think may occur in course of next spring; and before any such come on, they may, I hope, think it necessary to do me common justice. The old cry with them was: you are in parliament, therefore can take nothing. [But] ... if they will not give me anything, I have a son who can take it ...'.

18   [post 4 Jan.   Arthur French, Frenchpark, [Co. Roscommon], to Parsons.
        1806]   'Yours of the 4th inst I only received yesterday. Allow me to assure you I have not the least doubt of your good wishes to promote my views; but I feel that I have been so badly treated, that I do not mean to inconvenience myself at present by a journey to London for those who, as soon as [they] get their turn out [of] me, think no more of their promises. I hope to meet you there in March, when we will have some pleasant days together.'

19   5 Mar. 1806   Lady Downshire, Hanover Square, London, to Parsons.
'I regretted that I was from home when you did me the favour to call before you set out for Ireland, because I intended to mention more particularly the wishes I stated to you respecting Lord Forbes at the next election for the county of Longford. Those wishes have been repeated to me and I am anxious therefore again to introduce them to your attention, being assured that towards the personage I referred to [the Prince of Wales?] you will do all you can to serve the candidate he would wish to succeed. Perhaps you may write a line to authorise me to state that your support and the interest you may [?have] with your friends who have possessions in that county, will not be wanting on that occasion. I am sensible this would give great satisfaction and I am the more desirous therefore to show that the opinion I took the liberty to express and which was received with the greatest attention is proved by your kindness to have been well founded, because I know there are those who would be inclined, if in their power, to inculcate a contrary idea. It gave me great pleasure to think that the suggestions of a friend may have had the desired effect and that you are to continue a Commissioner of his Majesty's Treasury, which I mention only to congratulate you on that event. I should indeed have been better pleased if the arrangements could have been so made that you might have filled a situation in which notable abilities and integrity would have had greater scope in the

E/33/19 *contd.*		service of Ireland, for the prosperity of which I must naturally entertain very anxious wishes. You will have heard how well the business of Monday night went off. I have not yet heard from Mr Bernard but hope soon to hear him recovered and that I shall see him shortly in London.'
22	3 May 1806	Lady Downshire, Hanover Square, to Parsons. 'I have just heard that Mr Bernard is in opposition and a few evenings ago voted against the ministry; and as you, in one of our conversations, informed me I might depend upon Mr Bernard's being with the government, I trust you will excuse my expressing to you the surprise I felt upon receiving this information. Perhaps you can have the goodness to explain Mr Bernard's reasons for the line he has chosen. It is so long since I have heard from or seen him, though I find he has been some time in London, that I have no opportunity of hearing from himself.'
23	11 May 1806	Draft of a reply from Parsons to Lady Downshire. 'I do not think that Mr B[ernard] has joined the opposition as your Ladyship apprehends, or that he has any indisposition to the present administration, but I collect from his letters to me that he considered himself bound in consistency to support Mr Pitt's defence bill, having voted for it during the former administration. I also beg leave to state that, though Mr B. from his regard for me has been pleased to coincide with me in his political conduct, he is, however, perfectly an independent member and entirely free to take an opposite part whenever he chooses; at the same time I think that from his attachment to me he might be very unwilling to do so. This is exactly the language that I have always held respecting Mr Bernard when I have had occasion to speak of him, and if your Ladyship conceived from any conversation of mine that I possessed any further influence with him, you must certainly have misapprehended me.'
26	24 May 1806	Thomas Bernard, London, to Parsons. 'Windham has made some small changes in his military plan; it is to come on next week (Friday); it will be the only question of moment this session. I hope to leave this about the 5th June. Sir John Newport did not acquit himself at all well last night in [?the committee] and on the detail of the Irish taxes. Foster [?perplexed] and puzzled him much.'
29	7 Nov. 1806	John Bagwell, Marlfield, Co. Tipperary, to Parsons requesting his support in the forthcoming election for Co. Tipperary. He adds that he does not think that Colonel Mathew really has any chance of success.
30	17 Nov. 1806	The 2nd Earl Digby to Parsons promising to support him at the forthcoming election for King's County.

E/33/33 17 Nov. 1806   The 1st Earl of Malmesbury, Spring Garden, London, to Parsons, now Lord Rosse.

  'Lord Malmesbury presents his compliments to Lord Rosse. On reconsidering carefully and attentively the expressions employed in Lord Charleville's letter to Lord Hardwicke, it is impossible for him to look upon their meaning as ambiguous, and he should not discharge his duty as a referee conscientiously or with satisfaction to himself, if he did not declare it was his opinion that the agreement made between the Earl of Charleville and Mr Fred. Robinson has become null and void by a dissolution of parliament. Lord Malmesbury has communicated this his opinion to Lord Hardwicke and Mr Robinson. They assent to it and are perfectly contented to abide by it. Lord M[almesbury] hopes in writing as well that no time may be lost in its being made known to Lord Charleville, and to spare Lord Rosse the trouble of coming again to Spring Garden.'

34   29 Apr. 1807   Sir Arthur Wellesley, Chief Secretary for Ireland, Dublin Castle, to Rosse reporting that he has taken steps to support Hardress Lloyd in King's County. He also looks to the return of Sir Thomas Fetherston and Mr Newcomen for Co. Longford and feels that, if they support each other, Lord Forbes would be excluded.

36   14 June 1807   Joseph Marshall, 4 Devon Street, Liverpool, to John Hubert Kelly, Parsonstown, asking him to add lives to the leases of Marshall's tenants so that they could vote in Lord Rosse's interest at the forthcoming election for King's County.

38   29 Mar. 1808   Sir Arthur Wellesley to Rosse asking him to exert the influence which he must have over the members for King's County to attend their duty in parliament.

45   14 Jan. 1809   Wellesley, Dublin Castle, to Rosse.

  'Since I had the pleasure of seeing your Lordship yesterday, the Lord Lieutenant has received letters from his Majesty's ministers by which his Grace is informed that they consider themselves bound by an engagement made by the late Mr Pitt to give all the support which government can give to the claim of Lord Mountjoy to be the representative peer on the vacancy occasioned by the death of the late Marquess of Sligo. His Grace has at the same time desired me to inform you that he is happy to have it in his power to pledge to your Lordship the support of government to your claims upon the next vacancy which may occur.'

46   [late Mar. 1809]   Draft of a letter from Rosse to Hardress Lloyd.

  'I have just had a letter from Lady Rosse. She is so loyal and so much attached to the K[ing], and thinks, as indeed is the fact, that we all must stand or fall with that family, that she regrets much your voting against the D[uke] of Y[ork]. I have written to her to

E/33/46 *contd.*

assure her that no one was more loyal on [?general] principles than yourself and that nothing but the strongest sense of duty I knew compelled you to do so, and that it must have been very unpleasant to you, as it was in opposition even to the interest of a favourite brother that you had in the army. I have in short said what I could and indeed what I ought on the occasion; for I am sure she apprehended that I was in part the cause of it, and that it was because I have been passed over to make way for Lord Mountjoy [for a representative peerage]. But this I must be very sorry anyone could think, for even if I did feel any resentment on that account, I should never think of showing it in a way to hurt the old King's feelings and in a point so tender. I am sure however that others too think that it was in some measure by my advice, and for the same reason, for the D[uke] on my coming to town received me a little coolly. I hope however some questions will soon come on that will remove the impression.' [Lloyd had voted against the Duke of York and with the opposition in two separate divisions on 17 March 1809.]

E/34	DATE	DESCRIPTION
34/1–41	1811–20	Miscellaneous political, personal and general correspondence of the 2nd Earl. The correspondents include Robert Peel, Chief Secretary, 1812–18, and the topics, King's County politics, law and order, agriculture, etc [for a complete sub-section on the King's County election of 1818, see E/17]. Also included in this sub-section is a description, in the form of an original letter from the 2nd Earl to his brother, the Rev. William Parsons of Tullynisky Park, Birr, of a reception in London for the visiting Continental dignitaries in 1814.

The sub-section includes:

12	21 Sep. 1816	George Fenamore, Clonarlee, to Lord Rosse. He offers to support Lord Rosse at the next election for King's County with his tenantry: they appear to number between 6 and 12.
14	18 Dec. 1816	Richard Warburton, Garryhinch, to Rosse.

'It being mentioned in my presence that Hardress [Lloyd] had determined to decline a contest for the King's County, I wrote in consequence to his father, stating the report and that, though I wished to give my second votes to Malone, I had not bound myself by any promise that might prove injurious to Hardress. I received an answer from Mr Lloyd in which he said that he did not know what were his son's intentions. If he is determined not to stand a contest he ought to say so, as in that case you might wish to put forward one of your own family and I should [like] to give my humble assistance to forward your wishes. My father always supported your family, and, although I felt a pleasure in supporting Hardress from my long acquaintance with him, yet I assure [you] my principal motive for doing so was to assist in maintaining your interest in the county. If you are acquainted with his intentions, have the goodness to make them known to me as well as your own determination in the event of his declining a contest.'

19	24 May 1817	John Drought, Ballyboy, to Rosse.

'For your information I send you enclosed a list of the freeholders in the town and townland of Ballyboy, some of whom you addressed and some were not at home at the time your Lordship was here. Any communication you wish from me I will with every willingness obey [sic].' The list consists of 12 freeholders in Ballyboy itself, and another 26 on the 900 acres of the townland. Of the 26, 13 were Drought's own tenants; 6 were the tenants of a Mr James Haslam; and the final 7 the tenants of Mr Robert Delany.

E/34/26 1818   A statement of the expenses of the police in King's County.

31   15 Jan. 1820   Colonel L'Estrange, Moystown, King's County, to Rosse. He writes of the disturbances in the county and makes reference to groups of volunteers (both Roman Catholic and Protestant) which have been formed to keep the peace.

35   5 June 1820   Thomas Foster (a London-based Irish portrait painter – see D/22/6 and 9 and E/35), London, to Rosse.

'I have been to make enquiries about the coronation robes according to your Lordship's wishes. I went first to Fisher's in Duke Street who showed me robes he has now in hand for several Irish peers, and he says that the price of the whole dress, including coronet, sword, etc, etc, would amount to £250. From thence I went to Webb's in Holywell Street, Strand, who is the King's robe maker, where I saw a great number of robes making for English peers, and I think the velvet and ermine seem of a much finer and richer quality than Fisher's. As the King wishes some little alteration to be made in the shape of the coat, which he has not yet mentioned decisively, Webb could not tell me the exact price the robes will come to, but he says it may be as low as £250 and will not exceed £270. He engages to furnish every article of dress necessary for the coronation and will also give a cedar chest to preserve the robes from decay.'

37   7 Nov. 1820   Sir George Fetherston (3rd Bt), Dublin, to Rosse.

'I came to town yesterday on some business of my own. I called on Mrs Newcomen, sister of Lord Newcomen. She married Counsellor N[ewcomen], a connection of the family.

He died about six weeks ago. Both she and her husband were warm friends of ours at the contested election and exerted all their influence in our favour. I am much concerned to hear that her affairs are in a very embarrassed state. In fact she knows not how to extricate herself. She is desirous of obtaining apartments at Hampton Court or any of the palaces where she might reside until her affairs were put into some better state. If this is not obtainable immediately she hopes she might be put on the pension list.

I really feel much concerned for her, as I fear the part she and her husband took at the election served to irritate Lord N[ewcomen], who now shows his enmity. If your Lordship would have the goodness to interest yourself in her favour it would be an act of humanity, independent of the political considerations.'

38   24 Dec. 1820   Sir George Fetherston, Ardagh, Co. Longford, to Rosse. He refers again to his wish that Rosse should aid Mrs Newcomen, and adds:

'... For my own part, I am at a loss to discover the pleasures of being in parliament, as since I have had a seat in the House I have heard nothing but tales of misery and I have not the satisfaction of having been able to provide for any one individual.'

E/33/39 N.D. [*c.* 1820] Anonymous letter to Rosse: an interesting report by a distiller on the difficulties of his trade since the Union.

40–41 N.D. [*c.* 1820] Printed prospectus of 'The Protestant Association of the King's County'. This association had been formed to resist murder and outrage in the county and was signed by the following gentlemen: Thomas Johnson, Chairman; Thomas Drought; Randal Cooke; Thomas Norris; Thomas Faulkner; Thomas Mullock; William Parsons, Treasurer; Robert Mullock Junior; Nicholas Gamble; Samuel Abbott; John Blakely; John Drought Junior; George Peirce; W.B. Drought; Shaw Cartland; John Weldon Tarlton; Thomas Berry; Thomas Crofton; John Wakely; Edward Crow; Henry Pilkington; Edmond Armstrong; Andrew Armstrong; Edward King.

E/35	DATE	DESCRIPTION

1–44   1821–34

Miscellaneous political, personal and general correspondence of the 2nd Earl, and also of Lord Oxmantown, from miscellaneous correspondents, including Lord Norbury, the 2nd Earl of Liverpool (Prime Minister, 1812–27), the Marquess Wellesley (Lord Lieutenant, 1821–7), Lord Francis Leveson Gower (Chief Secretary, 1828–30), and Sir Benjamin Bloomfield (later 1st Lord Bloomfield). The topics include: King's County patronage, militia, law and order, and elections; the views of Thomas Foster (who had just finished the portrait of the 2nd Earl, in George IV coronation robes, which is in the dining room in Birr Castle), about his painting, 'Mazeppa', and other artistic matters, 1822; the desirability of having a pope of 'moderate principles' (in Lord Liverpool's view, expressed in 1823); the financial affairs of the late Capt. Hardress Lloyd (of the Gloster family, but not the namesake who was M.P. for King's County, 1807–18); etc, etc. [For other original correspondence of the 2nd Earl relating to the late Capt. Hardress Lloyd's affairs, 1823–5, see National Library, MS.13885. These particular papers appear not to be of Birr Castle provenance.]

The sub-section includes:

2–4   29 Jan. 1821

Printed letter and enclosures from W. Shaw Mason, Record Tower, Dublin Castle, concerning the holding of special sessions, in this instance in King's County, for the purpose of carrying into effect the provisions of the Population Act, 55 George III.

7   3 July 1822

Lord Norbury to Lord Rosse about the stolen letter from Saurin to Lord Norbury - see F/21.

'... As to our political sentiments, they have been no secret. You are too pure, too proud, and [too] perfect a gentleman to have ever intimated to any judge to do any act that could contaminate his judicial character.

I have no recollection of the letter in question, but though I have not been able to go to Saurin since my gout, I am ready to believe that such a letter may have passed to me amongst many others of private and sacred confidence of our mutual, honourable intimacy. ...

In many cases, the receiver [ie. O'Connell] is as bad as the thief ...'.

11   18 Sep. 1823

Lord Liverpool, Fife House, [Charing Cross], to Rosse.

'I am much obliged to you for your letter with its enclosures.

I feel the full importance, in the present state of the world, that a pope should be elected of moderate principles, and who will be disposed to conform to the temper and disposition of the times.

We cannot expect that English influence can have much weight in such an election and, indeed, I believe that it has almost

E/35/11 *contd.*   uniformly happened that the person elected by the conclave has
not been the individual who was expected to succeed, even by
those states which have necessarily the greatest influence. We have,
as you know, no resident Minister at Rome, but our Minister at
Florence has been directed to attend there and to watch the course
of events.'

12   20 Nov. 1823   Lord Wellesley, Woodstock, Inistiogue, Co. Kilkenny, to Rosse
(letter marked 'Private') about the colonelcy of the King's County
Militia.

'Some time since I had the honour of receiving a letter from
Lord Oxmantown expressing a wish to be appointed to the
command of the militia of the King's County. At that time no
vacancy existed, but Colonel L'Estrange has since resigned in
consequence of ill-health. I am convinced that it is unnecessary for
me to assure your Lordship of my sincere respect for you and your
family, or of my disposition on all occasions to manifest every just
and practicable degree of attention to your interests and welfare.
But on the present occasion, I have felt myself bound by the
obligations of justice and impartiality to give consideration to the
claims of Mr Bernard. ...'

27   23 Sep. 1828   Denis Hegan, Broakhann [*sic* – Brockernagh?], Moneygall, King's
County, to Rosse, Castle, Parsonstown, '... taking the liberty of
addressing you a few lines relative to [the] factions that have
disturbed the peace of this part of the county for the last three or
four years, and particularly so at Thurles, Templemore, Roscrea
and Parsonstown.

The Catholic Association, feeling a particular anxiety to preserve
the peace, to promote due respect for the laws, and to quash
differences between all his Majesty's subjects, is now and for many
months [past] using all their [*sic*] influence to restore good order
and kind feelings amongst the peasantry, and further to teach
them due respect for the law and to preserve harmony and love
towards their Protestant brethren of every class. With those
motives solely, many thousand persons have lately assembled in the
different towns of the county of Tipperary, and their peaceable
conduct on each of those occasions speak [*sic*] loudly for the
salutary advice they have received and still continue to receive
from the Catholic Association.

My Lord, the peasantry in those parts of the King's County wish
to meet on next Sunday for [?amical] reconciliation of their
quarrels both at Shinrone and Parsonstown, and as an humble
member of the Catholic Association, I take this liberty of soliciting
your Lordship's pleasure in stating if you see any legal or valid
objection to such a course being adopted, knowing as I do that
both Shinrone and Parsonstown is [*sic*] a property of your
Lordship and that of your friend, Colonel Lloyd.

E/35/27 *contd.*

Be assured, my Lord Ross [*sic*], when I looked through the debates on the Catholic Question in the late Irish parliament now before me, and read your eloquent, liberal and patriotic speeches on the Catholic Question, I fancy that already I hear from your Lordship in answer sentiments equally liberal and wise with those of your early exertions for the freedom of Ireland.

My Lord, I feel a duty I owe to the preservation of the peace of our country, as a member of the Catholic Association, thus to acquaint your Lordship in particular on this subject, in consequence of a false report abroad (as I believe) that your Lordship's tenantry of the Established Church intends to come in contact with the multitude at Shinrone. The result of such contact should be deeply deplored by all good friends to the true interest of Ireland.

I am sincerely anxious to concur in the adoption of any suggestion flowing from so pure and wise a source. I shall gratefully acknowledge and attend to your Lordship's reply, so far as my duty as a Catholic member of the Association may permit me prudently so [*sic*] to do. ...'

28–9   27 Sep. 1828   Two depositions concerning the impending clash at Shinrone.

30   1 Oct. 1828   Lord Francis Leveson Gower, the Chief Secretary, Dublin, to Lord Oxmantown, Parsonstown (letter marked 'Private'): the same.

'I am directed by his Excellency to communicate to your Lordship his high sense of the zeal and discretion evinced by your Lordship in the prevention of the expected meeting at Shinrone on Sunday the 27th, and to request your Lordship to communicate to your brother magistrates, by whom you were supported on that occasion, this expression of the Lord Lieutenant's approbation of their valuable services.

I have to thank your Lordship for your letter of the 29th. The service rendered to government and the country by furnishing such detailed information as is contained in that letter, is only second in value to your Lordship's active exertions in preserving the peace in your county. ...

A proclamation will reach your Lordship's county by this day's post, which his Excellency trusts will sufficiently declare to all parties concerned the intentions of government, and point out to the civil authorities the course which it is necessary to pursue and in which they will be supported, if necessary, by the whole force of government, with reference to the illegal assemblages of the people, should they unhappily be presevered in.'

31   9 Oct. 1828   John Darby, Marklye, to Rosse about the Catholic Question.

'... The present times must have occupied you so much as to draw your attention from private matters. You and I always thought alike but upon one subject, and now I see you are trying to subdue a spirit which I still think has been mistakenly withheld.

E/35/31 *contd.* But perhaps I am still in error. I yet think the law, not the opinion of factious men, should be our guide. ... What has given the turn to Lord Rossmore? If old Westenra got out of his grave, what would he say? I am now eighty or very near it, and I never remember a gift or concession to the papists that was not followed by some insurrection or violence. ...'

33   20 Sep. 1831   The 2nd Lord Rossmore, London, to Rosse commenting on
'... a resolution I had just seen in the papers with your name and that of some magistrates, etc, etc, appended to it, reflecting, evidently intentionally, upon me.

I beg leave to refer your Lordship to a copy of my letter to Sir John Harvey in my solicitor, Mr Cooke's, hands in Parsonstown, which fully explains that my reason for not attending a meeting of magistrates with your Lordship at their head, assembled in the manner they had been, did not proceed from any disinclination "to bring forward charges which had been preferred", imputed to me by your Lordship and those magistrates, and in which I conceive you and they volunteered a very unnecessary and, pardon me for saying, a very inappropriate remark or allusion to me.

Your Lordship immediately doing the insinuation away, as far as it relates to me, will relieve me from the necessity of any further observations. Capt. Richardson will convey this, to whom I refer your Lordship.'

35   1 Jan. 1832   'Copy of a [Ribbon] notice which was found posted up in Geashill.'

F/3	DATE	DESCRIPTION
1–2	1784–8	

Rough sketches by Parsons of some of the events of the Lord Lieutenancies of the Duke of Rutland and the Marquess of Buckingham, including the clashes between John Foster and Sir John Parnell, Chancellor of the Irish Exchequer, on the one hand, and John FitGibbon, the Attorney-General, on the other, over the bill for the lowering of the rate of interest from 6% to 5%.

'The bill for reducing the interest of money to 5% was yesterday rejected by the Lords on the motion for committing it. The numbers, with proxies, were 27 to 17.

In the course of the debate, its connection with the loan was frequently stated, and no one attempted to defend the loan. The job seems to be universally acknowledged. People were very slow in comprehending it. I omitted no opportunity of explaining it during the progress of the loan bill in the House, but it was not understood, not even in the City, until it had passed. I endeavoured to assemble a meeting of the City, to oppose the loan project, but though every merchant that was spoken to acknowledged the truth of the statement I made, yet they said it would be impossible to have the subject taken up with spirit, the citizens were so much dejected at the failure of their opposition to the police, and the influence of government is now so powerful.

The conduct of Foster and Parnell in this whole business, I believe, has offended the other members of our Cabinet. They took it up and endeavoured to carry it through by their own powers, without even consulting the other Ministers, who all strenuously opposed it – the Chancellor and Archbishop of Cashel in the Lords, the Attorney and Solicitor General in the Commons. Fitzherbert [the Chief Secretary] did not attend the debates. They all insinuated the gain that would accrue if it passed to the contractors for the loan. The principal men were jealous of the power that was usurped, and the subalterns of the profit which formerly was divided, each receiving a [?bulse] of tickets, and Parnell asserted that in former lotteries never more than 15m [*sic* – 15,000], and sometimes not more than £5m, resulted to the state, Even merchants who at first wished for the reduction of interest to 5 per cent seem now well pleased at the failure of the bill, because it has defeated so monstrous a job. I think, though, that this bill will pass in a year or two. The agitation for it now will produce some effect upon the interest of money and show whether the nation is fit for it or no.

I intend to speak again upon the loan. It remains still in the option of the Lord Lieutenant to execute the plan of the C[hancellor] of E[xchequer], and I think, if he persists in it, he will not serve his character in England as a financier who aspires to be at some future day a Prime Minister. It is wretched policy to

F/3/1–2 *contd.*   put the funds of a nation below par and thereby out of the
dominion of a Minister; for [text defective] ... reduce to $3^1/_2$%,
because the Minister can't call them in without a manifest loss ...'

'... The Duke of Rutland's administration was one of the most
exceptionable I remember in this country. Expense generated
expense and profusion outran profusion. Every office in the land
germinated daily with some new salary, and although £150,000 a
year was voted in one session to equalize Revenue to expense,
before the next session the expense had by more than that sum
outstripped the Revenue. Yet the people seemed insensible to all
this, and in the parliament it passed without opposition or
animadversion ... .

The Marquess of Buckingham came, and so little was the
disposition of the people then adverse to the government, that
they went to the shore to meet him and drew him in triumph to
this City. ... They expected from his attention to business, and
some indications of his disposition [text defective] ... which he had
given in his former administration here, that some check [would
be] given to that course of prodigality which had been pursued by
[text defective] ... . In this, however, the people as usual were
deceived. ... I believe his ... intentions were rendered illusory ...
[by] the corrupt and jobbing dispositions of those who
[?surrounded] him, and I am the more confirmed in this opinion
by the multitude of invectives I have heard against him from lips
that never inveighed against anything but public virtue and never
adulated anything but public vice. ...'

F/12   DATE   DESCRIPTION

1–2   [*c.* 1806]   Two sketches by Parsons, one concerning his own indifference to office and power, the other concerning the formation of Lord Grenville's 'Ministry of All the Talents'.

The first item is as follows:

'I am not an aspiring man. I am not ambitious of political power. I have never courted it. On the contrary, I have often wished to be released from all public situation; and if the sense of duty to my country did not impel me, I should not now have a seat in this House. But my reason, and my friends, always told me it was a duty, and what I believe to be a duty I will never avoid. Under the shade of science and of learning, I could pass a life more congenial with my disposition and in my mind of much greater felicity. It is not therefore a love of power that moves my voice upon this occasion. Were I sure that I could be of no service to my country in the situation I am now in, I should soon depose myself. A lust of more policital power is the political disease of the time. It rages through all denominations of people, fermenting and fevering their blood, and making them heated and unhappy in every situation. They are not satisfied with being well-governed, but they must be themselves governors. Yet, were they to know how uneasy a thing it is to be even on the first eminence of power to which weak, frail humanity can be exalted, they would not pant so after it.'

F/13

DATE	DESCRIPTION

[post
1816]

[Incomplete?] 'Political recollections' of Parsons, now 2nd Earl of Rosse,
covering the years 1777–81. [This document has been photostated by the
National Library (MS. 13841), and a second photostat has been placed
alongside the original.]

'I think it was in 1777 that I entered Dublin College. The Irish parliament
was then sitting, and the gentlemen of the College were allowed, whenever they
pleased, to go to the gallery of the House of Commons in their gowns to hear
the debates. The House was an octagon. A corridor opening with three arches
surrounded the House. The fourth arch was the principal entrance. The gallery
was all round, over the corridor, with beautiful Ionic columns, between which
there was an iron balustrade, and over which there was a dome. The spectacle
was magnificent, and good and graceful speakers appeared there to the greatest
advantage. How poor and confined the House of Commons of England
appeared to me after it!

There were at this time many distinguished orators. Mr Flood had the highest
reputation, but he was then Vice-Treasurer, and not approving much of the
conduct of the government, he seldom spoke. We knew little of him, but from
the report of those who had formerly heard him. Mr Grattan was then in the
maturity and vigour of his ability. He possessed great powers of delivery, and was
an accomplished actor of whatever he spoke -great variety of intonation, peculiar
but not ungraceful action. His declamation, rapid and vehement; his figures
often extravagant, yet partaking of the sublime. His most admired speech was on
moving a declaration of right that only the Irish parliament had the right to bind
Ireland by laws. He was dressed in full court dress on the occasion, as was usual
then for the principal speakers, especially those who were to make a motion. His
hair had many curls and was much powdered, but long before he concluded, the
powder was dissipated and his head dishevelled by the vehemence of his actions.
He spoke like one inspired, with the frenzy of a sybil. He frequently rose
completely off the ground, and advanced far on the floor from his seat. After he
concluded, no one attempted to rise to oppose his motion. The Speaker,
according to form, put the question twice. On putting it a second time, one
faint no was heard. It was from Mr John Scott, afterward Lord Clonmell; and a
debate then ensued as to whether the question had passed or no, for according to
the usual mode of proceeding, the question had been carried. But Mr Pery, the
Speaker, said that on so momentous a subject he did not think it would be right
to close a debate for a mere matter of form. Scott then, with much hesitation,
which was unusual, but evidently embarrassed by attempting to reply to such a
splendid effusion of eloquence, spoke against the motion. The debate lasted to a
very late hour, when Mr Flood arose [see C/6]. Though in office he spoke
strongly in favour of the principle of the resolution, went into a long historic
detail, asserting the right of Ireland to [be] bound by her own parliament alone,
argued this with great force, and concluded by recommending that the
resolution should be withdrawn, as a similar one, in substance the same, was
already on the Journals. This suggestion was finally adopted, It was in allusion to

F/13 *contd.* this he said on a subsequent occasion, in a reply to Mr Grattan, "that day when he declaimed, I argued". And on another occasion, "that day when declamation triumphed." And again, "I rescued his motion from the disgrace of postponement or the ruin of rejection."

In the course of the speech of Mr Grattan's which I have just been mentioning, he used a figure which, though incorrect, produced much emotion at the instant. In order to make it intelligible, it is necessary to state the facts alluded to. The English parliament had long claimed and fequently exercised the power of making laws binding on Ireland, in which the Irish courts of law acquiesced, partly because the principal judges were Englishmen, partly because the laws were frequently useful ones, principally because there lay an appeal from the Irish courts to the House of Lords in England, which House would of course enforce the English statutes. But about this time the right of the English parliament to bind Ireland by such laws began to be questioned. As to Ireland it was a question exactly the same as that with America, which caused the existing war, and as such a large party in England denied the right of her parliament to legislate for America, and as this was supported by much argument, the people of Ireland applied the same principles and arguments to their own case and were bold and open in doing so, backed thus by the authority of a great party in England. Ireland, too, was powerful at this moment, the army being withdrawn to the American service, and the people in arms, as Volunteer corps commanded by officers nominated by themselves, being very numerous. In a little time the right of the English parliament to legislate for Ireland had become so unpopular that the judges, participating in the sentiments of the people, did not venture to give an English law in charge to a jury, who would have treated it with contempt. Alluding to this, Mr Grattan said in his speech ... that the English law lay like a spent thunderbolt upon a desert island, which the Minister was afraid to touch and the people were fond to trample upon. Faulty as this figure is, it was so delivered that it electrified the House.

Mr Walter Hussey Burgh was also a very eloquent speaker at this time. He had a fine person – most graceful action – a full and sweet voice – fluent elocution – his periods sonorous and Ciceronian. I and the young men of my acquaintance who frequented the gallery, were charmed with his oratory, though he spoke for government, for he was their Prime Serjeant. But he was the only speaker on that side who we were glad to hear, for as is natural to young men, we supposed that all those who supported government were influence [*sic*] by interested and sordid considerations. The struggle between the government and opposition at the time was on subjects most likely to inflame young minds, or even old. The opposition were contending against the power of the English legislature and the government trying to uphold it. All the questions, too, respecting economy and retrenchment of expenses looked ulteriorly to this, as the number of places and pensions, etc, contributed to enable the government to procure a majority in support of those unpopular claims and powers. Burgh, however, in the course of the session resigned his office and joined the opposition. He made a most animated speech on the occasion, and at the conclusion, in allusion to the English laws, which often cramped the trade of Ireland, and to the Volunteer corps, he said, "they sowed their laws in serpents' teeth and they had sprung up

F/13 *contd.* aimed men". It is unnecesary to mention that this speech was received with great
acclamation. It was Mr Burgh in this session afforded a striking example of the
different views which men take of the same things, according as it suits the line
of argument of their respective party. For, near the commencement of the
session, when in office, he represented the country in a flourishing condition,
that content was singing in the cottages and agriculture smiling in the fields.
But, after he relinquished office, he described the country in a most wretched
state. Hope, he said, had forsaken the plough, the shuttle had fallen from the
hand of the manufacturer, etc, etc. He made a motion for an extenstion of trade,
for England had interdicted almost every branch of trade between Ireland and all
the rest of the world, except with herself, and even that lay under many heavy
and unequal restraints. When Burgh, after an eloquent speech, made his motion
for a great extension of trade, Mr Flood said in a loud and deep tone across the
House, why not a free trade, and these words were immediately substituted; and
such was the spirit of the time that the motion was carried by a great majority
against the Minister, and only a short money bill passed, to ensure its success. It
was, I think, in the following session that Mr Flood resigned his place as Vice-
Treasurer and joined the opposition. His resignation of so great an office
produced a considerable sensation.

Ireland was at this time very poor. The American war had exhausted the
country. The taxes became unproductive. Rents were badly paid. When the
government wished to change the quarters of the army, as it was usual to do
every year, although the number of troops was but small, there was not money
enough in the Treasury to do it, and the government borrowed £50,000 from
the English Treasury. Many members could not get money enough out of their
estates to bring their families to Dublin when they came to attend parliament,
and the attendance was consequently less than usual. This distress united the
members in their endeavour to relieve the country by an extension of trade. The
English Minister, Lord North, was also very willing to extend the commercial
privileges of Ireland, but the jealousy of England would not permit him to do so,
though it was obvious that the richer Ireland should be, the more wealth would
flow from it to England. All he could accomplish was a permission to the Irish to
cultivate tobacco, an herb which could not be brought to perfection in their
climate. This increased the indignation of the people against England, and
caused every man who opposed the government to be considered by them as a
patriot, and every man who supported it became peculiarly obnoxious. The
people began to think of intimidating the government by their numbers and
their arms; and though the armament of the people in the Volunteer corps began
without any such design, they suddenly began to feel their strength augmented
by arms and discipline; their ideas and objects accordingly enlarged.

The first Volunteer corps that was raised was in the county of Wexford by Mr
Ogle in the year 1776. He was member for the county. The object was to
preserve the peace against some insurgent peasants who were called whiteboys
and were committing depredations there. In April of the same year, a similar
corps was raised in Birr, in consequence of two gentlemen there who had lived in
Wexford and who had recently visited it, and gave an account of Mr Ogle's
which excited among the young men of Birr a wish to put on red coats and

F/13 *contd.* practise arms, especially as the papers were filled with accounts of military proceedings in America. I mention this so particularly, as it shows from what a slender cause events of much consequence originated. By degrees, a few other similar corps were formed, principally I think from the desire which the young men had for the dress, which was rather a novelty, being heretofore confined to the regular army, for there was then no militia. At length, the united hostile fleets being too powerful for the fleets of England, the Lord Lieutenant sent 500 stand of arms to each county, and called upon the people to be ready to defend themselves in case of an invasion from France, for there was not a sufficient army in the country to protect them, and the English fleet was no longer able to do so. This call was immediately obeyed. The martial spirit having been infused into the people here by the American war, all were eager now to appear in military parade. They everywhere chose their own officers, bought their own clothing and accoutrements, bought a great deal of arms in addition to those given by government, and being all commanded by the principal gentlemen of the country, and the privates as well as officers being nearly all Protestants, government had no apprehension of any improper use being made by them of the power which arms and discipline gave them; for government knew very well that the Protestants of Ireland were not sufficiently numerous and powerful to maintain the station which they held against the Catholics, unless supported by England. Still, however, in a little time the people became more powerful than was foreseen, and began to turn their thoughts to political subjects, and at their reviews used to enter into resolutions declaratory of their rights.

About the same time, the first bill for relaxing the penal code against the Catholics was introduced into the House of Commons. It was moved by Mr Gardiner, afterwards Lord Mountjoy, and seconded by Mr O'Neill, afterwards Lord O'Neill, both of whom were killed by the rebels in 1798. It was opposed by Mr Flood, and but coldly supported by Mr Grattan, who comprised his sentiments at that time on this subject in these words, "Catholic toleration: Protestant Ascendancy". At the same time the Test was repealed in favour of the Protestant Dissenters. This act of repeal passed with scarcely any observation, although in England the Test Act is considered as an act of vital consequence. However, numerous as the Dissenters are in Ireland, I never heard anyone say that any disadvantage or inconvenience proceed [*sic*] from the repeal, and I believe that few people in Ireland from that time to this have been aware of the fact or thought about it. It seems impossible that this measure, which had no effect of any kind in Ireland, could have much in England if adopted there, either good or bad. But the intellects of men upon many subjects, but especially politics, are miserably defective, as the predictions of the ablest, continually contradicted by events, proves. However, those who oppose change act, for this reason, the discreeter part. They who are so blind as not to be able to discern the objects immediately before them, had better sit still, if not compelled to move by some urgent necessity.

Mr Flood's office of Vice-Treasurer was given on his resignation to Lord Shannon, and the office of Muster Master General, which had been held by Lord Shannon, was given to Mr Denis Daly, who was a very distnguished public speaker. He spoke but seldom, but with great effect. His language was plain and

F/13 *contd.* pointed, his sentiments strong and manly, and all his observations replete with good sense and without any refinement. He imputed in a speech Mr Flood's resignation to *disappointed ambition*. Mr Flood took notice of this in reply. Mr Daly immediately arose and interrupted him, by assuring him that he did not mean to say anything unpleasant to his feelings. Mr Flood said that was not sufficient, that he understood the words as applied to him, and must do so if not retracted. Mr Daly wished, by some kind of apology which he made, to soften the expression. But Flood rose again and said, "That will not do", and began to take of his great coat, evidetly about to proceed to animadvert on Daly, when Daly once more arose, and in very complimentary language to Flood retracted the expression. I mention this, as it showed in what great awe so able a speaker as Daly stood of Mr Flood's abilities.

Mr Eden, afterwards Lord Auckland, was at this time the Lord Lieutenant's Secretary. He used to express himself fluently, but in a light, unimpressive manner; and speaking one night, in reply to Mr Flood, he said that anyone who took Johnson's Dictionary and put together some hard words, could make as good a speech. Flood said across the House in a deep tone, "try", which completely disconcerted Eden. Sir William Osborne was also a distinguished speaker at this time – a fine voice – very finely modulated – and his diction pointed and often splendid. His faculties were, however, now in their wane. Lord Yelverton, afterwards Chief Baron and Lord Avonmore, was a very forcible, but not an elegant, speaker. He had not the high polish of the others whom I have mentioned. Mr Scott, a lawyer, afterwards Lord Clonmell and Chief Justice of the King's Bench, was not a man of eloquence, but had great felicity in telling a story. He was a very entertaining companion and an admirable mimic. He at this time told one night in debate an amusing story ridiculing Flood, whom he described by the name of Harry Plantagenet, who was fond of hunting and who used to hunt with the King's hounds. ... [Here follows the well-known story at Flood's expense]. Some of the gentlemen about Flood told him, while it was going [on], that he ought to answer it, but Flood said, "How is it possible to reply to such stuff?" But they urging him, he got up and began by saying, it is true I have been fond of hunting, but I was never a whipper-in. To understand this, however, it is necessary to know that there was always two or three members employed by government to watch the government members, and to see that they were in their places at the time of a division, and to send to them for that purpose to the coffee houses, etc; and these were called, in reproach, whipper-in, and when Scott was first brought into parliament, he was employed in this way. Flood then drew a ludicrous picture of Scott and of a recent attack on his house by the mob, insinuating that he represented this as much more serious to government than it really was, in order to enhance his merits. He described him as going to the Castle to the Lord Lieutenant to state his sufferings, weeping in the ante-chamber, blubbering in the presence chamber, etc, and getting his windows repaired again with *crown* glass. He told it with so much wit and humour that he completely turned the laugh against Scott, and far exceeded in this impromptu in Scott's own style, Scott's prepared attack. Afterwards, while the debate was still going on, Flood went out to take some refereshment, and when he was returning by the arch behind the Speaker's chair,

F/13 *contd.*   there were many members standing there, so that it was not easy to pass, and among then he met Scott. So Scott said to him in a good-humoured way, laughing, "Well, how do you do, old Ironside." "Very well, I thank you, Hardicanute", says Flood in a deep, grave tone. Scott was so remarkable for his effrontry that he was called copper-face. He himself told me one day that the subjects debated in the Irish parliament had so little to do with the rest of the world, that no fame could be acquired by any display of abilities there; that he had early formed the decision that there no passion could be gratified but avarice; and that he had made the most he could of the situation. His income at the time he said this was from his Chief Justice's place, and also from another office which he held, £20,000 a year. I forget the name of the office, but it was afterwards held by the late Lord Buckinghamshire [the Clerkship of the Pleas in the Court of Exchequer].'

F/19

DATE	DESCRIPTION

[1794–8]   Folio commonplace book/scrapbook, which Parsons has begun to use to record
the dates of bills drawn by him or on him, but which is converted to other
purposes, particularly to an account of parliamentary and other political
transactions involving Parsons, January–March 1794 and January 1795; the
book also includes notes for speeches or pamphlets on the corn bounties,
parliamentary reform, 'The repeal of the Insurrection Bill', etc, and also the first
few pages of some political recollections along the lines of F/13, covering (in a
fairly uninformed fashion, since Parsons was very young at the time) the period
between the passing of the Octennial Act and the outbreak of the American War.
The book was the principal element in the Rosse papers drawn on by Stephen
Gwynn in his *Henry Grattan and his Times* (London, 1939), so subjoined to it
are Gwynn's letters to the 6th Earl of Rosse on the subject, 1938–9.

The followng is the part of the early reminiscences which relates to the forming
of the Volunteers. [It is also printed, with some blunders, in Gwynn's *Grattan*,
pp.58–60.]

'... The people arming themselves voluntarily during the American war was a
singular and pregnant event. As the origin of these armaments will hereafter be
assigned to many false causes, I will here record it, as I can speak of it from my
own knowledge. It began in the town of Wexford. It was a whim, I believe, of
some young men there who wished to put on red coats. Mr Ogle, representative
for the county [of Wexford], without any deep feelings, but partly probably to
amuse them, partly to amuse himself and perhaps with some view to repress
some petty disturbance of the peace in that neighbourhood [sentence
incomplete]. A Mr Tottenham, who had been in the army, and had an old
attachment to red clothes, lived then at Parsonstown. He was a native of
Wexford and, happening at this time to go there, returned full of desire to have
something of this kind constituted in Parsonstown. He accordingly proposed it
to several young men. They had a meeting, were delighted at the idea of wearing
red clothes and a cockade, and this martial spirt was perhaps excited by the war
which was then carried on in America, and the daily accounts of the exploits
there and the daily preparations that were making for it at home. Accordingly, in
April 1776 a light infantry company was formed and a uniform fixed upon, and
I happening to be from school just at that time, was elected one of the officers.
But the plan was soon enlarged. One or two battalion companies were formed,
and that very summer we were reviewed by my father, who was appointed the
General of that and all the neighbouring corps. For the spirit diffused itself
rapidly, first, as I say, from fashion, afterwards for the protection of the country,
as the war advanced.

The whole nation in a few years was thus arrayed. That is, every Protestant
capable of bearing arms and who was able to clothe and accoutre himself, besides
many who were not, who were equipped by public subscriptions. Government,
in order to spare the more men for America, encouraged it and distributed arms
among the people. I believe there might have ben 50 or 60,000 men thus raised,

F/19 *contd.* and they were soon tolerably well disciplined. But their spirit rose with their armament and discipline. And, beginning only to secure themselves, and proceeding to protect the country against France, they concluded by vindicating their constitution and liberty against the aspiration of England.'

The following is the parliamentary/political diary, 1794–5, [printed, also with blunders, in Gwynn, *Grattan*, pp.288–302].

'1794, January 21. A profound and awful silence reigned in parliament for some days after the opening of the session. The government during the sumer had made converts of many members who usually had voted in opposition. Lord Shannon and his numerous train, which from the time of the debates on the regency had been brought into opposition, now became partizans of the Court by his Lordship being gratified with the situation of the First Lord of the Treasury. Mr O'Neill and his two members also quitted the opposition, he being gratified with a peerage. Several of the county representatives, by being appointed to higher situations in the militia regiments, were become either wholly devoted or much inclined to the Court.

I moved for the last monthly return of the army. This occasioned much real and pretended alarm: that is, ministerial men insinuated everywhere that I would expose the paucity of our force to the French, as if the difference between the actual number of troops and the establishment, which amounted to but 1,302 men, would have any effect upon the determinations of the French in respect of an invasion. I did it to prevent any more men being sent out of the kingdom, as I knew it was the immediate intention of the government to send out two more regiments. The return I got was as follows. It was not made to the House of Commons, but to me privately. ...'

The return stated the cavalry at just over 3,000, of whom Parsons notes that one only regiment of 405 men afterwards embarked. The infantry were returned as totalling 9,390 effectives, '... from which deduct the flank companies on foreign service, being 6 officers, 12 non-commissioned officers and 140 rank-and-file from each regiment of infantry, in all 1,738 ...'. This left a total of 7,657 infantry which, added to the 3,041 cavalry, amounted to 10,698. The total militia was about 11,923, which meant a grand total of 22,621 effectives.

'... In point of artillery, the kingdom is still worse provided. From the war commenced, the number of men was about 300. These 300 were augmented by recruits, so as to enable government to send out of the kingdom 500 disciplined and half-disciplined men, and there is now left but 300, most of whom were but mere recruits. There were not arms in our stores sufficient for arming our militia, and what these were, were old and unfit for service. The reason given about the arms was that the stores were damp. Why not renew them? But all the money that could be wrung from the people of this country has been made a spoil of by its administration.

This army was principally composed out of recruits who were very young boys, much under size as well as under age for actual service, and only initiated in the rudiments of discipline. This arose from the order for the sudden augmentation of the regiments, on the declaration of war, and from the amputation they suffered in losing their flank companies, which were completed

F/19 *contd.* by men culled from the battalion and sent to the West Indies.

The militia establishment too was but in its infancy, the middle of the last year having given birth to it.

In the House of Commons, however, there seemed to be the greatest apprehension of discussing any subject, and particularly one which related to the army. There were, however, many reasons for apprehending that the French might invade this island. They were making great naval preparations, apparently with a hostile design against either England or Ireland. England had greater temptations, being nearer and richer. But, then, she was much more powerful, having a militia of, I believe, 30,000 men, having her Guards and some cavalry and all the army which had been intended under the command of Lord Moira to have relieved the royalists in Brittany, amounting to about 15,000 men, now garrisoned in her towns on her southern coast. Her people, besides, were all affected well to the government, and teemed with their ancient antipathies to the French nation. Not so Ireland. Much weaker in armed force, and abounding with people who were supposed to be disaffected; the Ministers very unpopular, from their long series of opposition to the wishes to the people; contemptible from their having, measure by measure, adopted what they had year after year represented in parliamentary debate as idle or mischievous, but which, the moment they adopted, they panegyricized as most useful and salutary; men of a low mediocrity of talents in general, of contracted knowledge not reaching beyond the little sphere of official sitAuation, and no public principle, but a determined system to acquiesce unlimitedly in the wishes of their English superiors. If ever they privately objected to anything which the primary planets in England required, it was only upon the mean ground that the people of Ireland or the opposition in parliament would be too much irritated by it, not upon defect of servility in themselves, or any assumption, real or feigned, of dignity or rectitude. Thus were they consequently despised and rewarded by the government and despised and hated by the Irish people.

February 4. This day I was to have made a motion in the House of Commons for putting this island into an adequate state of defence. Being a few minutes later than the hour of meeting, 4 o'clock, the members, who almost to a man pusillanimously dreaded any discussion, adjourned. I was detained by waiting for Mr Duquery, a lawyer, who had not at that time returned from the courts of justice, and who was to have seconded my motion. This evening, Mr D. and I agreed to postpone this motion for a few days until some more members had considered it, and in view of it, that I should move tomorrow for those treaties, etc, relative to the war, to be laid before our parliament, which had been laid before the parliament of England, and to preface the motion with a declaration of my sentiments on the imprudence of the war, and my determination speedily to give this great subject, which had hitherto been passed over in silence, a full and calm investigation in the Commons, and that Mr Tighe should second this motion, and Mr D. and Mr Curran speak to it also. We feared that parliament was sinking very low in the estimation of the public by observing so profound a silence upon every public measure, that it appeared as if parliament was intimidated and awestruck, and too many thought that it was totally and in all

F/19 *contd.* its parts and ramifications corrupted by the Ministers, and that the people would cease to look up with respect or confidence to parliament, and therefore would direct their views elsewhere.

February 5. I made the motion in the House of Commons, as had been concerted. It was opposed by the administration, and by Mr Grattan and Mr G. Ponsonby and their immediate connections, from which I suppose, either that one of the Portland party in England, probably Lord Spencer, it is determined shall succeed Lord Westmorland in the administration of this country, or perhaps on the more remote speculation that, if Mr Pitt shall be obliged to quit his station in England and that that country should find it necessary to treat with France for peace, the D. of Portland is to succeed Mr Pitt as First Lord of the Treasury. The ground upon which Mr Grattan opposed my motion was that this country was bound to rise or fall with Great Britain, and that the parliament was already pledged by the address voted the first day of the session – as if circumstances could not change and make prosecuting the war at one time advisable and a treaty for peace advisable at another time, as if our determining to support the executive power during the continuation of the war was inconsistent with our advising the executive power to negotiate for peace. But Mr Grattan himself had expressly the first day of the session stated several times that he did not mean by assenting to the address to pledge himself to an approbation of the principle or conduct of the war, and those gentlemen who thought the continuance of the war imprudent, felt themselves sheltered under this general exception, against any imputation of inconsistency, should they afterwards go into a discussion of the merits of the war, as it is usual to consider such an exception, especially when made by any leading and distinguished member of the House, as of general implication. I left the House before the question was put upon the address, because I thought that, as there were some expressions in the speech breathing a disposition to peace, it was better to let the address pass unanimously, as strengthening the arm of the executive power while treating for peace, and, as far as it could have any effect, auxiliary to good terms. As to the expression of standing or falling by Great Britain, which was echoed from his [*sic*] Grattan by almost everyone who spoke on both sides, I thought it a bad expression. It was figurative and indistinct, admitting of great latitude and graduated interpretation. I thought it undignified, representing this kingdom as such a dependent satellite that it can only exist with its primary orb. I thought it injurious to the public sentiment in favour of the connection, as annexing to it tremendous pains and penalties. I thought it idle, because England never called for it, neither did England ever say that she would rise or fall with Ireland. I thought it dangerous, because it will [be] construed by a government, all the springs of which are worked by Englishmen, to authorise every hazard to this country and the stripping it of all its arms and treasures, when England is supposed to be in any danger, by which it is very likely that Ireland may fall, and that perhaps soon, in order that England may rise. But, above all, I thought the interpretation given to it, viz. that it should preclude our parliament from all investigation of the war, and blindly support England [*sic*] without enquiring into its causes or conduct, as a surrender of that independence so gloriously

F/19 *contd.* achieved in 1782, or at least of the proudest part of it, a deliberative voice upon war of peace.

February 6. I intended this day to have made some observations on the report of the committee of supply, but the Speaker took the chair earlier than usual, and the House adjourned before I arrived there.

Feburary 7. I spoke with Mr Curran on the subject of the war. He seemed to disapprove of it as much as I had done, but he did not like to separate or even differ from Messrs Grattan and Ponsonby, and they decided against any proceeding in favour of peace, or even [any] motion which might stir at all the question of the war. Mr G. especially, I believe, considered any discussion of the kind as peculiarly mischievous to him, and therefore affected, and perhaps in some degree worked himself up to believe, that it was mischievous to the nation. He thought, I believe, that the war accorded with the sentiments of the House of Commons, but discorded with the sentiments of the people, and that his popularity would abate much with every discussion. Mr Curran had so long co-operated with him, had lived in such friendship, or thought or wished others to think that he lived in such friendship, with him, that he did not wish to differ from him. He talked to me of my ancient disagreements with Mr G. I told him I thought Mr G. could from his talents and situation be of much use to the public cause, and therefore that, if I did harbour any old antipathy to him, I should erase it from my mind for the benefit of the public and co-operate with him, could we agree on public subjects; but that I conceived the war to be the most important of all others, and that I could never approve of that or mitigate my opposition to it in any compliment to any man.

That evening, Messrs Duquery and Egan came to me. They despaired of being able to cntinue their connection with Mr G., they differed from him so diametrically on the subject of the war. They also doubted of the practicability of separating Mr Curran from him. It was resolved, however, that Duquery should see Grattan and bring him to an eccalircissement on this subject and on his general political sentiments, which we all thought were verging much to the Court. D. did so the next day, found him close, reserved, not willing to have any meeting of the party, and inflexible on the war. We consulted, therefore, what it would be best to do in the committee on ways and means which were [*sic*] to come forward the next day, and we thought that the best tax which could be proposed would be one on absentees, and D. resolved to move it, in lieu of such taxes as the Chancellor of the Exchequer should propose. It was reported at this time that we were a faction formed by Mr C. Fox for the purpose of breaking up the Portland party here, and this was credited by many men of consequence, whereas I had not, nor I believe had D., the least communication of any kind, mediately or immediately, with that gentleman on any political subject.

February 10. Mr Grattan on this day suggested the propriety of a bill being passed in this country similar to that which had been passed about ten years ago in England, to empower the Lord Lieutenant to raise independent companies. This appeared to be well received by the leaders on the Treasury Bench, and there were infallible marks in their conduct of a previous concert between them on this subject.

F/19 *contd.* February 12. Finding a great disinclination in the House of Commons to the discussion of any subject at all relative to the war, I gave notice that I should postpone bringing forward the state of the defence of this country until I should hear what the Minister had to propose for that purpose. Indeed, so corrupt, so servile to the Minister and so illiberal in their sentiments were most of the members of the House that I found, even from having intimated my difference from the government on the subject of the war, those I have been familiar with would scarcely speak to me, and that an under-current of calumny was everywhere beating against my character and endeavouring to undermine it. I expressed my approbation of all the new impositions proposed by the Chancellor of the Exchequer, except that upon leather as far as it extended to the peasantry. I wished that *brogues* should be exempted. The term caught the public mind, and the tax on *brogues* was repeatedly repeated [*sic*] through the popular newspapers. The government postponed the consideration of it, afraid that a word, as it often has done, might produce much commotion. The Speaker suggested to me in lieu of it to take off the inland and coasting carriage of corn to Dublin. The bounty on that brought castways last year amounted to £28,000 and on tht by inland carriage to £60,000. Afterwards, however, government determined to persevere in the tax.

February 18. The Chancellor of [the] Exchequer proposed the vote of credit, that there might be some money in the Treasury in case of any emergency. This was a suggestion of mine in the committee of supply.

Mr Grattan signified to me by Mr Vandeleur that he had no intention of interfering with me in the measure I proposed of putting the country into an adequate state of defence, or any other; but had casually thrown out the idea of independent companies. I therefore called upon the Secretary in the House to state whether any such measure would be brought forward by him. He said it was still under consideration. I then said it was too critical a moment to slumber over the state of the country. It was what my Lord Chatham called a flying moment, wherefore I would the next day bring forward a proposition respecting the state of our defences and how they might best be augmented. I stated also the necessity of some such measure, [from] the power of the French and the probability of an invasion. I never found the House more averse from a discussion. Every word stuck to them as if I was stabbing at their vitals. Murmurs, interruptions, gloom and consternation on every bench. I notwithstanding persevered.

February 19. I communicated with Mr Duquery on the subject I was to propose. He perfectly agreed with me on the necessity of it. I wrote to Mr Curran, who also came to the House to support me. I found, however, even while prayers were going on, the emissaries of the Court running among the members and alarming them against the discussion, and with the usual success. Lies have a great advantage over truth. They are unlimited. They can show everything in such various shapes, magnify or diminish, compound or dissolve, and with their plastic power deform or beautify whatever comes under their influence. While truth is but one, simple and unchangeable. The Secretary began by stating that, after the subject of raising independent companies had been

F/19 *contd.* well-weighed by his Majesty's Ministers, they had determined that the measure
was inexpedient. In consequence of this, every person from whom I expected
support, told me that the attempt had now been fruitless; that by persevering I
only manifested the strength of the enemy, and in some degree our own
weakness; and that it was better to postpone the measure still further and wait
for events. I yielded to necessity, not to conviction, and stated that I should once
more postpone the measure. I am now confident that they will be obliged to arm
at last the peasantry of the country, when it will be too late, indiscriminately and
promiscuously, instead of selecting and training now those who could be safely
entrusted with arms and putting them under wise regulations.

February 20. Mr Grattan proposed in the House of Commons a resolution "that
the duties on the importation of goods into England from Ireland should be
reduced to the standard of the same goods imported into Ireland from England".
He made a weak and complimentary speech to administration. He spoke like a
lawyer hired to oppose his friend. Popularity was the fee, government the friend
– a fee which will not be paid by this day's harangue, as I am certain it will excite
much popular disgust. I believe he had pledged himself to his constituents to
bring it forward, and he did do so, but in such a way as that it might be silently
stifled as soon as it was born. The Secretary, therefore, immediately rose to
suffocate it with the motion of adjournment. He conveyed it, however, in such a
gale of fulsome adulation on [*sic*] Mr G. as I have never heard breathed before
within the walls of parliament. We have not been used to the heavy odours of
Caledonian panegyric. The old, plain, sturdy, ardent expression of a member of
parliament was now laid aside by Mr G. for the gentle, bending, complimentary
courtier. Nothing that passed between the two had the air of debate. They might
as well have brought battledores and shutlecocks and played across the table, as
thus bandy from one to the other their feathered compliments. Mr Duquery
supported the motion with sense and spirit. Mr Curran with much fancy and
elegant diction made some good observations. I performed no part in the trash.

March 4. Nothing important had now occurred for some time. I received a letter
from the M[arquess] of Lansdowne [D/1/2] informing me that he had showed
my letter on the defenceless state of Ireland to a person of great property in
England and still greater in Ireland, and who, from circumstances, ought to have
great weight with the present administration – I suppose Lord Fitzwilliam. Lord
L. said also that he had some intention of communicating it to the Ministers,
but from the manner of their receiving some remonstrance from quarters of very
high consideration, he thought it would be unnecessary.

   The reform of parliament was this day proposed in the House of Commons.
The members were very unwilling to debate it. They seemed much more anxious
to go to dinner – I mean the principal government members, who were to have a
feast that day and had flattered themselves with the hopes that the panic at the
time and the wide diffusion of ministerial influence would on this, as it had on
every other, day and session soon have extinguished the debate. It lasted,
however, till after 12 o'clock this night. Nothing remarkable occurred in it.

This session closed without any other event worthy of notice.

F/19 *contd.* In the interval between it and the next session, the Viceroy was changed, and Lord Fitzwilliam succeeded Lord Westmorland. Being nearly connected with the Ponsonbys, it was supposed that they had prevailed upon him to accept of this station, to which he was much averse; and most people believe that an agreement was made between the D. of Portland and Mr Pitt at the time of their coalition that the Duke should have sole management of the government in Ireland, and that accordingly Lord Fitzwilliam came here with the utmost plenitude of power. Soon after his arrival, the Catholics presented to him a petition praying for a repeal of all the remaining penal laws against them, to which he gave as favourable an answer as they could desire.

The persons supposed to have most influence upon the mind of the new Viceroy were the two Ponsonbys, William and George; Mr Grattan; and [Chief] Baron Yelverton. They also persuaded, or endeavoured to persuade, Lord Charlemont and Mr Conolly that they also had much weight with them, though I believe they had not. Mr D.B. Daly, brother-in-law to the Ponsonbys, had much influence on them, and indeed was their principal councillor and manager, having more address and promptitude in dealing with men than any of their party.

A great gloom was now cast over the partizans of the former Viceroy. It was rumoured that most of them were to be removed from their offices, and a few days after the arrival of Lord Fitzwilliam, Mr D.B. Daly was sent to Mr Beresford, then First Commissioner, to inform him that he was not to continue in office, but that he should have a pension equivalent to his salary. Mr Cooke, Secretary of War [*sic*], and Mr Hamilton, who was Secretary in the Civil Department, were also removed. Sir L. O'Brien, who was Clerk of the Hanaper having died, Lord Glentworth, who had a patent to succeed him, granted by Lord Westmorland, was informed that that patent was revoked. The dismissions also of Arthur Wolfe, Attorney General, and John Toler, Solicitor General, were notified to them. The friends of the late Viceroy complained everywhere of this treatment. They said that they had supported all Mr Pitt's measures, and that while he continued Prime Minister of England, that [*sic*] it was very hard usage towards them to remove them from office only because they had supported the administration of the Viceroy he had sent here.

Two appointments at this time gave much satisfaction to the public: Dr Newcome, Bishop of Waterford, to the Primacy, and Dr Murray to the Provostship of Trinity College, Dublin, being both men of great learning and exemplary good conduct.

January 22 [1795]. Parliament met. Mr Duquery applied to me in the House to move or second the amendment he showed me to the address, expressing a desire for peace. Though I thought with him on [the] war, I did not like to take such a forward part as this: in the first place, because on a subject of such great magnitude it would have been necessary to have previously arranged or weighed the various topics which were included, otherwise I could not have expected to speak with effect. In the next place, I doubted D.'s sincerity on the subject, and apprehended that he was urged to the motion by private pique to the new Ministers, conceiving himself to have been slighted by them, as they did not

F/19 *contd.* notice him in their new arrangement nor summon him to the reading of the
Speech, as they did Mr Curran and Mr Browne. I also doubted whether he
would afterwards persevere in following up that motion with others of a similar
tendency during the course of the session, having found him reluctant to do
so in the last session, who was one of the most ardent men at the
commencement who supported me on that subject; and to promote the one
attempt only, and to execute that ill, I thought would only expose myself, and
not serve the public. But the consideration which weighed with me most was
the prudence of agitating so delicate a subject at so critical a time. There were
four cases with respect to the disposition of the English and French ministries
for peace, all which deserved to be well considered. 1st, the English ministry
might be disposed to peace and the French indisposed; or, 2, the French
ministry might be disposed and the English ministry indisposed; or, 3, they
might be both disposed; or, fourthly, they might be both indisposed. Now, in
the 1st and 4th of these cases, an address on our part would be of no avail.
Because the French ministers were indisposed of peace, our address could not
alter their sentiments: if it had any effect, it would be to elate them and give
them an idea of a dislike on our part to the war, which might embolden them
the more to make an aggression here, while the discussion of the subject would
tend to make our own people more averse to the war, more turbulent and
more reluctant, in case of invasion, to repel them. In the 3rd case, our address,
as far as it might have influence, would have a bad one; for, if the ministries
of both nations were disposed to treat, the higher language we held respecting
the war, the better terms the French would be inclined to accede to, and any
expression of disapprobation to the war would certainly, if it had any effect,
injure the terms for us; while, our ministry being themselves disposed to peace,
it would be superfluous as far as it was intended to have any effect on them.
That our ministry should be disposed to peace, I thought most probable,
considering the hopeless state of the war, the object of it being now evidently
impracticable, as every man must admit, viz., a restoration of monarchy in
France ... . As to the 2nd case, it was the only one in which such an address
could be useful, but, it being the most improbable of any at the present juncture,
it would be against all laws of probability to act upon that, against the other
three.

I therefore spoke a few words in the debate on the amendement, expressing
merely my disapprobation of the war, declining, however, for the present all
discussion of it, but reserving to myself the power of doing so without any
imputation of inconsistency in some future period of the session, should I deem
it necessary.'

The following are a couple of short extracts from Parsons's notes for a speech on
the 'Repeal of the Insurrection Bill.

I was one of those who originally opposed this law, and the imbecillity of its
operations since has satisfied me that I was not mistaken. I thought then and do
still that if the old laws of the land, seconded when necessary by military aid,
were insufficient to procure internal peace, that no accession of new laws would
answer that purpose. ...

F/19 *contd.*   The Insurrection Bill did not contribute to compose the internal counties. The Defenders [were] suppressed previous to its enaction.

Yeomanry [is] the best institution for that purpose. It was not adopted in time. I proposed it [in 1794]. Had it then been established, the country would never have been disturbed. ...

In my mind ... a wise government would employ its time rather in devising means to have the laws in being executed, than in the formation of new ones. ...'

F/20

DATE	DESCRIPTION

1791–
1819

Quarto commonplace book, bound in red morocco, containing copies (the paper of the book is marked 1811) of poems by Parsons, most of them expressing homesickness for Birr and Ireland generally, and variously titled 'The Absentees', 1801, 'Passage from Dublin to Holyhead, March 24 1804', 'Verses on quitting Birr Castle in 1812, written for Lord Oxmantown to turn into Latin verse', 'Passage from Holyhead to Dublin in December 1819', etc, etc; and also including poems on other subjects, particularly on the death of Flood in 1791, and on Parsons's resignation of the command of the King's County Militia in 1798. [The poem on the latter subject is accompanied by copies of the correspondence between Parsons and Lord Camden, the Lord Lieutenant, which will be found in E/32; the correspondene is also printed, from other copies, in the *H.M.C. Report on the Charlemont MSS*, ii, pp. 317–18.] The background information on the resignation from the militia colonelcy is as follows:

'... In the beginning of the year 1798, the King's County Regiment of Militia, of which I was the Colonel, was quartered in Dublin. Mr L'Estrange was Lt-Colonel and Mr Westenra, now Lord Rossmore, was Major. I appointed them both to these situations when I raised the regiment. Westenra was one of the most scheming men that I ever knew. His uncle, General Cunningham [*sic* – Cuninghame], afterwards Lord Rossmore, had been Commander-in-Chief a short time before. Through him, he had constant access to the Lord Lieutenant's ear, and he made representations disparaging me and the regiment, hoping that, if I was removed, he should, through General Cuninghame's interest, obtain it for himself. I had taken great pains with [the] regiment, and it was generally considered that I had it in a state of very high discipline. He represented me as being too lenient; that I did not execute corporal punishment on the men as often as was necessary, for at that time whipping them severely on the back with a cat-and [*sic*]-nine-tails for trivial offences was a common practice in some regiments, and to which Westenra had no reluctance. In consequence, however, of these continual and clandestine representations, the Lord Lieutenant sent Lord Charles Fitzroy to me to tell me that I did not govern the regiment with a sufficiently severe hand, and that it would be better if I would let the Lt-Colonel command it, and that I might have leave of absence. I immediately wrote to the Lord Lieutenant that, since the manner in which I commanded the King's County Regiment was not approved, that [*sic*] I requested leave to resign it altogether. I sent this letter to him by my friend, Lord Charleville, as I thought him the properest person to succeed me ... .

The Lord Lieutenant then gave the regiment to Colonel L'Estrange, induced probably to do so by Major Westenra, operating through the medium of General Cuninghame, when he found that he could not obtain it for himself. Westenra thought that, hawing got me out, he could not fail to remove L'Estrange; and this he attempted soon after. He prevailed himself on Major Rolleston and three other officers of the regiment to bring L'Estrange to a court martial. Westenra managed this business, making tools of the others, as they told me. They were put to great expense, in which Westenra did not assist them, and L'Estrange was

F/20 *contd.* continued Colonel of the Regiment. I met Lord Charles Fitzroy at this time, who began to understand the practices of Westenra, and he said to me, if Westenra now succeeds in getting out L'Estrange also, he will have accomplished his great object. Lord Charles was at the time going into Lord Cornwallis's chamber, who was then Lord Lieutenant, and probably his representation to Lord Cornwallis contributed to defeat Westenra's project. ...'

F/21

DATE	DESCRIPTION

1791–
[1765?]:
1795-8:
1822–8

Folio commonplace book/scrapbook, which originally must have been Flood's property, as the first item in it is a lengthy (c. 30 pages) draft, in Flood's handwriting, for his speech on the Address in October 1765?, in which he maintains that the British ministry is bent on destroying the liberties of America, Ireland and England, warns the House against falling into the trap of exaggerating the gravity of the Whiteboy disturbances, and asserts the pre-Norman antiquity of the Irish constitution and the pre-Norman civilisation of the Irish people. The rest of the book contains speech and other notes by Parsons, together with relevant newspaper cuttings inserted by him. These notes and cuttings particularly concern the work-up to the '98 Rebellion, in King's County and elsewhere, February-April 1798, and include copies of proclamations and circulars from Dublin Castle; there are also comments by Parsons on the 'Bill to prevent seditious assemblies, English parliament, November 17, 1795'. The rest of the book is devoted to the period 1822–8, and contains, among other things, a newspaper publication of the text of the stolen letter from Saurin to Lord Norbury [see F/14], 1822. Also included is a newspaper publication of a King's County address to Lord Wellesley in March 1822, which Parsons (now 2nd Earl) notes was composed by his younger brother, Thomas C. Parsons. There are a couple of papers about the death of Thomas C. Parsons and the local testimonial to him, and also notes and papers on the death of another brother, John C. Parsons, on 1 May 1826 at Roscommon, where he was on circuit with the Insolvent Debtors' Court. On a brighter note, there is a detailed account of an entertainment given in the yellow drawing room in Birr Castle on 4 July 1826. Further detail about the disputes and skirmishes in Birr between the factions supporting the rival parish priests of the 1820s [see E/11] is provided, and a newspaper controversy between Doctor Doyle (Roman Catholic Bishop of Kildare and Leighlin)and the 5th Lord Farnham causes the 2nd Earl to record some interesting notes on Flood's motives at the time of the drawing up of the Volunteer plan of parliamentary reform in November 1783. [One end of this volume is in dire need of conservation.]

Flood's speech of [1765?] is as follows:

'It is the custom, I know, to echo back from this House the speech from the throne – a custom but of recent introduction, however, and of little authority, unparliamentary and undignified. Undignified notwithstanding as it is, I am so far acquiesent in custom and submissive to prescription that I should not propose any deviation from the trite path of congratulatory repetition, if the matter and the occasion did not demand it. As to the promising part of it, I am content to accept it, with a resolution to believe it when I see it performed. Lest, however, this caution should seem ill-founded in me, or not be adopted by others who mean well to their country, I desire them to look back through the whole series of our Journals and to see whether there ever were a set of fairer and more promising speeches than those of our successive Lord Lieutenants, who seem in general to have adopted the Italian maxim that it is better for a man to break his promise an hundred times than his neck once. Is there in any one event

F/21 *contd.* the smallest hint at any of those multiplied jobs which have exhausted, or those unconstitutional measures which have degraded and injured, this country? If a job be wanted and is at all mentioned in these political manifestoes, as they may be called, it is sure to be mentioned as a work necessary and indispensable, and the most insidious or tyrannical measures are marked under the fairest and most flattering appellations. Did our governors from Henry II's time downwards, when tyranny and oppression so often unsettled this country, according to the weighty and candid Sir John Davi[e]s's observation, and who were in reality the authors of so many rebellions, though they charged them on the miserable natives – did they ever avow that they did this to monopolise the whole kingdom into the hands of a few families, and that they fomented rebellion to profit by forfeiture? Far from it. It was salutary rigour and wise discipline. The name of England and of Englishmen was held up, as the sacred name of religion also has been prostituted in later days to the same vile purposes. Did another governor, who came to betray you into a grant of your additional duties for one-and-twenty years, and which was carried against him – I shudder to think of it, but by one – did he tell the people that he came to annihilate their parliaments and make them betray and sell themselves and their posterity? Did another, who came at the command of a corrupt and insolent Minister to cram down your throats, as that Minister termed it, a patent for [the] utterance of base money, and which your ancestors bravely withstood – did he, I say, tell you what he meant to do, promulgate his intentions and forewarn you to beware of him? Did a later Chief Governor, when he desired a sum of money from you, tell you that he did not want it so much to repair your barracks as his own fortunes? Or when a noble Earl, not the last, submitted to the temporary exile of coming to this country, in order to serve it in the capacity of its Governor, and when he refused a parliamentary donative in increase of his salary from consideration of the inability and indigence of this country, as he alleged – did he tell you that he meant to make a momentary sacrifice to superficial popularity, while this country was not to benefit by his refusal of that constitutional offer, but, on the contrary, was afterwards to suffer by his impositions to a greater amount, and that, too, in an unconstitutional, odious and illegal mode of imposition?

Nay, with respect to the last government, though we were to trip over it with the lightness of a Camilla scouring a plain of corn in Hexamitir [*sic*], yet even in that, however chaste and liberal, what do we see? A letter from Lord Halifax read in a circle, to a Junto, that they might say that they had seen, or heard in a crowd, a letter promising something about pensions, which they could not remember a word of a year after, if desired, nor if they did, could not call upon any man for the performance of, of which the original was no longer to exist, and *de non apparentibus et non existentibus eadem est ratio* [*sic*], says the law – a maxim which courtiers, though not over-fond of the law, would doubtless embrace on this occasion, and which Patriots would the more readily admit in this particular, because so far as the memorable epistle, or to speak of him in a character of infallibility, the *Bull* of Lord Halifax, transpired, it seemed to be calculated rather to rob and to enslave than to disencumber or redress the nation. This poor expedient, this mean trap for credulity, this crutch to help the venal cripple over a style, could never have come from Lord Northumberland. It

F/21 *contd.* must have exhaled through a native. It must have been the *caput mortuum*, and
the last calx of an expiring and evaporated politician. Yet, thin and airy as it was,
this shabby and inapparent, this subtle and fugitive security, was sufficient to
pacify the suspicions and to lull the patriotism of some men. But to you who
mean well I speak – beware of government. Their instrument is dissimulation,
their views are not Irish, and their end is deception. They trade in deceipt and
traffic in seduction. Love and reverence your King. He is patriotic and
beneficent. Love and reverence the people of England. They are free and
magnanimous. But with respect to the Ministers of England and their under-
Ministers here and elsewhere, be cautious, circumspect, suspicious. Remember
your past unmanly injuries, and beware of future.

   With respect to the matter of this address, it is in one part highly
exceptionable in my mind, inasmuch as it gives a representation of this country
as false as impolitic – I mean that part which speaks of us as rebellious. Do the
English call themselves rebellious because the pitmen at Newcastle will not work,
because they enter into combinations certainly illegal, which it is necessary to
call in the military to quell? Do they call themselves rebellious because the
Spittal fields [*sic*] weavers have marched in array through the metropolis of the
kingdom, because some looms have been burnt and a house in the very heart of
the capital torn down. Did they speak of rebellion even when the avenues of
both Houses of Parliament were blocked up by an exasperated multitude, and
when a Minister of State and the favourtie of the crown was threatened to be
Buckinghamed in the open streets, when the same person was driven from the
ear of his sovereign by the terrors of a mob, when he skulked from coach to
coach to escape with safety, when he went through the hisses and execrations,
while the great persons he had dismissed from the conduct of the state passed
through the acclamations, of the people into the City, and that too in the
presence of the sovereign, when he is obliged to fly from the capital in terror,
and to return to it in disguise, when the army was obliged to be quartered in the
cider counties, who rose up to oppose the extension of the Excise – that is in
opposition to King, Lords and Commons in that instance – was this, I say, called
rebellion? They are not so light as to scatter the hand of rebellion so wantonly
about. They know there must be tumults in states, in free ones especially. They
know that, though freedom is sometimes endangered by, it never could subsist
without, them. They know that popular insurrections have generally been right
in their beginnings, though often otherwise in their end. They promise the
ringleaders, they repress the immediate violence, and then they endeavour to
redress the grievance which is always at the bottom of these eruptions. This they
do when they are wise, and when they do not, they suffer the penalty of their
folly; for, redress must be in one hand as well as punishment in the other, or
there never can be quiet, except by extirpation or slavery. It is true, indeed, that
politicians have made a temporary use of such violences, that they have carried
penal laws and riot acts in consequence of them, which otherwise they could
not, because there will always be old women of both sexes enough to be
frightened at such perils. Thus, Sir Robert Walpole got a riot law passed, got a
large standing army entailed on the English constitution, and what is still worse,
perhaps, long parliaments also, by continually talking of revolting colliers,

F/21 *contd.* unruly mobs, of popery and the Pretender; and yet, what was the truth? That if he and his party had not kept alive these distinctions by talking of them, by exasperating and persecuting their fellow-subjects, if, in short, they had not fomented these divisions on purpose in order to keep all power in their own hands by proscribing all others, and to govern by a faction – if they had not done this, those divisions would never have disturbed the state which by their wicked policy, the absurd virulence of their ignorant followers and the greater ambition of their opponents, broke out into two rebellions and threatened the existence of the state. Such reproaches between fellow-subjects, such proscriptions and persecutions of each other, and such dangerous suggestions, are of fatal consequence. They often beget the reality by propagating the name. They exacerbate and embitter. They make the prevailing side insolently insufferable, and the inferior dangerously desperate. They are always suspicious and almost always proceed, the infatuation of a few zealots excepted, from the crooked views and interested malignity of a few operating on the indolent and ignorant credulity of the many.

Here, the tumults which are magnified into rebellion began in the North – in our Protestant counties, where, though riots may sometimes arise, rebellion cannot. The justice of government interposed. Many were tried, scarcely any suffered, but the law was made known. Possibly some redress was promised where the grievance had foundation, and where it had not, expostulation and argument convinced them of their folly. Thus it ended, and no more has been heard of it; and yet, who does not remember at that time the frantic fears of many in the North, the absurd propositions of barracks and an augmentation of the army for the protection of that part of the kingdom, of the impossibility of their returning to their counties or living in their houses without they were thus garrisoned, and the constant predications of a second insurrection? Thank God, government was too prudent to listen to their frenzy! Otherwise, who knows what might have happened, when we know that, if [*sic*] some of the most intelligent of the gentlemen of the army who were sent down on the eruption of these disorders to quell them give strange accounts of I know not what rage and fury which prevailed in some parts of that country, inasmuch that, if the civil power had not in some instances been restrained by the military, I have been informed that some parts of that country, from the rashness of a few individuals, would have been made a scene of bloodshed and desolation. The wisdom of government repressed this temerity, and after having made the law known, and punished a few individuals, they left it wisely to the magistrates and principal gentlemen of the country by a mixture of authority and relaxation and remonstrance and redress to seize and pacify the minds of men who knew enough of their rights to have spirit and independency to expect to be treated like men. This was known, and therefore it was done.

But the same measures have not been taken in the South, where I presume it was not thought to be necessary, the ordinary inhabitants being in general ignorant and careless of their rights, poor and oppressed, and a herd almost as much as the cattle which they feed. Here, persecution only has been tried and the rod of iron extended, which is better to exterminate than reclaim. What has been the consequence? The beast has been goaded into greater resistance, and

F/21 *contd.* kicks, though it be against the pricks. What happened in and near the country in which I live whilst I was in England, which was at the beginning of this second tumult in the South, I know not. But I know that, when I heard in England that no less than 20,000 were regularly exercised by night in that part of the world, that they were regimented, armed, officered and paid from abroad, as was supposed, I laughed at first hearing at the rumour; for, who must not see that, if that were true, it must be as clear as the sun when it shines at noonday. In a country thinly peopled, as the Southern counties of this kingdom are, could 20,000 men be nightly exercised in different parts and in large bodies, and the proof of such a thing be doubtful or difficult? I will venture to say that the Kellymount gang, consisting of not above 50 men, appeared in as many places, and in as large bodies, by common report, which ever magnifies, as all the 20,000 men have done. Could 20,000 men have undergone military discipline all night and country labour all day? Impossible. And would not the labour of 20,000 men be missed and the pay of 20,000 be felt in every corner of the country? But this was exaggeration, it may be said, though in a degree the reality of these risings cannot be doubted. I allow it. But I say that this was such a degree of exaggeration of the commencement of this business, and to my knowledge, since I have resided in that country, there is so much virulence and ignorance and so little sober examination into this subject, that but little of what we hear is to be depended on. If a notice is posted up in any public place of a pattern or a hurling, the country rings with it in a moment, and you hear many men talk of it as a signal of rebellion. Some notices I have heard of, proclaiming expressly a meeting of Whiteboys, and I have seen people credulous enough to follow it, though every man must see that the Whiteboys must have other and more secret methods of assembling, that it is absurd to suppose they would ever post up such a notice as to mark themselves out industriously for the vengeance of the law, and to proclaim to the world where they might be seized. Any man of common sense and unprejudice [*sic*] must see that, if such a notice was ever posted, which I wholly disbelieve, that [*sic*] it must be done by prosecutors of Whiteboys, not by Whiteboys themselves, and that a tithe-proctor was more likely to have been the person than those whose names are usurped in all probability. Again, if any violence be committed of any kind in the country, the first fool you meet says, the Whiteboys were up last night. ... That there have been, are and will be outrages and offences committed, I doubt not, and I am equally clear that the magistracy of the country was laudably exerted to quell these disturbances on their commencement, and that it ought to continue vigilant to prevent a renewal of them. One of the persons principally concerned in opposing this licence, I honour, though he is unknown to me; the other, whom I know, I both love and honour. Of the sentiments of those whom I do not know and have never conversed with on the subject, I cannot speak. But the gentleman whose thoughts I did know had the most liberal ideas and the most correct sentiments of justice and of humanity on the subject. He thought there was a licentious spirit which, whatever was its denomination or among whatever society of men it appeared, he exerted himself like a magistrate to suppress. But he never minded the idle tales which would endeavour to make one believe that the air was filled with nothing but the soundings of horns and that the highways

F/21 *contd.* would be worn out by the paces of Whiteboys; and I do him this justice in this House the rather because it has not been done him elsewhere sufficiently.

But with respect to many persons in that country, I have seen a rage and fury and implacability which astonished and alarmed me. I attended the assizes when this matter was first brought to trial in the county to which I belong. I cannot speak of what passed in the grand jury room, but I may of what passed in public court and in public companies afterwards. I attended the trial of those who were accused as Whiteboys, 7 or 8 I think, and took notes minutely of the evidence. Their alleged crime was high treason, inferred and not expressed in the letter of the statute, and though not new to the law perhaps, yet certainly new in practice and not vulgarly known nor commonly understood till lately. In this consideration of it also, it required the fullest testimony of the actual guilt, at least as the intentional guilt might be something more uncertain than usual from the obscurity or at least little notoriety of the law [sense?]. Now, what was the evidence? The evidence of but one person in a case of *constructive* and *newly construed* high treason, and that one person a bearer of a bad character in general, an approver, and therefore of bad character in the very instance under contemplation, and doubly bribed to effect the conviction of these men, if possible, by a large pecuniary reward and by security to his own life. A testimony weak in every particular, except that inconsistency with himself was not added to its imperfection. The prisoners were acquitted. Who could have expected otherwise, that was a cool spectator of this transaction? Yet, numbers seemed to be struck dumb with astonishment, some talked of the impossibility of living in their houses, others that the Church was overthrown, and the deepest discontent and gloom hung upon many brows. This was not all. Three of the jury, it seems, were for convicting these men, improperly doubtless. The other nine, fearing the prevalent warmth and prepossessions of men on that subject, so far listened to the sentiments of these three who dissented from them as to come out of the jury room to consult the bench upon the subject and to ask the jusge whether the evidence of another against two or three of the prisoners, whom he charged, not with respect to the same offence nor even the same species of offence, not for high treason, but a misdemeanour – they asked the court, I say, whether this could be considered by them as a corroboration of the approver's testimony. The court were [*sic*] clear that it could not. Accordingly, they did not pay any regard to it in their verdict. But neither the reason of the thing nor the sanction of the court nor the charity and candour which is due to men acting on their oaths nor the number of the persons to be executed, if convicted, nor the singleness and incredibility of the testimony on which they were to be thus convicted, nor the atrocity of the crime which therefore requires proportionate evidence, nor the want of liberality or the constructiveness of the offence, nor the novelty of the construction and therefore in some sort the unblameable ignorance of the persons arraigned – not all these considerations together could stand against the current of the time. The three who had dissented and who in giving up their opinion could alone be considered as culpable, were applauded for a few hours in the madness of prejudice, and not only for a few hours, but the day after, if it had not been repressed, and partly by myself, an application would have been made to the grand jury of the most unparrelleled and unconstitutional kind – an

F/21 *contd.* application to destroy our constitution, in effect, in a material point, to destroy the distinction and total separation of the petty from the grand jury, to subject the latter to the former, to make the two trials by these two distinct juries but one, contrary to the wise intention of the law, and to give to the grand jury, generally struck on motives of rank or favour rather than on strictly judicial considerations, a power of revision with respect to the verdicts and a censorial authority with regard to the characters of petty jurors, which is not endured by the constitution – an application, I say, to condemn the 9 jurors who had acted in conformity to their convictions, by an address of compliment from the grand jury to the 3 petty jurors who had concurred in a verdict contrary to their convictions, though certainly a better verdict than that which they wished to have made. This is some key to the temper of the time and of that county, and some caution not to adopt too hastily what we hear on this topic. ...

Three or four gentlemen of the army, for one of whom I have a particular respect and honour and the rest of whom I do believe to be highly respectable, but whom I do not know, went for curiosity to a neighbouring patron in order to show the nature of it to one of the company, who was son to a respectable nobleman of England and never had been in Ireland before. Now, I ask any man at first sight whether he thinks that these gentlemen were in any probable danger from this adventure, whether the common Irish are not remarkably respectful to gentlemen, whether a lord may not do what he pleases among them almost, and whether a lord belonging to that country, living in that neighbourhood, and of manners which must endear him to any country in which he lived, whether a peer in these circumstances had any reason to expect any insult or indignity from the common Irish? Certainly not: and it is plain that the noble lord and the gentlemen who accompanied him did not expect any such thing, for otherwise they certainly would not have gone. It was clear, therefore, that what happened after was wholly unexpected and casual. Had these gentlemen gone to suppress this multitude, as magistrates, some resistance might have been possibly expected from a few rash or drunken men, and that would have been a resistance to magistracy of a very criminal kind. But this was not the case. The gentlemen went merely for amusement – that is on the same errand of almost every other man in the patron, and certainly, so far as going to a patron is faulty, were embarked in the offence. They had nothing, therefore, to expect but to go in and come out again, to see the humours of a patron as new to an Englishman as Bartholomew Fair to an Irishman, only perhaps to be treated with greater respect than usual from their address and from one of them being known and regarded in the country. I will not mention the rumour of the country, supported by nothing but the probability of it at first view perhaps, that a young gentleman of the party, not one of the gentlemen of the army, committed some indecency with respect to a girl who was engaged in paying a silly specimen of devotion at a sanctified well on that ground, as it is thought by the vulgar. The gentlemen deny this, I apprehend, and therefore I pay no credit to it. But this is certain, for the candour of the noble Lord acknowledges it, that the noble Lord did first make use of his hand, that the man, knowing or finding out who it was whom he had offended and from whom he had received a stroke in consequence of that offence, instead of persevering in anything offensive for returning the blow, went

F/21 *contd.* down upon his knees and begged the noble Lord's pardon. It would have been well and prudent if nothing more had been required. But a demand of further submission, and that from a young gentleman in the neighbourhood who was not so respectable as the noble Lord, did, as I am told, produce the altercation and difference which ended in the gentleman's being attacked. One circumstance, however, there is which is much spoken of and relied on, and which shows the root of that spirit by which this matter has been so much magnified in every part of its progress. It is that the mob cried out, down with the Sassanaghs [*sic*] means Englishman. I have heard it used in Wales to men who spoke English by those who did not. It is a term of national, not religious, distinction, and had here so fair an object in Colonel Harcourt, an Englishman just imported, who was known to be in the country at the noble Lord's house and who was then with him at the patron, that nothing but great blindness, from ignorance or prejudice, could have so far mistaken its application. Yet, two counties were in commotion on this subject. Some gentlemen in one county rode to the place of meeting, for a meeting was appointed to consider ways of measures on this important subject, with their forces larded with guns and pistols, though no possible danger or opposition was in the way. ...

Is this equality? Can you call the country free in which these things are done? Or shall men be called patriots for being forward on such an occasion? Is oppression become patriotism? Shall a man be called a patriot because he can drag his chariot wheels over the necks of miserable men, because he takes the cause of the strong against the weak, of an oligarchy against the whole? It is a cheap patriotism. Patriotism in general has been supposed to be a laborious virtue which encountered power in defence of weakness and prevented the tyranny of the few from overwhelming the many. Patriotism consists in relief, not in oppression, in moderation with respect to self-benefit, and a warm benevolence in promoting the benefit of others. It is a mild, a generous and a beneficent, not a narrow, persecuting, vindictive spirit. Away with such patriotism!

And what have been the immediate consequence of the spirit? That from magnifying a false terror we have diminished a real one, that we have relinquished the civil power, abandoned magistracy and thrown ourselves into the arms of the military. Can it be believed by those who did not see it, that at length we were so far gone in this infatuation that, if a petty constable were to be sent to jail for an arrear in his collection, he was sent with a party of the army to conduct him? ...

A time will come – I warn those who are industrious in propagating this doctrine – a time will come when we shall repent the wantonness with which we charge ourselves with rebellion. We may, to please ourselves, make what distinctions we will and except ourselves, if we please, from the reproach of disaffection. But if ever the time comes when it shall be the purpose of others to consider us as a rebellious nation in order to crush us with better pretence, we shall find our distinctions will not be adopted, though our charges will. ... Are we too popular among our neighbouring nations, or so much respected by England, that we should so labour in our own diminution, and endeavour to degrade ourselves to a level with the rest of the world? We need not be

F/21 *contd.* apprehensive. We have no exuberance of reputation to fear.

As to the occasion, was there ever a time when it was so necessary to this House to exert all its powers as when all its powers have been denied. The worm will turn when it is trod upon, and why should not the parliament of Ireland? If there be a deposit more sacred than any other, it is that which is lodged in the representatives of the people alone to tax the country which has sent them to parliament. Yet, even this right has been denied you by Ministers – by Ministers, I say, for the people of England are too wise, too bold and too free to wish to enslave you; and it is our business to teach all Ministers that this is a doctrine which, as honest men to our constituents or as freemen, we cannot endure. Does any man doubt that the doctrine has been held? I tell him that it has, that my ears tingle and my heart beats with indignation to hear it. But it has not been attempted in act. There is no man so mad as to attempt to rob a nation of its freedom till he see whether they are likely to bear it or not. It has been thrown out to sound [us]. The same doctrine was thrown out with respect to the American colonies before it was enacted. But shall any Minister consider this country in that light? This country which stands with Magna Charta in her hand for near 600 years, with the laws of England and the parliamentary constitution adopted at the instance of the Irish, as the record of Henry III expresses it, and by the fairest, the fullest, most ancient and best attested national compact which any nation has to boast as the ground of its constitution? Shall this nation be enslaved by the dictum of a First Lord of the Treasury? Shall its rights shrivel up at the breath of any man of whatever authority? Shall there be no faithful son to call upon his country in this House to show the spirit in this session which becomes them, and to show the world that they are not afraid to talk of their rights, and that whenever the day of trial comes, they are ready to abide it? ...

Unhappy country which we inhabit, what curse has been entailed upon it? Torn into petty principalities, it could have known little stability before the arrival of the English. Then we might have hoped, from the voluntary surrender of their traditional law by the inhabitants and their voluntary acceptance of the English constitution and liberties, that it might have seen a dawn of peace and establishment. But it was not so happy. The wicked policy of a succession of governors weakened and disturbed the country for the first ages by perpetual divisions between the aboriginal inhabitants and the English settlers. So inhuman was their tyranny as to monopolise the whole country in ten or twelve hands by a perversion of all law and justice, and, not content with beggaring the miserable natives, they had the barbarous injustice to acquit the robber or the perpetrator of murder, if he could prove that the person who was robbed or murdered was of Irish blood. That this is really the fact, however, astonishing, we cannot doubt, upon the authority of Sir John Davies, himself an Englishman, a man candid and able in the highest degree, and one who sat himself upon the bench of justice, though in better times; and, if his authority wanted confirmation, we have the confirmation of indisputable records. When this was the situation of this country, when the original inhabitants who had received the new settlers into their bosoms without resistance, in great measure found themselves so basely requited, when they saw one another beggared and murdered with impunity, when they found the ministers of justice the ratifiers of

F/21 *contd.* their wrongs and not the redressers, can you wonder that this country was harrased with perpetual insurrection? At length, however, the pacific reign of James held out a promise of tranquillity. The miseries, however, of the succeeding reign intercepted this prosperity in its beginning, and plunged us again into division and bloodshed. Again we revived with the Restoration, but so mangled with the wounds and worn down with the distempers of so many ages, that we scarcely had recovered when our miseries and our conflicts were renewed. The Revolution came. We hailed our Deliverer and promised ourselves from that time to this an establishment of our national rights and of a state of prosperity. We set out in the thirteenth century in every constitutional right equal to Britain, in some superior. We are now in the decline of the eighteenth century, but, alas, how different. In Henry VIII's time, where our declension commences, our judges were made dependent on the crown and their tenure changed into a tenure at will by statute instead of being for life, as they were originally. Our parliament at the same time, according to the construction of that act which seems prevalent, was made dependent on a dependent council. But of this hereafter. Illegal confiscations, rebellions fomented in order to produce forfeitures, a perversion of all law and justice with respect to the natives, and the public robbery of rapacious inquisitions into defective titles – I pass over, however atrocious, because they were but temporary evils, and though they were abuses of the soil, as it were, they left the boundaries of the constitution where they were. The era of liberty, the Revolution, came. But, instead of an era of liberty to this unfortunate country, as it was to Great Britin, it forms the second grand point of its declension. Since that time, we have seen one House of Parliament deprived of its judicature, and both, so far as a declaration of another body has validity, deprived of their independence and divested of their supremacy. We hoped that the reign of a patriot prince would restore to us the independence of our judges, who voluntarily increased that of the judges in England. We hoped that the favourable period was on the wing for which we had long waited with patience and resignation. And what do we now hear of – an aggravation of everything grievous, an annihilaton of our parliamentary rights, a deprivation of the last and most precious jewel remaining to us after former usurpations and an accumulation and completion of all that is ignominious and servile.

It is at length time to show some sensibility, to awaken out of the turbid state of inattention in which we seem to have been congealed, to remember that we are men, and to act as such. We see that there is occasion for it. Every year takes something away from us. If we do not put a stop to it, we shall soon have nothing left. Nothing can be objected to this but a supposed impracticability and a want of power to prevent it. And here indeed we have an old prejudice to contend with, artfully propagated by a few and ignorantly received by many. But, entrenched though it is in antiquity, it is so weak by its absurdity and so contradicted by fact, that when it is examined it must instantly give way to purer, nobler and more manly ideas. What? When Sir Robert Walpole sent over his patentee to debase the brass currency of this kingdom in order to indemnify for the bribes by which he had obtained his patent. Did the people suffer it to be crammed down their throats, or did they wisely, honestly and bravely reject it? ...

F/21 *contd.* And if on a later occasion, the administration of Mr Pelham, when the personal
character of the Minister, when the steadiness and sobriety of direction which
appeared in his councils and the address and moderation with which he managed
the national party for England, had produced there almost a national union – if, I
say, on a later occasion, when this powerful administration held the helm in
England and sent over a Governor [Dorset] to this kingdom strong in the former
favour he had been received with amongst us, strong in the abilities of his filial
Secretary [Lord George Sackville], strong in the talents of a political prelate
[Stone], strong too in the almost equal division of the representatives of the
people here, though by no means of the people themselves, and still further
strengthened in the particular point he was to carry by a manifesto, as it were, of
the whole Privy Council of England – if such an administration, both here and in
England, could not carry this point against national opposition, what have we to
fear from modern administrations? And if this nation, after all the threats that
were hurled against it, was not sunk into the bottom of the sea for its
magnanimous defence, if, on the contrary, we find nothing but Court strategem
and corruption employed, in order by the weakness of individuals to undermine
the strength of the nation, we have nothing to fear, it is plain, from national
weakness. On the contrary, we have everything to hope in a just cause from
national weight, and nothing to fear but private venality and perfidy amongst
ourselves, which every nation has to fear alike and which should no more
discourage us therefore than those nations who in spite of it are determined to be
free. And if, on a still more recent occasion, when a noble Duke [Bedford] was
our Governor, whose partinacity of disposition, whose illustrious connections and
princely influence, combined to make him a formidable person to contend with,
if, notwithstanding, this House with a dignified resentment stopped its
proceedings and compelled that haughty nobleman to retract an unconstitutional
indignity he had offered to parliament, to restore his [*sic*] privileges and disclaim
his declarations – if this be a fact within every man's memory, why should we fear
to show our resentment in some degree at least and in some mode against a
system which has set fire to all the dependencies of Great Britain, the evils of
which are as yet but in the womb, and of which the noble personage of whom I
speak and the late First Lord of the Treasury [Bute] were the principal concertors.
Let us show all Ministers, past, present and to come, that they are not to take
these liberties wantonly with two millions and an half of men with impunity. ...

The wiser and more intelligent of the people of England have long lamented
the decay of liberty in the dependencies of Britain as a melancholy presage of
their own slavery. They see too many at home ready to sell their country to the
highest bidder, and that an arbitrary Minister would have a large association to
assist him in an attempt upon the liberty of Great Britain itself; and if to these
intestine enemies the weight of all her enslaved dependencies and between four
and five millions of their enslaved inhabitants, together with the evil wishes of
every potentate in Europe, were added, it would be impossible for her to resist
the complicated calamity. This she knows must be fatal, and that it must be the
fact. ... Such are the fears of the wise in a neighbouring kingdom, if the
dependencies of Great Britain should ever be enslaved. They therefore wish your
freedom as ardently as their own, and consider the one as necessary to the other.

F/21 *contd.* They therefore trembled at the temerity of some late Ministers who seemed to have a formed design to subjugate all the exterior parts of the empire of Great Britain. They see at home placemen and pensioners without end, and a regular concatenation of ministerial spies spread throughout the kingdom. They see the Law, the Church, the State, the Army, all contributing in their different departments to the introduction of arbitrary sway. They see a national debt, the fruit of successive profusion, threatening their country with one stupendous ruin and involving in its consequences a ruin more certain perhaps, though not so apparent. They see it the pregant source of that mystery of iniquity, stock-jobbing, which infects from the lowest to the highest ranks of the community. They see the Minister presiding over this mystery and scattering like fortune millions amongst his dependants. They see this at home, whilst abroad they feel servitude like the coldness of death, creeping upon them from all their extremities. Amidst these conflicting difficulties, they call upon you and upon all their extremities for assistance, and desire you to preserve your own liberties that they may not be incapacitated from preserving theirs.

I have but a short life to promise to myself or to my country, but such as it is, it shall not be ignobly occupied; such as it is, it shall be dignified with freedom; and, weak as we are, we are not so weak but that we can defend the liberties of our country and consequentially the liberties of Great Britain, and consequentially those of mankind. The idea is captivating and the practice glorious. We have heard of men who have defied danger, death, poverty, reproach, pain – who have defied all evils of nature or of accident – in a magnanimous pursuit; and shall we think that this virtue is extinct – I ask you, and your eyes answer me that it is not – I ask my own heart, and it replies in the negative. We have heard of the freemen of Athens. We have heard of the freemen of Rome. We hear of those in America. Why should we not hear of the freemen of Ireland? Come then, my countrymen, let us be united. Like a band of brothers let us stand together, or like friends long separated by accident but reunited by distress, let us examine into the ills we have suffered, that we may intercept future. Let us with the piety of the Indian, disinter the remains and bind up the wounds of a mangled constitution. Let us gather around the throne, and with tears in our eyes and anguish at our hearts, there supplicate, there implore the justice and the mercy of our sovereign to [?repair] our past and prevent all future injuries.'

The 1798 newspaper cutting and commentaries include:
Cutting from *The Dublin Gazette* of 31 March 1798, consisting of the Lord Lieutenant's proclamation issuing '... the most direct and positive orders to the officers commanding his Majesty's forces to employ them with the utmost vigour and decision for the immediate suppression ... [of the traiterous conspiracy], and also to recover the arms which have been traiterously forced from his Majesty's peaceable and loyal subjects, and to disarm the rebels and all persons disaffected to his Majesty's government, by the most summary and effectual measures ...'.

At the foot of this cutting, Sir Laurence Parsons has noted: 'In consequence of the above, Lt-General Abercromby, Commander-in-Chief in Ireland, who had

F/21 *contd.* just before issued an order to the army not to act but by [the] orders of the civil
power, sent in his resignation, but felt notwithstanding that it was his duty, until
a successor should be appointed, to act agreeably to that proclamation. He
therefore accordingly issued the succeeding one ... for free-quartering the army
in the county of Kildare, King's County and Queen's County. ...'

'On Friday the [blank in the text], Sir L. Parsons gave notice in the House of
Commons that he would on the following Wednesday submit a motion to them
for the adoption of such measures as would tend to conciliate the affections of
the people to the government. The members of administration were very adverse
to the discussion of this subject and laboured incessantly in the interval by all
means of private cabal and every Court practice to prevail on as many members
as possible of the House of Commons to oppose the motion. However, when
Wednesday arrived, finding that they had not succeeded as completely as they
had hoped by these practices, they wished therefore for time for a few days more
to pursue their intrigues, and for this purpose desired all their members to delay
going to the House till after four o'clock. A few minutes before 4, the Speaker
had prayers said, and at the instant of 4 counted the House, and there not being
40 members, adjourned it. There was a great concourse of people to hear this
debate; the gallery, etc, quite full. To prevent a similar disappointment, Sir L.
moved next day that the House should be called over the Monday following,
when he commenced the debate with the following speech. The motion he made
was that the House should forthwith resolve itself into a committee of the
Whole House to take into consideration the cause or causes of the present
discontents, the means which have been adopted to assuage them, and the most
likely method of restoring public order and tranquillity. He was seconded by
Lord Caulfeild [soon to succeed as 2nd Earl of Charlemont]'.

What follows is a printed newspaper account:

'As several incorrect statements of Sir Lau[rence] Parson's late speech on
conciliation have appeared in the public papers, we present our readers with the
following more perfect representation of it.

"It is the duty of the legislators of a free state to attend to the desires of the
people, and as far as they are reasonable, to gratify them. This is true in all times,
but in times of the greatest difficulty and danger, when a general discontent
threatens our very being, not to do so would be the most criminal folly. I
therefore intend to propose to you this day an enquiry into the causes of the
present discontents, and the expediency of adopting those measures which we
know to be most ardently desired by the people. If they are right in the objects
of their desire, conciliate by conceding them: if they are wrong, prove that they
are so by your argument, and conciliate by convincing them.'

I know there are many whom I address adverse to this discussion, but I desire
you in the first place to recollect who you are, and by what authority you sit
here. You are not self-created legislators, you are not the representatives of
money, you are not the representatives of individuals called borough proprietors
– you are the representatives of the people, the deputies of the people, the agents
that their voices have sent here to speak their sentiments, and your first and
paramount duty, and that which transcends every other, is to consider their

F/21 *contd.* grievances and afford them redress. Do you think that you are sent here merely to vote a tax or frame a turnpike bill, or that it is only in ordinary times and about common transactions that you should deliberate, but that at a time when everything that is valuable to man is in the most imminent peril, you are to sit like mutes upon your benches and not exercise that intellect which the Deity has given you for your direction, and those organs by which he has empowered you to communicate the result of its reflections? When you, Sir, claimed for us on the first day of this session that freedom of speech which the representatives of the people have always enjoyed in parliament, I am sure it was not intended to be a barren privilege; on the contrary, we were told from the throne that our sovereign had at this important period assembled us here in order to resort to our deliberations and advice. But what have been our deliberations ever since? An address was voted, without any discussion, repeating verbatim the language of the speech, syllable for syllable, faithful as echo from the rock, and from that day to this nothing has been said or done but in the ordinary routine of business; while, as to the alarming discontents of the people, or the application of any remedy to remove them, we have remained in utter silence.

That the government of this country cannot go on as it proceeds at present, has been said by some in high station, and all seem to agree that a change is necessary. But what that change should be, you are now to decide. Some say that the powers of government should be augmented and a still severer system of coercion resorted to: others that without diminishing any of the legitimate energies of the government, conciliation should be tried. The two ways are open to you. It is your duty to examine both, and then determine which course you will take, and on the wisdom of that determination depends the fate of yourselves, your fortunes, your families and friends, the fate of Ireland, and with it of the British Empire. I shall freely, therefore, express my sentiments on this awful subject, unmoved by any consideration but the attachment I bear to truth and the public weal. And I here invoke that Diety who presides in the heavens to guide your minds to that decision which shall best ensure at this formidable crisis the safety and prosperity of our country.

The Irish people have been lately represented as a people never to be conciliated by concession; that, on the contrary, every new concession has only been productive of new demand, and historic facts have been appealed to in support of this opinion. It therefore deserves some examination, both to exonerate the Irish name from the opprobrium of such a character, and to prove that there is no occasion for apprehending now that conciliatory measures would be unproductive of content. In the American war, the trade and manufactures of this country were very much injured, both by the necessary consequences of the war and also by an embargo on the exportation of provisions, for at that time, linen excepted, there was scarcely any article but provisions the export of which was not interdicted by the British legislature. The people were, therefore, very soon reduced to great poverty and distress, and became clamorous for the freedom of trade which God and nature seemed to have peculiarly intended for the inhabitants of this island. I was not then a member of this House, but being a student of the University, I had an opportunity of which I constantly availed myself to attend to what was passing here. The English Minister then found that

F/21 *contd.* something in the shape of concession must be granted to Ireland. And what do you think was the first instance of his liberality? A permission to plant tobacco. And I remember well when, day after day during the course of a whole session, it was vociferated from that bench that the people of Ireland ought to be quiet and content, for that this licence to plant tobacco (a weed which would not grow in our soil) was an equivalent for a free trade. During the following summer, the distresses of the people increased. The tenants were no longer able to pay their rents. The country gentlemen, becoming sufferers as well as the people, coincided with the people in requiring a remedy. There were at that time in this House a very respectable and honourable body of men, of great weight and consequence in the country, who kept aloof from the Court and were never seen sighing after its toys or trimming for its petty patronage. There were also many men of virtuous and independent principles who usually voted with the Minister, for corruption had not then produced such a general debasement as in subsequent times. When, therefore, on the first day of the session of 1779 the late Chief Baron Burgh, one of the brightest luminaries that adorned this House, moved an amendment to the address, the words desiring an extension of trade not being deemed sufficiently comprehensive, and some difficulty arising about the expression which he proposed to substitute, Mr Flood, then in office, called out across the House, "Why not a free trade?", his words were adopted, and the amendment was carried.

The people of Ireland having thus obtained a free trade, were so unreasonable as to desire also a free constitution. They were not merely content with the liberty of becoming merchants and factors, they wished to be freemen; and for this they are stigmatised as an insatiable race, whom concession will never conciliate. The English parliament had long assumed the power of binding this country by its laws, and the Privy Council also exercised the power of originating, altering and rejecting the acts of our legislature. Against such a degraded and mutilated constitution as this, the people of Ireland raised their voices, and motion was made after motion for the assertion of our liberties. The influence of the Minister, however, continued to predominate, and large majorities resisted every proposition brought forward by the popular leaders. The people became inflamed. The authority of English laws here was denied. The Minister at length feared that the sentiment of the people would be communicated to the army, and as the army had been hiterto governed by an English mutiny bill, to prevent the risk of an unsubordinate [*sic*] soldiery, he had recourse to an Irish mutiny bill. This was considered as a point gained by the friends of Irish liberty, for it was an oblique admission of the invalidity of an English law. But the mutiny bill which was sent over to England from our parliament, a biennial act (as our parliament then met but every second year), was altered in England to a perpetual act; and thus was the power of the sword taken out of the hands of the British legislature and transferred forever, not to our parliament, but to the King. A more unconstitutional act or more perilous to the liberties of the people than this cannot well be conceived. Yet, the parasites of the Court through a whole session contended that this perpetual mutiny bill was an equivalent for a free constitution, as they had before contended that a liberty to plant tobacco was an equivalent for a free trade. The

F/21 *contd.* people of Ireland, however, were so insatiable as not to be contented even by this; and their voice ascending at last to the thone, not through the medium of their representatives but by some indirect reverberation, on a change of ministry, the sovereign required that the grievances of the people should be enquired into and the causes of them removed. Ireland then obtained the independency of her legislature.

But a doubt arose with respect to the sufficiency of the act by which the English parliament acknowledged that independence. One of the ablest men (Mr Flood) that ever enlightened any parliament, with an irresistible body of argument maintained that the mere repeal of the English statute which had asserted the right of the English parliament to bind this country by its laws, was inadequate, as it did not contain a renunciation of that right. The gentlemen of the bar were almost unanimously of the same opinion. They appointed a committee of some of the most respectable men among them, to state more precisely the imperfection of the repeal – some of those judges who now adorn our bench were members of that committee – and the people, not absurdly, as has been stated, presuming to decide an abstract question of law, but reluctantly by this weight of authority and argument, were persuaded of the inadequacy of the simple repeal. They, however, desired nothing new from England. They called for no further concession. They only required that that which [the] English parliament had professed to do it should do perfectly, and by such an explicit and infallible instrument as should remove all doubt and preclude the possibility of any further disagreement arising between the nations. Now was there anything unreasonable in this? Or is it fair for [*sic*] this to represent the nation of Ireland as one never to be satisfied? Soon after this, the decision of an appeal from Ireland in the King's Bench in England proved the inadequacy of the simple repeal, and the English parliament then passed an act of renunciation.

But it has been stated that the people of Ireland then found out that their parliament, which had thus redressed all their grievances, was itself a grievance, and desired that it should be reformed. The observation is more smart than just. The fact is that during this struggle of the people for their constitutional liberties, the House of Commons negatived every proposition that was offered to it for the assertion of them, and thus made the people feel their defective influence over their parliamentary organ. They sought a remedy, therefore, to repair this defect; and the subject of a reform in parliament being then much discussed in England, they saw in such a reform the remedy which they sought. They, therefore, urged the expediency of it. Was there anything unreasonable in this? Or who does not see that their conduct in so doing was perfectly conformable to the dictates of wisdom and good sense? They did not, however, urge it intemperately, and when it was refused, they remained quiescent. They are next accused of desiring protecting duties. The fact is thus. A great inequality of duties, to the disadvantage of Ireland, prevailed between the two kingdoms. I will trouble you with but one instance. A yard of woollen cloth imported here from England pays but sixpence duty, but the same quantity imported from this country into England pays forty shillings and sixpence. Thus is the English manufacturer admitted into our market, while the Irish manufacturer is excluded from theirs. Our manufacturers were at this time reduced to the

F/21 *contd.* greatest distress in consequence of the war. They were in multitudes begging about our streets. So great was their poverty that it was necessary by charitable contributions to feed them at public tables, and in this moment of misery they desired what? That the duty should be equalised between these co-equal kindoms, in order that they might earn their bread by honest industry. They only called upon their representatives to protect their manufactures with the same duties that the English parliament protected theirs. Was this unreasonable? Or are the people of Ireland to be represented as discontented and unconciliable because their manufacturers, contemplating the distant benefits of a free trade and a free constitution, did not submit in silence to the pressure of immediate calamities and lie down contentedly in the streets without employment and without food, to starve and to perish?

I repeat it again, that my object in reminding you of these transactions is to vindicate our national character from recent aspersions, and not to revive the ungracious topics of ancient jealousy against England. On the contrary, I applaud the conduct of England towards this country in the American war -its wisdom and its justice. It was, it has been truly observed, a series of continued concessions. And what was the effect? That it united all the enegies of our people in defence of the state; and when our armies were withdrawn, when the fleet was no longer able to defend you, conciliation alone defended you. If, therefore, the experience of that time is to influence the decision of this day, you must decide in favour of the conciliatory system. Mark but the difference between that period and this. In the American war your defence did not cost you £500,000 a year and you were safe: in this war it costs you near £4,000,000 a year and you are in the greatest danger. This is the difference between conciliation and coercion. In the American war you had not latterly 5,000 troops here in pay and you were in security: now you have 50,000, beside yeomanry, and you are in the most imminent peril. This is the difference between conciliation and coercion. In the American war the fleets of the enemy rode triumphant on your coasts and you laughed at their threats: now the British is mistress of the seas and you fear for your very existence. This is the difference between conciliation and coercion.

From the American war nothing of consequence occurred till the vote on the regency, an epoch of considerable moment in our political annals; for, then it was that the purchase of a majority of parliament was ostentatiously menaced, then it was that corruption began to be more widely extended and more openly avowed than at any former period, then was displayed in its most abandoned form the profligate system of augmenting places, splitting places, creating places and splitting them to the size and shape of every recruited mercenary that entered the ranks of administration, then it was that by this base traffic parliament became so disparaged in the esteem of [the] people as has been lately lamented, though the crime has been unjustly charged, not upon those who perpetrated the deed, but upon those who reprehended and resisted it. To restore, however, parliament to its purity and to its reputation, my Lord Fitzwilliam came here. He intended in the first instance to have destroyed all the recent corruptions of his predecessor.

But it is necessary, before I touch further on his administration, to notice the origin of a society which has since produced the most important influence upon the people of this country, and is the immediate cause of the alarm which

F/21 *contd.* prevails at present – I mean the society of United Irishmen. It was instituted in the year 1791. The professed and avowed object of it was merely the attainment of parliamentary reform embracing all the people of every religious description whatsoever. The founder of it certainly wished for a separation of these kingdoms, as appears by his letters in the report of the secret committee. But it does not appear that the people who were prevailed on to enter into the society had any such wish. On the contrary, the letter of the founder shows that they were of a different sentiment then, for he says in it that it would be too hardy then to propose to them a separation. Yet, much pains have been taken to affix upon every man who originally joined the society the character of a separatist – for no good or fair reason – but, as it seems, to confound reform with separation, and by so doing to bring into odium that measure which some men in power here apprehended would detract from their consequence. Whatever may have been the sentiments of Mr Tone, who founded the society, about separation, the people in general who joined it saw nothing, heard of nothing, but reform. There was not a syllable in their original test but for reform in parliament on the broad basis of including all religious persuasions. It contained no injunction of secrecy. I speak of the original institution and the original test – it was afterwards, and very lately, that the injunction of secrecy was added and the words, parliament, omitted, as you will see by the report of the secret committee of this House. This disingenuity [*sic*] of charging every man who belonged to this society originally with a desire of severing these kingdoms, and the virulent calumny with which reform and Catholic enfranchisement were termed the watchword of separation and rebellion, produced much mischief, by disgusting and irritating thousands who desired these measures merely as objects of rational liberty, without connecting with them any sentiment against the crown or the connection. The society of United Irishmen, however, in a little time fell almost entirely into oblivion. In Lord Fitzwilliam's administration it was scarcely ever heard of, nor could it, I am persuaded, have ever risen into note or consequence but for the recall of that nobleman, and the irritation thereby produced in the public mind.

I had no connection with Lord Fitzwilliam's administration, but acted as distinctly and independently as I do now. Yet, never was I more concerned at any political tidings than when I heard of his recall. I foresaw the discontent that would arise in the minds of the people at thus having all their hopes at once dashed away, just at the instant they were assured of their completion. I therefore, day after day, deprecated his recall; and you, Sir, may remember well that, when in foretelling the consequences which would ensue from it, I said that soon gentlemen would be obliged for their protection to have five or six soldiers stationed in every house, clamours burst forth here against me, the galleries were to be cleared, my words to be taken down, I was to be brought in custody to the bar. Yet, have not these words been long since literally verified, so that it has even become a subject of complaint with our generals that the discipline of the army has been impaired by its dispersion in the houses of individuals. Let, therefore, those in power take care lest what I utter this day, as it may be equally repugnant to their sentiments, may equally be disregarded by them now, and equally verified by events hereafter. ...

F/21 *contd.*   I do not believe that the gentlemen who plotted the recall of Lord Fitzwilliam
saw the extent of the fatal consequences that were to follow from it, much less
do I believe that my Lord Camden or the Rt Hon. Gent. who represents him
here, foresaw them. I believe they were persuaded that a very little time would
restore the people to tranquillity and good humour; they were taught, I am
confident, to believe that the Irish were a people lightly excited and lightly
appeased. This was the erroneous character with which they had long since been
dubbed, and the error of which now near three years unhappy experience has
evinced; during which time, so far from having succeeded in appeasing the
people, the Rt Hon. Member himself must admit that they are in a state of
irritation at this day far surpassing any former example, so miserably have some
men been mistaken in what is the first and most essential science of a statesman,
that is, a knowledge of the character of the people who are to be ruled.

Soon after my Lord Fitzwilliam departed, the system of coercion commenced,
the first striking instance of which was sending a general with military power
into the disturbed counties, who preceded the judges of assize and took out of
the gaols and out of the hovels every man he thought fit, and without any form
of trial sent them all aboard the fleet. This was the first flagrant violation of
justice. This was the first instance of the law of the land being publicly trampled
under foot. This was the first time that a person in high station, acting
immediately under the government, ventured to flout at, and turn his back
upon, those august tribunals which alone have a right to decide upon the
liberties and lives of the freemen of this land. This lawless and licentious
authority was soon assumed by many others, and in the following session of
parliament the representatives of the people, instead of enquiring into these
outrages upon the liberties of the people and arraigning the delinquents – what
did they do? They passed an act of indemnity, sheltering and sanctioning every
one of the enormities. This was the most fatal measure in the history of the
present times. ...

The indemnity bill was accompanied by the insurrection act, which
legitimised this arbitrary power of transportation. But still, as the coercion was
augmented, disturbances were extended. Then further and severer measures were
resorted to: burning houses, military executions – which may in some cases have
produced apparent tranquillity, but really have left lasting and incurable
discontents. No punishment is more illegal, none more iniquitous, than burning
the houses of the peasants, for it is not merely the offender that is injured, but
the aged parents, the innocent females, the helpless children, those who from
their age and their youth could not be parties in the crimes. This is such visible
and ostentatious injustice that every eye must see it. ... Are you surprised after
this at the progress of the popular discontents? ... Where is now the loyalty that
was your boast when the French were at Bantry? ... It was you by these severities
who irritated and exasperated the lower orders and, if I may use the expression,
prepared the raw material which the United Irishmen have thereby been since
enabled to manufacture into this web of organisation which is so formidable to
you at present. ... So much for the system of coercion.

But what would conciliate the people? In the first place, they say, a removal of
those in power, and others substituting the high offices of the state [*sic*] who

F/21 *contd.* have the confidence of the people, men from whom concession would not be attributed to fear, nor conciliation to hypocrisy. In the next place the adoption of the two measures desired by the people, the Catholic bill and parliamentary reform. As to the first, I consider it but as a feather. It is, however, a feather which the Catholic would be proud to wear, and which it is unwise in you any longer to withhold. As to the reform, it is the right of the people. It is their right to be fairly and fully represented in this House, and to have the constitution rendered in act what it is in theory. ... The people of this country may be distributed into three classes: one, who will in all events support the government, and this class is composed of a large body of men, some actuated by interest, others by principle; the latter of these think that, whatever may be the faults of administration, still it is better to uphold it than risk the perils of a contest. There is another class whom perhaps no modification of government would satisfy, discontented and ambitious spirits, or those who in the lowest ranks seek convulsion for the sake of spoil. But there is a third, and most considerable, class which is a mean between the other two and which has always existed in every state circumstanced as ours, men ardently attached to liberty, who look with disgust at the abuses of the Ministers, who pant for a more honest dispensation of government and a more perfect form of constitution, active, intelligent men, widely diffused over the nation, pervading principally that middle order which acts immediately on the multitude beneath, a class which is especially powerful in this metropolis and powerful in the North. This class, I am sure, could be conciliated and embodied with the government, and all its energies called forth in its support. ...

I therefore call upon the country gentlemen of Ireland, both in this House and out of this House, to weigh well our present situation. Let them recollect that they can have but one object in view, that is to preserve their country. But those in power have another and a distinct object, that is to preserve their places. These they think would be endangered by any reform. But you will be the most infatuated of all mankind if you suffer yourselves to be persuaded by them to stake your lives and fortunes and everything that is dear to man on the same desperate die with their places, instead of trying by reasonable measures to conciliate and incorporate with you the great body of the people, and so put your country in a fit state to abide securely this tremendous contest.

I shall now conclude, once more invoking that God in whose hands are the fates of nations, to guide your deliberations this day to that ultimate resolve which shall best promote the peace, the prosperity and the liberty of this island.'

'MR SAURIN'S LETTER.

The following is a copy of a letter which is said to have been addressed by the Rt Hon. William Saurin, when Attorney General, to Lord Norbury [see E/35/7]. ...

"Dear Lord Norbury, I transcribe for you a very sensible part of Lord Rosse's letter to me:

'As Lord Norbury goes our circuit, and as he is personally acquainted with the gentlemen of our country [*sic*], a hint to him may be of use. He is in the habit of talking individually to them in his chamber at Philipstown, and if he were to

F/21 *contd.* impress upon them the consequence of the measure, viz. that however they may think otherwise, the Catholics would in spite of them elect Catholic members (if such were eligible), that the Catholic members would then have the nomination of the sheriffs and in many instances perhaps of the judges, and that the Protestants would be put in the background, as the Catholics were formerly – I think he would bring the effect of the measure home to themselves, and satisfy them that they could scarcely submit to live in the country if it were passed.'

So far Lord Rosse; but what he suggests in another part of his letter [is]:
    "That, if Protestant gentlemen who have votes and influence and interest would give these venal members to understand that, if they will, [they may] purchase Catholic votes, but by betraying their country of its constitution they shall infallibly lose theirs, it would alter their conduct, though it could neither make them honest or [*sic*] respectable."
    If you will judiciously administer a little of this medicine to the King's County or any other members of parliament that may fall in your way, you will deserve well. ...'"

Beneath this, the 2nd Earl has noted: 'It is supposed that the above letter was written in the year 1812 and found in the year 1822 by a servant of Lord Norbury's, who gave it to Mr O'Connell.'

'1825. This year, the Catholic clergy first began openly to attend all meeting[s] respecting the representation of counties and to make speeches at them, and declare that they would exert all their influence over the voters. ...'

In the correspondence of 1827 between Dr Doyle and Lord Farnham, which is introduced in full in the form of newspaper cuttings, Lord Farnham remarks:
    '... If Lord Charlemont and Mr Grattan had concurred earnestly with Mr Flood at the time the Irish Convention first met in Dublin, ... separation would have been then attempted. ...'
    To this statement, understandably, the 2nd Earl takes strong exception. 'This assertion that Mr Flood wished to separate the kingdoms is utterly unfounded. I knew all his sentiments well at the time. His object in the convention was not to allow any alteration in the representation that he proposed to parliament which had not been previously sanctioned by the English parliament, such as opening a decayed borough to the adjacent district. He had then been just chosen for the first time a member of the English parliament, and he was impatient to go over and attend there. His mind never seemed to me to have glanced on the expediency or practicability of a separation. He was much attached to England, but more to Ireland. Weak as Ireland was, with a divided population, by religious differences, he could not have conceived that such a separation could be practicable, and, if practicable, that it could be desirable. As to Mr Grattan, he was not a member of the convention and had nothing to say to it, nor was he on terms of intercourse with Mr Flood.'

J/4	DATE	DESCRIPTION

1–12   1842–5: 1851: 1853: 1855: 1866

Letters to the 3rd Earl from the Conservative leaders, Sir Robert Peel and the Duke of Wellington, about elections to the Irish representative peerage, including the 3rd Earl's own, 1842 and 1844, and letters to him from them and other Ministers (Lords Aberdeen, Derby, Palmerston, etc) about miscellaneous political and patronage matters.

The sub-section includes:

2   11 Apr. 1842   Sir Robert Peel, 2nd Bt, Whitehall, to Lord Rosse (letter marked 'Confidential') about the representative peerage.

'I beg your padon for having so long neglected to reply to a letter which you addressed to me some time since. I do not plead my incessant occupation, for that alone ought not to have prevented me from writing to you, but I wished to ascertain if possible, what had passed with reference to Lord O'Neill when the last election took place for a representative peer.

We have of late years left the selection and support of candidates for that distinction very much to the resident peers of Ireland, interfering only with our opinion and advice when there was a risk of a conflict of opinions. I believe that on the last occasion many peers felt that, from the age of Lord O'Neill, his service of forty years in the House of Commons, his name and property, his pretensions were very strong, and many peers may have committed themselves to him.

Have the goodness to allow matters to remain in their present state until, by the arrival in London of some of the peers who took the most active part in reference to the election, I can ascertain more correctly how they stand. I certainly feel strongly – and on public grounds – that your accession to the House of Lords would be honourable to the Irish peerage and most useful to the country.'

3   29 Nov. 1842   The 1st Duke of Wellington, Stratfield Saye, Hampshire, to Rosse, Parsonstown.

'I beg leave to remind your Lordship that I have not a vote in the election of a peer [to] represent in the House of Lords the peerage of Ireland; nor have I any influence in such elections not due to the [word illegible] confidence of friends. I suggest to your Lordship that you should state your views to the Lord Lieutenant of Ireland and his Chief Secretary, and to the Queen's Minister, Sir Robert Peel.'

6   11 Dec. 1844   Peel, Whitehall, to Rosse, Coulson's Hotel, London.

'I have availed myself of the earliest opportunity after my return to London today to confer with the Duke of Wellington on the subject of your letter. You have our good wishes for your success at the election of a representative peer to succeed Lord Limerick.'

M/3	DATE	DESCRIPTION
1–16	1867–9	Letters to the 4th Earl from the Chief Secretary, Lord Mayo, and others about representative peerage elections, including that of the 4th Earl himself.

1   21 Nov. [1867]   Mayo, Irish Office, London, to Lord Rosse (letter marked 'Private').

'I hope you will excuse my writing to you so soon after the great affliction which you have sustained [the death of the 3rd Earl], and in which I hope I may be allowed to offer my most cordial sympathy.

But the subject matter of this somewhat [?presses], as a meeting of Irish peers is shortly to be held to choose a representative peer to fill the next vacancy, whenever it may occur. Lord Derby is anxious to know whether you would wish to be put in nomination, and I have little doubt that, if you express a wish for election, you would in all probability be named for the next vacancy.

I must of course make this communication in the most confidential manner, but, as I feel it would be of great advantage both to yourself and to the party that you should enter early into public life, I hope you will enable me to tell Lord Derby that you are willing to come forward as a candidate for the next representative peerage.

Lord Derby also desired me to say that he would have gladly offered you the Lieutenancy of the King's County, but that he has the greatest objection to make that office hereditary, and he thinks that it is but fair that the different families in the county should in different generations share in that honour.'

2   28 Nov. [1867]   Mayo, House of Commons, to Rosse (letter marked 'Private').

'I am very glad to hear that you are willing to come forward as a candidate for the next representative peerage. Allow me to suggest that you should cause immediate steps to be taken in the House of Lords to prove your right to vote, and that when that was done, you should address a letter to each Irish peer asking for his support.

I believe Sir Bernard Burke can give you all the necessary information as to the proper course you should take for proving your right to vote.'

3   29 Nov. 1867   The 4th Viscount Hawarden, Carlton Club, to Rosse (letter marked 'Private').

'As Headley is, I know, canvassing most actively, I think it right you should know his actual position, as many people may suppose that, from his having been told to canvass against Dunboyne, he has a claim to be selected for the next vacancy.

M/3/3 *contd.*

The determination come to at the last meeting was that Dunboyne was to be considered our candidate, unless Headley could show that he had a majority of promises. They were therefore both to canvass and report the result to me for Lord Derby's information. The result was that Dunboyne obtained 60 promises and Headley 32, and Dunboyne therefore became the candidate to be supported.

The meeting further decided, and I received directions to make known to both of them, that the unsuccessful candidate was not to consider that he had any claim to the support of the party at the next vacancy, but that a future meeting would decide who was to be our candidate at a future vacancy.

I think it right that you should know what occurred, as you were probably not aware of what passed at the meeting.'

4   3 Dec. 1867   Mayo, Irish Office, London, to Rosse (letter marked 'Private').

'I have received your letter of the 30th. As I am a member of the House of Commons, I am unable to vote in the election of a representative peer, but you may depend on my using any little influence I possess to secure your return at the next vacancy.'

5   5 Dec. [1867]   Mayo, Irish Office, to Rosse (letter marked 'Private').

'I thought it a matter of such importance that your right to vote should be proved in the House of Lords during this short session, that I wrote to Sir Bernard Burke myself on the subject. He very kindly came over at once, and got the affair arranged on Tuesday last. I hope there will now be no difficulty about your election to the next vacancy, whenever it takes place.'

6   21 Dec. 1867   Copy of a letter from Rosse, Birr Castle, Parsonstown, to Lord Hawarden.

'I have now, I think, received answers to my circulars from all who are likely to reply, and the following is the result.

Twenty intend to give their votes to Headley; twelve either promised me their votes or will be guided by the decision come to at Lord Derby's meeting; and [there are] 10 who either do not pledge themselves or merely acknowledge the receipt of my circular. These are all the answers which I have received, with the exception of 5 or 6 from peers who have not qualified and to whom circulars were sent before the arrival of the official list.

If these answers afford any indication at all of the way that the remaining peers are likely to vote, I do not see that I have very much chance next time. I should infer from the answers that many peers either have not heard of the decision come to at Lord Derby's meeting, or, if they have, do not intend to vote in accordance with it. Lord Headley in his reply (dated December 1st) to my circular says that he has received more than 50 promises, besides many letters unanswered.

M/3/6 *contd.*   I should be sorry if my coming forward for the *first* vacancy
should appear at all premature and unfair to Lord Headley, which
possibly it might, if the peers do not generally know what passed
at the meeting, more particularly as I came forward, not so much
in consequence of my own wishes on the subject, as at the earnest
request of leading members of the Conservative party, and in the
hope of being of some little service to them.

The meeting which, I understood, was to have taken place
shortly at Lord Derby's, does not appear to have been held yet, so
probably most of the peers are not aware of the wishes of the
government on the subject.'

7–8   [*c.* 21 Dec.   Lists of promises to support Lord Headley and himself, in
         1867]   Rosse's handwriting.

9   23 July 1868   Duplicated circular, signed by Lord Hawarden, Carlton Club,
                           and headed 'Irish representative peerage'.
                           'At a "preliminary" meeting of Irish peers, held at Chesterfield
                           House on 25 July 1868, present: Duke of Buckingham, Lords
                           Abercorn, Westmeath, Lucan, Verulam, Leitrim, Longford,
                           Henniker, Courtown, de Vesei, Limerick, Hawarden; on the
                           assumption that the Earl of Rosse will be elected (according to the
                           decision of the meeting held lately at Lord Derby's house) to fill
                           the existing vacancy in the Irish representative peerage, it was
                           voted by 11 votes against 1 vote that the Earl of Caledon be
                           recommended as well qualified for election to the next vacancy
                           that may occur after the Earl of Rosse's election.'

10   25 Aug. 1868   The 3rd Lord Headley, Aghadoe House, Killarney, Co. Kerry,
                           to Rosse.
                           'A suggestion occurs to me in consequence of the terrible calamity
                           that has just happended, causing a second vacancy by the death of
                           our lamented friend, Lord Farnham. It is this: that, as senior
                           candidate and so much longer in the field (since the early part of
                           1864), I should be allowed by our party (in order to stop further
                           division) to take the vacancy caused by the demise of Lord Bantry,
                           and that you should succeed to the one that has just come before us.
                           I put this to you for consultation with your friends, from no
                           other reason than that of a *very urgent feeling I entertain* against a
                           continuation of the present split in our camp.
                           You would be sure of the support of most of my present 68
                           friends, the greater number of whom have already signed, and
                           some of those abroad will soon do so. Indeed, I think your election
                           in succession to me would wellnigh be a nem. con. affair.'

11   25 Aug. 1868   Copy of the foregoing.

12   18 Sep. 1868   The 2nd Lord Oranmore, Castle Macgarrett, Ballindine,
                           Co. Galway, to Rosse.

M/3/12 *contd.*   'I seek to be a representative peer, and shall feel flattered by your vote and support. If returned, I should vote for that party which supports our Protestant institutions, which I believe to be the foundation and safeguards of the liberty we possess.'

13   25 Sep. 1868   Duplicated 'Private' circular from Thomas J. Farley, this copy addressed to Rosse, proposing, if assured of the co-operation of the peers themselves, to compile and print reports of the debates of the House of Lords alone, which would come out more swiftly and to a higher standard of accuracy than the present bicameral system of reporting; he encloses [M/3/14] printed copies of letters from the Duke of Argyll, and Lords Hardinge, Stanhope, Dufferin, Fortescue, etc, etc, expressing dissatisfaction at the present system and interest in Farley's proposal.

15   15 Nov. 1868   Lord Oranmore, Castle Macgarrett, to Rosse.
      'I'm obliged by your kind letter.
      I do not believe any change in land laws will benefit either landlord or tenant, though I fear revolutionary measure so much so [*sic*] that I let grass lands only as grazing.
      Lord Caledon is, I believe, hardly of age, and can wait, unless he really looks to take an active part in politics. I shall feel much obliged by your forwarding my candidature. While Disraeli is Conservative and Protestant, I should, as now, give the government any support I can.'

16   21 May 1869   The 4th Lord Ventry, Burnham, Dingle, Co. Kerry, to Rosse.
      '... I ground my claims [as a candidate for the representative peerage] on residence in Ireland and my family's constant support of the Conservative cause. In politics I am a decided Conservative, but I shall always regard the interests of Ireland as paramount to mere party considerations. I will only add that I am prepared to devote my best attention to the duties of the position I am seeking.'

R

DATE	DESCRIPTION

1869: 1884:   Artificial collection of letters, obituary and biographical notices, printed
1896–8: N.D.:   order for memorial services, photographs, etc, received or asssembled by
1902: 1905:   the 4th, 6th and 7th Earls of Rosse, the Hon. Geoffrey L. Parsons and Mr
1907–9: 1913:   Laurence Parsons, all concerning the inventor of the turbine, Sir Charles
1918: 1922:   Parsons, a younger brother of the 4th Earl
1927–8: 1931:   The following is a calendar of Sir Charles's letters to his nephew, the
1933–6: 1942–3   Hon. Geoffrey L. Parsons.
1950: 1952:
1954: 1956–9:
1968–82: 1984

22 June 1909   Letter from Charles Parsons to the Hon. Geoffrey L. Parsons.
     '... I am thunderstruck by the "conservatism", to use a mild term, of musicians in regard to the Auxetophone instruments. It is absolutely "Arkwright's Loom" over again (assuming the thing is any use at all). At last Carnegie Lane and I have arranged for Van Bene to play the Aux. cello at the Queens Hall on July 8th. It is to cost £365.0.0 with orchestra! And the admissions may bring back £100.0.0. I am weary of them and shall take a radical step shortly – I think give them shares, viz. to the musicians, and see what they will do! I don't suppose they will ever have been put in such a dilemma before! ...'

3 Sep. 1909   Letter from Parsons, Ray, Kirkwhelpington, Newcastle-on-Tyne, to the Hon. Geoffrey L. Parsons.
     'This letter will I hope reach you ... before sailing. We shall be glad to see you. You have not missed much in the grouse line as it has been a bad year on the moor ... .
     The works at Heaton have undergone some re-arrangement as regards shop management, and Armstrong is superintendant of piece work in electrical and turbine departments; costs are going down considerably.
     Wallsend is extremely slack and has been so for some months. Admiralty work going under cost, but we hope to get some more work shortly.
     Lau has a new car (a Talbot) which goes very well. 10–12 HP and Bedford has bought his former one. Tommy is also getting a similar Talbot. Our old Daimler is still going strong, but a bit noisy after some 17,000 miles, and must go in for an overhaul this winter ... .'

20 Sep. 1927   Letter from Parsons, Ray, to the Hon. Geoffrey L. Parsons.
     'Very many thanks for your kind letter of congratulations. I knew nothing about their thinking about giving me the O.M. till a letter reached me from Lord Stamfordham about ten days before it was in the papers. From the many letters that have reached me from engineers, they seem very pleased that their class for the first time has been considered, and I was surprized to receive a telegram of congratulations from Mussolini on behalf of the Italian Marines.

R/ *contd.* Willie may have told you about his beat-up of relations for a dinner at Claridges last week. Eighteen came, no speeches (thank goodness) and everybody seemed to enjoy themselves. Willie organised it spendidly. Poor Bishop of Newcastle and Mrs Wild left today. He has suffered a terible breakdown, a sort of paralysis of hands, throat, etc, from (it is said) over work. He came for a day or two's trout fishing in Sweethope, but was really too ill to catch more than three or four. He resigns next month.

Edward was at the dinner. He looks very dignified after his induction.

Yes, we should both like if we should be able to go to S. Africa the year after next, when the British Association meet there. ...'

T/1

DATE	DESCRIPTION

1923: 1936–8:   Letters to the 6th Earl and Countess of Rosse, some of them from Thomas
1941–2: 1945:   U. Sadleir of the Office of Arms, Dublin Castle, about Parsons, Boleyn,
1947: 1952:   Savage and Sprigge genealogy and family history, including: a typescript
1956: 1961:   copy of the well-known letter written by Francis Johnston in 1820 in
1967: 1969–71:   which Johnston itemises his architectural opera to date (and excludes Birr
1983   Castle from the list); extracts from Gilbert's *History of Dublin* concerning
the raffish life of the 1st Earl of Rosse (of the first creation) in Dublin in
the 1730s and his patronage of the portrait painter, James Worsdale; an
MS. copy of a poem by Sir Laurence Parsons, 5th Bt, *c.* 1793, on the
decadence of the Irish parliament, taken from Wolfe Tone's *Life*, by his
son; etc; etc. Also included are correspondence and papers about the 6th
Earl's establishing his right to vote in Irish representative peerage elections,
1936–7.

The poem by Sir Laurence Parsons, 5th Bt (extracted for the 6th Earl by a
Dublin record agent called James Fleming, 1937–8) is as follows:

'... What, though by virtue's trumpet late inspir'd,
Our Youth stood forth, in freedom's arms attir'd,
And peel'd in thunders to the British shore
The ills for ages we ignobly bore.
'Twas a brief dream, a meteor of an hour,
Fled is that spirit, gone its short-lived pow'r.
Look all the island round, and what's display'd?
Buyers and bought, betrayer and betray'd.
Self like a plague, through every class has ran,
Nor left one thought to dignify one man.

What, though a crown imperial now we claim,
And with the empty title gild our shame,
In rank co-ordinate with Britain vie,
Boast thrones and senates, pompous pageantry,
With all the playhouse trappings of a state.
Where are the acts or men which speak us great?
Who kings it here, or who our senate rules?
Or who, yet meaner, are of these [the] tools?
Their merits; stations; name them man by man;
And then vaunt of your country if you can.
First a raw peer, a creeping unknown thing,
In England flouted at, sent here a king.
A sorry aide-de-camp, with sage conceit,
Beneath him wields the thunders of the state;
And at his feet in humble rev'rence crawl
Ireland's proud nobles, prelates, Commons, all.
O glorious picture! Who would not be proud

T/1 *contd.*

To lick the dust with this right noble crowd!
To bask his crest in H[o]b[ar]t's haughty rays,
Or shine in W[e]stm[ore]l[an]d's mock royal blaze!
To crouch to such a twain, search all around,
No other people could on earth be found. ...'

APPENDIX

A DESCRIPTIVE LIST OF ALL THE
SEVENTEENTH-CENTURY MATERIAL
IN THE ROSSE ARCHIVE

by

AOIFE LEONARD

A DESCRIPTIVE LIST OF SEVENTEENTH-CENTURY MATERIAL

INTRODUCTION

INTRODUCTION

The 17th-century papers constitute only a fraction of the very large archive in Birr Castle, which in its entirety spans four hundred years. This section of the archive marks the arrival of the Parsonses in Birr and traces their early progress and development among the first settlers and later as Governors of the territory of Ely O'Carroll. Birr, alias Ely O'Carroll, had been in the possession of the O'Carrolls for generations prior to English occupation. The town was like many of the small rural settlements in the country at the time. There is no evidence among the records of the size or population of the town or indeed how many settlers came with the plantation though there is a good deal of evidence of its growth throughout the 17th century. In 1612 Sir Laurence records memoranda of agreements with tenants and copies of bonds (1612–16) which give a fair indication of the number of people in the town with whom he had dealings. The town must have been well populated to necessitate the establishment of ordinances for its regulation (see no. 1).

The Parsonses, particularly Sir Laurence, could be considered as benevolent Governors who were dedicated to their office and zealous in their loyalty to the sovereign (see no. 241). They were granted several lands in the King's County including the castle and town of Birr which became known as Parsonstown. Among the accounts of Sir Laurence (see no. 2, 1622–7) are several entries detailing work carried out in the town such as the erection of a market cross, widening of the bridge and work on the church, all of which were done at his own expense. There is a draft petition from William Parsons (c. 1643 – see no. 183) to Oliver Cromwell to reduce the taxes collected on houses, markets and mills to encourage regrowth in the town which had suffered badly during the Civil War. He states that it was burnt three times over the summer and that there were no tenants living there. Later, in 1692, Sir Laurence (1st Bt) wrote in a letter to a silver-smith (see no. 163) that '... if there be any persons aboute you that wants farmes and can bring stock with them I cann suplie them with land in Ireland on easy termes ... I have alsoe a want of good tradesmen in the town of Birr pray tell your neighbours and if any came over let them be such as are able for our Kingdom is over stock with beggars'. Sir Laurence (1st Bt) in 1689 took his tenants "into his castle for a time as their homes and goods had been plundered by a gang of robbers who were terrorising the area. For this act of kindness he Was suspected of setting up a garrison in the castle and narrowly escaped a charge of treason (see no. 228 – General Moore's report on his findings).

The 17th century was a particularly violent time for the Parsonses. They witnessed periods of bloodshed, the total destruction of the town, the ruination of the family fortune and the castle and estate laid waste. The castle was seized twice, in 1643 and 1689. Sir Laurence spent several years in captivity after 1689 and barely escaped being hung, drawn and quartered as a traitor. These episodes are well documented in the archives. Capt. William Parsons, who commanded the garrison at Birr in 1642, left a diary (no. 188, 1641–3), which gives a day to day account of the troubles leading up to the siege of the castle. In fact, the earliest evidence of a suspected rebellion was in 1639. An order was issued to Capt. William to search the house of John O'Carroll of Clonliske for ammunition (see no. 185) and the examination of O'Carroll's servants (see no. 187) revealed that some had been found together with a secret room in the house.

In April 1687 Sir Laurence was forced to leave Ireland with his wife and children due to a threat by a servant to impeach Lady Parsons for treason. He left his agent, Capt. Heward Oxburgh to manage his business and estate and returned to Cheshire. However on investigation he discovered that he was owed £3,000 from rents that had been collected by Oxburgh but never returned (see correspondence with Capt. Oxburgh, nos. 95–107). He came back to Ireland to rectify the situation and was faced with the siege of the castle (1689) by Oxburgh and his army (raised with Sir Laurence's money) and was forced to surrender. All is recorded in a journal (see no. 226) written in a later hand and probably copied from an original (not in the archive).

The several petitions of the Parsonses (see no. 240–1; Nos. 232–3) no. 233) seeking compensation after the rebellion of 1689 reveal the extent of their losses and sufferings.

Throughout the 17th century the Parsonses' relations with the rebels were, not surprisingly, strained and among the correspondence (see Section B, William Parsons 1638–45) are letters from some, namely Molloy, O'Kennedy and O'Moore, which express very articulately their side of the argument and their attitude towards the Parsonses. However, it appears that Governor William Parsons was on particularly good terms with his neighbours (see no. 176, 1642–3).

Turning to the Parsons castle and estate which were built and developed between 1623 and 1627, there is an account book (see no. 2) recording contracts and accounts for building and renovation work carried out on the property. They give a vivid insight into the original structure of the castle (which was a gatehouse extended) and the layout of the estate (i.e. which buildings, walls, cellars, dungeons and other features were remodelled or demolished) and what types of trees and shrubberies were planted in place of the original vegetation. One particular entry (which may be of interest to archaeologists) records the wages paid to labourers to bury a huge stone in the orchard, which could not be broken up. There is a detailed index to the entries in this book in Birr Castle (see Birr Castle: Renovations and Birr Castle: Estate and Gardens).

Equally well documented is the Parsonses' private life (see Administration of Home and Family Affairs). One item of particular interest is a recipé book written in the hand of Dorothy Parsons with recipés for various dishes, cures and cleaning solutions. Recorded is a successful cure for a cancerous growth, which it states was tried and recommended by the wife of the Archbishop of Dublin who was diagnosed as being incurable.

ARRANGEMENT AND DESCRIPTION

The material is arranged in a logical manner as near as possible to the original order, where this can be established. It is divided and described under four main sections, which mainly relate to the Parsonses of Parsonstown and the Parsonses of Bellamont, Co. Dublin, and Tomduff, Co. Wexford. Sub groups (section A) cover material relating to the administration of the estate and property, e.g. accounts, rentals, leases, letters, patents, etc, and also cover material in connection with the home and management of family affairs, e.g. account books, correspondence of a private nature, recipés, and bills for clothing and schooling, food, etc. The second section of the list relates to the personal careers and professional activities of some members of the Parsons family (only a few are represented). The type of document found here varies from letters patent (e.g. granting admiralty jurisdiction to Sir Laurence), letters from the rebels, marching orders and official despatches to Capt. William Parsons, orders for the plantation of Leinster, memoranda of transactions in the Houses of Parliament, etc. The covering dates given correspond to the period covered by the material and not the span of their careers. The third section (section C) relates to the Parsonses of Bellamont and Tomduff and contains a small quantity of material that did not warrant further division. The fourth section (section D) covers the 17th-century maps and plans of the archive (section O of the catalogue) and the fifth section (section E) covers the 17th-century material found among the papers which have no apparent relevance to the Parsonses. However, there are some interesting items among these.

The unit of description is generally the individual document although there are some volumes such as account books and diaries. In the 19th century a large portion of documents and letters were bound in two volumes (A/1 and A/5). Unfortunately there is little evidence that any attention was paid prior to the binding to the content or chronology of the documents. This has presented problems in a couple of cases, e.g. Sir George Preston's dispute with the Corporation (of Limerick) regarding his patent of the salmon weir in Limerick. The documents (29 in number) were not placed in chronological order in the volume. In order to avoid unnecessary confusion the letters have been listed in the descriptive list in the order in which they were found (and therefore not chronologically). Similar examples are the marching orders issued to Capt. William Parsons, which were found scattered throughout the book.

This rearrangement and descriptive list of the 17th-century material was created in 1988–9 and was made possible by the generosity of the Carroll Institute, who established a fund to finance the work. The numbers assigned to each document by A.P.W. Malcomson are given in round brackets underneath the descriptive list number. The descriptions themselves have been constructed to indicate in general terms the content of each item and to highlight the more significant items.

Aoife Leonard

December 1989

NO	DATE	DESCRIPTION

A   THE PARSONSES OF PARSONSTOWN, BIRR, KING'S COUNTY

I   ADMINISTRATION OF ESTATE AND PROPERTY

i.   *Accounts and rentals 1612–94*

1 (A/4)   1612–94   Bound volume recording the rentals of the Parsons' estate (1629–41; 1667–86, 1694), copies of bonds and memoranda of agreements with tenants (1612–16), and the accounts of rents received by Sir Laurence's estate agent (Captain Oxburgh), 1663–7. Included are miscellaneous items such as copies of various letters patent granted to the Parsonses, e.g. the patent of Birr (26 June 1620); a grant of 200 acres for the free school at Birr; a grant of the custodies of the castle and lands of Ballybritt to Sir Laurence and George Herbert; memoranda of Star Chamber procedures with notes on the cases heard; the ordinances for the regulation of the town of Birr devised by Sir Laurence (1626); Royal Orders and directions for the 'better settlings and preservations of his [the King's] rents and revenues within the realm of Ireland', together with the duties of the Officers of the Exchequer.

Includes: Herb remedies for wounds and other ills such as kidney stones.

Includes: A copy of the first letter patent for the plantation of Longford and the O'Carrolls' country (8 Aug. 1619). Also a 'brief certificate of the acres of land of several natures in the county of Longford and the territory of Ely O'Carroll' with instructions for the plantation of Longford.

Includes: Copy of 'the old deed of the Town of Birr granted by the Earl of Ormond to Hossey' (1620).

Includes: Copy of the custody of Bovine granted to Sir Laurence (6 May 1627).

Includes: A genealogy of the children born to Laurence Parsons.

2 (A/8)   1620–7   Sir Laurence Parsons' account book recording accounts and contracts mainly for the upkeep and maintenance of the castle and estate; details of farming transactions such as the purchase of cattle and exchange of livestock; leases (1625; 1635–41); a rental of the Parsonses' lands in the King's County (1620–27); examples of entries are as follows:

Accounts: Money lent to Thomas Glen, schoolmaster, towards Donagh Carroll's and Laurence Parsons's teaching to 'write fayre sett, roming and text hand and to cipher well' (5 June 1628); 15

'For the chardge of a guide and my owne chardge in goeing to
Portumary'; 'Paid for 2 tonnes of iron spent about my building
at Byrre and working thereof; 'paid for pulling down the walls
before the doore of the castle' (1621); 'my charges at
Phillipstowne Sessions 4 dales at 20 shillings per *dale*'(1621);
'Paid unto Dermoid O'Gavane for making the irons to hang the
great gate' (1622); 'Donnells charges goeing to Croghan for
Cherrie Fees' (1622); 'paid to Wm. Dier and his man for making
up the doors at Ballindowne Castle' (1623); 'Paid in part for 2
new mill stones' (1623); 'Paid to Dier and Willsome for making
the small cable end over the staires case and for breaking the wall
at the staire foot for the fail of a doore there' (1623); 'paid to
take downe the scaffiles and to take downe the gable end of the
stairecase for the raiseing of the stairecase higher' (1623); 'paid
for work done by Thomas Davies and his boy and Thomas
Evans in taking out the window at the stairehead and setting in
it the doorecase there...' (1623); 'paid unto John Marne for his
work about the new mill' (1623); 'paid unto Thomas Davies in
full paiement for his lathing work within the new castle' (1624);
'paid for fetching of young trees and grass from Portuming'
(1625); 'for making of the drawing table' (1625); 'for pulling
down the old walle and building the foundations for the new
kitchen chimnmey' (1625); 'for emtieing the well' (1625); 'paid
for pulling downe part of the south wall of the garden tower'
(1625); 'paid to them for burying the great stone within the
orchard that could not be broken' (1625); 'paid to Phillip
Traddy for willowe stakes and hedging for 192 perches of the
hedge of the orchard and the newe ditch towards Clonaghaul'
(1625); 'for rootinge the old apple trees and plum trees and
throwinge downe of those bankes and raisinge the ground at the
south corner of the orchard' (1625); 'paid to Patrick Condon
and Edward Renolds for theire charge and wages in fetching the
cherry trees and plum trees from Thorles' (1625); 'paid for
lewing and sawing more wainskotting my own bed chamber
next the hall' (1627); 'paid Brian McHugh and his company for
pulling downe the old castle by Mr Morley's appointment'
(1628).

Contracts: for a stone mill near the castle (3 June 1626); for a
watercourse (3 July 1626), including a list of stone masons and
labourers employed for the construction of the mill and
chimney; 'to colour and [?putty] sufficiently all my windows and
doores staires now made in my English house, the 3 great towers
[word 'flankers' has been crossed out] for the buttery, storehouse
and flanker, but also to refresh again the coloure and oyle, all the
windows, doores'and steares in my dwelling castle, called the
gatehouse' (1627); for pulling down the barn wall between the
old castle and the storehouse (1627); for pulling down part of

the old castle and the 'barn wall'. '... They shall out of hand take down 12 foot of the south east angle of the old castle, the dungeon there and the west wall within the old castle in the western end thereof; to take down also the inside wall of the north side of the old castle so low as may serve for the loft to be layed thereon, to take down the little flanker and that part of the barn wall that reacheth from thence to the dungeon; to sort the coignes and wall stones by the lime and gravel of the old castle walls inward within these walls...' (1627).

Includes: Reference to the purchase of the Manor of Newtown from Sir Thomas Roy Knight, Lord Baron of Bantry and Viscount Baltinglass, for £410 sterling.

Includes: Record of the day Francis Boyle, Earl of Cork, came to live with the Parsonses (p. 19, July 1623).

Includes: A record of the setting of the boundaries in the Kings county for plantation (1627), e.g. 'We began at the Laghan – Ballymanagh parcell of Cargindonell Doorus and fortland lyeing westwarde of that meare and there digged a hole and drove in a stake and from thence we went southwarde first to an old whitethorne tree...'* Approx. 150 pp

3 (A/l/72)	June 1687	Captain Oxburgh's account of money received and paid to Sir Laurence Parsons in England.
4 (A/l/152)	23 Nov. 1688	Particulars of payments made by Capt. Oxburgh to Sir Laurence and of the rents collected at Birr.

ii.   *Leases 1604–94*

5 (Q/l–3)	(1604)	Original lease (1604) and two non-contemporary copies of the lease of 'The Myrtle House" Youghal, Co. Cork (former home of Sir Walter Raleigh), to the Parsonses of Parsonstown from the 1st Earl of Cork, and the lease of one house and garden to William Dalton from Sir Richard Donovan. (Document is very fragile). 3 Items
6 (A/5/49)	14 Jan. 1636	Lease of the lands of Lattenboy and Knockportalaghan, Co. Tipperary, from Lady Anne Parsons to Donagh 0'Kennedy of Tirreglasse, Co. Tipperary, and Edward O'Kennedy of Portalaghan, Co. Tipperary. 1 p
7 (Q/24(2))	7 Feb. 1659	Parchment lease of Ballynanarge [Boolinarig], King's County, to Robert Pitt of Clonmel, Co. Tipperary. 1 membrane
8 (A/l/33)	7 May 1664	Articles of agreement for the leasing of the lands of Balmarrig [Boolinarig], King's County, between Mary Pitts of Limerick City and Robert Clark of Balmarrig. 1 p

---

*   For further details of the construction and renovation of the castle and estate recorded in this book, see the index under 'Birr Castle and Estate' in the muniment room.

9 (A/l/34)	21 Mar. 1666	Lease of the lands of Ballinary [Boolinarig], King's County, from John Marshall to Laurence Parsons. 1 p
10 (A/l/35)	1668	Bond between Mary Pitts and Horton Vaughan in respect of a lease of Ballinanage [Boolinarig], King's County, made (13 Aug. 1659) to her husband from James Marshall. 1 p
11 (0/32(1))	20 Apr. 1668	Parchment lease of the castle, hall, town and lands of Cloonelyon [Clonlyon] and also the town and lands of Glann in the Barony of Garrycastle, King's County, from Thomas Buckridge of Dublin to John Coghlan. 1 membrane
12 (0/24(1))	27 May 1668	Lease of Balinagg [Boolinarig] in the Barony of Eglish, King's County, from Hector Vaughan to Laurence Parsons. 1 p
13 (0/24(3))	27 May 1668	Lease of Ballinanage [Boolinarig], King's County, from Mary Pitts to Hector Vaughan. 1 p See also no. 10
14 (A/8/4)	16 Sep. 1672	Parchment confirmation and lease of the lands of Birr Castle, King's County, from Henry Harewell of Islington, Middlesex, England, to Abigail Harewell (mother). 1 membrane (Centre of document is torn and text is faded in parts).
15 (Q/32(2))	6 June 1673	Parchment lease of Clonlyon, King's County, from Elizabeth, Abigaile and Henry Harewell of Middlesex, England, to William Sands of Dublin. 1 membrane
16 (Q/24(4))	10 July 1673	Lease of Ballinanigge [Boolinarig], King's County, from John Marshall of Middlesex, England, to Ezekiell Webb of Parsonstown,Birr, King's County, for 'one pepper corn a year'. 1 p
17 (Q/75(1))	13 May 1685	Parchment lease of premises in Castle Street, Birr, King's County, from Sir Laurence and William Parsons to William Reade, a bricklayer of Birr. 1 membrane (Document is badly damaged at end).
18 (Q/90(1))	14 June 1679	Parchment lease of premises in Birr Town, King's County, from Sir Laurence to Philip Moore of Birr. 1 membrane
19 (Q/30(1))	May 1694	Parchment lease of Cloonad and Ballnamoddagh 1 in the Barony of Cullistowne, King's County, from William Sprigg[e] of Cloonevoe, King's County, to Edward Tayler of Dysart, Co. Westmeath. 1 membrane

iii.   *Title deeds 1625–90*

20 (A/25/2)	Circa. 1604	Fine of the lands of Ballindara [Ballindarra] and Krinkle [Crinkle] in the King's County. 1 membrane
21 (A/25/6)	Circa. 1611	Fine of the lands of Reban, Co. Kildare, property of Thomas Savage (presumably brother of Francis Savage, wife to Sir Laurence, 1st Bt). 1 membrane

22 (A/1/3)	25 July 1620	Deed of conveyance of the castle and town of Ballynagarragh and Caherknoghan, Co. Cork, between Garret Goulde, John Roche of Imericke, Co. Cork, and Edward Kendall (Deputy Escheator of Munster).
23 (A/5/69)	27 Nov. 1620	Agreement between Richard Roche Fitzdavid and William Parsons for the plowland of Shimanagh [Shinanagh, Co. Cork] (purchased by the Parsons), for payment of the purchase by the following May. 1 p
24 (A/5/67)	23 Oct. 1625	Receipt of £60 for the redemption of two plowlands in Whites land [Whiteland], Co. Tipperary, from Sir Laurence Parsons to Henry Hesnold. 1 p
25 (A/1/6)	21 June 1631	Copy of deed of confirmation of Fanenlobane [Fanenloslea], Phrehane [Preghane], Knocknanafe [Knocknanagh], Ballynolan [Ballynoran], in Cork from Philley Barry Ogres of Kincurran, Co. Cork, to Richard Parsons in respect of a mortgage made to Sir Laurence. 1 p
26 (A/25/5) See also no. 31	27 Aug. 1632	Parchment deed of sale of the lands of Crinkle and Ballindarragh [Ballindarra], King's County, to Lady Anne Parsons from Henry and Francis Suchevel [Sacheverell?]. 1 membrane
27 (A/1/9)	1636	Writ ordering that the rents granted to Lady Anne Parsons from the lands of Boytin, Clonbrone [King's County] and Shangannagh [Queen's County] be forfeited to the crown. 1 p
28 (A/5/87)	1636	Chancery order for the reversion of the rents from the lands of: Newtown, Ballynogan [Ballyknockan], Tullagh, Ballymacmurragh, Ballywilliam, Colin, Roscomroe and Claghroe, all in the King's County and the property of William Parsons, to be reverted to the former rent as laid down in the letters patent to William Sinclare. 1 p
29 (A/5/37) See also no. 39	20 May 1640	Acquittance of Arthur Coghlan to Laurence Parsons for £100 redemption of a mortgage of the towns of Tullaghneskeah [Tullaskeagh], Co. Tipperary.* (Signed by William Parsons)
30 (A/5/40)	20 May 1640	Mortgage deed of the lands of Tullasneskeagh [Tullaskeagh], Co. Tipperary, to William Parsons for £100. (Signed by Lady Anne Parsons)
31 (A/25/8)	1641	Deed of conveyance of the castle and lands of Ballindarragh [Ballindarra], King's County, to Henry and Francis Suchevel [Sacheverell?] from Lady Anne Parsons. (Wax seal is attached)
32 (A/1/142)	5 July 1664	'The Voluntary Disposission of William O'Ready' testifying that the title to the lands and meares of Shananagh [Shinanagh],

---

* Tullaskeagh is near Roscrea; equally, the townland referred to might be Tullynisky, which is on the King's County side of the Tipperary/King's County boundary.

Co. Cork, Ballytyna and Fasaghkeale, King's County, belongs to Laurence Parsons. 1 p

33 (A/5/61)	15 July 1665	Receipt of part payment for the purchase of the town and lands of Hedanmore [Fedamore], Fedanbeg and Clonbannon, Limerick, by Desmond Hamilton of Dublin City. 1 p
34 (A/25/9) See also no. 36 no. 38	[16 May 1666]	Parchment deed of conveyance of the lands of Fedanmore, Fedanbeg and Clonbanoe, Limerick, to William Hamilton from Edward Coghlan. 1 p
35 (A/18/5)	1669	Copy of the Chancery bill for the purchase by Laurence Parsons of an interest in the lands of Ballymerrig and Ballyduffe, King's County, from William L'Estrange. 10 pp
36 (A/18/6)	N.D.	Copy of an extract of a document bearing the articles of agreement between Thomas Scott of Sedan and William Hamilton in connection with the sale of Sedan to Scott. (Content of document is obscure due to a large portion of the text being missing). 1 p
37 (A/1/69)	13 Apr. 1681	Parchment 'Counterpart of the defeazance [sic] of the Statute Staple' between Matthew French of Dublin (Merchant) and Sir Laurence Parsons, for the sum of £3,000. 1 membrane
38 (A/5/78)	13 Feb. 1668	Bill of sale from Thomas Buckridge of the town, castle and lands of Clonlyon and Gleane, in the Barony of Garriscastle [Garrycastle], King's County, to William Hamilton. 1 p
39	25 Mar. [1690]	Receipt for £100 for the redemption of the mortgage of the lands of Ancillah, King's County, from Lady Anne Parsons to Arthur Coghlan. 1 p

iv.		*Bonds and receipts 1607–92*
40 (A/3)	1607	Parchment bond between John Netterville and William Talbot of Dowth, Co. Meath. 1 membrane
41 (A/1/4)	2 May 1629	Bill of sale of ten cows of 'English breed' to Lady Anne Parsons as security for a loan of £1000 to Samuel Smith of Birr, King's County. 1 pp
42 (A/1/7)	1631	Bond between Lady Anne Parsons and Owney O'Carroll. (Signed and sealed by O'Carroll) 1 p
43 (A/1/5)	1631–41	Four Bonds between Lady Anne Parsons and Owney O'Carroll, Con, John and Charles Coghlan, John Duigin and John Bryan. (Signed by all parties) 4 items

44 (A/1/10)	1636	Copy of two bonds between Lady Anne Parsons and Lewis, Turlagh, and James O'Carroll; Elizabeth Gough and Thomas Greene. (Signed by William and Fenton Parsons) 1 p
45 (A/5/64)	24 June 1636	Certificate of acknowledgement of £150 due by H. Sacheverell to Lady Anne Parsons. 1 p
46 (A/1/11)	1638	Bond between William Stockdale and Lady Anne Parsons. 1 p
47 (A/1/15)	1639	Bond between Edward Reynolds, Edward Harman, Edward Brereton and Lady Anne Parsons. 1 p
48 (A/1/16)	1640	Bond between Francis Medhope and Lady Anne Parsons. (Witnessed by John Carroll) 1 p
49 (A/1/18) See also no. 55	1640	Bond between Pierse Butler and Lady Anne Parsons. 1 p
50 (A/1/30)	1640	Bond between Richard Williams and William Parsons. 1 p
51 (A/1/17)	24 Mar. 1640	Bond between William Wharam and Lady Anne Parsons. Includes: Note of confirmation of security signed and sealed by Richard Heaton [the celebrated Irish botanist]. 1 p
52 (A/1/26)	29 Aug. 1641	Bond between Morris Tennell and William Parsons. 1 p
53 (A/1/25)	1641	Bond between Francis Medhope and Lady Anne Parsons. (Witnessed by John Carroll) 1 p
54 (A/1/24)	1641	Bond between Patrick Hogan, Thomas Roch and Lady Ann Parsons. 1 p
55 (A/1/23)	8 Oct. 1641	Bond between Pierse Butler and Lady Anne Parsons. 1 p
56 (A/1/27)	1643	Bond between Sir Adam Loftus and William Parsons. 1 p
57 (A/1/29) See also no. 58	1645	Bond between Peregin Banastre, Thomas Alcock and William Parsons. 1 p
58 (A/1/21)	1645	Bond between Peregin Banastre, Thomas Alcock and William Parsons.
59	26 Oct. 1648	Bond between Ann Gee and William Parsons (cousin of the Parsons) 1 p

60 (A/5/51)	14 Feb. 1652	Copy of abstract of debts due to Lady Anne Parsons. Several bonds are listed such as: bond with Teige O'Carroll of Ballistorell, King's County, and John O'Carroll of Leap, King's County; also Eaves O'Carroll of Glanne [Glan], Co. Cork, and Terlagh and James O'Carroll of Grange, Queen's County. 1 p
61 (A/1/68)	28 Sep. 1678	Receipt for £100 rent on Jenkins Mill, Limerick, from John Duroy. 1 p
62 (A/1/74) See Also no. 63	3 Jan. 1686	Bond between Sir Laurence Parsons, Heward Oxburgh, Lieut. Colonel Archibald Douglas and John Dawson. (Signed and sealed by Sir Laurence and Oxburgh. Back endorsed: 'Sir Laurence Parsons and Heward Oxburgh theire bond for payment of £300 of the penalty of £600 entered judgement on this bond for Lieut. Coll. Archibold Douglas and John Dawson by virtue of a warr(ant) of at the court on Pleas Trinity terme'.)
63 (A/1/146)	3 Jan. 1686	Bond between Heward Oxburgh, Sir Laurence Parsons and John Dawson, (Signed and sealed. Back endorsed: 'noe satisfaction on record acknowledged Judgement entered.') 1 p
64 (A/1/75)	5 Aug. 1690	Bond between Lady Frances Parsons and Henry Finch. 1 p
65	14 Nov. 1692	Bond between Francis Medycroft and Sir Laurence and William Parsons. 1 p

v.		***Testamentary and settlement deeds 1640–60***
66 (A/5/58)	[1640s]	Copy of the will of Lady Anne Parsons.
67 (A/25/1)	7 Jan. 1625	Parchment deed of settlement of Sir Laurence and Richard Parsons on William, Fenton, Gerard, Lowther, Ann and Katherine Parsons, of the castle, manor, lands, tenements and hereditaments of Parsonstown, King's County, and also lands in Co. Cork. 4 membranes
68 [A/1/28) See also no. 70	28 June 1643	Deed of settlement of Lady Anne Parsons on Fenton Parsons, Lincolns Inn, Middlesex (son), of the castle and lands of Bovine [Boveen], the town and lands of Clonibrony [Clonbrone] and Shangomath in the King's County. 7 pp
69 (A/11)	18 Feb. 1650	Copy of the will of Sir William Parsons [the Lord Justice]. '... If God should return me unto Ireland where if God please I would die then to be buried in my own vault in Patricks, Dublin, without charge or ceremony my present destitute condition not permitting it.' 6 pp
70 (A/5/79)	30 Sep. 1652	Clause in the will of Fenton Parsons concerning the settlement of the lands in Bovine [Boveen], King's County, given to him by his mother, Lady Anne Parsons. 1 p

71 (A/13)	14 Feb. 1660	Power of attorney to the Earl of Cork, Lord Digby and Sir John Cole, from Catherine Parsons (mother of Sir Richard, future 1st Viscount Rosse, of Bellamont, Co. Dublin), authorising them to act as guardians for Richard on her behalf. 1 membrane
72 (A/25/7/	29 May 1693	Parchment deed of settlement of Captain William Parsons to Gerard, Lowther and William Usher of the manor of Birr, King's County. 1 membrane

vi.   *Letters patent (for the grant of lands) 1595–1693*

73 (A/25/4) See also no. 76	N.D.	Copies of patents granting to the Parsons the markets and fairs at Parsonstown. 10 pp
74 (A/1/1)	14 May 1595	Grant of a lease of lands (not specified) to Richard Hardinge in consideration of 'losses and hinderances' sustained in services within the realm of England. (see no. 262.) 1 p
75 (A/5/46)	Circa. 1620	'A draught [sic] of the King's Leter [sic]...' to Sir Laurence Parsons providing for the grant of Birr, Newtowne and Laughlainbridge, King's County. 2 pp
76 (A/1/2)	Circa. 1620	Grant of the estate and lands of Parsonstown, Birr, King's County, to Sir Laurence Parsons and providing for the privilege to hold a Court of Record of Pleas in the manor and to establish a prison in the town. Also provides for theprivilege to hold a weekly market on Wednesdays and two yearly fairs on the 25th March and 20th August, to last for two days, one in Birr Laughlinbridge and Ballynockin, King's County. Lands granted:' Clonaghalls, Siffins, Derrinduff, Ballinee, Aghnasillagh, Krinkill, Clanlagga, Ballindarragh, Ballyduff, Newtowne, in the Barony of Ballybrett, King's County, together with the towns and lands of Ballindowne, Ballywilliam, Tulleneskeagh, Ballykeally, Ballinareage, Cooleges, Ballinalogg, Ardgogy, Shanbally, Carrigoones, Carrigedmond, Carrigdonnell, Gallrush, Derrinlough, Drinah, in the Barony of Eglish, King's County, 'to be known as' the mannor of Parsonstowne'. 2 pp
77 (A/5/91)	1 July 1667	Certified extract from the Chancery Rolls of Ireland of the letters patent granting Robert Bowyer, the castle, hall, town and lands of Clonlyon, Glean and Garry Castle in the King's County. 1 p
78 (A/5/53)	8 Apr. 1668	Copy of an extract from the Chancery Rolls of Ireland of the letters patent, granting to Elizabeth Harwell, 104 acres of Clonlyon and Garrycastle in the King's County. 1 p
79 (A/25/3)	3 Charles I	Copy of an extract from the letters patent to Laurence Parsons providing for the privilege to hold markets and fairs in Birr, Co. Offaly. (Text in Latin) 4 pp

vii.	*Schedules of property 1635–59*	
80 (A/1/8)	1635	Schedule of the lands and hereditaments of William Parsons in the King's County, as granted by letters patent. Includes: A copy of the letters patent. 3 pp
81 (A/5/40)	1636	Copy of the schedule of lands granted to Sir Laurence Parsons by letters patent (dated 25 June 1620) listed as follows: the castle, towns, lands and forts of Birr, the town and lands of Ballindarrage; Bealande and Cappaneale; the town of Ballindarragh; Sesseraghbrack; Sessin; Derrinduffe and Ballinury (Ballinry); Clonahill and the watermill, Ballyduffe; Killeran and Cappaneale, all in the King's County. 1 p
82 (A/1/139)	1641	List of lands escheated in Dublin and Cork with details of their denominations. Endorsed: 'A copy of the Lott in which I [William Parsons] am concerned.' 1 p
83 (A/1/22)	1641	Schedule of lands in Cos. Cork, Tipperary, Westmeath, Limerick and Longford, recording the individuals to whom the lands were granted and details of rent reserved thereof. Endorsed: 'Forfietors [sic] Sir Geo: Preston.' (Sir William Parsons, 2nd Bt married Sir George Preston's daughter, Elizabeth). 2 pp
84 (A/5/33)	15 June 1638	Schedule of the lands and hereditaments compounded (and granted to William Parsons), Imericke, Ballynoe, Classeganiffe (alias Classiganniffe) Shynanagh [Shinanagh], Co. Cork, Killyvalley [Co. Cork or Londonderry?], Killinvallige and the watermill of Killinvalley in the Barony of Fermoy, Co. Cork. 1 p
85 (A/5/44)	[1659]	Schedule of the lands in the Barony of Eglish for the 'Dominion wealth survey of the Barony of Eglish...'. Includes: names of tenants and the number of acres profitable. (Signed by the Surveyor General, Benedict Cookine). 2 pp
86 (A/18/1)	N.D.	Treasurer's account of the number of acres in King's County.

viii.	*Correspondence and other Documentation, 1636–92*	
87 (A/5/36)	4 Apr. 1636	Order of composition from the Commissioners on Defective Titles to William Parsons, for the increase of rent on the manor, castle and estate together with other lands in Parsonstown. 1 p
88 (A/5/89) See also no. 89	29 Sep. 1646	Letter from Robert Southwell to William Parsons in connection with his position as manager of the Parsons estate. '... I have willingly taken the charge of your business upon mee and I shall hereafter indeavor to give satisfactory account thereof.' 1 p

89 (A/5/75)	11 Jan. 1647	Letter from Robert Southwell to William Parsons declining to accept the tenancy of the lands of Barry Oge and others in Kinsale. States however that he would be willing to manage the property for him. 2 pp
90 (A/18/2–3)	13 Oct. 1671 7 Jan. 1672	Letter from John Marshall to Sir Laurence Parsons, in connection with their dispute regarding the title to the lands of Ballynary and Ballynarge, King's County. Includes: A copy of the proceedings in the case (Letter is torn in parts) 2 Items
91 (A/5/62)	[1670]	Order for the payment of the 'former' rent of the lands of Ballynadowne and Ballywilliam, King's County, to William Parsons, as granted by letters patent. 1 p
92 (A/l/37)	26 June 1675	Copy of a list of writings sent to Capt. Sloughter 'for the use of Douglas Savage' concerning Laughlinbridge, King's County, from Capt. Larky, e.g. copies of despatches to Edward Medhop; a book of" depositions from Laughlinbridge on behalf of Waiter, Earl of Ormond [d.1633], against. Sir Arthur Savage. (These documents as listed are not in the Archive. Sir Laurence Parsons, 1st Bt, was married to Frances Savage). 1 p
93 (A/1/148)	7 Apr. 1687	Agreement between Sir Laurence Parsons and Capt. Heward Oxburgh appointing him attorney for his estate and giving him the authority to collect rent on his behalf. (Signed and sealed by Oxburgh) Includes: A rent roll of Laughlinbridge, King's County, '... as it was lett by Sir Laurence Parsons ...' and a map of the houses and plots of Birr. 1 p
94 (A/1/71)	10–11 May 1688	Covering letter from Capt. Oxburgh to Sir Laurence Parsons, annexing a copy of a letter which he sent to Edward Burke in response to the latter's continuous assaults on their work at the coal pits on the Derringhey estate. Letter states 'that is not the first unkindness you have shewed me, though I am not contious of myself of ever deserving it ..., and still I say if it be decreed that I have noe right to the land soe as to make coale pits upon it I will leave to my Lord both the wood and the land and the receiving of the money due on Sir Harry according my bargaine with him, for I value not the matter in respect of my Lord of Clanrichards [sic] desatisfaction.' (This letter is written on the reverse side). 1 p
95 (A/1/147)	6 Apr. 1687	'Instructions for Capt. Oxburgh and memoranda', e.g. schedule of bonds and other papers in Sir Laurence Parsons' possession; also details of leases with names of lessees and in some cases additional information on the property leased. Includes: An explanation of Sir Laurence's behaviour towards Capt. Larkey's son, who he states attempted to '... cut Lady Parsons off from her inheritance ...'. 4 pp

96   10 Oct. 1687   Letter from Capt. Oxburgh to Sir Laurence Parsons reporting
(A/1/149)   on the general affairs of the estate. 2 pp

97   16 Oct. 1687   " 2 pp
(A/1/150)

98   15 Feb. 1688   Letter from Sir Laurence Parsons to Capt. Oxburgh, castigating
(A/1/155)   him for neglecting his duties and failing in his obligation to
                                 him. He expresses his bewilderment at Oxburgh's behaviour and
                                 states: '... what you intend I can't imagine unless to destroy me
                                 and my family by [?shaming] them in England and me heer ... .
                                 I think these things doe not looke like friendshipe though you
                                 wear pleased not long since to tell me you wear the only friend I
                                 had in the King's County.' 1 p

99   21 Feb. 1688   Letter from Capt. Oxburgh to Sir Laurence Parsons in response
(A/1/160)   to Sir Laurence's instruction to his tenants not to pay their rents
                                 to Oxburgh. '... I took it ill that you should send to your tenants
                                 not to pay me any of the rents in the nature of a proclamation,
                                 as if I was not fit to be trusted to ask for it

100   [Mar.] 1688   Letter from Capt. Oxburgh to Sir Laurence Parsons' reporting
(A/1/153)   on the affairs of the estate. 1 p

101   13 Mar. 1688   Letter from Capt. Oxburgh to Sir Laurence Parsons reporting
(A/1/154)   on the affairs of the estate. 1 p

102   20 July 1688   The same. Includes: Reference to the poverty endured by some
(A/1/157)   of the tenants on the Birr estate: '... if you weare here yourself I
                                 am sure you would pitty most of them.' 1 p

103   9 Oct. 1688   Letter from Capt. Oxburgh to Sir Laurence Parsons, defending
(A/1/158)   himself against accusations of dishonesty. '... Sir Laurence you
                                 never had a truer friend in the King's County but myself.' 1 p

104   11 Oct. 1680   Letter from Capt. Oxburgh to Sir Laurence reporting on the
(A/1/159)   affairs of the estate. 1 p

105   29 Mar. 1689   Letter from Richard Redy to Sir Laurence Parsons informing
(A/1/161)   him of Capt. Oxburgh's numerous requests for money which he
                                 claimed were sanctioned by Sir Laurence. 1 p

106   13 May 1689   Letter from Capt. Oxburgh to Sir Laurence Parsons reporting
(A/1/162)   on the affairs of the estate. 1 p

107   18 May 1689   The same. 1 p*
(A/1/163)

108   5 Aug. 1690   Petition of John Weaver for the return of sheep taken by him (in
(A/5/11)   lieu of rent) from Capt. Oxburgh for Clonkelly, King's County.
                                 States that the sheep were later seized by the sheriff as rebel
                                 goods.
                                 Includes: An order for their return 1 p

*   For particulars of rent received by Oxburgh from the Birr estate and money returned to Sir Laurence see:
      Accounts and Rentals (Nos 3, 4 1), and Household account book (No. 114), and for an account of their
      conflict see: No 224.

109 (A/5/47)	28 Aug. 1690	Receipt for a bond for £300 received from Thomas Piggott "... conditional for returning sheep if it appear they are the property of Col. Oxburgh.' 1 p
110 (A/5/13)	Sep. 1690	Copy of Sir Laurence Parsons' petition for an order to John Weaver to deliver to Sir Laurence the sheep and other livestock which had been taken from Col. Oxburgh. 1 p
111 (A/1/85)	3 Dec. 1692	Note from Samuel Taylor to Thomas Bagn[u]ley arranging a meeting to solve some business concerning Sir Laurence. 1 p
112 (A/1/145)	Circa. 1690	Lieutenant William Parsons' formal letter of acknowledgement for the receipt of £1,500 sterling received from Sir Laurence as the proceeds from the will of his late father, Capt. William Parsons. (Signed and sealed with three leopards heads, a star fish and a fleur de lis). 1 p
113 (A/5/18)	N.D.	Letter from Laurence Parsons to Teige Mcdonough O'Carroll of Rathmore, King's County, in connection with his interest in Tullahnasragh, King's County. (Document is badly torn, therefore text is obscure).

II ADMINISTRATION OF HOME AND FAMILY AFFAIRS

i. *Account book 1652–97*

114 (A/12)	1652–6: 1679–87: 1696–7	Bound volume (with entries for several generations) recording the family's personal expenditure such as accounts for schooling and clothing, an account of each person's personal allowance and other expenses including an account of rents received.

Examples of entries are as follows: 'An account of my brother Laurence his schooling and diet at Mr Frances Jacobs beginning January the 22, 1652'; 'an account of my brother Laurence his expenses for cloths and other necessarys beginning November the 11th, 1652'; 'an account of what money I received for my own use ...' (1652–4); 'an account of my Margarets expenses' (1653–8); 'an account of all the servants wages' (1652–3); 'an account of the cookmaid's wages' (1652–4); 'paid Doth Parsons for her wedding expense', 'a note of the money layde oute for my [Sir Laurence's] fathers funeral who died November 11th, 1652', 'for my sister Betty's funeral and spent in her sickness, died 24 December 1652,' 'for my brother John's funeral and spent in his sickness, died 4 January 1652'; 'Note of severall legacies my father left to be given to severall people' – e.g. – 'to a poore woman – 001–00–00; 'an exact account of all the money received either debts due to my father or else things sould since his death' – e.g. 'received of the Lady Padget for 3 rows of pearl which she bought 066–00–00 received for an ould coach ...', 'For a black shirt making and all when my father died (Nov. 11,

1652). Also copies of household bills for the butcher and baker, for coals and beer for the year (1656), and particulars of amounts received from the English Exchequer since the death of Capt. William Parsons.

Includes: 'A True note of what lands doth belonge unto Laurence Parsons in the Barony of Clonlisk and the townes of Furkleanan'.

Includes: Accounts of rent received by Capt. Oxburgh from 1686–87 and tenants' accounts recorded in detail, 1696–7, with such names as Teige Carroll, Charles Carroll and Keane Carroll.

Includes: On the reverse side of the book are copies of letters patent granting to the Parsons the lands of Parsonstowne, Newtowne, Ballindowne, Ballywilliam, Ardgogyes, Carrigedmond and Crinkle, King's County, and providing for the holding of a court at Parsonstown and Newtown and the rights to all fines thereof. approx. 150 pp

ii.		*Bills and receipts 1680–90*
115 (A/5/84)	1680	Draper's bill for material purchased by Sir Richard. Items included are: '8 yrds. of cherry culored sattin – 04–6–7^1/2,' 7 yrds. of green floral silk – 05–01–6.'
116	May 1681	Draper's bills for material, e.g. 1p '2 yrd. ^{1}/4 light cullered cloth 02–14–00 10 yrds. in green strip silk 03–05–2^1/2.' 2 Items
117 (A/1/134) (B)	1688	Draper's bill for material e.g. ' 2^1/2 yrds. & 3rd over of silver and gold lace, 5 yrd. mixt ferret, 3 yrds. and ¼ black ferret 0:2:10^1/2.'
118 (A/1/151)	1687	Solicitor's bill to Sir Laurence. 1 p
119 (A/1/156)	12 June 1688	'Mr John Beswell's bill' (items not listed) 1 p
120 (A/1/136)	4 May 1689	Bill for materials purchased by Madam Parsons. Items included are: '1 fine dress 00–12–00 1 fine fure 00–03–06 6 yrds of fine scarlet ribbin 00–08–00.' 1 p
121 (A/1/133)	6 July 1690	Dressmaker's bill. Items included are: 'for making you bloue briches 0–1–6, for making Mr John Parsons' briches 0–0–10, for covering your steys and all lening them 1–0–2, for bone for stomichers and steys 0–0–6.' 1 p
122 (A/1/73)	21 Feb. 1689	Dressmaker's bill for Madam Parsons, eg 'for making you childs cote for 10 gold buttons for silke and thred.' 1 p

123 (A/1/77)	23 Dec. 1689	Receipt for 4^1/$_2$ yrds of [Stur: feire]. 1 p
124 (A/1/6) (A)	1689	Receipt for medical supplies made out to William Parsons, eg. 'A purging infusion of gum arabic, and worms (ds) ointment.'
125 (A/5/86)	4 Jan. 1680	Receipt for £300 from Sir Laurence Parsons, payment received by William Parsons of Langley, Bucks, (signed and sealed by William Parsons)*

iii.	*Recipes*	
126 (A/17)	1666	Recipé book written in the hand of Dorothy Parsons and entitled: 'Dorothy Parsons her booke of choyce receipes all written with her owne hand in 1666 but those are most espeicaly excellent that are marked with E.P. being all a provd and tryed by the Lady Eliz. Parsons in her life time.'

Entries are indexed. The types of recipes listed are for cooking, preserving, herbal remedies and cures and some for cleaning solutions. Examples are as follows: 'for cleaning mahogany; to make inke; directions for cleaning coaches or chaises; cures for rhumatism; deafness; for the biting of a mad dog; for small pox, for a cancerous tumour most excellent; for the plague, a rare distilled water for a consumption'; and recipes for: 'making sausages, cheescake, custards, to dress a cod's head, to souce a pig, to collar a pig' and to make ' very good perfume.' Aprox. 200 pp

Includes: A pencil sketch of Parsonstowne house 1668 entitled 'An excellent receipe to spend 4,000 pounds.'

iv	*Correspondence 1649–93 and other documents*	

Four letters from the Countess of Kildare to the Parsonses.

127 (A/5/20)	1649	Requesting a loan of twenty pounds. 'Let this be in cobs and crownes for the money I have is.
128 (A/5/21)	1649	
129 (A/5/22)	15 Jan. 1649	
130 (A/5/23)	3 Feb. 1654	Letter to Lady Phillis and Dorothy Parsons about an agreement 1 with Capt. Williams Parsons regarding a lease. 1 p
131	5 Mar. 1650	Letter from William Davys (cousin) to William Parsons, beseeching him to lend him a sum of money to pay off a debt. States that his creditor has threatened to ruin his reputation

*   For further household bills see: Account Book (no. 114)
    For more herb remedies see: Account and Rental Book (no. 1)

both in Ireland and abroad '... and to make my very name odious to any gentlemen'. 1 p

132–3:
136–151:
153–162

The following 29 items are correspondence, notes and documents in connection with Sir George Preston's dispute with the Limerick Corporation over his patent of the salmon weir known as Laxweare in Limerick. The correspondence is between Sir George, his attorneys and the Duke and Duchess of Ormond who were endeavouring to assist him in the case. (Sir George Preston was the father of Elizabeth, wife of Sir William Parsons, 2nd Bt).

(The documents are listed below in the order in which they are found in A/1 and therefore not chronologically. See introduction to list.)

132 (A/1/36)	1673	Copy of Sir George Preston's letter soliciting the King's Bench in his case. (Text is in latin). 1 p
133 (A/1/38)	7 Jan. 1676	Draft notes in connection with the Corporation of Limerick's lease of the salmon weir to Fitzgerald of Laxweare. 1 p
134 (A/1/40)	26 Jan. [1688]	Letter from the Duke of Ormond to Lord Chief Justice Keating in which he refers to Sir Laurence Parsons' civility towards him in not pressing for 'his kinswoman's portion' and stating that he intends to send Sir Laurence the ten thousand pounds at easter on the occasion of their marriage.
135 (A/18/7)	23 Oct. 1688	Copy of a letter from Sir Laurence Parsons, Manchester, England, to the Duke of Ormond, requesting the payment of money due to Lady Parsons from her mother, Lady Preston. Refers to a legal suit in which he has been involved for some time with a Mr Henderson and Capt. Matthews. States that he desires his Grace to command Capt. Matthews to free him from the suit '... which I am troubled with ...' 1 p
136 (A/1/39)	27 Oct. 1688	Letter from the Duke of Ormond, Whitehall, to Sir George Preston acknowledging receipt of his letter. 1 p
137 (A/1/41)	N.D.	Letter from the Duchess of Ormond to Sir William Domville, Attorney General, requesting his advice on the case. 1 p
138 (A/1/42)	17 July 1688	Letter from the Duchess of Ormond to Sir George Preston regarding the dispute. 1 p
139 (A/1/43)	16 July 1688	Letter from Sir George to Lady Preston in connection with the case. 1 p
140 (A/1/44)	N.D.	Letter from the Duchess of Ormond to Martin Smith, requesting that he sends her the charter signed by the King in favour of Sir George Preston's patent. 1 p

141
[A/1/45]

N.D.

Covering letter from the Duchess of Ormond to Valentine Smith asking for a copy of Sir George's petition to the King and the Lord Lieutenant together with a report, in the hope that they will be of value in Sir George Prestons's defence. 1 p

142
(A/1/46)

11–12 Nov. 1675

Draft covering letter from the Duchess, then Countess, to Valentine Smith annexing a letter from the Attorney General in connection with the case. 1 p

143
(A/1/47)

30 Dec. 1675

Letter from the Duke, then Earl, of Ormond to his Counsellor requesting that he advises Sir George Preston on the case. 1 p

144
(A/1/48)

3 Nov. 1675

Letter from the Countess to Sir George Preston stating that it is the opinion of the King's Advocate and other lawyers in Scotland that she has a right to the Lordship of Dingwall. 1 p

145
(A/1/49)

13 Jan. 1676

Extract from Sir John Temple's (Solicitor General) letter to the Earl of Ormond in connection with Sir George's business with the corporation and stating that he will give Sir George assistance. 1 p

146
(A/1/50)

20 Jan. 1676

Draft letter from Sir George Preston to Valentine Smith informing him of a proclamation of rebellion issued against Sir [ ] Lynch for failing to pay rent and that his estate will be seized unless security is provided. 1 p

147
(A/1/51)

22 Jan. 1677

Letter from Sir George Preston to Valentine Smith, acknowledging receipt of Chief Justice Keating's letter and requesting his advice. 1 p

148
(A/1/52)

22 Jan. 1676

Letter from Sir George Preston to Valentine Smith, informing him of the dispute in which he is involved with the corporation. 1 p

149
(A/1/53)

20 Jan. 1676

Draft letter from Sir George Preston to Valentine Smith in connection with the case. 1 p

150
(A/1/54)

22 Oct. 1676

Letter from Sir George Preston to the Earl of Ormond regarding the case. 1 p

151
(A/1/55–6)

N.D.

Sir George Preston's personal notes on the case. 2 items

152
(A/1/57)

N.D.

Letter from the Countess to Sir George Preston, informing him of his daughter's miraculous escape from drowning, when the ship in which she was travelling was wrecked off the west coast [of England]. States 'she was brought on shore upon a man's backe'. 1 p

153
(A/1/58)

30 Mar. 1677

Letter from Sir George Preston (recipient unknown) informing him of the amount of rent which he received from the weir. 1 p

154 (A/1/59)	1 May 1677	Letter from Sir George Preston to Valentine Smith, informing him that the Earl of Ormond has spoken of passing a new patent in his interest, the meaning of which he is not sure about. 1 p
155 (A/1/60)	N.D.	Draft lease of the fishing rights to the Laxweare in the City of Limerick and to the river Shannon, from Sir George Preston to William King. 1 p
156 (A/1/61)	17 Oct. 1677	Letter from J[ohn] Keating [Lord Chief Justice] to George Matthew, giving an account of the conflict between Sir George Preston and the corporation. 2 p
157 (A/1/62)	N.D.	Note from Sir George Preston to [ ] Kennedy, explaining why his wife has decided to remain in Ireland rather than travelling to Scotland. 1 p
158 (A/1/63)	14 Oct. 1678	Draft note from Sir George Preston to John Sarsfield informing him of a letter he received from Capt. Matthew and Mr Clark, stating that they cannot employ Sarsfield at this time. 1 p
159 (A/1/64)	24 Sept. 1677	Letter from the Countess to Sir George Preston stating that the fishing rights to Laxweare and the mills are in his possession by virtue of previous acts of settlement. States (on another matter) that she would also like to know what he intends to give as 'preferment to his daughter'. 1 p
160 (A/1/65)	N.D.	Draft covering letter (for no. 161) from the Countess to Sir George Preston informing him that 'his friends' have brought the dispute to an end, by offering to lease the Laxweare for £260 a year. (Letter is incomplete). 1 p
161 (A/1/66)	6 Nov. 1675	Copy of a letter of attorney by the Countess, appointing herself arbitrator to preside over the leasing of the Laxweare and castle in Limerick to the Earl of Arran and George Matthew. 1 p
162 (A/1/67)	12 Aug. 1678	Note from Sir George to Valentine Smith informing him that he will be staying in Kilkenny for a few days. 1 p
163 (A/18/8)	2 July, 1692	Letter from Sir Laurence Parsons, Chester, England, to John Bagnuley, requesting that he applies to his attorney for the money owed to him for the silver goods. Also states: 'If there be any persons aboute you that wants farrnes and can bring stock with them I cann supplie them with land in Ireland on easy termes ... I have alsoe a want want of good tradesmen in the towne of Birr pray tell your neighbours and if any came over let them be such as are able for our Kingdom is over stock with beggars.'
164 (A/1/135)	N.D.	Note from Samuel Taylor to Thomas Bagn[u]ley in connection with plate requested by Sir Laurence. See also no. 163. 1 p
165 (A/1/76)	1 July 1693	Note from John Beswell requesting Sir Laurence Parsons to pay a bill for him. 1 p

B		THE PERSONAL CAREERS OF THE PARSONSES OF PARSONSTOWN
i		*Sir Laurence Parsons, 1619–26*

166 (A/7/2)	23 July 1619	Deputation from George Lowe, Vice Admiral of Munster and Leinster, to Laurence Parsons. (Written on parchment and signed by George Lowe) 1 membrane
167 (A/7/1)	28 July 1619	Letters patent from the Duke of Buckingham, Lord High Admiral, oppointing Laurence Parsons Judge of the Admiralty for Munster. (Written on parchment and signed and sealed by Buckingham). 1 membrane
168 (A/5/83)	3 July 1626	Order by Lord Deputy Falkland and the Council for the plantation of the Barony of Eglish, King's County, to deliver the lands of Eglish to John McFarrell (native of Eglish), '... and to remove from theire the former possessors and pretending proprieters thereoft ...'.* 1 p
169 (A/1/138)	N.D.	'The copie of the commission under the great seale of England for passing lands upon the first commission of defective titles in Ireland.' 3pp

ii		*Richard Parsons, 1624*

170 (A/1/164)	4 Nov. 1624	Letters patent to Richard and William Parsons and Sir Adam Loftus, appointing them to the office of General Surveyor and Surveyor of the Court of Wards as previously held by Sir William and Sir Laurence. lp

iii		*William Parsons, 1638–45*

171 (A/1/12)	15 Jan. 1638	Draft petition of William Parsons for the remedy of defective titles to lands in the Barony of Fermoy, Co. Cork. 2pp
172 (A/5/38)	28 Nov. 1638	Schedule of the lands and hereditaments compounded by William. Lands listed are: Imericke [Imphrick], Ballynoe, Classeganaffe [Clashanniv] , Shynanash. Keilyvallv (alias Killinvallage) and one watermill with watercourse in Killinvalley, Co. Cork. 2pp
173 (A/5/17)	17 Mar. 1641	Letter from Phelem Molloy, Catholic Camp, Eglish, King's County, to Governor William Parsons in response to his letter to Col. Moore which Molloy had intercepted. (The letter was an attempt by William Parsons to bring Col. Moore over to his side). Molloy in reply states: 'I intercepted your letter before it came to my Colonel's hands. You write to my Colonel forthwith to repair unto you and to help you in suppressing those who have offended his Majesty but who are the offenders the English or Irish. I say without any partiall regard of either nation that

---

* See: (No. 1) – The ordinances for the regulation of the town of Birr devised by Sir Laurence in his capacity as Attorney General for the province of Munster.

they are partely of the Irish and for the most parte the English officers and Governors who contrary to his Majesties gratious intention oppressed the poore subjects which bred a great scandal to the King's dignity and crown. If you [join] with them Mr Parsons we cannot in conscience [join] in an unlawful matter with you or with anybody of the faction or any factions else.' States that the reason why they were so '... mild and tender hearted towards you ...' was because of the kind reputation of his mother. He continues by advising him to join with them and in return he promises him protection and states that they have 100,000 men in arms '... and God is our guide.'

174 (A/5/43)	12 July 1641	Account of the subsidies charged in the King's County, 'Toward the paiement of the second subsidie of the foure intire subsidies within the county abovesaid. ' Townes listed are: Phillipstowne, Warrenstowne, Collenstowne, Colleistowne, Gomshee [Gormlee], Kilcoursey, Ballincowne, Ballybeg Granicastle [Garrycastle], Eglisses [Eglish], Cloanliske [Clonlisk], and Ballibritt. l p
175 (A/1/19)	30 Aug. 1641	Instructions from the freeholders of the King's County to William Parsons and John Coghlan of Streamstown, King's County, as to their conduct in parliament with regard to the holding of the assizes and the keeping of a gaol in Birr.
		Includes: An 18th century transcript of the original. (The instructions are written on parchment and signed by several including the O'Carrolls of the King's County). 1 membrane
176 (A/5/19) (A)	circa. 1642–3	Letter from William Parsons to Teige O'Carroll informing him that twenty thousand men have landed at Dublin: 'Good neighbour, I pray god defend you from your enemies and fear them not for the armie is landed at Dublin.' (Document is badly torn). lp
177 (A/5/1)	20 Jan. 1642	'Articles of agreement between the Right Honourable [the] Lord General of Leinster and William Parsons, Governor of Birr, upon surrender of the castle. Refers to the former articles of agreement (see no. 179). 'It is agreed that the governor shall freely have two drought of oxen to draw his caradges and his coach and horses with their ladyes shall goe freely unfreightened and unsearched given at the campe this 20th of Jan. 1642.' (Agreement is signed by George Preston and William Parsons). 1 p
178 (A/5/2)		Copy of 177.
179 (A/1/91)	20 Jan. 1642	Copy of the articles of agreement made between William Parsons and the Lord General of Leinster on the surrender of Birr Castle. '... and it is agreed that the Lady Phillippes and the Lady Parsons shall have to each of them 2 payres of sheetes and

the Governor's Lady and Captain Coote's Lady shall have each of them 2 paires of sheetes and the Governor's children 2 paires of sheetes and to each paire of sheetes a paire of pillow bearers and all their clothes of Lynon and woolen with their trunche and cheste to carrie them in and 2 fether beddes for his children and the redd bedd that is laced with willow colloured lace with its furniture that the soldiers and all other of their people shall carry away with them all their wearinge appell both lynen and woolen and their swords by their sides.'

180   28 July 1642   Letter from Farrell O'Kennedy to William Parsons, offering to
(A/5/16)   arrange a meeting with Col. Richard Butler. In reply to a complaint made by William with regard to the hindrance of the markets, he states: '... itt is not my doings but the general consent of the armie which I cannot forgoe without further directions from my superiors, as for sheddinge of blood specially of some sick people, women and children, we take it to our own hearts ...' He goes on to mention the arrival of Owen Roe O'Neill in the North with Spanish assistance and that Colonel Preston is at Wexford with ships loaded with arms and ammunition. Also included are references to other military developments. 1 p

181   5 Oct. 1642   Letter from Col. R. O'Moore to Lady Anne Parsons in response
(A/5/15)   to her request for the return of her carriages and horses which were taken by the rebels. He expresses his resentment and hostility towards her family and states that '... I find all the gentry and neighbours of these parts to much honour, esteeme and love you and in that degree that one would thinke you are of their blood and flesh and there detained against their wills ... and for your parte madam, though I think you have noe mallice to us yett are you the support and maintayner of that place and those that are with you being known as I heard to be malitious, will take anything you have to help their designes as they have used those horses now writt off and by liklihood would do again, so that if I should gett them restored I should arm or help my enemy against my selfe, in which case (if you weare a judge yourselfe) you would condemn me. But if I weare assured noe such use should be made of them I would endeavour to gett them restored ...'.

182   Circa. 1642–3   Copy of a memorial from the Lords of Ireland to the King in the
(A/1/137)   form of an appeal for peace in which they refer to the suffering they have endured by having been '... exposed to the merces of two powerful armies now in the fields, the one of the Confederatt Catholiques Partie ...'.

Endorsed 'A copy of a letter of Lords of Ireland to his Majestie for peace.' 2 pp

| 183 | Circa. 1643–4 | Draft petition (with amendments) of William Parsons to Oliver |
| (A/5/50) | | Cromwell, requesting that all the taxes collected on houses, |

markets and mills be eased to encourage the regrowth of the
town which had suffered badly from the rebellion. States that
the town of Birr had been thrice burnt over the summer and
that no tenants live there any more to help the garrison. '... and
yett they force the poore tenants left to pay as much
contribution as if the towne were not burnt .... that all those
that will build houses in my town of Birr or any other place or
your petitioners lands may be eased from any taxes or
contribution for their houses and gardens. And that the milles
may be eased from contribution ... and that the proffitts of the
faires and markets may be eased from contribution to encourage
the bringing in of provision to the garrison.' 1 p

184	10 Aug.–	Memorandum recording daily transactions and proceedings
(A/5/30)	25 Oct. 1645	during a visit by William Parsons to London. Examples of
entries are as		

follows: 'The 16th Oct. 1645 wee attended common counsell ...
The ... of September, 1645, wee received warrants for £6,000 for
the soldiers.'

(Text is badly faded and document torn in parts). 1 p

| iv | | *Captain William Parsons, 1639–63* |

| 185 | 30 Nov. 1639 | Copy of a warrant from the Lords Justices and Council to |
| (A/5/52) | | William Parsons and William Beisley, instructing them to |

search the house of John O'Carroll of Clonliske, King's County.
and to arrest him '... with the assistance of such of those soldiers
as you think fitt to entrust heerin doe search the said John
O'Carroll's house and such other places as you or either of you
shall find necessary and to seise what muskets, pikes and other
armes or provisions of warr.' 1 p

| 186 | Nov. 1639 | Examination of William Parsons and Captain William Beisley, |
| (A/1/14) | | concerning the find of arms at the house of John O'Carroll of |

Clonliske. 1 p

| 187 | 19 Dec. 1639 | Examination of John O'Carroll's servants: 'The examination of |
| (A/5/55) | | Hugh Grehane, Mr John O'Carroll's footman ... he further saith |

that he never saw nor heard of any muskettes or gunnes which
his master had but of some five or six which his master had in
his house to defend himself ...' 'The examination of John
McReadagh Callin, servant.' Includes details of some of the
rooms in Clonliske Castle, eg. 'There was a littell roome called
Chamber Arrigett which we did not see because nobody can goe
into the roome without a lather, stoole or stayer to help them up
to it and the entrance to the roome is like the tunnel of a
chemlye [chimney] ... the chamber Arrigett was he said that he

had heard it was a room which within old time they did use to coyne monie ...' 2pp

188 **(A/9)**	18 Oct. 1641 –20 Jan. 1643	Diary of Capt. William Parsons recording daily events in King's County, during the civil war. The type of detail recorded are the numerous attacks on his castle and livestock by the Carrolls and Molloys, the atrocities committed by therebels and the day to day operations of the force under his command. The diary is entitled: 'A booke of the memorable things and service done by the garrison consisting of .... [tear] ... the command of Capt. William Parsons and a 100 foot under the command of Capt ... at Parsonstowne alias Birr in the King's County from the first day of this unhappy event to the twentieth day of January Ano Domini 1642.' (This may be a later transcript of the original, a few loose sheets of which were found in the diary. Some annotations were added in the margins at a later date. There is also a 19th century transcript of the diary together with notes and transcripts of relevant documents in the Archives).
189 **(A/5/76)**	12 Nov. 1641	Order from the Lords Justices, Sir William Parsons and John Borlase, to Capt. William Parsons to gather an army of footmen and horsemen in the King's County and to lead them against the rebels. 1 p
190 **(A/1/20)**	20 Nov. 1641	Parchment commission from the Earl of OrMond to William Parsons appointing him Captain of a horse troop consisting of 35 mounted men. (Text is faded and badly stained and in parts illegible). 1 membrane
191 **(A/1/88–** **90)**	20 Nov. – 31 Dec. 1641	Receipts for money paid to the officers by William Parsons, Commander-in-Chief of the territory of Ely O'Carroll (alias Birr). Amount paid: £130–10–6 3 items
192 **(A/5/54)**	20 Nov. 1641– 20 Jan. 1642	Account of money paid to the troops and in maintenance of the garrison eg 'to the Lieutenant of the horse part payment of his entertainment for four hundreth and twenty seven dayes the sum of £85–8–0.' '... to the common troops for the said four hundreth and twenty seven dayes in parte payment of their entertainment the sum of £747–85–0.' 1 p
193 **(A/1/92–3)**	26 Nov. 1641– 20 Jan. 1642	Original and copy of the accounts of money paid to the soldiers under the command of Capt. John Carroll and for expenses such as for the maintenance of the garrison at Parsonstown, eg: '£1:3:3 paid to one Drummer for 31 dayspay; £18:15:0 laid out to mesengers I sent from place to place to gitt intelingence; for making scaffolds for the soldiers to fight on the walls.' 2 items

194 (A/5/41)	26 Nov. 1641– 20 Jan. 1642	Account of money paid to the soldiers (under the command of Capt. John Carroll) and in the maintenance of the garrison at Parsonstowne, eg: '12 great saddles for my troops which were made at Parsonstowne with all furniture to them; four barrells of salt to Mrs Carroll which was employed in salting of meats for the store.' 2pp
195 (A/5/42)	N.D.	Copy of an account of the expenses accrued in maintaining the garrison.
196 (A/1/87)	1641–43	'A list of my grandfather's [Capt. William Parsons] papers for the Duke of Ormond.' List comprises receipts for the payment of officers in Birr, all of whom are named. 1 p
197 (A/1/94– **118 and** **121–132**)	23 Jan. 1642– 25 Dec. 1643	Receipts and accounts for payments made to the soldiers and other expenses incurred in maintaining the garrison at Birr. (Originals and copies). 36 Items
198 (A/5/3)	16 Feb. 1642	Copy of an order from the Lords Justices and Council that commissions be granted to Capt. William Parsons and Capt. Chidl[e]y Coote and that their troops be listed as an army and paid accordingly from Nov. 1641; '... and pay as such Captaines,Officers, horses, troops and foote companes in his Majesties pay in this Kingdom are and shall be allowed.' (This was ordered twenty-seven days after the surrender of Birr Castle). 2pp
199 (A/5/77)	1 April, 1642	Commission instructing Capt. Parsons to keep the castle of Birr and to defend it, the town and surrounding countryside. 1 p
200 (A/5/4)	9 Sept. 1642	Order from the Council of War for the provision of a means of deterring the continuous theft of the army's ammunition. Signed by John Borlase, George Kildarp. Lambert and Fra[ncis] Willoughby. (Document is torn at the edge and part of the text is missing). 1 p
201 (A/5/56)	29 Oct. 1642	Receipt for £11.6.0 paid to officers under the command of Capt. Parsons. 1 p
202 (A/5/88)	1643	Petition of Capt. William Parsons to the Lord Lieutenant General of Ireland, requesting permission to equip his army with the necessary ammunition from his Majesty's stores. 1 p
203 (A/5/57)	23 May, 1643	Copy of the order from the Council [of War] for the payment of money to the officers and troops of Capt. William Parson's army and for the expense of maintaining the sick and the wounded. 2 pp
204–210		Warrants issued to Capt. William as follows:
204 (A/5/27)	20 June 1643	To march with his army to Monasterevin, Co. Kildare. 1 p

205
(A/1/119–
20)

8 Mar. 1643

Original and copy warrant for the disbanding of the troops under the command of Capt. William Parsons. Signed by Edward Brabazon, John Borlase, Francis Willoughby and others. 2 items

206
(A/5/28)

8 Mar. 1643

To disband his horse troops. 1 p

207
(A/5/29)

3 June 1643

To march with his army to Jobstown, Co. Dublin. 1 p

208
(A/5/25)

5 July 1643

To leave Jobstown, Co. Dublin, and march with his troops to Kiliabbans in Co. Dublin, '... wheare you are to remaine in garrison till further direction. And vou are also required to take speciall care that none of them troope take away from Jobstowne afforesaid any thing but what shall properly appertaine to themselves ...'. Signed by Ormond.

209
(A/5/26)

14 Oct. 1643

To march with his troops '... in full nomber and completely armed and to march from your new garrison at the Naas Co. Kildare to this citv Dublin where you are to remayne in garrison till further order.' Signed by Ormond.

210
(A/5/90)

27 Oct. 1646

From the Council of Ireland to march with his troops from York, Nottingham and Lancaster '... towards West Chester to the place appointed by the Lord Lieutenant for his shipping'. 1 p

211
(A/5/31)

25 May 1644

Memorandum by Capt. William Parsons '... of occurances from the 25 of Maye 1644. Mundays the 27th Maye some of the Paralment Troops tooke me awaye prisoner to one Captain Duke and sent me to my Lord Generall who commanded me to wayght on the Parlament.

... 5 of June, being Wednesdaye. I wayted on Sir John Clotworthy and Mr Renolds and shewed them how far I had done, where I herd strange stories from them and advised the forebarance of a declaration for a time untill my fellow agents came heather.

... 28 of June 1644. The Committee of house of commons came to our lodging and there wee gave them a narrative of the proceedings of the protestant agents.' 1 p

212
(A/5/85)

3 Aug. 1645

Order for the payment of money to Capt. William Parsons for his troops. 1 p

213
(A/5/48)

Circa. 1645

Copy of a petition from Capt. William Parsons to Parliament, requesting repayment of 2,185–5–05 spent by him for the support of the army during the rebellion. 1 p

214
(A/5/80–
81)

13 Sept. 1645:
18 May 1646

Proceedings at meetings of the Committee of the Lords and Commons of Ireland to consider petition and demands of Captain William Parsons for compensation for the expenses he had incurred in maintaining the army and garrison under his command. 2 items

215 **(A/10)**	7 July 1646	Royal commission appointing Capt. William Parsons captain of a troop of horse in the Regiment of Col. Jones '... to serve in this present expedition for Ireland'. (Written on parchment, signed and sealed). 1 membrane
216 **(A/5/24)**	Nov. 1646	Order from the Committee of the Lords and Commons of Ireland for the repayment of money due to Capt. William Parsons '... for raysing, arming and transporting a troope ...'. 1 p
217 **(A/5/14)**	10 Mar. 1663	Order for payment of sums in arrears to Capt. William Parsons for his service as Captain of 'a troope of horse' and in accordance with the act entitled 'an act for the better execution of his Majesties gracious declaration for the settlement of his Kingdom of Ireland and the satisfaction of several interests of adventureres, soldiers and other subjects there.' (Signed and sealed) 1 p

Orders for the payment of money to Capt. William Parsons' troops and his own expenses.

218	13 May 1647	1 p
219	N.D.	1 p
220	26 Aug. 1652	1 p
221	2 Sept. 1652	1 p

v	*Sir* Laurence ***Parsons (1st Bt), 1663–92***	
222 **(A/5/45)**	5 July 1663	'Instructions to bee observed by the Commissioners appointed for the assessing and ordering of the fifth, sixth, seaventh and eighth subsidies of eight intire subsidies of the temporality granted by an act of this present parliament. Firstly you are required to give charge to the assessores that they take speciall care in theire assessments that there bee all equality and indifference used with such moderation and respect of the poorer sort ... .'

(Signed by several including the Earl of Kildare) 2 pp

223 **(A/1/70)**	6 Dec. 1683	Letters patent appointing Sir Laurence Governor of the King's County and all its militia forces.
224 **(A/19)**	1672–81: 1688–9	Bound volume recording several memoranda in relation to Sir Laurence's position as Governor of Birr and all the militia forces and Trustee of the Forty-Nine Officers, eg. the rules and orders of the Committee appointed for the 'assessing and leavying of the [deficiency] of the yares value', charged upon

King's County and other counties. Also recorded are: the minutes of the proceedings of the committee's meetings (13 April 1672, 10 July 1672, 20 Aug. 1672, 1679–81) held at Parsonstown and Killeigh, King's County (with much mention of Sir Laurence' and Heward Oxburgh); a copy of the warrants issued to the collectors appointed (eg Heward Oxburgh and Francis Coghlan), giving details such as the name of the landowner, the number of acres and amount to be paid by each; an assessment of the levies in various baronies including Meath, Dublin, Louth, Ossory, Rathdown, Wicklow, Shillelagh, Salt, and Ikeathy and Oughterany. At the reverse end of the book is a record of the distribution of the '... 2 troops and three companies upon the several baronyes of the county allowing 600 acres for a horseman and 300 acres for a foote soldier of Sir Laurence Parsons' troops and Captain Daniel Gahan his company.' Also at the end of the book is a copy of a letter from the Lord Lieutenant and Council of Ireland (dated 7 Feb. 1680), instructing Sir Laurence, Sir Francis Blundell and Richard Barry, 'to carry out a survey of all the troops and soldiers in the area for the purpose of establishing how much ammunition is required by them and the reasons why and also to provide details of each soldiers' earnings and the amount of exercise they have.'

Includes: Diary entries from April–May 1689, recording the daily atrocities of Lieutenant Heward Oxburgh and the rebels and their attack on the castle (part of the entry is crossed out). Also recorded is a list of the witnesses who were brought against Sir Laurence in testimony to the charge of treason and the evidence they gave. States that the articles of agreement signed upon the surrender of the castle (see no. 227) were written by Owen Carroll. It outlines the start of the conflict between Sir Laurence and Lieutenant Oxburgh, which led to the seizing of the castle in 1689, eg '... [Lieutenant] Oxburgh['s] regiment being quartered in the castle of Birr made great wast burning everything they could lay their hands on and twice set the castle on fire .... The 14th April '89, Lutt Oxburgh and his Lady etc. came to the castle of Birr to prepare for the entertainment of the Duke of Terconell [Tyrconnel] who was expected to [join] the Lutt. Regiment, till this time Ray Cousen, John Phillips and his wife were permitted to live in the castle but now they are turned out and have not a house to put thear heads in his owne being destroied by Lutt. Oxburgh soldiers.'

225 (A/5/10)	15 Feb. 1688	Despatch from Oxburgh to Darby Ryan (Constable) and the town watchman issuing orders for the watch in Birr. 'Let 3 men watch at the fronte reare northside house, Let 3 men watch towards his castle above Coghlan.' 1 p

226 (A/24)	1689	Journal of the troubles leading up to the siege of Birr Castle in 1689 by Capt. Oxburgh and his forces. It is written in a 19th century hand and presumably copied from an original not now in the Archives. It includes several references to the gardens of Birr Castle and the layout of the estate, e.g. in connection with the seizure of the castle, it records that a battery was raised '... just by the pond, then they lined all the hedges by the green, Godsella Park and behind the almshouse and the little cabins on the green. ...' Includes: A list of several tenants whose houses were burnt during the siege. (p. 168) Includes: Plan of the castle and town '... as besieged by General Sarsfield in 1691'. 199 pp
227 (A/5/5)	20 Feb. 1689	Copy of the articles of agreement made between Sir Laurence and Heward Oxburgh upon the surrender of Birr Castle. 1 p
228 (A/5/12)	8 Mar. 1689	Report from General Moore in response to orders received from the Duke of Tyrconnel to enquire if Sir Laurence '... was fortefieing and making a garrison of his house at Birr'. States that he met with Sir Laurence who claimed that he had taken in his tenants for their own protection as they feared for their lives; their homes and goods had been plundered by a gang of robbers who were terrorising the area. (The order was issued after Oxburgh reported that Sir Laurence had set up a fortress and had 1500 men in arms). 1 p
229 (A/5/6)	8 Mar. 1689	Order issued for the reprieve of Sir Laurence's death sentence. 1 p
230 (A/5/7)	22 May 1689	The same. 1 p
231 (A/5/8)	7 Aug. 1689	The same. 1 p
232 (A/1/80)	1690	Petition of Sir Laurence outlining the misfortunes which he suffered during the war. States that he was sentenced to be hung, ... drawn and quartered, '... for endevoring [sic] to preserve himself and his English tenants from violence,' and that his family in England have been reduced to a low condition and are much in debt, '... which they now must sinke under unless releved by his Most Gracious Majesty.' 1 p
233 (A/1/78)	20 Nov. 1690	Certificate presenting the case of Sir Laurence with a list of '... the troubles, losses and dangers which occurred in the late wars in Ireland and signed by many of the nobility, clergy and gentlemen of that Kingdom.' States that Sir Laurence has suffered imprisonment and that his estate amounting to £1,500 a year is all laid waste, most of his orchards and gardens were cut

down and destroyed and his house which cost £3,000 so badly ruined that it is uninhabitable; '... and many of his tenants houseless in the town of Birr and the farms adjacent are burnt ... and he was neer loosing his life being shott through the brim of his hatt and severall of his party killed.'

Includes: A list of the houses that were burnt and pulled down together with the names of the tenants.

234 (A/5/9)	27 Feb. 1692	Order from Dublin Castle to Sir Laurence to implement penalties for the abuse of the late proclamation whereby the militia were empowered to distrain all manner of stock and household goods. '... We have therefore resolved all such unwarranted proceedings shall be examined into by the next judges of Assizes and severely punished – this we direct shall be published forthwith.'

vi	*Sir William Parsons (2nd Bt), 1682–94*

235 (A/21)	1682	Grant of arms to Sir William by Richard St. George, Ulster King of Arms. Written on parchment and illuminated with the arms described as follows: 'Two leopards Argent, spotted sable, collared Gules studded or supporting a shield of his paternall coate of Arms ... and to be by him and every of them respectively borne at all times and upon all occasions.' 1 membrane
236 (A/1/82)	4 June 1692	Report from John Beswell, Dublin, to Sir William, of the capture and sinking of a fleet of ships some of which were '... split upon the rock at Jersey towne – 13 great shipps sunk and burnt in one place six in another ten in another besides some transport ships and to give it the greater emphasis done in King James plea performed with the greatest bravery in the world by a fireship and boats ...'. 1 p
237 (A/1/83)	19 Aug. 1693	Letter from John Beswell to Sir William requesting payment due to him. 1 p
238 (A/1/84)	23 Sep. 1693	" " 1 p
239 (A/5/93)	12 Oct. 1694	Orders issued to Sir William to instruct the colonels and officers in charge of the several regiments of foot and dragoons in the Low Countries to '... be furnisht in their respective garrisons and quarters with the usual allowance of bread by the contractors Machada and Pereira during the present winter quarters in like manner as in the field.' 1 p
240 (A/1/140)	N.D.	Draft petition from Sir William to the Duke of Ormond requesting financial relief and compensation for the losses

sustained by his father during the war and also for the several
sums of his father's money advanced before the war of 1640 for
'reducing of this Kingdom to the obedience of the crown of
England ...'. 1 p

241   N.D.   Petition from Sir William to Parliament outlining the losses
(A/1/141)   sustained by him and also his father Sir Laurence during the war
                            and the expenses he incurred and paid for out of his own
                            personal fortune in containing the enemy for two years. States
                            that he (the petitioner) '... voluntarily consented to the burning
                            most part of his town of Birr, alias Parsonstowne together with
                            several out houses belonging to his castle when it was thought
                            serviceable for the English against the Irish in the late rebellion
                            ...'. Petition is endorsed: 'Later Duke of Ormond prayed me not
                            give this petition and he'd serve me with the King.'

C   THE PARSONSES OF BELLAMONT, CO. DUBLIN AND TOMDUFFE, CO. WEXFORD

i   *Sir William Parsons, 1641–66*

242   26 Feb. 1641   Letters patent granting Concordatum money to Sir William and
(A/1/165)   Sir John Berlase [Borlase] for the exercise of their duties as Lords
                                Justices of Ireland. 1 pp

243   12 June 1641   Instructions to Sir William and Sir John Berlase [Borlase], to
(A/1/186)   implement the reduction of rent granted to Brian MacConnell
                                (a footman). 1 p

244   20 Aug. 1642   Instructions from the Lords Justices and Council of Ireland to
(A/1/167)   demand from the parishioners of St Michael's [Dublin?] a
                                contribution to the fortification of the town and that all names
                                and amounts contributed are to be recorded. 1 p

245   26 Sep. 1666   Certificate (from the Exchequer) stating 'That this is the thirty
(A/5/74)   six lott of the debt to which are drawn the eightieth lott of the
                                creditt.' Records amounts paid to severall including William
                                Parsons, the Earl of Montrate [sic] and Colonel Chidley Coote.
                                1 p

ii   *Sir Richard, 1681–2*

                            Accounts of money lent to Sir Richard and paid out in his
                            name, e.g. 'Paid Gregory Doyle of Tomduffe by Sir Richard's
                            order when he agreed with Doyle for surveying his lands. 05–
                            01–00. Lent Sir Richard to give to the poore, 00–03–00'.

246   Aug. 1680–   "   "   5 p
(A/1/143) 1682

247
(A/1/144)

7 May 1681

Accounts of money lent to Sir Richard. 1 p

248

2 July 33
Charles II
[1681]

Illuminated patent granting Richard Parsons the dignities of
Baron of Oxmantown and Viscount Rosse. 1 p

249
(A/22)

Circa. 1680

File containing a memorandum and a letter (written by Arthur
Parsons of Tomduffe) outlining a feud between Sir Richard
Parsons, Sir Arthur Parsons, Sir Adam Loftus and one
Whitehead in connection with Loftus' attempts to deprive Sir
Richard of his inheritance before he came of age. The letter
records how Sir Richard had employed Arthur to manage his
estate for him. The agreement was that Arthur was to receive
£1,000 per annum of his estate together with some land. He
describes how he set about running the estate and making
improvements until Loftus took over the management and tried
to discredit Arthur and his motives, stating that he had heard
that it was Arthur's intention to kill Sir Richard. The
memorandum (presumably written by Sir Richard) outlines how
he and Arthur had decided to surrender the original deeds to the
estate and have new ones drawn up as Sir Richard regarded
them as being too severe in their expectation of his performance
(see Lodge's *Peerage*, Vol. II, p. 574). These new deeds were to
favour Arthur with a large part of the estate. It was Sir Richard's
intention to keep the estate in the family as he had as yet
produced no heirs. It recounts how Loftus and Whitehead
arranged to trick the two.

Includes: A copy of the Chancery bill presented by Sir Richard
in connection with the dispute which gives a detailed schedule
of the lands owned by the Parsons.

250
(A/25/11)

2 June 1682

Deed of conveyance from Richard, Lord Baron of Oxmantown
and Lord Viscount of Rosse, to Arthur Parsons of Tomduffe,
Co. Wexford, of the manor and lands of Parsonstown
(Tomduff), Co. Wexford, for a yearly rent of £7.15s. (Signed by
Arthur Parsons) 1 membrane

iii   *Bonds and leases, 1638–96*

251
(A/1/13)

1 Dec. 1638

Bond between Phelem Redmond of Tingar, Co. Wexford, and
Walsingham Cook of Tomduffe, Co. Wexford. (Signed and
sealed by Phelem Redmond)

252
(A/25/10)

23 June 1682

Parchment indenture between William Mathews of Templelyne,
Co. Wicklow, and Arthur Parsons of Tomduffe (alias Ne-nam),
Co. Wexford, in connection with an indenture of release bearing
the same date. 1 membrane

253 (A/25/12)	19 Mar. 1694	Parchment deed of conveyance of Cullenragh and Ballyduffe, Co. Wexford, from William Mathews of Templelyne, Co. Wicklow, to John Grogan of Johnstowne, Co. Wexford, as mortgaged by Arthur Parsons. 1 membrane
254 (A/25/13)	26 June 1692	Parchment deed of surrender from William Parsons (family of St John's), Co. Wexford, to Walter Bunbury of Dublin, of a decree obtained by Sir Laurence in 1675 for the payment of £676 from the estate of Elizabeth (his sister-in-law) and her second husband Henry Piers, for the maintenance and education of William and Sandy Parsons (his nephews), the payment to be continued for 28 years. 1 membrane
255 (A/1/86)	1699	Parchment deed concerning Michael Parsons, (son and heir of Arthur of Tomduffe), William Parsons, and Clotilda Parsons (Michael's wife). (Written in Latin). 1 membrane
256 (Q/4(1))	25 Mar. 1674	Lease of lands of Tomduffe, Co. Wexford, to Robert Marsh by Arthur Parsons for a term of 21 years. (Signed and sealed by Robert Marsh). 2 pp
257 (Q/4(2))	18 Nov. 1675	Parchment lease of lands of Ballyduff, Co. Wexford, to William Peargiter by Arthur Parsons. 2 membranes
258 (Q/4(3))	18 Nov. 1698	Lease of Garranoe and Ballyduff, Co. Wexford, to Thomas Taylor by Michael Parsons of Co. Wexford (brother to Arthur), for one year for one pepper corn.
259 (Q/4(4))	[1696]	Lease of lands of Tomduffe, Co. Wexford, to John Redmond by Michael Parsons for 21 years. (Date is rubbed).

D   MAPS AND PLANS

260 (O/1)	1638	Coloured map of John Crew's Park in Siffinwood, Parsonstown, King's County, by Francis Morley. (Damaged and incomplete)
261 (O/2)	Circa. 1691	Photostat of a plan of Birr Castle and its defences, by Michael Richards. (The original is among the papers of George Clarke, William III's Secretary at War, and held in Worcester College, Oxford).

See also Recipe Book, A/17 – Pencil sketch of Parsonstown House.

See also A/24 – Journal with plan of the castle and town, 1691.

E   OTHER SEVENTEENTH-CENTURY MATERIAL

262 (A/5/94)	Circa. 1558–1603	Confirmation of the grant of a lease to Richard Hardinge by Queen Elizabeth, of all the monasteries, abbies, priories, castles, Manors, lands, tenements, rectories, tithes and hereditaments within the realm of Ireland. (See no. 74.) 1 p

263 (A/5/63)	N.D.	Grant of the Monastery and lands of Lurghodin, Co. Tipperary, to William Dongun. 1 p
264 (A/5/92)	N.D.	Copy of a letter from the Council to Sir John Croke and the Solicitor General, instructing them to report (with the assistance of Sir Robert Gardener), on the findings of their investigation into the lands of Henry Lea in Ireland.
265 (A/5/72)	N.D.	'A remonstrance humbly presented to the Honourable Counsell of State for the speedy raising of money in an ancient way by subsidi and without partiality and that some grievances of the people may be eased, that they may pay the more ceerfully ... This account or valuation will produce sixteen hundred thousand pounds a yeare or there abouts. ... The way of rating the taxes is an arbitrary way, but this way be subsidies is a vesable way and an ancient parlement way.' 1 p
266 (A/5/60)	Circa. 1646	Copy of a grant of the lands of the '... late dissolved Monastery or Abbey called St Mary's Abbey neere Dublin and all the landes, tenentes rentes, service tithes and heredita[me]nts' to Richard Wakeman. 1 p
267 (A/15)	1641–66	Book of State Papers and petitions concerning the Acts of Settlement and Explanation. Recorded are several petitions from the 'Catholic subjects' of Ireland together with the Royal response, e.g.: a response to '... certaine exceptions against the clause and proviso tendered on [behalf] of his Majesties loyall subjects the Roman Catholiques of Ireland'; 'Answeares at large to certaine proposals offered in order to the settlement of Ireland'; The answeare to the declaration and instructions'; 'A briefe as well of certaine proposalls presented to his Majesty on behalfe of the English in relation to the settlement of Ireland. As also of the severall answeares by the Irish [Commanders] given thereunto.' Includes: A brief narrative of the sufferings of the Irish under Cromwell, printed in 1660. 93 pp
268 (A/5/71)	25 Aug. 1643	Declaration to the farmers, plowmen and others within three miles of Monasterevin, Co. Kildare, with the exception of those involved in the rebellion, that they may '...without interruption, plowe, manure, and sow theire grounds, fields, gardens within the said lands and limits.' 1 p
269 (A/5/32)	May 1644	Copy of the King's reply to the Irish delegation and their propositions delivered at Oxford, e.g.: In reply to the 14th grievance – 'His Majesty doth not admitt that the long continuance of the chiefe government of the Kingdom in that place hath bin occasion of much tyranny and oppression or that any tyranny or oppression hath bin executed upon his majesty subjects of that Kingdom, however His Majesty will be carefull

such govenours shall not continue longer in those places then he shall find good for his people there....' 2 pp

270   2 Aug. 1648   Copy of an extract from the Journal of the House of Commons
(A/5/68)   recording receipt of numerous orders, among which are
                               mentioned: 'An order declaring those that invited the Scotch into
                               England Traytors'; 'An order for sequesting and compounding
                               with delinquents in the late insurrection in Kent.' 1 p

271   N.D.   Ordinances devised by the Mayor and Corporation of Galway
(A/14)   for the regulation of companies or guilds in the town.
                               (Document is badly damaged in the centre and part of the text
                               is therefore illegible).

272   1668-75   Account book of David Johnston, merchant of Dublin,
(A/16)   recording particulars of accounts with e.g. Captain Claud
                               Hamilton, Thomas Langton, Bartholomew Hamlen, Lieutenant
                               John Charlton and Thomas Bligh. Types of entries are as
                               follows: '...severall disbursements don at Mr Adam Stokes
                               weading 18 Sept. 1669; for tobacco; Turkey; mutton; wine;
                               glasses; nail and Spanish iron; An account of divers charges don
                               at the funeral of Mrs Elizabeth Vincent – 6 yrds of ribin to tie
                               her; 2 hundred branches of rosemary, The Countess of Mount
                               Alexanders coatch with 6 horses which carryed the hearse, paid
                               for wine, beere, bread, sugar and tobacco and pipes. So much
                               left myselfe to buy a mourning ring.'

ROSSE PAPERS

INDEX OF NAMES

(The references are to sub-sections or piece numbers in the archival arrangement, not to pages of the book, since the former almost always provide a more precise reference-point. A sub-section number without suffix refers to the summary list; a sub-section or piece number with the suffix * refers to the detailed calendar; a sub-section or piece number with the suffix • refers to the appendix of 17th-century material.)

Armstrong, Mr, R*

Armstrong, [Mr], (of Clara, King's Co.), B/8/10*

Armstrong, Mr, (of Gallen), E/11/1-70*

Armstrong, Sir Nesbitt, Q/383

Armstrong, [Thomas St George?], E/17/6*

Armstrong-Jones, Anthony, Earl of Snowdon, S, T/125, T/169

Armstrong-Jones, Ronald Owen, S, S/7, T/169

Armstrong-Jones, Susan, see Vesey, Susan, Viscountess de Vesci

Arran, Earl of, see Butler, Richard

Ash, Thomas, B/1/1/6*

Ashbourne, 1st Lord, see Gibson, Edward

Ashenhurst, Mr, E/31/9*

Ashley-Cooper, Anthony, 9th Earl of Shaftesbury, T/90

Ashley Cooper, Lady Mary, T/90

Ashton, Sir Frederick U/34

Aslet, Clive, S/12

Astaire, Adele, see Cavendish, Adele, Lady Charles

Astaire, Fred, T/105

Aston, William, B/1/1/6*

Atholl, 4th Duke of, see Murray, John

Atkinson, Mrs Judith, G/43

Atkinson, Norman D., A/26, C/13

Atkinson, Robert, H/104, H/111, H/112

Attwood, Thomas, D/22/10*

Auckland, 1st Lord, see Eden, William

Avonmore, 1st Viscount, see Yelverton, Barry

Babbage, Charles, J/1

Bacon, Francis ('Lord Bacon, Lord Verulam, Viscount St Albans'), C/6*

Bagnuley, John, 163•

Bagn[u]ley, Thomas, 111•, 164•

Bagot, Charles, E/25/6*, E/25/26*

Bagwell, John, B/7/5*, E/33/29*

[?Bagwell], William, B/7/5*

Bainbridge, Mr [of Messrs Puget & Bainbridge, bankers, London?], D/7/99*

Baker, William, B/7/5*

Baldrusski, Edward Raphael, R/11

Baldwin, Charles B., V/1

Baldwin, John, junior, A/23*

Balfour, John Patrick Douglas, 3rd Lord Kinross, T/83

Balfour, William, B/1/1/6* Ball, B., & Co., bankers, D/12

Ball, Ensign, A/23*

[Ball], Mr, (of Co. Longford), D/7/66*

Ball, Robert, K/36B

Ball, Robert Stawell, K/35, L/6/1

Banastre, Peregin, 57•, 58•

Bandon, Earl of, etc. see under Bernard

Banks, Sir Joseph, H/89

Banon family, Q/390

Banon, Christopher J.B., V/2

Bantry, 3rd Earl of, see White, William Henry Hare Hedges-,

Barclay, Tritton & Bevans, H/88

Baring, Mr, D/22/2*, D/22/10*

Barker, William, B/7/5*

Barnard, E.E., K/36

Baron, Rev. Edward, B/7/5*

Barr, John, T/154A

Barraclough, see Evans, Barraclough & Co., (solicitors)

Barran, Sir David, T/103, U/22

Barrett family, Q/393

Barrett, J.S.P. Malone, V/7

Barrington, Sir Charles, H/117, T/19

Barrington, Mr, E/32/22*

Barry, James, B/1/1/6*

Barry, Redmond, B/1/1/6*

Barry, Richard, 224•

Barry, Richard F., & Son (solicitors), Q/384

Barton, Henry, B/4

Barton, William, B/7/5*

Baskerville family, G/17

Bate Dudley, Rev. Sir Henry, D/7/66*

Batey, Mrs Mavis, T/25/1

Bath, Marchioness of, see Fielding, Daphne Winifred Louise

Bath, 6th Marquess of, see Thynne, Henry

Bathurst, Henry, 3rd Earl Bathurst, D/14/6*

Bayley, John, B/7/5*

Beaton, Sir Cecil, T/142, U/32

Beaty, Francis, A/8*

Beauchamp, Earls, etc. see under Lygon

Beauchamp, John, B/1/1/6*

Beaulieu, Earl of, see Hussey-Montagu, Edward

Beaumont, Rex, T/83, T/125

Beck, William, H/31, H/32

Bective, 1st Earl, see Taylour, Thomas

Bedford, Dukes of, see under Russell

Beecham, Sir Thomas, T/111

Beere, John, A/4*

Beetenson, William, A/8*

Beisley, Captain William, A/5*, 185•, 186• see also Peisley

Beit, Sir Alfred, 2nd Bt, T/130

Beit, Clementine Mabell Kitty, Lady, T/130

Beith, Sir John, T/61/1

Belfield, Viscount, see Rochfort, Robert

Denny family, F/11

De Noailles, Vicomte, T/25/4

Derby, Lords, *see under* Stanley

Dering, Edward, A/5*

Dermod, Provincial King of Leinster, C/6*

Derry, Bishops of, *see* Barnard, William; and
   Hervey, Frederick; *and* King, William; and
   Knox, William

Derwent, 4th Lord, *see* Johnstone, Patrick Robin
   Gilbert Vanden-Bempde-

Desart, Lady, *see* Cuffe, Anne

Despard, Francis Green, B/7/5*

Despard, William, B/7/5*

D'Esterre, Mr, D/5/42*

De Valera, Eamon, K/38, R/6, T/63

Deverell, Anne, (Mrs R.B.), E/42/1, D/7/100*,
   D/7/142*

Deverell, R.B., E/42/1, [D/7/97*], D/7/100*

De Vesci, Viscountess, *see* Parsons, Frances Lois

De Vesci, Viscounts of, *etc. see under* Vesey

De Vilmorin, Lulu, T/25/1

Devonshire, 10th Duke of, *see* Cavendish,
Edward William Spencer

Dibb, Christopher, G/10

Dickens, Charles, J/15

Dier, William, 2•

Digby, Edward, 2nd Earl of Digby, E/33/30*

Digby, Henry, 1st Earl of Digby, B/8/10*

Digby, Kildare, 2nd Baron Digby, A/13, A/5*

Digby, Dean William, B/8/10*, E/32/4*

Dillon, George, E/25/12*

Dillon, Robert, A/4*

Dillon, Thomas, A/23*

Dillon-Lee, Charles, 12th Viscount Dillon,
   D/14/1*

Disney, William, E/14/49*

Dixon, Robert, B/1/1/6*

Dobbin, Rev. Dr, B/9/3*, C/12/1*

Dodd, Captain, D/14/1*

Doherty, Edmond, B/7/5*

Dolly (employee of 2nd Earl of Rosse), D/10/1*

Domville, William, (Attorney General), 137•, 142•

Doneraile, Viscounts, *see under* St Leger

Dongon, William, A/5*

Dongun, William, 263•

Donnell, 2•

Donoughmore, Earls of, *see under* Hutchinson

Donovan, Sir Richard, 5•

Doolan, Mrs K.M., T/41B

Doria family, T/8, N/36

Doria, Princess, *see* Emily Augusta Mary, Princes
   Doria

Doria-Pamphili-Landi, Prince Alonso, N/36,
   N32/1

Doria-Pamphili-Landi, Prince Filippo, N/36,
   N32/1

Doria-Pamphili-Landi, Princess Orielta, N/10,
   N/13, N/32/1, N/36, T8

Dorset, 1st Duke of, *see* Sackville, Lionel
   Cranfield

Douglas, Lieutenant Colonel Archibald, 62•

Douglas, Charles, 3rd Duke of Queensberry, H/2

Douglas, Sir Howard, J/21

Douglas, J.W., H/115

Douglas, Lieutenant Colonel, A/23*

Douglas, Sylvester, 1st Lord Glenbervie,
   (Secretary of Irish House of Commons),
   D/1/4*, F/19*

Douglas-Home, Henry, T/92

Downer, Maurice, Q/34

Downes, 2nd Lord, *see* Burgh, General Sir
   Ulysses

Downes, William, 1st Lord Downes, D/8

Downey, Michael, E/11/1-70*

Downshire, Marquesses of, etc., *see under* Hill

Doyle, Dr James Warren, R.C. Bishop of
   Leighlin and Ferns, F/14, F/21, F/21*

Doyne, Philip, B/1/1/6*

Drew, Sir Arthur, T/56/3, T/60/3

Drew, Sir Thomas, O/56

Dreyer, John Louis Emile, K/26

Drought family, E/25/4*, E/37, O/57A, V/11

Drought, Captain Alec, Q/328-Q/394, T/33,
   V/1 1

Drought, George, E/11/1-70*, E/25/4*

Drought, John, E/11*, E/34/19*

Drought, John, junior, E/34/40-41*

Drought, Mr, D/4/13*, D/20/2*

Drought, Mr, (of Droughtville), E/17/1*

Drought, Mr, (of Whigsborough), E/17/6*

Drought, Rev. R., E/17/1*

Drought, Thomas, E/34/40-41*

Drought, W.B., E/34/40-41*

Drummond, John, 1st Earl and titular (Jacobite)
   Duke of Melfort, A/5*

Drummond, William, A/4*

Drummonds, (seedsmen), T/13

Drury family, T/110B

Drury, Mabel, T/110B

Dryden, John, H/40

Dryden, Sir John *see* Turner, Sir John

Dublin, Archbishop of, *see* Bulkeley, Lancelot,
   and King, William; *and* Simms, George Otto;
   and Whately, Richard

Foster, [Anthony, Chief Baron of the Exchequer], C/1/7*

Foster, Charles Wilmer, G

Foster, John, H/71, C/15*, D/2/2*, D/4/11*, D/8/63*, C/14/1-5*, C/15*, D/5/6*, D/7/55*, D/7/107*, D/14/1, E/31/5*, E/31/6*, F/10*

Fowler, John, T/25/1, T/61/9

Fox, Charles James, H/71, C/8/38*, C/8/40*, C/8/42*, C/8/46*, C/8/54*, C/8/63*, C/14/1-5*, C/15*, D/5/6*, D/7/55*, D/7/107*, D/14/1*, E/31/5*, E/31/6*, F/19*

Fox, Rev. [Francis, of Fox Hall, Co. Longford], D/7/99*

Fox, Henry Richard, 3rd Lord Holland, E/27

Fox, [Luke, Judge of the Common Pleas], D/7/28*

Fox, Colonel Richard, of Fox Hall, Co. Longford, D/7/95*, D/7/96*, D/7/99*, D/13/9*

[?Fox], Wilfrid, T/22

Fox-Strangways, Edward Henry Charles James, 7th Earl of Ilchester, 1778

Fox-Strangways, Giles Stephen Holland, 6th Earl of Ilchester, T/55/5

Fox-Strangways, Hon. John, T/81

Fox Talbot, William Henry, P Foyle, Christina, T/136A

Foyle, W. & G., Ltd., T/163A

Fraser, William, C.E., O/31, O/49

Francis, Sir Frank, T/60/1

Frederick Augustus, Duke of York, (brother of Duke of Kent) E/33, [D/14/1*], E/33/46*

Freeman, Samuel, B/1/1/6*

Freke, Lady Catherine, C/8/45*

Freke, John Evans -, later 6th Lord Carbery, C/8/45*

French & French (solicitors), Q/387

French, Arthur, E/33, B/1/1/6*, E/33/18*

French, Sir John, B/1/1/6*

French, Matthew, of Dublin, (merchant), 37•

Furlong, George, A/42

Gaghan, Daniel, A/23*

Gahan, Captain Daniel, 224•

Gahan, Daniel, B/7/5*

Galbraith, Major Richard, V/12

Gale, Benjamin, H/97

Galtrim, Baron of, A/4*

Galway, Lord, see Bourke, Ulick

Gamble, Nicholas, E/34/40-41*

Gardener, Sir Robert, see Gardiner, Sir Robert

Gardiner, Charles John, Viscount Mountjoy, Earl of Blesington, 264•, E/33/45*, E/33/46*

Gardiner, Luke, 4th Viscount Mountjoy, F/13*

Gardiner, Sir Robert, 264*, A/5*

Garrett, George, T/63, T/115

Garrett, Mrs George, T/63, T/115

Garstin, Mrs, E/2/2*

Garvey family, Q/56

Garvey, George, V

Garvey, Toler R., junior, Q/328-Q/394, T/31, T/32, V

Garvey, Toler R., senior, M/23, Q/318, Q/328, Q/382, V

Gascoyne-Cecil, Robert Arthur James, 5th Marquess of Salisbury, T/44/2

Gason, Richard, B/7/5*

Gassiot, John Peter, K/17

Gavan, Dermot, A/8*

Geary, Admiral Francis, H/12

Gee, Ann, 59•

Geering, Richard, B/1/1/6*

Gell, William, G/27

Genée/Isitt, Adeline, T/141

Geoghegan, Colonel, A/23*

Geoghegan, Walpole, J/19

George II, C/8/32*, H/2

George III, C/1/1*, C/2/7*, C/2/28*, C/2/36*, C/2/37*, C/6*, C/8/41*, C/8/47*, C/8/49*, C/8/59*, D/4/11*, D/7/7*, [D/7/71*], D/7/74*, D/10/3*, E/33/46*

George IV, E/35, D/2/16*, D/23/4*

George, Prince of Wales, (George IV), C/8/51*, C/8/54*, D/7/51*, D/10/9*, D/14/1*

George V, M/10, N/10

George VI, T/162

Gibb, James, A/4*

Gibbs, Miss Anne, H/57

Gibson, Daniel, B/9/3*

Gibson, Edward, 1st Baron Ashbourne, M/19

Gibson, Elisabeth Dione, Lady, T/61/5

Gibson, Richard Patrick Tallentyre, Lord Gibson, T/24, T/61/5

Giffard, [John], D/2/1*

Giffard, John Anthony Hardinge, 3rd Earl of Halsbury, T/58/1, T/60/4

Gifford, John, A/5*

Gilbert, Sir John, A/5, C/11

Gilbert, J.T., A/15*

Gilbert, Sir John T., A/26

Gilbert, [Sir John Thomas], T/1

Gilbert, St Leger, B/1/1/6*

Gilhane, Hugh, A/5*

Gillam, Justice, D/20/2*